INN SPOTS

SPOTS

& IN THE SOUTHEAST
SPECIAL
PLACES

A guide to where to go, stay, eat and enjoy in 26 of the region's choicest areas.

Wood Pond Press
West Hartford, Conn.

The authors value their reputation for credibility and have personally visited the places included in this book. They have seen them all, which gives them a rare perspective in the field. Unlike others, they do not ask the owners to fill out information forms or to approve the final copy. Nor do they rely on researchers or field inspectors with varying perspectives and loyalties to do their leg work. They make their recommendations based on their experiences and findings. No fees are accepted or charged for inclusion.

Prices, hours and menu offerings at inns and restaurants change seasonally and with business conditions. Readers should confirm to avoid disappointment. The prices and hours reported in this book were correct at press time. They are offered as a relative guide to what to expect. Lodging rates quoted are for bed and breakfast, unless otherwise specified (MAP, Modified American Plan, breakfast and dinner; AP, American Plan, breakfast, lunch and dinner). Restaurant prices generally show the range for dinner entrées.

The authors welcome readers' reactions and suggestions.

Cover Design by Robert V. Smith.

Cover Photo: Breakfast table at Casablanca Inn, St. Augustine, Fla.

Graphics by Jay Woodworth

Contents

Introduction

This is yet another inn book. But it's far more, too.

We enjoy reading others, but they rarely tell us what we *really* want to know – which inns and B&Bs are especially good and what they are like, where to get a good meal and what there is to do in the area. No inn is an island – they are part of their locale. With their neighbors, they share a sense of place.

These insights are what we now share with you. We start not with the inn but with the area (of course, the existence of inns or lack thereof helped determine the 26 special destination areas to be included). Then we tour each area, with the eyes and ears of the first-time visitor and the perspective of seasoned travelers and journalists. We visit the inns, the restaurants and the attractions. We *work* these areas as roving journalists, always seeking out the best and most interesting. We also *live* them – staying in, eating in, and experiencing as many places as time and resources allow.

The result is this book, a companion to our existing series covering the New England and Mid-Atlantic regions. It's a selective compendium of what we think are the best and most interesting places to stay, eat and enjoy in these 26 special areas – some of them the Southeast's best-known and some not widely known at all.

The book reflects our tastes. We want creature comforts like private bathrooms, oversize beds and comfortable reading areas in our rooms. We like to meet other inn guests, but we also value our privacy. We seek interesting and creative food and pleasant settings for meals. We enjoy different, enlightening things to do and places to see. We expect to receive value for time and money spent.

While touring the past year to research this book, we were struck by how new the inn and B&B phenomenon is in many areas in the Southeast. In New England and the Mid-Atlantic region, inns have been around a long time. So have inn-goers. In many Southeastern areas, inns and B&Bs have only emerged in the last few years. Only a minority of those we detail here even existed a decade ago. Inn guest books are full of comments from guests who report that this was their first time at a B&B and how much they enjoyed it.

The inn experience is highly personal, both for the innkeeper and for the inn-goer. The listing services, the advertising and the Web site hype cannot convey the personality of the place. Nor do they give an objective perspective.

That's the role of experienced guidebook writers who make the rounds and report things as they see them. Yes, the schedule is hectic and we do keep busy on these, our working trips that everyone thinks must be nothing but fun. One of us says she never again wants to climb to the third or fourth floor of an inn to view "just a couple more rooms" for the umpteenth time that day. The other doesn't care if he never eats another bedside chocolate or has to cope with a strange bathroom in the middle of the night.

Nonetheless, it's rewarding both to experience a great inn and to discover a promising B&B. We also enjoy a good meal, touring a choice museum, poking through an unusual store and meeting so many interesting people along the way. The Southeast proved to be full of special places, most of them quite seductive and beckoning us to return.

That's what this book is all about. We hope that you enjoy its findings as much as we did the finding.

Nancy and Richard Woodworth

About the Authors

Nancy Webster Woodworth began her travel and dining experiences in her native Montreal and as a waitress in summer resorts across Canada during her McGill University years. She worked in London and hitchhiked through Europe on $3 a day before her marriage to Richard Woodworth, whom she met while skiing at Mont Tremblant. They have lived in upstate New York and New England since. They became familiar with the Southeast during explorations while driving to and from their winter condominium in New Smyrna Beach, Fla. She started writing her "Roaming the Restaurants" column for the West Hartford (Conn.) News in 1972. That led to half of the book, *Daytripping & Dining in Southern New England,* written in collaboration with Betsy Wittemann in 1978. She since has co-authored *Inn Spots & Special Places in New England, Inn Spots & Special Places in the Mid-Atlantic, Weekending in New England, Getaways for Gourmets in the Northeast, Waterside Escapes in the Northeast,* and *The Restaurants of New England.* She and her husband have two grown sons and live in West Hartford.

Richard Woodworth has been an inveterate traveler since his youth in suburban Syracuse, N.Y., where his birthday outings often involved train trips with friends for the day to nearby Utica or Rochester. After graduation from Middlebury College, he was a reporter for newspapers in Geneva and Rochester before moving to Connecticut to become editor of the West Hartford News and eventually executive editor of Imprint Newspapers. With his wife and their sons, he has traveled to the four corners of this country, Canada and portions of Europe, writing their findings for newspapers and magazines. He and his wife have co-authored five editions *of Inn Spots & Special Places in New England* and *Getaways for Gourmets in the Northeast,* and three editions of *Inn Spots & Special Places / Mid-Atlantic.* They also have written two editions of *The Restaurants of New England.* With this new book, the couple have experienced and reported on more than 1,000 inns and 2,000 restaurants up and down the East Coast from Cape Breton Island, N.S., to Key West, Fla. Between travels and duties as publisher of Wood Pond Press, he tries to find time to ski in the winter and weed the garden in summer.

Excerpts from several of the authors' guidebooks may be seen on-line at www.getawayguides.com.

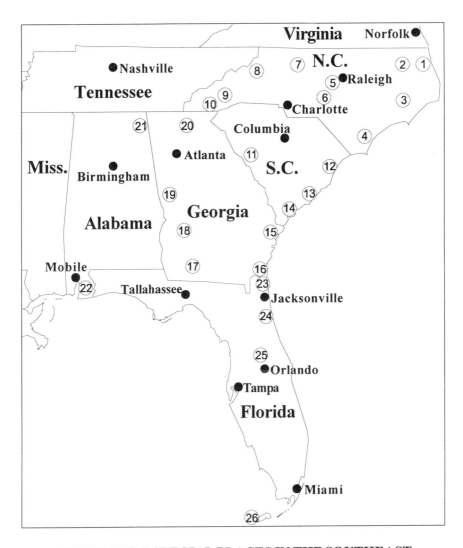

INN SPOTS & SPECIAL PLACES IN THE SOUTHEAST

1. Manteo/Roanoke Island
2. Edenton
3. New Bern
4. Wilmington
5. Chapel Hill
6. Pinehurst/Southern Pines
7. Winston-Salem
8. Blowing Rock
9. Asheville
10. Highlands/Cashiers
11. Aiken
12. Georgetown
13. Charleston
14. Beaufort
15. Savannah
16. St. Mary's
17. Thomasville
18. Americus/Plains
19. Warm Springs
20. Dahlonega
21. Mentone
22. Fairhope
23. Fernandina Beach
24. St. Augustine
25. Mount Dora
26. Key West

Dare County Tourist Bureau Photo

Cape Hatteras Lighthouse is landmark for sailors and travelers along Outer Banks.

Manteo/Roanoke Island, N.C.
Jewel of the Outer Banks

A couple of entries in the guest book at a Roanoke Island B&B are telling: "Reading the guidebooks in England, we planned a quiet two weeks looking at the wildlife of the Outer Banks. We were shocked to find the wildlife of Nags Head was the human variety."

And another: "We planned a beach weekend, but exploring this wonderful island became our priority."

This "wonderful island" is a new destination of choice for people in search of the Outer Banks of yore. Only lately being "discovered," Roanoke Island stands in contrast to much of the Outer Banks. The traditional simplicity of the famed barrier island off the coast of northeastern North Carolina, especially the busiest stretch between Nags Head and Kill Devil Hills, has been forever altered by commercial and residential development in the last decade.

Sure, the extremities of the Outer Banks still have places for escape: The unspoiled southern stretches around Cape Hatteras and Ocracoke Island, if you can get to them. The luxury northern stretches around Duck, Sanderling and Corolla, if you can afford them. But for most of the annual six million visitors a year, the Outer Banks means days on the beach, evenings at miniature golf courses or bars, and nights in motels, condos or house shares.

A change of pace is offered by Roanoke Island, a few miles back toward the mainland across a causeway from Nags Head and bordered by the Intracoastal Waterway. Here, on a more sheltered island twelve miles long and several miles wide, Sir Walter Raleigh's party of adventurers founded the first English-speaking settlement in America in 1587 – before Jamestown and Plymouth Rock. The settlement mysteriously disappeared and is remembered as the lost colony.

Historic Manteo (pronounced MAN-te-o) survives as the county seat and lately has blossomed as a waterfront resort of character.

"This is quiet and quaint, a refuge amid the hustle and bustle," says Bebe Woody, a native and retired National Park Service ranger-turned-innkeeper on Roanoke Island. "We have retained what the Outer Banks has lost."

People staying at her B&B or at others in Manteo can walk to three good restaurants and a 1950s-style theater showing movies for $3 a night. They wander the boardwalks around the waterfront and enjoy the new Roanoke Island Festival Park. They enjoy the famed outdoor pageant "The Lost Colony." They visit museums and formal English gardens. They bike or hike along a new six-mile bicycle trail from bridge to bridge or down to the sleepy fishing community of Wanchese. Just across the causeway lie Nags Head, the beaches, the national seashore and all the other attractions of the Outer Banks.

Roanoke Island gives visitors a respite and a sampling of a vanishing way of life.

Inn Spots

This being essentially an area of motels, condos and family rentals, there are precious few inns and B&Bs. These are clustered in Manteo and in Nags Head, just across the causeway. We also include a sophisticated beachy B&B in Duck and an upgraded B&B under new ownership on Ocracoke Island.

First Colony Inn, 6720 South Virginia Dare Trail, Nags Head 27959.

The last of the old beach-style hotels along the Outer Banks, the First Colony is an anomaly. Its location is the farthest south in the United States for a shingle-style building in the coastal vernacular style. "It's actually a northern New England-type Victorian building, a pretty weird animal around here," according to Camille Lawrence, the woman responsible for its survival today.

The structure was built in 1932 as a 60-room, two-bath inn on the oceanfront near Jockey's Ridge. A developer had it slated for demolition in 1988 when Camille, her husband Richard and their four grown offspring stepped in. Camille tells a gripping tale of a long Memorial Day holiday weekend of maneuvers as this far-flung family of architects, preservationists and entrepreneurs resolved to stave off the wreckers. A special Planning Board meeting allowed the Lawrences to move the structure against the utility company's wishes. After the inn was cut into three sections and loaded on trucks, it was moved nearly four miles down the road to family-owned land between the main highway and the coastal road. Here they reconfigured the three-story structure into 26 spacious guestrooms, rebuilt two floors of wraparound porches and completed a meticulous rehab that placed the structure on the National Register.

Three years later, appropriately on Memorial Day weekend, the Lawrences opened. Guestrooms vary in size, view and bed configuration. Each is furnished with English antiques and reproductions. A tiled bath with English toiletries and a

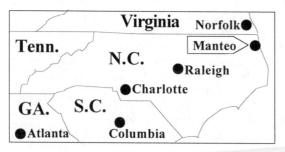

heated towel rack are standard. So are television, telephone and a refrigerator. Our rear-corner room on the third floor was extra-large, with a view of the ocean. It came with a kingsize fishnet canopy bed, a day bed, a wet bar with a microwave, two

Outdoor pool in sand dunes awaits guests at First Colony Inn.

armchairs in the dormer, a writing desk and good marine art on the walls. And, thank goodness, the windows opened to let in the sea air. The bathroom, though lacking one of the inn's several jacuzzis, was sumptuous, from the shaving mirror to the oversize towels. The second-floor veranda that wraps around the inn is great for relaxing. So is a handsome second-floor sitting room/library with old beams, fireplace, a pump organ, games and considerable memorabilia regarding the inn's history and its move. Iced tea, wine, crackers and cheese are offered here in the afternoon.

In the morning, guests gather for a substantial continental breakfast in a snug dining room with fresh flowers in a cream pitcher on each linened table. Sideboards at either end hold juices, pastries and fresh fruit, along with the day's special: broccoli and bacon quiche one morning, cheese strata the next.

A large outdoor pool lies in the rear dunes just beyond the main-floor veranda. A private boardwalk leads past some rental cottages owned by the Lawrences across the road to the ocean beach.

(252) 441-2343 or (800) 368-9390. Fax (252) 441-9234. Twenty-six rooms with private baths. Memorial Day to Labor Day: doubles, $175 to $265 weekends, $150 to $240 midweek. Spring and fall: $130 to $205 weekends, $110 to $185 midweek. November-March: $90 to $165 weekends, $75 to $150 midweek. Two-night minimum weekends most of year, three-night minimum on holidays. No smoking.

The Tranquil House Inn, 405 Queen Elizabeth St., Box 2045, Manteo 27954.
Like most of its compatriots, the old Tranquil House Inn, built in 1885, burned in the 1950s. This was rebuilt in 1988 and occupies a prime spot alongside Shallowbag Bay, across from the illuminated tourist attraction Elizabeth II, a reproduction of the ship that brought the first colonists to America.

Owners Don and Lauri Just from Richmond, who scoured the East Coast for their first innkeeping venture, liken the experience to "being a flight attendant on an airplane that never lands." Their chatty welcome letter admits "we were eager, if not informed."

The guest would not know it, although some rooms do have their idiosyncrasies and some in the front look over the parking lot. Ten come with two double beds and a single wing chair. Some suites have queen beds and small sitting rooms. There's no "typical" room. Decor includes stained and beveled glass, designer wallpapers, hardwood floors with oriental rugs, berber carpets and dried flower arrangements. Ours was a huge third-floor room with king bed, a sofabed, three wing chairs scattered around the perimeter, a large dressing room/closet and a double vanity just outside the bathroom. Cheery in blue and mauve, the layout was nonetheless peculiar. There was a great water view but from windows so high you had to stand to see out. The bed was backed against the wall beneath.

No matter. We simply helped ourselves to the welcoming wine, cheese and crackers put out in the service area and joined everyone else out on the second-floor balcony facing the waterfront. Dinner in the **1587** restaurant on the main floor was a treat (see Dining Spots).

Continental breakfast the next morning from the same service area turned out to be special, too. Fresh fruit, two kinds of cereal and sausage biscuits made for a filling repast. We worked it off by climbing to the fourth-floor observation tower, which is furnished like a library and has doors open on two sides.

(252) 473-1404 or (800) 458-7069. Fax (252) 473-1526. Twenty-five rooms with private baths. Doubles, $129 to $169 in summer, $89 to $139 in spring and fall, $79 to $99 in winter.

The White Doe Inn, 319 Sir Walter Raleigh St., Manteo 27954.

A couple of park rangers loved the Outer Banks too much to accept a promotion that would have meant a move to Atlanta or Washington. Bob and Bebe Woody decided instead that a B&B would be a good retirement project. They acquired a landmark Queen Anne residence on Bebe's native Roanoke Island and converted it in 1995 into a B&B listed on the National Register.

"The house had been vacant three years and needed the attention we could give it," said Bebe. The hospitality business also was a natural for the veteran National Park Service rangers who like to promote Roanoke Island as "the way the Outer Banks used to be."

Visitors could have no better guide than Bebe, who retired after 31 years with the Cape Hatteras National Seashore, Fort Raleigh National Historic Site and Wright Brothers National Memorial. She manages the inn and serves on the Roanoke Island Commission to preserve the island's heritage. Bob does some of the breakfast preparation, carves award-winning decoys and continues as chief of interpretation and visitor services for the parks' Cape Hatteras Group.

The couple spent two years renovating the turreted 1898 Victorian, adding ten bathrooms and a gas fireplace in every bedroom. Each room has a queensize bed.

Silky linens dressed the bed in our second-floor Turret Room, pretty with white Victorian furnishings and sea-blue wallpaper flecked with delicate peach flowers. Other decorating motifs vary from one with green with gold damask and East Lake furniture to another with earthy colors, sloped ceiling, brass bed, cozy sitting area and clawfoot soaking tub. The third floor holds a large room with two queensize beds and another where the fireplace is on view both from the bed and the double jacuzzi in the bathroom. A tower suite was in the works for 1999.

Clocks tick-tock methodically in the former Victorian parlor with white walls and the darker den/library with TV and stereo, on either side of the front entry hall.

Curving wraparound porch and tower embellish Queen Anne facade of White Doe Inn.

Breakfast is served at a table with eight hand-carved chairs in the chandeliered dining room. A wraparound porch and deck allow for seating six more outside. The fare when we were there included gingered pears, sweet-potato biscuits, bagels and french toast with a side of grits.

The B&B's name derives from an Indian love legend about Virginia Dare and the Lost Colony. "It's local, the building is white and has a romantic aura about it, and it just went with the house," says Bebe. "You sit on the front porch and think this is the way life used to be."

(252) 473-9851 or (800) 473-6091. Fax (252) 473-4708. Seven rooms with private baths. Doubles, $140 to $195, Memorial Day to Labor Day; $130 to $180, spring and fall; $120 to $170, January to early April. Two-night minimum weekends most of year. Children over 12. No smoking.

Roanoke Island Inn, 305 Fernando St., Manteo 27954.

There is artistry behind the laid-back air and image of this old inn. It stems from owner John F. Wilson, an architect and eleventh-generation islander whose great-great grandmother built what was then a small, simple island house in the 1860s. Later enlarged, it was renovated as an inn in 1982 and expanded again in 1990 to provide eight comfortable guest rooms, a cottage and a second-floor breezeway porch that's to die for.

The inn's brochure is so simple as to be overlooked. The breakfast is help-yourself. The owner turns over day-to-day operations to resident manager Ada Hadley, whose car license proclaims "Newfie" for her native Newfoundland. And the rate schedule says "open Easter 'til we're tired!" So one does not expect to find such style and whimsy inside and around the grounds.

The lobby bears a fascinating ceiling with three-dimensional molding painted by an artist in 1976. The library contains replicas of a boat and a village, plus lamps fashioned from coffeepots. The second-floor breezeway porch connecting the two buildings holds rockers in which one could spend all day facing the gardens and Shallowbag Bay across the street. Birdhouses and squirrel feeders are spread around the lush grounds. A lily pond with fountain and koi is screened from view by six-foot-tall iris. Beyond is a gazebo-like affair that John built. It contains a dining table and a hammock and is said to be popular for weddings.

John also built the unusual hand-carved beds and furnished the guestrooms with this and that, in an arty cross between old lodge and beach style. Dark green is a favorite color and handsome quilts the norm. One room with a king canopy bed has a round table with three chairs, an armchair and a full bath with separate vanity. Another room with a quilted king bed with a ship replica on the dresser adjoins a small room with a twin bed and a lawn chair. A two-bedroom suite has a king poster bed, two twins and two antique loveseats, with a carved lighthouse and a rowboat on the side table. A two-bedroom cottage offers a wet bar, a clawfoot tub and a modern shower.

Continental breakfast and beverages are available in a small kitchen off the reception lobby. It was stocked with mini-muffins, danish and cereals the day we were there.

(252) 473-5511. Eight rooms and one cottage with private bath. Doubles, $128 in July and August, $88 to $118 in spring and fall. Two-night minimum stay in most rooms. Open Easter to Halloween.

Scarborough House Inn, 323 Fernando St., Manteo 27954.

Sally Scarborough was "born two streets over from here" and her husband Phil came from Wanchese, a few miles down island. They ran the Scarborough Inn on Highway 64 before selling it to their son. Now they offer five bedrooms with continental breakfast in the room in their simple shingled residence, in a quieter location and with gardens that had just won a local award at our visit.

The Scarboroughs are known for "offering a good room for the price," as a colleague put it. "We provide a refrigerator and microwave, coffee and tea, fruit and bagels, so people can eat in their rooms to keep costs down," explains Sally. Each room has a TV, a small bathroom and homey antique furnishings. One has a kingsize lace canopy bed and a table and side chairs. Two have a queen and a single bed each, small tables and one or two chairs.

The Scarboroughs refer to their premier accommodation as a cottage bungalow. A large upstairs loft has a king bed, stained-glass windows and a full bath. A downstairs workshop area with a jacuzzi tub may or may not be rented with the room.

Although there's little guest interaction, guests can mingle in a small common room or on a side porch beside the gardens and a fishpond with a waterfall.

(252) 473-3849. Four rooms and a cottage with private baths. Memorial Day to Labor Day: doubles $67, loft cottage $85 with jacuzzi ($72 without). Rest of year: doubles $60, loft $75 with jacuzzi ($65 without).

Advice 5¢, 111 Scarborough Lane, Duck 27949.

A nickel jar at the foot of the stairway in the entry to this inn is getting so heavy that Nancy Caviness and Donna Black can barely move it. The nickels are for all the advice they have dispensed since opening their sophisticated dream of a B&B beach house in 1995. They had escaped to the Outer Banks for a respite from winter in Ithaca, N.Y. Donna, a Donald Duck fan, wanted to stay at a B&B in Duck and couldn't believe there wasn't one. Friends had tried earlier to cajole Nancy

Decks and big windows are features of contemporary structure housing Advice 5¢.

into buying an old shack in upstate New York and run it as a muffin and coffee shop called Advice 5¢.

The name stuck. The B&B idea jelled while the women were in Toronto to run in a marathon. There they "brainstormed on the proverbial cocktail napkin" in a pub. An architect designed their shingled, contemporary Nags Head-style house as a B&B, nicely located in an upscale residential neighborhood midway between downtown Duck and the ocean.

All five guest quarters are on the lower floor of the striking house, which is built on pilings above the sand dunes. Each is identified by a sign, painted artistically on the door. All have private decks or porches, oak floors, contemporary cottage-style furnishings and designer linens, down comforters and duvet covers. Beds are queensize except for one room with twins. Daybreak, the largest and the only one with TV and stereo, has a bed with a shuttered headboard, a plush wicker sitting area and a spacious bath with oversize shower, double vanity and a wonderful mural of an egret in a marsh on the surround of a jacuzzi tub.

The upstairs is a great room that lives up to the name. Paneled partly in juniper wood, it opens into a vaulted ceiling and a side mezzanine. Here, with a table for four and windows on three sides, you can see both ocean and sound, sunrise and sunset. A deck stretches off the living room, and a dining room holds three tables for four. People leave the beach to return for afternoon tea, lemonade and "cookie time." The innkeepers bake everything from scratch. Breakfast begins with fresh fruit cup, fruit salad or parfait with yogurt and granola, juices, an array of baked goods and English tea or their own blend of coffee (french roast with Columbian and Mexican), so good that they sell it in a shop. The main event could be wholegrain banana-pecan pancakes or ginger or pumpkin french toast doused with fruits.

The decks provide plenty of space for relaxation. Guests also can enjoy the neighborhood association's pool and tennis court, as well as a private walkway to the beach. And yes, the innkeepers will give you plenty of advice. Just put your nickel in the jar, please.

(252) 255-1050 or (800) 238-4235. Five rooms with private baths. Doubles, May-September, $140 to $175; rest of year, $95 to $120. Children over 16. No smoking.

Berkley Manor Bed & Breakfast, Silver Lake Road (Highway 12), Box 220, Ocracoke Island 27960.

Remote Ocracoke Island finally got a good place to stay in 1998. Robert and

Amy Attaway moved from Raleigh to give the aging Berkley Center Country Inn additional rooms and infused the establishment with new comforts and amenities.

The heart of the secluded harborfront complex on several acres is the main, weathered-shingled manor house topped by a tower four-and-one-half stories high. With a spectacular island and water view, the observation tower is made for sunset watching. Five guestrooms are on the first two floors of the manor house, which is listed on the National Register. Seven more are in an adjacent two-story house.

Each of the twelve guestrooms is named for a Caribbean island, in keeping with Ocracoke's description as offering a taste of the Caribbean on the East Coast. All rooms now have private baths, three with double jacuzzis. Each room has a king or queen bed, and two have fireplaces. The premier rooms are three new ones on the main floor of the manor house, one of which has a private patio with water view. The Attaways redecorated all the rooms in what Robert calls "Caribbean plantation style." Berber carpeting, bed covers and window treatments brighten up the interiors, which are otherwise an expanse of wood from floors to walls to ceilings.

Twin, mirror-image lounges flank the central staircase in the lobby of the manor house. A full breakfast is served at two seatings in the dining room. The fare could be eggs soufflé, crab quiche, shrimp and grits or stuffed french toast. Afternoon beverages, cookies and cakes are put out in the dining room. Guests help themselves and repair to the lobby lounges or climb the five flights of stairs to the observation tower.

(252) 928-5911 or (800) 832-1223. Doubles, $125 to $175, June-September; $75 to $150 rest of year. Children over 12. No smoking.

Dining Spots

Like similar resort areas, the Outer Banks presents a staggering array of dining options. We concentrate on those nearest Manteo and Roanoke Island.

1587, At the Tranquil House Inn, 405 Queen Elizabeth St., Manteo.

The restaurant on the main floor of The Tranquil House Inn is known for some of the best food in the Outer Banks area.

Big windows face the waterfront. Peach sponge-painted walls, polished tables crossed by colorful runners, red oak flooring, blond wood trim and warm copper accents cast a mellow glow across the airy interior at nightfall. It's an appealing setting for food billed as "global fusion." Honey wheat bread with butter bearing a hint of cinnamon and a superior salad of spinach and gorgonzola with pecans, pears and roasted peppers got our dinner off to a good start. The evening's main-course choices ranged from grilled North Atlantic salmon over a wild mushroom soufflé to pan-seared pork loin medallions atop southwestern crawfish and silver queen corn hash. Among them were an excellent Asian-style lacquered mahi mahi on a bed of wilted greens and spring vegetables, plus an interesting shrimp and chicken phad thai over sesame cappellini. A bottle of Mirassou riesling accompanied from a well-chosen wine list.

Desserts included banana crème brûlée, frozen chocolate marquis, almond-cappuccino cheesecake and, our choice, Mexican tarragon ice cream in a puff pastry sandwich. Young chef Donny King from Virginia Beach made the rounds after dinner to chat with patrons.

(252) 473-1587. Entrées, $15.95 to $20.95. Dinner nightly, 5 to 10, mid-February through November. Closed Monday-Tuesday in spring and fall.

1587 restaurant faces Manteo waterfront from main floor of Tranquil House Inn.

Clara's Steam Bar & Seafood Grill, Waterfront Shops, Manteo.

Clara Shannon, part of the oldest and most ubiquitous restaurant family in the Outer Banks, runs this large, with-it establishment in the Waterfront Shoppes and condominium complex. Her parents own the venerable Owens restaurant and her cousin owns RV's restaurant, both in Nags Head. Here are a yellow bar area favored by young women at our visit, a rear dining room with booths and black tables onto the water and, a bit away from the action, a large side dining room with an art deco motif.

The last was our choice for a casual dinner that included Clara's signature tuna kabob and Mediterranean shrimp with feta cheese over angel-hair pasta. She-crab soup and a salad accompanied. Key lime pie was the least filling of the rich desserts.

The wide-ranging menu offers something for everyone. The fried calamari and grilled portobello mushroom are highly recommended appetizers. Typical of main courses are Greek chicken, prime rib, grilled Japanese salmon and something called broiled shadboat, a combination of shrimp, scallops, fish and crab cakes based on a family recipe.

(252) 473-1727. Entrées, $9.99 to $18.99. Open daily, 11:30 to 8:30 or 9.

Full Moon Café, Waterfront Shops, Manteo.

Outdoor tables in the courtyard are the seating of choice at this establishment with a vaguely tearoom atmosphere inside. White trellis dividers break up the expanse of glass-topped tables, and cobalt blue vases and mauve walls lend color.

The menu is extensive, particularly for lunch, when the Full Moon is said to be at its best with exotic sandwiches (how about a black bean burger?) salads, quiche, eggplant napoleon and pasta.

The dinner menu changes nightly. The dozen entrées when we were there ranged from Low Country shrimp and polenta ("the house version of shrimp and grits") and salmon topped with lump crab to pan-seared pork tenderloin with raspberry coulis and beef charron, both served over polenta. The shrimp and crab enchilada is a local favorite.

(252) 473-6666. Entrées, $8.95 to $18.95. Open daily, 11:30 to 9. No dinner Monday-Wednesday in off-season.

The Lone Cedar Café, Manteo Causeway, Nags Head.

Overlooking Roanoke Sound, this newcomer is one of the few Outer Banks restaurants with a water view. It's named for the former Lone Cedar hunt club across the road, which was favored by fishermen and duck hunters for communal hunt-club meals.

The family-run restaurant is built in the Nags Head style with wraparound porches on the outside and a spacious paneled dining room with green and white checked oilcloths at booths and tables.

The chefs know how to cook fish and game, according to the local clientele, and the cornbread is exceptional. Much of the seafood comes broiled or fried, an exception being the grilled tuna steak served on a sweet corn salsa and a special of grilled dolphin topped with crabmeat and asparagus. The crab cakes, soft-shell crabs and oysters are favorites on the extensive menu.

The house specialty is Cedar Island game pie, a blend of duck, game hen and sirloin tips with vegetables and sweet potato crust. The mixed grill teams tuna, honey-dijon chicken and filet mignon.

(252) 441-5495. Entrées, $10.95 to $19.95. Lunch daily, 11:30 to 3; dinner, 5 to 10.

Owens' Restaurant, Beach Road, Nags Head.

This is the granddaddy of Outer Banks restaurants, started by owner Clara Owens Shannon's grandmother in the 1947. It's large, locally popular and consistent, Clara still watching every plate that comes out of the kitchen and her husband Lionel seating patrons who sometimes endure long waits in the gift shop (no reservations are taken). We found it far more polished and with better food than similarly large and touristy seafood establishments that we have learned to avoid.

White-clothed tables, vases of roses, oil lamps and low lighting lend glamour to a series of dining rooms that seem to ramble on and on. Each intimate room has its own staff. The family's collection of early seafaring and Outer Banks memorabilia convey a sense of place.

The encyclopedic dinner menu features "classic coastal cuisine." That translates to almost every conceivable choice from pecan-encrusted Carolina catfish to Maine lobster to Smithfield pork ribs to tenderloin of beef wellington. Crackers with wispride cheese and a bread basket of hushpuppies staved off hunger before our main dishes arrived: delectable fried oysters with rémoulade sauce, shoe-string potatoes and apple coleslaw and the Hatteras combination: a mix of broiled shrimp, sea scallops and lump crabmeat. From a pretty dessert tray lined with roses came blueberry cheesecake and key lime mousse with belgian chocolate.

(252) 441-7309. Entrées, $14.95 to $27.95. Dinner nightly, 5 to 10. Closed January to mid-February.

Other Choices. Father afield from Roanoke Island are more good dining spots. Among the best are the top-rated **Ocean Boulevard** in Kitty Hawk, its sister restaurant **Blue Point Bar & Grill** in Duck, **Flying Fish Café and Colington Café** in Kill Devil Hills, and **Elizabeth's Café** in Duck.

Diversions

The Outer Banks are a family vacation destination, famed particularly for their beaches. Everyone should visit the **Wright Brothers National Memorial** at Kill Devil Hills, where the intrepid brothers launched man's first powered flight. **Jockey's Ridge State Park,** site of the East Coast's highest sand dunes, is known for great sunset views, kite flying and hang gliding. The **Cape Hatteras National Seashore,** a 75-mile strand, is the country's first national seashore. As opposed to a beach playground, Roanoke Island promotes itself as an educational and historical experience.

Fort Raleigh National Historic Site, Roanoke Island.

The park service oversees the 143-acre property where Sir Walter Raleigh's explorers and colonists settled in 1585, about three miles northwest of Manteo. In the visitor center, a seventeen-minute movie details the fascinating drama of the lost colonists, who disappeared without a trace three years after their arrival from Britain. Beyond the center, trails lead to the restored fort, which amounts to little more than earthen embankments. A nature trail winds through the woods past the site of the long-gone dwellings built by the colonists outside the fort.

(252) 473-5772. Open daily, 9 to 5, to 6 in summer. Free.

"The Lost Colony," the nation's oldest outdoor pageant, is performed under the stars in the Fort Raleigh National Historic Site's newly refurbished Waterside Theater. First produced in 1937, the pageant proved so successful it has played every summer since, attracting more than three million spectators and inspiring the creation of other pageants. The symphonic drama of song and dance is constantly evolving, recreating itself with new talent and technical improvements.

(252) 473-3414 or (800) 488-5012. Nightly except Saturday at 8:30, early June to late August. All seating reserved. Tickets, $14.

North Carolina Aquarium/Roanoke Island, Airport Road, Manteo.

One of three state-supported aquariums, this is a place for families, who were out in force at our visit. There are touch tables, small tanks and all kinds of hands-on and audio-visual exhibits. For us the highlight was the outdoor courtyard with a pond, a "turtle crossing" and three languid alligators. The grounds extend to Croaton Sound. The aquarium was closed in 1999 for renovations and a major addition. It was scheduled to reopen in spring 2000.

(252) 473-3493 or (800) 832-3474. Open Monday-Saturday 9 to 7 in summer, to 5 rest of year. Adults $3, children $1.

Roanoke Island Festival Park, Manteo.

Opened in 1998, this new festival park occupies 26 acres fronting Shallowbag Bay across from the Manteo waterfront. It represents the expansion of the Elizabeth II State Historic Site. The Elizabeth II, a 69-foot sailing ship moored along the waterfront, is a reproduction built in 1984 of the 16th-century vessels that brought the first colonists to Roanoke Island and America. Costumed guides explain the intricacies of the ship and the lifestyles of those who sailed it. A new exhibit hall is a hands-on, interactive museum. Visitors enter through the facade of a tall ship to walk through four centuries of history, including an Elizabethan parlor, an English colony, the Freedman colony, and boat building and fishing exhibits. A 50-minute movie, "The Legend of Two Paths," portrays Native American culture during the early English settlement. The Roanoke Island Institute of the North Carolina School of the Arts presents cultural arts programs in the new amphitheater pavilion near the water. Boardwalks connect the main building to nature paths and bike trails throughout the park.

(252) 475-1500. Open daily, 9 to 5, April-October; 10 to 4, rest of year. Adults, $8.

In Manteo, the **George Washington Creef Memorial Park,** on waterfront land donated by local families, contains a boardwalk extending from the marshlands across from the Roanoke Island Inn to the bridge to the festival park next to the Tranquil House Inn. The Davis Boatworks building on Queen Elizabeth Street is becoming the **North Carolina Maritime History Museum on Roanoke Island.** It's linked with the Roanoke Island Festival Park but under auspices of the North Carolina Maritime Museum at Beaufort. The museum opened in 1998 with several small race boats built by the Davis brothers and two of the only four surviving shad boats built locally by George Washington Creef. It's open daily in summer; free.

Shopping. New stores seem to pop up every year in downtown Manteo. Most of the action is centered around the Waterfront Shoppes. Grouped around an interior courtyard are stores like the **Island Trading Co.** with artworks and dinnerware, **Island Nautical** with antique lanterns and life preservers, and **Charlotte's,** a women's apparel boutique. Across the street are the new **Carriage House** for flowers and gifts and **Water Street Station**, an apparel and gift shop. The large **Manteo Bookstore** has strong regional and nature sections. Candles incorporating shells are featured at the **Candle Factory.** We admired the cute painted birdhouses at **My Secret Garden. Clemmons on Budleigh** is a good new antiques shop. Bonnie and Bob Morrill, who have a studio in Wanchese, sell their delightful **Wanchese Pottery** in a retail shop in a former boat shed at 107 Fernando St.

Manteo is also home of the world-famous **Christmas Shop** and the **Island Gallery,** a complex of seven multi-level buildings along Highway 64 on the east side of town. Here you'll find an extravaganza of 33 rooms, decorated Christmas trees, thousands of ornaments, gifts, collectibles and artworks.

Otherwise, the area's most interesting specialty stores and boutiques are in Duck.

Extra Special

The **Elizabethan Gardens,** Fort Raleigh National Historic Site, Roanoke Island.

This formal English garden is a shady and tranquil waterside retreat away from the hubbub. The Garden Club of North Carolina created the 16th-century-style garden as a living memorial to the ill-fated lost colonists. From a brick gatehouse furnished with period furniture and English portraits, you wander along pine-needled walkways through a variety of gardens and trees. Antique statuary, fountains, a sunken parterre garden and herb and rose beds are among the highlights. Relax and listen to the bird songs in an English thatched-roof gazebo near the shore of Roanoke Sound. Then check out the ancient live oak, believed to have been alive in 1585 when the first colonists landed.

(252) 473-3234. Open daily 9 to 5, to 8 in summer when "The Lost Colony" is playing next door. Adults $3.

Historic Barker House (center) backs up to waterfront in heart of Edenton.

Edenton, N.C.

Eden Off the Beaten Path

They call it "the prettiest town in the South." And who'd challenge the claim? Especially after enjoying an early-morning bicycle ride through the streets of this aptly named Eden.

This off-the-beaten-path community of 5,000, North Carolina's second oldest, is nestled around a bay along Albemarle Sound in the northeastern corner of the state. It could be the epitome of an old Southern town, except that when natives refer to "The War" they mean not the War between the States but the Revolution. Here in 1774, area women staged the Edenton Tea Party, a forerunner of the Boston event. Edenton, which was incorporated in 1722 as the first capital of the colony of North Carolina, was named for Lords Proprietary governor Charles Eden. It could just as well have been named for the Eden of Adam and Eve.

Nicely situated along a beautifully open waterfront, it is a quiet backwater town of parklands and gardens, old homes and stately buildings. Nothing intrudes on the reverie. The imposing 1758 Cupola House and Gardens stand right across from commercial buildings at the foot a main street that hasn't changed all that much in more than 200 years. The landmark 1782 Barker House is up against the water on a point in the bay. The impressive Georgian county courthouse faces a green extending to the bay. Scores of old homes are sited close to the street; a few occupy broad lawns. No particular architectural style predominates. "The tremendous diversity of architecture is one of our treasures," according to Historic Edenton tour guide Bill Strong. Many share a common feature generally found farther South: no basements, and double porches, upstairs and down.

There's a palpable air of tranquility. Nothing hustles or bustles in this town. People fish beside three cannons facing the placid waterfront. They picnic in the waterfront park. The last commercial intrusions, some oil tanks, were razed in 1997. The wide-open waterscape now stretches across virtually the entire town.

Cypress trees grow starkly out of the water, and a wreck of a boat lies tilted near the pier. The stunning view across Edenton Bay and Albemarle Sound from the waterfront parks, the tree-lined streets graced by fine homes from earlier eras and the courthouse green all combine for a storybook, small-town scene dripping with atmosphere and charm.

"Edenton Is a Special Place" is the name of the introductory video shown at the visitor center. Indeed it is.

Inns Spots

The Lords Proprietors' Inn, 300 North Broad St., Edenton 27932.

Arch and Jane Edwards moved their family from a high-powered life in Washington, D.C., to open one of the first of the South's new breed of inns in 1982. They bought a late Queen Anne house built of Edenton brick in 1901 and opened an eight-room B&B on the main street. They outgrew it as soon as they opened the doors, so quickly expanded next door into the much older (1801) Satterfield House. The venture has since grown to a complex of five buildings with twenty gracious guest rooms and an exceptional restaurant.

Bedrooms are outfitted with king or queen beds (except for two with twins). They are sedately elegant with antiques, good artworks and interesting window treatments. TV/VCRs and telephones are the norm. Expect the odd stenciling and hooked rug. The most striking thing about those in the main house may be their color schemes: pink and mint in one, coffee brown in another, bright wedgwood blue and yellow in a third. The ground floor is big enough for two guest rooms as well as a guest parlor with port and sherry awaiting in decanters, a help-yourself guest kitchen for soft drinks and homemade cookies, an office and a gift shop owned by a local woman. The four bedrooms in the adjacent Satterfield House are crisp and colorful and share a living room painted dark blue.

The prized accommodations are in the rear Pack House, a converted tobacco packing structure that was moved to the property. Here, Arch designed a huge double parlor with two fireplaces and a soaring ceiling, flanked by a mezzanine leading to the second-floor rooms. Four large guest rooms are on each floor. Most have canopy beds and armoires made by famed cabinetmaker Ben Hobbs from nearby Hertford. One in front looks rather Vermonty and another has a Pennsylvania Dutch feeling. Three premium upstairs rooms with high sloping ceilings have kingsize beds, seating areas with sofas and plump chairs, baths with tubs and separate showers (one big enough for two). Two in back have outdoor decks.

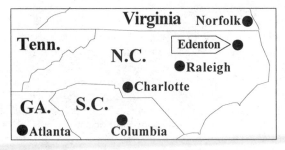

Dinner is served Tuesday-Saturday at 7 or 7:30 and is included in the rates. Chef Kevin Yokley, formerly an assistant at the acclaimed Fearrington House Restaurant near

Brick house at Lords Proprietors' Inn was among first of South's new breed of inns.

Chapel Hill, has been with the Edwardses since they added dinner service in 1992. Arch designed and built the Whedbee House with palladian windows and white damask-linened tables for the purpose. Colorful in blue/gray and yellow, it's an elegant setting for candlelit dinners. The four-course meal changes nightly. At our visit, it opened with roasted quail with red onion slaw and goat cheese, followed by the inn's salad. There was a choice of entrée: crab cakes with sherry dipping sauce or medallions of beef with portobello mushroom sauce. Dessert was cranberry bread with butterscotch and vanilla ice cream or chocolate extravaganza.

(Dinner is open by reservation to the public for $45 prix-fixe, plus a fee for membership in a dining club that allows outsiders to be served alcoholic beverages.)

This room or its adjacent patio is the setting for a southern breakfast, the fare changing daily. The inn is known for its soufflé pancakes, waffles and french toast.

(252) 482-3641 or (888) 394-7722. Fax (252) 482-2432. Twenty rooms with private baths. Rates include gratuities. Doubles, Tuesday-Saturday, $185 to $235 MAP; Sunday and Monday, $125 to $175, B&B. Children welcome. Smoking restricted. No credit cards.

Granville Queen Themed Inn, 108 South Granville St., Edenton 27932.

A rowboat is suspended from the sloping ceiling above the antique double bed in the Captain Queen's Quarters in this inn that's themed within an inch of its life. Innkeepers Marge and Ken Dunne call this their masculine room, with heavy carved furnishings, a window seat and a private balcony off a small sitting room.

For feminine, consider the Queen of Queens Room, which has a massive carved queen bed with matching armoire and bureaus. "Isn't this exquisite?" asks Marge. Perhaps, though not according to the usual definition. Try stately and overwhelming. She moves on to the bathroom, which "is even prettier than the room," with palms at either end of the tub beside a window. Or how about the Queen Victoria, lacy in pink and blue? The centerpiece of the bathroom is a "throne" draped in lacy canopy.

Just when you think you've seen everything you're shown to the Egyptian Queen Room. Two 800-pound bronze sphinxes rest beside two carved black chairs, another type of throne backed by fabric canopy. Ahead is an extra-low kingsize bed covered with a leopard-skin throw. A TV faces the bed, which must be the viewing area of choice for the throne chairs appear rather useless. The sink in the luxurious bathroom has cobra-handled faucets. This room is so themed it has its own web site, Marge advises, and so popular it has a waiting list.

There's more. In the Peaches and Queen Room with handcrafted furniture from an estate in Italy, the bath is done in glass and marble. Water spews out of the wall in the sit-down shower section of a soaking tub for two, with a chandelier overhead. The Queen's Highness Room comes with two inlaid walnut double beds, a gas fireplace, a tub paneled in mahogany and marble, and faucets of sculptured fish.

And still more. Breakfast is a five-course affair, from homemade apple crunch and fresh fruit cup through entrée of folded eggs, rosemary potatoes and a choice of grilled chicken or filet mignon. Dessert is a Southern pancake resembling a soufflé, sprinkled with sugar and pecans, or a blueberry and crème cheese crêpe. Marge and Ken cook and, they say, people eat every bit.

The Dunnes moved from Long Island in 1991 to acquire the inn, which had just been opened by Californians who spent a bundle on the renovating the 1907 house, not to mention the imported furnishings from Italy, China, Holland, Thailand and England. "We liked the themes so continued them," said Marge, who obviously relishes the role.

The chandeliered dining room contains butterfly chairs from Spain at pink-clothed tables, but breakfast generally is taken at seven wrought-iron tables with big wicker chairs on the enclosed Plantation Porch. The living room has an ornate carved ceiling, recessed lights and an antique square piano dating to 1800. The theme idea may overwhelm, but there's an aura of taste and elegance and, thankfully, no clutter. Young people, in particular, like the air of fantasy

All rooms have TV with VCR and telephones. Many have fireplaces and private balconies. This is a comfortable place with lots of common space and a wrap-around porch in which to spread out. Amazingly, the rates are about half what you might expect.

(252) 482-5296. Nine rooms with private baths. Doubles, $95 to $105. No children. No credit cards. No smoking.

Trestle House Inn, 632 Soundside Road, Edenton 27932.

Several miles out in the country is this lodge-style B&B built of 400-year-old California redwood that had been railroad trestles. Where the in-town inns exude history, this caters to eco-tourism. Peter Bogus and Wendy Jewett, 1996 transplants from Connecticut, are nothing if not versatile. While she works in town, he keeps the inn, leads canoeing and fishing expeditions, and makes Peter's Piping Hot Sauce, marmalades and herbal vinegars from organic materials they grow outside and sell under their private Willow Tree Farm label across the country.

The sprawling, contemporary-style house, built in 1972 as a hunting retreat, sits on five acres overlooking a wildlife refuge and a large pond fed by nearby Albemarle Sound. The pair undertook a total renovation of what had been an off-again, on-again B&B.

They named five guest rooms, equipped with private baths and TVs, for birds sighted from their windows. The largest is the Egret with a kingsize sleigh bed of

Bronze sphinxes flank chairs in Egyptian Queen Room at Granville Queen Themed Inn.

solid chestnut. Also on the second floor are the twin-bedded Mallard with some amazing sponge-painted walls done by Peter and the Heron with a queensize sleigh bed. The main floor holds the Osprey with two double antique oak beds and the Cormorant with a queensize bed and an Italian-tiled bathroom containing a commode with a molded seat ("so comfortable the guests rave about it," says Peter).

Also on the main floor beneath the redwood beamed ceiling is a lodge-like family room with a fieldstone fireplace. A large game room offers a billiards table and wet bar. There's also a small exercise room with steam bath.

Peter serves complimentary wine at check-in. Guests often take it to the spacious rear deck overlooking the pond, where we paused to watch a great blue heron. They can play with the inn's goats and canoe into the Sound.

A gourmet breakfast is served in the side Cook Room, full of plants and colorful with pottery and baskets. It has an open barbecue grill and wet bar. The morning fare might be baked stuffed blueberry french toast or Dr. Seuss's green eggs and ham. Peter may interrupt your reverie to point out rare birds that aren't supposed to be in this region.

(252) 482-2282 or (800) 645-8466. Five rooms with private baths. Doubles, $80 to $95. No smoking.

Captain's Quarters Inn, 202 West Queen St., Edenton 27932.

A nautical theme prevails in this 1907 Colonial Revival house, renovated in 1994 from an apartment house by Bill and Phyllis Pepper. They offer eight guest rooms with a sailing captain theme. Each has TV, telephone and a king, queen or two twin beds.

The second outside entry off the pillared porch testifies to the building's apartment heritage. It leads to upstairs rooms like the front Captain's Cabin by the Sea, colorful in orange and mint green, with a canopied queen bed made by area cabinetmaker Ben Hobbs. The Capt. Dennis Connors Room is Phyllis's tribute to

San Diego, with sailing posters, lots of florals, an extra day bed and a bathroom converted from a kitchen. She stuffed a treasure chest full of jewelry and gold coins at the foot of the poster bed in Blackbeard's Room. She decorated Captain Quilt's Room to show off a handmade friendship quilt on wall. The rear clipper ship Cutty Sark Room is paneled in dark birch to look like a stateroom, with portholes in a side wall . The premier Captain of Her Heart Room, romantic in pink and burgundy, has a raised corner jacuzzi in what had been a kitchen, plus a huge, tiled shower for two.

Guests enjoy a large living room with library, an informal gathering room and a 65-foot-long wraparound porch with swings and rockers.

Bill offers daily cruises as well as sailing weekends on his 34-foot-foot sloop "Sandpiper." Phyllis stays home to ready afternoon refreshments, including tea cakes and cookies, cheese and crackers to go with tea, lemonade, wine or beer. She serves guests dinner by reservation on sailing and mystery weekends.

A three-course breakfast is served in the dining room. Juice and fruit are followed by a choice of omelets, blueberry pancakes or raspberry stuffed french toast. Breakfast trifle is the dessert. A lavish buffet is featured on Sunday mornings.

(252) 482-8945 or (800) 482-8945. Eight rooms with private baths. Doubles $80 to $95. No smoking.

The Albemarle House, 204 West Queen St., Edenton 27932.

The newest in a lineup of B&Bs along Queen Street, this circa 1900 house also is relatively new by Edenton standards. Marijane and Reuel Schappel moved from Rochester, N.Y., in 1995 to convert the private residence into a B&B. There are enough antiques, stenciling, lace curtains, clock chimes, woven shawls and collections to qualify it as a much older house – perhaps like your great-grandmother's from the 19th century.

An old crank victrola resides in the parlor, along with an enormous collection of June McKenna Collectibles. Flag bunting decorated the hall stairway rail at our visit, although Marijane changes it seasonally to Williamsburg greens. Quilts and more collections shared the upstairs hall with stuffed animals and family photos.

All rooms come with queensize beds, TVs and private baths. The front blue room has a lace canopy bed, a wing chair, an old Ansco camera on the bureau and a TV atop an old radio. A rear suite has a queen sleigh bed in one room and a quilted double in a second room. We slept well in the cherry sleigh bed in the James Iredell Room, named for a justice on the first U.S. Supreme Court.

An early-morning ride on one of the Schappels' bicycles around the town ablaze with crape myrtle and shiny magnolia foliage proved enjoyable. Residents waved as we passed by. The exercise worked up an appetite for breakfast by candlelight with classical music in the dining room. Marijane served cantaloupe, "yum yum coffeecake" and ham and cheese omelets with a pansy garnish. Blueberry pancakes, pecan waffles and strawberry french toast are offered other days.

Reuel, a sailor of note, offers guests three-hour cruises on Albemarle Sound on his 28-foot cruising sloop "Wanderer." He also gives midweek "Learn to Sail" classes. He finds sailing the sound much more palatable than his former venue, Lake Ontario. "It's almost deserted," he says. "If you find more than half a dozen boats at any time, you know it's a holiday."

(252) 482-8204. Three rooms and one suite with private baths. Doubles, $80. Suite, $125 for four. Children over 10. No smoking.

Pillars and wraparound porch grace facade of Governor Eden Inn.

Governor Eden Inn, 304 North Broad St., Box 1145, Edenton 27932.

This lovely house of neoclassical design is fronted by massive Ionic columns, oval beveled-glass portals and a majestic wraparound porch. The curving upper balcony overlooks tree-lined Broad Street, the old Virginia Post Road.

Ruth Shackelford and her late husband opened it as a B&B in 1988 after their three children left home, and its sale as a B&B was pending as this book went to press.

The main floor has a fireplaced foyer with a grand staircase, a living room and a dining room with a table set for ten. Here is where breakfast of pancakes or bacon and eggs is served. Afternoon refreshments are offered on the upper balcony.

The upstairs holds four guest rooms, all with private baths and TV. One of the two in the front corners has twin beds. The other has a queen bed with an Empire dresser.

Toward the rear is a queen room with a bath in which the clawfoot tub is raised on a platform and framed by pink and white curtains. Women are partial to this room, while men like its counterpart across the hall. It has a queen canopy bed and two comfy platform rockers in front of the TV.

(252) 482-2072. Four rooms with private baths. Doubles, $80. No smoking.

Dining Spots

Waterman's Grill, 427 South Broad St., Edenton.

The most versatile restaurant in town is this nautical haunt in a brick storefront near the foot of Broad Street. Dining is on two floors amid brick walls, covered with nautical photos and artifacts, a spiral staircase in the center and a paneled bar at the end.

It's a lively, pleasing setting for such seafood specialties as crab cakes with hushpuppies, the waterman's trio (steamed crabmeat, shrimp and scallops), fried shrimp and fried oysters. Cashew-crusted tilapia with beurre blanc, cajun tuna shrimp, and shrimp and crawfish étouffée were specials the night we dined. We tried the last, an assertive concoction served over rice. The meal comes with steamed broccoli or two vegetables from a selection of usual suspects. The waitress talked us into the specialty steamed broccoli – "it's good, and something green." It arrived on a side plate covered with a big saucer and a bowl of hollandaise sauce, with a saw-tooth knife for cutting. The ice water contained a slice of lemon; the crusty roll came without butter. The short wine list is quite good and nicely priced in the teens.

Crab bites, tuna bites, hush puppies, chilled crab dip with crackers and afore-mentioned steamed broccoli comprise most of the appetizers. Seafood is available from a raw bar. Featured desserts are "liquor milkshakes," topped with whipped cream. The bill comes with a chocolate mint.

(252) 482-7733. Entrées, $9.95 to $15.95. Lunch, Monday 11 to 3. Lunch and dinner, Tuesday-Saturday 11:30 to 10.

Dram Tree Restaurant, 112 West Water St., Edenton.

The fanciest restaurant in town is this large complex that started life as a bottling shop. The main, high-ceilinged dining room is pleasant in gray and burgundy. It features a stunning mural of a dram tree in Albemarle Sound. More diners can be seated in the side Garden Room overlooking a courtyard and fountain.

The extensive dinner menu offers something for everyone. Among starters are coconut shrimp, seafood crêpes, baked brie and crab cakes. Main courses range widely from shrimp scampi and crab imperial to roast duck with orange sauce, veal dijon, filet mignon and rack of lamb. Martha Collier, owner with her husband Ron, makes the desserts. The wine list is quite serviceable and affordably priced.

Next door, the Colliers offer two overnight suites to groups and families, plus a third single room for business people. The two suites are entered off a main-floor living room. Doubles are $75, plus $10 for each extra person. Rates include a full breakfast in the Garden Room.

(252) 482-2711. Entrées, $12.95 to $21.95. Dinner, Friday-Tuesday 5 to 9. Sunday brunch, 11:30 to 2.

Creekside Restaurant & Bar, 406 West Queen St., Edenton.

This welcome newcomer opened in late 1998 in the quarters that formerly housed the popular Boswell's. Owner Gail Finan renovated the large restaurant into a 100-seat dining room plus a banquet facility. Executive chef Delbert White Jr., a former Wall Street trader, exercises his culinary skills acquired through world-wide travels.

His opening dinner menu contained such entrées as "drunken" Gulf shrimp marinated in lime and tequila, pan-fried crab cake, blackened catfish, smothered fried chicken, grilled pork medallions with peach and ginger sauce and prime rib with grilled mushrooms and roasted garlic. Among starters were a beer-battered bloomin' onion, grilled portobello mushroom over mixed greens, wood-smoked salmon and a basket of Southern fries (sweet-potato fries with fried onions and jalapeño peppers). Desserts, based on the chef's family recipes, included Chowan peanut pie, peach cobbler, chocolate layer cake and wild berry sorbet with three-berry compote.

Innovative salads and sandwiches are offered for lunch at bargain prices.

(252) 482-0118. Entrées, $8.95 to $16.95. Lunch, Monday-Friday 11 to 2. Dinner, Monday-Saturday 5 to 10 or 11.

Diversions

History and the water are the hallmarks of Edenton. The town is always interesting, but at its best when houses are open for the biennial spring Pilgrimage and the annual Christmas tour, when it's decked out in Williamsburg style. Edenton Bay opens onto Albemarle Sound, the largest fresh-water sound in the country and a paradise for sailors.

Historic Edenton State Historic Site, 108 North Broad St., Edenton. (252) 482-2637.

Several notable Colonial buildings are located on this site at the north end of downtown. Tours begin at the visitor center, a late 19th-century house, where a fourteen-minute orientation video relates the fascinating history of "a special place." A map for a 1.5-mile walking tour details 28 designated historic sites. A variety of guided tours also are offered for a fee. The best is the Historic Edenton overview tour, offered Monday-Saturday 9:30 to 11:30 and 2 to 4, April-October; Tuesday-Saturday 10:30 to 12:30 rest of year (adults $7).

Among tour sites:

The Cupola House, 408 South Broad St., was long thought to be the oldest house in town. Lately it was found to have been built not in 1725 but rather in 1758. The oldest title is now held by the privately owned Edmund Hatch House, built in 1744. Built in the Jacobean style with a cupola on top, the house is unusual in that no additions have been built. The interior is notable for period furnishings and fine woodwork. Guides point out a three-sided crib at the foot of the parents' bed, eliminating the need for slats on the fourth side. In an early example of graffiti, a young resident left her tiny mark on the window pane of the children's room, inscribing the rhyme "When this you see, Remember me," her initials and the date, April 15, 1835. The gardens have been re-created from a 1769 map.

The **Chowan County Courthouse** on East King Street, dating to 1767, is considered the finest Georgian courthouse in the South and one of the outstanding buildings of Colonial America. Closed for renovations at our visit, it faces a wonderful green laid out in 1712 and stretching down to the bay. The green is flanked by handsome houses.

The **Edenton Teapot** on the green commemorates the Edenton Tea Party, the earliest known instance of political activity on the part of women in the American colonies. A marker tells how 51 women resolved in 1774 to discontinue "that pernicious custom of drinking tea" and voted not to buy any more goods from England.

St. Paul's Episcopal Church, Broad and Church streets, is one of the finest Colonial churches in the South. Built from 1736 to 1766, North Carolina's oldest chartered church is unusual in that it does not face the street but rather inward onto a magnolia-shaded churchyard filled with monuments dating from Colonial times, including the graves of three Colonial governors. A solid brass chandelier from the 15th Century and communion silver from 1725 are still in use.

James Iredell House, 105 East Church St., was built in 1773 by North Carolina's first attorney general, who was appointed by George Washington to the first U.S. Supreme Court. Visitors see the intricate and ornate desk in the law office of his son, who served as a governor. A rare rope bed is found in the west bedroom.

A walking tour turns up other interesting sites and more than two centuries of architectural styles. The most obvious landmark is the 1782 **Elizabeth Barker House,** on a point jutting out into the water. Once home to an organizer of the Edenton Tea Party, it was moved three blocks to the site in 1952. The Edenton Historical Commission opens it for tea on the third Wednesday of each month. There's a wonderful block of mansions along West King Street. South Granville Street also has a variety of substantial residences of interest.

The **Chowan Arts Council Gallery & Museum,** 200 East Church St.

The old E.A. Swain School has been turned into a gallery and museum. Photos illustrating a century of Chowan County from 1850 were on display at our visit. Works of fine artists are shown in a gallery and shop.

(252) 482-8005. Open Monday-Saturday 10 to 4, Sunday 1 to 4. Free.

Shopping. The three blocks of Broad Street that make up Edenton's downtown are typically small-town, and there are no empty storefronts. The biggest store in town is **Byrum's Hardware and Gifts,** where every bride registers and George Byrum will sell you just about anything. The next biggest is **Sound Feet Shoes** (uniforms and safety shoes). The norm is typified by **The Betty Shoppe** ("smart fashions") and **Jovon Fashions,** "the perfect outfit for the perfect lady." Next door is **Ann & Andy's** children's shop, side by side with the **Fame Men's Shop.** Of interest to visitors are **Magnolia's,** with great apparel and accessories for women, and the adjacent **Made by Hand,** with fine gifts, baskets and crafts made in Edenton. **Marion's Boutique** is a high-fashion dress store that also carries antiques that the owner gathers on shopping trips to England. **Pembroke Landing Antiques** stocks beautiful antique linens, furniture and china. **Fancy That** offers items that are more affordable. **The Lovin' Oven** bakery produces breads and pastries.

Extra Special

Edenton Mill Village, 420 Elliott St., Edenton. The old brick Edenton Cotton Mill was closed in 1995, and the small, tin-roofed houses where mill workers lived alongside stood vacant. But the blighted neighborhood on the wrong side of the tracks at the edge of the Edenton historic district is alive today. The 44-acre mill village was donated by the Greensboro corporate owners to Preservation North Carolina. A master plan calls for condominiums and artist studios in the mill, which was built of one million bricks, all made locally. The workers' houses are being sold to people who restore them for personal residences under strict covenants. More than 40 houses that were not grandfathered to tenants have been sold and restored, prompting PNC to do the same for another cotton mill village near Burlington. The colorful structures, ranging from modest three-room mill workers' cottages to the Colonial Revival overseer's house, are well worth seeing as an example of affordable housing and adaptive re-use. Signs mark some of the houses; the owner called one Messington, circa 1909, because it was such a mess. A cluttered mill museum in the PNC site office shows all kinds of collections owned by a local man.

(252) 482-7455. Site office and museum open Monday-Friday, 8:30 to 5:30.

Tryon Palace is reproduction of royal governor's 18th-century capitol and residence.

New Bern, N.C.

Town of Firsts

A clock tower atop City Hall is one of New Bern's striking features, just as it is in the Swiss capital of Bern. And, as in Bern, the city makes the most of its name, which is the old Germanic word for bear. Black bear signs welcome visitors at highway entrances to the city. Two bears stand above the entry of City Hall. Three wooden bear sculptures dominate the downtown Bear Plaza. Bear symbols designate city vehicles and uniforms.

The Swiss accent reflects the heritage of North Carolina's second oldest town. Swiss and German adventurers settled at the confluence of the Trent and Neuse rivers in 1710. In 1765, British Royal Governor William Tryon made New Bern, by then the biggest town, the capital of the Carolina colony. Tryon Palace, the reproduction of his 18th-century capitol and residence, is the focal point of a fourteen-acre museum and garden complex that today draws tourists by the thousands.

Tryon Palace is not the only attraction in this, a town of firsts. The 40-block historic district and waterfront contain several museums and more than 150 sites dating to the 18th and 19th centuries. The early 19th-century Federal period is especially well represented. New Bern is the site of the state's first public school. The state's first printing press produced the first book and the first newspaper in North Carolina. The state's first bookstore was opened here in 1783. New Bern has the oldest movie theater in America still in regular operation. George Washington's birthday was first celebrated officially in New Bern. And a local pharmacist invented "Brad's Drink," forerunner of Pepsi Cola.

Not all is history in this town of 17,500, however. The Swiss Bear Downtown Redevelopment Group is rejuvenating downtown, which is nicely focused around a landmark Episcopal church whose property occupies an entire city block. The utilities are being buried underground. Antiques shops abound. The Union Point Park and waterfront promenade were rebuilt following hurricanes. A New Orleans paddleboat carries tourists along the riverfront And a new high-rise bridge over the Neuse River was about to reroute Route 17 through traffic around town and away from the historic district.

Harmony House Inn is actually two houses joined as one.

That's good for the historic district. But unknowing travelers won't realize what they are missing.

Inn Spots

The Aerie, 509 Pollock St., New Bern 28560.

Nicely situated in the historic district a block from Tryon Palace, this handsome 1880 Victorian was a private residence for nearly a century. Now owners Dee and Howard Smith from Frederick, Md., offer some of New Bern's most comfortable accommodations.

"We're not into frou-frou Victorian," says energetic Dee, a grandmother of four. "We lean more toward Colonial decor."

There's a player piano in living room, where two long sofas face each other in front of the fireplace. Four sturdy tables are set for two to four in the dining room, scene of a memorable morning breakfast.

All bedrooms come with private baths, one occupying what had been the first indoor kitchen in New Bern. Rooms also have TVs, sitting areas, writing desks and diverse bed configurations from twins to kingsize. They vary from the Pencil Post with a queensize bed and loveseat to the Bay Window with a queen bed and two wing chairs in the window. The largest is Cricket's, with a handcarved Eastlake kingsize bed, Victorian sofa and coffee table. Jack's Room is more masculine, done in a horse motif in

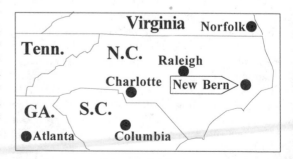

rust and navy blue. We were happily ensconced in the rear Hidden Room, so named because it is hidden off a rooftop deck above the kitchen. A victim of the 1996 hurricanes that roared through New Bern, it was rebuilt and appointed in Dee's favorite Williamsburg toile. Although we liked the tiered deck, most guests gathered on the terrace beside the back-yard garden.

Dee is known for gourmet breakfasts, with three hot entrées offered daily. Ours was a choice of tarragon eggs with bacon, french toast with apple syrup and belgian waffles with strawberries. Orange juice, strawberries and coffee cake preceded. The eggs were garnished with mint and pansies. Hazelnut-flavored French roast coffee accompanied.

Teapots from Bermuda are employed for afternoon tea, served Friday and Saturday from 2 to 5. It's complimentary to guests and open to the public for $3.95. All kinds of tea are available, served with sweets like apple dumplings, scones with clotted cream and strawberry jam and, at our visit, lemon coconut cake.

Prospective new owners Donna and Doug Bennetts were at the inn serving an internship as this book went to press.

(252) 636-5553 or (800) 849-5553. Seven rooms with private baths. Doubles, $89 to $99. Children accepted. No smoking.

Harmony House Inn, 215 Pollack St., New Bern 28560.

Except for the two side-by-side front doors, the facade of this B&B gives little hint of the unusual interior. What began in 1809 as a four-room Greek Revival house is really two houses joined as one. After nearly a century's worth of additions, the house was sawed in half and the western portion was moved nine feet away. A new hall and stairs were built beside the original, and a wall divided the reconnected house into two sections. One of the corridors now serves as a gift shop featuring unusual needlework crafted at the inn by Sooki Kirkpatrick, innkeeper with her husband Ed.

The main floor of one side of the house holds a living room and a dining room, where a full breakfast buffet is presented on an antique sideboard. The fare the day of our visit included fresh fruit sundae with low-fat yogurt, homemade coffeecake, homemade granola and a baked egg and cheese casserole. Baked stuffed french toast with blueberry-maple syrup was on tap the next day.

The second floor and most of the main floor on the other side of the house are devoted to guest bedrooms, including a couple of suites. All have TVs, telephones, decorative fireplaces and queen poster (some canopy), king or twin beds. Top of the line is the Eliza Ellis Suite with a quilt-covered king bed, two armchairs, formal swag draperies and a bath with a double jacuzzi in the corner. The Benjamin Ellis Suite downstairs offers a queen canopy bedroom and a sitting room with a queen sofabed. Decor is traditional, and furnishings are a mix of antiques and reproductions.

The Kirkpatricks offer afternoon wine or soft drinks in the parlor or on the small front porch. Sherry or port are available in the evening..

(252) 636-3810 or (800) 636-3113. Eight rooms and two suites with private baths. Doubles, $89 to $99. Suites, $140. Children accepted. No smoking.

King's Arms Inn, 212 Pollock St., New Bern 28560.

Established in 1980 as New Bern's first B&B, this took its name from an old New Bern tavern said to have hosted members of the First Continental Congress.

Owners Pat and Richard Gulley describe the 1848 beige house with black trim as Greek Revival combined with Second Empire. But they decided to redecorate in the Colonial style.

The main floor has a small parlor converted from what previously had been a guest bedroom. That's the only common area, except for a small back porch furnished in wicker. That explains why the Gulleys make quite a production of delivering breakfast by candlelight on a silver tray to guest bedrooms. It includes cinnamon coffee, fresh fruit, muffins and quiche, generally ham and cheese, accompanied by the morning newspaper.

Three pleasant bedrooms on the main floor and four on the second are furnished with a mix of antiques and reproductions. One has a king bed, three contain two doubles and the rest are queensize. Most in demand is the third-floor suite enclosed behind the mansard roof. It offers a large sitting room with TV, a queensize brass bed, a full bath and a view of the Neuse River. The original bead-board walls and ceiling are painted white, and the entire expanse has four colors of wall-to-wall carpeting.

Complimentary sherry, pink lemonade, fruit and homemade cookies are offered in the afternoon. For special-occasion celebrants, the Gulleys fly a banner from the front porch and say "the champagne is on us."

(252) 638-4409 or (800) 872-9306. Fax (252) 638-2191. Eight rooms with private baths. Doubles, $100. Suite, $145. No smoking.

Howard House, 207 Pollock St., New Bern 28560.

Steven and Kimberly Wynn had experience building and selling new houses in Raleigh before they bought a Victorian structure here in 1997. "But this old apartment house was a whole new ballgame," Kim recalled. They undertook six months of renovations, doing most of the work themselves, before opening their B&B with four guest rooms, luxury amenities, family heirlooms and an emphasis on good food and drink.

Beige with rust trim, the 1890 house is listed on the National Register. The Wynns have enhanced its historic character with such room niceties as fresh flowers, 250-count Egyptian cotton sheets ("which I have to iron," Kim relates), private baths with terrycloth robes and hair dryers, bottled spring water, cable TV, telephone and nightly turndown with a chocolate on the pillow.

The Victorian Blue Room with a view of the river has a queensize rice plantation poster bed and a private hall bath with a soaking tub. The rear Yellow Rose Room contains a turn-of-century sleigh bed that belonged to an aunt. When it's not occupied, Kim likes to read the newspaper beside the stained-glass windows in the spacious Turret Room above the parlor. It comes with an authentic Victorian double bed with a giant eight-foot headboard and matching dresser, plus a velvet parlor set inherited from Kim's great aunt and previously used only at Christmas. The newest room is the handsome downstairs Plantation Green Room with a queensize plantation bed.

Cookies and fudge on a tray await guests in their rooms. That's in addition to the afternoon lemonade, fruit, cheese and crackers set out in the turreted parlor, furnished with unusual corner chairs obtained from an old church. Not to mention the fancy desserts – perhaps strawberries and pound cake from her mother's family recipe – that Kim presents on the front porch in the evenings.

Breakfast is served by candlelight in the dining room. A favorite granola fruit

King's Arms Inn takes its name and theme from a Colonial tavern.

parfait might precede a bacon omelet presented in a muffin cup, followed by orange french toast. Another day might bring a sausage casserole with mozzarella cheese and apple-pecan pancakes.

(252) 514-6709 or (800) 705-5261. Fax (252) 514-6710. Four rooms with private baths. Doubles, $89 to $99. Children over 12. No smoking.

The Harvey Mansion, 221 South Front St., New Bern 28560.

Built in 1797, this white-brick beauty is the last surviving historic structure facing the water and reflects New Bern's early days as a seaport. The lower floors house a thriving restaurant (see Dining Spots). In 1998, owners Carolyn and Beat Zuttel opened three guest rooms on the third floor as well, and were planning to add a fourth room in 1999.

The bed chambers are spacious by New Bern standards and quite luxurious. The spiffy furnishings include prized antiques. Oriental rugs accent the wall-to-wall carpeting. Two beds are kingsize posters and one is queensize, each extra-plush with a pillow-top mattress. TV/VCRs and a computer shelf are hidden in the armoires. Two closets in the Commandant's Room have been converted into bath facilities – one with a retrofit jacuzzi bath and shower massage accessed from the short end of the tub. Two river-view rooms have jacuzzi tubs and showers in private hall baths reached through a common room. The common room comes with a stocked snack refrigerator and a balcony onto the river.

Swiss-born chef Beat makes all the breakfast breads for the hearty continental breakfast offered in the first-floor dining room. The fare includes fresh orange juice, fruit compote, Swiss muesli and oatmeal. Complimentary teas, wines and beers are offered in the afternoon in the atmospheric Cellar pub.

(252) 638-3205 or (800) 638-3205. Fax (252) 638-3206. Three rooms with private baths. Doubles, $125 to $145, includes $20 dinner allowance. Smoking restricted.

New Berne House, 709 Broad St., New Bern 28560.
A handsome brick Colonial Revival house of newer vintage along busy Broad Street holds an unusual variety of guest rooms on three floors.
Although each has private bath, telephone and flouncy window treatments, there's no such thing as typical. A room at the rear of the main floor comes with kingsize bed, two armchairs, well-worn oriental rug and a 1940s bathtub with the faucets on the side wall. A second-floor room with queen poster bed has a shower enclosed in 1950s-style opaque glass blocks. The biggest room is a third-floor hideaway with a kingsize bed against a wall canopied in fabric, a chaise lounge and two wood chairs with cushioned seats. Marcia Drum, innkeeper with Howard Bronson, a retired ship captain who traveled the world, made this wall canopy as well as one for a second room with a queen brass bed and hooked rug. She calls the decor English country, seasoned with antiques and antique treasures.
Breakfast is taken between 8 and 9 o'clock in a dining room with three tables. Belgian waffles with praline cream sauce and spiced bacon might be one day's fare, and strata with balsamic potatoes and homemade coffeecake the next. Afternoon tea is offered in the pleasant front parlor with TV or in the library. Beyond the side porch is a garden harboring an old swing and oversize hammocks.
The inn sponsors monthly mystery weekends, mixing food and intrigue.
(252) 636-2250 or (800) 842-7688. Seven rooms with private baths. Doubles, $88. No smoking.

Dining Spots

The Harvey Mansion, 221 South Front St., New Bern.
The builder of this imposing 1797 mansion was ship owner and merchant John Harvey of Somerset, England, whose family is known for producing Harvey's Bristol Cream sherry. Since 1991 it has showcased the continental fare of chef Beat Zuttel, coincidentally a native of Bern, Switzerland, after which New Bern was named.
His American wife Carolyn oversees the front of the house, the changing artworks on the walls and the new overnight guest quarters on the third floor. She even designed a self-guided tour of the historic building, which was saved from demolition in 1979 because of its National Register status. The tour's eleven stops offer elaborate written descriptions (one details a creamware chamber pot unearthed during archeological renovations).
Dining is in six small, elegant, high-ceilinged rooms. They're notable for decorative fireplaces, hand-carved crown moldings and interior shutters open for views through floor-to-ceiling windows toward parkland and riverfront. We were seated in a room known as the art gallery for a leisurely dinner. A vegetable tartlet with three cheeses and salads incorporating no fewer than twelve exotic greens from the chef's garden proved an auspicious start. Berner roësti with sautéed veal morsels and mushrooms is a fixture among continental entrées on the menu, which changes seasonally. The chef is known for his grilled entrecôte soubise, filet mignon, rack of lamb and fresh seafood specials. We were well satisfied with the roasted chicken with ginger sauce and fried polenta and the fan of duck martinique sauced with rum, bell peppers and bananas and teamed with handmade spaëtzle. A key lime-berry tartlet and strawberry-yogurt mousse cake were worthy endings.
Downstairs is the **Cellar Pub** with a low beamed ceiling, copper-topped bar

and a dart room. It features a short menu of focaccia sandwiches and light entrées – perhaps ragoût of salmon and grouper or satay of beef, both served with rice. *(252) 638-3205 or (800) 638-3205. Entrées, $12.95 to $25.95; Cellar, $6.50. Dinner nightly from 5 (from 6 in summer). Cellar from 5.*

Henderson House, 216 Pollock St., New Bern.
For a splurge, well-heeled locals recommend this elegant restaurant. It has attracted knowing diners from far and wide since the Weaver family bought it in 1983.

Matthew Weaver is a classically trained French chef. He offers a traditional French menu with Southern accents in three dining rooms of a brick, center-hall Federal home with a well-documented pedigree dating to the 18th century. His mother, Betty, often greets diners at the door. The paintings of his late father, Robert Weaver, a noted Indiana artist, hang on the walls and are shown in his former studio on the second floor.

The stunning artworks, crisp table linens and fine antiques provide a refined backdrop for Matthew's culinary artistry. Dinner might begin with the house pâté blending goose, pork and chicken livers or a substantial jumbo lump crab cocktail. Exemplary house salads enriched with a brandied vinaigrette precede the main courses. They range widely from crab norfolk and lobster au whisky to pheasant sesame and veal chop with chanterelles. The carpetbagger steak with oysters and sauce poivrade is a signature dish. The house combo for two pairs a South African lobster tail with a choice of lamb chops, tournedos or entrecôte with herbed butter sauce.

Save room for one of Matthew's "entremets," classic desserts spiked freely with liqueurs. Favorites are a kahlua-flavored coffee and chocolate ice cream and graham cracker concoction called coco moco pie, strawberries sabayon, meringue glacé, profiteroles and white chocolate mousse. The extensive wine list favors the better French vintages.

(252) 637-4784. Entrées, $17.95 to $34.50. Dinner, Tuesday-Saturday 6 to 9. No smoking.

The Chelsea, 335 Middle St., New Bern.
This lively restaurant began life as the second drug store of Caleb Bradham, the inventor of Pepsi-Cola. Later known as the Williams Restaurant, it was a landmark for travelers from New England to Florida. In 1991 it was renovated and became The Chelsea. It was doubled in size in 1996 to seat 140 on two floors – casual on the main floor, which retains the feeling of a turn-of-the-century drug store, and a tad more elegant with Tiffany lights and Victorian accents upstairs.

The cuisine is billed as regional, international and fusion, and the menu is the kind upon which everything appeals. For lunch, we sampled the signature appetizer called blue chip stacks, an overwhelming plateful of homemade chips baked with garlic herb butter, bacon, scallions and two cheeses. It was so much we couldn't possibly finish our other orders, an appetizer of dynamite Asian dumplings for one and the specialty "coastalina" shrimp and grits. These came on huge white plates, each decorated with garnishes and served in far too generous portions. We couldn't even think of indulging in the day's dessert offerings of key lime pie, banana cream pie and pound cake with strawberries.

The midday appetizers, focaccia sandwiches and flatbreads also are offered at night. Dinner entrées range widely from pecan-crusted catfish and shrimp sonoma to liver with onions and steak and mushroom pie. But most people hold out for the wonderful coastalina shrimp and grits, which turns up on the dinner menu as well.

(252) 637-5469. Entrées, $10.95 to $16.95. Lunch and dinner 11 to 9, weekends to 10. Closed Sunday.

Sonny's Raw Bar & Grill, 235 Craven St., New Bern.

The biggest restaurant in town has to be this establishment fashioned from an old garage turned playhouse turned El Mex restaurant. Looks deceive. From the small entry, an interior corridor winds to a cavernous hall with high wood-beamed ceiling, brick walls and even little casa rooms with a Mexican theme, greenery and cactus. The prodigious menu is as expansive as the space.

It's a good place for a quick lunch or a casual supper. A basket of hush puppies arrived as we sat down for lunch. The oyster burger with french fries and coleslaw was tasty and a bargain for $4.99. Less successful was a chicken salad plate.

The dinner menu offers something for everyone: six scallop or shrimp specialties, chicken and ribs, pasta dishes, seafood and combination platters, steamed and raw shellfish, Mexican standards and Sonny's "downtown grill." Desserts run to key lime cheesecake and fried ice cream.

(252) 637-9000. Entrées, $7.95 to $13.99. Open daily from 11:30.

Pollock Street Delicatessen, 208 Pollock St., New Bern.

For a casual meal, locals swear by this casual establishment they refer to as "The Deli." The old house offers dining on the main floor, upstairs and on the patio. The fare ranges widely from bagels with cream cheese to complete seafood, veal and chicken dinners with appetizers, salad and dessert for a bargain $10.25 to $13.45. The New York deli-style foods are fresh and homemade. The specials are said to be really special. One night's included seafood alfredo, jumbo sea scallops parmesan, chicken à la swiss and sliced london broil with brandied mushroom gravy. Among desserts are Kentucky pie, chocolate mousse pie, brownies and eclairs.

The deli has a beer and wine license.

(252) 637-2480. Entrées, $6.75 to $9.25 Open Monday, 7 to 4; Tuesday-Thursday 7 to 8, Friday 7 to 9, Saturday 8 to 9, Sunday 11 to 4. No credit cards.

Diversions

Most of New Bern's attractions and activities are focused in the 40-block historic district that forms a triangle between Tryon Palace and the Trent and Neuse rivers.

Tour guides call New Bern "The Town on Wheels," because so many structures have been moved – one of them twice. Even Tryon Palace is not a restoration but a re-creation.

Self-guiding maps and walking tours are available through the Craven County Convention and Visitors Bureau, 314 South Front St., (800) 437-5767. The bureau's audio-tape walking tour covers 50 sites and takes longer than most anticipate, about three hours.

An overview is provided by **New Bern Tours,** which offers informative 90-

minute trolley tours of the historic district. With much verbiage and detail on this house and that, the tour is of special interest to architectural historians, as one might expect in a "Treasure Town of Exquisite Architecture," as once described by The New York Times. You get to view and learn about sites you might otherwise miss, including the First Presbyterian Church – unique in the Carolinas and built in the Congregational meeting-house style of New England – and choice sections of New and Johnson streets. Passengers disembark at the Cedar Grove Cemetery, site of ghost tours on Halloween, and outside Christ Church, to which we returned later for a view of the interior.

(252) 637-7316 or (800) 849-7316. Tours April-October, Thursday-Saturday and Monday at 11 a.m. and 2 p.m., Sunday at 2. Adults $10.

Tryon Palace Historic Sites and Gardens, Pollock and George Streets.

Considered the finest government building in Colonial America when it was completed in 1770, most of Royal Governor William Tryon's short-lived palace was reduced to rubble in a fire in 1798. Hence the magnificent red brick, Georgian-style mansion and capitol is a re-creation, rebuilt to its early glory in the 1950s on its original foundation and furnished to the period. A semi-guided, two-hour tour includes several other sites and expansive gardens.

You are expected to spend half an hour each in the first two houses to which you are directed. The John Wright Stanly House, built in 1779 by the Revolutionary War patriot, was later moved, became a library and then moved a third time. The portrait of George Washington, who stayed here two nights to attend a ball at the palace in 1791, hangs in the hallway. He described it as "exceeding good lodging," and we must say that the large, well-furnished upstairs bedrooms would rank with those of New Bern's choicest B&Bs today. The Dixon-Stevenson House (circa 1826) is noted for important furniture among its Neo-Classical antiques. A costumed guide pointed out that the nose on the portrait of its second owner seems to follow you as you pass.

The tour high point is the palace, rebuilt with 30-inch-thick walls on the foundation uncovered beneath the rubble. The stable is the only original structure. A cook was baking in the palace kitchen and a weaver was spinning at a loom in a room above during our tour. The interior is notable for rare English and American antique furnishings, a library with fifteen-foot-high ceiling, and a prized oil by French artist Claude Rouen in the drawing room. We were struck by prolific flower and vegetable gardens at midsummer stage at our early May visit, and an intricate 18th-century English parterre garden among fourteen acres of period gardens.

The Tryon properties include the 1806 New Bern Academy Museum (the oldest school in the state) a few blocks away at Hancock and New streets, and the 1810 home of craftsman Robert Hay. The complex also offers a modern visitor center, a fine museum shop in the 1809 Jones House, and a small craft and garden shop behind the palace kitchen office.

(252) 514-4900 or (800) 514-4900. Open Monday-Saturday 9 to 4, Sunday 1 to 3. Adults, $12.

Other Attractions. Local memorabilia, dolls and Civil War artifacts are displayed in the 1790 **Attmore-Oliver House,** home of the New Bern Historical Society, at 511 Broad St. The manager-historian often dresses in Confederate uniform for tours of **The New Bern Civil War Museum,** 301 Metcalf St. It houses one of the largest private collections of war memorabilia and weapons in the country. Early firefighting equipment, rare photos, Civil War relics and even the mounted head of a faithful old fire horse named Fred are shown in the **Firemen's Museum,** 408 Hancock St.

Pepsi-Cola Tour. Yes, there's a Pepsi Walking Tour, a printed guide developed by the New Bern Preservation Foundation for the town's 1998 celebration of Pepsi's centennial. The humble drug store where young pharmacist Caleb Bradham developed "Brad's Drink," which he later patented as Pepsi-Cola, still stands at the southeast corner of Pollock and Middle streets. It's now officially known as The Birthplace of Pepsi, a gift shop and museum where Pepsi is dispensed from a fountain. An elaborate Pepsi mural, painted by a former New York police officer-turned-artist, is on view at The Chelsea restaurant, the site of Bradham's second drug store. The site of Pepsi's first home office and bottling plant (1902-1923) is at the northwest corner of Johnson and Hancock streets. Houses of early Pepsi workers stand on either side. In 1908, the by-then prosperous druggist moved into New Bern's grandest Greek Revival residence, an 1850 beauty at 201 Johnson St. His grave is in Cedar Grove Cemetery.

Shopping. Downtown New Bern is a pleasant area with pocket parks, a bear plaza featuring carved bear sculptures and an oasis of greenery surrounding historic Christ Episcopal Church. **Carolina Creations** stocks wonderful artworks, crafts and gifts fashioned by regional artisans. **Elusive Treasures** is known for award-winning jewelry. We liked the wood carvings, ceramics and sculptures at **Art of the Wild. Peacock Plume** has suave clothing, as does **Panache. New Berne Antiques & Collectibles** features Pepsi memorabilia. The 700 block of Pollock Street, diagonally across from Tryon Palace, offers treats like **Backyard Bears** for animals and fudge, **Chateau Monroe** for French country fashions and **Cherishables** for antiques and collectibles.

For a shopping break, the **Trent River Coffee Company** offers cappuccino, espresso, pastries and such in an historic, coffeehouse atmosphere. **Mustard's Last Stand,** a movable concession stand last seen at the corner of Tryon Place Drive and East Front Street, dispenses hot dogs and Polish sausages.

Extra Special

Christ Episcopal Church, 320 Pollock St.

Other than Tryon Palace, the town's most notable property may be the square occupied by Christ Church, successor to the old King's Chapel, in the center of downtown. The remarkable brick Gothic Revival edifice is surrounded by trees, the odd gravestone and, off to one side, playground equipment. Built in 1875, it incorporates the walls of an 1824 church that burned in 1871. Foundations of the first church (1750) are preserved in a corner of the churchyard. Displayed in a recessed glass case at one side of the altar area are a silver communion service, a prayer book and a Bible printed in 1717 at Oxford. All were presented to the parish in 1752 by King George III. The gently curved ceiling and dark wood pews are notable. Across the street is a pocket park, which replaced a pool hall so parishioners would not have to look at people playing pool as they left services. *(252) 633-2109. Open Monday-Friday 9 to 5, Saturday 9 to noon. Free.*

Wilmington's downtown and historic district are on view from waterfront.

Wilmington, N.C.

Hip and Happening

Until a few years ago, you might have passed off Wilmington as a decaying port city best bypassed on the way to the ocean beaches.

No more. The pleasantly ramshackle waterfront – a once gritty melange of wharves and warehouses along the Cape Fear River – is undergoing conversion into a people place of shops, restaurants, condominiums and open spaces. Portions of a downtown that formerly looked like an urban renewal war zone and the adjacent residential areas are being restored. The 200-block National Register historic district, one of the largest in the country, is alive with an obvious back-to-the-city residential movement and an ongoing flurry of new inns, restaurants and shops.

And, you may not have realized, a strong heritage of performing arts activity has helped turn Wilmington into a film capital. Its studio complex is the largest east of Hollywood.

Quite suddenly, the revitalized port city – in its early heyday the largest in North Carolina – is hip and happening. Wilmington in the 1990s has turned into one of the nation's fastest-growing areas.

"In the early '90s we were called pioneers," says Jay Rhodes, who moved with his wife Stefany and family from Cape Cod to open the Front Street Inn. "There have been dramatic changes since, but you can still get in on the ground floor."

The influx of newcomers, many of them young to middle-aged, have bolstered the area's economy and boosted tourism. Everyone but the vanishing breed of the Old Guard hails the new dynamic. They tell of countless visitors who have come for a weekend and decided to stay.

Tourists find the riverfront historic district a pleasant combination of business, civic and residential uses. It's compact enough that you can explore and get everywhere that matters by foot. Yet the city is less than a dozen miles from the ocean. Inn-goers who tire of history can go to the beach for the day and return to town for a sophisticated dinner and a night of top-flight theater.

How many other cities can offer the same?

Inn Spots

So recent and rapid was the growth of inns and B&Bs in Wilmington's historic district that a 1997 zoning controversy led to the imposition of a rule limiting new establishments to one per block and a requirement of owner-occupancy. Yet innkeepers see a growing demand based on the historic downtown ambiance and proximity to the beaches.

Graystone Inn, 100 South Third St., Wilmington 28401.

The grandest accommodations in town are found in the imposing Bridgers Mansion built in 1905 of gray stone by the widow of a local merchant whose father was president of the Atlantic Coast Line Railway. Paul and Yolanda Bolda, originally from Detroit, undertook a total renovation and opened in 1998 with a showplace that numbers among its guests the notables who use it as a movie set.

"This was our eighteenth house in nineteen years," said Paul, a marketing executive who was in charge of expansion for Enterprise Rent-a-Car and spent much of his twenty-year career traveling and staying in inns and B&Bs. "Yolanda said this was our last house, so we might as well do it up big."

Moving from London with furniture collected in their travels, they found a lot of house to fill – 14,300 square feet on four floors, to be exact. The Boldas occupy the walk-out ground level, where Yolanda has her interior design studio. Paul, the genial host, turns over the lavish main-floor common areas and two upper floors to overnight guests.

An enormous great hall is open to a pillared living room and music room that fills most of one side of the house. On the other side is a smaller sitting room and a dining room with a breakfast table set for twelve, plus two tables for two in the window. To the rear is a cozy library paneled in Honduran mahogany. The drawers of the tables here look like books. Outside are a side porch, a terrace and a lower patio for guests.

A staircase of carved oak rises two stories to a ballroom, now converted for use as a conference room and party facility accommodating 100. Also on the third floor is the smallest guest room as well as the Bellevue Suite. The latter has a kingsize poster bed and a settee in the bedroom, plus a queen sofabed in a sitting room dressed in French toile wallpapers and fabrics and, surprise, two leopard pillows. The bathroom comes with – a new one to us – an oversize clawfoot tub for two as well as a walk-in shower for two. "This just shouts romance," claims Paul.

Subdued elegance is the hallmark of other accommodations, including the second-floor Latimer Suite, arrayed in pale yellow with a window seat and a queen sofabed in the

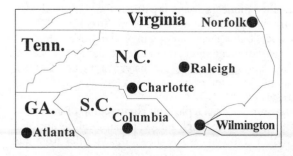

Graystone Inn occupies grand mansion in historic district.

large sitting room and a king bed plus a sitting area in the bedroom. The bathroom here is the inn's only one without a clawfoot tub. It has a rare Victorian cage shower instead.

Our quarters in the junior suite were comfortable and utterly quiet. A queensize sleigh bed, a sitting area with a couch and two upholstered Victorian chairs facing the fireplace, two window seats, a writing desk/table and a bureau holding the TV barely began to fill the space. The room, with pale green walls and dark green carpeting, came with not one but two walk-in closets. As in the other quarters, the ironed sheets were 320-count pima, the closets held all-cotton robes and ironing equipment, and mints were on the pillow after evening turndown.

Breakfast the next morning began with fresh fruit, blueberry crumble bread and homemade jams, set out on the sideboard with a special blend of coffee. Yolanda, who did the interior decorating, prepared a cheese omelet with ham and toast. Belgian waffles were on tap the next day.

(910) 763-2000 or (888) 763-4773. Fax (910) 763-5555. Four rooms and three suites with private baths. Doubles, $165. Suites, $225 to $265. Children over 10. Smoking restricted.

Front Street Inn, 215 South Front St., Wilmington 28401.

Stunning artworks, healthful breakfasts and a Spanish breakfast room and bar called Sol y Sombra set this appealing inn apart. Stefany and Jay Rhodes moved in 1993 from Cape Cod to convert an office/apartment building that began life as a Salvation Army building in 1923. Jay had been an architectural builder, so the required major rehab was right down his alley. Stefany, an art enthusiast, decorated with verve. She named and decorated each room for "someone I like." The theme? "Fun and relaxed, a place where you can put your feet up."

Everywhere is vibrant American art gathered from galleries, fairs, auctions and attics. Or perhaps a bird, perched in a cage beneath the outside staircase. Or the sailboat Jay was restoring in the back yard behind the family quarters.

Two snowshoes on the wall are fanned around a pan as accent art in the Molly Brown Suite. A shawl was draped over the deco chair and a vine painted on the wall and draped around the wrought-iron bed of the Monet Room. We stayed in the brick-walled Segovia Room, whose theme was obscure beyond the guitars on the bedspread. "I'm still looking for the perfect guitar for the wall," Stefany said. "But don't you love the leather chair and ottoman?" Beside the queen bed, facing the recessed TV and separated from the room's wet bar and dining area, the chair could not have been more comfortable. Stefany thinks the nicest room is the Georgia O'Keeffe Suite, with a king bed and jacuzzi bath. All have updated bathrooms, TV, telephones and king or queensize beds. Suites add kitchenettes, fireplaces and jacuzzis.

Suites on the second floor are reached by an outside staircase. They share a wide balcony with a distant view of the battleship North Carolina. The thick brick walls, arched windows, iron balconies and landscaping convey a look of the Southwest, a feeling heightened by the colorful little Sol y Sombra bar, enshrouded in painted grapes and vines (one of which continues into the Monet Room nearby). Here is where guests – many of them businessmen and women – gather for beverages, including beers and wines from an honor bar. In the morning it is transformed from moody and intimate to bright and airy for an unusual continental breakfast spread. The bar and sideboard are laden with juices, dried fruits, cut-up fruits, muesli, interesting breads for toasting and great coffee.

Downstairs is a game room for pool and darts, a small exercise facility and a room employed by an in-house massage therapist on call. "The inn is still on-going," says Stefany. "We're having fun."

(910) 762-6442. Fax (910) 762-8991. Five rooms and four suites with private baths. Weekends: doubles $105, suites $125 to $155. Midweek: doubles $95, suites $110 to $140. Smoking restricted.

The Verandas, 202 Nun St., Wilmington 28401.

Two years of renovations to this 1853 Victorian Italianate mansion paid off for Dennis Madsen and Chuck Pennington. Knowledgeable inn-goers, the pair bought the former convent-turned-boarding house that had been abandoned after its third fire, gutted the interior down to the studs and eventually opened as a B&B in 1997. They quickly earned the annual preservation award of the Historic Wilmington Foundation.

The restoration – and the state-of-the-art, sophisticated B&B – reflect a labor of love for the partners from Washington, D.C., who visited Wilmington for a weekend and decided to stay. Dennis was an interior designer for an architectural firm and Chuck managed an office building. They produced an elegant, comfortable house that cossets overnight guests in splendor.

The main floor is a beauty in pale yellow and white. Crystal chandeliers hang from the twelve-foot ceilings, floor-length windows let in light and floral arrangements provide color. On one side of the center hallway is a quiet music room and library. On the other, the living room opens like a double parlor into the dining room. At our visit, a remarkable collection of antique bird figurines was spread out around the table for twelve. "We decorate for the holidays," explained Dennis, and these were for the next one. There had been shrimp boats for Labor Day and porcelain boxes with bunnies for Easter.

Breakfast is a social event, with seatings at 7:30 and 8:30 weekdays and at 9 on

Spanish-style Sol y Sombra breakfast room and bar is a favorite of guests at Front Street Inn.

weekends. Dennis prepares such treats as exotic fruit compotes, croissants stuffed with peaches, thick oatmeal-mincemeat pancakes or scrambled eggs with sour cream and herbs from the garden. The meal can be taken in the dining room or on a rear screened porch, overlooking a circular patio and gardens.

Pampering touches abound. The partners French-press the coffee for breakfast. Wine is complimentary in the evening. Chocolates are at bedside. The sheets and linens are hand-ironed. Unusual oatmeal-almond soaps are among the toiletries. Built-in night lights illuminate the bathrooms.

Each of the second and third floors holds four corner guest rooms. Five have kingsize beds and three are queensize. Bathrooms with garden-size soaking tubs and marble floors, vanity tops and detailing around the showers are the norm. So are original artworks, TVs and telephones. Every room comes with "at least two pieces of lounge furniture," says Dennis. Even the smallest with a queensize bed has a loveseat and a club chair with ottoman. One room with white walls and dark stained floors is fancy in black and brown. Another with pearl gray walls is dramatic in gold and black. Morning glories are painted on the furniture of a third-floor room. The walls of its neighbor, painted with scenes from *The Wind in the Willows,* so charmed visitors from Switzerland that they wanted to take them home. Chuck's favorite room has a king brass bed, a sofa and two chairs, a carved bear in a corner and handpainted birds beside the door with a nest painted atop the thermostat.

A spiral staircase winds to the rooftop cupola, 60 feet high, from which guests can see the downtown skyline and river.

Four verandas give the place its name. Front and back, upstairs and down, they are lit by twinkling lights and lanterns and outfitted with Adirondack chairs, rockers and a swing.

(910) 251-2212. Fax (910) 251-1396. Eight rooms with private baths. Doubles, $160. Two-night minimum weekends. Children over 12. No smoking.

Catherine's Inn, 410 South Front St., Wilmington 28401.

This handsome 1883 Italian/Federal house backs up to a sunken garden, sloping lawn and an unobstructed view of the Cape Fear River. It is Wilmington's only B&B with a water view.

Catherine and Walter Ackiss retired here from Virginia specifically to run a B&B. They were among the first innkeepers, opening Catherine's Inn on Orange Street in 1988. They sold that in 1994 to purchase this residence. "We were raised on the Chesapeake Bay and wanted to be on the water," Catherine explained.

Although the front has a porch wrapping around the main floor, the main attraction is the screened porch off the rear of the second floor. Here Catherine has placed a "welcome tree to welcome guests." She decorates the artificial HanChristmas tree for the seasons, but the porch is welcoming enough with its wicker furniture, a stocked refrigerator "for continuous refreshments" and a vista of the passing river traffic. "This is where guests live," she says.

Not that they have to. The nicely decorated interior holds two small, elegant front parlors with Indian-shuttered windows. A table is set for ten in a large mauve dining room, where Catherine serves juice, fruit and banana french toast one morning, a tomato-egg casserole the next – "something different every day."

Coffee is placed outside the door of each of the five bedrooms. Two have kingsize canopy beds and the others are queens. All have desks and loveseats or comfortable chairs. A welcome basket on each bed contains mints, an inn postcard and a flower. A trunk is at the foot of one bed. An armoire and an in-room washstand are in another room. Off the rear porch is the prized Waterview Room, so named for its bay window onto the river. It's purple with yellow accessories and comes with a queensize iron bed and a loveseat.

At night, Catherine leaves bedside liqueurs during turndown service.

(910) 251-0863 or (800) 476-0723. Five rooms with private baths. Doubles, $85 to $109. Children over 12. Smoking restricted.

Rosehill Inn, 114 South Third St., Wilmington 28401.

Some of the best breakfasts in town, served in a breathtaking dining room, are the hallmarks of this engaging B&B in an 1848 mansion that was once the home of the architect for the Lincoln Memorial. Laurel Jones and Dennis Fietsch visited from Kansas City on vacation and fell in love with Wilmington and this house, which needed a lot of work. "I always wanted a Victorian house," Laurel said. They bought this, which predates the period and started ongoing renovations and cosmetic improvements in 1995.

Dennis, a self-taught cook, learned from his parents, "who were incredibly good cooks." He has a repertoire of 30 breakfasts. The meal is served at 9 o'clock at a custom-made table for fourteen – with an extra leaf for four more – in a setting that draws gasps from first-time visitors. A chandelier hangs overhead, and a lighted display case along the side holds a rotating collection of Czech glass. The signature dish is eggs benedict done in a ramekin with rustic bread and topped with shrimp. Others are a crustless vegetable quiche, cornmeal waffles with cranberries and pecans, grand marnier-stuffed french toast, Mexican-style eggs with salsa and Andalusian baked eggs. Fresh fruits, muffins, biscuits and perhaps Caribbean banana-nut bread with tart lime sauce accompany.

Laurel, who commutes to Kansas City to oversee her two retail stores, did the decorating here. Two parlors set the stage. "It's not Victorian but eclectic," she says.

Handsome Italian/Federal riverfront residence is home of Catherine's Inn.

Upstairs are five comfortable guest rooms. Side by side in front corners are the oriental Indochine dressed in pink and yellow florals, with a settee and two chairs at the foot of the queen bed, and the Heritage with a British club look. The headboard and footboard for its kingsize bed are made of New Orleans-style cast-iron gates. The side Carolina Room is dainty with the queen bed's comforter matching the floral wallpaper and a reading corner in the bay window. Two large rear bedrooms offer kingsize beds, one a four-poster angled from the corner with three armchairs nearby. The cozy Tea Rose Room on the main floor has a queensize walnut bed, two wing chairs and a settee, and a vanity in the room. Beds are covered with hypoallergenic comforters, which Laurel obtained from Canada as "godsends to those allergic to feathers," she said.

Outside are a wraparound porch with a glider swing, a walled terrace and a rear lawn with a pergola. A fountain with reflecting pool was in the plans.

(910) 815-0250 or (800) 815-0250. Fax (910) 815-0350. Six rooms with private baths. Mid-March through October: doubles $135 to $195 weekends, $119 to $175. Rest of year: $99 to $155. Children over 12. No smoking.

The Curran House, 312 South Third St., Wilmington 28401.
This 1837 house in the Victorian Italianate and Queen Anne styles provides all the comforts of home and then some. Vickie and Greg Stringer bought the property known as the Kingsleigh Inn in 1996 and renamed it for his mother. They upgraded the three spacious upstairs guest rooms, furnished them with flair and set about providing hospitable amenities. All have TVs and private baths, one newly enclosed to meet AAA standards. "This old house is my boss," says Greg, who did most of the work himself. "There's always so much to do."

You'd never know it, so full of raves are the room diaries. "You have thought of everything to make your guests comfortable," wrote a previous guest, citing the fluffy down pillows and the neat stacks of books beneath the lamps by the bedside tables. We were staying in the front Blue Harbor Room, which has a queensize iron scroll bed, Hawaiian art, an Oriental wardrobe and marble-top dresser. Best of all, it opens onto a private front balcony shaded by a spreading live oak.

The rear of the house holds two more guest rooms with strikingly different themes. The Gentlemen's Room has a kingsize sleigh bed, leather sofa and a burgundy and green polo motif. Greg made shadow boxes for the walls to display his great-grandfather's hunting and golfing equipment. A baseball glove with a ball rests on the mantelpiece. Across the hall is the Southern Ladies Room with a kingsize canopy bed, armoire, two wing chairs and a pink and white bathroom with a walk-in shower. Figurines of Scarlett O'Hara and Rhett Butler on the mantelpiece personify the *Gone with the Wind* theme.

The living room and dining room are appointed in English furnishings. The latter is the setting for an elaborate breakfast, served by candlelight with ornate silver, crystal and china. Delicate cut-up fruit with yogurt, two kinds of juices and strawberry bread preceded our main courses: an egg and cheese casserole with zesty homemade "South of the Border" potatoes that lived up to Greg's billing as waker-uppers. The couple grind their own coffee.

There's a ping-pong table on the back porch. Most recently, Greg built a gazebo in the back yard and furnished it with four wicker rockers.

(910) 763-6603 or (800) 763-6603. Fax (910) 763-5116. Three rooms with private baths. April-September, doubles, $119 weekends, $89 midweek. Rest of year: doubles, $95 weekends, $79 midweek. Two-night minimum most weekends. Children over 12. No smoking.

The Worth House, 412 South Third St., Wilmington 28401.

This 1883 Queen Anne-style house with wraparound porch, rounded bay windows and turrets looks ever so Victorian on the outside. The interior is less so, especially in some of the guest rooms, where innkeepers Francie and John Miller from California have fashioned, in her words, "a place where people make themselves at home."

There's a pump organ in the front turreted parlor, which has velvet Victorian seating. A larger and more frequent hangout is the corner library/den with a big-screen TV. The liveliest haunt is the third-floor recreation room, with a modern sectional sofa, games and videos.

Four guest rooms on the second floor have working fireplaces and most have sitting areas. The front Azalea Suite, with a kingsize poster bed, has an enclosed porch and a bath with clawfoot tub off the porch. The rear Rose Suite, with king rice canopy bed, also has a sunporch and a bath with tub and separate shower. The Louisiana has a king bed and sleeper sofa along with rattan cushioned chairs and French-style wallpaper.

Upstairs off that great recreation room are three more guest rooms. The kingsize Gardenia is carpeted to disguise a sloping floor. The kingsize Turret Room in the turret over the bay is attractive in wicker. The Magnolia has one of the inn's two queensize poster beds.

Besides the common rooms, guests enjoy the wraparound front porch and a rear porch appointed in wicker, overlooking a pleasant back yard with gardens and a fountain. That porch or the chandeliered dining room is the setting for a substantial breakfast, perhaps scrambled eggs with ham and an apple pancake or orange french toast. Fresh fruit, juice and fresh-ground coffee accompany. Tea,

Rounded bay windows and turrets enhance The Worth House.

soft drinks and snacks are available around the clock in a refreshment area – a standard amenity in many Wilmington B&Bs.

(910) 762-8562 or (800) 340-8559. Seven rooms with private baths. Doubles, $80 to $125. No smoking.

Live Oaks, 318 South Third St., Wilmington 28401.

Established in 1996, says the sign over this unassuming gray 1883 Victorian with black and white trim, which has had only three owners in 115 years. Doug and Margi Erickson from New Jersey acquired the private residence in 1996 and undertook major renovations. A pump organ and an antique victrola are attractions in the formal front parlor. A rear library is more casual with a TV/VCR. The unusual dining room chairs were obtained at auction from a film studio. They appeared in a dining car scene in the movie, *Road to Wellville.* Here is where Margi serves a full breakfast at 9 o'clock. Fruit and muffins precede a main dish, perhaps her specialty artichoke-mushroom quiche or eggs florentine.

Upstairs are three guest rooms with queen beds and private baths. The pink and burgundy Victorian Room is notable for original heart-pine floors and carved walnut furniture. The Blue Room has a poster bed, an Eastlake armoire with TV, a sink in a dresser, and two comfortable chairs. Margi's favorite rear Garden Room is small and secluded, entered off a shared back porch furnished in wicker. Fresh in white and yellow, it contains an iron bed and a single armchair.

The porch overlooks a back yard with a brick patio, a hammock and a pond and waterfall in the corner.

The Ericksons had the place up for sale as a B&B. "We love what we do and want to do more of it," said Margi. They were hoping to acquire a larger B&B in town.

(910) 762-6733 or (888) 762-6732. Three rooms with private baths. Doubles, $90 to $125. Two-night minimum peak weekends.

Dining Spots

Wilmington offers more sophisticated dining options than many North Carolina cities, and people tend to dine late here. Some of the better restaurants are in residential areas or on the outskirts toward Wrightsville Beach, including Bocci, Tomatoz, Brenner and Rialto. We focus on those in the historic district.

Deluxe, 114 Market St., Wilmington.

This is the new hip spot in downtown. Owner John Malejan upscaled what had been a late-night coffee and dessert house into a restaurant of distinction in 1997. Different colored wall sections of the extra-long, narrow storefront have a distressed look and are hung with showy art. Back-lit glass in the ceiling and the stained-glass accents around the 30-foot-long bar come from the owner's glass business in Raleigh.

Chef Arron Peterson favors eclectic dishes he declines to categorize. Consider such contemporary dinner dishes as ginger-seared black grouper with a spicy Asian plum sauce, smoked chile fettuccine with cumin-roasted tomatoes on a bed of creamy corn puree, pan-roasted duck breast with gorgonzola and port wine demi-glace, and filet mignon encrusted with pistachio nuts and peppercorns. You might start with cilantro-lime tempura shrimp with a spicy cashew dipping sauce or sweet corn and apple cakes garnished with smoked salmon, black lumpfish caviar and vodka crème fraîche. Chocolate crème brûlée, tirami su and homemade coffee and vanilla ice creams are worthy endings.

The pesto-rubbed salmon, grilled and served over a toasted pimento cheese bruschetta and organic greens, highlighted a super lunch. The Sunday brunch also is considered outstanding.

(910) 251-0333. Entrées, $12.95 to $18.95. Lunch, Monday-Saturday 11:30 to 2:30. Dinner nightly, 5 to 10 or 11. Sunday brunch, 10:30 to 2:30.

Caffe Phoenix, 9 South Front St., Wilmington.

Also hip and staffed by film actors and wannabes is this often noisy spot where you can see and be seen, especially on the sidewalk patio out front. The interior is convivial and chic in white and black, with a small bar in the center, an upper-level balcony and lights in ficus trees soaring toward the high ceiling.

Candles and bottles of olive oil are on each table, the better for dipping some really good home-baked breads. The short contemporary Mediterranean menu is strong on pastas, pizzettes and torta rustica. A handful of more substantial dishes range from horseradish-encrusted salmon with dill-butter sauce to beef tenderloin chargrilled with garlic and peppercorns. Three salads come in large and half sizes. We were well satisfied with the house caesar salad and a special called tortellini alexander, combining roma tomatoes, artichoke bottoms, olives and sundried tomatoes with ricotta-stuffed tortellini, feta cheese and pinenuts. The portion was too filling to even think about dessert.

(910) 343-1395. Entrées, $13.50 to $21.75. Open Monday-Saturday 11:30 to 10:30 or 11, Sunday 5 to 10:30.

The Pilot House, Chandler's Wharf, Wilmington.

If you prefer "happening" to hip, Chandler's Wharf is where it's happening. Few places in Wilmington are more atmospheric than the restored area beside the Cape Fear River. The Pilot House and its sister Elijah's restaurant are at its heart.

The Pilot House is the more elegant, quietly ensconced in the 1870 Craig House. The consistently good food is billed as "innovations on Southern cuisine." It's a large place, seating 150, but tables are well spaced, the main dining area looks like a porch and the place settings are elegant with white linens, pewter service plates and shaded oil lamps. We chose the canopied waterfront deck, lit by oil lamps and lanterns. It's jaunty with blue and white chairs at vinyl-covered tables, perfect for observing the passing river scene. The pleasant backdrop did nothing to detract from the food. A shared appetizer of baked oysters preceded two stellar entrées, grilled salmon with dill-sour cream sauce atop a crisp fried grits cake and sweet potato-crusted grouper, served on mixed organic greens with mushroom ravioli. Although seafood appeals most along the river, there are plenty of meat and fowl dishes, among them jerk-seasoned pork tenderloin, veal chop forestière and a country medley of grilled chicken, pork and flank steak, served with collard greens and red-skin mashed potatoes with spicy tasso gravy. Among desserts were lemon sorbet, Southern coconut cake and key lime pie.

(910) 343-0200. Entrées, $13.95 to $24.95. Lunch, Monday-Saturday 11:30 to 3. Dinner, nightly 5 to 10. Sunday brunch, 11:30 to 3.

Elijah's, Chandler's Wharf, Wilmington.
Many visitors to Chandler's Wharf happen across Elijah's first and proceed no farther. For here is an appealing establishment with an enormous menu, a large nautical dining room with windows onto the water, and a canopied and umbrellaed side deck called the Oyster Bar, open to the water.

Jointly owned with the adjacent Pilot House, this is more casual and – except for prime rib on weekends and a handful of steak and chicken dishes – definitely into seafood. Oysters, clams, shrimp and crab legs are available from the raw bar. You can order anything from mussels and calamari to a salad of shrimp louie, a crab cake sandwich, barbecued shrimp skewers, cajun catfish or a Carolina bucket of steamed practically everything, served with new potatoes and corn. As if this weren't enough, they even posted specials of peppercorn-encrusted salmon and mahi mahi the night we passed by.

(910) 343-1448. Entrées, $13.95 to $18.95. Lunch, Tuesday-Sunday 11:30 to 3. Dinner 5 to 10 or 11. Also open Monday in summer. Oyster bar, 11:30 to midnight.

Saxon's By the River, 138 South Front St., Wilmington.
The space vacated by Crook's By the River, an offshoot of a Chapel Hill standby, gave way in 1998 to this promising newcomer. Saxon is the middle name of one of the owner/partners.

The dinner menu is short but serious. We wanted to order the cast-iron skillet purloo with chicken, andouille sausage, mussels, clams and shrimp, until we learned it took 25 minutes. The waitress suggested the cornmeal-fried catfish with lemon slaw and jalapeño-tomato meunière instead. It proved a good choice, the assertive slaw on top a zesty counterpoint to the succulent catfish beneath. A basket of mini-biscuits and cornbread preceded. Intense cantaloupe and honeydew sorbets with pecan shortbread followed. We'd gladly return to try the grilled rainbow trout BLT style, which the waitress advised is just what it sounds like, served over greens, or the smoked angus filet with barbecued oysters, tasso and sweet-potato griddle cakes.

The wine list is with-it, and the bar is into single malts. The brick-walled dining room, white and black and deco glitzy by day, turns dark and romantic at night. The tablecloths are black, and there's a wall of liquid bubbles. Out back on a lower level is a casual dining patio.

(910) 251-0333. Entrées, $15 to $22. Lunch in summer. Dinner nightly, from 5.

Paleo Sun Café, 35 North Front St., Wilmington
Dark and colorful with Southwest accents, this offbeat café with a few sidewalk tables specializes in adventuresome food. It operates on odd hours, Thursday-Sunday late into the evening, and features nightly entertainment.

You might expect to find the menu and the place in high-country Taos, not in downtown Wilmington. But locals recommend it for offbeat dishes like vegetarian fettuccine in a spicy Thai peanut sauce, grilled mahi-mahi tacos, chicken cacciatore, and shrimp, artichoke, spinach and cream cheese crêpes. The menu ranges widely from garden burgers, black bean burritos and turkey salad pitas to salmon in a red wine sauce with grilled polenta. Hot herbal teas, house-blended coffees and a full bar are featured.

(910) 762-7700. Entrées, $11.95 to $16.95. Dinner, Thursday-Sunday 4:30 to 10. Bar menu, 10 to 1:30 a.m.

Grouper Nancy's, 501 Nut St., Wilmington.
For a change of pace, consider this high-ceilinged brick space in the restored railroad station called the Coast Line Center. It's casual with exposed pipes and beams, black and white checked oil cloths and accents of greenery. An arched window yields a glimpse of the Cape Fear River beyond a covered side dining porch.

Owners Mark and Nancy Moore previously had Mark's Café in Chapel Hill. Grouper Nancy, the signature dish there, became the restaurant's name here. The dish arose from a bit of experimenting when Mark and a sidekick started throwing everything they had on the line into a sauté pan. Now grouper Nancy is a tasty blend of sautéed grouper fillet with shrimp, scallions, tomatoes, black olives and green peppercorns over angel-hair pasta. Szechuan yellowfin tuna, firebird salmon, chicken New Orleans, blackened steaks and a number of pastas also are featured.

(910) 251-8009. Entrées, $9.95 to $15.95. Dinner, Tuesday-Saturday from 5:30.

Diversions

Riverfront Park, along Water Street at the foot of Market Street, is the downtown gathering place, with a helpful visitor information center. You can rest on benches here and watch all the activity, both on land and water. There are bus tours, riverboat tours, walking tours, trolley tours and horse-drawn carriage tours.

Wilmington Trolley Co. Tour, South Water Street and Dock Street.
This is the newest and perhaps the best tour for over-all orientation purposes because of the distance it covers. The 45-minute tour leaves the historic waterfront, where you learn the Wilmington Iron Works, oldest in North Carolina, is to be razed to make way for riverfront condos. Up Baptist Hill are streets lined with substantial homes, some converted into B&Bs. They're quite in contrast with the humble cottages along Church Street, where two homes are so close together that workmen couldn't hammer to make repairs. People wave at young trolley operator Wes Moore, as he trundles along the bumpy brick streets beloved by

Historic District residents, who pick away at the new asphalt in the middle of the night whenever the city tries to repave. The tour passes the state's oldest Jewish temple and St. James Episcopal Church, understated like much of Wilmington, adjoining one of the oldest graveyards. On Fifth Avenue, you learn that early residents who traveled to New York opted to change its name from Fifth Street. The guide points out early preservationist David Brinkley's birthplace, since torn down for a low-slung office building. As he tells how Wilmington was discovered by Hollywood, you find that Shirley McLean was filming in the area that very day. You learn from historic tours that Whistler's mother was born here, Woodrow Wilson spent his youth here and church founder Mary Baker Eddy lived here. You may not know that more recently Charles Kuralt came from here. Ditto for Sammy Davis Jr. and basketball superstar Michael Jordan. All the visiting movie stars have nothing on the native sons and daughters.

(910) 343-1611 or (800) 676-0162. Tours daily at 10, 1, 3 and 5. Adults, $8.

Historic Sites. If historic houses are your thing, Wilmington has plenty, many posted with plaques that are a bit difficult to get close enough to read. Three of the most historic houses are open to the public under different auspices. The **Burgwin-Wright House** at 224 Market St., a substantial 1770 Georgian built on the massive stone walls of the old town jail, is a good example of a Colonial plantation owner's townhouse. A bright yellow "supper room" is located upstairs above the parlor, which represented quite a hike from the outside kitchen and craft room. A back porch overlooks terraced gardens, including an "orchard garden" of fig, pear, pecan and pomegranate trees. Two blocks away is the **Zebulon Latimer House** at 126 South Third St., furnished in Victoriana to reflect the 1852 Italianate home's beginnings. Three generations of Latimers lived here, and some original furnishings remain. Of particular interest are the costumes of the day shown in the sewing room, and the original kitchen now serving as an occasional Victorian tea room. The biggest house is the **Bellamy Mansion** at 503 Market St., an imposing 1859 residence wrapped in corinthian columns combining Greek Revival and Italianate styles. A restoration in progress, it is a museum of history and regional design arts that will improve with time.

Tour hours vary: Burgwin-Wright, Tuesday-Saturday 10 to 4, admission $3. Latimer Monday-Friday 10 to 3:30, weekends noon to 5, admission $5. Bellamy Mansion, Wednesday-Saturday 10 to 5, Sunday 1 to 5, admission $6. Combination ticket, $12.75.

Wilmington Railroad Museum, 501 Nutt St.

The old Atlantic Coast Line Railroad freight office has been turned into an idiosyncratic museum tracing the important history of railroading in this area until the trains stopped in the late 1950s. In 1840, the 161-mile track of the Wilmington & Weldon Railroad was the longest in the world. Shipping had turned the port city into an early railroad center and for more than a century, railroading was its chief industry. Some of the guides, many of them former railroad employees, are walking histories. Besides exhibits, artifacts and photos, you'll find model trains running in an enormous railroad diorama upstairs. You can board a steam locomotive, boxcar and caboose. Visitors share their favorite train memories in the museum's "memories book."

(910) 763-2634. Open Monday-Saturday 10 to 5, Sunday 1 to 5. Adults $3.

Thalian Hall, 310 Chestnut St.

Built in 1855 as a combined City Hall and theater, this is one of the oldest and most beautiful opera houses in America. Guided tours go backstage and cover much of what's still one of the most flourishing theater complexes in the country. Events often occur simultaneously on three stages. The main 682-seat theater is intimate and special, with red corduroy cushioned seats on the main floor and lower balcony and the original, not particularly comfortable wood benches on the steep upper balcony. As executive director Tony Rivenbank led a tour, the 100-seat Studio Theater was ready for a cabaret-in-the-round performance and 200 chairs were being set up in the city council chambers/ballroom for a concert of folk music. "It's amazing the quality of attractions we draw," he said. Visitors who may not have come to Wilmington for theater are "stunned by the performances." The oldest community theater group in the country – one of 22 local troupes – performs here. In Wilmington you find TV and film actors doing community theater, which gives it special professionalism. What with local performances and touring entertainers, the Thalian is dark only ten or so nights a year. Further expansion was planned: an adjacent site was earmarked for an 1,800-seat concert hall.

(910) 343-3664 or (800) 523-2820. Performances most nights. Guided tours, Monday-Friday 11 to 3, Saturday at 2. Adults $5.

EUE/Screen Gems Studio, 1223 North 23rd St., Wilmington.

In 1983, Frank Capra Jr. visited Wilmington for his boss, Dino DeLaurentiis, to see whether the town would be a suitable location for their next movie. It was, and Capra stayed to oversee the development in "Wilmywood" of the largest film studio east of Hollywood. Eight-going-on-nine stages and sound studios are rented to film and video outfits. Feature films, made-for-TV movies, TV series and commercials are often in production at the studios and around the Cape Fear area. The variety of settings attracted the filmmakers, as did the quality of local talent assembled over the years in this mecca for the performing arts. There are spin-offs: Wilmington has a monthly journal of film and video called Reel Carolina, and restaurant staffers are apt to be dabbling in filmdom – or is it vice-versa? A monumental Reel Café with rooftop courtyard, sidewalk patio, indoor dining and entertainment was emerging at a key downtown location at our 1998 visit.

(910) 675-8479. Tours by reservation, Saturday and Sunday at 10, noon and 2

Shopping. Chandler's Wharf and the Cotton Exchange anchor either end of what promoters tout as "Wilmington's largest open-air mall," its Riverwalk along the riverfront. Paralleling it, Water, Front and Second streets have their share of interesting shops, although the number of vacant storefronts attest to changes in retailing patterns. Local specialty boutiques, antiques shops and galleries – and nary a chain store – cater mostly to visitors. At atmospheric Chandler's Wharf, once a supply center for ships, the **Gifted Gourmet** and the **Spectrum Gallery** appeal. The Old Wilmington City Market (1880) is full of grocers and vendors. A few specialty retailers like **Island Passage** (gifts and clothing) occupy space in the newly restored Jacobi Warehouse. More action is concentrated at the other end of the Riverwalk at the Cotton Exchange, the first historic downtown complex in North Carolina to adapt to retail and restaurant use. Eight small buildings that formerly housed the world's largest cotton exporting company hold 30 shops of predictable variety. The colorful ceramics and hand-blown glass at **Makado Gallery** caught our eye. So did every kind of stuffed animal, bird and fish at **Zoo.**

Among other shops are **Down Island Traders** for clothing, jewelry and handicrafts, **River Galleries Antiques, Twice Baked Pottery Studio** (buy pottery here and paint it yourself), **Ad-Lib Home** (for Mexican furniture and accents) and **Ad-Lib Body & Soul** (women's items).

A special store is **The Red Dinette** at 5 North Third Street. You'd have to know about it to venture inside the old auto repair garage, but the interior is a showplace of furniture and domestic arts. The furnishings are new but many look old, slipcovered in the English style. Apparently there are plenty of people who will pay $4,600 for a sofa, $1,063 for a chair or $264 for a pillow that looked like vintage hand-me-downs. The establishment, which the owner named for an old dinette, started in a 1,000-square-foot gasoline station. It now is ten times the size.

There are no fewer than four espresso and coffee houses spread across the downtown area. And the **Pheeza Juice Bar** occupies a principal corner at Front and Market streets.

Battleship North Carolina, off Hwys. 17/74/64/21 in the Cape Fear River, Wilmington.

If ever a ship were a tourist attraction, this is it – and appropriately so, in the Port City. In 1961, North Carolina school children saved their coins to return as a memorial World War II's most decorated battleship, which served in every major naval offensive in the Pacific. An hour-long tour takes visitors onto three decks to view the crew's quarters, galley, sick quarters, gun turrets and a rare Kingfisher float plane. A more strenuous, two-hour also takes in the engine room, ammunition storage areas, bridge and admiral's cabin. Authentic shipboard announcements add realism. Museum exhibits display war photos and artifacts. A water taxi shuttles visitors from Wilmington's downtown Riverwalk every half hour to the ship berthed on Eagle Island across the river.

(910) 251-5797. Open daily 8 to 8, mid-May to mid-September; 8 to 5, rest of year. Adults, $8.

Extra-Special

Wilmington Adventure Walking Tour, Foot of Market St., Wilmington.

You may not see as much of Wilmington as on other tours, but you see it up close and certainly get to sense the place. Robert Jenkins makes sure you do. The showman in bermuda shorts with straw hat and cane *is* the performance. He walks fast but talks eloquently about his hometown. "My family has been here since 1617," says the well-connected native, a retired interior designer who restored the first downtown building in the 1970s and lived above his design store. He describes the river pilots, who were all born and reared here ("we don't say raised – you raise hogs and chickens, you rear people.") He pauses to watch tugboats guide freighters up the river after passing through the "Cape of Fear" with its dangerous shifting shoals. To show the valuable pine trees that led to the colonization of Cape Fear, he takes over the Water Street Tavern as the staff sets up for lunch, pointing out the beams and passing out samples of pine oil and tar. He herds his followers into Island Passage Elixir to show more pine oils, then hastens up town, showing points of interest along the way. After a pit stop at Mollye's for coffee and snacks, the tour hustles off to see the ins and outs of City Hall/Thalian Hall and St. James Episcopal Church. "There's nothing very pretentious here because we're a different breed of Southerners," he stresses. At tour's end, he announces with a theatrical flourish: "So now you know who we are."

(910) 763-1785. Tours daily at 10 and 2, April-October. Adults, $10.

Old Well, landmark on Chapel Hill campus, is symbol of University of North Carolina.

Chapel Hill, N.C.

The Southern Part of Heaven

As a university town, Chapel Hill has long been known as a hotbed of liberalism – the Southern equivalent of, say, Cambridge or Berkeley. No less an antagonist than Jesse Helms, then a state senator, once suggested that rather than waste tax dollars on a new state zoo, the state could just build a fence around Chapel Hill.

The state did not build a fence, but it did create a rural strip that has shielded Chapel Hill from some of the urban encroachments of Raleigh, Durham and the rest of the burgeoning Research Triangle.

The town derives its name from its highest point, where a church called New Hope Chapel was located at a Colonial crossroads. The name later was shortened to Chapel Hill, and the site became part of the nation's first state university, chartered in 1789. Since then a college town, first and foremost, Chapel Hill has been nicknamed – Jesse Helms not withstanding – "The Southern Part of Heaven," after a book of the same title by William Meade Prince, published in 1950.

The University of North Carolina is the dominant presence. Its campus covers 729 acres. Its 24,000 students account for more than half the town's population. There's a lot of tradition, from the Old Well, the campus landmark, and the Dean Dome basketball arena to the Carolina Coffee Shop and the Rathskeller, a pair of Franklin Street restaurant institutions.

Most of the area's attractions are connected with the university. Among them are the Morehead Planetarium, the North Carolina Collection, an art museum and a couple of gardens.

Chapel Hill's sister community of Carrboro, a former railroad and mill town, has an eclectic mix of shops and restaurants and a growing arts community. Beyond is the new community of Fearrington, one of the more upscale destinations anywhere.

A bit removed – and as different as can be – is sleepy Hillsborough, the well-preserved Orange County seat. Historical markers everywhere convey the age of this pre-Revolutionary War enclave, which some call a museum without walls. Together they make up a slice of heaven.

Inn Spots

Chapel Hill's residential zoning regulations limit the number of rooms that live-in owners can rent to two, which accounts for a dearth of inns and B&Bs.

The Fearrington House Inn, 2000 Fearrington Village Center, Pittsboro 27312.

When R.B. and Jenny Fitch of Chapel Hill bought a 1,100-acre dairy farm eight miles south of town in 1974, they started fulfilling their vision of a country village like those they knew in the British Cotswolds. The centerpiece for visitors interested in a luxury getaway is now one of the few AAA five-diamond inns and restaurants in the country.

Dairy farmer Jesse Fearrington probably wouldn't recognize the area, although his original silo and barn remain prominent and three of the village's signature Belted Galloway cows were cooling off beneath a shade tree near the entrance as we arrived. An upscale shopping village, two restaurants, a swim and croquet club, a park and more than 800 homes and townhouses surround the village center. The village masks its urbane amenities in favor of a country look in the midst of rolling farmlands.

Even the Relais & Chateaux inn and its widely acclaimed restaurant are not immediately apparent to the arriving visitor. The restaurant (see Dining Spots) occupies the original Fearrington family homestead, hidden behind hedges, vines, white fences and a knot garden. The inn's original thirteen guest rooms – now fourteen with the conversion of the Fitches' early apartment – open off a courtyard sequestered behind a white fence and the inn's office. Eighteen more, situated above stores and commercial enterprises, face a seventeen-acre park with gardens and pond. The newest is a secluded jacuzzi suite located above a bank.

Fearrington House started in the courtyard area with Jenny Fitch as the first chef of the restaurant, which opened in 1980. She also was the decorator, hand-stenciling several guest rooms for the inn that opened in 1986. Legend has it that she never used the same fabric twice. The pine floors in several bathrooms came from an old London warehouse. The rooms vary from standard to deluxe to superior, differentiated mainly by size and by the size and configuration of sitting areas.

With a bow to contemporary wants, five of the newest contain fireplaces and jacuzzi tubs. And lucky No. 13 has a large living room in pale yellow and green, a jacuzzi tub and separate shower, and two rockers on its own private screened porch.

Each is decorated in restful florals with under-stated luxury. There are an antique camera here, a brass lunchbox there and English pine everywhere. Distinctive touches include ecclesiastical doors used as bed headboards, marble vanities and separate dressing areas, heated towel racks and individual sound systems from which classical music emanates for arriving guests. The closets are complete with robes, umbrellas and a bathroom scale. S. Pellegrino water is complimentary in each room. A lavish basket of gourmet snacks and juices, from trail mix to Nantucket Nectars, carries a charge for each.

Not that you'd likely need them. Tea is served daily starting at 3 in the Garden Room, sort of a one-room cottage with a plush sitting area reserved for guests. Dinner and a gourmet breakfast are offered in the dining rooms of the original homestead.

In the early days, Jenny Fitch also was the head of what is now a staff of twelve full-time gardeners tending an array worthy of the guided walking tours offered to groups of twelve or more. Their work is most evident in the formal Jenny's Garden, devoted to all white flowers and centered by a water sculpture by North Caroline artist Wayne Trapp, just off the south-facing Sun Room and Terrace, another guest common area.

Kelley Fitch continues her late mother's artistic tradition as she injects her own style in decorating the newest rooms. Suave Richard Delany, with a touch of British accent, is the ever-present innkeeper. He turned up at the check-in desk at our visit and later manned the cash register in the Market Café located in the farm's former grainery. "I wear many hats," he said in an understatement.

Developer R.B. Fitch of Chapel Hill's Fitch Lumber Co. family calls it hospitality. "We wanted to create a place where people could sort of punch out," he said. "Folks are looking for a place to cocoon, to wrap themselves up and be treated nicely. Maybe they can't go far, but you don' have to go far to feel like you are away. It's not so much where you go, but how you're treated that is hospitality."

(919) 542-2121. Fax (919) 542-4202. Sixteen rooms and fifteen suites with private baths. Doubles, $165 to $225. Suites, $275 to $325. Children over 12. No smoking.

The Inn at Bingham School, 6720 Mebane Oaks Road, Mebane 27302 (Box 267, Chapel Hill 27514).

The sign on the fence here as you leave says "outside world." It's appropriate, for this historic B&B out in the country eleven miles west of Chapel Hill exists in its own world – ten acres of lawn, hammocks strung beneath pecan trees and well-preserved tranquility from another era.

The B&B – the first North Carolina house to be entered in the National Trust – was the headmaster's house in the mid-19th century for a preparatory school for boys seeking entrance to the University of North Carolina at Chapel Hill. Started as a log cabin in 1790 and expanded in stages, it had been abandoned before it was converted into a B&B in 1985. François and Christina Deprez, a young couple with two toddlers, took over in 1994 and infused it with new energy.

"This is the newest part of the house," François said as he showed the main 1835 Greek Revival section. It holds a grand living room with its original windows, Prussian blue ceiling, and cream colored walls above the wainscoting. Here also is the dining room, historic-looking as can be with an enormous cabinet/armoire that suits the room. Upstairs is the Headmaster's Room, a guest room with windows on three sides, a queen canopy bed, fireplace, and a raised clawfoot tub and pedestal sink in the bathroom.

The Inn at Bingham School is based in former headmaster's house.

The rest of the structure was built in the Federal style in 1801. It rambles around the original log cabin, which is now a guest room with quilts on the double bed and the wall, a corner closet and hooked rugs on flooring with a noticeable tilt. Adjacent on one side the owners' quarters and kitchen. On the other side is the 1801 Room, a spacious ground-floor beauty with cream-colored walls accented by bright red wainscoting and molding color-coordinated with the floral comforter on the queensize canopy bed. Accoutrements include a fireplace, wing chair, rocker and a writing desk, plus the hair dryer, fluffy towels, robes and TV common to all rooms. It proved to be a most comfortable place in which to stay. François says Rusty's Room upstairs has the most character, with its antique double and three-quarter rope beds and a two-part bath fashioned from closets. For privacy and romance, there's the separate brick Milkhouse with a sitting room, a jacuzzi tub and a queensize rear bedroom with full-length windows on three sides. Fireplaces were added to all rooms in 1998.

The only remnants of the onetime school are three sturdy green benches placed on the open, L-shaped porch and the inn's separate office that served as the school office. The room diaries are school composition books in which guests pen their thoughts about the sense of history and the innkeepers' hospitality.

The Deprezes place a plate of chocolate-chip cookies in each bedroom and offer wine and cheese on the back terrace in the late afternoon. Breakfast at our visit was fresh orange juice, grapefruit and a baked German apple puff pancake. Quiche lorraine, pear-almond waffles and huevos rancheros are other favorites. The last reflect the owners' background in Texas and Mexico. They moved here from Mexico City when François tired of his French family-owned cotton brokerage business.

(919) 563-5583 or (800) 566-5583. Fax (919) 563-9826. Five rooms with private baths. Doubles, $75 to $120. Children welcome. No smoking.

Hillsborough House, 209 East Tryon St., Box 880, Hillsborough 27278.

Part of this imposing house tucked away on seven acres in Hillsborough's historic district was built in 1790. Descendants of the town's founding families lived in the house nearly 140 years and turned it into a stylish B&B. Artist Katherine

Webb, who built the stunning gallery that forms part of the rear of the house in 1990, and her husband sold the B&B in 1998.

New owners Lauri and Kirk Michel from New York carry on the innkeeping tradition in sophisticated common areas and guest rooms notable for their walls of different colors. The previous owner handpainted the bamboo trees on the walls of the large white and gray dining room. Across the foyer is a library/parlor with tangerine walls, a TV/VCR in the armoire, a fireplace and sliding pocket doors onto a screened side porch, which complements the 80-foot-long open veranda across the front of the house. A private haunt with its own stone porch overlooking a fish pond is the side Kate's Room. Its dark gray walls are lightened with white trim and a kingsize bed dressed in white. Much of the rear of the main floor is devoted to a skylit gallery showing the works of local artists and a spacious new conference room for business meetings and corporate retreats.

Upstairs are four large guest rooms, all with unusual touch-top lights that one turns on with a flick of the hand. The front corner Elizabeth's Room is light and airy in robin's egg blue, with tall windows and a high queen canopy bed draped in blue and white. All the queen rooms have gas fireplaces and the rooms with king beds have porches. One of the latter is the rear Joe's Room, masculine in gray with a window seat, two chairs in recessed alcoves and a step-down porch overlooking the inn's otherwise hidden swimming pool. The biggest room with the highest ceiling is the pink and gray Miss Eliza's, where the queen bed is canopied in fabric hung from the ceiling. Sitting on the plump Victorian feather couch here is like sitting on a pillow of feathers.

Outside in the 1790 summer kitchen beside the pool is a three-room suite with three fireplaces and a jacuzzi tub. Its queen bed, canopied in a bower of budding white poplar branches, is quite a sight.

A continental buffet breakfast is taken on the front porch or at individual tables in the dining room. Fruit, cheese and a loaf of cinnamon-apple bread were supplemented at our visit by a rich chocolate pound cake. Complimentary juices, sodas, popcorn and homemade cookies are available at all hours in the guest kitchenette. Fruit and bottled water in guest rooms are typical of the amenities found in this luxuriously comfortable B&B.

(919) 644-1600 or (800) 616-1660. Five rooms and one suite with private baths. Doubles, $95 to $125. Suite, $200. Children over 10. No smoking.

The Village Bed & Breakfast, 401 Parkside Cir., Chapel Hill 27516.

When Cindy Burnham prepared to retire after 26 years in nursing management at the University of North Carolina Hospital, she bought a house in the pioneering new planned community called Southern Village on the outskirts of Chapel Hill. The problem was how to maintain it "in the style to which I'd grown accustomed." She called a friend and suggested they run a B&B. "Great," was Susan Laswell's response. "What's a B&B?"

She quickly found out, as the pair overcame Chapel Hill's stringent guest-house regulations and set up a two-room B&B in Cindy's house in a territory planned for annexation to the town. The developer and neighbors are enthused about the B&B, Cindy said, since theirs is an old-fashioned community of neighborhoods, front porches and back-alley garages. Like Disney's ballyhooed Celebration in Florida, it is a self-contained town in the true sense of the word, with lodging, restaurants and shops mixed in with residences, townhouses and condominiums.

Hillsborough House occupies seven-acre site in historic district.

Cindy's corner property is given over to a free-form garden. The front porch faces Arlen Park across the street. Enter what appears to be an ordinary house and find yourself in the middle a two-story living room and dining area, furnished in a mix of traditional and family antiques.

At the rear is the master suite called the Garden Room. Its queen bed bears a lace patterned coverlet. Roses from the garden turn up in vases. The glamorous bathroom contains a double vanity, jacuzzi tub and separate shower. Upstairs is the Basket Room, with a king bed, rattan couch, TV and hall bath. It's named for the baskets that Susan planned to make for decorative accents.

Susan, who's raising a family in nearby Carrboro, comes here to prepare breakfast for guests. Fresh orange juice and fruit salad or baked bananas might accompany a main dish like scrambled eggs and hash with baked cheese grits. Chicken crêpes are offered occasionally.

Cindy pours "sweet iced tea in the Southern tradition" for guests in the late afternoon as they sit on the porch, admire the gardens and watch Southern Village's growing little world pass by.

You get the impression her two-room enterprise is just the beginning for this vivacious woman who's "too young to retire." After her first year of operation, she hoped to add another house, and to do business on a larger scale.

(919) 968-9984. Two rooms with private baths. Doubles, $110. No smoking.

The Inn at Teardrop, 175 West King St., Hillsborough 27278.

The teardrop-shaped beveled windows in the front door and the molding around the eaves account for the name of this circa 1768 house that once was an adjunct for the nearby Colonial Inn, one of the country's oldest. In 1987, owner Tom Roberts converted what had recently been a private residence into a six-room B&B as a showcase for his antiques business endeavors.

An itemized list details the heritage of some of the more important furnishings in the public rooms. The large living room holds a grand piano, while the back parlor/library adds a TV to its antiquities. A full Southern breakfast – perhaps featuring an egg-sausage-cheese casserole with baked cheese grits – is taken at a long oval table for eight in the chandeliered dining room. The corner cupboard is full of silver goblets, mugs and trays.

A staircase lined with family portraits leads to four second-floor bedrooms with private baths. One front-corner room has a canopied double bed, a floral carpet atop the wide-board floor, a shower in a tight closet, one easy chair and a desk chair, but no reading lamp. The other front-corner room has two double poster beds, a full bath, a sofa and two chairs and oriental rugs. The rear rooms with shower baths vary similarly. One has a queen poster bed topped by a colorful quilt. The other has a double poster bed, a fireplace and a portable clothing rack. On the third floor are two attic rooms sharing a shower bath. One has a double bed and the other has two twins and a chaise lounge.

Tom likes to point out salient finds, such as the usual 1850s swing butter churn that could pass for a cradle in the upstairs hallway. He offers a decanter of port or sherry in the living room or bedrooms. The shady back lawn contains a couple of pleasant patios.

(919) 732-1120. Four rooms with private baths and two rooms with shared bath. Doubles, $90 to $110 private, $85 shared. Children welcome. No smoking.

The Carolina Inn, 211 Pittsboro St., Chapel Hill 27516.

There's a lot of history in this Chapel Hill landmark on the edge of the University of North Carolina campus. The chapel on the hill that gave the town its name once stood on this spot. The old faculty club used to dine here, and several generations of parents and alumni have made it the university's living room.

So it's a surprise to learn that the sprawling 184-room inn opened only in 1924 and that it had deteriorated to the point that it lost its AAA rating. The turnaround came after the Doubletree hotel corporation was retained to manage the university-owned facility. The hotel was totally closed in 1995 for a year's renovations and expansion. Now 50 rooms larger but retaining its Mount Vernon-style portico and some of its original Colonial Revival look, the red-brick inn is imbued with a four-diamond sense of service and award-winning public space renovations.

One would never guess the sumptuous lobby was once the inn's cafeteria. It's now a lavish, pillared space with large potted plants, showy flower arrangements and countless plush sitting areas. With additions over the years, the inn rambles like Topsy. The original lobby is now an elegant bar across from the acclaimed Carolina Crossroads restaurant (see Dining Spots). The grand ballroom with its black and white checkerboard floor is the ultimate in Southern graciousness. The inn is so popular for functions that it offers far more meeting and party space than the norm. Luckily, the renovation produced a quiet little guest parlor where those inclined can retreat for privacy.

Not that many are so inclined. The guest rooms are charmingly different, and particularly in the older section come in various shapes and sizes. "You may find a large room, or a view, or a small bath," says Margaret Skinner, the inn's longtime sales director and institutional memory. Our corner room was comfortable and attractive in beige and mauve with olive green accents. The queensize bed was turned down almost upon arrival, the closet had removable coat hangers, the armoire held not only a TV but a stash of bottled waters, and the bathroom was laden with amenities. Best of all was the bag of chocolate chip cookies presented at check-in. The only frustration was a dim-watted reading lamp between the two armchairs.

Plantings surround Mount Vernon-style portico of Carolina Inn.

Rooms in the newest wing are larger and contain two double beds rather than the single queen common to the others.

A plaque in the lobby reveals something of the ambiance of the inn, given to UNC by an alumnus in 1935: "This generous gift affords a cheerful inn for visitors, a town hall for the state and a home for returning sons and daughters of Alma Mater."

(919) 933-2001 or (800) 962-8519. Fax (919) 962-3400. One hundred seventy-six rooms and seven suites with private baths. Doubles, $159. Suites, $239 to $289.

The Siena Hotel, 1505 East Franklin St., Chapel Hill 27514.

Handsome in Mediterranean yellow and beige, this four-story boutique hotel was built in 1987 by local developer Sam Longiotti, who wanted to bring a bit of his homeland to North Carolina. He and his wife Susan modeled their hotel after a Tuscan villa in Siena. "The exuberant spirit of the Sienese is contagious," says Susan. "We have always loved Siena because of its warm people and beautiful Tuscan landscape."

The owners return often to Italy to bring back embellishments for their pride and joy. New things show up after every trip, says their marketing manager. You'll find grand public spaces, stunning artworks, a distinguished restaurant, and plenty of books on Siena and Tuscany scattered about the marble-floor lobby.

The 80 guest quarters come in four configurations, including standard, corner kings, six large studio suites and six small suites. Interesting touches abound. The king bed is offset in an alcove of a studio suite, where french doors open off the living/dining area onto a European balcony that's decorative rather than functional. Round roman tubs are featured in small suites. Marble baths and good paintings inspired by the Italian renaissance are featured in every room. Turndown service and waffle weave robes are standard.

(919) 929-4000 or (800) 223-7379. Fax (919) 968-8527. Sixty-eight rooms and twelve suites with private baths. Doubles, $165 to $175. Suites, $195 to $235.

Dining Spots

The Fearrington House Restaurant, 2000 Fearrington Village Center, Pittsboro.

Mention Chapel Hill to anyone familiar with the area and you're bound to be steered toward Fearrington for a meal and an experience to remember. The reputation and appeal of this Relais & Chateaux inn extends far beyond the borders of the country village launched two decades ago on an old dairy farm in the gently rolling hills south of Chapel Hill.

The only AAA five-diamond establishment in North Carolina, the restaurant occupies the original Fearrington farmhouse, built in 1927. Off the entry is a stylish lounge with plump bar chairs in gray and black and, on the bar, a selection of cigars to take outside. The main dining room is a beauty in white and moss green. Each table bears fresh flowers, white chargers and three stemmed glasses per place setting. It and smaller dining rooms are furnished with original art, antiques and colorful fabrics. Window tables look out on trellised gardens or, on one side, what the staff calls the wedding terrace.

Executive chef Cory Mattson oversees an extensive menu of what he describes as "classic regional cuisine." Dinners are prix-fixe, $59 for three courses and extras.

Dinner begin with an amuse-gueule and soup of the day, followed by a choice among eight appetizers. Typical are crispy sweetbreads with red wine-truffle vinaigrette and warm potato salad; air-cured antelope carpaccio with tomato and basil concasse, and sautéed soft-shell crayfish with orange-creole butter sauce and grits.

An intermezzo of buttermilk sorbet or orange-fennel salad prepares the palate for the main course. How about rice paper-wrapped yellowfin tuna with ginger sauce and Asian slaw? Or seared snapper fillet with lobster-fennel fricassee and lobster sauce? Or rabbit tenderloin wrapped in country ham with rabbit ravioli and an orange jus? Or braised leg of lamb and roast lamb loin with apple chutney? The descriptions belie the complexity of ingredients and presentations.

The same goes for desserts, perhaps a cherry bon-bon cake, hot chocolate soufflé with chocolate sauce or chilled passionfruit broth with fresh fruit, served with tangerine, key lime and grapefruit-ginger sorbets. More than 350 selections are carried on the Wine Spectator award-winning wine list.

If you can't get here for dinner or prefer a meal of less dramatic proportions, the nearby Market Café fills the bill. Interesting fare is offered for lunch, brunch and dinner, and whenever we've been there the café has been filled to overflowing. Twice we've had to settle for sandwiches in the deli, where you place your order and hear your first name called out in most un-Fearrington-like fashion.

(919) 542-2121. Prix-fixe, $59. Dinner, Tuesday-Saturday 6 to 9, Sunday to 8. Café: lunch, Monday-Friday 11:30 to 2:30; brunch, weekends 9:30 to 3; dinner, Monday-Friday 6 to 8:30.

Crook's Corner, 610 West Franklin St., Chapel Hill.

With a pink pig on the roof and a herd of folk art animals all around, this one-time barbecue joint has been a culinary destination since the days of the late Bill Neal, chef and cookbook author who won the praise of food critic Craig Claiborne. Neal, who first founded La Residence (see below), brought fine dining to the area

Acclaimed Fearrington House Restaurant lies behind pillared portico.

and, through reputation, to the Southeast. Many are the restaurateurs who worked with Neal at Crook's, including the current chef, Bill Smith.

Flowers, cacti, a cinderblock wall of hubcaps with softballs for eyes, and a log sculpture shaped like a pig are among the exterior attributes at Crook's. The inside is haute casual with a bar on the left and a snug dining room with a deco look on the right. The place to be in season is on the large outdoor courtyard. It's partly canopied around the perimeter and well screened from the street. Bamboo trees, gardens, sculptures and fountains provide the backdrop for little green tables and black ice-cream parlor chairs.

The menu changes daily. First courses range from andouille gumbo and jalapeño-cheddar hushpuppies to fried oysters with roasted garlic mayonnaise. The shrimp and grits, sautéed with bacon, mushrooms and scallions, is a signature dish. Not to be overlooked are the pan-fried catfish with homemade tartar sauce and collard greens, the chicken livers with avocado and onions and wilted spinach, or the garlic-pepper sirloin with Jerusalem artichoke relish and grilled asparagus. Those into barbecue enjoy the hickory-smoked, pit-cooked pork. Others simply hang out with a Crook's hamburger and a glass of wine or beer or a cup of "counter culture coffee" and enjoy a special place.

(919) 929-7643. Entrées, $9.95 to $17.95. Dinner nightly from 6. Sunday brunch 10:30 to 2.

La Résidence, 202 West Rosemary St., Chapel Hill.

This charming gray house opens up to the sunny look of Provence, with gardens outside giving way to a series of dining rooms dressed in yellow with blue accents. Tall candles, fresh flowers and starched napkins standing in cone shapes enhance the well spaced tables, each pristine in white over patterned undercloths. The walls are a veritable art gallery.

The place has been going strong since it was founded in 1976 by the late Bill Neal of Crook's Corner. The contemporary French/American menu is short but sweet. Look for starters like cream of sweet red pepper soup with goat cheese pesto, a classic beef tartare, and scallops au poivre wrapped with prosciutto and grilled citrus shrimp with a chipotle vinaigrette and a passionfruit beurre blanc.

Typical entrées are grilled sushi-grade tuna with oriental barbecue glaze and smoked tomato soy sauce, pan-seared grouper with porcini mushroom sauce, and osso buco with white truffle-oil mashed potatoes and haricots verts. Finish with kalouga (the signature chocolate soufflé cake), espresso ice cream with a splash of kahlua or the assorted sorbets with homemade cookies.

The wine list is distinguished, with reserve selections that could set you back as much as $180. There may be no better place to sample one of them than at the elegant bar or on the garden patio called Café La Rez.

(919) 967-2506. Entrées, $17.95 to $24.95. Dinner nightly, 6 to 9:30, Sunday to 8:30.

Four Eleven West, 411 West Franklin St., Chapel Hill.

When the locals advised that this sleek Italian café is wildly popular, little did we realize how much. Arriving about 8 on a weekday night, the lines extended out the door and we were told the best bet was to await an opening at the marble bar. There they were standing two and three deep, each with the same thought of getting a drink while awaiting a table. It took the hostess half an hour and several false starts to find a vacant bar stool with enough elbow room to eat.

Established in 1990, it's an expansive mix with a bistro look, Mediterranean colors, bare wood tables and a wood-fired pizza oven in front. Ficus trees thrive in a side solarium, and an enclosed rear courtyard harbors a fountain and plants.

The clientele is a wide mix of university types, young professionals, downtown shoppers, soccer moms and retirees. The menu follows suit – or is it the other way around? Pizzettes and pastas are the mainstays, accompanied by trendy appetizers, salads and weekly specials. When finally seated amidst the noisy bar crowd, we were impressed with the speed of service and the artistry of presentation. Assertive, peppery rolls and a good house salad preceded a huge plate of chicken marsala pasta, served with grilled vegetables.

Desserts are typical of the Italian ilk. Many folks seem to drop in for coffee and dessert or a snack at the cappuccino and pizza bar. Probably around 4 o'clock or after 10, when the mealtime crowds clear out.

(919) 967-2782. Entrées, $6.25 to $16.95. Lunch, Monday-Friday 11:30 to 2:30, Saturday to 4; dinner, nightly, 5 to 10 or 10:30, Sunday to 9:30. Cappuccino and pizza bar, 11:30 to close. No smoking.

Carolina CrossRoads, The Carolina Inn, 211 Pittsboro St., Chapel Hill.

Handsome in pale yellow with blue accents, this is the elegant restaurant in the storied Carolina Inn, the university's longtime "living room" and dining room of choice for returning alums. Contemporary Southern cuisine is featured, to go along with the new look of the restaurant and the plush adjacent bar, fashioned from what had been a meeting room and originally was the lobby. Both restaurant and bar adjoin a pillared veranda, where a few tables are set up for outdoor dining and imbibing.

The crowd was a mix of romantic tête-à-têtes and family gatherings – one with three generations and two lively toddlers – the Friday night we dined in the fairly bright yet romantic dining room. Addictive herbed butter and honey butter in big crocks arrived with the bread basket. Good starters were chilled diver scallops with a white bean and tropical fruit salad and a goat cheese terrine served with mesclun greens. Main courses ranged from the ubiquitous shrimp and grits to fricassee of baby hen and grilled New York angus steak. The smoked breast of duck, served over baby spinach with a tomato and orzo salad, was a winner. Polished waitresses crumbed the table between courses, making way for a dessert tray bearing raspberry swirl cheesecake, blueberry mascarpone tart, banana cream cake and pot de crème.

(919) 918-2777. Entrées, $17 to $23. Lunch daily, 11 to 2. Dinner nightly, 5 to 10. No smoking.

Il Palio Ristorante, 1505 East Franklin St., Chapel Hill.
A small open bar/lounge at one end of the marble-floored lobby stands beside the entrance to this distinguished restaurant in the posh Siena Hotel. The hotel is modeled after a Tuscan villa, and its arched and pillared dining room follows suit. Small dining areas are set off nicely at angles, creating intimacy amid the subdued opulence.

Chef Brian Stapleton is known for innovative, light "new Tuscan cuisine." The antipasti sampler of regional appetizers and the caesar salad prepared tableside get dinner off to a good start. Exotic pastas and risottos come in two sizes. The short list of main courses range from pan-seared monkfish and grilled halibut to braised lamb shanks and osso buco. The wine list merits the Wine Spectator award of excellence.

Classical guitar or piano music is presented nightly in the lounge.

(919) 929-4000 or (800) 223-7379. Entrées, $18.25 to $21.50. Lunch, Monday-Saturday 11:30 to 2. Dinner nightly 6 to 10. Sunday brunch, 11:30 to 2.

Top of the Hill, 100 West Franklin St., Chapel Hill.
Atop the First Union bank building is this large, mod restaurant with a bar in the center and dining areas built around a brewery. Best of all is the huge rooftop porch, where you can sit at high perches beside a railing and overlook the busy intersection of Franklin and South Columbia streets.

University types by the score gather here at all hours. Many were on hand when we stopped for a late lunch of crispy chicken spinach salad, which turned out to be a large and tasty concoction of fried chicken strips atop the usual spinach salad and accompaniments, and a grilled tuna fillet with roasted red peppers, ginger aioli, and caramelized onions on a sesame roll, accompanied by french fries. A couple of glasses of the house-made Kenan summer ale and Lake Hogan hefeweisen hit the spot.

The dinner menu offers much the same kind of contemporary American fare. It's supplemented by a range of entrées from home-style meatloaf to filet mignon stuffed with boursin cheese.

(919) 929-8676. Entrées, $10.95 to $21.95. Open daily from 11:30 for lunch, dinner and late night. Sunday brunch, 10 to 3.

Diversions

Culture and sporting events star in Chapel Hill, as in most university towns. Two icons that say Chapel Hill to the traditional South are the Old Well and the Morehead-Patterson Bell Tower on the University of North Carolina campus. The latter-day icon is the 21,572-seat Dean E. Smith Center, dubbed the Dean Dome as the home of national basketball champions.

University of North Carolina. The 729-acre campus stretches south from Franklin Street in downtown Chapel Hill. The visitor center in the west lobby of Morehead Planetarium offers a map for a short campus walking tour. It takes visitors past the principal sites, including the nation's two oldest state university buildings, Old East (1795) and Person Hall (1797). Outside Old East residence hall is the Old Well, the early source of water and the unofficial symbol of the university. The broad, tree-shaded lawns nearby are marked by the Davie Poplar Tree and the Caldwell and Silent Sam monuments.

Morehead Planetarium, 250 East Franklin St.

One of the largest planetariums in the country, this was the first owned by a university. It served as a NASA training center and contains art and science exhibits and a walk-in model of the solar system. The domed, 330-seat Star Theater presents star shows nightly and matinees on weekends.

(919) 962-1236. Open daily 12:30 to 5 and 7 to 9:45, Saturday from 10. Exhibits free. Programs, $3.50.

The Coker Arboretum, adjacent to the Morehead Planetarium. About 580 species of trees and shrubs grace the campus landscape, thanks to the vision of the university's first professor of botany, who also chaired its first buildings and grounds committee. He developed a five-acre boggy pasture alongside the campus into an outdoor classroom for the study of plants native to North Carolina, supplemented by many exotic East Asian trees and shrubs that are close relatives of the indigenous species. It's a pleasant, though somewhat abused refuge, as noted by a sign at an entry: "Frisbee players, dog owners and smokers take note. This is not a park, rather a collection of plants to be used by students, educators and the public as a resource." The gardens were to be restored for their 100th anniversary in 2003.

Ackland Art Museum, South Columbia Street.

Rather forbidding on the outside, the interior holds more than 7,000 works of art from a wide range of cultures, from ancient Greek bronzes to 20th-century abstract paintings. The Ackland claims one of the strongest collections of Indian art and Western prints, drawings and photographs in the Southeast.

(919) 966-5736. Open Wednesday-Saturday 10 to 5, Sunday 1 to 5. Donation, $3.

The North Carolina Collection Gallery, in the Wilson Library on UNC campus.

This is considered the best collection of state literature in the country. Most of the more than 250,000 volumes are housed on five levels of closed stacks. Highlights for the casual visitor are museum exhibits devoted to band leader Kay Keyser, Sir Walter Raleigh and – surprise – the original Siamese twins. The fascinating story of twins Eng and Chang, who immigrated to North Carolina in the late 1830s after traveling the world as celebrities, is recounted here. The Thomas Wolfe Room is based on his boyhood home in Asheville and contains a scholarly exhibit of the state's most celebrated writer.

(919) 962-1172. Open Monday-Friday 9 to 5, Saturday 9 to 1, Sunday 1 to 5. Free.

North Carolina Botanical Garden, Old Mason Farm Road.

The UNC-owned garden is a cool refuge of picnic tables and plantings within earshot of Highway Bypass 15/501. Paths and plants surround the Totten Center headquarters. Native Southeastern plants are arranged by coastal plain, sandhill and mountain habitats. A boardwalk traverses lily ponds and trails pass wildflowers, herbs and ferns. Across the street, nature trails lead through 80 acres of Piedmont woodlands.

(919) 962-0522. Open Monday-Friday 10 to 5, Saturday 9 to 6, Sunday 1 to 6. Free.

Historic Hillsborough. What Chapel Hill lacks in visible history (only one historic house open to the public, the circa 1840 Horace William House), this small town of 4,300 offers in spades. As a capital of Colonial and Revolutionary North Carolina, the town was the scene of several dramatic events prior to the Revolutionary War. The laid-back historic district, listed on the National Register, contains more than 100 surviving late 18th- and early 19th-century structures, some of which can be viewed on guided or self-guided walking tours. The visitor center, a 1790 house, once served as headquarters for Gen. Joseph E. Johnston, who negotiated the surrender that led to the end of the Civil War. The Colonial Inn, dating to 1759, is one of the oldest continuous operating inns in North America. It looks and feels it.

Shopping. Chapel Hill's Franklin Street, passing the UNC campus, is the main street for both town and gown. The stores and eateries, naturally, are of primary interest to the university community. Franklin Street is full of surprises, from the venerable and unexpectedly elegant Carolina Coffee Shop, whose dark paneling conveys look of a Victorian library, to the funky Caribou Coffee in a former Pure gasoline station. Another institution is **Julian's,** a men's clothing store since 1942. Clothing designer Alexander Julian grew up in his father's store and now hand picks the best from his collection to show in his hometown. Sister Missy, who runs the store, calls the result "traditional with a twist."

Carrboro is home to the Carr Mill Town Center Shops in a restored mill. The rambling layout offers **Talbots, O'Neill's** men's apparel, **A New Attitude** women's clothing, **Benchmark** furnishings and **Gallery Americas,** which displays some stunning contemporary art, crafts, furniture and accessories.

Extra-Special

A Southern Season, Eastgate Shopping Center, Chapel Hill.

This sprawling specialty store is legendary for its blend of gourmet foods, coffees, cheeses, candy, breads and more. You'd never guess that it started in 1975 in a little lean-to – "like a large walk-in closet," says Michael Barefoot, local farmboy-hippie turned entrepreneur. He roasted coffees and sold bulk spices and imported cheeses and wines, all "considered quite esoteric locally at the time." The South caught up with the times and A Southern Season led the way, evolving into one of the largest specialty food shops in the Southeast. A brisk mail-order catalog business focuses on its North Carolina roots. Half an acre of space holds chrome shelves and glass display cases laden with treats, from the candy fantasyland at the front to the 270-seat Weathervane Cafe in the rear. The growing enterprise is composed of nine departments, each personally run by a manager in a proprietary way. In a world of franchises and super stores, A Southern Season is content to continue following its magic formula: great products, warm ambiance and personal, small-town service.

(919) 929-7133 or (800) 253-3663. Open Monday-Saturday 10 to 7, Sunday noon to 6.

Pinehurst/Southern Pines, N.C.

Golf Capital of the World

The pine-clad sandhills of North Carolina weren't good for much more than tar and tannin when Boston philanthropist James Walker Tufts purchased 5,000 acres of ravaged timberland in 1895. The land was bare and sandy, but Tufts had a vision. He commissioned Frederick Law Olmsted to create a town of curving streets and open spaces to provide a luxury health resort for Northerners retreating from winter's cold. Olmsted transplanted the charm of a New England village to the sandhills of North Carolina. They called it Pinehurst.

The barren farmlands had long reminded the early Scot settlers around Aberdeen a bit of home. And no less a Scotsman than golf professional Donald James Ross moved here in 1900 to design the famed Pinehurst No. 2 course. He remained here until his death in 1948, opening an inn and designing about 400 other golf courses.

These days, 26 golf clubs and resorts with a total of 40 courses draw thousands to a sportsman's paradise known as the cradle of American golf. So intertwined are golf and Pinehurst that the village was designated a national historic landmark in 1997. The designation was based on its prominence in the development of American golf and its integrity today as a remarkably intact planned recreational resort community.

Golf is, of course, paramount in this area that spawned not only the famed Pinehurst resort but also the first driving range and the first miniature golf course. "There is perhaps no other spot on earth as devoted to golf, and the leisure to play it, as Pinehurst," according to history as interpreted by the Pinehurst resort.

But the leisure lifestyle pursued here extends beyond: to horses, harness racing, polo and foxhunting. To shopping, in some of the South's finest stores. To arts and crafts, as epitomized by the nearby Seagrove potteries. To restaurants that cater to high living well into the evenings. And to gardening, as represented in one of the more appealing horticultural ventures we know of.

Stately Midland Road, its parkway median shaded by towering pines, spans much of the area's leisure spectrum. It follows the six-mile-long path of the original trolley line that transported golfers to the infant Pinehurst resort from the train depot in the middle of the main street of Southern Pines, now an arty equestrian community. It passes the manicured lawns of pine needles, grass or both surrounding substantial homes as well as the lush fairways of ten golf courses. It terminates at the edge of downtown Pinehurst, just a few yards from the second green of the legendary Pinehurst No. 2 course, site of the U.S. Open in 1999.

The area is nirvana for golfers. One of the strengths of the place is its attractions for non-golfers, too.

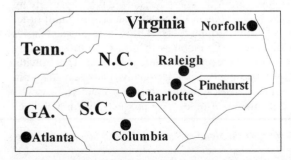

Elegant Knollwood House backs up to 15th fairway of famed Mid Pines Golf Club.

Inn Spots

As owner Ned Darby of the Magnolia Inn tells it: "We have some guests who are here just for a romantic getaway weekend. And there's a thoroughbred horse group, the occasional tourist and others. But golfers are far and away our most frequent guests." That explains the emphasis on package deals and the multiple bed configurations indigenous to area inns and B&Bs.

Knollwood House, 1495 West Connecticut Ave., Southern Pines 28387.

Inn-going golfers can't get much closer to a golf club than this elegant English manor house that adjoins the 15th fairway of the famed Mid Pines Golf Club. Yet the accommodations in the main house and the newly renovated carriage house exist in their own private world – a shady, residential expanse of five acres bearing gardens, longleaf pines, towering holly trees and showy azaleas. The only sounds are those of the birds and – at our visit – a power mower readying the Mid Pines fairways for the day's play.

The B&B is the expanding retirement project of Dick Beatty, a former officer of the Manhattan-based advertising agency, Ogilvie and Mather. He and wife Mimi moved here from Southport, Conn. He and their right hand, Cora, run the B&B while Mimi commutes to her fund-raising job at the University of North Carolina in Chapel Hill.

The Beattys share their sophisticated home with guests in two rooms and four suites. And what a home! The front door opens into a large, elegant living room cheery in yellow and outfitted in chintzes, tapestry and needlepoint. There's plush seating in no fewer than three conversation areas. Jutting beyond is a large, three-sided screened porch that ends in an enclosed garden area for potted plants. Also decked out in lounge chairs is an equally large and glamorous outdoor patio beside. Here is where breakfast is served, unless the weather forces the meal inside. We were seated amidst late 18th-century antiques in a formal dining room for a feast of fresh orange juice, cantaloupe and sausage strata, accompanied by baked, sliced granny smith apples and Amish bread. Possibilities on other days include cheese soufflé, chicken hash and a Viennese breakfast pudding.

Large back porches turn two of the four upstairs bedrooms into suites. The Toile Suite, named for the wallpaper, is handsome in white and green with a queen bed and a rear porch with a couple of day beds and a TV. The dressing table bearing family silver pieces and the bathroom with Mimi's monogrammed towels gave the feeling of staying as a family guest in a private home. When we were there, the adjacent suite with twin beds was occupied by two young golfing buddies here on a bargain package plan that included greens fees and dinners at the Beattys' favorite restaurants. A retired couple who also were playing golf were ensconced in the new suite in the front carriage house, converted in 1997 from what had been a garage. They enjoyed a queen bed, plump loveseat and chair, wet bar in the sitting/dressing room and a walk-in shower. A smaller suite next door in the carriage house holds twin beds and a loveseat in the sitting area. All accommodations have TVs and are comfortably furnished with understated family pieces and antiques gathered from around the world.

The Beattys bill the Knollwood House as "very civilized." Given its history as a holiday house for a prominent Philadelphia family, who entertained the likes of Walter Hagen and Ben Hogan, you'd not be surprised to learn that Glenn Miller's Orchestra once played a concert on the back terrace.

(910) 692-9390. Fax (910) 692-0609.Two rooms and four suites with private baths. Doubles, $115. Suites, $135 to $150. Two-night minimum stay or $25 surcharge on weekends. Children over 10.

Covington House, 1855 Camp Easter Road, Southern Pines 28387.

Prepare to be overwhelmed. This contemporary showplace based on Frank Lloyd Wright designs could pass for a decorator showhouse, and frequently is a setting for benefit galas. So the fact that owner Linda Covington runs it as a B&B with four guest rooms is a surprise.

"This is rather spectacular," we told her upon arrival. "It's home," she countered. Home for a 40-something woman who sold her credit reporting agencies in Raleigh to move back to the property across the street from where she grew up. Home for her nine horses, which she and guests ride around the rural, 35-acre property. Home for her bridal and B&B guests, who fill the guest book displayed in the soaring foyer with accolades amounting to "we could not have felt more at home."

Some home. But a tribute to the hospitality with which Linda shares it. The 10,000 square feet of interior space spreads outward and upward from the foyer, so big with so much for the visitor to take in that you could fail to notice the big painting of a lion whose eyes follow you whichever way you go. Go into the 40-foot-high living room, where a Christmas tree with 10,000 lights stands sentry in a corner year-round. A massive fireplace and chimney of Pennsylvania stone soars to the ceiling. Above the seating areas and a rear sunroom is a loft with a grand piano and more seating. From its tall windows you discover the large, free-form swimming pool tucked beside a manmade lake in the back yard, hidden from view at ground level. Move on to the side library/TV den, which Linda calls "my jungle room," with a kangaroo skin on the floor and a stuffed tiger in the corner. A glass breakfast room leads to the two-story-high designer kitchen, which opens onto a

Rear of contemporary Covington House is on view from landscaped pool area.

plush sitting area with a fireplace. Off the kitchen in the front of the house is a chandeliered dining room with full-length windows at one end and a gold inlaid brass credenza that matches the long table. The table, flanked by white fabric chairs, is covered with a white damask pleated cloth Linda designed and made herself.

The other end of the foyer leads to the guest quarters. At our visit, Linda was converting her master suite into a bridal suite. A plump white kingsize bed lies beneath a semi-circular opening in the ceiling topped by a skylight, with an exercise room on the loft above. Marble is everywhere in the breathtaking series of bath/dressing/vanity areas with a whirlpool tub and a walk-in shower big enough for an entire wedding party.

Linda named the other bedrooms for her sons and a niece. The Shannon Leigh Room has a kingsize canopy bed with a mirrored top and the plumpest feather-bed mattress we ever saw, draped in damask with white fabric all around. The James Edwin has a loveseat and a white damask queen bed laden with pillows. The bath includes a jacuzzi, dressing area, vanity and closet. The Bradley Davis has a separate sitting room, a queen bed and a beige and tan masculine air, complete with the son's golf trophies and football memorabilia.

The contemporary décor throughout is splashy, mostly white and of the California designer variety. Artworks and statuary, plants and fresh orchids and roses provide color. The idyllic pool area is a refuge of lounge chairs, stone work and tranquility from which we could barely pry ourselves away. Off to one side, beyond gardens ablaze with a small nursery's worth of impatiens plants, is a building that Linda planned to convert into a two-bedroom cottage with living room and fireplace in the future.

You might think breakfast here would be an afterthought. Not so. Linda cooks eggs, quiche or pancakes to accompany a fresh fruit tray, oatmeal, croissants and muffins.

"Camelot," one guest called the place.

(910) 695-0352. Fax (910) 695-1040. Three rooms and one suite with private baths. Doubles, $150. Suite, $200.

Page Manor House, 300 Page St., Aberdeen 28315.

Some view Aberdeen as little more than the busy commercial strip for Pinehurst and Southern Pines. Seasoned travelers Sharon and Russell Cogan from Connecticut had a different vision for their property hidden in the woods above the aging town center. With great taste and hard work, the Cogans finished the conversion of the abandoned home of one of the town's founding families into an elegant B&B of uncommon appeal.

The rambling, three-story Victorian cottage was built in the early 1900s by the son of business mogul Henry A. Page, who lived in an adjacent mansion and gave his name to the street known locally as Millionaire's Row. The seven acres of grounds include a pool with a garden cabana, a lighted tennis court, wooded trails and elaborate English gardens centered by a fountain and fish pond. Inside are elegant, comfortable common rooms and four guest bedrooms with all the amenities.

Russell decorated the house, Sharon does the cooking and cleaning, and together they mow four acres of lawn with his and her power mowers. Together they were finishing the fourth day of painting the inside of their 20-by-40-foot swimming pool at our visit.

Russell's decor is, in his word, eclectic. The spacious living room is handsome in dark green, with a huge aviarium of finches set into the front window. Beside the living room is a cheerful sunporch. Across the foyer are a large dining room with an oriental dining set and a cozy den of Southern pine with plush loveseats, TV and a big mirrored bar.

The Cogans designed the colorful carpet runner that goes up the stairway and had it custom-made to match the wallpaper and artworks. Sharon spent five weeks wallpapering the hallway alone. The names of the bedrooms are understated and chosen because of the prevailing colors. Each has an oversize bed, working fireplace, down pillows, duvets and 310-count bed linens. The Mauve is a refuge for romance. It has a kingsize French iron bed canopied in white fabric, two wing chairs and a day bed, a working fireplace and – as in the other bedrooms – wallpaper where one expects wainscoting and mauve painted walls above. Here as elsewhere, the TV/VCR is hidden in an armoire. Two wing chairs, a fireplace and a queensize cherry sleigh bed grace the Blue Room, which took the couple ten months to redo. In the canopied-queen Green Room, they made a couple of closets into a two-part bathroom with a washstand between. Oriental fans accent the attic penthouse room, in which Russell ingeniously sawed out a recessed ceiling above the kingsize bed for airiness and ventilation.

"I try to decorate to give a relaxing feeling – just like home," says Russell. "We have a helluva time getting guests off the front porch to go home." Which is understandable after you have experienced one of Sharon's gourmet breakfasts by candlelight. Ours began with fresh orange juice and a pineapple boat drizzled with low-fat caramel sauce and featured a smashing eggs benedict on toasted Italian tomato bread spread with pesto sauce, layered with tomatoes and dusted with reggiano-parmegiano cheese. Guests are offered a changing selection of three exotic choices for the fruit course and four for the main course (from a repertoire of 27). They make their choices the night before.

Page Manor caters not to golfers but to romance, says Sharon. "Our guests want to get away and be well fed."

*(910) 944-5970. Fax (910) 944-1172. **Four rooms with private baths. Doubles, $150 weekends, $125 midweek, tax included. No smoking.***

Rambling Victorian cottage has been transformed into Page Manor House.

The Magnolia Inn, 65 Magnolia St., Pinehurst 28374.

This 1896 Victorian – the second structure to be erected in the new village of Pinehurst – was built as an inn. It offers three floors of faded 19th-century elegance, Victorian antiques and accessories, and a prime location facing the main shopping district from behind a shield of magnolia trees.

Fully renovated in 1990 and since partially redecorated, the accommodations are geared to the golfing clientele that the inn attracts. The first second-floor room we saw was described as typical. It contains a queensize pine bed with an extra single bed, an armoire with a TV on top, a shower but no bathtub, two chairs and oriental scatter rugs. Another room with one of the inn's two in-room working fireplaces has a queen bed, a full bath and a single velvet rocking chair. The Dogwood suite has a queen bed in the main room, a twin bed in a side room and a clawfoot tub. Four smaller rooms on the third floor, each with twin beds and a single chair, appear plain but serviceable.

Since taking over in 1991, golfing innkeepers Jan and Ned Darby have added a restaurant (see Dining Spots). They installed a commercial kitchen and converted the parlor into a formal dining room and a back bedroom into a cozy, English-style pub. A full country Southern breakfast includes eggs any style or omelets, grits, sausage and biscuits.

(910) 295-6900 or (800) 526-5562. Fax (910) 215-0858. Eleven rooms with private baths. Doubles, $140. Add $30 for MAP.

The Old Buggy Inn, 301 McReynolds St. (Hwy. 24-27), Box 707, Carthage 28327.

"Authentic Victorian," reads the sign above the doorway to this good-looking Queen Anne house, painted gray with moss green and rose gingerbread trim. And how. From the wraparound porch up close to the road to the twin parlors to the upstairs guest quarters that look like a museum, Victoriana reigns.

Owners Royce and Susan Smith moved with two daughters from Raleigh in 1990 and undertook a painstaking restoration prior to opening in 1996. Victorian antiques, wallpapers and carpeting prevail throughout.

Chirping birds in four cages ensconced in the turret greet new arrivals in the library/TV room. A leather sofa faces the fireplace in the gentlemen's parlor. Lace curtains grace the ladies' parlor. The sideboard in the dining room was laden with cantaloupe, cereals and frosted donuts at our weekday visit.

An ornate, white-trimmed staircase leads from the large entry foyer to the second-floor landing, where seating is offered amid collections of Victorian purses and canes. Whimsical angels and a rug painted on the floor decorate the front-corner Angel Room with a queen brass bed and a loveseat in the bay window. The front Tower Room with a double bed has a circular sitting area in the turret, which was given over to a twin bed when we were there. Eastlake-style furniture and a roses and ribbons motif dignify the Romantic Rendezvous Room, which may connect with the Tower Room to form a suite. The white iron and brass antique bed in Amanda's Midnight Retreat is almost upstaged by the canopied day bed, not to mention the Victorian gloves and shoes on display. The french doors of the down-stairs Veranda View open onto a large back porch overlooking decks and a swimming pool. Altogether there are five guest rooms that come with carved fireplaces, sleeping porches and queen, double or twin beds. In early 1999, the Smiths added three bathrooms so all rooms would have private baths, some down the hall.

The outside of the property is handsome as well. Besides the pool, there are rose gardens and elaborate landscaping. Although both Smiths work by day, at night they offer wine and cheese, coffee and cookies. Breakfast on weekends might be baked fruit and eggs soufflé or strawberry waffles.

(910) 947-1901 or (800) 553-5247. Five rooms with private baths. Doubles, $80 to $95. Suite, $160. Children accepted. Smoking restricted.

Pinehurst, Carolina Vista Drive, Box 4000, Pinehurst 28374.

The bellhops are in golf knickers at the entry and the public corridors are a veritable museum of golf at this grand hotel, now bearing its original name, **The Carolina.** The national historic landmark has changed precious little since it opened in 1901 as the largest wood-frame hotel in North Carolina. Conceived as the centerpiece of what became the model golf community in the country, the hotel at the edge of downtown Pinehurst is surrounded by eight golf courses. It offers a total of 144 holes of golf, more than any resort in the world. Little wonder Pinehurst has been called "The Queen of the South" and "The White House of Golf."

The rambling, four-story hotel topped with a cupola has been updated over the years by its Dallas-based owner, Club Resorts Inc., a golf and conference resort company. It contains 220 rooms and nine suites that have been totally renovated. Bed configurations vary, from one queen to two doubles, two queens or one king. Rose and forest green is the color motif, and furnishings are dark wood. Gold fixtures gleam in the bathrooms.

Meals are included in the rates. The public is welcome as well. The Carolina Dining Room, elegant and formal, offers an $11 breakfast buffet said to be worth a trip from anywhere. The menu for the five-course prix-fixe dinner ($37) changes nightly.

The hotel is considered the hub of the Pinehurst resort. Pinehurst also runs the less formal **Manor Inn,** a 46-room facility two blocks away that its publicity

Stately Carolina hotel, a national historic landmark, is hub of Pinehurst resort.

likens to a B&B. Its newest, most deluxe and intimate facility is the renovated **Holly Inn** (see below). The resort also rents 135 condominiums and 40 villas.

(910) 295-6811 or (800) 487-4653. Fax (910) 295-8503. Hotel, 220 rooms and nine suites with private baths. Rates MAP: doubles, $410 in spring and fall, $344 in summer, $306 in winter.

Holly Inn, 2300 Cherokee Road, Pinehurst, 28374.
The first inn in Pinehurst underwent a multi-million-dollar upgrade for reopening in April 1999.

The original five-story inn was designed in 1895 by James Walker Tufts, the resort area's founder, to resemble those on Cape Cod in his native Massachusetts. Situated at the head of the village green, the 75-room inn with pillared portico had experienced its ups and downs over its first century.

It was acquired by Resorts of Pinehurst Inc. in 1997. Pinehurst closed the inn for 1998 and launched a massive renovation to produce 79 rooms and six suites, two of them bi-level with upstairs bedrooms. The deluxe, full-service inn is billed as the resort's premier facility.

Guest rooms have custom-made Victorian furnishings, including rocking chairs, full-length cheval mirrors, work desks and two armchairs, and porcelain pedestal sinks in the bathrooms.

The inn's main floor contains a dining room and tavern. Noon and afternoon tea are served in the lobby, which has been expanded to include a library. The Holly's original octagonal-shaped music room was restored for business meetings. A new outdoor swimming pool is surrounded by a manicured English courtyard.

(910) 295-6811 or (800) 487-4653. Seventy-nine rooms and six suites with private baths. Rates MAP: doubles $500 in spring and fall, $360 in winter, $300 in summer. Two-night minimum stay peak weekends.

Pine Crest Inn, Dogwood Road, Box 879, Pinehurst 28370.
Nestled among tall pines near the center of the village, this gray stone building

topped by a wood third floor is a favorite among golfers. It was owned by Donald Ross, the legendary golf course architect, from 1921 until his death in 1948. Frankly, it has not changed much since.

For traditionalists, it's a convivial and unpretentious home away from home. To others it appears to have seen better days.

Enter the dark lobby and step into the past, a past full of golf atmosphere and personality. The 40 guest quarters vary, and some are frayed around the edges. The smallest rooms contain two twin beds. The majority are standard rooms, which the owners claim would be called deluxe at many other hotels. They have two beds – a queen and a double or twin – and an occasional chair or two. The five corner rooms are larger and contain a king and a twin bed or two queens plus a sofa. The prime accommodations are in the Telephone Cottage, so named because it was once a telephone switching station on the grounds of the inn. It has two queen beds and a smaller bedroom for an extra person, a jacuzzi, large shower, easy chairs, dining table, refrigerator and wet bar. All rooms have TV and telephones.

Most of the basic rooms are not the kind in which to linger. At any rate, most guests spend time in the lobby's piano bar, Mr. B's Lounge, which owner Bob Barrett calls "one of the great watering holes in all of golf."

The old-fashioned dining room is pillared and dark in mauve colors. The cuisine – "nothing fancy, and just like mom's" – has been a tradition for some since the inn's inception in 1913. Locals liken it to going out for Sunday dinner every day, and some do. The short menu ranges from basic (meatloaf, roast turkey and ham steak) to a little more fancy (coquilles St. Jacques and broiled filet mignon). For the public, soup, salad and beverages come with. Desserts like peach melba, crème de menthe sundae and pecan pie are extra. Gentlemen are requested to wear jackets at dinner.

(910) 295-6121 or (800) 371-2545. Fax (910) 295-4880. Thirty-nine rooms and one cottage with private baths. Rates, MAP: $75 to $100 per person in spring, $58 to $88 in fall, $49 to $70 in summer and winter.

Dining Spots

The wide spectrum in the area's dining situation is illustrated by innkeeper Russell Cogan of Page Manor: "If the weather's nice, visitors play 36 holes of golf and food is not a factor. If the weather's crummy, people go out to eat."

Chef Warren's, 215 N.E. Broad St., Southern Pines.

Local chef Warren Lewis opened this upscale bistro in 1998 to critical acclaim. His fans pack the place nightly, for contemporary fare served in a renovated storefront across from the train station. Wife Maureen Lewis oversees the front of the house, where the 60 seats are primarily at side banquettes with a few tables in the center for larger parties. She decorated in a cross between arts and crafts and art nouveau styles to achieve the look of a turn-of-the-century French bistro. "People tell me they think they're back in New York, New Orleans or Paris," says Maureen.

A dining bar surrounds the open kitchen at the rear, where diners can watch the well-traveled (Manhattan, Boston and Miami) chef at work. With-it specials supplement the short menu, which is affordably priced, although the specials like pan-seared Maine diver scallops and grilled filet of ostrich are more expensive. The treats begin with such starters as a lobster eggroll with a trio of Asian dipping sauces, a delicate roasted crab cake with a charred corn and scallion relish and chipotle mayonnaise, confit of duck salad, and chèvre and potato gnocchi with roasted tomato coulis.

Typical main courses are sesame-crusted ahi tuna with mango ketchup, pan-seared fillet of rainbow trout, pecan-crusted rack of pork with maple-rosemary glaze, braised lamb shanks with root vegetables on creamy polenta, and an unusually flavorful grilled skirt steak with wild mushrooms. Warren's specialty is duck, in several variations – if it's available, Maureen strongly recommends it.

The signature dessert is crème brûlée. Pecan pie based on her mother's recipe and blueberry cobbler are other favorites. The wine list is choice, and with less of a markup than the norm.

(910) 692-5240. Entrées, $15.95 to $18.50. Dinner, Monday-Saturday 6 to 9:30 or 10. Closed Mondays in December-February and July-August.

Ashten's, 140 East New Hampshire Ave., Southern Pines.

Sisters Ashley and Quinten Van Camp were born and raised here but went their separate ways. Ashley trained in cooking and restaurant management in New York and Quinten returned home. The idea for a restaurant arose "to get Ashley back here," her sister said. Teaming with chef Steven Bigger from Pennsylvania, a Culinary Institute of America graduate, they opened the area's most stylish restaurant in 1997.

The name incorporates portions of the sisters' names and the decor represents their vision of an English country manor. The main-floor dining room is elegant in pale yellow and burgundy beneath a pressed-tin ceiling. Downstairs is a cigar bar/wine cellar where Quinten mixes "a killer martini" and folks hang out in an English library setting.

The changing menu offers three courses of appetizers, soups and salads before the main course. You might start with fried sea scallops with a lemon-ginger sauce over radicchio or smoked salmon cheesecake with a dill-sour cream sauce and an herbed scone. Soup could be cream of asparagus with a pureed salmon swirl or smoked chicken with sundried tomatoes, wild mushrooms and asparagus. Typical of the exotic salads is one with watercress, avocado, jìcama and toasted almonds, tossed with a lime vinaigrette.

Main dishes range from dijon-crusted fillet of Atlantic salmon with a dilled risotto, sautéed arugula and baby carrots to tournedos of angus beef with a garlic and shallot sauce, served with a horseradish and chive croquette, haricots verts and sundried tomatoes. Desserts, listed under "pudding course," might be a creamy frozen lemon soufflé or chocolate chunk bread pudding with a wild berry sauce.

Service is formal in the European tradition. Tables are crumbed between courses and napkins refolded if diners get up from their chairs.

(910) 695-1019. Entrées, $16 to $30. Dinner nightly, 6 to 10. Sunday brunch, 11 to 2.

The Jefferson Inn, 150 West New Hampshire Ave., Southern Pines.

A hotelier from Long Island took over this old inn in 1997 and quickly put its restaurant on the culinary map. Local chef Lloyd Manning's food is at the cutting edge, the dining room and bar decor is nostalgic Victorian and the outdoor dining courtyard and tiki bar is idyllic on a pleasant evening.

The terrace/tiki bar is where we chose to eat, perched on bar stools at tall tables for two, surrounded by greenery and twinkling white lights. The steak house pub menu offered an appealing choice of appetizers and main dishes, whose simple names belied the complexity of presentation. An exemplary house salad of mesclun, slivered monsego cheese, walnuts and oven-dried tomatoes arrived on an oversize dinner plate. The main course, blackened catfish, came on piping hot white show plates. Rice and tasty grilled vegetables accompanied, as did excellent roasted red pepper bread.

The pub meal was an ample test of the chef's talents, which are more formally showcased in two dining rooms on either side of a rich wood bar/lounge called **T. Patrick's Steak and Chop House and Pub.** There the fare is billed as Southern plantation cuisine. You might start with bahamian rock shrimp seviche, confit of duck or carpaccio of lamb. Main courses range from a simple grilled breast of chicken with mashed potatoes and pan gravy to New York strip steak au poivre in a cognac cream sauce with a wedge of potato pie.

Owner Jollyn Erickson calls her restaurant and inn "a work in progress." Undergoing extensive renovations were twenty guest rooms and three suites with king, queen or two double beds, televisions, telephones and a mix of "found" furnishings. Two rooms have jacuzzi tubs. Rates include a basic continental breakfast.

(910) 692-5300 or (888) 703-4272. Fax (910) 692-8300. Entrées, $14.95 to $28.95. Pub, $14.95 to $24.95. Lunch daily, 11;30 to 2. Dinner nightly, 5:30 to 10. Doubles, $65 to $125; off-season, $45 to $99.

Theos Taverna, 140 Chinquapin Road, Pinehurst.
Greek and Mediterranean fare play starring roles in this large yet intimate downtown restaurant and lounge owned by Theos Dalitsouris. Upwards of 200 people can be seated in a two-story dining room with a wraparound balcony overlooking the scene and in an elegant lounge. Fifty more are accommodated at umbrellaed tables on a shady front patio banked in geraniums.

The extensive menu offers something for everyone, from light fare and pizzettes to pastas and meats. Lamb is the specialty in a variety of presentations. Among them are moussaka, lamb in phyllo, Theos' lamb slowly cooked in herbs, root vegetables and tomato wine sauce, and rack of lamb for two with Theos' lemon potatoes.

We'd planned to make a dinner of an appetizer of fried oysters over greens and a grilled pizzette with smoked salmon, until we were informed that appetizers served as entrées are charged $3 extra. A special of crab cake over angel-hair pasta was a satisfactory substitute, artistically presented on an oversize plate speckled with herbs and bearing al dente broccoli, carrots, snow peas and cauliflower around the perimeter. Greek house wine accompanied from a large wine list, far more affordable than the area's norm. A reserve list offers fine Italian vintages. Greek music played softly in the background.

(910) 295-0780. Entrées, $10.95 to $23.95. Lunch, Monday-Saturday 11:30 to 2:30. Dinner, Monday-Saturday 5 to 10.

The Magnolia Inn, 65 Magnolia St., Pinehurst 28374.
Two formal, wainscoted dining rooms in beige and burgundy impart an elegant, refined feeling to the well regarded restaurant on the main floor of this lately restored inn in the heart of Pinehurst. Owners Ned and Jan Darby added the restaurant and a cozy rear pub after they took over the inn in 1991.

Chef Mark Elliott from England offers a contemporary American menu with

Magnolia Inn in center of Pinehurst village is known for elegant dining.

innovative twists. For main courses, sautéed salmon arrives on a red onion-maple confit with a cider-saffron sauce. Tournedos of ostrich are presented on a potato and pear gâteau with a fig-honey sauce. Venison loin is roasted in wine and rosemary and set on a parsnip and potato puree. Veal medallions are stuffed with southern sausage and complemented with a potato hash. Look for appetizers like zesty duck spring rolls, mushrooms and scallops au gratin, and ravioli stuffed with goat cheese and arugula.

(910) 295-6900 or (800) 526-5562. Entrées, $13.95 to $28. Lunch, Tuesday-Saturday 11:30 to 2:30. Dinner nightly, 6 to 9:30.

La Terrace, 270 South Broad St., Southern Pines.
French people run this small, classic restaurant that looks as if it would be at home in the countryside of Provence. Mirrors, wainscoting and lots of lattice work provide a summery backdrop for traditional French fare refreshingly lacking in nouvelle conceits and haute pricing.

The menu starts with duck and pork pâté "like in France with toast," "beautiful large shrimp cocktail cooked to order," Norwegian smoked salmon "with all garnishes and cream cheese," escargots bourguignonne, French onion soup gratinée and classic vichyssoise.

Among the loyal clientele are people who order the stellar dover sole meunière every chance they get. Others prefer the coquille neptune (three seashells filled with crabmeat, lobster and scallops, each in a distinctive sauce), the signature boneless breast of duck albarine and the filet mignon with béarnaise sauce.

Dessert could be caramel custard, a pecan ball with chocolate sauce or a chocolate truffle with English cream sauce.

(910) 692-5622. Entrées, $12.50 to $19.50. Dinner, Monday-Saturday 6 to 9:30.

Sleddon's, 275 South Bennett St., Southern Pines.
An old Southern Pines stucco residence, this has been converted into a restaurant of distinction. Much of the distinction revolves around the boneless breast of duck specialty, served by reservation only and slow-roasted in advance for $14.

"This will be the best duck you have ever tasted," the menu advises, but only those who call ahead will get to try it. Similarly, only those who pick the right time will get to order the live Maine lobster. It's flown in and offered as a special the last week of every month. Chicken, pork, beef and lamb are staples on the limited menu, their presentation changing from week to week but the renditions consistently good. The same goes for the salmon, scallops, shrimp and swordfish.

Dinner begins with homemade bread, soup of the day or salad. Desserts, like everything else here, are homemade.

Dining is by candlelight in one of five small dining rooms. Each different, they and the cozy lounge convey the feeling of being in a private home.

(910) 692-4480. Entrées, $12 to $19.50. Dinner, Tuesday-Saturday from 6.

Sweet Basil, 134 N.W. Broad St., Southern Pines.

This sweet garden spot featuring Mediterranean and California cuisine is everyone's favorite for lunch. Sprightly in yellow and green with a potted plant on every table, the place is bigger than it looks on the outside and packs in the crowds for all of four hours a day.

Chef John Davis is credited on the menu for the innovative salads, pizzas, pastas and sandwiches on wonderful, rustic breads baked in house. The sweet Virginia ham and swiss cheese sandwich on focaccia is a winner, teamed with a side mesclun salad dressed with balsamic. Desserts here are special and available as a sampler or as a mini-dessert. We were smitten by a delectable strawberry shortcake with whipped cream, just like mother used to make.

(910) 693-1487. Entrées, $5.25 to $6.95. Open 11 to 3, Saturday 11:30 to 3.

Diversions

To the uninitiated, the village of Pinehurst and Southern Pines are usually synonymous, meaning golf. (Aberdeen, the oldest of the three communities that make up the Sandhills region), is virtually unknown outside the area.)

To others, the village of Pinehurst is an artificial – as in planned, albeit historic and beautiful – golf enclave. Southern Pines, also historic and beautiful, is more earthy (the railroad track still runs up the middle of Broad Street), cultural and varied.

As noted by novelist James Boyd in 1927 in a letter to the Raleigh News & Observer, which had mistakenly identified him as a resident of Pinehurst: "The difference is immense. Pinehurst is a resort visited by golfers. Southern Pines is a town inhabited by foxhunters. In the summer, Pinehurst ceases to exist. It is merely a deserted village haunted by the ghosts of departed golfers. But all the year round, Southern Pines may be seen vigorously flourishing, its noble civic life distinguished by all the attributes of organized metropolitan society."

Golf. Pinehurst, the new umbrella name for the resort and country club, is the most famous. The eight eighteen-hole courses qualify it as the world's largest golf resort. Its legendary No. 2 course, designed by Scot transplant Donald Ross, was selected as the site for the U.S. Open championship in 1999 to cap the centennial celebration of Pinehurst as the cradle of American golf. But more than 40 fine golf courses, including MidPines and Pine Needles, are located within a fifteen-mile radius. Most lodging establishments offer package plans that permit guests to play leading courses.

Tufts Archives, 150 Cherokee Road, Pinehurst.

The rear wing of Givens Memorial Library, on the green in the center of Pinehurst, is the repository of more than a century of Pinehurst history, as well as of its founding Tufts family and of Donald Ross, America's leading golf course architect. Most of the arcane books and memorabilia are of principal interest to golfers, of course. But there are fascinating tidbits for anyone interested in social history: an early menu from the Holly Inn, the first light bulb used at Pinehurst, a Tufts family soda fountain, an Annie Oakley shooter, a harness racing program and tickets to a Harvard-Yale football game in 1925.

(910) 2295-3642. Open Monday-Friday, 9:30 to 5, Saturday 9:30 to 12:30. Free.

Weymouth Center for the Arts & Humanities, 555 East Connecticut Ave., Southern Pines.

On 24 acres, the Georgian-style estate of the late historical novelist James Boyd is the site of special literary, musical, lecture and garden events. The author's former study was once the literary gathering place that Raleigh editor Jonathan Daniels declared "launched the Southern Literary Renaissance" in the 1920s and '30s. It is now the home of the **North Carolina Literary Hall of Fame,** devoted to memorabilia of Thomas Wolfe, O. Henry, Paul Green, Daniels, Boyd and ten others.

(910) 692-6261. Open Monday-Friday 10 to 4. Free.

Weymouth Woods Sandhills Nature Preserve, 1024 Fort Bragg Road, Southern Pines.

In the midst of a regenerating longleaf pine forest, a 676-acre nature preserve features a visitor center, natural history museum and 4.5 miles of hiking trails beloved by plant and bird watchers. The museum traces local history from 1740 when Highland Scots settled the area into the 1800s, when the Tar Heel State was living up to its name with 1,500-plus distilleries producing one-third of the world's turpentine. Many trees were bled to death for their valuable resin and the forests were lost. The once majestic virgin longleaf pine forest was barren by the end of the century, with only a few remnants to provide seed for a second-generation forest being nurtured at Weymouth Woods. Outside, you can walk through the pines and perhaps see a red-cockaded woodpecker, an endangered species that lives in loblolly pines. At a recent bird count, 82 were sighted, a national record.

(910) 692-2167. Open Monday-Saturday 9 to 6, Sunday noon to 5.

History. The **Pinehurst Harness Track,** founded in 1915 and listed in the National Register, is open daily and visitors may see horses put through their paces early in the day. The three **Shaw House Properties** at Morganton and Broad Streets in Southern Pines depict daily life of early settlers from 1770 to 1850. The Shaw House, the town's oldest house on its original foundation and home of its first mayor, features early area pottery and "plain-style" furniture. Also open for tours are the Britt Sanders Cabin (1770) and the Garner House, a log structure with heart-pine paneling, hand-forged hinges and board doors. Near Aberdeen, the **Malcolm Blue Farm & Museum** recreates farm life from the early 19th century.

Seagrove Area Potteries. Dozens of potters – some of them nationally recognized – still employ their craft as it has been done for generations around Seagrove, a dot on the map off I-73/74 northwest of Pinehurst. Upwards of 100 potteries are listed in a guide provided by the Friends of the Pottery Center. Most are concentrated along or just off Route 705 between Seagrove and Robbins. This is a rural, seemingly impoverished area, strangely uncommercialized given the fame of its potteries. Most are located in houses and sheds. The quite sophisticated Blue Moon Gallery/Walton's Pottery, representing leading contemporary American craftsmen, departs from the norm. More typical is the family-owned Nichols Pottery, where a couple and their daughter sign "God Bless You" to each colorful, handpainted pot produced in a rustic shed and studio beside their manufactured home.

Shopping. Trains still run down the middle of tree-shaded Broad Street in Southern Pines. On either side of the street, but difficult to get to back and forth across the raised tracks, are excellent stores and galleries. The golf section is bigger than the travel section in **The Country Bookshop. The Cook's Choice** is an unusually good kitchen store, and the hand-painted furnishings and accessories caught our eye at **Arabesque.** Giraffes in all guises and greenery are the themes for house and garden gifts at **The Green Giraffe.** Designer ladies' fashions are featured at **Morgan Miller.** One of the state's biggest wine selections is carried at the **Wine Cellar & Tasting Room,** which has a tasting bar with up to a dozen wines available by taste or glass.

The options are fewer and a bit pricier in Pinehurst, a quaint center of seemingly concentric circles that could be in New Canaan or Winnetka. On or around the Chinquapin Road centerpiece is **Razook's** for women's apparel, **The Book Place, Old Sport & Gallery, Burchfield's Golf Gallery** and **Midland Crafters Too.** The last is an offshoot of the exceptional **Midland Crafters,** a sprawling gallery of traditional and contemporary handcrafts – many with a bird or floral theme – at 2220 Midland Road. Another must stop is the **Sandhills Woman's Exchange,** across from the Village Chapel on Azalea Road. The 1810 log cabin houses some second-hand items but mostly locally made handicrafts, quilts, dolls and sweaters. The rustic tea room offers soups, sandwiches and salads in the $4.25 to $5.95 range.

Extra-Special

Sandhills Horticultural Gardens, 2200 Airport Road, Pinehurst.

Where larger and better-known gardens tend to overwhelm, this gallery of gardens is manageable, presented to scale and really quite extraordinary. Located on the Sandhills Community College campus behind Heutte Hall, 25 acres of themed gardens include the largest holly collection on the East Coast, exotic conifers, roses, rhododendron and azaleas, a formal English garden and much more. What makes it so unusual is the setting of plants against the brown pine needles. Individually identified, each is spaced well apart against a natural backdrop, and stands out rather like an individual artwork among many on a gallery wall. There are topiaries, metal sculptures in an "art field" and a delightful herb garden in which a purple giraffe sculpture anchors a corner. You'll find lilies and roses next to red Texas sage and monkey flowers. A waterfall cascades into a fish pond surrounded by petite pink Scottish roses. A holly garden slopes down a hillside to a native wetland area, a shady refuge on a sunny day. The gardens are designed and maintained by SCC's Landscape Gardening School.

(910) 695-3882. Open daily, sunrise to sunset. Free.

Old Salem is a living museum beneath backdrop of downtown skyline.

Winston-Salem, N.C.

A Tale of Two Cities

The hyphenated nature of Winston-Salem tells something about the place.

Locals call it Winston for short – or perhaps out of tradition. For this really was two municipalities that consolidated into one in 1913.

The first was Salem, founded in the Carolina wilderness in 1766 by a group of Moravians as the center for their commercial and religious efforts. Over the years, Salem became surrounded by the industrial city of Winston, where R.J. Reynolds created a tobacco empire.

Old Salem – a mini-Williamsburg of original homes, shops, gardens, a church and cemetery – survives today as a jewel in the middle of a prosperous, cultured city built by tobacco and textiles.

Moravians founded the Wachovia Bank, now headquartered in a 34-story landmark towering above Old Salem. The Reynolds legacy endures in the wonderful Reynolda House, Museum of American Art and the surrounding Reynolda Village support complex. Across Reynolda Road, the Tudor estate of the late industrialist James G. Hanes is now the Southeastern Center for Contemporary Art. The Piedmont Craftsmen Gallery and Shop inspires contemporary crafts. A leading benefactor of Old Salem founded the unique Museum of Early Southern Decorative

Arts. Wake Forest University, drawn to Winston-Salem by the Reynolds interests, adds the Museum of Anthropology to a mix that has led the city to be called the Arts Capital of the Carolinas.

Reynolda Road, one of the prettiest tree-canopied streets in America, reflects Winston-Salem from the era of its early country estates. So does Tanglewood, a county park given by the Reynolds family. The city's West End, a roller-coaster of hills and curving streets, adds a Victorian enclave of restaurants and B&Bs.

In the midst of it all is Old Salem, which draws 300,000 visitors a year to enjoy its historic structures, tidy gardens and working evidence of an earlier lifestyle.

Inn Spots

The Augustus T. Zevely Inn, 803 South Main St., Winston-Salem 27101.

This handsome brick house, built for a physician in 1844, is in the midst of the Old Salem restoration area. Its front door is usually locked, such is the appeal of the house for Old Salem passersby who think it's part of the restoration and would otherwise be trooping through at all hours. Faithfully restored and furnished to the era, the inn is a tranquil refuge.

"It's like living in another world," says Linda Anderson, innkeeper for the five investors who restored the four-story structure in 1994. Downtown Winston-Salem is only a few blocks to the north, but Old Salem is a place apart – a place where guinea fowl roam and a fox is in residence.

A stay here is truly to experience yesteryear, albeit with modern-day comforts. Guests enjoy a cozy parlor with overstuffed chairs and a corner fireplace as well as a two-story, ell-shaped porch in back. Here you can look out over heirloom gardens – brightened at our visit by many colors of sweet william – toward neighboring residences, all privately owned and occupied. A mural of Old Salem decorates the rear wall of the formal dining room. A smaller front dining room is where wine and cheese are served in the early evening and where a wet bar in an alcove holds tea and soft drinks. Cookies await guests arriving back from dinner, and sherry or brandy are offered in cool weather. Breakfast is presented buffet style on a sideboard in the foyer. The fare is continental-plus during the week. A hot entrée, perhaps scrambled eggs with hash browns or cinnamon french toast with sausage, is added on weekends.

Guests are cosseted in quarters that are unusually comfortable for so old a building. The Winter Kitchen Suite on the main floor was most inviting. It had a kingsize poster bed dressed in an Amish quilt, an enormous armoire hiding a TV set, an oversize cooking fireplace whose gas logs could be lighted with the flip of a switch, and a cozy sitting room with a plush loveseat, wing chair and another TV in an armoire. Capel carpets dotted the old wood floors. The bathroom was equipped with a jetted tub. And the windows blessedly opened, although the tiny "authentic homemade beeswax electrified candles" in each were too fragile to be turned off at night.

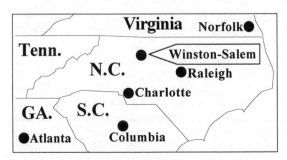

Two others of the twelve

Evening lighting bathes ornate Henry F. Shaffner House in rich glow.

accommodations on four floors have kingsize beds. The rest are queensize. All have private baths, TVs and telephones, clock radios and hair dryers. Furnishings are from Lexington's Old Salem Collection and by local artist Bob Timberlake. The second-floor, front-corner Augustus T. Zeveley Room has a kingsize Carolina backcountry bed, chaise lounge and one of the inn's three in-room working fireplaces. Two garret end rooms on the third floor offer jetted soaking tubs and refrigerator/microwaves.

All the charms of Old Salem lie just outside, and the historic Salem Tavern restaurant is across the street. "Guests can leave their cars and walk everywhere," says Linda. There are few more atmospheric places to walk than around here.

(336) 748-9299 or (800) 928-9299. Fax (336) 721-2211. Eleven rooms and one two-bedroom suite with private baths. Doubles, $80 to $135. Suite, $205.

The Henry F. Shaffner House, 150 South Marshall St., Winston-Salem 27101.

A manmade waterfall tumbles off the rear porch of this dramatic Queen Anne-style Victorian at the edge of downtown. It's an example of the showy enhancements undertaken in 1992 by local residents.

Built in 1907 by the co-founder of the Wachovia Bank, the abandoned residence-turned-boarding house had stood empty and condemned. Betty and Henry Falls Jr. meticulously restored the interior with its fine tiger oak woodwork, brass fixtures and nine ornate fireplaces.

The common spaces are beauties. From the porte cochere a grand foyer opens into a chintz-furnished parlor with grand piano and coffered ceiling, a library stocked with the finest reading materials, and a large and stylish sunporch decked out in rich green and white wicker. The latter is where innkeeper Shirley Ackeret pours the local Westbend Vineyard chardonnay and presents fresh fruit and cheeses during the late-afternoon social hour. Upstairs, the second-floor hall holds another sitting area, and a rooftop deck goes off a side hallway. Outside is a broad wraparound porch that's made for relaxation, despite traffic noise from the expressway adjacent.

The eight guest quarters vary from the merely spacious to enormous. The Piedmont suite stretches across most of the third floor. Here is a contemporary expanse in beige and black, with a plush sitting area, a kingsize canopy bed and a mirrored bath with double jacuzzi and separate shower. Another winner is the large front Wachovia Room with kingsize poster bed, pretty in mauve and black with two wing chairs, dressing alcove and large bath with clawfoot tub and separate shower. We were quite content in the quiet, front-corner Reynolda Room with queensize bed. Its only drawback was that to reach its private bath meant quite a trek through a common area and down a hall. Three suites with small sitting rooms and wet bars on the ground level are much in demand. All rooms have TVs and telephones.

Breakfast is a continental-plus feast of fresh fruit, granola, cereals, muffins, bread and bagels, put out on two sideboards in a dining room with individual tables. Quiches and omelets are added on weekends.

In 1998, the inn started offering dinner to house guests and the public in the dining room called **Emil's**. The night's six entrées might include sautéed chicken with béarnaise sauce, peppered beef tenderloin with portobello mushrooms and rack of lamb with smoked tomato sauce. Shrimp and rice cake with spicy coleslaw is typical of starters. Desserts include pecan pie à la mode, triple chocolate cake and tirami su.

(336) 777-0052 or (800) 952-2256. Fax (336) 777-1188. Six rooms and three suites with private baths. Doubles, $99 to $219. Suites, $129 to $169. No smoking.

Entrées, $12 to $20. Dinner, Wednesday-Sunday 5:30 to 8. Sunday brunch, 11 to 2.

Colonel Ludlow Inn, 434 Summit St., Winston Salem 27101.

Winston-Salem's longest-running B&B opened in 1982 in the Queen Anne-style Ludlow House in the city's hilly West End. It expanded six years later with the addition of the columned brick Neo-Romanesque Sheppard House next door. Together the two National Register properties occupy an entire city block.

Whirlpool tubs, kingsize beds and business amenities assure a high occupancy rate. Eight of the nine rooms offer double jacuzzi tubs, and four have working fireplaces. Each is fully equipped to be a private cocoon, with microwave, refrigerator, stereo, TV/VCR, telephone and in-room breakfast. "Some people check into their rooms and never come out," says Constance Creasman, longtime innkeeper for owner Ken Land. Those who do find a small parlor with a Chickering piano in the Ludlow House, and a billiards room with big-screen TV and a well-equipped exercise room in the Sheppard House.

Rooms run the gamut. One at the rear of the main floor of the Ludlow House has an Eastlake half-canopy king bed, a showplace of a sunken bath complete with TV, and one of the dining tables for two that characterize each room. Upstairs in the Sheppard House is a dark room with kingsize bed, working fireplace, a whirlpool tub in the bedroom, well-worn oriental rugs on the original wood floor, and a TV on a table at the foot of the bed. At the rear of the Sheppard House is a large bedroom flanked by a three-part bath. Here, the whirlpool tub is right beside the table in a room that doubles as a kitchenette/dining area and the other necessities are in adjacent closets.

Constance calls the inn a renovation in progress. That may explain the masculine

Brick walls and quilt-covered poster beds lend atmosphere to Brookstown Inn.

aura, the jungly look to the side porch of the Ludlow House and the still unpainted, unfinished ceilings above the stairway in the Sheppard House at our visit.

Breakfast, stocked in the rooms the night before, includes juice, fresh fruit, yogurt and granola, two types of quiche (spinach and bacon), and assorted breads and bagels. French toast is also an option. Room service is available for drinks, and dinner from selected fast-food restaurants can be delivered to one's room.

(336) 777-1887 or (800) 301-1887. Nine rooms with private baths. Doubles, weekends, $159 to $209; midweek, $139 to $169. Small queen room without jacuzzi: $109 weekends, $95 midweek. Children over 12.

Brookstown Inn, 200 Brookstown Ave., Winston-Salem 27101.

This modern inn capitalizes on its illustrious past. It began in 1985 in an abandoned cotton mill, which the Moravians had established in 1837 at the edge of Old Salem. The mill was later placed on the National Register as the community's first factory.

The four-story Brookstown reveals its origins in its brick walls, exposed beams and rafters, and tall windows and ceilings. Not to mention the fourth-floor graffiti wall, upon which young mill workers etched their names and thoughts in concrete, now screened behind glass for posterity.

Each of the 71 guest accommodations is slightly different. Standard rooms are unusually spacious, with queen, king or two double poster beds and sitting areas that might include two plush cchairs or a sofabed. Handmade quilts cover the beds, TVs are hidden in armoires, and Capel rugs dot the floors of the bathrooms, fifteen of which contain round garden tubs or jacuzzis.

The inn expanded across a shady brick courtyard in 1990 and 1991 into a similar mill building. Here are 31 bi-level suites with a mix of white and brick walls and the odd column. Eight have refrigerators and microwaves in sunken sitting areas and a king bed with TV above.

The Brookstown aims to convey a B&B atmosphere, albeit on a larger than usual scale. Wine and cheese are offered from 5 to 7 p.m. in a large and handsome, high-ceilinged parlor. Milk and cookies follow at 8, and the beds are turned down at night. Breakfast is billed curiously as continental but includes waffles, french toast, sausage and biscuits – everything but bacon and eggs, according to our guide. It's offered in a pleasant dining room seating 50 at individual tables.

A portion of the lobby of the newer building has been converted into an exercise facility for guests. Upstairs under separate ownership is a large, casual restaurant called **Darryl's**. The old boiler in its center once powered the entire complex.

(336) 725-1120 or (800) 845-4262. Fax (336) 773-0147. Forty rooms and 31 suites with private baths. Doubles, $90 to $155. Suites, $100 to $155.

Lady Anne's, 612 Summit St., Winston-Salem 27101.

Gray with pink and white gingerbread trim, this gabled house in the West End is a fantasy of Victoriana. The ornate exterior barely hints of all the antiques and doodads inside. Owner Shelley Kirley named it partly for its Queen Anne style but primarily for her late mother, who served as her inspiration when others said the 1890 apartment house was beyond repair. Twelve years of renovations, one room at a time, justified her mother's faith.

From a rambling front porch, an etched-glass door with stained-glass windows leads into a world of vintage hats, flowing lace, frilly tassels and family portraits. The purple walls of the parlor hold quite a collection of butterflies. Beyond is a dining room where Shelley presents a breakfast of french toast made with home-made bread or eggs with spinach and a basket of breads.

Upstairs in front is the Magnolia Room, blessed with a private balcony under a magnolia tree. It has a lace canopy queensize bed and the TV, cassette player, coffee maker, telephone, refrigerator, microwave, ironing board and lights on dimmer switches common to all guest rooms. It also has an extra-large tiled bath with double jacuzzi and separate shower. The premier Summit Suite has a burl and walnut bed angled in the corner, a Victorian sitting area, a big window in the bathroom overlooking the rear gardens, and dark wood trim that matches the Indian shutters screening the windows.

The Victoria Suite on the first floor has a private entrance and sunporch. A fiddle is on the wall above an antique victrola in the living room. Lace curtains puddle to the floor in the bedroom, which has an ornate burl and walnut double bed. Tassels hang from the doorways.

Shelley decorated her ground-floor Garden Suite in the rear in "Victorian log cabin style." With dark paneling and brick walls, it is an open expanse with living room, efficiency kitchen, a queen bed and a sofabed. The bathroom has a two-headed shower with two seats.

Besides cooking, Shelley likes to garden – a talent that shows around her rear brick patio with fountain beside.

(336) 724-1074. One room and three suites with private baths. Doubles, $110 to $165 weekends, $85 to $95 midweek. Children over 12. No smoking.

Tanglewood Manor House, Highway 158 West, Box 1040, Clemmons 27012.

The majestic former home of Kate and William Neal Reynolds, brother of tobacco magnate R.J. Reynolds, is situated in Tanglewood Park, about ten miles southwest of downtown Winston-Salem.

Formerly a restaurant and a mini-hotel, it is now a B&B, operated by the Forsyth County Park Authority.

The Reynoldses raised and raced thoroughbred horses and established profuse gardens on the 1,100-acre estate, which they willed in 1952 to the county. The golf courses, Olympic-size pool, bridle trails and entertainment venue make the park North Carolina's third most-visited tourist attraction.

Set apart from any hubbub is the 28-room, white brick manor house, built in sections dating to 1859. It offers ten substantial guest rooms, each with private bath, telephone and TV. The rooms we saw contained queen beds with a loveseat and two armchairs, crystal chandeliers and thick carpeting. Rich floral comforters and fabrics accented the yellow décor.

The main floor holds a function room and Will Reynolds's "Trophy Room." The latter is a parlor/library with a silver trophy case and plaques and equine photos on the walls. Across the hallway is a room with a big old stone fireplace. The continental breakfast served here includes fruit, cereal, breads, bagels and croissants. A pillared front porch overlooks the sloping front lawn and award-winning rose gardens.

Overnight guests get free entrance to the park ($2 a car) and reduced greens fees.

The complex also includes a motel-like lodge with eighteen additional guest rooms, a guest house sleeping up to eight people and four rustic cottages overlooking Mallard Lake.

(336) 778-6370. Fax (336) 778-6379. Ten rooms with private baths. Doubles, $77 to $107. Lodge, $45 to $65. Guest house and cottages, $325 to $575 weekly.

Dining Spots

For a city its size (143,000), Winston-Salem has a disproportionate number of highly rated restaurants. Many are considered good value because, as one restaurateur put it, the clientele is affluent but thrifty: "When they go out, they like to see how much money they can save." Most restaurants are smoker-friendly because, in tobacco land, they know what pays the rent.

Fabian's, 1100 Reynolda Road, Winston-Salem.

The best, most sophisticated restaurant in the city is located in an old Gulf station and run by an Italian from Argentina. In 1996, chef-owner Fabian Botta transformed the main floor of what still looks on the outside like a service station. Inside is a diminutive yet opulent dining room. Here, up to 30 diners are seated at white-clothed tables with mismatched chairs for a five-course, prix-fixe meal costing a bargain $35. Overhead in an atrium is a crystal chandelier with a gold medallion. Beyond is a wine cellar for private dining.

Upstairs is a candlelit martini bar with a Tuscan feeling, a painting of the Mona Lisa smoking a cigar and an outdoor deck with a tiki bar. Only one brand of beer is offered, says Fabian, but there are ten vodkas, fifteen single-malts, caviars – just "high-end stuff" for the local high-rollers who pack the place.

Dinner begins with an amuse-gueule, followed at our visit by shrimp bisque, an organic salad and an appetizer of spinach empanadas. Fabian recites the main-course choices: fresh North Carolina tuna, ostrich, rack of lamb or veal, each prepared in "the continental old world style with a Mediterranean influence." Dessert when we were there was a white chocolate bread pudding.

Then, if they haven't spent their wad on the select but pricey wine list, those in the know adjourn upstairs to the cigar bar for an after-dinner cognac or single-malt. *(336) 723-7700. Prix-fixe, $35. Dinner by reservation, Monday-Saturday at 7:30.*

Southbound Bistro & Grille, 300 South Liberty St., Winston-Salem.
A section of the 1913 freight warehouse and office known as the Railroad Building has been transformed into an innovative restaurant, located a scant two blocks from Old Salem. The high-ceilinged interior is a stylish mix of brick and mirrors, booths and white-clothed tables.

The signature dish is grilled North Carolina ostrich, described by our waitress as "like filet mignon and better for you." Other choices include grilled yellowfin tuna with a scallion wasabi sauce and grilled muscovy duck breast with cran-blackberry sauce. We succumbed to the ostrich and found it a memorable treat, served with rosemary-shiitake sauce over a cannellini ragoût with grilled asparagus. Fried oysters with baby greens and pepper-sesame shrimp with fried spinach in a toasted flour tortilla made good starters. Desserts were strawberry and almond roulade with caramel ice cream and frozen chocolate mousse with white chocolate lace and chocolate-chip cookies. Like the rest of the meal, they were presented with architectural flourishes.

(336) 723-0322. Entrées, $15 to $27. Lunch, Monday-Friday 11:30 to 2:30. Dinner, Monday-Saturday 5:30 to 10.

Leon's Café, 924 South Marshall St., Winston-Salem.
When Louise Thomas and her ex-husband opened this popular spot in 1983, they named it in tribute to his late father, who ran the Bear & Castle restaurant in Greensboro for 50 years. Taking over what she called a greasy spoon, Louise created on the main floor a bar and a mirrored dining room attractive in cranberry and pale green, an upstairs with more seating and an idyllic front courtyard terrace hidden behind greenery from the street.

The handwritten menu offers a mix of contemporary/continental fare. Among appetizers are escargots in puff pastry and lamb loin brochette on a painted palette of raspberry and citrus beurre blancs. Main courses could be broiled mahi mahi with tequila-chive cream sauce, pan-seared lamb chops with mango-mint chutney and grilled filet mignon with béarnaise sauce. Desserts run the gamut from black-berry tart to crème caramel.

(336) 725-9593. Entrées, $15 to $21. Dinner nightly from 6.

B 900 and The Cellar, 900 South Marshall St., Winston-Salem.
Spirited cooking and spirited ambiance prevail at this popular haunt – a food and jazz club on the lower level and two funky, brightly colored dining rooms with an open kitchen upstairs. Chef-owner Ken Martin decorated the outside wall with musical instruments salvaged from a repair shop. His wife, Lynn Byrd, planted the tiered gardens that make dining on the outdoor courtyard so pleasurable.

Ken, a classically trained French chef, offers a blend of American, Vietnamese and Southern fare with a bow to vegetarians and vegans. Fried spinach is a signature appetizer. Other choices are Asian spiced shrimp, crab and artichoke dip, and potato cake with sour cream and caviar. Main courses include potato-crusted catfish sauced with dijonnaise sauce, shrimp and cheese grits, and flank steak marinated in beer and black peppercorns. Ken recited some of the night's specials – beef stroganoff, salt pork loin smothered in apple gravy and mixed grill of venison, duck and quail breast with plum sauce – to give an idea of the range. Dessert could be chocolate-pecan pie or lemon ricotta soufflé with citrus sauce. Incidentally, B stands for Bistro 900, which is what the place used to be called. *(336) 721-1336. Entrées, $13.95 to $15.95. Dinner, Wednesday-Saturday 6 to 9:30 or 10:30; Cellar, Thursday-Saturday.*

Noble's Grille, 380 Knollwood St., Winston Salem.

Sophisticates consider this sleek, contemporary restaurant in the Nations Bank office building among the city's best. The interior is urbane, with tall glass windows and high ceilings, and there's a terrace for outdoor dining. Open oak-hickory wood grills and ovens give a California accent to the assertive French-Mediterranean cuisine.

Main courses range widely from grilled black grouper with a sorrel-apple-parmesan pesto and wood-fire roasted mussels to grilled rabbit, pan-seared veal sweetbreads and grilled veal tenderloin with sherry aioli. Start with a fried oyster salad with Asian greens, a morel mushroom pizza or roasted penne with duck and sundried tomatoes in a rosemary cream sauce. Dessert could be guava-lemon sorbet, tangerine-cinnamon cheesecake or Noble's currant-raisin and Courvoisier bread pudding. The wine list has been honored by Wine Spectator.

One of three Noble's restaurants in the Piedmont Triad area, the restaurant sells olive oil and balsamic vinegar from Tuscany as well as T-shirts and the chain's cookbook. *(336) 777-8477. Entrées, $16 to $27. Lunch, Monday-Saturday 11:30 to 2:30. Dinner, Monday-Saturday 5:30 to 10 or 11.*

South by Southwest, 241 Marshall St., Winston-Salem.

For a casual meal, consider Patrick Burke's large establishment, full of adobe colors, Southwestern decor and a variety of seating.

The oversize menu offers the usual suspects with novel accents, perhaps black bean-corn soup or chiles rellenos with smoked salmon and walnut sauce. The chips, ordered extra, come with blackened tomato-chipotle or chile verde-tomatillo salsas.

Main courses include grilled salmon with chipotle-pinenut sauce, mixed seafood with roasted red pepper-saffron sauce in a grilled tortilla and angus ribeye steak with smoked chile-roasted tomato sauce.

On a busy weeknight, a seat in the bar hit the spot. We were well satisfied with a Corona Light and the grilled adobe chicken with green chile-mashed potatoes and grilled vegetables. The assertive after-taste was barely assuaged by a couple of cookies back at our B&B. *(336) 727-0800. Entrées, $10.50 to $16.50. Dinner, Monday-Saturday 6 to 9:30 or 10.*

Zevely House, 901 West Fourth St., Winston-Salem.

This restored 1815 house is not to be confused with the Augustus T. Zevely Inn in Old Salem. That's a B&B named for a physician, and this was the home of his father, Van Neman Zevely, a Moravian cabinetmaker. It was moved to its present site in the West End in 1974. The small house, hidden in the trees, offers tables by the fireplace in winter and outside patio dining in summer.

The handwritten menu is short but sweet. Typical appetizers are the locally

Old Salem Tavern is on view from main entrance to Augustus T. Zevely Inn.

popular fried spinach, pan-fried oysters with tomato-cumin sauce and baked cream cheese with pistachios and raspberry puree. Expect main courses like sea scallops gratinée with apricots and jarlsberg cheese, Moravian chicken pie with sage gravy, and a mixed grill of roasted pork loin and grilled chicken breast with wild mushroom bordelaise. The signature beef Van Neman comes with chutney sauce, bacon and sesame seeds.

One of the few local restaurants open on Sundays, this is known for a good brunch.
(336) 725-6666. Entrées, $14.95 to $21. Dinner, Tuesday-Saturday 5:30 to 9. Sunday brunch, 11 to 2.

The Vineyards Restaurant, 120 Reynolda Village, Winston-Salem.

Housed in the original boiler building for the estate at Reynolda Village is this ramble of rooms with a vaguely Mediterranean look. Owner Nick Graczyk went for uplifting bright colors in five dining areas with terra-cotta floors. The side courtyard is popular with visitors to the nearby Reynolda House, Museum of American Art.

The extensive menu has something for everyone, from stuffed ravioli with saffron vermouth sauce and penne vodka to veal dijon, tenderloin tips bourguignonne and rack of lamb with a roasted garlic-rosemary-beaujolais sauce. How often do you see a "spa menu" (grilled swordfish topped with winter pesto on a bed of blackeyed pea salsa) alongside "from the barbecue pit" (New Orleans-style back ribs). Or apple beignets on a dessert menu touting a hot fudge sundae? The homemade bread pudding with berries and crème anglaise was voted Winston-Salem's best.
(336) 748-0269. Entrées, $7.95 to $21.95. Dinner, Monday-Saturday 5 to 10.

Old Salem Tavern, 736 South Main St., Old Salem.

A favorite with visitors to Old Salem, this fulfills everyone's idea of an historic tavern. Established in 1772, it harbors smooth soapstone hearths, beautiful chairboards and prized antiques in three small dining rooms downstairs and three upstairs. A rear porch offers five more tables, with still more available on a trellis-covered patio.

Inside, candles flicker in glass boxes as you partake of the specialty Moravian chicken pie or sauerkraut stew. Some of the old standbys have been updated, as in appetizers of crawfish fritters, barbecued duck quesadilla and fried goat cheese. Expect main courses like shrimp and sausage tossed with tasso gravy on creamy grits, sautéed grouper with a crawfish-leek sauce and sautéed lamb medallions topped with blackeyed pea chili.

Moravian gingerbread with homemade lemon ice cream is the dessert specialty. The beer selection is better than the wine list.

(336) 748-8585. Entrées, $14.95 to $19. Lunch daily, 11:30 to 2. Dinner, Monday-Saturday 5 to 9 or 9:30.

West End Café, 926 West Fourth St., Winston-Salem.

Come here early or late, or expect a wait on the sidewalk outside. People are lined up at all hours for the mix-and-match fare in which this establishment specializes. It moved in 1998 from what looked like a train car to large and modern quarters with a mix of booths and tables in two dining areas and a big counter for dining at the bar.

The enormous soup, salad and sandwich menu even lists a liverwurst sandwich. We sampled Rob's choice, a salad with tuna, chicken, curried chicken, vidalia onions and a little of everything else that moved him, and a turkey sandwich with three fixings.

A local hangout, the place is known for its potato pancakes, black bean burritos, sea bass, and shrimp and lobster quesadillas.

(336) 723-4774. Dinner entrées, $12 to $20. Open Monday-Saturday 11 to 10 or 11.

Diversions

Old Salem is what draws most visitors to Winston-Salem. Once there, the arts attractions exert their pull. As publicist Judith Smith of Reynolda House says, "visitors say they didn't know Winston has so much to offer."

Old Salem, Old Salem Road at East Academy Street, Old Salem.

Just south of Interstate 40 and downtown Winston-Salem lies the living history town of Salem, settled by Moravians from Pennsylvania in 1766. Today, this oasis in a city many times its size lives on. Its 90 restored and reconstructed buildings, all original, rank it among the most authentic restorations in the country. Although most structures are private residences, one is the Augustus T. Zevely Inn and another the Old Salem Tavern restaurant.

Self-guided tours begin with a twelve-minute slide presentation at the Visitor Center. Costumed interpreters, some of them Moravians, are posted at key spots to answer questions and demonstrate early domestic activities and trades. Some appear taciturn; others talk at length..

The admission ticket gives access to seven buildings, including a school, a watchmaker's house, a shoemaker's shop and the Miksch House – the first private family home in Salem and, curiously, the oldest tobacco shop in America. Chief among them is the Single Brothers House, a three-story structure that was home to 60 men and boys aged 12 to 72. It's now an expanse of crafts rooms, a dining room and a large religious room displaying a 1788 Bible translated by the Brethren. The Winkler Bakery (see Extra-Special) carries on the Moravian tradition of baking breads and cookies. Eight reconstructed gardens are open for viewing. Moravian products and mementos are on sale in the preservation corporation's gift shops. A children's museum opened in 1998.

Much of the charm of Old Salem can be enjoyed gratis, simply by walking around Salem Square, Main and Church Streets and their cross streets. The Home Moravian Church, built in 1800 and not officially part of Old Salem, is the largest of 53 Moravian congregations in the South. Adjacent is the tranquil, beautiful campus of Salem College, an outgrowth of the school for girls established by the Moravians in 1772 and the oldest college for women in the country. Its 750 students add contemporary flavor to Old Salem, whose visitors may wander among the brick buildings, brick walks, gardens, pergolas and benches of the intimate campus. Another treat is God's Acre, the 1771 graveyard with perfect rows of flat burial stones arranged in uniform simplicity, symbolizing the Moravian belief in equality in death. The graves are decorated with flowers for the Easter sunrise service, observed with fanfare here since 1772, with members of a brass band playing to one another from various parts of the cemetery. Among the historic district's treasures are the private homes, from tiny to substantial, most with well-tended gardens. At district's edge is the Museum of Early Southern Decorative Arts.

(336) 721-7300 or (888) 653-7253. Exhibit buildings open Monday-Saturday 9:30 to 4:30, Sunday 1 to 4:30. Adults, $15.

Museum of Early Southern Decorative Arts, 924 South Main St., Old Salem.

Appropriately sited at the edge of Old Salem is this 1965 structure, the only museum dedicated to researching and exhibiting the decorative arts of the early South. The nucleus of the collection was donated by Frank L. Horton, who spearheaded the restoration of Old Salem. He believed in the merits of Southern crafts from an era when others thought nothing of artistic value was produced south of Baltimore. Hour-long guided tours show 30 period rooms and galleries arranged in room settings. All the furniture, paintings, textiles, ceramics, silver and other metal wares were made in the Southern Colonies (1645-1850) and are shown chronologically. You can walk through a 17th-century Virginia great hall, a one-room Maryland plantation dwelling, a log house from the North Carolina backcountry, an elegant Charleston living room and a Virginia Eastern Shore parlor from the Federal period. The museum is unusual in that the displays are not roped off, so visitors can poke around as if in a furniture showroom. There's also plenty of space for more rooms to be furnished as the finds continue.

(336) 721-7360. Open Monday-Saturday 9 to 5, Sunday 1 to 5. Adults, $10. Combination ticket with Old Salem, $20.

Historic Bethabara Park, 2147 Bethabara Road, Winston-Salem.

This reflects the original settlement of Moravians in 1753 amid Indians and wild animals in the Piedmont wilderness. Located on the northwestern outskirts of Winston-Salem, it looks far more rustic than Old Salem, which its settlers founded in 1766 as the permanent town. Bethabara – pronounced Be-THA-ba-ra and meaning "House of Passage" – was meant to be a temporary farming and crafts community. The wooded 110-acre site features restored buildings, a 1788

Showy gardens front Reynolda House, Museum of American Art.

Moravian church, a 1752 cabin, a 1756 French and Indian War fort, reconstructed community gardens and a visitor center with a video presentation.

(336) 924-8191. Park open daily, dawn to dusk. Buildings open April-November, Monday-Friday 9:30 to 4:30, Saturday and Sunday 1:30 to 4:30. Free.

Reynolda House, Museum of American Art, Reynolda Road, Winston-Salem.

This treasure of a place was built in 1914-17 by Richard J. and Katharine Reynolds as their country home, the centerpiece of a 1,067-acre estate complete with a model farm and a self-supporting village. The art, shown in a country house setting, has been added since its opening to the public in 1965. The original furnishings reflect the taste of the owners. The art collection gathered by nationally known director Nicholas Bragg is distinguished.

The low-slung stucco exterior belies the elaborate Colonial Revival interior of the 40,000-square-foot house. Affectionately christened "the bungalow" in the modest manner of old money, it is built around a two-story living room with comfortable furniture and a cantilevered balcony. As architectural historian Brendan Gill notes in the museum's brochure, the house was built to be lived in, not to show off – "a pleasing novelty" in the early 20th century.

Paintings hang unobtrusively in many of the 64 rooms. The concentration of Hudson River School artists is particularly strong. But the visitor quickly realizes the furnishings and the ambiance are as much a part of the experience as the art. On the balcony, Flemish tapestries conceal the 2,500 pipes of an Aeolian organ. Tiffany glass shines in Chippendale corner cabinets. American pottery is on display. The upper floor exhibits the extensive wardrobe of Katharine Reynolds, including the wedding dress she made herself, plus the clothes and toys of their children. A later wing added by the Reynoldses' daughter and son-in-law contains a bowling alley, an art deco bar, a squash court, a shooting gallery and an indoor pool.

Behind the house, Reynolda Village (see shopping) was designed as an English country village to make Reynolda a self-supporting community. The resident cottages, greenhouses, offices, a school and utility buildings have served as shops and restaurants since the 1970s.

(336) 725-5325. Open Tuesday-Saturday 9:30 to 4:30, Sunday 1:30 to 4:30. Adults, $6.

Southeastern Center for Contemporary Art, 750 Marguerite Dr., off Reynolda Road, Winston-Salem.

Old meets new in the gallery addition to the 1929 Tudor-style mansion on the 32-acre wooded property of industrialist James G. Hanes. Visitors enter through the Centershop, a quirky place with choice contemporary crafts. How about a unique seatbelt fashioned from beer-bottle caps or albums crafted from license plates? Changing exhibitions are mounted on the soaring walls of a series of spare, cascading galleries. There's no permanent collection, but rather several temporary exhibits are shown simultaneously. Those we saw were definitely at the cutting edge.

(336) 725-1904. Open Tuesday-Saturday 10 to 5, Sunday 2 to 5. Adults, $3.

Piedmont Craftsmen Gallery & Shop, 1204 Reynolda Road, Winston-Salem.

More than 350 professional craftsmen from across the South show their works in this stunning gallery and shop. The members, juried in for life, show and sell in ten media. Many are represented in the White House collection. While the famed Southern Highland Craft Guild favors traditional Appalachian crafts, the emphasis here is on the contemporary. We coveted almost everything we saw.

(336) 725-1516. Open Tuesday-Saturday 10 to 6, Sunday 1 to 5. Free.

Shopping. As in most cities, downtown stores have fled to the suburbs. The Hanes Mall on the southwest side of town is among the South's largest.

Most visitors will be content with browsing through **Reynolda Village,** a pastoral campus of outbuildings and formal gardens on the former estate of R.J. Reynolds. The white stucco buildings with green tiled roofs match the facade of the main Reynolda House. Here you'll find two dozen stores and galleries, including **The Stocked Pot** (a large kitchen shop with a cooking demonstration area), **Gazebo** fashions, **Little Women** (petite apparel), **Village Book Shop, La Cache** and **The Niche** for gifts, and four restaurants.

Extra-Special

Winkler Bakery, 525 Main Street, Old Salem.

The aroma of breads baked in a brick wood oven lures everyone into this bakery, still operating much as it did upon opening in 1800. Staffers come in at 2 in the morning to light the fires in the unusual domed bake oven, nine feet wide, seven feet deep and two feet high. The bakers follow about 7, rake out the wood coals and employ the residual heat of the bricks. Ninety-six loaves are baked in 22 minutes at 400 degrees, our guide said, and four batches can be made before the bricks cool. The loaves are often snapped up by regular customers before museum visitors get there. The front shop sells many items associated with the bakery, including tins of the authentic, paper-thin Moravian cookies (ginger, sugar, lemon and black walnut). The shelves are stocked with mixes for pancakes, biscuits, hushpuppies and sweet potato muffins, as well as yellow grits and cheese straws.

(336) 721-7302. Open Monday-Saturday 9 to 5, Sunday 12:30 to 5.

Vistors relax with view of mountains outside craft center at Moses H. Cone Memorial Park.

Blowing Rock, N.C.

High Country Refuge

Four thousand feet up in the heart of North Carolina's High Country sits Blowing Rock, a mountain village of uncommon sophistication alongside a crest of the Blue Ridge Parkway.

Here, at the Eastern Continental Divide, the population swells from 1,300 to 7,000 in summer, when temperatures are usually twenty degrees cooler than in the flatlands below. Winter arrives early and stays late at eight ski areas nearby.

The only full-service town along the scenic, 470-mile-long parkway, Blowing Rock is a mountain community from yesteryear. Picture Aspen without the pretense, or Lake Placid without the Olympics. Here, amid several square miles of forests and lakes, are a few resort hotels, good inns and B&Bs, innovative restaurants, posh homes and residential developments, inviting parks, upscale shopping and summer culture. It's a thoroughly appealing, small-town atmosphere. As restaurateur Ann Esposito put it, "when I moved here from South Florida, I thought this would be a pretty good place to be poor."

The town powers that be banded together long ago to prohibit high-rise hotels and condos as well as neon and illuminated signs. The result is a refreshing naturalness to the carved wooden markers denoting the entrances to Blowing Rock. The churches are picturesque, and the motels are enveloped in lush landscaping. The town parks in the center and the welcoming 8,000 acres of the Moses H. Cone estate typify Blowing Rock more than the touristy Linville Caverns and Tweetsie Railroad theme park nearby.

There are mountain pursuits and tourist attractions aplenty for those so inclined in this area with the highest average land elevation in the Eastern United States. Mount Mitchell is the highest mountain and Linville Gorge the deepest canyon east of the Mississippi. Nearby are Boone, a rough-edged college town, and quiet Valle Crucis, a crossroads valley hamlet known for an Episcopal mission and an old general store. Beyond is Banner Elk, a frontier-style community catering to skiers.

The principal resting place for visitors seeking peace and quiet is Blowing Rock, a refuge of tranquility in the High Country.

Inn Spots

Gideon Ridge Inn, 6148 Gideon Ridge Road, Box 1929, Blowing Rock 28605.

When Cobb and Jane Milner converted a private residence into a B&B in 1984, it was a hit from the start. "They offered the right combination of rustic and elegant," said their son, Cobb III.

And what a combination! The stone house is perched on a bluff with mountain views on three sides. It overlooks five acres of perennial gardens that change colors with the seasons. There's a broad flagstone porch outfitted in comfortable wicker and wrought iron for taking it all in. Inside are handsome common rooms and ten inviting guest rooms, all richly furnished in a style that befits mountain elegance. Rather as you'd expect in a home built by a nephew from Boston of the wife of textile tycoon Moses H.Cone. And rather as conveyed in the inn's distinctive, understated brochure, written suavely in the narrative style by author Jan Karon, a friend of the family.

Three prized guest quarters in the Terrace Wing claim their own terraces. The Old Master Bedroom has a carved plantation bed and one of the ten in-room fireplaces. The Victorian offers an antique Edwardian bed original to the house as well as a fireplace in both bathroom and bedroom. All rooms have queensize beds except for two with king beds at either end of the house. Each of the latter has a whirlpool tub as well. The Carriage Room at the near end has a cast-iron whirlpool tub for two in a corner of the bedroom, a bathroom with tub and shower, and an idyllic garden patio. The Sunrise Room at the far end of the house was converted from a laundry area in which clothing was hung to dry from beams beneath the vaulted ceiling. Now the room is lodge-like with stone and pine walls, a potbelly stove, a cedar-lined bathroom and a jacuzzi in the corner. From the kingsize bed you can watch the sun rise.

Upstairs bedrooms in the Terrace Wing are smaller but comfortable and notable for unusual window treatments in the dormers. All beds are outfitted with frette cotton sheets. "We go first class because we want our guests to have at least as nice a room as they have at home," says the younger Cobb. He and wife Cindy have taken over innkeeping duties from his parents.

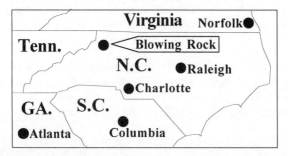

Surely few homes have as nice living areas, starting with that great back porch/terrace that looks onto a changing landscape of azaleas, rhododendron, mountain laurel and summer perennials. The beamed, lodge-style living room has a huge fireplace

Rare chestnut bark siding graces exterior of Inn at Ragged Gardens.

with part of the Milners' collection of model trains on the mantle and a grand piano in a corner. The breakfast room with its crystal chandelier and original art opens onto a tiled porch, which opens in turn onto a side patio. Sturdy individual tables are set for a substantial breakfast – perhaps cornmeal pancakes with Vermont maple syrup or egg and cheese strata with applewood-smoked bacon.

In the afternoon, tea from silver pots is offered in the English style, with home-made shortbread, scones and finger sandwiches. Iced tea is substituted on hot days.

There's plenty of room in which to spread out. "Most of our guests come for privacy," says Cobb. "They can mix if they wish, but they also can be anonymous."

(828) 295-3644. Ten rooms with private baths. Doubles, $120 to $220. Children over 12. No smoking.

The Inn at Ragged Gardens, 203 Sunset Drive, Box 1927, Blowing Rock 28605.

His construction background, her decorating ingenuity and lots of hard work have turned this renovated mansion into a luxurious hideaway in the heart of Blowing Rock. The previous owners had run it as an Italian restaurant with seasonal rooms overhead. Lee and Jama Hyett took over in 1996, closed the restaurant and redecorated with flair. They added several bathrooms and fireplaces for all guest rooms. They also built a rear wing with five suites bearing the same rare chestnut bark siding as that on the original edifice.

The interior of the turn-of-the-century manor house is stunning. A flagstone foyer/sunporch with massed flowers serves as the entry. The great hall, paneled in chestnut, is big enough for a dining area and a parlor with three Victorian sofas grouped in front of a stone fireplace. Wormy chestnut folding doors lead into a handsome library, which the Hyetts converted from a former dining room. They enclosed the side porch for a larger dining area to serve additional guests housed in the new suites in back.

A rare stone staircase, made of granite from nearby Grandfather Mountain, leads to six upstairs guest quarters. The biggest is the Camelot Suite, named for the camelot lily. It reflects a medieval theme with silk wallpaper, wrought-iron furnishings and a stone fireplace. The queen bed, graced with a coat of arms, bears a fancy fabric headboard typical of Jama's ingenuity in recycling leftovers into showy decor. A huge balcony is an asset in Monet's Garden, a trove of mauve and green. It has a corner fireplace paneled in beadboard and an ingenious headboard that Lee crafted out of Victorian porch parts for the kingsize bed. Flowing fabric, down comforters and an abundance of pillows typify the electric blue Blue Wisteria Room and the soothing English Lavender. Lee's favorite room in the main house is the secluded Rock Garden Garret, the largest of two third-floor rooms. It comes with a king bed under a skylight in the eaves, a window seat, a jacuzzi, a twig rocker in the sitting room, and a little rock garden and fountain.

His newest favorite is the third-floor treehouse in the new wing, so named because guests feel as if they're in the trees. All suites here have fireplaces visible in both bathroom and sitting room or bedroom, balconies, double jacuzzis and separate steam showers.

Breakfast in the new dining porch beside a formal rock-walled garden begins with fresh fruit cup, cereal and toasting breads. The main even could be egg puff casserole, quiche or stuffed french toast. A butler's pantry is stocked with home-made cookies, soft drinks and decanters of port and sherry.

(828) 295-9703. Five rooms and seven suites with private baths. Doubles, $125. Suites, $150 to $200. Two-night minimum weekends. Children 12 and older. No smoking.

The Mast Farm Inn, 2543 Broadstone Road, Box 704, Valle Crucis 28691.

The feeling of earlier days pervades the historic Mast Farm Inn, one of the area's more interesting and enduring lodging establishments. The farm began in 1812 with a log cabin that's still in use as a two-room guest cottage beloved by city slickers for its rustic antiquity. When her frame farmhouse was built in the 1880s, Josie Mast turned the original log cabin into a loom house and began weaving coverlets, rugs and handbags, some of which found their way into Woodrow Wilson's White House and are shown in the Smithsonian today. By the turn of the century, she and her husband Finley started offering rooms and meals to passing tourists.

Wanda Hinshaw and Kay Hinshaw Philipp, sisters who are natives of the area, bought the inn in 1996. They made cosmetic improvements – "reupholstering everything in sight" – to enhance the comforts of what the National Register lists as one of the most complete and best preserved groups of 19th-century farm buildings in North Carolina. They also upgraded the restaurant into one of the best in the area (see Dining Spots).

Wood signs on the doors, hooked rugs on the original wood floors, dark paneling and plenty of antique furnishings authenticate the age of the nine guest rooms in the three-story farmhouse. They offer comforts like the occasional gas fireplace, step-up king or queen beds and a fainting couch here, a soaking tub for two there. There's a common room on every floor. One is a former sleeping porch with a window seat and a table for checkers. The third floor's is a game room and the main floor's is a country Victorian parlor with fireplace.

Across the street is the two-bedroom Granary, the former owners' quarters, which the sisters now open for guests. Light and airy and relatively contemporary in feeling, it has a wonderful rear deck, a queen bedroom and an upstairs king bedroom with a jacuzzi tub in the room and a separate shower.

Restored farmhouse is at center of Mast Farm Inn complex.

Beside the main inn is the Loom House, one of the oldest inhabitable log cabins in western North Carolina and lately turned into the inn's ultimate getaway cottage for two. The cabin retains its log walls and an old potty (for decorative purposes) from the early days when the inn had one bath for thirteen bedrooms. It offers a downstairs sitting area with original fireplace, wet bar and a new massage tub and a queen bedroom upstairs. Out back is the weathered Dog Trot Building, where two detached cottages back up to a farm pond. Our quarters in the Woodwork Shop here conveyed what the Mast Farm experience is all about. Although it looked like a shack from the outside, the interior accommodations were thoroughly up-to-date. The sitting room had a vaulted ceiling, exposed timber studs along the walls and a hooked rug on the floor, with a new wet bar at one end. Small farm implements accented the walls. A loveseat and two rockers faced an old trunk doubling as a coffee table. The king bed came with a fine comforter and quilt, and a loft contained an extra bed. The modern bathroom had a shower, and there was a clawfoot tub in an alcove off the bedroom. We relaxed on the covered porch and read ever-so-realistic reminiscences in *Step Back in Time* by author Elizabeth Gray Vining, who visited Mast Farm when it was a boarding house and has a room named after her. That evening, the gas fireplace took the chill off a rainy night. Wake-up coffee was delivered in a basket to our door the next morning.

In the inn, a fire was blazing in the breakfast room, where Appalachian quilts hang on the walls. A feast of scrambled eggs with salmon and capers, grilled redskin potatoes and buttermilk-raisin scones capped an experience to remember.

(828) 963-5857 or (888) 963-5857. Fax (828) 963-6404. Nine rooms, three cottages and a two-bedroom house with private baths. Weekends and peak season (May-October): doubles $125 to $165, cottages $175 to $215, Granary $310 to $330 for four. Midweek discounts in off-season. Families with small children welcome in cottages. No smoking.

The Inn at the Taylor House, Highway 194, Valley Crucis 28691.

Comfortable rooms, stylish decor and lavish breakfasts are the hallmarks of this delightful B&B, set on twelve rural, forested acres at the Valley Crucis end of one of the High Country's more hair-raising roads, the twisting and narrow Mast Gap Road (Highway 194) to Banner Elk.

Carol (Chip) Schwab, then an Atlanta caterer and restaurateur, bought the 1911 farmhouse when the last of the Taylor family put it on the market in 1987. Four months of renovations preceded its opening as a B&B.

The house contains five guest rooms and two suites. The Main Suite, opposite the living room on the ground floor, comes with a kingsize bed, a European clawfoot tub and a sitting room furnished with antiques and family photos. Five rooms on the second floor have thick carpeting and beds wrapped in European duvets and goose down comforters. With a decorator's eye, Chip incorporates Waverly floral balloon shades and Brunschwig & Fils fabrics. Amenities include terrycloth robes and French milled soaps. The third floor holds a luxury suite with a king bed, English floral linens, a bathroom with an oversize tiled shower and a private balcony overlooking the woods in back. A former shed barn at the side of the house serves as a honeymoon cottage.

In the stylish and spacious living room of the farmhouse, a white sofa, two plush blue armchairs and an ottoman flank a glass coffee table. A corner cabinet displays plates and pottery. All around are artworks and treasures that Chip has collected on her travels.

Three glass tables in the dining room are set with floral mats for breakfast, delivered from Chip's dream of a kitchen just beyond. Typical fare includes orange juice, small sour-cream pancakes with raspberry sauce and a main dish of scrambled eggs with chives, zucchini, parmesan cheese and vidalia onions with toasted homemade bread. Eggs benedict, chili puffed eggs, eggs rolled in tortillas with salsa and zucchini-parmesan pancakes are other specialties.

Guests relax on the wraparound porch, a colorful expanse of cushioned wicker and hanging plants, or at her spa with a massage therapist. They browse in Chip's Old Milkhouse shop for gifts, specialty foods and garden accessories. Herb and vegetable gardens, sheds and a handful of animals contribute to a farm feeling. Chip's Jersey giant rooster, named Jose Carreras after the opera singer, issues a wake-up call at dawn.

(828) 963-5581. Fax (828) 963-5818. Five rooms, two suites and one cottage with private baths. Doubles, $150 to $175. Suites, $200. Cottage, $285. No smoking. Closed early December through March.

Crippen's Country Inn, 239 Sunset Drive, Box 528, Blowing Rock 28605.

A striking painting over the parlor fireplace depicts this inn in various seasons that blend one into the next across the façade. Until owner Jimmy Crippen explained it, we wouldn't have guessed that it was done sight unseen from a photograph by an artist friend in Miami.

The painting typifies the style of the inn and restaurant, run with flair and personality by Jimmy and his wife Carolyn, a Sheraton dropout, with the considerable input of James Welch, their talented chef (see Dining Spots).

The Crippens bought the old Sunshine Inn B&B, built as a Victorian boarding house, in 1994 when he was 28. He had spent nineteen summers at his family's horse farm in Blowing Rock, and "every time it became harder to leave." Backed by his father, a retired Miami auto dealer, the couple began eight months of renovations. They enlarged eight bedrooms to hold king or queensize beds and added private baths. They converted two main-floor bedrooms into bathrooms for the restaurant. "You can judge a restaurant by its rest rooms," Jimmy said knowingly, as he showed off his.

Four upstairs bedrooms are considered deluxe, with kingsize beds and sofabeds for seating. Restored hardwood floors, painted walls, period furnishings, colorful quilts and simple window treatments are among their attributes. Jimmy says the aim was for "homespun elegance." Four queen bedrooms are considered standard. Two on the third floor have hall baths.

We lucked into the side cottage, a two-room affair that was both stylish and comfortable. It had a queen bedroom and a sitting room with sofabed and the inn's only in-room TV. Carolyn offered a refreshing passionfruit iced tea, enjoyed on the front porch of the inn. Overnight guests share two small front parlors with arriving dinner patrons. The walls of the small mahogany bar at the rear of one parlor are accented with sports equipment. The other parlor has an unobtrusive TV.

Breakfast the next morning was a continental buffet put out in a sunny corner of the restaurant. The spread included juice, cereal, fresh blackberries, bagels and English muffins.

(828) 295-3487. Fax (828) 295-0388. Eight rooms and one cottage with private baths. May-December: doubles $99 to $129, cottage $159. January-April: doubles $79 to $109, cottage $139. Children over 12. No smoking.

Maple Lodge, 152 Sunset Drive, Box 1236, Blowing Rock 28605.

The front of Blowing Rock's oldest operating B&B is deceptive. Built in 1946 as a village inn, it looks like a small house, except for the Mobil and AAA ratings in the windows beside the front door. But the inside meanders on and on, opening up to two parlors, a colorful breakfast sunporch and eleven guest rooms.

Since purchasing the B&B in 1993, Marilyn and David Bateman totally redecorated. The result is an altogether appealing place to stay, one that conveys the feeling of a tasteful home. The front of the house has two pine-paneled parlors. One is a library with a stone fireplace for fireside reading. The other is bigger and more formal with oriental rugs and a pump organ.

Pine ceilings, antiques, family heirlooms, lace and down comforters typify the guest rooms, which vary in size and decor. All wallpapers match the room names. The Bridal Wreath offers a king canopy bed, TV and refrigerator, while Queen Anne's Lace and Lilac have queen canopy beds and two wing chairs. Four rooms in a former garage in the rear include two of the nicest. The Dogwood Room has a king bed and a bathroom beyond a dressing room with an oriental rug on the floor. The Rhododendron Suite has a king bed and a sitting room with a TV in the armoire.

A substantial breakfast buffet is put out in a large, slate-floored side sunporch overlooking wildflower and perennial gardens. The fare includes fruit crisp, home-made granola, muesli, homemade muffins and bagels. The main event could be ricotta cheese pie served with sautéed smoked turkey, sausage frittatas, blueberry pancakes or orange-pecan french toast.

The Batemans keep guests informed in a chatty newsletter, "The Maple Leaflet."

(828) 295-3331. Ten rooms and one suite with private baths. Doubles $85 to $150. Suite $160. Two-night minimum most weekends, three-night minimum on holiday weekends. Children over 12. No smoking. Closed January-February.

Lovill House Inn, 404 Old Bristol Road, Boone 28607.

This 1875 farmhouse on the outskirts of Boone is the oldest in town. It was built by Captain Edward F. Lovill, a lawyer, state senator and founding trustee of the Appalachian Training School, forerunner of Appalachian State University here. Indeed, Captain Lovill drafted the papers that established the university in the front parlor of his house.

Drawn to this historic site were ex-banker Tim Shahen and his wife Lori, who restored the house to its original luster and opened it as a B&B in 1993. Unusual wormy chestnut arches join the living and dining rooms. Beyond is a big kitchen in which guests like to munch on Tim's homemade cookies and hang out with the owners, whose avowed purpose is "to make guests feel at home." As Tim tells it, "our close relationship with guests" is what prompted its four-diamond rating from the AAA. That includes a "hosted social hour" in which the Shahens get guests to interact over wine, beer and a changing array of snacks, from crackers and cheese to quesadillas..

The breakfast fare at tables for six in the dining room changes daily. Fresh orange juice, homemade granola and toasted bagels and English muffins are standard. The main event could be apricot smoothie, zucchini bread and macadamia nut french toast with bacon one day, and strawberry smoothie, pumpkin muffins and cornmeal apple pancakes with sausage patties and apple cider syrup the next.

The five bedrooms have oversize beds, designer linens and comforters, robes, hidden TVs, telephones and hair dryers. The largest is the Bristol, downstairs and across the hall from the living room. It comes with a beamed ceiling of wormy chestnut, kingsize bed, huge woodburning fireplace, loveseat, coffee table and desk, and a floral comforter that matches the draperies. Upstairs are four queensize rooms. They vary from the rear Hickory, the smallest room with a two-room hall bath that happens to be the largest and nicest in the house, to Tim's favorite Lenoir with a poster bed and a loveseat in the corner.

In 1998, the Shahens added a large new luxury room in a rear cabin with queen bed, fireplace and its own deck overlooking some of the perennial gardens.

Guests enjoy a wraparound porch with a lineup of white high-back rockers. A stream runs along the side of the eleven-acre property, and there's a waterfall in the woods beyond a barn.

(828) 264-4204 or (800) 849-9466. Six rooms with private baths. Doubles, $115 to $185. Children over 12. No smoking.

Chetola Resort, North Main Street (Box 17), Blowing Rock 28605.

The setting for this 78-acre gated resort lodge and conference center is tough to beat. It's surrounded by mountains and set back from the highway at the edge of Blowing Rock, facing its own little lake. Its Cherokee name, meaning "Haven of Rest," sums it up. No wonder the North Carolina Symphony uses the lakeside gazebo on the resort's grounds for summer concerts.

The three-story main lodge, built in 1988 in contemporary alpine style, offers 42 rooms and suites in the hotel idiom. Thirty contain two queen beds and the rest have one king. Most have wet bars and microwaves. The largest offer sitting areas with sofabeds. Reproduction furniture and plush carpeting are standard. The 27 choicest rooms, most with balconies, face the lake. The rest face a rear parking lot and hillside.

The resort's recreation center has a huge indoor pool, a fitness center, regulation

Chef James Welch and innkeepers Carolyn and Jimmy Crippens on porch at Crippens Country Inn.

racquetball court and a spa therapy center. The **Manor House Restaurant** serves three meals a day in the original turn-of-the-century mansion around which the resort developed. Three dining rooms and a new outdoor patio offer lovely water views. The traditional dinner menu is priced from $17.95 to $26.95. A casual new restaurant called **Snyder's Soda Shoppe** has opened in the resort's Highlands Sports and Recreation Center.

The resort also rents out 62 condominiums of one to four bedrooms.

(828) 295-5500 or (800) 243-8652. Fax (828) 295-5529. Thirty-seven rooms and five suites with private baths. May-December: weekends, doubles $125 to $171, suites $176 to $219; midweek, doubles $110 to $153, suites $160 to $209. January-April: weekends, doubles $95 to $145, suites $155 to $195; midweek, doubles $89 to $130, suites $140 to $184.

Dining Spots

The town's restaurants are said to be better than the norm because Blowing Rock was the first mountain town to allow them to offer liquor by the drink.

Crippen's Country Inn & Restaurant, 239 Sunset Drive, Blowing Rock.

The restaurant here is so good and so central a part of the operation that it tends to overshadow the inn. People come from miles around to sample the cooking of chef James Welch and the suave hospitality of Jimmy Crippen, the omnipresent owner and polished host. They worked together for seven years at one of the best restaurants in Florida, Mark's Place in North Miami, before launching this venture. Their state-of-the-art kitchen produces what a reviewer from Welch's native Greensboro publicized as the best food North Carolina. The James Beard Foundation quickly invited the pair to prepare a dinner in New York.

The restful, 70-seat rear dining room has cranberry-colored walls and decorative accents related to food (the sconces are trout). Our dinner began with complimentary nippy scotch bonnet pepper and white bean spreads to be lathered on wasabi potato bread. Softshell crab tempura and braised Pacific oysters with wild mushrooms and spinach in cognac cream sauce were stellar appetizers. We could have stopped right there or sampled one of the exotic pastas and been happily sated, but this was not the night. The chef suggested the rare yellowfin tuna and the banana leaf-wrapped swordfish stuffed with poblano chiles and ginger. But we had already decided on the grilled flank steak with goat cheese flan and the grilled angus ribeye steak with merlot sauce to accompany a bottle of McDowell petite sirah from a choice wine list.

A sampling of homemade sorbets (orange-mint and strawberry rum) and warm chocolate cake with espresso meringue capped off a memorable meal.

In 1998, Crippen's began offering gourmet pizzas at the South Marke shopping complex..

(828) 295-3487. Entrées, $16.95 to $24.95. Dinner nightly from 6, Thursday-Sunday from 6 in off-season.

The Riverwood, 7179 Valley Blvd., Blowing Rock.

One of North Carolina's few totally smoke-free environments is provided by this decade-old restaurant ensconced in a restored, 70-year-old stone and brown frame house on the side of a hill northwest of town.

Innovative culinary creations are featured, as in such appetizers as grilled venison sausage with pickled radicchio and black mission figs sautéed in bacon vinaigrette over sliced stilton with mixed greens. Main courses might be New Zealand mussels in roasted yellow pepper saffron cream over pasta, grilled grouper with hoisin-raspberry glaze, roast cornish game hen rubbed with a ginger spice blend and served with a prickly pear-molasses sauce, and grilled beef tenderloin marinated in herbs and wine. The chef prepares a "five-alarm, dangerously hot" spicy dish that changes nightly.

The gourmet vegetarian specials here are said to be exceptional, as are the homemade cheesecakes and chocolate desserts.

Dining is by candlelight in three cozy rooms. A strong wine list is featured.

(828) 295-4162. Entrées, $14.95 to $19.95. Dinner, Monday-Friday 6 to 9, Saturday 5:30 to 10. Closed Sunday, also Monday-Tuesday November-March.

Twig's Restaurant & Lounge, Highway 321 Bypass, Blowing Rock.

Although known for its lounge, Mather Ward's longtime restaurant here has its devotees. Count us among them. A twig banister leads people inside, where the pine-paneled dining room features a charming twiggy divider. There are Audubon prints and plates on the walls, and white linens and sleek oil lamps on the tables.

The contemporary regional menu, with international overtones, is strong on seafood. House salads are dressed with unusual vinaigrettes, in our case apple curry and roasted tomato with garlic. Main courses were the signature crab cakes, two huge and exemplary renditions with nantua sauce, accompanied by garlicky mashed new potatoes, and an enormous plate of Low Country shrimp and andouille sausage, topped with lobster cream sauce and served over cheese grits. Choices ranged from linguini tossed with smoked trout, cilantro, tomatoes and baby corn to T-bone steak topped with a roasted garlic, onion and gorgonzola compound butter.

The pastry chef's desserts tempted, but we already had overindulged. The polished staff, who knew what was what, served us a dish of neopolitan ice cream to share.

(828) 295-5050. Entrées, $13.95 to $19.95. Dinner, Tuesday-Sunday from 5.

The Best Cellar, Little Springs Road, Blowing Rock.

Hidden off Highway 321 behind the Food Lion supermarket is this oldtimer that started as a sandwich and book shop on the lower level, inspiring the name.

Founders Ira and Lani Wilson, who had a knack for food, retired in 1997 after 28 years and turned over the reins to Lisa Strippling and Rob Dyer, who had been dining room manager and wine bar manager respectively at Twig's.

They continued the tradition in the log house they call a lodge, nestled against a hillside. Five candlelit dining rooms on several levels have been joined by a new outside deck.

The fare is continental, with a dose of contemporary offerings such as the specialty grilled tuna marinated in soy and ginger and the grouper stuffed with smoked gouda and roasted almonds. Otherwise expect the predictable shrimp provençal, chicken marsala, roast duckling, veal oscar, prime rib and filet au poivre. Oysters and shrimp from the raw bar make good starters. The homemade desserts change daily.

(828) 295-3466. Entrées, $14.95 to $18.95. Dinner, Monday-Saturday 6 to 9:30, May-October. Rest of year, Friday-Saturday 6 to 9:30. No smoking.

Navelli's Cucina Italiana, 537 North Main St., Blowing Rock.

Chef Kevin Rounsvelli trained in the old world Italian tradition in New York and gave up a top culinary post there to open a tiny restaurant in Blowing Rock. Backed by a local woman, he converted a small beige house with olive trim into an authentic country Italian restaurant. The interior holds about a dozen tables amid artworks and framed photos on the walls and swagged floral draperies around the windows.

The menu, in the classic Italian tradition, is prodigious – everything from pasta with soup and salad to a seven-course, prix-fixe extravaganza from antipasti to cappuccino. Among entrées are five poultry dishes, six veal choices, lobster fra diavolo and New York strip steak encrusted with gorgonzola, to mention a few.

Those in the know opt for the leisurely, prix-fixe option, which takes about three hours and yields enough food that you may not be able to eat again before dinner the next day. A typical meal brings antipasti and an appetizer of jumbo shrimp wrapped in prosciutto, penne with marinara sauce, rack of lamb, salad, a fruit plate of sliced watermelon and cantaloupe over a honey cream sauce, a dessert of tirami su and a choice of coffees.

The wine list is all Italian.

(828) 295-6004. Entrées, $15.95 to $27.95. Dinner nightly except Sunday.

The Village Café, off Main Street, Blowing Rock.

Everyone's favorite luncheon spot is this stylish place in an old Episcopal church reading room, with a shady courtyard outside. The Historic Register building is hidden down an alley off Main Street, but well worth seeking out.

Owner Ann Esposito moved her establishment here in 1990 after she outgrew her original quarters in nearby Foscoe. She since has "semi-retired" from cooking, turning over chef duties to Andy Whatley and doing a few specials and desserts between hostessing duties.

We were seated in one of the simple upstairs dining rooms as the locals felt it was too cold for lunch outside that spring day. Word of the specialty crêpes preceded our visit, and the day's Creole shrimp crêpe with tasso and a cup of sweet corn soup with roasted poblano puree turned out to be very good indeed. The vodka-cured salmon in cream sauce over angel-hair pasta was one of the best pasta dishes ever. The toasted fugasa bread, based on a traditional Argentinean sourdough recipe, is a house specialty. It was so good that we decided to sample a couple of desserts: warm apple oatmeal crisp à la mode and espresso pot de crème.

We'd gladly return to try the Greek chicken salad, the crab cakes, the grilled shrimp and polenta or the exotic sandwiches made with fugasa bread. Not to mention the fugasa french toast, the montrachet eggs florentine or the Scandinavian eggs with that vodka-cured salmon for an indulgent breakfast.

(828) 295-3769. Entrées, $7.95 to $10.95. Breakfast and lunch daily except Wednesday, 8 to 3. Closed January to late April.

The Mast Farm Inn, 2543 Broadstone Road, Valle Crucis.

This old-timer, traditionally a favorite of the locals, has been enhanced by new owners Kay Hinshaw and Wanda Phillipp. They hired as chef Scott Haulman, who trained in Greensboro restaurants before redefining Southern cuisine here.

Dining is in a couple of simple, historic rooms with Appalachian quilts on the walls and on an outdoor terrace. Specialties are sautéed shrimp with white cheddar grits over zesty rosemary tomato sauce, steamed asparagus tips and corn relish, and herbed mountain trout pecan with parsley-lime butter. They're so popular they show up on the brunch menu as well. For starters, try the black bean jicama, chorizo and cheddar spring rolls or the crispy backfin crab and rice croquettes. If you're a meat-eater, consider the grilled bourbon-barbecued ribeye or the grilled mustard-rosemary lamb loin. Not into meat? How about seared tofu triangles with brown texmati rice? The dessert tray stars a homemade fruit cobbler.

Herbs and vegetables come from the farm's garden across the road. This is the latest in contemporary Southern fare, served in the endearing surroundings of an 1880s farm home.

The restaurant also stages periodic wine dinners.

(828) 963-5857 or (888) 963-5857. Entrées, $13.75 to $24.95. Dinner, Monday-Saturday 5:30 to 8:45, May-October; weekends in off-season. Sunday brunch, 11:30 to 2. Lunch on weekends in summer. BYOB.

A variety of restaurants serve other interests. Just east of Blowing Rock, **The Original Emporium Restaurant** has a smoky bar and a family dining room that's a sea of pine, but a window table or the small outside deck yields an awesome view of the John's River Gorge. The **Speckled Trout Cafe** offers mountain trout in two rustic rooms and a porch overlooking downtown Blowing Rock.

In downtown Boone, the vivid pink **Caribbean Cafe** is a favorite of the college crowd, at least on the "25-cent Wing Night" we stopped by to try the tequila chicken and the specialty catfish. Three restaurants are highly recommended for fine dining in Banner Elk: **Morel's, Louisiana Purchase** and **The Black Diamond Bistro and Grill.**

Diversions

Relatively tranquil much of the year, Blowing Rock is at its busiest in summer. Daytrippers and weekenders jam the downtown sidewalks, savoring ice cream cones while sitting on benches in the town's Memorial Park and watching the passing parade. A block beyond are the Annie Cannon Memorial Gardens with a gazebo, Broyhill Park and the start of the Glen Burney Trail to three sets of waterfalls. Across town is scenic Crystal Lake. A Blowing Rock visitors' guide includes an historical walking tour of 22 points of interest in the center of town.

A sign opposite the historic Green Park Inn on the town's eastern outskirts marks the Eastern Continental Divide. The New River in the heart of town is said to be the only one in the East to flow north and west. Grandfather Mountain, the highest peak in the Blue Ridge, is close by. The rhododendrons flanking the Blue Ridge Parkway bloom in June, while the fall foliage is at its best in mid-October.

The North Carolina Symphony Orchestra plays summer concerts beside the lake at Chetola Lodge and at Appalachian State University in Boone. The Blowing Rock Stage Company has presented summer stock productions since 1986. The town park is the site of free outdoor concerts and monthly Art in the Park festivals, as detailed in the weekly newspaper, The Blowing Rocket. "The Horn in the West" in Boone is one of the nation's oldest outdoor pageants.

The Blowing Rock, Highway 321 South, Blowing Rock.

Yes, there is a blowing rock. It's a large protruding rock formation overhanging the Johns River Gorge 3,000 feet below. Indian legend has it that a Chickasaw maiden lost her lover as he leapt from the rock, only to be returned with an upward gust of wind. Ripley's Believe It or Not cartoon portrayed this as a place so windy that the snow falls upside down. There are gardens, a visitor center and an observation tower with a view of the rock, gorge and mountains. (A similar view, free with drinks or a meal, is afforded from the Original Emporium Restaurant and Lounge nearby.)

(828) 295-7111. Open daily, 8 to 8 May-October, 9 to 5 weekends rest of year. Adults $4.

Parkway Craft Center and Moses H. Cone Memorial Park, Milepost 294, Blue Ridge Parkway.

Flat Top Manor, the turn-of-the-century country home of textile magnate Moses Cone, overlooks Bass Lake and a 3,600-acre estate three miles west of Blowing Rock. Twenty-five miles of gentle carriage trails wind through the park for the enjoyment of walkers, hikers and cross-country skiers, and horses may be rented by reservation from Blowing Rock Stables. The fine offerings of the Southern Highland Craft Guild's craft center are nicely displayed in various rooms of the manor house. A weaver was spinning on the porch at our visit, and a National Park Service ranger pointed out the various hiking trails.

(828) 295-7938. Center open daily, 9 to 6. Closed in February. Free.

Boone. Named for western pioneer Daniel Boone, who had a cabin in the area in the 1760s, bustling Boone is the home of Appalachian State University. It's the site of An Appalachian Summer Festival, a lively performing festival every July. Visitor attractions include the Daniel Boone Native Gardens and the adjacent "The Horn in the West," a musical drama portraying the struggles of Daniel Boone and his pioneers. It's presented nightly except Monday from late June to mid-August in an outdoor amphitheater in Daniel Boone Park. Downtown offers the

Cottonwood Brewery and the **Wilcox Emporium,** an interesting complex of vendor kiosks, shops and restaurants fashioned in 1996 from an old warehouse.

Valle Crucis. Three mountain streams converge from different directions in the shape of a cross at quaint Valle Crucis, whose Latin name means vale of the cross. Founded by Scottish highlanders, the hamlet is known for its Episcopal Mission School and the **Mast General Store,** established in 1883 and still looking about the same. It's listed on the National Register as one of the best remaining examples of an old general store. Country hams hang from the ceiling and a pot-bellied stove warms the musty interior. Nearby are the **Mast Annex & Candy Barrel,** featuring clothing and a deli, and the **School House Shop & Museum,** a gift shop and small museum.

Shopping. Stores of considerable appeal are located along Main Street and Sunset Drive. **Ashe Wine & Cheese** is the place to pick up fine cheeses, produced in the factory at West Jefferson, as well as wines and picnic supplies. **High Mountain Expeditions** offers equipment and information on canoeing, kayaking, tubing and whitewater rafting on the scenic New River. **Pandora's Box** has a great selection of cards and local music, while **Pleasant Papers** is a lovely stationery shop. Neat banners and twig furniture caught our eye at **The Last Straw.** **Appalachian Rustic Furnishings** had a twig table in the window to die for. Colorful clothing is featured at **Almost Rodeo Drive,** while **The Fig Leaf** has casual clothes. **Trading Roots** stocks "gifts with a conscience." Designer home accents are offered at **My Favorite Things** and hard-to-find kitchen items at **My Favorite Kitchen Things,** both upstairs in the historic Martin House. **Chickory Suite** is one of several coffee shops. Look for the green turrets of **South Marke,** a cluster of boutiques in a Victorian shopping village just off Main Street. **Serves You Right** has smashing accessories and gifts for the kitchen and dining room. **Sarah Peck** offers classic and spirited apparel for women. **Starwood Gallery** and **Crestwood Galleries** are two of the better galleries. At the edge of town are 35 outlet stores at **The Shoppes on the Parkway.**

Extra-Special

Roger's Trading Post, 3679 U.S. Hwy 321 South, Blowing Rock.

You could spend hours poking through all the stuff at this roadside emporium that you'd probably pass by, unless you knew about it. Roger Reedy's specialty is birdhouses – more than 25,000 of every description. They're made of wood, bark and moss by 45 local families. They look like doll houses, chalets, churches, school houses, even an ark. The most expensive at our visit was a 16-room affair for $350 – "any bird would be proud to call this home," proclaimed a staffer. He then showed us the nest a wren had made in a jewel box in the chicken coop that houses an array of collectibles – from tools to books, you name it. The sign calls it "literary archives and kitchen department." No less an authority than radio newscaster Paul Harvey touted Roger's as the best place in America to buy a birdhouse. We departed with a cute but fragile $6 model whose handle fell off on the way home, rendering it decorative rather than functional.

(828) 265-1944. Open seasonally.

Some of East's highest mountains provide backdrop for downtown Asheville skyline.

Asheville, N.C.
Home, Grand Home

When George W. Vanderbilt, grandson of railroad titan Cornelius Vanderbilt, set out to build the largest private home in America, he chose a site just outside Asheville.

The widely traveled young Vanderbilt thought it one of the most beautiful places in the world. These days, many of the 850,000 visitors who are drawn annually to his Biltmore Estate would agree.

The estate enjoys a sweeping view of Mount Pisgah and the Great Smokies, and almost nowhere in that great expanse is a sign of civilization. Although it is less than four miles from downtown Asheville, the Biltmore is not readily visible from the city and vice-versa.

Asheville, which native-son novelist Thomas Wolfe described as a town existing within the rim of an enormous cup,.is surrounded by the East's highest mountains. It blends the friendly, small-town feeling of a somewhat remote Appalachian town with the sophistication of the worldly transplants who have settled here.

The city, whose minor-league baseball team bears the appropriate nickname the Tourists, has been created by and for outsiders. A number of its current attractions were built by people like Vanderbilt who visited and decided to stay.

The beauty and spirit lure the affluent, artists and New Agers to what some liken to an energy vortex, as in the Sedona of the East. The arts and crafts scene is unrivaled in the Southeast. Bohemian coffee shops abound. A downtown sidewalk vendor does a brisk business in vegetarian hot dogs.

Asheville owes its cachet today not only to its spectacular location. Rather than default on its loans after the Depression, it chose to pay back every dollar, a burden that took until 1976. The city was thus spared the bulldozing of urban renewal, and retains much of the look of its 1920s heyday.

Its flashy art deco city hall in pink and green sits side by side with the staid county courthouse at one end of wide-open Pack Square. Alongside is contemporary Pack Place, developed by the city as an arts and cultural center. Curving, one-way Wall Street is the nucleus of a revitalized downtown. Though surrounded by office buildings, novelist Wolfe's childhood home remains rather homey (and was planned for reopening after a 1998 fire). Not at all homey is the sprawling Grove Park Inn, one of the South's grand resort hotels carved out of boulders on the side of a mountain.

The last decade has spawned a number of inns and B&Bs, where visitors can quickly feel at home. Many of them find Asheville to be a livable city that they might like to call home.

Inn Spots

Asheville claims to have more inns and B&Bs than any town between Cape May and Charleston. Although their brochures do not necessarily specify, most require two-night minimum stays weekends in season and during the month of October.

Richmond Hill Inn, 87 Richmond Hill Lane, Asheville 28806.

For people seeking to take part in a luxurious Biltmore House lifestyle, the stately 1889 mansion, cozy duplex cottages and a sumptuous new building that make up this complex offer an appealing choice of places to stay. Showy parterre gardens, a manmade brook with a waterfall and an award-winning restaurant conspire to round out a most satisfying inn experience.

Although the Queen Anne-style mansion is its centerpiece, the Richmond Hill is really a "campus" unto itself, perched on a hill on the northwestern outskirts of Asheville.

Listed on the National Register, the mansion was built for Richmond Pearson, former congressman and ambassador, and his socialite wife Gabrielle. Eventually abandoned, its land was sold for a Baptist retirement home and the mansion was moved by the local preservation society 600 feet to the east to await a buyer. The saviors were Dr. Albert Michel and his wife Margaret, owners of the Education Center Inc. in Greensboro. They undertook a painstaking, $3 million restoration and reopened the mansion as a full-service inn in 1989, its 100th birthday year.

The hillside inn complex has been growing and improving ever since. In 1990, nine Victorian cottages were built around a manicured croquet court to the west of the mansion. In 1996, fifteen more rooms were added in a new Garden Pavilion below and to the east of the mansion.

The accommodations differ one from the other and between buildings. Purists prefer the twelve antiques-filled rooms and suites – some quite opulent and a few more basic – upstairs in the mansion. Here they hark back to the good life as experienced a century ago with canopy beds and clawfoot tubs. Those with more modern tastes like the newest quarters in the

Croquet cottages, mansion and Garden Pavilion make up Richmond Hill Inn complex.

pavilion with refrigerators and fireplaces. A few there have jetted tubs and garden terraces.

We were more than content in the sweet Laurel Cottage, one of eight duplex units and a suite grouped around the croquet lawn. A pencil-post queen bed, two comfy blue and white checked swivel club chairs in the front bay window, a tiled gas fireplace, TV and a huge skylit bathroom with a tub and separate oversize shower fulfilled the basics. Waffle-weave robes, a mini-refrigerator stocked with sodas, a stunning watercolor above the fireplace and white decor with arty accents came with. The icing on the cake was the front porch, made for whiling away the afternoon on rockers facing a mountain panorama that more than compensated for the sounds of the highway below.

Afternoon tea is a treat in the mansion. It's put out at 3 o'clock in Gabrielle's restaurant and whisked away promptly at 5 so the restaurant can be set for dinner (see Dining Spots). We arrived just in time for the pastry chef's daily extravaganza, a tiered tray of addictive sweets including chocolate caramel nut crunch and lemon curd tarts with blackberries. A tour of the mansion's majestic Oak Hall and grand staircase paneled in rich native oak, the library harboring 200 original volumes from the Pearson collection and the six-sided front parlor with octagonal bay helped work off the calories. So did walking up and down the path along the cascading brook to the parterre gardens. Here is an exquisite array of white, blue, purple and yellow flowers, varying with the season.

Breakfast the next morning in the dining room at the Garden Pavilion provided a choice of three treats. Exemplary were a three-egg frittata with smoked ham and a toasted brioche with a spiced rum and berry compote and sweet cream, both accompanied by grits du jour.

(828) 252-7313 or (800) 545-9238. Fax (828) 252-8726. Thirty-three rooms and three suites with private baths. Weekends, holidays and October: doubles $195 to $375, suites $450. Midweek: doubles $135 to $240, suites $285. Two-night minimum weekends. No smoking.

The Inn at Wintersun, One Wintersun Lane, Fairview 28730.

With a grand entrance not unlike that at the Biltmore, a three-quarter-mile driveway winds up to this hillside manse on 80 private acres in the mountains seven miles southeast of Asheville. Susan Sluyter and Judy Carter built the house as a potential wellness center, but thought they'd try a B&B first.

Asheville's newest B&B is its most luxurious, from the 24-foot-high, manmade waterfall in the stone garden in back to the marble spa and salon that comes with the Wintersun suite. The owners built the house for guests, since they occupy a house near the stables, where Judy fulfills her dream of raising horses.

The decor is the work of Susan, a clinical psychologist from New York, who continues to practice here. "Decorating is my hobby," she said, "although I never had a canvas this big." She splashed floral chintzes around the living room, a most welcoming space with zillions of books and family pictures. She covered the five tables in the dining wing with tapestry fabrics, and produced a charming family-room retreat off the open kitchen. Colorful geraniums and lush ferns brighten the front veranda, furnished in dark green wicker that matches the facade of the house.

Beautiful artworks and handpainted furnishings dignify the foyer and the hallways leading to the four second-floor bedrooms stretching across the front of the house. Stone fireplaces, plush seating, queensize beds (one kingsize), antiques and oriental rugs are their hallmarks. Each is stylishly accessorized to the max. The two corner rooms are larger, and have larger bathrooms with windows.

Nice as they are, these rooms pale next to the main-floor Wintersun suite, so big it has three entrances – off the main living room, off the rear veranda and off the waterfall garden. The bedroom is like the others, but with the additional advantage of opening onto a private section of the front veranda. Its adjacent spa is "a new way to define decadence," in Susan's words. Architectural balance required a wing the size of the dining room, filled with windows, marble and greenery. Its centerpiece is a 500-gallon spa sunk in a marble surround facing the fireplace. Marble vanities line one side. A display of hats identifies a corner shower that doubles as a steam bath and is big enough for a basketball team. An alcove holds not one but two lavatories, each with its own door.

Succumb to self-indulgence, or retreat to the private veranda, the rear garden, the sumptuous living room (where wine and champagne are poured in the late afternoon) or the cozy sitting area beside the fireplace off the kitchen. That's where we found the brightest lights for pre-dinner reading. There's no television, but taped music wafted throughout the house which, with no other guests that evening, was ours for the duration. A nicer home away from home would be hard to imagine.

We awoke the next day to a memorable breakfast. Orange juice and cut-up fruit with yogurt preceded an artistic array of treats: a portobello quiche, artichoke-stuffed tomatoes, blueberry yeast rolls and ham. Susan said she had tried to serve bacon and sausage, but guests seemed to want only the ham. It all tasted as good as it looked, and we left ready to take on the day.

(828) 628-7890 or (888) 628-1628. Fax (704) 628-7891. Four rooms and one suite with private baths. Doubles, $190 to $210. Suite, $375. No smoking.

Abbingdon Green, 46 and 48 Cumberland Circle, Asheville 28801.

An English garden theme prevails at this comfortable B&B, run with flair and enthusiasm by transplanted New Yorker Valerie Larrea. A series of events conspired to lead the high-powered bank executive to vacation in Asheville, which she found "grabs you by the collar and says 'pay attention.'" Drawn by its spell, she moved here with no idea of what she wanted to do and found a rundown boarding house hidden behind overgrown trees and brush. She saw its immediate potential as a B&B and its possibilities for future expansion. After five months of

Photo by J. Weiland

Marble fireplaces in bedroom and luxurious spa are feature of suite at Inn at Wintersun.

renovations she opened with a preservation award in hand. Soon, this one-woman dynamo had transformed the overgrown property into her first-ever gardens, a feat that garnered the best new garden award for Buncome County in 1997.

The English theme is a natural for Valerie, whose father's family lived in England. Her brother lives there now and her daughter studied at Oxford. Current British magazines grace the front parlor/TV room, which conveys an English hunt look. The larger living room across the back is furnished in the English-style Sheraton and Chippendale antiques and reproduction pieces characteristic of the rest of the house. A library of garden books here provided inspiration for her handiwork outside.

Three lace-covered tables in the front dining room are the setting for breakfast. One of Valerie's fruit soups and homemade bread or cake precede a hot entrée such as eggs benedict, quiche florentine or orange croissant amandine. "I like to cook for a crowd," says the hostess, for whom entertaining is a natural.

Upstairs, she cossets overnight guests in six rooms named for parks and gardens around London. Each is tastefully decorated in florals and bears an underlying theme: topiary in Regents Park, royals in St. James's Park, golf in Kensington Gardens.

Amazingly, Valerie made all the draperies and bed canopies, hung the wallpapers and hand-cut the borders to extend floral designs onto the painted walls. All the beds are queensize, except for one twin room in the rear, two-bedroom carriage house. Besides the twin bedroom, this comes with a main room with kingsize bed, a living/dining/kitchen area and an outside deck beside the boxwood garden.

Landscaped lawn and front veranda greet guests at The Lion & The Rose.

The boxwoods, more than 300 in all, also are on view from the large rear porch off the second floor of the main house.

(828) 251-2454 or (800) 251-2454. Fax (828) 251-2872. Six rooms and one two-bedroom cottage with private baths. Doubles, $110 to $155. Cottage, $185. No smoking.

The Lion & The Rose, 276 Montford Ave., Asheville 28801.

The first president of the fledgling Historic Asheville B&B Association has imbued her handsome Queen Anne/Georgian home in the historic Montford district with "all the amenities you find in a five-star hotel." The result is a comfortable, winning B&B with uncommon style.

Lisa Yorty and her husband Rice took over an existing B&B in 1995 and "redecorated everything in sight." They retained the name, which reflected an English theme and coincidentally matched the initials of their first names.

The main floor holds both a formal parlor with an antique Steinway piano that guests like to play and a more casual parlor with a TV. Morning coffee is set out beside a fireplace in an inglenook in the entry foyer. Guests then adjourn to a chandeliered dining room for a gourmet breakfast at 9. The meal at our visit was fresh fruit with yogurt, followed by a pear bavarian puff pancake. Blintz soufflé with granola on the side is Lisa's personal favorite. Afternoon tea is put out on an 1860 sideboard. Scones, datenut bars and fresh lemon cake typically accompany. More sweets are put out at night on a shelf in the kitchen, where the refrigerator is stocked with complimentary beverages. Decanters of sherry and port await those who prefer.

The treats continue in the five upstairs guest quarters, all with private baths and TVs. The queensize beds are turned down with chocolates and lemon water. Bedside clock radios are programmed with a choice of "white noise," from woodland sounds to ocean surf. Fresh flowers brighten the bureaus. Bathrooms have hair dryers and terrycloth robes, and the tissue is embossed with the Lion & Rose logo.

A seven-foot headboard of tiger oak matches the dresser in the master suite. Here, two tapestry wing chairs are set into a bay window overlooking the front gardens and a built-in bookcase harbors the TV. The Fannie Rice Room holds a draped canopy bed from England. The Holger-Nielsen Room has a step-up oak bed in the corner and rich wallpaper borders over painted red walls. Most of the third floor is given over to the Bridal Suite, which Lisa decorated with a light and airy, cottagey feeling. A dressing room contains a day bed and wicker chairs, the main room has a wicker bed, a corner fireplace, and a front balcony with two wrought-iron chairs. The decoupage on portions of the walls replicates the wallpaper border pattern. A huge walk-in shower is built into a back dormer, and the skylit bathroom has a whirlpool tub. A local artist painted a mural of an Asheville garden, complete with lion and rose, beside the tub.

You might not notice, but posted in the entry vestibule is the state agency's seal of sanitary and health approval. Lisa is proud of hers, because it notes a perfect 100 percent rating, the only one in Asheville.

(828) 255-7673 or (800) 546-6988. Fax (828) 285-9810. Four rooms and one suite with private baths. Doubles, $135 to $175. Suite, $225. Children over 12. No smoking.

The Inn on Montford, 296 Montford Ave., Asheville 28801.

This Arts & Crafts style house, designed in 1900 by the supervising architect for the Biltmore House and listed on the National Register, has a lot going for it: Four comfortable guest rooms. Four common rooms. Sumptuous decor. Eight fireplaces. Antique collections. Gourmet breakfasts.

Lynn and Ron Carlson acquired in 1997 a B&B created four years earlier by Ripley Hatch, an inn consultant. They redecorated and furnished with English and American antiques dating from 1730.

Hidden behind trees and a wide front porch full of green wicker, the house is a beauty. The large foyer has a stone fireplace in a corner and chunky wainscoting on the staircase. The Germanic dining room provides display areas for Lynn's prized collection of Georgian silver napkin rings, tea caddies, Staffordshire pottery, decanters and antique glassware.

"Antiquers sometimes feel they know me," she says. She attributes that to her appearance on Public Television's Antiques Road Show, when her two Chinese teacups were valued at $1,200.

The front corner parlor holds a Victorian fireplace and a loveseat. A side sunporch is made for TV and music and contains a guest refrigerator. The rear library, furnished in plush leather, is home to the couple's collection of antique maps and Baxter prints.

Upstairs are four corner guest rooms with queen beds, fireplaces, private baths (three with whirlpool tubs), heated towel bars and unusually good soundproofing. O'Henry, the least expensive, has a poster bed, two armchairs, oriental rugs on the hardwood floor and an antique medicine cabinet above the original clawfoot tub. The black and red florals of the rear Edith Wharton convey something of a bordello feeling. The F. Scott Fitzgerald is the biggest, with two plump chairs and a desk in the window.

The Carlsons host a social hour at 6:30 to talk about food and restaurants over a glass of wine. The next morning, Lynn delivers coffee service in a bag, which she hangs on the door knobs of guest rooms. She then sets a lavish table for eight in the dining room at 9 o'clock. When we were there, the three-course meal included baked pears with raspberry sauce, a dish called eggs in straw (a nest of potatoes and bacon) and cinnamon rolls.

(828) 254-9569 or (800) 254-9569. Fax (828) 254-9518. Four rooms with private baths. Doubles, $135 to $180. No smoking.

The Wright Inn, 235 Pearson Drive, Asheville 28801.

Lovely gardens surround this handsome Victorian, one of the finest examples of Queen Anne architecture in historic Montford. The gardens are the work of Art Wenczel, resident owner-innkeeper with his wife Carol. The interior décor reflects the touch of Carol, who raised their family in a typical one-story ranch house but "came to love Victorian." The Wenczels took over a B&B with a museum feeling befitting its status on the National Register and added warmth, cosmetic enhancements and creature comforts. They changed many of the beds to queensize, installed a couple of gas fireplaces and furnished with Victorian antiques in a light as opposed to dark and heavy style.

The nine guest quarters each come with down quilts, TV, telephone and a hair dryer in the bathroom. The prized Wright Suite on the ground floor, pretty in pale yellow, has a carved mahogany bed with a step stool, fainting couch and rocker, fireplace and a private breakfast room for intimate tête-à-têtes. Other favorites are the Green Room, which has a private balcony accessible through one of the triple windows, and the spacious Powell Room with a rose loveseat that matches the oriental carpet. Three bedrooms on the third floor open off a sitting room. With the feel of a casual Victorian cottage, the two-story rear carriage house can accommodate eight guests in three bedrooms, a living room with a queen sofabed, dining room, kitchen and two baths.

The rich lincrusta walls in the entry hallway look like the Spanish tuile leather in the breakfast room at the Biltmore House. Here is where Carol puts out delectable cookies and brownies along with crackers and cheese for afternoon tea. Guests gather in an elegant parlor and a drawing room, or move outside to the wraparound porch with its corner gazebo.

Breakfast is a substantial affair, served by candlelight amid china and crystal at 8:30. The printed menu changes daily. The day of our visit it started with fresh orange juice, mixed fruit, granola or cereal, Scottish oat scones and banana pecan bread. The main event was Bermuda pancakes with blackberry syrup. Eggs benedict was on tap for the next day.

(828) 251-0789 or (800) 552-5724. Fax (828) 251-0929. Eight rooms and one suite with private bath, plus a three-bedroom carriage house. Doubles, $110 to $135. Suite $155. Carriage house $235. Children over 12. No smoking.

Beaufort House, 61 North Liberty St., Asheville 28801.

Robert and Jacqueline Glasgow attended a seminar for prospective innkeepers in Florida and stopped in Asheville on their way home to Ontario. "We wanted to convert a private home into an inn and saw this house for sale," says Rob, son of a Niagara Falls builder. In the vanguard of Asheville's B&B movement, they opened the 1894 Queen Anne Victorian atop a sloping two-acre property in a residential section in 1992.

The National Register house contains eight guest quarters, and a rear carriage house was transformed in 1998 into three attached "cottage" units. All but three have double jacuzzis and most have wood-burning fireplaces. Each has a TV/VCR

Wright Inn in historic Montford section is fine example of Queen Anne architecture.

(the B&B touts an extensive video library), telephone and – in the main house – sturdy, high Victorian furnishings. The rooms vary from the smallest Ivy Terrace Room with a queensize antique bed dressed in handpainted floral linens and a double jacuzzi to the light and airy Sarah Davidson Suite occupying the entire third floor. It has a king canopy bed, a day-bed couch and a double jacuzzi. The main-floor Arbor Room with queen poster bed, fireplace and jacuzzi is accessed from a private porch overlooking the rose arbor. The Garden Room, appointed in mint green and peach florals, has a high antique oak queen bed, fireplace and clawfoot tub and comes with a private balcony.

For seclusion, romantics opt for the new cottage quarters with high peaked ceilings and contemporary flair. Each has a private deck with rocking chairs facing a wooded area in back. The TV/VCR is on a swivel shelf above the jacuzzi tub in a corner of the pine-paneled Savannah, the largest. Its queen bed is enveloped in a drapery canopy. The Willow, decorated in taupe and black, conveys a Romanesque theme in keeping with its sunken jacuzzi and hand-held shower in a corner.

The Glasgows, who live with their children in a house behind the cottages, are usually on hand to offer afternoon refreshments, including wine and cheese and chocolate truffles, which Jackie was preparing in the kitchen when we stopped by. She's also known for lavish breakfasts served at a table for twelve and three smaller tables in the dining room. Egg soufflé with roasted potatoes is a specialty. So are eggs benedict, belgian waffles, pear dumplings and zucchini bread. Versatile Jackie, a potter, also makes many of the craft items she sells along with her homemade jams and preserves in the inn's gift shop.

Guests gather around the fireplace in the Victorian parlor in the winter and on the wraparound porch in warm weather.

(828) 254-8334 or (800) 261-2221. Fax (828) 251-2082. Seven rooms, one suite and three cottages, all with private baths. Doubles, $65 to $175. Suite, $195. No smoking.

Albemarle Inn, 86 Edgemont Road, Asheville 28801.

New life is being imparted to this pillared Greek Revival mansion, hidden behind Norway spruce trees in a posh residential area not far from the famed Grove Park Inn.

Lawyers Cathy and Larry Sklar moved from Rye, N.Y., to take over the inn in 1998. They had stayed at the Albemarle for a week in 1997 while investigating the possibility of practicing law in Asheville. It was their first B&B experience. As chance would have it, the inn changed hands while the Sklars were there, and "that event planted the seed in my wife's mind that perhaps it was time for a lifestyle change," Larry recalled. They returned to Asheville several months later to begin looking seriously at inns when they were advised that the Albemarle was again for sale. "Since Cathy had fallen in love with the inn from the outset," said Larry, "we commenced negotiations and bought it." Was it serendipity? "Absolutely," he responded.

The Sklars recognized the B&B's potential. They repainted the faded façade and upgraded the property's landscaping, adding a stone patio and stone entry columns. They began renovating two first-floor bedrooms into more luxurious guest quarters and redecorated several rooms upstairs.

Guest rooms on three floors vary in size. The skylit, third-floor Shangri-La is cozy and private with a queen brass and enamel bed and two rattan armchairs. The nearby Royal Hideaway has a carved oak queen bed, matching marble-top dresser and bedside tables, a spacious sitting area with Queen Anne loveseat and chairs, and a twin bed in a dormer alcove. Tops on the second floor are the redecorated Sunrise Suite with a kingsize carved mahogany poster bed and sunporch outfitted in wicker and Juliet's Chamber, a corner space with rice-carved queen poster bed, armoire, two wing chairs and a private balcony. We were happily ensconced in Cathy's favorite, Pink Parfait, a spacious confection of pink florals with queen canopy bed, complementary dresser and loveseat and the telephone and TV standard in all rooms. The two-first-floor rooms were originally parlors, each with twelve-foot ceilings and tall windows overlooking the veranda.

The Sklars serve afternoon refreshments in the large, L-shaped foyer/parlor at the foot of a handsome, carved oak stairway. In good weather guests move to the broad front veranda beneath 30-foot-high pillars overlooking the lawn and gardens.

Breakfast is served from 8 to 9 in a chandeliered dining room or the large rear sunporch, a pretty expanse of wicker and white lace that would do a restaurant proud. Ours started with a choice of juices, broiled grapefruit and a multi-grain roll. The main course was eggs Albemarle with feta cheese, zucchini and sliced ham. Another morning might feature Cathy's stuffed french toast with applesauce or apple-cheddar quiche with sour cream raisin muffins.

The songs of the birds outside inspired Bela Bartok to compose his Third Piano Concerto during a stay here in 1944.

(828) 255-0027 or (800) 621-7435. Fax (828) 236-3397. Ten rooms and one suite with private baths. Doubles, $115 to $210. Suite, $235. Two-night minimum weekends. Children over 14. No smoking.

Cedar Crest Victorian Inn, 674 Biltmore Ave., Asheville 28803.

Among the first of Asheville's B&Bs, this is also the closest to the Biltmore House. Hotelier Jack McEwan and his wife Barbara turned the showy Queen Anne landmark on a hillside above busy Biltmore Avenue into a Victorian fantasy in 1984.

The turreted exterior is imposing – almost formidable until it was softened by landscaping – in pale yellow with dark green trim. The interior is ornate and opulent, especially the extravagant main-floor woodwork. The entry foyer is paneled in carved dark oak contrasted by fluted pilasters with Ionic capitols and original stained-glass windows. The parlor is notable for a corner fireplace with three-dimensional carved woodwork, fluted columns buttressing a denticulated frieze and a beveled mirror canted forward. In contrast to this and the ornate dining room, the cozy, oak-trimmed study with TV comes almost as a relief.

The ten guest rooms on the second and third floors are wallpapered, furnished and dressed within an inch of their lives. Four have gas fireplaces. All have queen beds except for one canopied double in the small Garden Room. The McEwans did the decorating themselves, installing a lace canopied ceiling in the Romeo and Juliet Room and wallpapering the ceiling of the Tower Room. The Celebration Suite has a front sitting room with TV, a black jacuzzi tub encased in oak that matches the wainscoting of the bathroom, and a bedroom with a feather bed and a canopy of wisteria vines sporting little white lights.

On the far side of the four-acre property, across from formal gardens and a croquet court, is a guest house of more recent vintage. One section has two bedrooms, each with double bed, and a parlor/dining area. The other has one queen bedroom and a small sitting room. The two suites share a kitchen.

The McEwans, who live in a carriage house on the property, offer iced tea, lemonade, cookies and little snacks in the afternoon, and tea, coffee and hot chocolate at night. In the morning, a breakfast buffet includes juice, fresh fruit, homemade pastries and a hot entrée, perhaps egg casserole, french toast or belgian waffles.

(828) 252-1389 or (800) 252-0310. Fax (828) 253-7667. Nine rooms and three suites with private baths. Doubles, $130 to $170. Suites, $130 to $220. Children over 10. No smoking.

The Black Walnut Bed and Breakfast Inn, 288 Montford Ave., Asheville 28801.

His brother Rob showed him most of Asheville's B&Bs before Randy and Sandy Glasgow from Canada settled on this turreted, Shingle-style home designed in 1899 by Richard Sharp Smith, architect for the Biltmore House. The resemblance between this and Rob Glasgow's Beaufort House is marked. The Glasgows are identical twins, and Randy freely admits to trading on his brother's expertise, from poising the TV/VCR on a swivel above the bed in a guest room to serving pear dumplings for breakfast.

The Black Walnut contains seven guest quarters, each with TV/VCR. Just opened at our visit was the Ivy Garden Room, a showy main-floor space with a king bed awash in ruffled pillows and comforter, two window seats around the fireplace and a jacuzzi tub open to the room through a travertine marble arch. The fireplaced Walnut Room with king bed and clawfoot tub is the former master bedroom. The Azalea Room offers a whirlpool tub and queen sleigh bed, while the Holly Room has a mahogany rooster-tail queen bed and an enclosed steam shower. The smallest Dogwood, originally a room for linens, is some guests' favorite. Housed in a turret, it has a brass double bed, a clawfoot tub and a ceiling painted with clouds. Out back past the shrubs and trees that give the rooms their names is a carriage house suite that looks like an apartment with a high, mod black and yellow living room/kitchen/dining area and a raised queen bedroom.

In the main house, guests enjoy a sitting area in the upstairs foyer as well as the main-floor living room, casual and simple in the Arts and Crafts style. Afternoon tea with English trifle is served here.

Breakfast is taken by candlelight at a locally handmade table for ten in the dining room, with overflow in what was a small sewing room. Eggs benedict and belgian waffles are the specialties.

(828) 254-3878 or (800) 381-3878. Fax (828) 236-0393. Six rooms and one suite with private baths. Doubles, $125 to $175. Suite, $140. Children accepted. No smoking.

The Grove Park Inn Resort, 290 Macon Ave., Asheville 28804.

No report on Asheville lodging would be complete without at least a mention of this legendary resort hotel with five restaurants and a conference-center atmosphere.

Built of local granite boulders on the side of a mountain, it's a destination in itself. You surely should come at least for a drink on the Sunset Terrace or in the Great Hall Bar as the sun sets over the Great Smokies. The hotel was conceived by successful tonic salesman E.W. Grove and brought to reality in 1913 by his son-in-law Fred Seely, who constructed it in eleven months from blueprints in his head. The sprawling inn on nine floors has expanded to 498 rooms and twelve suites since then, but it remains a tribute to Arts and Crafts style. The famed Roycrofters of New York made many of its original custom-built furniture and hand-hammered copper lighting fixtures. Visitors gather around two massive stone fireplaces at either end of the great hall lobby or on the terrace, where dozens of rockers yield a panoramic view of distant mountains. Deluxe guest rooms on the club floor feature jacuzzis and a private lounge.

(828) 252-2711 or (800) 438-5800. Fax (828) 253-7053. Five hundred ten rooms with private baths. Doubles, $190 to $335, mid-April through December; $140 to $285, rest of year.

Inn on Biltmore Estate, Highway 25, Asheville.

A 224-room deluxe hotel on the grounds of the Biltmore estate is to be opened in the summer of 2000 by the Biltmore Company. The building, comprised of three wings five to seven stories high, is located on a hill above and within walking distance of the Biltmore Estate Winery.

The $31 million hotel will include a variety of guest rooms and suites affording mountain vistas from porches and balconies. The facility also will incorporate a 150-seat restaurant, a library, a lobby bar, an exterior swimming pool with cabana and bar, a health club and a children's activities area.

Planned amenities include activities reminiscent of guest activities during the George Vanderbilt years: walking and hiking trails, carriage rides and horseback riding, biking and croquet.

Design of the property echoes other estate structures, incorporating materials such as gray fieldstone and stucco and a slate roof. A turn-of-the-century resort atmosphere is planned.

"My great-grandfather enjoyed entertaining guests here a century ago," said William A.V. Cecil Jr., CEO of the Biltmore Company. "Now, we'll be able to offer many of the same amenities, including an inviting place to stay the night."

(800) 543-2961. Two-hundred twenty-four rooms and suites with private baths. Doubles, about $200. Opening summer of 2000.

New Inn on Biltmore Estate, as shown in artist's rendering.

Dining Spots

Gabrielle's, Richmond Hill Inn, 87 Richmond Hill Drive, Asheville.

The elegant restaurant in the famed Richmond Hill Inn lives up to the rest of the setting. One of the half-dozen four-diamond restaurants in North Carolina, Gabrielle's serves dinner nightly for inn guests and the public, who favor it for special occasions.

The setting is formal in the mansion's stately dining room and less so in the intimate, glass-enclosed sunporch.

The contemporary menu changes frequently. Expect main courses like lobster-crusted trout, salmon steak wrapped in prosciutto, roasted pheasant stuffed with andouille sausage and chipotle-glazed caribou loin with dried cherry-tarragon sauce. The signature dish is lump crab cake and seafood sausage sauced with lobster-fennel cream on a smoked tomato coulis.

Favorite starters include a wild mushroom and sweetbread strudel, roasted quail stuffed with a grilled fig chutney and served in a potato nest, and grilled shrimp on a rosemary skewer with Asian slaw and sesame-ginger vinaigrette.

Typical desserts are chocolate truffle torte with oven-roasted bananas and blood-orange caramel sauce, granny smith apple crème brûlée and tropical fruit cheesecake with pineapple sorbet.

(828) 252-7313 or (800) 545-9238. Entrées, $26 to $42. Dinner nightly by reservation, 6 to 10. No smoking.

The Market Place, 20 Wall St., Asheville.

Chef-owner Mark Rosenstein and his wife Kim have been producing "nationally recognized creative cuisine" since 1979. They also are known locally for the most consistent food in town.

Their urbane restaurant derives its name from its original location on North Market Street. The larger quarters here include a black and white dining room in front and, our choice, a multi-colored, curving rear dining room with a high ceiling. Cushioned rattan chairs at well-spaced tables, glass oil lamps and delicate pink-stemmed glasses convey a sophisticated look.

The menu follows suit. Mark is known for such dishes as oven-roasted salmon with red onion and apple crust, pan-seared duck breast with sundried blueberry sauce and roasted rack of lamb on a bed of zucchini, rosemary and goat cheese. Several of the main dishes can be ordered in light portions at about half the price.

One of us made a satisfying dinner of a pair of appetizers: grilled shrimp with a crispy herbed polenta and a duck and sundried tomato ravioli with a white wine and leek reduction. The other enjoyed a spinach salad with olives and feta cheese prior to digging into the grilled trout stuffed with spinach, lime, dill and capers. A Preston fumé blanc accompanied from a well-chosen wine list. Dessert was a refreshing port wine shortcake with cinnamon plums.

(828) 252-4162. Entrées, $14.95 to $27.95. Dinner, Monday-Saturday 6 to 9:30.

Possum Trot Grill, 8 Wall St., Asheville.

One of the most memorable meals we've had in a long time transpired at a weekday lunch in this somewhat funky haunt. Roland Schaerer, a classically trained Swiss chef who formerly cooked at the Grove Park Inn, returned in 1994 from a stint in New Orleans with a new lease on culinary life. From his open lunch-counter-style kitchen here come a variety of treats in the refined New Orleans – as opposed to assertive cajun – idiom.

Specials here are truly special. Two appetizers, a roasted sweet onion and goat cheese bouché and the signature black bean and crawfish cakes, made a dynamite lunch for one. The bouché, presented like the other dishes in the architectural style, came with two chives as ears and was one of the tastiest dishes we've ever had. A main-course special of penne with crawfish tails and andouille left the mouth on fire, and the smoky sauce was good to the last bit of penne.

Cheesecakes, the dessert specialty, are not to be missed. The mango cheesecake, with a chocolate doodle on top and swirls of mango coulis beneath, was so light and ethereal it spoiled us for any other version.

The short dinner menu ranges from shrimp creole to New York strip steak with shiitake sauce. The catch of the day is blackened or grilled. There's a short beer and wine list.

A washboard and musical instruments in the front window and the lineup of hot sauces at the entry set the stage for the treats beyond. The rear dining room is simple with pale yellow walls and colorful circular cutouts in the windows.

(828) 253-0062. Entrées, $11.95 to $15.95. Lunch, Tuesday-Saturday 11:30 to 2:30. Dinner, Tuesday-Saturday from 5:30. No smoking.

The Bistro, Biltmore Estate Winery, Asheville.

The three restaurants spread across the far-flung Biltmore Estate each have their devotees. The casual Stable Café is located in what was used as the stable, adjacent to the courtyard shopping area outside the mansion. Deerpark, the lovely, breezy courtyard restaurant with a California look and feeling, pleased us at our first visit with a couple of exotic salads. It now offers luncheon buffets for $13.95 and Sunday brunch for $15.95 from 11 to 3, April-December.

As of our last visit, we're partial to the Bistro. The newest restaurant, it's a joy to behold: a rustic yet elegant, high-ceilinged space with a variety of dining areas around a central open kitchen. Herbs in clay pots top tables covered with blue and white checked cloths, and you could easily imagine you were dining in the countryside of Tuscany.

The food contributes to the illusion. Wood-fired pizzas, homemade pastas and Biltmore-raised beef and trout are the stars. After a morning's tour of the Biltmore Estate, the Bistro makes a perfect stop for lunch – away from the crowds, who have yet to reach the winery. Sensational herbed focaccia bread was served with help-yourself bottles of extra-virgin olive oil and balsamic vinegar. The Blue Ridge pizza with wild mushrooms, garlic, spinach and goat cheese was a huge and gooey, knife-and-fork extravaganza. A cup of the day's roasted garlic and eggplant soup and a bruschetta with gorgonzola also went down well, as did a glass of the Biltmore riesling. Dessert could have been a vanilla bean crème brûlée, flourless chocolate torte with white chocolate mousse or the Bistro apple cake, but we couldn't manage any more.

(828) 274-6340. Lunch entrées, $8.25 to $14.95; dinner entrées, $11.25 to $19.95. Lunch daily, 11 to 5. Dinner, 5 to 9. Restaurants open to paying Biltmore Estate visitors and twelve-month passholders only.

Grovewood Café, 111 Grovewood Road, Asheville.

This stucco English cottage with a red roof is set among lofty evergreens on a slope beneath the Grove Park Inn Resort. Its two highly recommended dining rooms are pretty in cream and dark green, although we would prefer to eat on the outside flagstone terrace or the upper deck, which inexplicably were not open at our May visit. Actually, we were lucky to eat at all, waiting interminably in the entry foyer trying to attract the attention of a hostess, a waitress, a busboy – anyone at all. Only the word of three Grove Park guests waiting ahead of us prevented a premature departure. They said their lunch here the day before was so good they were returning for an encore.

Finally seated, we fared better than the couple who arrived behind us and were informed after a fifteen-minute wait that the kitchen was closed. The lunch menu ranged from pork schnitzel over spaëtzle to a hot crab sandwich with roasted potatoes and grilled vegetables. A harassed waitress took pity and scouted up a bowl of corn and crab soup, a cobb salad and a pecan chicken salad. Each was adequate, and held out promise for better meals ahead.

The short dinner menu offers nine main courses, four of them vegetarian. Others range from poached salmon with potato-leek cake to grilled filet of beef with wine sauce. Two spa cuisine entrées are offered at lunch. The dessert tray held pies, tortes and a delectable blackberry crumble.

(828) 258-8956. Entrées, $14.50 to $19.95. Lunch daily, 11 to 2, Sunday to 4. Dinner nightly, 5 to 9.

Flying Frog Café, 76 Haywood St., Asheville.

The chef is in the kitchen and his father out front in this unlikely looking hole in the wall at the edge of downtown. This was once the home of the Windmill European Grill, which provided our best meal during an Asheville stay a decade ago.

Praised by natives, the Flying Frog makes up in gutsy food for what it lacks in ambiance. From an open kitchen, Vijay Shastri offers an extensive repertoire of French, Cajun and Indian fare. Expect worldly renditions of bouillabaisse and chicken française, jambalaya and cajun filet, coconut curried shrimp and lamb korma. The Flying Frog is many people's favorite for a reasonably priced dinner now that the Windmill has gone suburban (see below).

(828) 254-9411. Entrées, $14 to $20. Dinner, Wednesday-Monday from 5:30.

The Windmill European Grill/Il Pescatore, 85 Tunnel Road, Asheville.

Flying Frog partisans feel that chef Cathie Shastri and her husband Jay, who is from India, lost something in moving to the grotto-like lower level of the Innsbrook

Mall. But they continue to pack in regulars for a creative mix of East Indian, German, Italian and European food.

The fettuccine Tuscany with calamari, baby shrimp, clams and scallops along with artichoke hearts and mushrooms proved an early winner, as was a perfectly spiced Indian dish of beef and lamb korma in an onion tomato curry, with all the proper accompaniments like raita and naan. It's rare to find escargots bourguignonne, wiener schnitzel with sour cream and dark cherries, samosas, Russian pashka and crème brûlée all on the same prodigious menu, but that's the Shastri family's stock in trade. As if that weren't enough, the night we were there they added thirteen specials.

Host Jay proudly advised that a customer had called his wife "the Picasso of culinary art."

(828) 253-5285. Entrées, $11.99 to $18.99. Dinner nightly, 5:30 to 9:30 or 10.

Other Choices. Asheville has more than its share of interesting restaurants. A few others often recommended include **23 Page at Haywood Park,** a fine dining establishment with a new upstairs French bar and patisserie. It is said to have slipped following a move to the Haywood Park Hotel and a change in ownership since we first reveled in its new American cuisine at 23 Page Ave. **The Savoy** at 641 Merriman Ave. is a noisy neighborhood Italian haunt favored by Montford folks for heaping pastas and seafood. **Café on the Square** at 1 Biltmore Ave., known for contemporary fare and great people-watching, helped spark the rebirth of Pack Square. **Salsa,** a casual Mexican-Caribbean eatery, is decked out in tropical colors and sidewalk tables at 6 Payton Ave. The famed **Laughing Seed** features a huge vegetarian menu and juice bar in a sleek, high-ceilinged space at 40 Wall St.

Diversions

Because the Biltmore Estate is so central to the Asheville experience, we concentrate upon it here. That is not to demean the city's other attractions.

Biltmore Estate, Highway 25, Asheville.

The three-mile-long approach to the nation's largest private residence is tiered in stair-step fashion to heighten the sense of drama, the feeling that something grand lies ahead. The road rises as it winds through forested ravines abloom seasonally with azaleas and rhododendron, passing woods and farmlands beneath a curtain of mountains all around. Beyond the final turn, iron gates and pillars topped by stone sphinxes open onto a massive front lawn leading to the Biltmore House.

No ordinary house, this. George Washington Vanderbilt, grandson of the Commodore, wanted a private mansion in what he considered one of the most beautiful places in the world. Young Vanderbilt commissioned a friend, celebrity New York architect Richard Morris Hunt, to build the 250-room chateau in the style of those in France's Loire Valley. Landscape architect Frederick Law Olmsted surrounded the house with more than 8,000 acres of forests, parks and gardens. Six years and millions of dollars later, the house opened in 1895 as what the New York Times reported at the time was "the most valuable as well as most extensive private property in America."

It makes the Breakers at Newport and San Simeon in California, both more showy and opulent, pale in size. Biltmore House, one suspects, could be America's Versailles. The youngest of Vanderbilts, at age 33, outdid them all.

Biltmore Company Photo by J. Valentine

George W. Vanderbilt's 250-room Biltmore Estate is largest private home in America.

Legion were the famous guests entertained by George and his wife, Edith Stuyvesant Dresser, until his death of complications from an appendectomy in 1914 at age 52. Their only child, Cornelia, lived here with her husband, John Francis Amherst Cecil, until 1930 when they opened the Biltmore House and Gardens to the public at the request of city officials, who hoped it would spur tourism in the area during the Depression..

The house is no longer lived in, and visitor fees and sales of Biltmore memorabilia and products pay the hefty operating costs (more than $40 million of estate earnings in the last fifteen years have been reinvested for the preservation of Vanderbilt's original concept of a self-supporting European estate). The Cecils' son, William Amherst Vanderbilt Cecil, who was born in his grandfather's Biltmore House, surprised his New York banking colleagues in the early 1960s when he came home to oversee the Biltmore property and, against all bets, turned his first profit of $16 in 1968. He and his wife live in a smaller house that his mother built when she tired of the Biltmore. He heads the family's Biltmore Company, whose principals now are his two grown children.

The key to the Biltmore's success is at least partly due to marketing, which is obvious from its slick web site to all the Biltmore products and memorabilia for sale in its various shops.

Despite its size, the Biltmore House surprises by its lack of ostentation, except perhaps for its pedigreed furnishings and art objects. Not to mention the awesome 70-foot-high banquet hall with a table seating 64, the winter garden conservatory and the 90-foot-long Tapestry Gallery. Or the towering library with 10,000 volumes in eight languages that took curators four years to catalog. Or the billiards room that is bigger and taller than a small house.

Many of the 85 rooms open to the public are more modest, given the circumstances, although the fact that most of the 34 bedrooms had private baths was unheard of at the time. (If the beds look small, we're told, it's because the rooms are so large. Even the servants' quarters are the size of some of the smaller bedrooms at today's B&Bs.) The downstairs kitchens and pantries overwhelm only in the aggregate; each is given over to a specialized function. The bowling alley, gymnasium and indoor swimming pool are less remarkable than the fact of their seventeen dressing rooms.

Biltmore is unusual in that tours are self-guided, allowing visitors to browse at their own pace. Audio tape cassettes are available ($4 and worth it) to point out the nuances and detail the treasures the Vanderbilts collected across the world to fill their house.

Tours end in the stable/courtyard area, where an array of shops, an ice cream parlor, a new bake shop and the Stable Café beckon.

After touring the house, visit the 75 acres of Biltmore gardens, some considered the finest of their type in the land. The Azalea Garden, for instance, contains one of the nation's most complete collections of native azaleas. Altogether, they comprise Olmsted's biggest, most important and last work.

Also worth a visit is the **Biltmore Estate Winery.** It's based in renovated structures at the site of the original Biltmore Dairy, part of the most successful self-supporting historical property in America. Though one of the youngest wineries, the Biltmore is America's most visited. It produces 75,000 cases of wine annually under three labels. The state-of-the-art facility is open for self-guided tours, followed by tastings in an excellent wine and gourmet shop.

(828) 274-6333 or (800) 543-2961. Open daily except Thanksgiving and Christmas, 9 to 5. Adults, $29.95.

Thomas Wolfe Memorial State Historic Site, 52 North Market St.

His mother's boarding house, in which the novelist grew up, is one of American literature's most famous landmarks. In his epic autobiographical novel *Look Homeward, Angel*, Wolfe immortalized the 1883 Victorian structure originally called "Old Kentucky Home." Now eerily surrounded by encroaching office buildings at the edge of downtown, the interior is homey and full of memorabilia of the man and his times. The roof and exterior was somewhat shabby looking even before a damaging fire in 1998. An audio-visual program is shown on the hour in the modern visitor center off North Market Street. A half-hour tour of the house at 48 Spruce St. traditionally follows. The house was closed for an indefinite period following the fire.

(828) 253-8304. Open April-October, Monday-Saturday 9 to 5, Sunday 1 to 5. Rest of year, Tuesday-Saturday 10 to 4, Sunday 1 to 4. Adults $1.

The Asheville Urban Trail, downtown Asheville.

Asheville was a sleepy little town in 1880, when the railroad breached the Blue Ridge Mountains and brought people of wealth and influence. It entered a boom period that lasted 50 years. The 27 stops on the Urban Trail show the results of that boom and its effect on the city today. An informative map guides the way, although you may find the small-type text difficult to read while walking the 1.6-mile route. Squares, sculptures and fountains are interspersed among such historic sites and architectural sights as the deco S&W Cafeteria building, the original Woolworth's (now a Family Dollar store), the Grove Arcade and the Battery Park Hotel in which George Vanderbilt stayed with his mother before building his Biltmore estate. Most striking is the red brick Moorish Basilica of St. Lawrence, with its large elliptical dome, statues and minarets looking straight out of Europe. Most unexpected is the I.M. Pei-designed executive offices of the Biltmore enterprises at One North Pack Square.

North Carolina Arboretum, off Blue Ridge Parkway at Hwy. 191, (828) 665-2492. The evolving new arboretum, run by the University of North Carolina, is envisioned as one of the state's premiere attractions. It is located southwest of town off the Blue Ridge Parkway at the edge of the Pisgah National Forest in what promoters describe as the most beautiful natural setting of any public garden in America. The 424-acre arboretum formally opened in 1996, but the visitor center was locked up tight the May afternoon we tried to visit. We did not get to see the state-of-the-art greenhouse or find any sign of the vaunted spring, stream and quilt gardens, the loop trail or any of the advertised 3,000 types of plants in landscaped settings. Instead we headed across town to an older facility, the **Botanical Gardens of Asheville,** on a ten-acre wooded site next to the campus of the University of North Carolina at Asheville. It's very low-key and not as showy as we expected, but at least it was open – free, from dawn to dusk.

Shopping. Reborn downtown Asheville has interesting shops and galleries, especially along Wall Street, Battery Park and Biltmore Avenue. The relocated and expanded **Malaprops Bookstore/Café** is a symbol of the rebirth. The real action for most visitors, however, is south of town at historic **Biltmore Village,** built in the late 1890s as a planned community opposite the entrance to the Biltmore Estate. Twelve square blocks of restored Tudor-style homes and buildings have been converted into shops, galleries and restaurants.

Extra Special

Crafts Galleries. The Southern Highlands is at the center of a long tradition of exceptional mountain handcrafts. The famed Penland School and John C. Campbell Folk School, the nation's oldest, have attracted artists since the 1920s. The emphasis has shifted from the preservation of traditional forms to creative expression in a variety of media.

The largest showcase is the Southern Highland Craft Guild's famed **Folk Art Center,** a must destination along the Blue Ridge Parkway at Milepost 382 just east of town. The main floor is devoted to the retail Allanstand Craft Shop, an offshoot of the nation's first craft shop, which began a century ago in a rural community near Asheville. The upper level contains museum space, traveling exhibits, guild offices and a library. The guild also operates the **Guild Crafts** shop at 930 Tunnel Road.

Also rewarding is the **New Morning Gallery,** a treasury of fine arts and crafts at 7 Boston Way in Biltmore Village. Owner John Cram, a leader in the area's crafts movement, also runs the nearby **Bellagio** featuring "art to wear" in handcrafted jewelry and clothing, and two downtown galleries, **Blue Spiral 1** at 38 Biltmore Ave. and **American Folk Art & Antiques** at 64 Biltmore Ave.

Best of all perhaps is the **Grovewood Gallery** complex at the Homespun Shops, 111 Grovewood Road, near the Grove Park Inn Resort. Above the main gallery is a floor devoted to contemporary furniture made of exotic and native wood and iron, where one could pick up a couple of maple and leather gargoyle chairs for $1,600 each. Wonderful sculptures are on the lawns leading to the **North Carolina Homespun Museum,** a repository of the handwoven homespun cloth tradition founded by George and Edith Vanderbilt of Biltmore Industries. Inside the Grove Park inn, the **Gallery of the Mountains** displays fine crafts.

Cashiers/Highlands, NC
The High Life

The roads into the Cashiers/Highlands area of southwestern North Carolina generally lead up. Up from North Carolina's Piedmont. Up from South Carolina's Upcountry. Up from the northern Georgia mountains. Even up from Tennessee's Smokies.

Here, at the southern crest of the Blue Ridge Mountains, the rivers part from the Eastern Continental Divide. Far off the beaten path, this is wilderness mountain country. It's also waterfall country. The locals liken their area to a rain forest. Upwards of 90 inches of rain a year nourish banks of wild rhododendron and mountain laurel.

Here is where folks from points south converge to escape summer's heat. At an average elevation of 4,000 feet, temperatures are ten to twenty degrees cooler than in the lowlands. Air conditioning is unnecessary, and windows open to catch the breezes.

Folks converge on Cashiers and Highlands, two appealing yet quite different communities.

Cashiers is pronounced CASH-ers – accent on the first syllable. The unincorporated community in a verdant valley is known for resorts and second homes. It has only one traffic light and claims the smallest post office in the United States. There's a new village "green" at the crossroads and a pedestrian trail in the making to link the increasing numbers of fashionable shops and restaurants scattered in wooded clusters for half a mile in all directions. Most didn't even exist a decade ago. The majority on the planning board is ardently anti-planning, for better or worse. Most of the 600 people who make Cashiers their year-round home like it as it is: laid-back, friendly and low-key.

From Cashiers, the road twists steadily up – in attitude as well as altitude to Highlands, ten miles to the west. Perched on a mountaintop plateau at 4,118 feet, this is one of the highest towns east of the Rockies. Highlands is incorporated and well planned, for better or worse. It's a summer resort created by Midwestern land developers, who bought 839 wilderness acres in 1875 and sold lots to investors. "No better climate in the world for health, comfort and enjoyment," they advertised. Today there are about 2,000 year-round residents. Ten times that many visitors crowd the town on summer weekends. Cultural amenities, shopping and restaurants are the draw.

There are no go-cart tracks or amusement parks in these verdant highlands where people enjoy the good life. The roadside attractions are of the natural variety: spectacular mountain vistas, countless waterfalls, scenic overlooks and hiking trails.

The only tour of note is not of historic attractions, and is certainly not taken by bus or trolley. It's a walking guide to trees in the Town of Highlands.

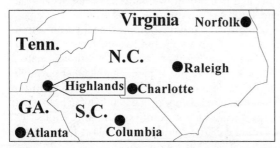

Mountain panorama is on view from lounge chairs on grounds of Millstone Inn.

Inn Spots

Millstone Inn, Highway 64 West, Box 949, Cashiers 28717.

This mountain lodge began life in 1933 as the home and office of the town physician. Now it offers rest and respite for the traveler.

Paul and Patricia Collins, British transplants by way of Atlanta, had stopped one bleak January day for lunch at the Market Basket and quickly fell for the charms of Cashiers. Looking to buy a country inn or B&B, they put in a bid for the Millstone, which had been extensively renovated in 1987. The Collinses added their personal hospitality to a going operation for a successful combination indeed.

The Millstone is best described as a rustically elegant mountain lodge. It's named for the ten millstones from a former mill on the property, located atop a secluded knoll a half mile off Highway 64. Said knoll commands a wraparound view of famed Whiteside Mountain and the hills and dales of the Nantahala National Forest. The only sounds are the chirping of countless varieties of birds and the roar of Silver Slip Falls below.

The main lodge holds five bedrooms and two suites, all bearing their original pine paneling and beamed ceilings. Queensize beds, televisions, hair dryers and refrigerators provide modern comforts. Most prized are two suites, one on the second floor with its bedroom facing the mountain view and the other below, with a double-barreled view from its living room and from its side patio.

Four more guest quarters are in the Garden Annex. We thought the best accommodation of all was its commodious ground-floor suite. There was plenty of space in which to spread out: a living room with TV and sofabed, a kingsize bedroom, a kitchen with dining area and a back porch with a view. It was easy to understand why some repeat guests book for a week or longer.

A brisk walk the next morning brought us down through the woods to the foot of Silver Slip Falls, actually two side-by-side waterfalls with two hundred-foot cascades each – quite a sight with a contemporary house perched in the middle.

The half-hour round trip heightened the appetite for breakfast in the main lodge's expansive dining porch with wraparound windows. Countless birds were feeding at the feeders as we stoked up on a choice of juices, homemade muffins and croissants, and a Southwestern egg and mushroom casserole. Between courses, Pat identified the various species, some quite rare. For further information, we had only to settle in front of the huge window in the lodge's comfortable living room with field guide and binoculars at hand. A fire in the stone hearth took the chill off the early morning air. Lounge chairs were scattered around the back lawns for taking in the sounds and sights of birds, waterfall and mountains all around. It was all we could do to tear ourselves away.

(828) 743-2737 or (888) 645-5786. Fax (828) 743-0208. Seven rooms and four suites with private baths. Doubles, $149 to $161 weekends, $114 to $126 midweek. Suites, $169 to $179 weekends, $134 to $144 midweek. Children over 12. No smoking.

Innisfree Victorian Inn, 7 Lakeside Knoll, Cashiers (Box 469, Glenville 28736).

The lakeside hamlet of Glenville, six miles north of Cashiers, is home to this anomaly – a new, built-to-look-old Victorian B&B designed flamboyantly by owner Henry Hoche for the self-indulgence and luxury of guests. Towered, turreted and trimmed within an inch of its life, it offers posh suites with fireplaces, jacuzzi tubs, gourmet treats and other creature comforts for the AAA four-diamond rating it wears proudly.

The gas fireplace was lit, music was playing and an oversize teddy bear was on the queensize French sleigh bed upon our arrival in Lord Tennyson's Suite, the association to whom was not readily obvious. Also on display were a gilt-framed mirror above the bed, a dining table for breakfast in the suite's tower, a complicated-to-operate satellite TV in the armoire, a wet bar with coffee and soft drinks, and an enormous, showy garden tub for two in a corner window in the bathroom. Glistening in green marble, the bathroom also came with a walk-in glass shower, a w.c. in its own little room, a sitting area with the best reading lamp in the suite, an oriental rug on the floor and a view of the bedroom through the see-through fireplace. Secluded on the top level of the house, the suite included a nifty rear porch made for sunset-viewing. There were enough power switches and dimmers to light up Rockefeller Center. The lights were dimmed, the bed turned down and Godiva chocolates at bedside upon our return from dinner.

Other accommodations, though similar, are not quite so grand. Except perhaps for Victoria's Grand Suite, billed as "one of the most luxuriously romantic suites anywhere." It measures up with a lace-canopy, hand-carved mahogany poster bed, a bay window, and a bathroom with jacuzzi, two marble vanities, oversize Italian tiled shower and a separate chamber for bidet and w.c. The suite is the largest of five accommodations in the main house. Four suites join Lord Tennyson's in the Garden House, down a steep hill, where breakfast is delivered to one's room. The suites come with wet bar, TV and telephone. All but one have garden tubs for two.

Breakfast in the main building is by candlelight in the tower dining room, a Victorian extravaganza in burgundy and florals. A round table for ten gleams in gold plating, from the gold-rimmed plates set three deep to the gold utensils (otherwise called silverware) to the water goblets. The sideboard at our visit was

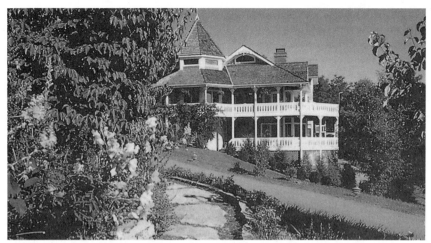

Tower and wraparound porches are features at Innisfree Victorian Inn.

laden with cut-up fresh fruit, granola, cereal, and banana and pumpkin breads. The main course was oven-baked french toast with blackberries picked on the property, served with a slab of ham in a caramel sauce. The entrée varies according to which staffer is cooking that day. The repertoire includes vegetarian quiche, Southwestern casserole and "cheddar nest," eggs and cheese cooked in french toast.

Expect to be well fed throughout your stay here. Afternoon wine is offered in the cathedral-ceilinged living room of the main house or on the veranda. Accompaniments include fancy crackers and cheeses, olives, marinated mushrooms and the like. A decanter of sherry is in each bedroom. Irish coffee is offered beside the main inn's fireplace nightly at 9.

The only television in the main house is in the upstairs "observatory," a pleasant sitting room with games, videos and books. The observatory has big windows onto the mountains and the best view – actually a glimpse – of the highest lake east of the Rockies in the distance. On the main floor, a wraparound veranda overlooks terraced gardens, the inn's Garden House and some of the area's more substantial homes.

(828) 743-2946. Three rooms and seven suites with private baths. June-October and all weekends: doubles $150, suites $175 to $290. Midweek, November-May: doubles $119, suites $159 to $249. Two-night minimum weekends, three-night minimum holiday weekends. No children. No smoking.

Toad Hall, 61 Sequoyah Point Way, Highlands 28741.

Enter through a driveway canopied in rhododendrons into this delightful lakeside compound built in 1949 by the Wrigley family of chewing gum fame. The main house, guest house and cottage on a peninsula surrounded by Lake Sequoyah were greatly transformed in 1998 by Rebecca and Jeff Krida from New Orleans. Here, in the manner of Mr. Toad in Kenneth Grahame's *The Wind in the Willows,* the Kridas entertain guests in a waterfront estate "with lavish abandon."

The Kridas redid the main house as their home and share common areas with guests. A log-walled great room is the gathering area, with a loveseat facing windows onto an outdoor terrace to view the lake head-on. This is the setting for a sumptuous breakfast as well as afternoon tea and scones or wine and cheese.

Guests adjourn to private quarters in the adjacent Badger House and the Cottage. Straddling a hillside, the former Wrigley guest house has been reborn with a screened porch, sunporch with fireplace, guest kitchen and a common room with fireplace, piano and again a loveseat positioned for viewing the lake head-on. Two guest rooms are on the main floor and two on the walk-out floor beneath. Rebecca decorated each in upscale mountain lodge style. Each comes with a king or queensize bed, TV/VCR and an idyllic private deck or balcony overlooking the lake. Three have double jacuzzi tubs bordered in patterned tiles and separate showers. The other has a single jacuzzi with a built-in shower.

The Cottage, which is popular with honeymooners, lacks a lake view but compensates with a fireplaced living/dining area, a corner jacuzzi in the bathroom, an efficiency kitchen and a front deck. The spectacular queensize "forest bed," made on the site, surprises with its canopy of branches and copper-colored leaves.

All guests have plenty of room to spread out in the Great Room of the main house, the common rooms and porches of the Badger House or on the broad patio behind the main house. Canoeing and fishing may be enjoyed from the peninsula's 1,000 feet of private shoreline. Hammocks, a deer sculptured from vines and critters from ducks to chipmunks vie for attention.

Breakfast the day of our visit started with juice and a mix of cantaloupe and honeydew melons with kiwi. The main course was french toast stuffed with bananas and pecans with a side of sausage. Other favorite dishes are omelets and blueberry pancakes.

"This has been a dream of ours for twenty years," says vivacious Rebecca. Her husband, former head of the Delta Queen steamboat lines, was involved in his new River Barge excursion lines in New Orleans and able to join her only on weekends. Son Ryan moved in as manager in the meantime.

(828) 526-3889 or (888) 891-3889. Fax (828) 526-9343. Four rooms and one cottage with private baths. Doubles, $127 to $139 weekends, $105 to $117 midweek. Cottage, $157 weekends, $135 midweek. Two-night minimum weekends and in July and October. No young children. No smoking.

Morning Star Inn, 480 Flat Mountain Estates Road, Highlands 28741.

A woodsy location on two acres near the ranger station atop Flat Mountain, comfortable accommodations and gourmet breakfasts are hallmarks of this B&B. Patricia Allen and her surgeon-husband, Patrick, opened it in 1994 as a retirement project.

Food is a principal interest of both Pats. At our visit, the Allens were in the Napa Valley, where she was attending a cooking school. She had just self-published a chatty cookbook, "Whisk Upon a Star." (We bought a copy and immediately tried the tortilla soup, which was delicious.) Patricia also gives cooking classes in spring and fall in the expansive rear sunporch, where participants get to dine on what they prepare while enjoying an awesome view toward Whiteside Mountain. The porch is big enough for several dining tables and a sitting area. You might never leave, except to try the broad front porch or the lower side yard dotted with bird feeders, hammocks, a glider and a goldfish pond with fountain.

Morning Star granola and Dr. Pat's grits are staples at breakfast. The main course could be caramel french toast, southwestern eggs with chile peppers or baked spinach egg "nests," a house specialty topped with hollandaise sauce. Caribbean pears, banana muffins and mini-biscuits might accompany.

Soaring stone fireplace and antique billiards table are features of great hall at River Lodge.

Collections are another of Patricia's interests. Stuffed animals and dolls crowd a high-back bench in a hallway. A lineup of stuffed bears overflows a bench in the dining area.

Guest rooms furnished in traditional style are scattered about this sprawling house on three levels. On the main floor are the Starburst Room, the master bedroom with a king poster bed and flowery pink and green decor. The Star-Gaze with queensize sleigh bed follows a sports motif. The Evening Star has a four-poster queensize bed so high a two-step stool is provided. The upstairs Starry Eyes honeymoon room comes with a kingsize wrought-iron bed, chaise lounge, TV and a huge bath with a double jacuzzi and separate shower. On the lower level is a kingsize bedroom with TV and private entrance.

A huge stone fireplace in the parlor is the focal point of the weekend hospitality hour. Wine and hors d'oeuvres are served to the accompaniment of classical music.

(828) 526-1009. Five rooms with private baths. Doubles, $135 to $175. Children over 12. No smoking.

The River Lodge, 619 Roy Tritt Road, Cullowhee 28723.

Cathy and Anthony Sgambato from The Bronx looked far and wide for a B&B like the Adirondack great camps they were familiar with in upstate New York. They found it in an unlikely spot – a hillside on a river bend some twenty miles north of Cashiers. The house had been built in 1974 of century-old hand-hewn logs by a Floridian who tried to run a construction business here and failed. The Sgambatos "found it by fluke" – it had been for sale for five years, and was never marketed as anything other than a house. What no one else wanted suited them to a T.

The great hall focuses on a twelve-foot-wide stone fireplace, soaring 30 feet high in the "dry stack" style (no mortar showing between stones). Plush leather sofas face the fireplace, and an antique Brunswick billiards table awaits nearby. Tall windows let in plenty of light.

A rustic stairway built of wormy chestnut leads to five snug guest rooms on the second floor. Three open onto a balcony that runs the width of the house and looks toward the river across meadows where belted galloway and other cattle graze. The biggest, the Victoriana, has a queensize bed made from a willow tree. The bathroom with clawfoot tub and separate shower is notable for its quarry stone floor and wainscoted ceiling. The other rooms feature mountain-made log beds (three of them queensize and one with twins). Decor lives up to their names (Trout and Creel, Mallards in Flight). Unusual window treatments, American Indian accents, distinctive furniture and excellent artworks abound.

Some of the art is by Tony, an accomplished painter who has a studio off the dining room. He moved here to paint, although so far has not found the time. At our visit he was about to start renovations for a sixth guest room on the main floor.

Outside are a front porch and a rear terrace within earshot of a trickling waterfall. Adirondack chairs beckon beside a little pond. The rural setting is quite idyllic.

Both innkeepers are involved in the preparation of a four-course breakfast. Yours might be the Italian country breakfast with a vegetable-cheese frittata, Italian sweet sausage, pan-fried sliced tomatoes and a side of focaccia, with a béarnaise sauce for dipping. Afternoon treats include cookies or biscotti, cheese and fruit, wine and beer.

(828) 293-5431 or (877) 384-4400. Five rooms with private baths. Doubles, $105 to $135 June-August and October; $95 to $125, rest of year. Two-night minimum peak weekends. Children over 13. No smoking.

4½ Street Inn, 55 4½ St., Highlands 28741.

This structure has been an inn and boarding house since the 1920s, and the original Fairview Inn sign is posted along the stairway. Abandoned for ten years, it underwent a major renovation in 1990 that preserved the integrity of the original house. "There are wonderful memories in this house," say new owners Helene and Rick Siegel from Atlanta, hands-on innkeepers known for warmth and an unpretentious, easygoing style.

They added decorative touches to ten guest rooms on three floors. Rooms come in a variety of sizes and bed configurations. Three are kingsize, five are queensize, one has two double beds and another a double and a twin. All have TVs, and three have working fireplaces.

Decor is simple and light in this long, narrow house on one acre between Fourth and Fifth streets, thus called 4½ Street. One room has a kingsize twig mountain bed, and another a king bed draped in fabric canopy. A third-floor room with an exposed stone chimney in the bathroom is a favorite. Front rooms on the second floor are close to a tiny balcony outfitted with a couple of chairs.

The fireplace is often lit in the cozy main-floor parlor, which is furnished in the mountain lodge style. In good weather, the place to be is the expansive side deck, overlooking restored gardens and banks of rhododendron. Beyond is an outdoor spa.

A hearty breakfast is served in a rear dining area with six tables and something of a summer camp look. The day of our visit produced fresh fruit, homemade granola, spinach frittata with salsa, cheese grits soufflé and apple-coconut muffins. Stuffed french toast strata was on tap the next day.

Helene puts out addictive cookies in the afternoon, and offers wine and hors

House with pillared portico is home of Colonial Pines Inn, area's oldest B&B.

d'oeuvres on the side deck in the afternoon. "People have fun here," she says, summing up the comments in the guest-room journals.

(828) 526-4464. Ten rooms with private baths. Doubles, $110 to $125, weekends and October; $95 to $110 midweek. Children over 12. No smoking.

Colonial Pines Inn, 541 Hickory St., Highlands 28741.

Quite a variety of accommodations is offered by Donna and Chris Alley in this, the area's first B&B. The Alleys opened in 1983, adding breakfast to what had been a tourist home and expanding and upgrading ever since.

Among the original bedrooms are three upstairs, each paneled in pine and appearing quite lodge-like. One has a king bed and another a double and a twin bed. The two smallest rooms were converted into a suite with a sofabed in the sitting room, a queen bed, and his and her bathrooms. The master bedroom on the main floor has a queen bed with a fabric canopy and an enormous walk-in closet. The newest suite is in a rear addition. Bigger and more contemporary, it has a kingsize wicker bed with a floral duvet comforter beneath a vaulted ceiling, a sitting room with sofabed and TV and a dollhouse on the loft overhead, a minifridge and a microwave, a skylit bath and a private deck with a view onto Satulah Mountain.

Two more accommodations are in an adjacent guest house. Upstairs is a two-bedroom apartment with efficiency kitchen, sleeping three. Downstairs is a guest room with kingsize brass bed. The Alleys also rent an elegant, fully equipped three-bedroom apartment, Miss Rebecca's Cottage, in downtown Highlands.

Breakfast for those not in the apartments is a hearty affair, served at three tables covered with plaid runners and bouquets of Scottish thistle in the dining room (Chris is Scottish, and occasionally dons a kilt). The fare the day of our visit was baked pears, a corn-egg-cheese flan with bacon, and cranberry-nut and whole grain breads. Various breakfast casseroles are featured other mornings.

The Alleys offer a menu book in which guests paste on stars for items they recommend. That and the reviews they write in a restaurant diary make for interesting reading in the pine-paneled living room or on the wraparound porch outside. *(828) 526-2060. Four rooms, two suites and two cottages with private baths. Doubles, $85 to $120. Suites, $110 and $140. Cottages, $105 to $250. Two-night minimum peak weekends. No smoking.*

The 1891 Stewart House, 425 Hickory St., Highlands 28741.

Antiques and collectibles lend an authentic, historic air to this B&B that's literally surrounded by a "forest" of rhododendron. Barbara Werder and her husband, who had a vacation home in Cashiers for years, moved here from Clearwater, Fla. They undertook an extensive restoration before opening in 1995 as "a semi-retirement project."

Barbara has furnished four guest rooms in keeping with the style of a Victorian farmhouse. All are painted in historic colors and have featherbeds and duvet comforters that she changes with the seasons. The Blue Room on the main floor, done in royal blue and white, has a queensize brass bed, fireplace and a chaise lounge. Upstairs, the front Fay Room with king bed is pretty in a pinkish mauve. The pale green Middle Room can sleep up to four in a queen brass bed and an antique double bed. The Loft Room is all sloping walls with a queen bed, a twin bed and hooked rugs on the original floors.

Among collections of note is a display of Franklin Mint plates. Barbara collects china, which accounts for the fact she can use a different set every morning for a month without repeating a pattern. A full breakfast is served at two tables for four in the dining room. Eggs benedict, fruit-stuffed french toast or soufflé egg casserole might be the main dish.

Barbara, whose avocation is cooking, prepares elaborate hors d'oeuvres to serve with afternoon wine. She also offers a homemade dessert in the evening. Guests enjoy a delightful sunporch, a guest living room with original fireplace and TV, and a wide front porch overlooking massed rhododendron that bloom in stages from May into August. *(828) 526-8067. Four rooms with private baths. Doubles, $110 to $120. Children over 12. No smoking.*

The Greystone Inn, Greystone Lane, Lake Toxaway 28747.

Miles off the beaten path in the heart of an exclusive resort community lies this lakefront inn ringed by several thousand acres of wilderness that residents call "Little Switzerland." The legendary Toxaway Inn hosted the likes of Henry Ford, Thomas Edison and John D. Rockefeller before its demise in 1916. Here was where Savannah heiress Lucy Armstrong Moltz built a six-level Swiss Revival mansion, the heart of what is now the Greystone Inn.

Owners Tim and Boo Boo Lovelace oversee a posh resort compound on a shady peninsula overlooking the lake. A front sunporch and a side slate terrace take full advantage of the water views. Leather sofas and a grand piano in the oak-paneled parlor focus on a flagstone fireplace, and a wonderful library-bar area opens through french doors onto the terrace.

The mansion holds nineteen guest rooms that ramble off various levels. Each is furnished with antiques and reproductions in a style befitting the mansion's historic status on the National Register. All have jacuzzi baths. Four have balconies overlooking the lake, and some have fireplaces.

Boats docked at Greystone Inn take guests onto Lake Toxaway.

Twelve more luxurious rooms are in the Hilmont Building, erected in 1988 at lakeside. Each has a private balcony, gas fireplace, jacuzzi tub, sitting area and wet bar.

Two lakeside suites with vaulted ceilings were added in 1995. Each has a kingsize bedroom, sitting room with sleeper sofa, screened porch, fireplace, wet bar and an oversize jacuzzi. The book-lined Presidential Suite, fashioned from the former library, features mullioned windows, a granite fireplace, 25-foot vaulted ceilings, a kingsize bed and a private deck overlooking the lake.

Tea and cakes are served each afternoon on the sunporch. The flower-bedecked terrace is favored for cocktails and hors d'oeuvres, prior to a six-course dinner by candlelight in the waterside dining room (jackets required).

Several choices are offered for each course on the dinner menu, which changes nightly. A typical meal might be salmon and shrimp terrine, three-bean soup, salade niçoise, an intermezzo sorbet, grilled backfin tuna and bananas foster prepared tableside. A hearty breakfast is offered in the morning.

Sailboats, canoes and paddle boats are moored at the dock for lake explorations. The day's highlight is the innkeeper's traditional sunset champagne cruise on the Greystone's pontoon boat outfitted with lawn chairs. Tim points out sights and details the history of the enclave. On Monday evenings, the Lovelaces host guests at a wine and cheese party on the boathouse deck at their lake house.

Other amenities are a spa, swimming pool, hiking trails, tennis courts and golf privileges at the nearby Lake Toxaway Country Club. Among the activities are group hikes and tours of homes under construction in the Lake Toxaway Community for those guests so smitten by the setting they might like to buy.

(828) 966-4700 or (800) 824-5766. Fax (828) 862-5689. Thirty rooms and three suites with private baths. Rates MAP: May-October: doubles, $300 to $540 weekends, $235 to $400 midweek. Rest of year: $265 to $350. Fifteen percent service charge. Two-night minimum weekends.

High Hampton Inn & Country Club, State Route 107, Box 338, Cashiers 28717.

"This is what High Hampton is all about," said general manager Mark Jones as he led a tour of this inn and resort beloved by generations of Southerners. We had paused on the balcony at the far end of the main building, overlooking a private lake and the aptly named Rock Mountain. The vista was breathtaking.

Until you experience the view and the tranquility, you may not understand the appeal of this rustic family resort that clings to its old ways. Its rooms are plainer than plain, the accompaniments are standard-issue motel (down to the brown plastic ice containers and the plastic glasses wrapped in cellophane), the seating is pretty much confined to porches and a great lodge-style lobby. There are no televisions or telephones, let alone jacuzzis. You dress up for dinner at family-style tables in a dining hall that's an expanse of chestnut-paneled walls, floors and ceiling. It all looks like the summer camps of our youth – which is exactly the way octogenarian owner William D. McKee, son of the founder, envisioned it. And the way the loyal repeat customers want it.

The main lodge contains 32 rooms, serviceable but not exactly the kind in which you would spend much time. Better are the 90 rooms in a dozen outlying cottages, which contain four to fourteen rooms each. Most of these come with porches, sitting areas and fireplaces, and we saw plenty of people relaxing on their porches at our visit. Outside are streams, a private lake, a swimming area, tennis courts, hiking trails up the mountains and an eighteen-hole golf course.

Three meals a day are served buffet-style in the dining room. The precise fare changes daily but is quintessentially Southern. You start with soup in the lobby or on the porch – a "social custom," we were told. Then you move inside to an assigned table and help yourself to mountains of salads, a couple of entrées (at our lunch, beef stew and grilled chicken) and an array of desserts that defy finishing. The iced tea flows (only lately has the resort been able to serve liquor). The waitress removes your finished plates but in our case left the dirty silverware for re-use with the next course. The dining room seats 375, and up to 1,000 meals a day are served in summer to inn guests and a ravenous public. "Please fix some food not so spicy," one recent visitor wrote in the guest register at the front desk. Did we eat in the same place?

"Not everyone will like High Hampton," the resort literature concedes. "But fortunately, most people do like it and come back season after season. High Hampton is unique in that it is both a country inn and a complete resort: a place where time seems to stand still and very little changes except the seasons."

(828) 743-2411 or (800) 334-2551. Fax (828) 743-5991. Thirty-two lodge rooms and 90 cottage rooms, all with private baths. Rates: Full American Plan. July-August: Doubles, $176 to $198 weekends, $162 to $192 midweek. Rest of year: $168 to $190 weekends, $156 to $176 midweek. No service charge and no tipping. Closed December-March.

Dining Spots

This area is known for fine restaurants, some of which seem to come and go every year. Some restaurants have liquor or wine licenses. Others let you "brown-bag" your own.

Market Basket/The Hot Rock Cafe, Highway 107 South, Cashiers.
The menu comes attached to a paper bag at this upscale grocery store that turns

into a full-service restaurant at night. The well-spaced tables are set with votive candles, assorted bottles of sauces and mats painted with vegetables. You eat beside shelves of foodstuffs beneath lamps fashioned from pails and colanders. Your wine is iced in a pail set on the floor, and guitarist Cy Timmons sings at one side. It's a folksy, altogether endearing setting appropriate for a sophisticated mountain area. Hot-rock cooking, in which the diner cooks vegetables and main course on a heated slab of North Carolina granite at the table, is featured. The extensive menu, printed weekly, ranges from pasta portobello to grilled filet mignon or shrimp and grits. The blackened chicken Santa Fe, served with homemade corn salsa and jalapeño fettuccine, was assertive. And the mountain trout sautéed in white wine was superb. Our only complaint – one apparently heard frequently in the area – was the over-abundance of side dishes crowding the plate: fettuccine *and* garlic mashed potatoes in one case, mashed potatoes *and* wild rice in the other, plus cauliflower, broccoli, carrots and haricots verts for both. The market basket salad yielded strawberries, mandarin oranges and mushrooms along with leaf lettuces.

The desert of choice is a brownie with ice cream and strawberries. Two chocolate twigs came with the bill.

(828) 743-2216. Entrées, $16.95 to $21.95. Lunch, Monday-Saturday 10 to 3. Dinner nightly except Wednesday, 6 to 10. BYOB.

Horacio's Restaurante, Chestnut Square, Cashiers.

Chef Horacio Repetto from Portofino came here in 1995 with $1,000 in his pocket and bought an abandoned building for a restaurant. Now he has a restaurant and catering service plus a casual cafe. Business seems to be thriving. At the end of a long evening in the kitchen, Horacio, chief cook and raconteur, showed off his infant son and had our party roaring over the tale of how he got to North Carolina.

Horacio bills his main restaurant as "European traditional." That translates to an ambitious menu ranging from baked trout catalonia to hoisin chicken to grilled veal ribeye. "I can cook anything," he says. Alas, he had run out of two items that particularly appealed the night we were there, grilled rabbit tenders and venison filet. We settled for a special of pompano and shrimp française, an odd combination that worked better without the shrimp, and a tasty fillet of red snapper encrusted with basil, pinenuts and walnuts. Mashed potatoes, properly lumpy, and pasta with greens and house salads accompanied. These were substantial enough that we were glad we had skipped the appetizers, which were few and pricey. Desserts included chocolate tirami su, a delicious lemon blossom tart that four of us shared, and a double chocolate torte.

The setting in an enclosed side porch and a rear dining room is rustic and pleasant.

(828) 743-2792. Entrées. $18.99 to $26.99. Dinner, Monday-Saturday from 5:30. BYOB.

On the Verandah, Highway 64 West, Highlands.

The best location and the most exciting menu in Highlands are offered by this large restaurant and wine bar overlooking Lake Sequoyah. Pine tables set with distinctive On the Verandah pottery showplates are well spaced on the enclosed lakeside veranda as well as in the interior dining room. A wine and cigar bar in front dispenses wines by the glass from a Wine Spectator award-winning cellar.

More than 900 bottles of hot sauce, each different, are displayed on shelves outside the kitchen. Among them are owner Alan Figel's prize-winning "mania hot sauce."

Not that the fare presented by son Andrew, the executive chef, lacks kick. Typical main courses are sautéed yellowtail snapper with crawfish americaine sauce, spicy Thai coconut ginger shrimp, pan-seared medallions of duck with apricot-curry glaze, poblano chile-stuffed filet mignon, and ancho chile and pecan-crusted lamb chops with mint aioli. A wild game sampler of buffalo sausage, barbecued quail and venison was offered the night we were there. Starters include smoked salmon quesadillas, a baked goat cheese salad and something rather odd as an appetizer, roasted garlic mashed potatoes. Godiva chocolate crème brûlée is the signature dessert.

The $17.50 champagne brunch on the veranda is deservedly popular.

(828) 526-2338. Entrées, $17.50 to $28. Dinner nightly, from 6. Sunday brunch, noon to 2:30.

Lakeside Restaurant, Smallwood Avenue, Highlands.

"More than fish," say the T-shirts on the staff at this small and immensely popular restaurant known for its fresh fish. Colorful fish are the decorative theme, from the carved wooden lamp at the reception desk to the chandelier of fish in the dining room to the fish stenciling in the men's room. The dining room is cute and colorful, but fails to take advantage of the view of Harris Lake outside.

Fish is featured on the dinner menu. We hear good reports about the grouper maison, sautéed with artichoke hearts and mushrooms, and the Louisiana redfish topped with a crawfish étouffée sauce. One well-traveled diner said the steak au poivre was the best he'd ever had.

We were here for lunch, when many of the nighttime entrées are available in smaller portions. We tried a super autumn duck and pumpkin soup, an oyster po-boy served with creole mayonnaise and a salmon B.L.T., a knife-and-fork affair paired with a surprisingly bland pasta salad. The highlight was the signature bread pudding with hot buttered whiskey sauce, a decadent indulgence that left little appetite for dinner.

Since obtaining a wine license, the Lakeside charges a corkage fee of $15 per bottle for any wine brown-bagged into the restaurant.

(828) 526-9419. Entrées, $16.75 to $23.50. Lunch, Wednesday-Saturday from 11:30. Dinner from 5:30. No smoking.

Paoletti's, 440 East Main Street, Highlands.

"A true Italian restaurant worthy of New York." That's how one food connoisseur who grew up in New York describes this small operation, a fixture here since 1984. The Paoletti family moved from Florida to open an intimate storefront establishment with a green ceiling of pressed tin, mauve walls and something of an Old World Victorian atmosphere. Wine Spectator awards and fine oils adorn the walls and hanging plants are suspended from the ceiling.

Chef Kevin Paoletti's fare is northern Italian. Entrées range form grilled mountain trout and shrimp fra diavolo to rack of Colorado lamb and veal chop stuffed with portobello mushroom, spinach and mozzarella cheese. Penne alla russe (spiked with vodka and topped with caviar) is a favorite pasta dish. Appetizers

run the gamut from crispy fried calamari to caesar salad to escargots bourguignonne.
(828) 526-4906. Entrées, $18.95 to $28.95. Lunch in season, Monday-Saturday noon to 2:30. Dinner, Monday-Saturday from 5:30. Closed in January. No smoking.

Wolfgang's on Main, East Main Street, Highlands..
Bavarian and New Orleans specialties co-exist at Wolfgang Green's popular restaurant in a Victorian house with a garden pavilion out front. Wolfgang touts his credentials on his menu: former executive chef at Brennan's, member of Texas Culinary Olympic team, voted Texas chef and Jamaican chef of the year, among them.
Among the specialties are crawfish étouffée, cajun shrimp, wiener schnitzel and a Bavarian sampler. But there are many other choices, from apricot honey chicken to châteaubriand. The chef's favorites are simple: calves liver and onions and andouille sausage with red beans and rice.
Eggs sardou and eggs hussarde are featured at a New Orleans-style Sunday brunch.
(828) 526-3807. Entrées, $16.95 to $24.95. Lunch in season, 11:30 to 2:30. Dinner from 6. Sunday brunch, 11:30 to 2:30.

Cornucopia, Highway 107 South, Cashiers.
The oldest restaurant in Cashiers is this casual eatery, established in 1979 in a former general store built in 1892, the second oldest structure in the Cashiers Valley. Owner Scott Peterkin has preserved the building as it was. There's a mix of booths and tables inside. Most of the seating is outside on a sprawling deck outlined and divided by picket fencing.
The mixed bag of a dinner menu comes on a double set of brown bags. Open it up book-style and find appetizers like crab cakes, barbecued ribs and a fried chicken salad with banana chips and fried onions. Main courses could be coconut shrimp, pork Jack Daniels, Jamaican jerk chicken with raspberry coulis and tournedos of beef with béarnaise sauce. An Octoberfest plate of knockwurst, bratwurst and pork schnitzel was featured at our visit.
Interesting salads, vegetarian items and deli sandwiches are offered on the lunch menu.
(828) 743-3750. Entrées, $14.95 to $19.95. Open daily, March-October: Breakfast, 8 to 10:30, lunch 11:30 to 2:30, dinner 6 to 9. Sunday brunch 11:30 to 3:30. BYOB.

Diversions

Nature lovers find this a wonderland or, as the publicists would have it, "Cashiers is beautiful – by nature. And "Come up to Heavenly Highlands."
The southern crest of the Blue Ridge Mountains produce layer after layer of mountains, stretching endlessly on all sides. The major mountain landmark is **Whiteside Mountain,** located between Cashiers and Highlands and presenting a different face toward each. It's named for the highest cliffs in eastern America, which stretch from 400 to 750 feet high some 2,000 feet above the dark Chattooga River valley below. The cliffs, formed of white granite, are home to peregrine falcons. Geologists theorize this is one of the oldest mountains on earth. A two-mile loop trail leads along the ridge from the Whiteside Mountain parking area off Highway 64. Other hikes and trails are readily available locally.

Waterfalls. Almost every guide to the area details the area's waterfalls. **Whitewater Falls,** a dozen miles southeast of Cashiers, is the highest in the East. The upper cascade of 411 feet meets others along an 800-foot drop that ends in South Carolina. A scenic view of the upper falls is a five-minute walk via a paved trail from the parking lot. An old roadbed leads to the top, but signs warn of danger. You'll get the idea if you try the easier trail nearly a mile down a steep, primitive path to a lower overlook. After hanging onto tree limbs and roots to keep from falling, you'll be rewarded with another view of the falls. Hikers also enjoy the three-mile **Horsepasture River Falls Trail** for views of Drift, Rainbow, Turtle and Bust-Your-Butt falls, located on the Horsepasture River halfway between Whitewater Falls and Cashiers. Closer to Cashiers, **Silver Run Falls,** a 40-foot cascade, ends in a pool for swimming. Just west of Highlands, you can detour off Highway 64 to drive your car behind the 120-foot-high **Bridal Veil Falls.** A mile or so beyond, you can park your car and descend an easy trail to walk behind 75-foot-high **Dry Falls,** which isn't dry at all. It's enough of a torrent off an overhang that you'll surely get damp from the spray. The Cullasaja River Gorge to the northwest produces many more cascades, culminating in the 250-foot-high **Lower Cullasaja Falls,** one of the South's most picturesque.

Culture. Highlands is the kind of place where you expect to find cultural attractions. The **Highlands Playhouse,** honored as one of the nation's ten best, has been producing summer theater since 1941. Four plays run for two weeks each from late June to late August. The **Highlands Chamber Music Festival** has been presenting summer performances since 1981. The award-winning **Highlands Pipes and Drums Band** plays periodically, lending the look and music of the Scottish Highlands. Local and regional artists exhibit in the **Bascom-Louise Gallery** in the Hudson Library. The **Center for Life Enrichment** presents numerous lectures and special events in summer. The **Highlands Nature Center and Biological Station** offers programs and walking trails. An unlikely looking log structure along Chestnut Street is the home of the **Museum of American Cut and Engraved Glass.** George and Bonnie Siek display over 400 pieces of antique glass from their private collection.

Shopping is big business and a major pastime in this area – obviously, in Highlands, and less so in Cashiers. That's because of their layout. They're scattered in houses strung out in the woods around the center of Cashiers. A couple we liked were **Wild Possessions** in an adorable shingled house in Chestnut Square, where the Aussie hats and pretty vests appealed, and the **Olde Home Place Shop** on Highway 107, with birdhouses, windsocks, local foods and cookbooks. We nearly bought a sweatshirt depicting Mom and Pop cardinals.

Stores line Main Street and side streets in Highlands in typical downtown fashion. We could begin and end every shopping expedition at **Southern Hands,** a remarkable emporium in Wright Square. We admired the richly colored chenille throws and scarves, the carved black bears, the quilts and the small fountains. The pottery here is especially good. In 1998, Southern Hands opened a smaller offshoot in Cashiers. Also in Wright Square are **Masterworks** with some great jewelry, **Rarities,** also with lovely gold jewelry and where we were fascinated with the bright blue butterflies in the window, and **Great Things!** for home decor. Fashionable women are well served at **Nancy's Fancys, Highlands Sportswear,**

Wit's End Shop and **Le Pavilion. T.J. Bailey** is the store for men. **McCulley's** claims the largest selection of Scottish cashmere in this country.

We liked the art (expensive!) at the **Ann Jacob Gallery** and many paintings at **John Collette Fine Art.** Other favorites are **Mountain Memories,** which speaks for itself, and the **Spring Street Gallery and Gardens,** which includes a little espresso bar. In a small arcade called Oak Square, you can find special coffees, teas and frozen yogurt at the **Highlands House of Coffee,** and books and cards at **Chapter 2 Too.** Check out the elaborate electric train setup at **Christmas Cottage** nearby. Little Highlands actually has two bookstores; the other is **Cyrano's Bookshop,** with books for the "mind, heart and spirit."

For a break from shopping, stop for a delicious sandwich and/or a cappuccino at **Wild Thyme Bakery-Cafe** on Carolina Way. If you want to take a picnic to one of the nearby lakes or waterfalls, try the **Rosewood Market,** which is run by the folks from the Lakeside Restaurant.

For antiquers, the event not to miss is the nightly evening auction at **Scudder's Auction Galleries.** Wide rows of bilious green theater seats await bidders, who can preview the wares at 7:30. The auctions begin at 8. Estate catalog sales are held in summer at 11 a.m. on second and fourth Saturdays.

Extra-Special

Ezekiel's Barn, Highway 107 North, Cashiers.

Eating here is a hoot. Doug and Debbie Wilgus built this small barn in 1996 and named it for their young son. They offer a five-course, prix-fixe dinner, the fare for which changes weekly. You call ahead to see what's on for the week, and if it doesn't appeal, you wait for another time. There will be plenty of takers after you. Artists both (their works hang in the barn gallery), Debbie does the cooking and Doug entertains, with occasional assistance from Ezekiel. Doug sings with the waiters and waitresses, tells jokes and encourages people to play games (such as guessing ten items stuffed inside a sock, with pastries as prizes). The meal when we were there included stuffed mushroom caps, popovers with honey butter, caesar salad, filet mignon wellington and a sampling of two desserts, strawberry tirami su and chocolate mocha torte. The experience takes about three hours. It's all quite elegant and intimate – like going to a dinner party at someone's house.

(828) 743-0185. Prix-fixe, $29.50. Dinner by reservation, Wednesday-Saturday at 7. *BYOB.*

Aiken, S.C.

A Rare Breed

They call Aiken County "a rare breed," and not just for the horses that give Aiken the air of a Saratoga of the South.

The longest railroad in the world at the time – all of 136 miles from Charleston to the Savannah River at Hamburg – made Aiken a health resort starting in the 1830s. At 500 feet above sea level in the sandhills of western South Carolina, it became for wealthy Charlestonians "a place of retreat from the heat and malaria of unhealthier regions." Railroad engineers laid out a town of wide parkways and named it for William Aiken Sr., cotton merchant and railroad builder. The town was divided into quadrants. On the north side of Boundary Avenue are 175 parkway blocks totaling more than fifteen miles in length. They're planted with live oaks and enough rare trees to warrant a Colleton Avenue Trail Guide – a guide to 48 varieties of trees.

South of Boundary, many of the more prestigious streets remained unpaved, the better for the hooves of the horses that outnumber residents in this section. On the south side, back yards are more likely to have stables than garages. Horses and carriages are berthed inside, and autos are relegated to carports.

The wide parkways and dirt roads testify to Aiken's heritage as a "Winter Colony" for some of America's wealthiest families. After the Civil War, the mild climate lured Northerners for polo, fox hunting and horse racing. Trains ran daily from New York to Aiken carrying winter visitors and horses. The Vanderbilts and Astors built mansions across the street from one another. The Whitneys and Hitchcocks turned Aiken into the sports center of the South.

The equestrian tradition continues to this day. It's obvious from the street signs shaped as horse's heads and the blinking traffic lights for horses along Whiskey Avenue on the way to the tracks. (The horsehead sign at Whiskey Road and Easy Street is the best-selling postcard here). Polo is still played on Sunday afternoons in spring and fall at Whitney Field, the oldest continuously operating polo field in the nation. Horsemen from across the country converge on Aiken in March for three successive weekends of the Triple Crown to watch Aiken-trained horses participate in harness, flat and steeplechase races.

Golf rivals horseback riding as the favorite participatory sport. The Palmetto Golf Course, founded in 1892 by Thomas Hitchcock and William C. Whitney, is almost as old as golf in America. The Highland Park Country Club course was opened in 1903. Just fifteen miles to the west is Augusta, Ga., home of the Augusta National Golf Course and the famed Masters golf tournament in April.

There's more than sport to this town of 20,000, as you might suspect if you happen to arrive here as we did for the

Horses and carriages are frequent sight along live oak-canopied streets of Aiken's Winter Colony.

annual spring Lobster Race. Young and old alike crowd the downtown Alley to race real lobsters in a cherished spoof of the Kentucky Derby the next day. Regional arts and crafts are shown on the downtown parkways during the annual Aiken's Makin festival in September. The downtown is a compact few blocks graced with shady trees and wonderful plantings down the parkway medians. Hitchcock Woods, a 2,000-acre forested preserve within walking distance of downtown, is bigger than New York's Central Park. The entire town merits the designation Tree City USA for its citywide arboretum project.

Located away from the mainstream, Aiken is a rare slice of living history: the small-town America that existed before Wal-Marts and freeways. People – and horses – come first here.

Inn Spots

The Willcox Inn, 100 Colleton Ave. S.W., Aiken 29801.

In the heart of the Winter Colony historic district, this gleaming white inn with its six-columned portico seems almost as traditional as Aiken itself. It was established in 1898 by English immigrant Frederick Willcox, who endeared himself to the winter set. Over the years the inn became a destination for dignitaries, including Winston Churchill, Franklin D. Roosevelt, Averill Harriman and Elizabeth Arden. Legend has it that the early Willcox would not admit gentlemen unless their shoes were of the right quality and shined to a high luster.

Such is not the case today, despite a multi-million-dollar restoration that returned the Willcox to its former elegance in 1987. The initial four-diamond rating in 1988 – still posted in the lobby – has been reduced to three diamonds. Yet the Willcox conveys the dignified, well-maintained look of an older hotel.

The inn offers 24 comfortable guest rooms with one queensize or two twin beds on the second and third floors. Those we saw had modern baths, poster beds, two armchairs, decorative fireplaces and a light and airy look with subdued floral fabrics. A mini-suite came with queensize poster bed, TV hidden in an armoire and a large bathroom with a clawfoot tub in the middle and a separate shower on the side. Six larger suites have queen or kingsize beds, porches, ceiling fans and window seats.

A low-key equestrian theme is evident throughout. Seating areas in the rich, beamed and paneled lobby focus on a wood-burning fireplace. The Polo Pub lounge is evocative of an English library with leather chairs and rich wood paneling. The skylit Pheasant Room, pleasant in green and white, overlooks the rear woods. It offers continental specialties with a southern accent for lunch and dinner. Rates include a complimentary continental breakfast. A full breakfast also is available.

(803) 649-1377 or (800) 368-1047 Fax (803) 643-0971. Twenty-four rooms and six suites with private baths. Doubles, $90 to $100 weekends, $95 to $105 midweek. Suites, $110 to $125 weekends, $120 to $135 midweek.

Sandhurst Estate, 215 Dupree Place S.W., Aiken 29801.

One of the early (1883) Winter Colony mansions, this was designed by noted architect Stanford White for a wealthy New York banker. It was "bulldozer-ready" when acquired by a latter-day New York banker, Sandra Croy, who took early retirement from Chase Manhattan after a career involving world-wide travel. She moved here to raise horses, spent two years restoring the mansion and opened it as a B&B and function facility in 1997.

There's no sign to mark the Sandhurst Estate, although its stately white facade and Corinthian pillars are hard to miss. It's the biggest private house and property on the street, with five acres sandwiched between Hopland Gardens and Hitchcock Woods.

The grand foyer, with a baby grand piano tucked beneath the staircase, hints of surprises to come.

Not one to dwell on formality, the down-to-earth hostess is likely to greet guests in a sweater and jeans. The visitor might almost think she's a stand-in for the real owner, especially as she frequently says "we" as she refers to her staff of chef, handymen and stablehands. But Sandra is the owner, the decorator, the party-giver, the fun lover. The furnishings and artworks and prized antiques are hers – "we had a bigger house than this in New Jersey" – so it was simply a matter of finding the right space and readying it for possessions collected over the years. "We're bringing back the Golden Days of the Winter Colony so people can see what that era was like," she says.

Off the foyer are a front library furnished in dark leather, a rear parlor whose sofas are white, a sumptuous sun room for morning coffee or afternoon cocktails under the watchful gaze of three carved giraffes, and a majestic, chandeliered dining room, where two tables are set for twenty.

The second floor holds six guest rooms and suites. The most striking features may be their new white marble bathrooms with crystal chandeliers and gilt-framed mirrors. Sandra named one room the Countess because her first guest was the Duchess of Westmoreland. The countess slept regally in a hand-carved Belgian kingsize bed with matching armoire and, we imagine, bathed in a double jacuzzi with a separate, oversize glass shower. Another suite is named for Elizabeth Dole, a friend of the hostess, who stayed here. Beyond its bedroom with queensize poster bed of golden teak is a sitting room with a front balcony perched between the pillars and an antique bookcase displaying a prized collection of fine glass. Windows on three sides enhance the Grand Master Suite, which features a queensize poster bed in the bedroom and a fireplace in the living room. Three smaller rooms here and on the third floor follow the theme, although most have clawfoot tubs instead of jacuzzis. Some rooms look rather spare in the fashion of the mid-1800s era that Sandra sought to replicate. You may find a zebra sculpture

Sandhurst Estate, designed by Stanford White, is one of early Winter Colony mansions.

in a bedroom or one of her 32 carousel horses in the bathroom. Down comforters, fine linens, terrycloth robes and plush towels are standard. Turndown service brings handmade chocolates.

Breakfast is served on one of Sandra's 47 sets of china amidst much crystal and silver. Eggs benedict is the signature dish, and Sandra and young chef Peter Allen from Maine have a running battle over whose hollandaise sauce is better. Blueberry pancakes is another favorite.

After breakfast, Sandra or one of her stablehands takes guests on horse-drawn carriage rides through Hitchcock Woods or the Aiken horse district. She raises driving ponies and miniature horses in her back-yard pasture. They're on view from the elaborate circular patio and fountain, home for Molly the cockatiel.

(803) 642-9259. Eight rooms and two suites with private baths. Doubles, $90 to $150. Suites, $175 and $200.

The Briar Patch, 544 Magnolia Lane S.E., Aiken 29801.

Another look at Aiken's equestrian life is offered at this novel B&B, the first to open in Aiken back in 1982 when B&Bs were not yet heard of here. Martha Hair bought the main house, which once was a stable and carriage house, as a residence for her and her daughter Trisha (now Mrs. Thomas Anderson III). They turned the former tack room out back into two guest rooms, each with separate entrance, private bath, fireplace and TV.

One room contains a step-up double spool bed plus a single bed and is nicely furnished in wicker. The copper horse weathervane above the fireplace mantel was rescued from a trash pile. The second room is slightly larger, with two canopied twin beds, a plush chair and two high-back wicker chairs in a bay window sitting alcove. Oriental rugs top the rare cork floors.

The lovely grounds in back include a brick patio and a tennis court for guests to use. Continental breakfast is served on the patio or at a round oak table in the homey kitchen of the main house. Martha's specialty is bran-pecan muffins, "the best you ever had in your life" – a claim we do not doubt. The beautiful square living room belongs to the hosts, but they might let you peek.

The accommodations are stylish and comfortable and represent good value. Martha professes surprise that four men fly in by private jet every spring for the Masters tournament and rent her rooms. "They don't even want breakfast and pay all that money just to sleep."

(803) 649-2010. Two rooms with private baths. Doubles, $50.

Town & Country Inn, 2340 Sizemore Cir., Aiken 29803.

"Bed, breakfast and barn" is the billing for this new B&B, in a rather contemporary brick and wood house with pillared entrance in a residential area south of Aiken. The barn refers to the five-stall barn out back, where owners Marlene and David Jones board horses for their guests.

A fountain trickles out front, and gliders on the first and second-story verandas overlook a pine grove. The Joneses aim for a home-like atmosphere, and have a house that conveys it.

Guests enjoy the main-floor living room with TV and fireplace, and a homey dining room, as well as an upstairs sitting area. Tea and soft drinks are offered in the afternoon. Of their five guest rooms, one has a king bed and a jacuzzi tub.

A bonus for summertime guests is use of the large swimming pool with cabana, kitchen and bath.

(803) 642-0270. Fax (803) 642-1299. Five rooms with private baths. Doubles, $65 to $95. No smoking.

Annie's Inn, 3083 Charleston Highway, Box 200, Montmorenci 29839.

Five miles east of Aiken is this old-fashioned B&B that originated in the 1830s as a cotton plantation home, with the requisite pillars and wraparound veranda. Owner Scottie C. Peck offers six guest rooms in the house, plus six cottages rented by the month.

The main floor has a formal parlor with a piano and an appealing library/den with plush chairs and a TV in the entertainment center. But most guests end up in the large country kitchen, gathered around the old wood cook stove. A full breakfast is served in the formal dining room. The fare varies daily. "Quiches, eggs benedict, blueberry waffles, ham and eggs – we do it all," says Scottie.

One bedroom with queen bed and large full bath is on the main floor. The others are on the second. Most have TVs and sprightly decor. Furnishings include country antiques, homemade quilts, feather pillows and oriental rugs. One in front has a queen bed, plush sofa, armoire and a washstand in the room. Another with twin beds contains an armoire and a decorative fireplace. The smallest room in the rear has a double bed.

The pine floors are original, from planks sawed on the plantation.

(803) 649-6836. Fax (803) 642-6709. Six rooms with private baths. Doubles, $75.

Dining Spots

Malia's Restaurant, 120 Laurens St. S.W., Aiken.

Chef-owner Malia Koelker started in 1988 with a cafe at the rear of a dress shop. When the shop closed, she took over the entire space and has been going strong since. Her quarters are quite stylish, with brick walls, beamed ceiling, track lighting and plush chairs flanking white-clothed tables.

This is the best place in town for dinner on weekends, according to all reports.

Annie's Inn occupies 1830s cotton plantation home in Montmorenci.

Malia only offers the evening meal on Friday and Saturday, but what a meal it is. We wanted to try everything on the menu.

For starters there were baked artichoke hearts stuffed with basil and chèvre, sautéed shrimp cakes topped with spicy avocado mayonnaise and tempura-fried portobello mushrooms with a sweet and sour soy dipping sauce. Among main dishes were baked halibut topped with caper-basil vinaigrette and sundried tomatoes, chicken provençal, pork punjab and New Zealand rack of lamb with a rosemary-port wine sauce. Desserts change nightly.

If you can't get there for dinner, consider the weekday lunch. The menu is short but sweet: things like crabmeat bisque, steak salad, strawberry chicken salad, souvlaki, portobello mushroom quesadilla and three sandwiches, served with soup or salad.

(803) 643-3086. Entrées, $13 to $20. Lunch, Monday-Friday 11:30 to 2:30. Dinner, Friday-Saturday 6 to 10.

Up Your Alley, 222 The Alley, Aiken.

Traditional Southern/American fare for Aiken's old-money horse set has been the hallmark of this old-timer run with TLC by Connecticut transplant Bruce Shipman and partner Janny Bijas. They undertook major renovations in 1997, producing a dark, pleasant series of rooms with brick walls, wainscoting, exposed ducts and stained glass. There's also a bar with separate entrance and a casual bar menu.

Shaded oil lamps flickered around our booth as we started with homemade rolls and the signature house salad, served family style in a big bowl, topped with sesame seeds and dressed with oil and vinegar. Main courses that night ranged from stuffed cornish game hen to charbroiled cowboy steak and roasted Australian lamb chops. We liked the broiled scallops with lemon-butter sauce and twin crab cakes swathed in mustard cream. Al dente carrots, squash, broccoli and roasted potatoes came with. White chocolate bread pudding with white chocolate sauce and profiteroles were among the tempting desserts. We settled for a refreshing raspberry sorbet, served with a wafer. Mint candies came with the bill.

An appetizer called Connecticut seafood chowder recalls to the owner's days in Stonington, where moneyed Fishers Island friends urged him to open a restaurant in Aiken. He did and couldn't be happier. "This is a great little town."

(803) 649-2603. Entrées, $11.95 to $19.95. Dinner nightly, from 5.

No. 10 Downing St., 241 Laurens St. S.W., Aiken.

Set back from the street amidst gardens and trees is this yellow and green Colonial house with the atmosphere of an English cottage. Dating to 1837, it once belonged to the parents of James Mathews Legare, poet and artist, whose works hang in the studio that forms one of the restaurant's four dining rooms. The British connection comes from co-owner Jan Waugh. She and partner Ginny Huckabee make the desserts that led to the opening of an adjoining bakery and a small shop where Ginny sells her calligraphy and works of local artists.

Wide-board floors, green-clothed tables and votive candles are the setting for dinners of distinction. Main courses run from almond baked sea bass, shrimp tasso and grilled swordfish with salsa fresca to chicken piccata, cumin-roasted pork loin and beef tenderloin with gorgonzola butter. Appetizers take a continental turn, as in pâté with French bread, Scotch egg with stone-ground mustard, lox spread with bagel chips and caponata with French bread. Save room for dessert, perhaps sabayon with fresh fruit, peanut butter pie or "very lemon pie." Choices are as elaborate as bananas foster and as simple as frozen yogurt with fresh fruit or "a cookie from the bakery."

There are lots of fancy salads and sandwiches for lunch. Or settle for the pub lunch of Scotch egg, mustard, cheddar cheese and English bread.

(803) 642-9062. Entrées, $13.95 to $18.95. Lunch, Tuesday-Friday 11:30 to 2:30. Saturday brunch, 10 to 2. Dinner, Tuesday-Saturday 6 to 9:30.

Riley's Whitby Bull, 218 York St. S.E., Aiken.

Restaurateurs Will and Lorraine Riley made a name for themselves in leased space at Aiken's downtown Holley Inn. Their fans followed when the couple, both Culinary Institute of America grads, opened their own 22-seat restaurant in this bright blue renovated house where they live upstairs.

Their charming, country-pretty dining room is colorful in peach, mauve and aqua. Orchids are on the tables, drapped in white over pink. Little wonder theirs was voted best for romantic dining two years in a row by readers of Aiken County magazine.

Their customers wanted breakfast all day, so the Rileys oblige with a lunch menu that's strong on egg dishes (omelets, eggs benedict and an Irish pub treat with hot sliced filet, scrambled eggs, cheese and port wine sauce served open-faced on a French loaf). Their specialty is crêpes, perhaps chicken and artichoke hearts or spinach and ricotta, served with Will's Irish soda bread. The choices expand for Sunday breakfast, which has become something of a local tradition.

The Rileys also offer table d'hôte dinners. The short menu changes weekly and is priced at $27.50 for seven courses, or $21.50 for the abbreviated version with soup or salad, entrée and coffee. The works might yield clear mushroom soup, chicken pesto bruschetta, a salad of asparagus vinaigrette and a choice of baked salmon, duck breast, filet of beef or grilled lamb chops. Dessert, perhaps chocolate pâté with raspberry sauce or strawberry-rhubarb crisp, is followed by fruit and stilton cheese.

(803) 641-6227. Table d'hôte, $27.50. Lunch, Wednesday-Friday 11:30 to 2. Dinner, Wednesday-Saturday 5 to 9. Sunday, breakfast 8:30 to 2, dinner 11:30 to 2. No smoking.

Olive Oils Restaurant, 233 Chesterfield St. S., Aiken.

An offshoot of his successful Up Your Alley, this Italian-American restaurant was opened by Bruce Shipman and Janny Bijas in small yellow house with several small dining rooms, a veranda and a front patio. It's wildly popular, at least the autumn weeknight we stopped by, when every table was occupied and the kitchen was running behind.

The wait was worth it for delectable garlic bread, the signature family-style salad enough for two to share, and a succulent pasta dish with pesto chicken and pinenuts in a creamy white sauce. The menu ranges widely from basic pastas to parmesan shrimp, chicken pancetta, filet gorgonzola, roasted veal chop and veal saltimbocca. Calzones, pizzas and vegetarian dishes also are available.

(803) 649-9062. Entrées, $9.95 to $18.95. Dinner nightly, 4:30 to 9:30.

Mango's, 149 Laurens St., Aiken.

A Florida-Caribbean theme enhances this tropical cafe, opened by chef-owner Lou Cerullo from Florida. He found he had to tone down the early Caribbean emphasis to suit more traditional Aiken tastes, but still offers things like conch chowder, Caribbean pizzas, Jamaican-jerk seafood and Cuban green chili. A specialty is shrimp sautéed in a curried margarita sauce and served over rice.

The menu ranges widely, from cajun jambalaya to grilled ribeye steak. Lou renovated the structure to convey the look of an old Key West house, with rooms painted in tropical colors and a Parrothead Bar where a Jimmy Buffett Fan Club meets monthly. In nice weather, diners spill outside onto a pleasant deck flanked by palm trees.

(803) 643-0620. Entrées, $10.95 to $15.95. Lunch, Tuesday-Friday 11:30 to 2:30, Saturday from noon. Dinner, Tuesday-Saturday 5 to 9:30.

Diversions

Equine sports remain Aiken's chief attraction. Activity is at its busiest from late November to mid-April. The Fall Steeplechase, fox hunting, polo tournaments and the Thanksgiving Blessing of the Hounds are draws in the fall. The spring highlight is the Aiken Triple Crown, three successive weekends in late March and early April featuring the Aiken Trials, the Aiken Steeplechase and the Harness Races. Thoroughbred farms are scattered around Aiken's Winter Colony district. The chief sites of public interest are concentrated on the southeastern side of town between South Boundary Avenue and Whiskey Road. Visitors can view the Aiken Training Track, home since 1942 of the Aiken Trials flat-racing events; the Ford Conger Field, site of the Aiken Steeplechase, and the city-owned Aiken Mile Track, a harness racing site known nationally as a training center for standardbred horses. An elaborate Horseman's Guide to Aiken brochure details training and riding facilities, horse farms and stables, tack shops and equine events.

Another guide describes the days when Aiken was the Polo Center of the South. Polo was launched here by William C. Whitney in 1882. At one time the town had sixteen polo fields and Mrs. Thomas Hitchcock started a boys' school that turned out some of the best polo players in the country. Polo is still played at Whitney Field Sunday afternoons March-July and September-November.

The **Citywide Arboretum of Aiken** was established by the city in 1995 to provide "a natural learning lab for those interested in discovering more about one of our greatest assets." From the magnolias along Park Avenue to the canopy of live oaks strewn with Spanish moss along South Boundary, trees have played an important role in the planning of Aiken's streets and parkways. The city has been awarded the National Arbor Day Foundation's Tree City USA award every year since 1985. Forty-eight species of trees are pinpointed and detailed in the Colleton Avenue Trail Guide, part of the Citywide Arboretum. The city and the Chamber of Commerce publish a map and guide to 78 historic points of interest.

Aiken Tours. The City of Aiken sponsors a guided 90-minute bus tour of the city, pointing out attractions, horse training areas and historic homes and buildings. The bus leaves from the Aiken Municipal Building in the Alley every Saturday at 10 a.m. Reservations are recommended (803) 641-1111. Tickets, $5.

Hopeland Gardens, Dupree Place, Aiken.

Hidden behind a serpentine brick wall beneath a canopy of ancient oaks and magnolias is this fourteen-acre estate that's a public garden, open-air concert venue and more. It was bequeathed to the city by Mrs. C. Oliver Iselin. Reflecting pools shimmer in the sun where the Iselin mansion once stood. The carriage house is the home of the **Thoroughbred Racing Hall of Fame,** which celebrates Aiken-trained horses that have become national champions. The Hall of Fame includes Kentucky derby winners Pleasant Colony and Sea Hero, Preakness winner Summer Squall and Kelso (horse of the year winner for five consecutive years). Visitors view an exhibit donated by Mrs. G.H. Bostwick featuring trophies and photographs from the career of the late Pete Bostwick, noted polo player and steeplechase rider. A large collection of Engelhard silver trophies is also on display. Radiating from the museum are networks of sandy paths and garden borders. A Touch and Scent Trail for the visually impaired leads to an amphitheater with a performing arts stage, the site for free Monday evening concerts from May through August. A bridge leads across a wetlands area to the Rye Patch Reception Center, part of a ten-acre estate donated to the city by the children of Dorothy Goodyear Rogers.

(803) 642-7630. Gardens open daily, 10 to dusk. Hall of Fame open Tuesday-Sunday 2 to 5, September-June. Donation.

Aiken County Historical Museum, 433 Newberry St. SW, Aiken.

Banksia, an impressive 32-room Winter Colony mansion built in 1931 by New York industrialist Richard Howe, was named for the Banksia rose. Rooms depict life in Aiken from the late 18th century. Exhibits include a handmade scale model of a miniature circus with 1,700 pieces, American Indian artifacts and an 1880s steam-powered fire engine. Also on view are a drugstore from the former town of Dunbarton, a furnished one-room schoolhouse, a medicinal herb garden and an 1808 log house. The grounds are being developed into an arboretum and nature trail. The museum property adjoins Hitchcock Woods (see below).

(803) 642-2015. Open Tuesday-Friday 9:30 to 4:30, Saturday-Sunday 2 to 5. Donation.

Shopping. Tree-lined, flower bedecked Laurens Street is the heart of Aiken's compact shopping district. Here you'll find places as diverse as the **Aiken Brewing Co.,** a brew pub with a bar and grill full of young people, and **Alvario's Restaurant,**

where we breakfasted with regulars who take over the back section every morning "and solve the problems of Aiken," in the words of a waitress. A restaurant of the old school, it's oddly juxtaposed next to the **New Moon Cafe,** which serves lattes and quiches. Another relative newcomer is **Gourmet Creations,** a good bakery and lunch spot. The fledgling **Aiken Center for the Arts** is a big, long and – at least at our visit – a somewhat sparse showcase of local arts and crafts. Our favorite store is **Tea Garden Gifts,** a fabulous shop with great magnets, cards and acrylic salad bowls and servers. Among its latest offerings was a huge acrylic platter in the form of a turtle for a cool $125. **Plum Pudding** bills itself as a gallery of gifts, gourmet items and curiosities. **Bear Hollow** specializes in collectibles, many of them stuffed bears. **Birds & Butterflies** offers garden accents, gifts and nature products. **The Loft at Laurens** carries colorful clothing, while **K.R. Smythe & Co.** upholds traditional women's apparel. **Lionel Smith Ltd.** stocks clothing for the horseman.

The Alley, a tree-shaded mews between Laurens and York streets, is a neat place to wander. Depending on your taste, stop at the **À La Carte Gourmet & Cafe** or at **Mud & Stogies,** a "cigar-smoking coffee bar."

Montmorenci Vineyards, 2989 Charleston Hwy., Aiken.

Cute best describes this little stucco and brick house along the highway east of Aiken. It's the showroom for a vineyard established in 1988, the second in the state. Winemaker Robert E. Scott Jr. converted a nearby peanut and cotton farm into a vineyard and turned a hobby into a thriving business. The output ranges from a light, dry Savannah white to a traditional French méthode-champenoise brut. The Triple Crown Blush is the best-seller. It's the only one of the thirteen vintages not to have won an award, the sales agent advised. The premier chambourcin, a big red wine, won a gold medal. This being new territory for wine tasting, much of the sales pitch involves suggestions for the pairing of wine with food.

(803) 649-4870. Open Wednesday-Saturday, 10 to 6. Closed first two weeks of January.

Extra-Special _____

Hitchcock Woods, off South Boundary Avenue, Aiken.

Almost at the edge of downtown Aiken is this 2,000-acre preserve of protected woodlands. Larger than New York's Central Park, it's the largest urban forest in the United States – a unique Southern forest in the midst of a city. The tranquil equine playground was once the private preserve of sportsmen Thomas Hitchcock and William C. Whitney. Now the public enjoys sixty-five miles of riding trails, where horses have the right of way but walkers may venture. Trails carpeted with pine straw trace the gentle ridges and valleys of the woods and hunt lines criss-cross through tall stands of pines. You may see the Ridge Mile Track where Thomas Hitchcock trained his race horses and the former site of the tea cottage where his aunt once entertained. You'll certainly see a lot of the Aiken-style jumping fences and countless people riding their horses. Cathedral Aisle follows the former railbed of the Charleston to Hamburg railroad. The Kalmia Trail follows a ridge abundant with rare kalmia, which blooms from late April to mid-May. A mysterious river of sand also winds through the forest. Wildlife and rare plants abound.

Open daily, dawn to dusk. No motorized vehicles.

Georgetown, S.C.
Gardens of Gold

"The Tidelands of Georgetown – A Natural Attraction," is how the Chamber of Commerce touts this area in its slick visitor guide. That captures one facet of this low-key area overshadowed by its bigger neighbors, Myrtle Beach to the north and Charleston to the south.

Here you find a small riverfront town blossoming around a charming historic district, antebellum rice plantations, a world-class sculpture garden and Pawleys Island, an early beach resort. The video in the local Rice Museum is called "Garden of Gold," referring to 200 years of rice-growing riches and the plantation aristocracy they inspired. Make that Gardens of Gold, for although rice growing is long gone, its heritage endures all around Georgetown. Today, the Midas touch is at Brookhaven Garden, which has turned sculptures to gold, and at Pawleys Island, where the proverbial rope hammocks live on in the posh Hammock Shops.

Georgetown, South Carolina's third oldest city, is the probable site of the first European settlement in North America. Spaniards landed here in 1526 before St. Augustine, Jamestown and Plymouth Rock were even thought of. The settlement vanished, but Englishman Elisha Screven laid out a town in 1729 at the point where four rivers converge on broad Winyah Bay funneling into the Atlantic. It was named in honor of King George II.

The predictable tidewaters and rivers surrounding Georgetown made irrigation practical, and the indigo and rice culture flourished in the 19th century. In summer, the early planters and merchants moved their families across the Waccamaw River onto breezy Pawleys Island to escape heat and humidity. Pawleys became one of America's first seaside resorts.

Hidden behind today's outward show of paper and steel mills is a tranquil historic district of sixteen square blocks reflecting Georgetown's status as one of the nation's richest areas in the mid-19th century. More than 60 structures are listed on the National Register. Guided carriage, tram and walking tours lead visitors along oak-lined streets, and boats take passengers through the rice plantation lands. A Harborwalk flanks the Sampit River along Front Street, site of pastel-colored shops, galleries and waterside restaurants.

For reasons not necessarily evident, Georgetown is reputed to be one of the nation's most haunted places. More than 100 known ghosts have inhabited the area, including some at inns detailed below. The annual Ghost Hunt in October is one of the Southeast's more popular events.

Centrally located yet off the beaten path, Georgetown (population 10,000) makes a good jumping off place for day trips to Charleston and the Grand Strand. After a busy day touring, it's a pleasant refuge to which to return. A

Double verandas overlook grounds and pool at DuPre House.

young man came here from Virginia in 1996 and purchased an inn, having fallen in love with the town. "We fit like a glove," said Marshall Wile. He'd found his garden of gold.

Inn Spots

DuPre House, 921 Prince St., Georgetown 29440.

The area's most pleasing all-around B&B, to our way of thinking, is this historical beauty in a residential section a block from the heart of town. That's due in no small measure to Marshall Wile, a former Virginia hotelier who scoured the South for the perfect B&B before discovering Georgetown. "It was the perfect fit," he said. After working for the Williamsburg Inn and the Ritz-Carlton Hotel in Kansas City, "I knew I could handle five rooms by myself."

Energetic Marshall, whose experience belies his youth, inherited a renovated B&B in need of TLC but ready to take off. He repainted and reconfigured the exterior to make it more welcoming, hung artworks with a childhood fantasy theme inside, and added personal effects and plenty of personality.

Bears and bunnies are the low-key theme. The stuffed-animal varieties serve as door stops and perch on a loft above a stairwell. Artworks convey familiar story themes and memories from childhood. "Georgetown reminded me of going home to Grandma's," Marshall said. So he decorated suavely in light pastels with darker accents. All is light and airy and crisp. Flashlights are hung on the doorknobs of each room for décor and use in case of power failure.

Creature comforts are paramount. Beds are queensize and dressed in fine linens and fabrics. Modern baths contain all the amenities. Three bedrooms have fireplaces. The other two on the third floor have soaking tubs. Nightly turndown is offered, and coffee is presented with a newspaper at your door in the morning. The Caine Room in which we stayed has access both to a second-floor parlor with TV and a broad front veranda running the width of the second floor.

The original main-floor parlor has been converted into a guest bedroom. The foyer and a small room adjacent now serve as a sitting area, open to a large and dramatic, contemporary-looking kitchen/dining area/butler's pantry that's the heart of the house. Marshall puts his hotel restaurant background to good use in preparing elaborate breakfasts. Ours was an artistic feast of french toast laden with fresh strawberries, kiwis and blackberries, accompanied by sausages. He usually serves items he can prepare the night before in order to spend time doing what he likes best – chatting with guests.

The rockers on the first-floor veranda are perfect for taking in the tranquil scene. The extra-deep lot contains a substantial swimming pool and a hot tub, with plenty of lounge chairs for relaxing. Beyond the rear parking area are a bocce court, a couple of hammocks beneath the trees and an herb garden. On vacant property next door is the oldest live oak in town – estimated at 400 to 500 years, and actually three trees in one.

(843) 546-0298 or (800) 921-3877. Fax (803) 520-0771. Five rooms with private baths. Doubles, $75 to $115. No children. No smoking.

King's Inn at Georgetown, 230 Broad St., Georgetown 29440.

Thanks to a total rehabilitation inside and out, this four-square Federal-style mansion built in 1825 by rice plantation mill owner Benjamin King has been converted into a B&B of great appeal. Former Missourians Marilyn and Jerry Burkhardt, who moved here in 1993 from Greensboro, N.C., transformed its 7,000 square feet into a refuge of bygone elegance, beckoning visitors to experience "the true South."

Marilyn did all the interior design and even made the full-length draperies, which in many cases puddle to the floor. She put antique mirrors in the bathrooms, and employed antiques and family heirlooms throughout. Even the downstairs powder room is outfitted with original art and a crystal chandelier.

Crystal chandeliers also hang from the twelve-foot-high ceilings in two fancy parlors. Each is notable for French plaster moldings and ornate ceiling medallions, triple-sash windows and original heart-pine floors. One is a music room with a grand piano. A less formal parlor is dressed in lavender and florals to serve as a comfortable TV room. Works by Low Country artists are for sale in the gallery/tea room, where guests are treated to tea, sherry, tea sandwiches and sweets like pound cake with raspberry curd.

Upstairs are seven guest rooms, each with private bath, telephone, designer linens and terry robes. Beds vary from twin to kingsize. The corner Blue Room has a French provincial king bed canopied in blue floral chintz with matching duvet cover. It opens onto the upper of two piazzas running the width of the house. The aptly named Linens & Lace comes with a queensize poster bed and an in-room jacuzzi tub for two. Marilyn fashioned the masculine Scheherazade from what had been a lawyer's library. It has windows on three sides and its shelves are stocked with books. Deco furnishings highlight a novel room called Decor Deco. Its kingsize iron bed is draped in filmy white fabric and the swag curtains bear trailing ivy.

The Burkhardts turn down the beds at night and put coffee outside the door in the morning. Breakfast is served on Haviland china at a table for fourteen in the formal dining room, at individual tables in the garden tea room or on the screened side veranda. The meal varies from wine and cheese soufflé to exotic quiches to

Arched doorway of Bermuda rock coral is under front porch of 1790 House.

shrimp and grits. Eggs benedict was the fare at our visit. Guests can work off the calories in a small lap pool in the side yard.

(843) 527-6937 or (800) 251-8805. Seven rooms with private baths. Doubles, $89 to $139. Children accepted. No smoking.

1790 House, 630 Highmarket St., Georgetown 29440.

This architecturally significant house in the West Indies style spoke to Californians John and Pat Wiley. On an inn-hunting tour of the Southeast Coast in 1992, this was their third of six stops. "We fell in love with this house and this town," John recalls. "We never got to our other destinations."

The Wileys kept the rear keeping room with its fireplace, TV, books on local lore, guest refrigerator and hooked rug in a cozy Colonial style, but furnished the rest of the substantial house in haute Victoriana. There's a lot of décor to look at, John acknowledges. "My wife collects dolls and angels."

The dolls show up everywhere, especially in the elegant fireplaced dining room with its long Chippendale table and matching chairs. Here we took breakfast under the watchful gaze of several, not to mention a ticking grandfather's clock and a wall display of silver spoons. Ours started with a baked pear topped with strawberry sauce and chocolate cream muffins. The main event was apple dutch baby with curried fruit mix.

The six accommodations are all quite different. Our room, Gabrielle's Library, was at the rear of the main floor. It was frilly and feminine in shades of lavender, with a queen iron and brass bed. On the second floor are the Indigo and the Rice Planters. The former, with twin pencil-post beds joined as a king and a single sleigh bed, is cheerful with lace curtains, a sitting area and decor in red and blue. The latter is a huge room with a queen canopy step-up bed, two wing chairs and a beautiful blue carpet.

The Prince George Suite, a hideaway under the eaves on the third floor, has a white iron queen bedstead entwined with pink flowers in the bedroom. In the middle is the bathroom with an old-fashioned tub, and in the second room a sitting area and a trundle bed. "Little girls love this room," said John. The Slave Quarters room in the walkout basement has the original wood beamed ceiling and a slate floor. It's done in masculine dark green and burgundy and has a queen bed, a game table and chairs. The bathroom walls are of knotty pine.

Through a pretty garden with winding brick paths, a gazebo and ivy ground cover is the Dependency Cottage. It comes with a brick floor, patterned rugs, a queen bed, two swivel rockers, jacuzzi and separate shower, and dolls everywhere. Guests here may have breakfast delivered to their own patio.

Three bedrooms have cable TV. Sherry is put out in all.

A wraparound porch is a great place to read, perhaps with the companionship of Boots, the inn cat, have a soda from the guest refrigerator, or a drink before going out to dinner. Just off the slave quarters is an outdoor space under the front porch (the facade of which is made of Bermuda rock coral used as ships' ballast from the 1700s). Here you'll find a ping-pong table, hammock and bikes to borrow.

In the inn's **Angel's Touch Tea Room,** a proper British tea is served by reservation Tuesday, Thursday and Saturday from noon to 3.

(843) 546-4821 or (800) 890-7432. Fax (843) 520-0609. Five rooms and one cottage with private baths. Doubles, $85 to $110. Cottage, $135. No smoking.

Alexandra's Inn, 620 Prince St., Georgetown 29440.

A "Gone With the Wind" theme and up-to-date amenities are the hallmarks of this new B&B converted from a private home in 1997 by New Jersey transplants Sandy (Alexandra) and Rob Kempe. They knew exactly what they wanted in a B&B and set about providing it. Rob, a former heating and air-conditioning contractor, can "fix anything," his wife says, "and I'm a people person. So running a B&B fits our lifestyle."

The narrow house, built in 1880, occupies one of historic Georgetown's largest lots, although you'd never know it from the front. The rear of the house opens onto a hidden yard with a pool, a carriage house suite, brick paths, gardens and an array of walnut, fig and magnolia trees, plus a 300-year-old pecan tree. The yard is on view from the back porch, which opens off a large family room.

The five bedrooms come with private baths, working fireplaces, TVs and telephones. The front-corner Scarlett's Room on the main floor has a loveseat at the foot of the step-up queensize mahogany pencil-post bed and an in-room jacuzzi surrounded by three bay windows. Upstairs is Rhett's Room. The large bathroom has a double jacuzzi in one corner, a shower in another corner and a toilet in a third corner. The room, dressed in pale aqua and florals, contains a kingsize cherry sleigh bed and a Victorian loveseat. Across the hall in emerald green is Melanie's Room, with a kingsize cherry rice bed. The front Ashley's Room has an oak queensize poster bed and a double shower complete with seats. All bedrooms have windows that open and seating for two rather than one, resolving two pet peeves of ours and of the Kempes at other inns.

The rear carriage house suite has two bedrooms, living room, kitchen and a new jacuzzi tub for two. It's favored by honeymooners and families.

Breakfast is a hearty affair, served in a dining room with a table for eight plus a deuce.

(843) 527-0233 or (888) 557-0233. Fax (843) 520-0718. Five rooms and two-bedroom carriage house with private baths. Doubles, $95 to $135. Carriage house, $165. Older children accepted. No smoking.

The Shaw House, 613 Cypess Court, Georgetown 29440.

When empty-nesters Mary and Joe Shaw wanted to open Georgetown's first B&B in 1984, the idea was so new hereabouts that "the city didn't know what to do with us," as Mary tells it. "We had never been to a B&B, but thought we could do it." Do it they have ever since, and "we've loved every minute of it."

The Shaws share their rambling, Georgian-looking white house with pillars and black shutters with guests in three large bedrooms, each with queen or kingsize rice beds. Ivy trailed around the lace canopy of the queen bed in the room we saw at one end of the main floor. It came with a sofa, thick carpeting and the antiques, telephone, TV and fresh roses typical in all rooms. The king bedroom upstairs is much larger and has an extra dressing room.

Guests enjoy the run of the house, which is at the end of a shaded residential neighborhood adjacent to the marshlands that typify rice-plantation country. Beyond a formal living room of traditional vintage lies an expansive family room that claims "the best view in town." Big windows look onto a vista of the marshes, where birds and wildlife entertain guests. Bird-watchers are in their element here. "We also have a little family of foxes who pass by," reports Mary.

Ever the gracious Southern hostess, she plies guests with tea, wine and banana bread and pound cake in the afternoon and puts out chocolates during nightly turndown. The morning meal includes lots of quiches (shrimp the day of our visit), pancakes, grits casserole or corned beef on toast, accompanied by juice, fresh fruit and biscuits. Depending on the number of guests in house, it's taken at a table for six in the chandeliered dining room, a table for four on the rear sunporch or, quite romantically, a table for two beside the window in that great family room.

(843) 546-9663. Three rooms with private baths. Doubles, $65 to $70.

Dozier Guest House, 220 Queen St., Georgetown 29440.

Antiquity reigns but comforts abound in this charming B&B built about 1770 for Captain John Dozier. Tom and Chris Roach, doing much of the work themselves, converted what had been a private home with an apartment in a lengthy renovation starting in 1989.

They offer three comfortable guest rooms upstairs. Guests are welcomed in the main house via an entrance from the side veranda, but later may access their rooms through a separate outside entrance that allows for a mix of conviviality or privacy as they wish. "With only three rooms," says Chris, who is full-time innkeeper while her husband works, "we get to enjoy our guests."

Their guests enjoy a handsome living room painted a rich green, with a well-worn step down to a chandeliered dining room painted a carnation pink. Chris likes to point out the heart-pine floors "that people would kill for these days" and – not in the same breath – a rare "coffin door" off the side porch.

A spinning wheel from her grandmother's family sets the tone in the upstairs hallway. Each guest room has a private bath with clawfoot tub and shower, TV and fireplace. The largest is the John Dozier in front, which opens to the second-floor porch with its Pawleys Island hammock. Its kingsize poster bed is covered with no fewer than 21 pillows and shams – each carefully put aside when Chris turns down the bed and leaves a treat of cookies or mints. Three steps descend to the original bathroom with pressed-tin walls and ceilings. Its considerable renovation took six months of Tom's life. Also accessible to the porch is the rear Elizabeth Giles Room with a queen brass bed and a sofabed. An airy bathroom has been created in what had been a corner sunporch. The rear Lydia White Room lacks porch access but comes with a king bed – and another twenty or so pillows – as well as a small sitting room.

Banana french toast with praline syrup is Chris's breakfast specialty, served in the dining room with china and silver or, weather permitting, on the side porch. Egg casseroles and belgian waffles are other possibilities. Homemade muffins, coffeecake or cream-cheese danish pastries and fresh orange juice accompany.

(843) 527-1350 or (800) 640-1350. Three rooms with private baths. Doubles, $90 to $110, all taxes included. Children accepted. No smoking.

Mansfield Plantation, 1776 Mansfield Road, Georgetown 29440.

A two-mile dirt driveway through a forest five miles north of town leads to this antebellum plantation considered "the most architecturally intact in Georgetown County." On 900 private acres beside the Black River marshlands, the circa 1800 National Historic Landmark offers spiffy and comfortable accommodations in three dependencies as well the experience of residing on an authentic rice plantation complete with the somewhat dilapidated remains of a slave village.

Sally and Jim Cahalan inherited the property with its low-slung, white brick and wood frame main house from her parents, who vacationed here from Columbia. Sally, who had been director for eighteen years of the Wheatland house museum in Lancaster, Pa., jumped at the chance to do something in her native South Carolina. Like other modern-day plantation owners, she needed to find a way for the vast property to support itself. Group tours and special events (a wine festival and concerts on the lawn) helped, but the Cahalans took the bull by the horns and moved here in 1994 to run it full-time as a B&B with a planned restaurant.

Sally's passion for antiques – she "started buying Victorian furniture when it was dirt cheap" – served her well in furnishing the main house. Ornate molding adorns the ceiling of the main parlor with a 19th-century piano and 19th-century paintings, which opens onto a rear library with a TV. On the other side of the main hall is a second parlor with an ante room, both best described as *very* Victorian. Off the main parlor is a dining room where an enormous table for twelve sits beneath a brass chandelier. Shunning the original kitchen below, Sally worked out of a closet to serve breakfasts to guests, pending completion of her newly built professional kitchen that was under construction at our visit. That kitchen opens onto a new rear sunporch overlooking the marshlands, a perfect spot for her planned dinners for groups by reservation.

Guest accommodations are in three nearby dependencies, each built of handsome red brick with green shutters. The old kitchen building and a schoolhouse built by the rice planter for his children are original. What is called the North Guest House was built in the 1930s in the Colonial Revival style of the main house.

All eight large bedrooms have original coal-burning fireplaces with carved mantelpieces and the fancy woodwork characteristic of the main house. Arguably the most choice are the two upstairs and two downstairs in the guest house, which has a Charleston-style curving outside staircase to the second floor in the rear and a large brick terrace shaped like a palm-leaf fan in front. Three rooms here have kingsize beds and one has two doubles. One on the first floor adds a sitting area with sofa and two chairs. Designer sheets match the bedspreads and floral chintz fabrics here and on the three antique four-poster double beds and a king bed in bedrooms in the other dependencies. A hanging swing and a hammock

Overnight guests stay in dependencies surrounding main house at Mansfield Plantation.

caught our attention outside rooms in the old kitchen. A front veranda with wicker rockers drew us to the schoolhouse.

A plantation-style breakfast starts with a fruit course, perhaps pears and cream, apple crisp or blueberry cobbler. Cereal, muffins, homemade biscuits, and cheese and grits accompany the main event, which could be belgian waffles, quiche or egg casserole with venison sausage made from the plantation's own deer, which sometimes startle guests as they bound across the dirt road at night.

(843) 546-6961 or (800) 355-3223. Fax (803) 546-6961. Eight rooms with private baths. Doubles, $95 to $115. Children and pets welcome.

Litchfield Plantation Inn, King's River Road, Box 290, Pawleys Island 29585.

So you want to stay in a real plantation? Perhaps have it all to yourself? Try this for size.

The stately Litchfield Plantation house, circa 1750, is set in the midst of 600 acres at the end of a quarter-mile avenue of live oaks. Once the heart of one of the area's more thriving rice plantations, it overlooks the former rice fields along the Waccamaw River.

It's the "inn" portion of the posh Litchfield Plantation golf resort and residential community, which also offers 26 other accommodations in cottages and villas.

Guests stay overnight in four substantial bed chambers in the house, which has been restored to the era with its original floors, mantels and chair rails. Two are on the main floor off a handsome living room with windows onto the rear brick patio and rice fields, Intracoastal Waterway and river beyond. They offer queen beds, thick carpeting and plush sitting areas, and the Gun Room Suite has a library/ sitting room amid a collection of guns. Up a curving staircase are two more accommodations with kingsize rice poster beds. The Ballroom Suite in the North Wing is breathtaking: a front living room opens onto a private veranda facing the "Avenue of Oaks." The rear bedroom overlooks the rice fields and offers more plush chairs plus an enormous bath containing a double jacuzzi complete with pillows and a step-in shower.

Guests here are on their own. They register at the Litchfield Plantation Visitor Center three miles away along Route 17. Afternoon refreshments and the makings for a continental breakfast are put out in the full kitchen of the plantation house. Brick paths lead to a swimming pool, tennis courts and the nearby Carriage House Club restaurant, which offers dinner to the public nightly.

Guests here like the privacy and seclusion. They have the run of the house and grounds. They also may encounter signs of a ghost. What other explanation for the occasional sound of bells ringing outside in the middle of the night?

(843) 237-9121 or (800) 869-1410. Fax (843) 237-8558. Two rooms and two suites with private baths. March-November: doubles $185, suites $220. Rest of year: doubles $150, suites $175. Two-night minimum weekends. No children. No smoking.

Dining Spots

Rice Paddy, 819 Front St., Georgetown.

After a dozen years on Duke Street, owners Susan Hibbs and Susan Felder moved their highly rated restaurant in 1996 to a waterfront location overlooking the Sampit River and the Harborwalk. The dining areas are casually elegant, their laminated wood tables left uncovered to show off their tops painted variously with tomatoes, fish, oysters and such. Service is polished and the food, first-rate.

Seafood, lamb and veal dishes star on the interesting menu. Appetizers include conch fritters with tomato salsa, deep-fried oysters wrapped in bacon and goat cheese croustades with tapenade and smoked salmon. Our dinner got off to a good start with hot sourdough rolls served with sweet butter and a tossed salad dressed with raspberry vinaigrette, blue cheese and pinenuts. Main courses range widely from pan-roased snapper with wild mushrooms and leeks to pan-fried quail with country ham gravy and grits and roast rack of lamb moutarde. Seasonal specialties include deep-fried soft-shell crabs and bacon-wrapped shad roe served with grits. We were well satisfied with the signature crab cakes and the bahamian grouper, accompanied by rice and brussels sprouts. Crème brûlée, fruit cobbler and lemon mousse with berries were among the desserts.

The Rice Paddy to Go store offers takeout meals.

(843) 546-2021. Entrées, $15.95 to $20.95. Lunch, Tuesday-Saturday 11:30 to 2:30. Dinner, Monday-Saturday 6 to 10.

The River Room, 801 Front St., Georgetown.

Serious seafood is the billing for this casual establishment, a dark and nautical square dining room jutting toward the water. An aquarium is at the entry, and the walls wear wooden oars and pictures of steamers and sailing boats. Owner Sid Hood relished the history of a Union gunboat sunk in Winyah Bay so much that he gave its name to his ice cream shop, the Harvest Moon.

Here the short printed menu, accented with pictures of colorful tropical fish, is supplemented by a host of specials. Grilled tuna with basil cream sauce, grilled dolphin with cucumber-caper relish, herb-encrusted grouper and grilled pork tenderloin with honey soy sauce were among the additions to the standard fare of sautéed local shrimp, crab cakes, shrimp and scallop tasso, Santa Fe chicken and ribeye oscar (grilled steak topped with Alaskan king crab). There are fried seafood

Broad avenue of live oaks leads to Litchfield Plantation Inn.

platters for those who prefer. Local shrimp and grits, oysters rockefeller and McClellanville crab balls are signature appetizers.

(843) 527-4110. Entrées, $11.95 to $19.95. Lunch, Monday-Saturday 11 to 2:30. Dinner, Monday-Saturday 5 to 10.

Orange Blossom Café, 107 Orange St., Georgetown.

Greek music plays softly in the two dining rooms where the tables are covered with assorted business cards under glass. Andy Thomopolous bills his as the Grand Strand's only authentic Greek restaurant. The Greek accent is decidedly that, for the other themes are "sizzling steaks with ladies' specials," a basic "Italian corner" and "seafood specialties." Andy covers all the bases and is beloved by locals for his large portions and reasonable prices. Everyone raves over his Greek flounder. And he reputedly makes the rounds of every table every night.

Although he was nowhere in evidence the Wednesday night we were there, we can attest to the large portions and reasonable prices. The Greek leg of lamb with Greek potatoes ($9.95) was a heaping mound that failed to do justice to either. The accompanying Greek salad was better. Best was the thick and juicy prime rib, far tastier than its $9.95 price tag would indicate. Southern vegetables and a basket of crackers accompanied. A leaden baklava followed.

From the short Greek/Italian wine list, a Kouros red for $18.50 cost almost as much as the meal. The oil lamps flickered, all the other patrons seemed to know each other, and the price was right.

(843) 527-5060. Entrées, $7.95 to $13.95. Lunch, Monday-Saturday 11 to 3. Dinner, Wednesday-Saturday 5 to 9.

The Pink Magnolia, 719 Front St., Georgetown.

"Good choice, you've picked the best thing on the menu," volunteered the waitress as one of us ordered the fried chicken salad for lunch. And as for our other choice, chicken magnolia, "that's the next best thing on the menu."

Who knows whether she would have said the same thing had the orders been for

160   South Carolina

the shrimp salad sandwich on a croissant, the crab quiche or even a burger or a grilled cheese sandwich? The fried chicken salad must be an acquired taste, for it left us unimpressed. And the chicken magnolia, a grilled breast topped with crab au gratin served over pasta, struck us as overkill. The best thing was the accompanying house salad with its pepper-parmesan dressing.

That, and the view from the shaded portion of the large rear deck, watching the parade of boats on the Samprit River and the pedestrians moseying along the Harborwalk. Sunworshippers were in their element in the uncovered portion of the deck that warm spring day. Others were content inside the long, narrow dining room, nondescript but for its dark feeling and air conditioning.

The menu touts its "fine Southern cuisine," mainly fried. Local skeptics believe the restaurant is riding on a reputation boosted by a blurb in Southern Living magazine. Yet its catering services and private evening parties are in demand.

(843) 527-6506. Entrées, $4.95 to $7.50. Lunch, Monday-Saturday 11:30 to 2. Full liquor license.

Frank's Restaurant & Bar, 10434 Highway 17 North, Pawleys Island.

Creative American cuisine and an extensive wine list are featured in this wildly popular restaurant and bar, for which reservations are difficult to come by.

The main restaurant in front is more formal. The changing menu ranges widely from roasted garlic and rosemary chicken to pan-roasted veal chop. Typical choices are seared sea scallops on a bed of spiced lentils, grilled swordfish on tobacco onions and lamb chops with braised shiitake mushrooms and new potato hash browns.

We're partial to **Frank's Outback,** a tree-shaded outdoor courtyard connected to a bar and bistro beyond. The atmosphere is ever-so Key Westy, made even more so by the three tail-less stray cats we saw wandering about. (The staff feed the strays and go through 40 pounds of cat food a week, a waitress advised.)

The extensive menu here is contemporary international, from the sushi of the day to the carpaccio of beef and the conch fritters offered as appetizers. Wood-fired pizzas, exotic salads and assertive pastas are offered. Main courses could be salmon baked in parchment with julienned vegetables and grilled pork tenderloin on black beans with chipotle sauce.

(843) 237-3030. Entrées, Frank's $12.50 to $22.50; Outback, $14.95 to $19.95. Dinner, Monday-Saturday 6 to 9:30.

The Mayor's House Restaurant, 2614 Highway 17 South, Litchfield.

A Myrtle Beach restaurateur took over the old mayor's house beside a pond and converted it into one of the area's better restaurants.

The extensive menu runs the gamut from regional Southern to continental. For starters, how about blackened green tomatoes with stone-ground grits cake and goat cheese sauce or oysters rockefeller? Low Country shrimp and grits shares top billing among entrées with such classics as bouillabaisse, coquilles st. jacques, lobster cardinale, duckling à l'orange, steak au poivre and veal oscar. Rack of lamb and châteaubriand are carved tableside.

Flamed tableside are desserts like bananas foster and cherries jubilee. The praline-pecan ice cream pie is highly rated.

(843) 237-9082. Entrées, $12.95 to $25.95. Dinner, Monday-Saturday 6 to 10, Sunday from 5.

Diversions

Busy Highway 17 traffic bypasses the heart of historic Georgetown, and the casual traveler might remember Georgetown more for its International Paper and Georgetown Steel Corp. mills as viewed from the bridge over the Sampit River at the southern entrance to town. You have only to detour a block off the main highway to find the historic district, where the southern charm is everywhere apparent.

The sixteen-block historic district is eminently walkable and embraces elegant homes, museums and landmarks like the large Prince George Winyah Episcopal Church, built about 1750 with old bricks from British ships' ballasts. Three informative tours, including a walk led by town native Nell Morris Cribb, leave from Front Street locations.

Excursion boats take visitors past rice plantations along the four rivers that converge on Georgetown. The Jolly Roger tall ship schooner gives two-hour harbor tours along the Winyah Bay. Several nearby plantations are open for tours.

The Harborwalk, a 1,100-foot-long boardwalk protruding over the Sampit River, allows pedestrians to browse along the waterfront where tall-masted sailing ships once arrived with goods from Europe and left with Low Country indigo, rice and lumber. Hidden behind downtown stores, the Harborwalk is connected to Front Street via pleasant little parks and greenways.

Artists are turning Georgetown into what one innkeeper calls "an artsy little town." She cites the Made in the Shade lawn concerts, a "gallery crawl" and a new cooperative, The Georgetown Art Gallery at 732 Front St. The Swamp Fox Players present four plays a year in the art-deco Strand Theater.

The Rice Museum, 633 Front St., Georgetown.

Located behind the landmark 1842 town clock in the Old Market Building is this musty museum that portrays the area's unusual heritage of rice plantations. A video called "Garden of Gold" compares the preparation of dikes for ricelands along six rivers with the building of the pyramids in Egypt, and notes that abolition of slavery after the Civil War meant the eventual demise of the local rice culture. By the 1840s about half the rice consumed in the United States was grown at 170 rice plantations around Georgetown. The last commercial crop was harvested in 1908. "No other area was so dependent upon one crop for so long," the narration intones. The video may be of more general interest than all the artifacts, photos and maps from the rice culture era.

(843) 546-7423. Open Monday-Saturday 9:30 to 4:30. Adults, $3.

Kaminski House Museum, 1003 Front St., Georgetown.

On a bluff with a sweeping view of the Sampit River at the other end of Front Street is this 1760s sea captain's home filled with antiques collected by local businessman and mayor Harold Kaminski, who willed the house to the city. The rooms are full of primarily American antiques, silver and crystal, with emphasis on American furniture, such as a Chippendale dining room table crafted in Charleston. A 15th-century Spanish wedding chest is a highlight. The museum offers visitors a chance to experience life in a townhouse as opposed to rural independent plantation lifestyle. An observation deck overlooks the river.

(843) 546-7706. Tours, Monday-Saturday 10 to 4, Sunday 1 to 4. Adults, $5.

Hobcaw Barony, 22 Hobcaw Road, Georgetown.

Some 17,500 acres of dormant rice plantations were purchased in 1907 by financier Bernard M. Baruch. Three-hour tours of the property, offered Tuesday and Thursday on four-wheel drive vehicles, include stops at the stately Baruch home facing Winyah Bay, where he entertained the likes of Franklin Roosevelt, Winston Churchill, Henry Clare Booth Luce and Gen. George Marshall. The focal point is the visitor center (formerly the **Bellefield Nature Center),** a plantation home and stables he built for his tomboy daughter Belle, who willed the entire property to the state. The off-again, on-again center at the entrance to Hobcaw Barony was revived in 1998 by new managers Richard and Caroline Camlin. They scheduled wildlife tours, birdwatching and kayak expeditions to North Inlet. The nature center has plant and animal displays, a saltwater touch tank with local sea life, and exhibits about the research activities of the Baruch Institutes. An audio-visual program details the Baruch family history there.

(843) 546-4623. Center open Monday-Friday 10 to 5, Saturday 10 to 2, free. Property tours Tuesday and Thursday at 10 and 1, $15.

Huntington Beach State Park, Highway 17 South, Murrells Inlet.
The pristine, nearly deserted three-mile-long ocean beach is viewed locally as the kind of place that no longer exists along the developed East Coast. The 2,500-acre park has four miles of nature trails, a saltwater marsh and a freshwater lagoon, and offers a busy schedule of nature events. A boardwalk winding far into the salt marsh enables visitors to watch tall wading birds and raptors seeking their prey. The less adventurous may get to see the 200 alligators the park ranger told us haunt the waters along the west causeway out to the beach (we saw part of only one alligator at our visit).
A park highlight is **Atalaya,** a forbidding looking, low-slung Moorish-style castle. It was built in 1931 in the form of a square with a 40-foot-high water tower by Archer and Anna Huntington of Brookgreen Gardens (see Extra-Special). Those in the know find the 55 rooms occupied by the couple, their numerous servants and Mrs. Huntington's sculpture studios fascinating. Others find them ugly and creepy. The castle grounds include an indoor courtyard, a former stable, dog kennels and bear pens. Guided tours are available daily in summer, or visitors may wander on their own. The place is at its best during the annual juried Atalaya Arts and Crafts Festival in late September.

(843) 237-4440. Park open daily 6 a.m. to 10 p.m., April-September, to 6 p.m. rest of year. Admission $4, March-November, free rest of year. Atalaya open daily 9 to 5 with park admission, plus 50 cents in summer, free rest of year.

Shopping. Some of the rainbow-colored stores along Georgetown's Front Street back up to the Harborwalk, a twelve-foot-wide boardwalk paralleling the Sampit River. **The Added Touch** is a ladies' boutique, and **Plum Pretty** offers pretty clothing. Shop for children at **The Calico Closet** and **Hareloom Toys. Pinckney's Exchange** stocks gifts, china and specialty foods. **The Osprey's Nest** is the largest gift and collectibles shop. Huge vases and fancy antiques caught our eye at **Augustus Carolina. The Prevost Gallery** adjoins the Rice Museum.
The delightful **Hammock Shops** complex along Highway 17 on Pawleys Island take its name from the world-famous Pawleys Island rope hammocks, which are featured at The Original Hammock Shop. Nearly two dozen fashionable specialty shops occupy restored buildings that once served as a schoolhouse, a post office and a mercantile store for the nearby rice plantation community.

Fountain of the Muses is among attractions at Brookgreen Gardens.

Extra-Special

Brookgreen Gardens, Highway 17, Pawleys Island.

The site of four 18th-century rice plantations, Brookgreen was acquired in 1930 by railroad magnate Archer Huntington as a setting for the works of his sculptress wife, Anna Hyatt Huntington. It has evolved over the years into the world's largest outdoor sculpture garden, plus a wildlife park that protects the habitats of indigenous animals and plants in their native settings. Brookgreen's 9,100 acres stretch from the Atlantic Ocean to the historic ricefields along the Waccamaw River. "Gray Oaks of Mystery, a ten-minute film shown in the large visitor center, sets the stage for the experience to come.

The remarkable complex is home to more than 500 examples of American figurative sculpture by 237 sculptors, gracefully displayed among 2,000 species of plants in a series of exceptionally attractive botanical gardens that surprise and delight at every turn. They range from a huge Pegasus and a fifteen-piece extravaganza called the Fountain of the Muses to little nymphs resting and a pint-size greyhound reclining in the plantings. Classical music plays in the background and it's an altogether peaceful place. In the 23-acre wildlife park, a trail leads through a huge cypress aviary of native wildfowl and past an otter pond and alligator swamp, where we found two alligators and, surprise, an alligator sculpture.

In a new endeavor with an extra $6 charge, the Springfield, a 50-passenger pontoon boat, winds through the scenic creeks and marshes of ricefields never before accessible to the public as a Brookgreen naturalist relates their story. The creek excursions are a precursor of an ambitious plan expanding the 300-acre outdoor museum into a 3,000-acre managed habitat connected by trails, trams and boats weaving through waterways, swamps, rice fields and uplands called the Low Country at Brookgreen Gardens. Meanwhile, for sustenance, snacks are available in the outlying Old Kitchen Garden, and lunch with interesting sandwiches and specialty dishes in the appealing Terrace Café. Keepsakes is the large gift shop. In season, Brookgreen is open at night for sunset boat cruises, suppers in the Terrace Café, wildlife park strolls and walks through softly lit gardens.

(843) 247-4218 or (800) 849-1931. Open daily, 9:30 to 4:45; summer until dark. Adults, $7.50.

Front piazza at Two Meeting Street Inn overlooks The Battery in typical Charleston scene.

Charleston, S.C.

Cosmopolitan Charmer

Remember the Charleston dance craze? Porgy & Bess? The Battery? Charleston she-crab soup? Fort Sumter? The Spoleto Festival?

Few cities its size have left more legacies than Charleston, an early flowering settlement that played a pivotal role in the nation's infancy. Founded in 1670 by English colonists and named Charlestowne for King Charles II, the waterfront city at the confluence of the Ashley and Cooper rivers quickly grew to become the largest south of Philadelphia. Thanks to seafaring trade and a plantation economy, it also was America's wealthiest. The arts were early and enduring beneficiaries.

Charleston won for America the first decisive victory of the Revolutionary War and fired the shot that started the Civil War. Through subsequent occupation, earthquakes, fires and hurricanes, Charleston has always bounced back, especially after Hurricane Hugo in 1989.

Today more than ever, this proud old port city – heart of South Carolina's Low Country – is chic and cosmopolitan. It's imbued with a sophisticated sense of place for residents as well as mystical allure for visitors. Readers of Condé Nast Traveler voted it one of the top twenty destinations in the world.

For the visitor, a walk along Charleston's cobblestone streets and alleys unveils three centuries of history. Antique cannons along the Battery evoke memories of war. Merchant ships ply the waters of Charleston Harbor, much as they have since the 1700's. Church bells toll the hour. Charleston, "the holy city," is the only one of size in America where church steeples dominate the skyline.

Magnificent antebellum mansions and unique Charleston "single houses" placed sideways stand in nicely preserved grandeur. In fact, the houses and gardens of Charleston are its most cherished legacies. The square mile from Broad Street to the Battery, between King and East Bay streets, offers more architectural landmarks and genteel charm than perhaps any place in America. It is in Charleston that you learn that porches are not verandas but piazzas. The lovely walled gardens of the city are as compelling in their own way as are the famed plantation gardens of the surrounding Low Country.

Take a horse-drawn carriage ride. Walk along the Battery and the harbor. Admire the pastel houses of Rainbow Row. Meander at will down historic alleys. Enjoy the scene at the new Waterfront Park. Shop the haute stores of King Street and Charleston Place. Visit the plantations. Stay in a small inn or B&B. Eat very well.

Savor the charms of a city like no other.

Inn Spots

Most of Charleston's inns are bigger than the norm. Some are not as warm and welcoming as reputation would have them, but rather curt and commercial. Few are owner-occupied. It is a challenge to find the "right" places to stay because many have the required ratings and the visitor center (and sometimes innkeepers themselves) decline to get specific in referrals. "We recommend everybody" is a frequent response – or sometimes nobody, other than themselves. Availability of parking may be a consideration.

Two Meeting Street Inn, 2 Meeting St., Charleston 29401.

They don't need to advertise, they don't accept credit cards and their brochure is a simple blue cardboard strip printed in black. What the Spell family have is location, location, location.

That's the key to this long-running B&B's success, although the deft hospitality imparted by the Spells and their staff pays off, too. This is one of Charleston's few inns with an owner presence. The 1892 Queen Anne-style structure is at the apex of the historic district at the foot of Meeting Street, facing the Battery park and the harbor. An arched veranda takes full advantage of the view.

"We have a great location and a great house," concedes Peter Spell, innkeeper with his wife Jean and, until lately, their eldest daughter, Karen Spell Shaw. "And our guests get to use all the common areas just like the people did when it was first built."

The structure became a guest house in 1931, and has been in the Spell family since 1946. Peter's aunt willed it to his older brother David, who added breakfast service in 1980. David, a bachelor, ran it as a B&B for ten years before tiring of the pace. He sold it in 1990 to Peter, who retired after 31 years as a civil engineer. He and Jean were assisted by Karen and her husband Rob, who opened The Governor's House Inn (see below) in 1998. Meanwhile, David Spell continues the family tradition with three meticulously appointed guest rooms at the Belvedere B&B at 40 Rutledge Ave., overlooking tiny Colonial Lake.

Built as a wedding gift for a daughter, this house features twelve-foot ceilings, hardwood floors and seven Tiffany stained-glass windows. The builder was a friend of Lewis Comfort Tiffany, who signed two windows behind the piano in the parlor. Another Tiffany window graces the dining room, paneled in old English oak. The feeling is definitely Victorian in a city that generally is not.

The nine bedrooms come with private baths, queensize beds (except for one with two doubles) and oriental rugs. TVs are secreted in armoires; there are no telephones. A main-floor guest room off the entry foyer has a canopy bed backed by floral fabric, two wing chairs in a turret and a working fireplace. Overhead is another room with a fireplace and a sofa, this one with an antique desk in the window of the turret and one of the inn's two private porches. The four other rooms on the second floor include a side room, a carbon copy of the dining room configuration below, with a curved window and walls and the original bathroom with a slab marble vanity and a clawfoot tub. A rear guest room with fireplace has a private balcony overlooking the garden and a similar bathroom, which was the first in the house. Three smaller rooms with sloping ceilings occupy third-floor dormer areas and command lower rates.

Sweets, cheese and finger foods accompany afternoon tea, served on the broad veranda that wraps around the house. Flavored coffee and sherry also are served. In the morning, the staff bakes Texas-size muffins (cranberry-orange, blueberry, cinnamon twirl) to augment fresh fruit for continental breakfast. It's enjoyed in the elegant dining room, on the veranda or in the rear garden. If you can possibly tear yourself away, the most evocative section of Charleston lies just outside.

(843) 723-7322. Nine rooms with private baths. Doubles, $155 to $265. Two-night minimum weekends. Children over 12. No smoking. No credit cards.

The Governor's House Inn, 117 Broad St., Charleston 29401.

Where its sister B&B has location, the Spell family's newly opened inn claims history. The 1760 National Historic Landmark was the residence of Gov. Edward Rutledge, the youngest signer of the Declaration of Independence. This block was spared in the 1860 fire, so it's one of the few pre-Revolutionary buildings surviving in Charleston.

Karen Spell Shaw, who was innkeeper for her parents' Two Meeting Street Inn, took on this venture in 1998 with her husband, Robert Hill Shaw III. "This is their project," her mother Jean insisted as she led a tour shortly before opening. "Karen designed and decorated – she has a wonderful eye."

One could sense it in the fabrics, the furnishings and the artworks resting beneath plastic coverings as contractors rushed the renovation toward completion.

For 25 years, the house had been the residence of a couple whom Jean Spell knew from college days. They raised five children in the house and were happy to sell to their longtime friends. They even sold some of their prized antiques, including a dining table expandable to seat sixteen. But the rest of the furnishings are newly acquired and deluxe, from king or queensize Charleston rice poster beds to wicker furniture for the south piazza.

Guests enter from a garden courtyard off the rear parking area. A sizable living room with yellow walls and a Colonial feeling harbors a grand piano, which Rob plays. The front library is appointed in cranberry red. Seasonal muffins and local

Governor's House Inn is one of few pre-Revolutionary War structures surviving in Charleston.

fruits are served for continental breakfast in the chandeliered dining room or on the piazza. Afternoon tea is taken here as well. Evening sherry is decanted in the living room.

A graceful curving staircase leads to the second floor, which has four spacious corner bedrooms with crown moldings along the ceilings. All have marble baths with separate showers, televisions and telephones. Triple-hung, floor-length windows open to the upper piazza from two rooms. One mini-suite has a library/ sitting area in a small entry hall. The master bedroom with a king poster bed has its own porch, a jacuzzi tub and a wet bar with refrigerator. A smaller room with a queen canopy bed angled from the corner is painted a bright red.

Atop the stairs on the third floor is a sitting area with a view across the rooftops toward the historic St. Michael's Episcopal Church steeple, a local icon. "It's a bit of a climb to get here but a great feeling," said Jean, barely pausing to catch her breath. The three rooms on this floor are nicely tucked beneath sloping ceilings.

More romantic accommodations are found in a rear carriage and kitchen house. The main-floor suite contains the original brick baking oven (a portion was left exposed behind glass), floral fabric upholstered furniture in the pale green living room, a gas fireplace, a dining area with wet bar, a queen pencil-post bed in the bedroom and a jacuzzi bath. Upstairs is a second jacuzzi suite with exposed rafters and beige grass-cloth walls bearing large Audubon prints that pick up the colors of the fabrics.

Three more rooms on the lower garden level of the main house were to be ready by the spring of 1999.

"I've got innkeeping in my blood," says Karen. "We're not building an empire, but this is such a spectacular property. It's our last hurrah."

(843) 720-2070 or (800) 720-9812. Ten rooms and two suites with private baths. Doubles, $165 to $305. Suites, $305 to $330. Two-night minimum weekends. No smoking. No credit cards.

John Rutledge House Inn, 116 Broad St., Charleston 29401.

This 1763 National Historic Landmark bills itself as "America's most historic inn." That's not so much a testament to its accommodations, which are thoroughly up to date and luxurious, as to its heritage as the home of John Rutledge. He was president of South Carolina when it was a republic, commander-in-chief of the South Carolina militia during the Revolutionary War, a signer of the U.S. constitution and chief justice of the U.S. Supreme Court. Yes, George Washington called here in 1791 and breakfasted with Mrs. Rutledge. The second-floor ballroom and library where guests now sip evening wine, sherry and brandy hosted many an early patriot and statesman.

The house had been abandoned for ten years when local hotelier Richard Widman got his hands on it. He had come to Charleston in 1979 as general manager of the Mills House Hotel and went on to develop the Kings Courtyard Inn, an early 41-room historic hotel on King Street. A major renovation in 1989 turned the Rutledge and two outbuildings into what hotel evaluators quickly rated the top inn in the city.

Check out South Carolina's palmetto tree symbol and the Federal eagle embedded in the intricate green ironwork along the facades of the two front porches that look as if they'd be at home in the French Quarter of New Orleans. Inside, you may be seated in a front parlor off the foyer – that is, if the William Moultrie suite is not otherwise occupied. It was not until sometime later that we learned that the parlor with working fireplace opened into a large bedroom with kingsize canopy bed, plus a bathroom with jacuzzi tub and separate shower. Ditto for the John Rutledge suite on the other side of the hall, where another parlor showcases one of the home's elaborate parquet floors – different in each room – and a bedroom holds a queen canopy rice bed.

The genuine common room is the aforementioned ballroom, upstairs in front and described as "the grand sitting room and library." A display case in a far corner holds items unearthed in an archaeological dig before the renovation, but guests are more likely to savor the less obvious feeling of history in a room where visitors helped determine a nation's destiny more than two centuries ago.

Not that all that many guests feel the need to spend much time in so imposing a room. Occupants of the nine other handsomely furnished rooms in the house have kingsize, queen or two double beds, sitting areas with an armchair and ottoman and perhaps two other chairs or a loveseat, telephones and TVs ensconced in armoires. The Thomas Heyward mini-suite appeals with its dark green walls and cream moldings, a marble fireplace, king bed and whirlpool tub. The bathrooms here are illuminated with mirrored candle sconces on dimmer switches. Three bedrooms on the lower level of the house, which is called the wine cellar, come with brick floors, king or two double beds and plush seating.

Less elaborate are guest quarters in the two rear carriage houses across a nondescript terrace behind the main inn. One building is original, and the other is rebuilt on the foundation of the early kitchen. These are small but comfortable, favored for their "charm and seclusion."

The staff serves a continental breakfast to the rooms, on the terrace or in the bar room. The signature dish is hot sherried fruit served with Rutledge biscuits, both of which we found worthy of their requested publication in Bon Appetit magazine. Innkeeper Linda Bishop is partial to the cinnamon swirl french toast and the shrimp with grits, part of the full breakfast available for an additional

Ornate second-floor piazza at John Rutledge House Inn looks out on Broad Street.

charge. Although the service is first-rate, some guests wish the Rutledge had more of an "inn" feeling and a personal touch.

(843) 723-7999 or (800) 476-9741. Fax (843) 720-2615. Sixteen rooms and three suites with private baths. All weekends and midweek spring and fall: doubles $235 to $275, suites $345. Midweek, winter and summer: doubles $170 to $235, suites $275.

Wentworth Mansion, 149 Wentworth St., Charleston 29401.

The latest feather in local hotel impresario Rick Widman's cap is this grandiose Second Empire mansion built in 1886 by a wealthy cotton merchant and considered locally at the time an example of the excesses of the new rich. Last serving as offices for the headquarters of an insurance company, it retains a solid aura. No ordinary inn, this. It's Charleston's tribute to the Gilded Age. A bit removed from the historic area, it's more a grand country house hotel – albeit in the midst of a city – on the order of Vanderbilt Hall in Newport, R.I., or Keswick Hall in Charlottesville, Va.

After a $6 million restoration, The Wentworth opened in the fall of 1998 with 21 luxury guest rooms and a restaurant in the works. Both were designed to appeal to Charleston's most affluent visitors.

Crystal chandeliers and parquet floors glisten in the main-floor common areas with walls of mahogany, fireplaces of sculpted marble, original Tiffany stained-glass windows and, literally, never-ending detail. A small parlor is the setting for afternoon tea and lemonade, followed by wine tastings from 5 to 7. One of the original back porches has been enclosed for a library, where decanters of port, sherry and brandy are at the ready. Another enclosed porch is now a tiled, light and airy haunt for what is called an upscale continental breakfast of fresh fruits, breads, croissants and cinnamon rolls. The walls here contain photos of the original family and rooms to impart a human scale.

Heavy oak doors open into guest quarters best described as stately, even regal. Beige and gray fabrics that look like ultra-suede but we're told are a type of velvet dignify the windows and form canopies for the kingsize sleigh beds. Thick oriental carpets accent the parquet floors. All rooms have baths with oversize jacuzzi tubs, most with separate, walk-in glass showers. Dimmer switches, weigh scales, hair dryers and closets with automatic lights, waffle-weave robes, safes and irons are standard. Armoires hold large-screen TVs, VCRs and cassette players. One fourth-floor room has a jacuzzi tub in the attic window open to the bedroom. Three rooms in the East Wing, otherwise known as the servants' quarters, are smaller and comforting. Two we saw were blessed with private outdoor porches (six mansion rooms come with enclosed sunporches).

Several rooms have day beds or sofabeds for extra guests. We're certain they have chairs for seating, though frankly we did not notice them. Truth be told, the appointments, though rich, come across as rather bland. "We were looking for understated elegance, not Victorian gaudy," said Rick Widman, who was setting his sights on producing a five-diamond, five-star establishment. To that end, he hired as managers Scott and Louise Williams, who already knew that level from Virginia's Inn at Little Washington.

One of the perks of the place is a lofty cupola. Climb the spiral staircase from the fourth floor and step out onto a (fortunately) railed rooftop deck with a view of the historic skyline and both the Cooper and Ashley rivers.

Outside, a manicured garden leads to a 50-seat restaurant and meeting facility in the former carriage house and stable along the side of the property. Well traveled chef Patrick Ramsey was preparing a dinner menu of Low Country cuisine for a setting that was to be casually elegant and open to the public. The stable was being considered for conversion into a spa.

(843) 853-1886 or (888) 466-1886. Fax (843) 720-5290. Eighteen rooms and three suites. Doubles, $275 to $350. Suites, $450 to $625. Smoking restricted.

The Hayne House, 30 King St., Charleston 29401.

Perhaps most like the personally run B&Bs with ample breakfasts found elsewhere in the country but lacking in Charleston is this low-key property in the heart of the quiet residential historic district, about a block from the Battery. In 1994, local preservationist Brian McGreevy, who worked for Historic Charleston Foundation and the National Trust, started reconfiguring a National Register house that had been a B&B off and on since the 1930s. "When I grew up here, there were lots of real B&Bs," said Brian, "so we're trying to bring one back." He and wife Jane prepare a family-style Southern breakfast. Each of their three youngsters has little jobs to do, like polishing table legs and keeping the baseboards clean.

The McGreevys also share countless, illustrious family heirlooms and offer amenities like full baths, fresh flowers, Turkish cotton robes and Ralph Lauren cotton sheets that need to be hand-ironed – "the kind of experience you used to get in the old days when you came to Charleston and your hosts had lots of help," Brian says.

The common rooms and family quarters are in the original wooden 1755 Colonial portion built in the Charleston single-house style and joined to an 1820s

Hayne House offers illustrious family heirlooms and personal touch.

Regency wing by a Victorian stair tower and entry. Here also are the high-ceilinged Wisteria Room with a raised queensize rice poster bed and a day bed. The queen-bedded Magnolia Room contains memorabilia of *Gone with the Wind* author Margaret Mitchell, a school classmate of Brian's great aunt. Both have gas fireplaces and the original or limited-edition prints of Charleston found in each guest room.

Four more private quarters are across a rear piazza and garden courtyard in a Colonial kitchen house, believed to be the oldest wooden kitchen house surviving in Charleston. The wainscoted Ginkgo Suite in the original kitchen has a queen poster bed, two wicker chairs, a fireplace, a kitchenette/wet bar and one of the establishment's two jacuzzi tubs, this one with a separate shower. It shares a porch with the smallest Wicker Room, outfitted in wicker and sporting a king bed that can be divided into twins.

Upstairs in the "hyphen" connecting the kitchen house to the main house is the Plantation Suite, with old cypress paneling and Brian's childhood furnishings from his mother's family plantation, pictured above the carved mahogany queensize bed. Upstairs in the kitchen house is the Cypress Suite, a dream of a retreat with kingsize bed, double jacuzzi, a painting over the fireplace of the Porgy House (where George Gershwin lived while working on *Porgy and Bess)* and a cypress closet. Its balcony offers idyllic garden views and the sounds of birds and church bells.

The McGreevys pamper guests with an informative welcome kit and nightly turndown service to the accompaniment of chocolates, benne wafers and shooting sherry ("because that's what is appropriate in Charleston"). Breakfast is indigenous as well. Served family-style in the dining room between 8:30 and 10, it includes fresh fruit, cereals and yogurts, cheese grits or an egg dish, biscuits with local preserves and Charleston Tea Plantation teas. Guests enjoy a formal drawing room and library with a blue brick fireplace surround and early Chickering piano, as well as a rear piazza with a swing and a private garden terrace.

(843) 577-2633. Fax (843) 577-5906. Four rooms and two suites with private baths. Weekends and peak season: doubles $140 to $185, suites $170 to $265. Midweek off-season: doubles $115 to $155, suites $145 to $195. Children welcome. No smoking.

Twenty-Seven State Street Bed & Breakfast, 27 State St., Charleston 29401.
Ring the doorbell at the black iron gate to this graystone townhouse built about
1800 in the French Quarter of the original walled city. Upon entry, you'll be in an
odd, covered courtyard area linking the main house and a carriage house, both
smack up against the street. Climb the staircase lit by twinkling white lights to the
balcony overhead – an atmospheric setting for the movie *Scarlett* – and you may
feel as if you're in Europe. Resident-owners Joye and Paul Craven, whose
establishment is widely recommended by their peers, capitalize on what they call
"a pronounced Old World influence."

Their B&B is as urban as it is urbane. Its location, at a prime residential/
commercial location of State and Queen streets, is arguably the most central in
town for access to points of interest, restaurants and shops, with the waterfront
two blocks away. Their rooms, large enough to be called suites and often booked
for longer stays, come with queensize beds, kitchen facilities, televisions and
telephones. Fresh fruit, flowers and the morning newspaper are among the
amenities. Furnishings are a mix of antiques and reproductions.

The main house has a chandeliered living room on the second floor for guests'
use. That floor also contains a two-bedroom suite opening off the covered balcony,
the two rooms joined by double doors. Upstairs are the largest quarters, an elegant
suite with two queen poster beds in one room, a sitting room and a full kitchen. A
smaller suite is across the hall.

Most in demand are two suites opening off the courtyard or balcony on the first
and second floors of the carriage house. The brick-walled lower floor has a sitting
area, a small but full kitchen, a queensize bed, a bath in the rear and oriental rugs
on the heart-pine floors. The upper floor has a sitting room with a sofabed, a
bedroom with queensize poster bed and TV, a skylit bathroom and a tiny kitchenette.

A continental-plus breakfast is taken in the rooms or on the balcony. A cheese
tray supplements the usual juices, fruits, breads and pastries.

*(843) 722-4243. Fax (803) 722-6030. Five suites with private baths. Doubles, $110
to $180. Two-night minimum weekends. Parking charge. Children accepted. No smoking.
No credit cards.*

Brasington House Bed & Breakfast, 328 East Bay St., Charleston 29401.
A grand Greek Revival example of a restored Charleston single house that's
one room wide, this is run with T.L.C. by Dalton and Judy Brasington. They opened
one of Charleston's early B&Bs in 1987 after a year's renovation and are among
the few live-in, hands-on innkeepers.

Theirs is a beauty of a house, turned sideways and facing a narrow walled garden
in the Ansonborough neighborhood, near the water some blocks north of the
historic district. Entry is through a locked door onto the open front piazza, from
which two doors open into the house.

The front of the main floor holds a formal Victorian living room, mauve with
white molding and trim, and a chandeliered dining room, where a leisurely Southern
breakfast is served family style amidst much silver and china at a table for eight.

Four guest quarters are found upstairs in the main house and rear kitchen house.
Three have king beds convertible to twins. All have private baths, telephones,
television and the makings for tea, coffee and hot chocolate. "After traveling in
England I love my tea," says Dalton, a retired travel agent, "and I expect to have it
in my room."

The bedroom at the rear of the kitchen house enjoys a private piazza. Restful in green, it has matching furniture of New York State Victorian oak, including a settee and a rocker. An oriental rug accents the original wood floor. Above are two dormer rooms holding a honeymoon suite with sitting room and kingsize bedroom.

The Adams Room, second-floor front, is dressed in more shades of green and florals. An antique sewing machine that belonged to Dalton's grandmother is employed as a table, and Victorian lamps light two armchairs. Plexiglas window coverings diminish the street noise. Dalton's favorite space is the aptly named Victorian Room, furnished with his grandmother's pieces. Included are a queen bed with an ornate headboard, a settee and rockers facing the fireplace. He points out the showy reproduction Victorian commode, "one of the few reproductions in the house."

Although there's tea in the rooms, lemonade or fruit punch are served on the piazzas. Wine and cheese are offered later in the living room as the hosts help orient guests to the city. Liqueurs and chocolates are available in the evening.

Breakfast at 9 is an elaborate affair, starting with five help-yourself fruits (cinnamon apples, strawberries, peaches, bananas and watermelon at our visit) and three cereals. Lemon squares and homemade biscuits accompanied. The main course alternates between cheese grits and an egg dish, perhaps scrambled eggs with cheddar and chives. Judy changes the china daily, employing one of fourteen sets she obtained from her family's jewelry store in North Carolina.

(843) 722-1274 or (800) 722-1274. Three rooms and one suite with private baths, Doubles, $134 to $154. Midweek in off-season, $115. No smoking.

Thirty-Six Meeting Street, 36 Meeting St., Charleston 29401.

Three large quarters with efficiency kitchens are hidden behind this Georgian-style Charleston single house, built in 1740 in what is now the most exclusive part of Charleston's historic residential district. This also is now one of the few local B&Bs that are run by native Charlestonians and that accept children.

Ann Brandt, a calligrapher and artist, and her husband Vic, a real-estate agent, have lived with their three children in the main house since 1992. Ann welcomes guests with a tour of the dark and elegant interior, which contains some of the finest Georgian detailing in the city (the music clef carved on the stairway is unique). The small front parlor with original heart-pine flooring, crystal chandelier and fireplace is furnished much as it must have been in Colonial times. Legend has it that this was the site of the first Christmas tree in Colonial Charlestowne when Hessian soldiers quartered in the home launched what was then a European tradition.

The rear guest rooms are reached via a gated brick driveway along the side piazza. They look comfortable with queensize rice beds, antique furnishings, kitchenettes, television and telephone. The Moultrie on the ground floor of the old kitchen is notable for its original 1740 beehive oven in addition to a smaller kitchen fireplace with a carved mantel and cornice molding. It has a private porch, as does the Marion upstairs, larger and a bit more formal looking, with a pleasant sitting area. Up a spiral staircase next to the main house is a third room with a new bath, a striped loveseat with plump floral pillows, peach walls and handsome artworks.

Continental breakfast is furnished in the kitchenettes. The fare includes cereals, English muffins, homemade breads and pastries.

Thirty-Six Meeting Street B&B occupies Georgian-style Charleston single house.

Gradually upgrading, Ann was redecorating at our visit and showed some elegant new curtains she had just embroidered to match the oriental rugs in the Marion room. She also showed the old privy, now a shed, where bicycles are stored for guests to use.

When filled, Ann refers callers to the nearby home in which she was raised. Her father and stepmother started taking in her overflow in the 1735 Thomas Lamboll House at 19 King St., (888) 874-0793. They now offer two spacious bedrooms with private baths for $125 to $155.

(843) 722-1034. Three rooms with private baths. Doubles, $130 to $170 weekends, $115 to $155 midweek. Winter: $95 to $135. Children welcome. No smoking.

The Cannonboro Inn, 184 Ashley Ave., Charleston 29403.

Sally and Bud Allen, whose names keep cropping up around South Carolina as leading Charleston innkeepers, opened this B&B in 1990. They moved from Michigan to relocate Bud's building business and renovated the 1853 house – a Victorian-style Charleston single house in miniature – inside and out. So successful was the restoration (and business) that the neighborhood association asked them in 1993 to do the same for the 1832 Ashley House. It's now the **Ashley Inn B&B** at 201 Ashley Ave., corner of Bee Street.

The Allens are involved innkeepers and retain quarters in both houses. They recently moved to a house on Kiawah Island, where Bud likes to golf and fish.

Located apart from the historic district in the midst of the hospital area, the two B&Bs cater to business people as well as tourists. Both houses are comfortably furnished with antiques and reproductions. Clocks ticked away in the Cannonboro parlor as Bud detailed the inns' assets and chronology. "Staying here is like staying at Grandma's house," he said. "Staying at the Ashley is like staying with a rich aunt."

The Cannonboro is a tad more humble, although you wouldn't know it from its curving double piazza alongside. Its six guest rooms contain poster and canopied beds and are decorated in florals and prints with a Midwestern accent. All have private baths and TVs. Those are also standard at the Ashley, which has six rooms in the main house and a two-bedroom carriage house in which the Allens resided during renovations. The furnishings here are more formal and the beds antique pencil-post or rice canopies.

Both inns and their resident managers pride themselves on their lavish breakfasts. Favorite recipes have been printed in a little cookbook sold at each inn. "Breakfast is like nothing you'll have at home," Bud said. One guest advised that the raspberry crêpes she'd had that morning at the Ashley Inn were the best she'd ever had. Your breakfast might be Mexicali eggs, a potato/tomato bake, Carolina sausage casserole, cheese soufflé, Welsh rarebit or sweet stuffed waffles. Praline bananas or blueberry cobbler, homemade biscuits and sausages could accompany.

Tea is served each afternoon with tea sandwiches and homemade sweets. The innkeepers meet halfway between each inn to exchange treats so guests get more variety. Sherry and port are offered in the parlors or taken to the porches.

Cannonboro: (843) 723-8572 or (800) 235-8039. Fax (843) 723-8007. Six rooms with private baths. March-November, doubles $110 to $165, suite $185. Rest of year: weekends, doubles, $79 to $109, suite $140; midweek, doubles $69 to $99, suite $130. Children over 10. No smoking.

Ashley: (843) 723-1848 or (800) 581-6658. Seven rooms and one suite with private baths. March-November, doubles $110 to $165, suite $190. Rest of year: weekends, doubles $79 to $99, suite $140; midweek, doubles $69 to $89, suite $130. Children over 10. No smoking.

Dining Spots

Over the years, Spanish, British, American and Creole cooking styles have influenced Low Country cuisine. Charleston is an eating city, more like New Orleans than neighboring Savannah, and quite sophisticated. One inn claims more than 230 restaurants within walking distance. The addition of Johnson & Wales Culinary Academy has enhanced the Charleston dining scene.

Magnolias, 185 East Bay St., Charleston.

Managing partner Donald Barickman, formerly the executive chef, is credited with redefining contemporary Southern cuisine at this magnolia-themed establishment in the heart of Charleston's restaurant district. Southern Living calls this the city's most celebrated restaurant, which may be a stretch, given the competition. But there's no denying its dependability, success or appeal. Located at the site of the original 1739 Customs House, the high-ceilinged, raftered space has big front windows, original magnolia art on the walls (and Charleston murals in the restrooms) and a bar along one side.

Its "uptown Down South" motif works its charm. A window table was an altogether pleasant setting for a late lunch that included a succulent panfried soft-shell crab po-boy sandwich made with a homemade benne seed bun. It was teamed with addictive sweet potato fries and a side of jalapeño-peach slaw that surprisingly lacked kick.

We'd gladly return at night to sample the spicy shrimp, sausage and grits (a signature dish here, as it seems to be everywhere in the Low Country). The all-day menu devotes a section to pasta, grits and eggs, as in grilled salmon fillet served over creamy white grits and chicken and sage hash with poached eggs and cream biscuits. Heartier appetites are appeased with the likes of shellfish over grits topped with fried spinach, coriander-seared tuna with a jalapeño and mango vinaigrette, grilled dolphin topped with crabmeat and ham, grilled game hen with spicy tomato chutney, and New York strip steak with a green peppercorn, mushroom and shallot demi-glace. Blackened green tomatoes, a house-smoked seafood sampler and a Southern egg roll stuffed with collard greens, chicken and tasso are among tempting starters.

(843) 577-7771. Entrées, $14.50 to $24.95. Open daily, 11:30 to 11 or midnight.

Carolina's, 10 Exchange St., Charleston.
This old-timer consists of three dining venues: an intimate enclosed sidewalk café with the look of New Orleans, a larger bar and dining area with a tile floor, a Mediterranean atmosphere, an open kitchen at the back, and an overflow or private dining area called the Perdita Room. The last was the only giveaway to the fact that here was the former Perdita's, an early restaurant mainstay that we enjoyed so much at our first visit in the 1960s to Charleston that we returned for an encore the next night. At that time, Charleston's exciting dining options were few and far between, and Perdita's stood out. Carolina's is a worthy successor, one that Golf Digest calls the best restaurant this side of New Orleans.

Vietnamese chef Rose Durden, known as Mama Rose to her staff, married a serviceman from the South. Her background and travels to California and the Mediterranean have inspired an eclectic regional cuisine (her Carolina Rose chutneys, relishes, sauces and jams prompted a thriving mail-order and catering business).

The extensive menu starts with treats like shrimp and crabmeat wontons on a lime-ginger sauce, spicy Thai crêpes laden with beef tenderloin tips and shiitake mushrooms, black-eyed pea cakes with sour cream and avocado salsa, and grilled andouille sausage with golden grits.

For main dishes, consider crawfish tails in a spicy tasso cream sauce over fettuccine, a Charleston seafood pot in a tomato-saffron broth, sautéed almond-crusted grouper topped with crabmeat and tropical fruit chutney, or grilled beef tenderloin with grilled shrimp and scallops and a Southern bean ragoût. Or you can opt for a Carolina burger or a penne pasta with tomatoes, garlic and herbs.

A pecan brittle basket filled with vanilla bean ice cream and fresh fruits and berries makes a sophisticated ending. Locals fancy the bourbon-chocolate pecan pie with ice cream.

(843) 724-3800 or (888) 486-7673. Entrées, $10.95 to $22.95. Dinner nightly, from 5:30.

Anson, 12 Anson St., Charleston.
The original Charleston Ice House has been transformed into one of the city's most sophisticated, casually elegant restaurants. The Balish family, who own Garibaldi's here and three restaurants in Savannah, outdid themselves with two floors appointed in yellows and golds, with white linens and brown accents. Cypress column pilasters, a preacher's pulpit, a solid cypress bar, marble floors and tapestry booths and banquettes are among the accoutrements.

The well-executed fare is a match for the refined setting. Crispy flounder and two versions of Low Country grouper are the signature dishes. The menu ranges widely from scallops in caviar sauce over angel-hair pasta to braised lamb shanks with sundried currant demi-glace. Seared pork tenderloin is served with local white shrimp, and pecan-crusted chicken with blackberry-bourbon sauce. Carolina gold rice is served here exclusively.

Starters include crackling calamari with apricot sauce, crispy crab and crawfish cakes with sweet pepper relish, and fried cornbread oysters with a potato cake. Desserts run from banana cream pie to a crisp benne almond basket filled with berries and vanilla bean ice cream.

(843) 577-0551. Entrées, $15.95 to $23.95. Dinner nightly, 5:30 to 11 or midnight.

Blossom Café, 171 East Bay St., Charleston.
This large offshoot of Magnolia's is located across the parking lot they share. Blossom is bigger and slightly more versatile. A chic art deco lounge with neon squiggles on the ceiling follows the lines of the circular bar in front. Next comes an exhibition kitchen with a wood oven facing the rear dining room with a dramatic vaulted ceiling. Best of all is the romantic walled outdoor patio, canopied by day and open to the stars at night.

Executive chef Donald Barickman's theatrics here involve modern American cuisine with Italian and Mediterranean influences. The all-day menu ranges widely from antipasto of shrimp on bruschetta to spicy lamb sausage pizzas to sautéed grouper niçoise to grilled lamb chops on a porcini mushroom and parmesan risotto to a rich chocolate crème brûlée. We supped on an appetizer portion of the acclaimed Carolina crab raviolis, an ethereal dish topped with porcini mushroom cream, and a man-size salad of grilled chicken over spinach with roasted peppers and toasted herb bread. The latter was a portion so large that no one could possibly finish a main course afterward. Everyone seemed to be departing with doggy bags, sometimes two or three each. We decided on a half portion of the homemade mango and berry sorbets for dessert.

With a fountain trickling, a searchlight scanning and billowing white clouds scudding across the darkened sky, the dining backdrop was Charleston the way it's meant to be.

(843) 722-9200. Entrées, $13.95 to $21.95. Open daily, 11:30 to midnight.

Slightly North of Broad, 192 East Bay St., Charleston.
The name is a takeoff on local directions, most of which use Broad Street as their compass and points south are the most choice. It's abbreviated S.N.O.B, but you won't find an attitude. Rather it's "a maverick Southern kitchen," one of three run by the Elliot Group restaurants (the newest is Slightly Up the Creek in suburban Mount Pleasant).

The pillared room with a dark beamed ceiling, plants and wrought iron conveys a New Orleans look. A bar is up front, dining is at banquettes and tables, and there's an open kitchen in back.

Innovative regional fare, with an emphasis on seafood and game, is featured on the shorter-than-the-local-norm dinner menu. You might start with red bean soup, oven-roasted clams with smoked sausage or a sauté of shiitake mushrooms stuffed with foie gras mousse on spinach. Some make a meal of small plates of maverick grits with shrimp and country ham, sesame-crusted tuna medallions with nori rolls and homemade kimchee, or the grilled Southern medley of chicken, zucchini, eggplant, tomatoes and goat cheese croutons, dressed with pecorino romano and balsamic vinaigrette.

Others continue with main courses – some available in smaller portions – like "coastalina" deviled crab cakes on spicy creole sauce, sautéed palmetto squab with foie gras over country cabbage or bacon-wrapped lamb tenderloin with a red wine sauce. The Low Country sampler yields grilled quail, smoked sausage, grilled pork tenderloin, butter beans, cabbage and rice.

Desserts include sherbets, sour cream apple pie and triple chocolate cake.

(843) 723-3424. Entrées, $14.75 to $24. Lunch, Monday-Friday 11:30 to 3. Dinner nightly from 5:30.

Peninsula Grill, 112 North Market St., Charleston.

National publicity accolades are posted all over the entries to this clubby, hotel-style dining room at the side and rear of the downtown Planters Inn. They testify to the successes of celebrity chef Robert Carter, a partner in the grill that opened in 1997. Velvet walls, 19th-century landscape paintings and sea-grass carpeting are the backdrop for inventive contemporary Southern cuisine.

The staff in black and white serve up specialties like wild mushroom grits with oyster stew, a signature appetizer, and spicy shrimp and sausage with tasso gravy over creamy white grits for a main course. Other good bets are black grouper with ginger-lime beurre blanc, pan-roasted breast of muscovy duck with a duck confit spring roll, and rack of lamb crusted with benne seeds and served with coconut-mint pesto. Accompaniments vary from sundried tomato grits fritters and truffled cornbread to sweet potato flan and "teene weene benne beans."

The champagne bar menu offers such exotica as a lobster martini with tomato rémoulade, a lobster skillet cake and Charleston crab cake with arugula salad, an oyster sampler, Argentine steak tartare and ossetra caviar "with Southern service."

Finish with a flourish from the dessert selection, perhaps banana pudding with milk chocolate ganache, vanilla bean-ginger brûlée, assorted sorbets on a signature cookie plate or a treat called "lemon!!!" – lemon tart, lemon sorbet, lemon crisp and candied lemon.

(843) 723-0700 or (800) 845-7082. Entrées, $16.50 to $26. Dinner nightly, 5:30 to 10:30 or 11.

Market East Bistro, 14 North Market St., Charleston.

For a change of pace, this small and unpretentious bistro fits the bill. Locals like it for its down-to-earth European-American cooking and reasonable prices.

The dinner menu features main dishes like crab cake with lobster coulis, almond-crusted grouper with ginger sauce, Moroccan couscous with sautéed shrimp, scallops and mussels, roulade of chicken rolled with goat cheese and rosemary ham, and grilled lamb chops with herb-mustard crust. Pastas like penne with crawfish and jumbo shrimp with Asian vegetables and wasabi caviar appeal. So do starters of smoked salmon on a potato cake and a crispy oyster and spinach salad with honey-bacon dressing.

Dessert could be orange crème brûlée or chocolate mousse with raspberry coulis.

(843) 577-5080. Entrées, $10.95 to $16.95. Open Monday-Saturday, 11:30 to 10 or 11, Sunday 10:30 to 3 and 5 to 9.

There are myriad other choices. On the high end is the **Charleston Grill** at Charleston Place, 224 King St., now under the auspices of the Orient-Express

Hotels and new chef Robert Waggoner. Soft orange linens are an elegant counterpoint to the prevailing dark mahogany; the French take on Low Country cuisine is highly rated. Departing from Louis's Charleston Grill, pioneering chef Louis Osteen opened **Louis's Restaurant** to mixed reviews in the NationsBank building at 200 Meeting St. Gourmands in the know also head out to suburban Summerville and the newish **Woodlands Resort & Inn**, whose creative restaurant earns a rare AAA five-diamond rating. The elegant **Charleston Chops**, 188 East Bay St., is touted as the city's best steak house. The old Farmers & Exchange Bank is now a highly rated continental restaurant called **Saracen**, 141 East Bay St.

Less formidable are pleasing restaurants like **Mint Juleps**, 68 Queen St., with a short dinner menu of California/Southern fare, and **Pinckney Café & Espresso**, Pinckney Street at Motley Lane, an affordable favorite for lunch and dinner. **Gaulart & Maliclet/Fast & French** speaks for itself at 98 Broad St. The outdoor raw bar and courtyard are fine for lunch and dinner at **82 Queen**, a relative old-timer at 82 Queen St. **The Library at Vendue Inn**, 23 Vendue Range, would be just another good restaurant without its new **Rooftop Bar** for lunch and drinks. Good food goes along with the drinks at **McCrady's Tavern**, 2 Unity Alley, a 1778 tavern where George Washington once supped. **Sonoma Café & Winebar**, 203 King St., offers innovative California and Pacific Rim cuisine. Northern Italian cuisine and cozy ambiance are the hallmarks of **Fulton Five**, 5 Fulton St. Contemporary Mediterranean fare is featured at **Papillon**, an all-day café and bakery at 32 North Market St.

Coffee, dessert and drinks in the European style are served up in a dark and decadent Victorian setting at **Mirabel**, 213A East Bay St.

Diversions

Charleston is impossibly difficult for first-time visitors to find their way around. The overly commercialized new Charleston visitor center is not much help for anyone but the most clueless tourist. (It even charges $2.50 for its 24-minute, multimedia orientation program for visitors.) The best advice is to take one of literally dozens of tours available all around the historic district, especially the carriage tours in the vicinity of the Old City Market. Get the lay of the land, and then strike out on your own.

Charleston began as a pedestrian city in 1670, and walking remains the best way to get around. Bound by the Ashley River on the west and the Cooper River on the east, the peninsula contains a 1,000-acre historic district that can be traversed from one river to the other in a half hour – or far longer. (And if you drive through on major Highway 17, you'll miss historic Charleston just to the east and wonder what all the fuss is about). Three centuries of noble architecture are on display. Wander away from the tour buses and the crowds to explore the maze of small alleys, lanes and courts that seem to pop up everywhere. Among the prettiest are Prices, Stolls and ZigZag alleys and Longitude Lane. Old, narrow and often cobbled, these are off-limits to carriages and buses. You'll be rewarded by architectural embellishments and secret gardens. You may be frustrated by historic plaques so small and discreet that they are impossible to read from the sidewalk. But that's the Charleston way, part of the Charleston attitude. Signs placed by the Preservation Society of Charleston are more readable.

The heart of the historic residential district is along Meeting Street south of Broad. Meeting Street, East Battery and East Bay are must-see thoroughfares. The commercial district lies north of Broad Street along Meeting and especially King Street, which shows how urbane the city has become of late. One of the nicest over-all areas – chockablock inns, restaurants, townhouses and shops – is the area around East Bay, Vendue Range and the new waterfront park.

Highlights are **The Battery,** the harborfront park with a forest of palmettos and live oaks facing Fort Sumter, and **Rainbow Row,** a row of pastel-hued stuccoed brick houses at 79-107 East Bay Street. **Cabbage Row** at 89-91 Church St. was the model for DuBose Heyward's Catfish Row, the locale of the operetta *Porgy and Bess.*

Charleston houses, like those in the rest of the Low Country, have raised piazzas. The unique Charleston single-style houses, placed sideways, are one room wide and two or three rooms deep. You enter a gate or a portal from the sidewalk onto the piazza that runs the depth of the house.

Historic Charleston Foundation, founded in 1947 before preservation was generally accepted, has been in the forefront of efforts to preserve Charleston's architectural treasures. It oversees three national historic landmarks: the palatial 1818 **Aiken-Rhett House** at 48 Elizabeth St., the **Powder Magazine** on Cumberland Street, and the **Nathaniel Russell House** at 51 Meeting St. The last is Charleston's most elaborate mansion, an 1808 Federal beauty with oval drawing and music rooms and an astonishing flying staircase spiraling unsupported three stories high.

The **Calhoun Mansion,** 16 Meeting St., is one of the most opulent Italianate Victorians in the South. The imposing 1825 Federal **Edmonston-Alson House** overlooks the harbor at 21 East Battery St. (It's still the family home of the owners of Middleton Place Plantation. Rembrandt Peale's Bombardment of Fort Sumter was painted from its piazza.) George Washington stayed at the 1772 **Heyward-Washington House,** home of a signer of the Declaration of Independence. Full of fine antiques, its tall Holmes bookcase, crafted in Charleston before 1785, is considered the finest extant piece of American-made furniture. The 1803 **Joseph Manigault House,** 350 Meeting St., is a notable example of the Scottish-influenced Adam style.

Churches. Charleston bears the nickname the "Holy City" because its church spires dwarf its office buildings. The oldest is **St. Michael's Episcopal Church** at Broad and Meeting streets. The eight bells in its clock tower have chimed since 1764. Most unusual is the **Circular Congregational Church,** 150 Meeting St., dating to 1681 and shaped in a circle. **St. Mary's Church,** 89 Hasell St., was established in 1789 as the Mother Church of the Roman Catholic diocese of the Carolinas and Georgia. The 1822 **First Baptist Church,** 61 Church St., is a fine example of Greek Revival architecture. The 1844 Gothic-style **Huguenot Church,** 136 Church St., is one of the last surviving French Protestant churches in the country. **St. Philip's Episcopal Church,** 146 Church St., known as the lighthouse church for the light in its steeple that helped guide ships to port, originated as the Mother Church of the province in 1670.

The churchyards at St. Michael's, St. Philip's and the French Huguenot church give a flavor of the true Charleston.

Imposing residences and palm trees typify East Bay Street scene in historic district.

Museums and Arts. The Charleston Museum, 360 Meeting St., is the nation's oldest (1773). Now housed in an award-winning $6 million complex, it focuses on Charleston and the Low Country, including silver made in Charleston in the 18th Century. The **Old Exchange and Provost Dungeon,** 122 East Bay St., was built by the British in 1771 as the Customs House and Exchange. George Washington was entertained at a gala ball in the great hall. Patriots were imprisoned in the cellars, where you can see the old city wall (Charleston was the only English walled city in America). The 1703 **Powder Museum,** 79 Cumberland St., the oldest surviving public building in the Carolinas, offers fascinating exhibits on the city's early history. **Gibbes Museum of Art,** 135 Meeting St., has a fine collection of American paintings, a terrific portrait gallery and miniature room displays.

Spoleto Festival U.S.A., founded here in 1977 by Gian Carlo Menotti, is a seventeen-day extravaganza of performances and exhibitions staged throughout the city the last week in May and the first week in June. Against its world-class backdrop, the outreach **Piccolo Spoleto** showcases regional arts and entertainers during the same period.

Plantations in the Low Country around Charleston entice visitors out of the city, especially along River Road (Route 61) along the Ashley River. We'll never forget the showy camellias and azaleas against the dark black waters of **Magnolia Plantation and Gardens** at our first Charleston visit three decades ago. Several rolls of slides bring back the memories. The one plantation not to miss is **Middleton Place,** a meticulously preserved 18th-century plantation encompassing America's oldest landscaped gardens. It shares a combination ticket with the unfurnished **Drayton Hall,** still in virtually its original 1738 condition and one of the finest examples of Georgian Palladian architecture in America. Between the two plantations along Route 61 is **Old St. Andrew's Church,** the oldest extant church building (1706) south of Virginia. East of the city, a half-mile avenue of Spanish moss-draped live oaks leads to **Boone Hall Plantation,** dating to 1681. The mansion, rebuilt in 1935, disappoints purists. Nine original brick cabins stand on one of the Southeast's few intact slave streets.

Shopping. Some local shops and galleries provide a way to get a flavor of the city without paying admission fees. Typical is **Charleston Gardens** at 61 Queen St., which displays garden and home furnishings and accessories in an exceptional setting. Another is the **Elizabeth O'Neill Vernier Gallery,** studio of the late artist at Church and Tradd streets, where reproductions of her works are for sale. On Church north of Tradd is **Southern Literary Tradition,** a tiny 18th-century building featuring Southern authors and an upstairs reading room. Charleston rice spoons and jewelry based on local wrought iron are among items for sale at **Historic Charleston Reproductions Shop,** 105 Broad St. Charleston books and gifts are highlighted at the **Historic Charleston Foundation Museum Shop,** 108 Meeting St.

Souvenir vendors upstage any farmers left at the **Old City Market,** a bustling area of shops and eateries favored by tourists along North and South Market streets. You'll find Gullah sweet-grass baskets and handmade crafts. Countless specialty shops, art galleries and antique shops are nearby. Orient-Express Hotels have upgraded the Omni Hotel and **The Shops at Charleston Place,** where Gucci, Laura Ashley, Crabtree & Evelyn, Talbots, Brookstone and the like show their wares. A new **Saks Fifth Avenue** occupies a prime corner at King and Market. Across the street is a local favorite, **Christian Michi,** with stylish acquisitions for house or wardrobe. In recent years, King Street has become very suave. Look for **Claire Murray Lifestyles, Palais Royal** French linens, **The Audubon Shop** for nature items, the **Silver Puffin** for one-of-a-kind gifts and household accents and several men's clothiers, including **Granger Owings.**

Extra-Special

Robert's of Charleston, 182 East Bay St., Charleston.

Chef-opera singer Robert Dickson opened his popular Robert's on Market Street in 1976. After taking a respite for a few years and traveling to Italy, he reopened in 1998 along East Bay Street's Restaurant Row. He says he's back where he belongs – "behind the kitchen range and in the dining room." Fans think he's better than ever. Robert is cooking a new version of his classical menu for a four-course dinner as he entertains with Broadway show tunes. The $65 tab includes wine and entertainment; tax and gratuity are extra. About 40 people get to share the intimate experience each night.

(843) 577-7565 or (800) 977-7065. Prix-fixe, $65. Dinner by reservation, Tuesday-Saturday at 8.

Horse-drawn carriage passes imposing Bay Street Inn in Beaufort's historic district.

Beaufort, S.C.

Queen of the Low Country

Life is slow-paced and tranquil in the coastal plain of sea islands, salt marshes and tidal estuaries called the Low Country. In these watery habitats sea turtles and wildlife nest, resorts and golf courses thrive and the African-American Gullah dialect is spoken in the shadow of the vast Parris Island Marine Corps recruit training center.

At its heart is Beaufort, off the beaten path roughly midway between Charleston and Savannah. Pronounced BYOO-fert – in contrast with its North Carolina cousin, BO-fert – this is "the queen of the Carolina Sea Islands."

Beaufort lies on Port Royal Island, facing the broad Beaufort River and Port Royal Sound, part of the Intracoastal Waterway. Founded in 1711, the town is the second oldest in South Carolina. It prospered particularly from 1820 to 1860 when cotton was king and Beaufort was the wealthiest, most aristocratic town of its size in America. This was the getaway place for wealthy plantation owners, who built elaborate second homes along the waterfront to escape, if only by a few degrees, the torrid inland summer heat.

Here was where South Carolina decided to secede from the Union. Its residents fled as Union forces took Beaufort early in the Civil War. It became the Union

Army base in the Deep South and its houses were turned into hospitals. This was one of few Southern cities to escape Sherman's touch.

The grand houses remain, testaments to a way of life still cherished by generations of Beaufort families. With few contemporary intrusions, the entire downtown is designated a national historic district. It's said to comprise the single richest concentration of antebellum dwellings in America.

Dripping with Southern charm, much like the spanish moss strewn from its trees, Beaufort became the Newport of the South in the early 20th century. Relatively recently, newcomers attracted by its cultivated, laid-back lifestyle have opened inns, restaurants and shops as the area doubled in population since 1970.

Beaufort was heralded as the South's hottest small town by Vogue magazine in the 1990s. The town of 9,600 is big enough to support a daily newspaper and a quarterly magazine but small enough to be ignored by most chain stores and hotels.

Its antebellum and subtropical charms fulfill filmmakers' dreams. Best-selling hometown author Pat Conroy's books come alive as you walk through the legendary streets of *The Prince of Tides* and *The Great Santini,* as well as of *The Big Chill* and *Forrest Gump.* Beaufort is the perfect movie set because it looks and feels like one.

Inn Spots

Though undiscovered by innkeepers until the 1980s, Beaufort really entered the realm of inn spots in the 1990s. Its inns and B&Bs command the highest average room rates in South Carolina.

The Rhett House Inn, 1009 Craven St., Beaufort 29902.

It took only a weekend stay in Beaufort to convince Steve and Marianne Harrison to leave Manhattan and open what is now considered a model Southern inn. While visiting a former Wall Street friend who ran the Bay Street Inn at the time, they bicycled around town and saw a for-sale sign on a B&B that had been open barely six months. Ready for a change of pace from their fashion design careers (her father co-founded Anne Klein and Steve was its CEO), they bought the classic 1820 plantation house once occupied by Southern aristocrat Thomas Rhett and his well-connected wife, Caroline Barnwell. They eliminated what Steve called "the very Victorian, drapey decor" and offered five guest rooms starting in 1986. They have since expanded to seventeen in two buildings, and have vacated their inn quarters for a charming, red-roofed house they built at the rear of the inn property.

Enveloped in live oaks dripping with spanish moss, the landmark main house with its corinthian columns and sprawling double verandas is a near twin to the famed Secession House down the street. That was were local notables drafted the South Carolina ordinance to secede from the Union.

The living room, painted a pale yellow-green color, was quite a sight with its palms and plants and all-white

Corinthian columns and wide verandas dignify Rhett House Inn.

stuffed chairs and sofas at our summer visit. Changing seasonally, the designer white look gives way to brown velvet in the fall. The breakfast room with eight white-clothed tables is elegant in pale yellow and white. It looks like the restaurant it was until the Harrisons stopped dinner service in 1996 to add more guest rooms in an annex they call "The Cottage" up the street. The favorite guest spaces are the verandas, awash in wicker and accented with prolific hanging begonias.

Furnishings are primarily English and American antiques. All guest rooms come with TVs, telephones, compact disc players featuring the area Gullah singers, and private baths equipped with robes and hair dryers. Many have fireplaces and half have jacuzzi tubs and separate steam showers. Beds are king or queensize. Sitting areas generally have plump chairs with an ottoman. During a filming expedition, Barbra Streisand slept in the kingsize rice four-poster in the largest bedroom overlooking the front veranda. The lower floor holds a secluded room opening onto an idyllic brick patio focusing on gardens and a fountain. The rear honeymoon room, daintily decorated with cherry furnishings and a king bed, has a whirlpool tub and its own screened porch overlooking the grounds.

In 1997, the Harrisons added seven romantic rooms in a cottage built in 1850 for freed slaves and now favored by the film celebrities attracted to the inn. Spiffily decorated, these come with private porches and entrances, modern gas fireplaces and bathrooms with jacuzzis, steam showers and lighting adjusted by dimmer switches. One with a kingsize wall-canopy headboard and a loveseat that converts into a twin bed has a porch overlooking the pastoral St. Helena's Episcopal churchyard.

Tea, lemonade, cookies and brownies are available at all hours in the kitchen of the main house. The staff puts out spanakopita and cheese treats at 5 o'clock in the parlor, where mini-bottles of alcoholic beverages may be purchased for $3. Mints accompany nightly turndown. Those inclined may order a tray of homemade desserts for $5.

Breakfast includes fresh fruit and a changing entrée of eggs, french toast or pancakes and grits.

(843) 524-9030 or (888) 480-9530. Fax (843) 524-1310. Seventeen rooms with private baths. Doubles, $150 to $225, March-May and October-November; $125 to $200, rest of year. Children over 5. No smoking.

The Cuthbert House Inn, 1203 Bay St., Beaufort 29902.

Refined accommodations and Southern charm are the hallmarks of this welcoming B&B, the largest historic mansion on the waterfront and the second largest in town. Gary and Sharon Groves moved in 1995 from Washington, D.C., to occupy and convert the private residence. It was built in 1790 and bears quite a history.

The house had been sawed in half and moved four blocks to a bluff overlooking the Beaufort River in 1810. A Union general used the house as his headquarters during the Civil War, and General Sherman spent a night here on his march northward from Savannah.in 1865. Several Union soldiers etched their signatures and home states for posterity on a marble fireplace mantle in what is now the Eastlake Suite.

Gary, a former military helicopter pilot and lawyer, did the bulk of the room renovations himself. The spacious rooms blend original carved moldings, heart-pine floors, clawfoot tubs and period furniture with such conveniences as TVs, telephones, stocked refrigerators and updated bathrooms. "People like old houses but new baths," Gary acknowledged.

The prime accommodation is the Eastlake Suite on the main floor at the front of the house. It harbors a large bay-view sitting room, a bedroom with antique Eastlake cherry queensize bed with hand-carved headboard, and a bathroom with a six-foot-long footed soaking tub, separate shower and vanity.

The Garden Room offers a queensize cannonball rope bed, an antique double bed at the side, a couple of leather chairs and a view of the garden. Two wicker chairs, a writing desk and a queensize mahogany sleigh bed grace the Victoria Room, which opens onto a porch with rockers. The Mariner Suite on the ground level has a kingsize mahogany rice poster bed, a sitting room and a two-person whirlpool tub. At our visit, Gary was finishing another suite with a queen bed.

Guests enjoy a handsome parlor, a cozy side sunporch stocked with newspapers and magazines, and the wraparound veranda. A side breakfast room in pale green yields a water view from four tables. A formal dining room in back is used for special occasions. Gary cooks the breakfast, served amid china and sterling at two seatings, 8 and 9:30. The fare at our visit was fruit salad, creamed yogurt with apricot preserves and belgian waffles with pecans and sausage. Eggs Cuthbert (a variation on eggs benedict with béarnaise rather than hollandaise sauce and sausage on the side), orange grand marnier pancakes and scrambled eggs with stone-ground cheese grits and homemade scones are other favorites.

(843) 521-1315 or (800) 327-9275. Fax (843) 521-1314. Two rooms and three suites with private baths. Doubles, $165 to $205. January-February and September: $135 to $150. Children over 12. No smoking.

TwoSuns Inn Bed & Breakfast, 1705 Bay St., Beaufort 29902.

Ron and Carrol Kay converted an abandoned Neoclassic Revival-style home facing the Beaufort River into a homey, hospitable B&B full of personality.

Cuthbert House Inn is largest historic mansion facing Beaufort's waterfront.

Relocating after twenty years in South Florida, they were heading for the North Carolina mountains in 1989 when they happened on Beaufort and decided to stay.

Their establishment defines the essence of a B&B as categorized by Ron, who was founding president of the South Carolina Bed & Breakfast Association and drafted the legislation for the South Carolina Bed & Breakfast Act of 1998. It is run by hands-on resident owners, has common rooms for gathering purposes and breakfast, and delivers a high level of personal service. Guests respond with glowing accounts of "great hospitality" and keep TwoSuns filled most of the time. Remarkably, the Kays do all the work themselves.

A large parlor across the front is the heart of the house, built in 1917 and bearer of a state preservation award in 1998. One side is a comfortable living room, where Carrol is apt to serve guests iced tea in Mason jar mugs or wine, sherry and brandy poured from decanters. Here is where Ron holds forth on topics great and small (not for naught is he the founder of the Eastern Bunch of the International Banana Club, the criteria for which include maintaining a sense of humor and having fun in a hectic world). Bananas are a low-key decorative motif. More obvious are the two looms occupying the other side of the parlor. Here is where Carrol, a juried weaver, produces her TwoSuns Handwovens creations. Her wearable art and home accessories are displayed at the South Carolina Artisans Center in Walterboro.

Her showy window treatments and bed coverings are evident in the six guest rooms. Furnished with antiques, all have private baths and king or queensize beds. Two contain extra day beds. Country quilts characterize one room and an Oriental motif another. A third has a Victorian library feeling. Chamber D is known for its rare full-body brass shower that sprays from every direction. The newest is the third-floor Skylight Room, where a pair of queensize wicker beds are placed beneath an elaborate greenhouse skylight created originally for ventilation. Two window seats are in dormers at either end. Decorated in dusty rose and mauve, this room comes with a TV and a guest refrigerator.

Neoclassic Revival house has been converted into TwoSuns Inn.

Two upstairs bedrooms open onto a screened front sleeping porch.

Carrol does the baking and Ron cooks the breakfast, a convivial affair taken at three tables for four in the dining room. Fruits and breads precede the main event, perhaps thick, wedge-shaped french toast with peach and strawberry glaze, accompanied by a mixed grill of turkey ham and turkey sausage. Ron is well known for his crêpes and his *le croissant deux soleil,* a specialty layered with shrimp or turkey ham, cheese and perhaps asparagus or artichoke hearts, "depending on how adventurous the guests are."

Ron, a raconteur, is always on the go. He's the omnipresent host, a B&B consultant, an artist/musician, and a sponsor of an annual community Halloween event and cartoon carnival, among others. Ask about the inn's obscure name and be mystified. Ask about the Banana Club and be entertained.

(843) 522-1122 or (800) 532-4244. Six rooms with private baths. Doubles, $128 to $151, March-November; $95 to $195 rest of year. No smoking. Children over 12.

Bay Street Inn, 601 Bay St., Beaufort 29902.

Opened in 1982 as the first B&B in town, this Federal mansion occupies a prime corner location in the heart of the historic district, with a panoramic view of the broad river and Intracoastal Waterway across the street. It was built in 1852 as a townhouse for a plantation owner named Fripp, whose property is now the Dataw Island gated community. It retains somewhat the same distinction under new owners Robert and Judy Lievense, New Yorkers who have an island home nearby. The Lievenses brought Peter Steciak, a business colleague, out of retirement to manage the inn when it reopened in 1997 after five months of renovations.

A signed Baccarat chandelier hangs over the soaring stairway foyer of this majestic house, which was one of the filming sites for "The Prince of Tides."

The common rooms with heart-pine floors are beauties. They range from a Federal parlor where tea and dessert are offered at 4 to a cozy cypress-paneled library where wine and cheese are put out at 6. Three tables are set for six in the chandeliered rear breakfast room, where the staff serves a buffet spread of fruits, omelets, pancakes or casseroles. We can vouch for the spicy Low Country casserole of rice, sausage and mushrooms, teamed with melt-in-the-mouth biscuits.

Guest rooms on three floors come in a variety of bed configurations – mostly queensize but two kingsize and two with two double beds. A couple add extra sofabeds. They are named for the nine Fripp children. All have TVs and phones, and all but one have working fireplaces. Furnishings are a mix of antiques and reproductions. Beds are turned down at night with chocolates. Caswell-Massey toiletries and hair dryers enhance the bathrooms.

The Lewis, main-floor front, is attractive in red and beige with a kingsize mahogany bed, armoire, writing desk, a sofa and two chairs. The queensize Graham, second-floor rear, compensates for lack of water view with windows on three sides. Also with windows on three sides is the Phoebe with two double beds, a convertible loveseat and a wing chair. The front Calhoun and Elizabeth rooms have queen poster beds and some of the best water views in town. An artist-neighbor did the floral stenciling around the bathroom in one of two guest rooms on the lower garden level, which claim the lowest rates.

"We have guests who come and never leave the front verandas," says Peter. There are two, upstairs and down, furnished in green wicker and yielding great views of the water.

(843) 522-0050 or (800) 256-9285. Fax (843) 521-4086. Nine rooms with private baths. Doubles, $125 to $225. Children over 8. No smoking.

The Beaufort Inn, 809 Port Republic Street, Beaufort 29902.

Built in 1897 as an attorney's second home, this became Beaufort's earliest inn in the 1930s. It was later a boarding house and a hospice before being salvaged from ruin. Except for its front facade, the building was essentially gutted and rebuilt, which explains its lack of patina in a town where age is cherished. "That's the beauty of it," says innkeeper Debbie Fielden, who grew up in Beaufort. "It looks old but is brand new."

She and her husband Rusty, a contractor, bought the renovated property in 1993 and quickly redecorated and expanded. They converted two main-floor guest rooms into an enlarged dining room for their restaurant, added a wine bar and turned their own two-bedroom cottage at the side into guest quarters.

Some of the thirteen guest rooms – particularly those at the lower end of the price scale – are smallish, at least in Beaufort terms. Each is named after a Low Country plantation, whose individual history is detailed in the room. Furnishings are reproduction – "all different," says Debbie. "I went through High Point, N.C., like I was shopping for groceries."

All rooms have modern baths (two with jacuzzi tubs), telephones, TVs and VCRs (all the movies made in Beaufort are available from the front desk). Fancy Victorian wallpapers, window treatments and plump chairs are the norm. Three rooms have fireplaces and four have wet bars. Two billed as junior suites have convertible loveseats in sitting areas. Two share a large porch. The Oak Grove comes with a private front porch overlooking the town.

Outside off a fountain courtyard and an elaborate landscaped terrace are a carriage house with queen-bedded guest quarters up and down as well as the apartment-like cottage vacated by the Fieldens. The latter has front and back porches, an open living/dining room and kitchen, two bedrooms and two bathrooms and is rented as one unit.

The most striking feature, no doubt, is the soaring rear foyer graced by a crystal chandelier hung from the ceiling three stories above.

A full breakfast and afternoon tea are included in the rates. Each room is equipped with a stocked refrigerator.

(843) 521-9000. Fax (843) 521-9500. Thirteen rooms. Doubles, $125 to $195. Children over 8. No smoking.

Old Point Inn, 212 New St., Beaufort 29902.

This deceptively small 1898 Victorian house is a low-key, traditional B&B imbued with flavor by founding innkeepers Joe and Joan Carpentiere from Connecticut.

Located in the edge of the posh historic district known as the Point, it's built in the Beaufort style that has its roots in the plantation houses of Barbados. With raised foundations, their arcades and double verandas catch the southwest breeze. Because it was the builder's wedding gift to his wife, it's known locally as, simply, the "Wedding Gift House."

Dressed in lace curtains and gingham-style wallpapers, the four guest rooms vary widely in size and price. The Nicholas Nickleby has a queensize mahogany bed, a single sleigh bed and access to the front veranda. It is accented as are all rooms with collections here and there. The third-floor Jane Austen has a unique eyelash window above the kingsize wicker bed. Lace surrounds the queensize pencil-post canopy bed in the premier Molly Bloom Room, which also has a single sleigh bed and a separate dressing area and overlooks the rear patio and garden. The cozy side Lucy Honeychurch Room with its antique white iron double bed is the best value in town.

Guests gather in the front parlor with a grand piano or upstairs in a corner library with a game table and four leather chairs. Breakfast is communal at a lace-covered table for ten in the dining room. Breakfast at our visit was broccoli and cheese quiche with chicken, fried potatoes, biscuits and fruit salad. Apple pancakes and sausage are another favorite.

Complimentary wine and soft drinks are offered in the afternoon by the hospitable hosts. And, bless their hearts: Most of their inn brochure is devoted to a helpful map tour of local historic sites.

(843) 524-3177. Fax (843) 525-6544. Four rooms with private baths. Doubles, $65 to $110. Children welcome. No smoking.

Dining Spots

Beaufort restaurants underwent a major shakeup in the year before this book went to press. One Bay Street structure that held The Gadsby became Nick's, then La Sirena and for a week or two the BackStreet Café. At our visit, that had suddenly closed and a sign in the window advised the space was about to be taken over by Ollie's, an offshoot of a seafood grill and bar across the river on Lady's Island. The popular Factory Creek Landing on Lady's Island also closed. The historic Anchorage was catering to tour buses and was closed the weekend we were there – a frequent occurrence, we were advised.

The best of the remaining players at the time:

Restored Beaufort Inn is known for fine dining as well as lodging.

The Beaufort Inn, 809 Port Republic Street, Beaufort.

Widely considered the top restaurant in town is this elegant establishment that owner Debbie Fielden likes to call "Beaufort's Inn – because it's so popular with locals." The dining operation was given its cachet by founding chef Peter de Jong, who was featured on PBS Television's Great Chefs of the South series before leaving in 1998 to open his own restaurant (see below). Much of the menu and spirit remained under new chef Chip Ulbrich and kitchen crew.

Forty-eight wines are offered by the glass or flight (a tasting of three) in the mahogany-paneled wine bar and grill room, original site of the inn's restaurant. In 1998, two guest rooms at the front of the house were converted into fancy dining rooms. They more than doubling the restaurant's size to the point where it takes up most of the inn's main floor.

The wine bar and grill menu is strong on starters, salads and flatbreads, and offers about six special entrées.

The main dining room offers fewer appetizers and more main courses at heftier prices. Look for starters like she-crab soup flavored with sherry, a blended crab and crawfish cake with roasted red pepper rémoulade and pan-fried tomatoes filled with goat cheese. Typical main dishes are whole crisped flounder served with a warm gazpacho sauce on yucca chips, grilled scallop and bacon satay served on lemon-pepper penne with a banana-mango ketchup, sliced duck breast on a blueberry gastrique with "forbidden black rice" and grilled ribeye steak flamed with cognac. Fresh bread and a house salad come with.

Dessert could be key lime tart, lemon sorbet coupe or coconut-banana crème brûlée.

(843) 521-9000. Entrées, $15.95 to $25.50; wine bar and grill, $14 to $19.25. Dinner nightly, 6 to 10, wine bar from 5. Sunday brunch, 10 to 2.

Bistro de Jong, 205 West St., Beaufort.

After putting the Beaufort Inn on the culinary map, Dutch chef Peter de Jong left in 1998 to open this European-style bistro showcasing modern Southern cuisine. It also consists of a patisserie and a sushi and satay bar, and is known for its cooking classes and wine dinners.

The look of the long and narrow downtown restaurant is vaguely Mediterranean, with arty local murals painted on the walls and sculptures and fish gracing the entry. Dining is by candlelight. The feeling is warm and casual.

Dinner might begin with a bowl of sherried she-crab soup, shrimp and jalapeño grit cakes or a caramelized apple and pecan chicken pâté with peach chutney. Or you could sample a dozen kinds of five satays from the bistro bar. Fresh blue crab sushi was a sensational special the night we dined. Main courses ranged from a crisp whole flounder with caramelized banana and a watermelon-strawberry chutney over basmati rice to grilled beef tenderloin with a wild mushroom ragoût over fried green tomato and sundried tomato-basil mashed potato. We liked the crusty bread better than the house salad, but were most impressed with the grilled chicken served with a superior cilantro-mango sauce over roasted fennel couscous and teamed with ratatouille. Dessert from the patisserie was a light cheesecake garnished with raspberries and blueberries.

Wednesdays are ethnic nights at this happening place, where you can stop in for coffee and dessert after an evening walk or take out sushi from the bar. At our visit Peter was about to launch limited lunch service.

(843) 524-4994. Entrées, $13 to $18. Lunch, Thursday and Friday 11:30 to 2:30. Dinner, Tuesday-Saturday from 5:30.

Emily's Restaurant & Tapas Bar, 906 Port Republic St., Beaufort.

There is no Emily and owner Peter Nilsson is Swedish. He's partial to the tapas of Spain, which proved so popular that he was thinking of dropping the rest of his extensive continental menu.

Three dozen tapas are offered at $7 each, and most patrons make them a meal. The locally ubiquitous shrimp turns up in seven variations, but also offered are Italian sausages, grilled quail, antelope sausage, alligator ribs and peppered ostrich steak. You also can opt for spinach terrine or crabmeat rangoon in puff pastry.

The rest of the menu is classic continental, from duck à l'orange to wiener schnitzel, beef tartare and steak au poivre. Exceptions might be the "bronzed tuna" (yellowfin lightly blackened) or Peter's favorite soft-shell crabs simmered in butter and cajun sauces. Desserts run to New York-style cheesecake, strawberry-amaretto torte and chocolate mousse pie.

The setting is small, intimate and quite urbane, with dark Honduran mahogany walls, booths and high-back chairs and tiny white lights twinkling overhead.

(843) 522-1866. Entrées, $20 to $23. Dinner, Monday-Saturday 6 to 10; tapas, 4:30 to 11.

11th Street Dockside, 11th Street West, Port Royal.

Everybody's favorite for fresh seafood with a water view is this out-of-the-way, atmospheric place beside Port Royal Seafood Inc., about six miles south of town. Shrimp boats are tied up at the docks near the confluence of Battery Creek and the Beaufort River. They vie with the sunsets to provide interest for diners at window tables or the clusters of waiting patrons outside. The place is cavernous with a rustic bar, a nautical dining room and, our choice, an enclosed porch with a tropical look.

The menu is fairly predictable, from fried shrimp and farm-raised catfish to grilled swordfish and sautéed crab cakes. Baked grouper topped with lump crab and a special of pan-seared tuna with mango-pineapple salsa and soy-ginger sauce appealed at our visit. A couple of steaks and southwest chicken are the only non-seafood items. Start with a pot of steamed oysters, steamed shrimp or fried green tomatoes. Finish with chocolate mousse cake or homemade pecan pie.

(843) 524-7433. Entrées, $10.95 to $15.95. Dinner, Tuesday-Sunday 4:30 to 9:30 or 10.

Plums, 904½ Bay Street, Beaufort.

Hidden down an alley behind stores and backing up to the waterfront park is this casual establishment, favored for lunch or a casual dinner on the rear porch looking toward the river. It's next door to Plumage, an elegant boutique, but otherwise the name is obscure.

Interesting salads and sandwiches are offered in a nondescript high-ceilinged yellow dining room open to the bar and on the back porch. The extensive dinner menu has international flair, as in starters of Tuscany antipasti, Cuban nachos, black bean quesadilla and steamed Prince Edward Island mussels. The adventure continues with such main dishes as a special of rare yellowfin tuna over Asian noodles with a Vietnamese chili sauce topping and Chilean salmon on a painted plate with wasabi, pineapple, rum and curry sauces. Lump crab cakes are topped with a cool key lime-jalapeño tartar sauce. Angus filet mignon is sauced with spiked béarnaise. Pastas, substantial salads and sandwiches round out the dinner menu. Desserts come from the owner's ice cream factory in Port Royal.

(843) 525-1946. Entrées, $11.95 to $17.95. Lunch daily, 11 to 5. Dinner nightly, 5 to 10.

The Bank Waterfront Grill & Bar, 926 Bay St., Beaufort.

Behind the columned facade of the old Beaufort Bank is this two-story establishment with a wraparound mezzanine and a neat rear courtyard patio. Tables topped with globe candles and lots of greenery help fill the high-ceilinged space. Tables of choice are the twelve on the patio surrounded by hibiscus, oleander and crape myrtle.

The enormous all-day menu offers something for everyone. There are two dozen appetizers, an equal number of specialty salads (from blackened salmon caesar to "grilled chicken healthy"), countless sandwiches and burgers, fried seafood baskets and platters, pastas, and ten black angus steak dishes. The choices nearly overwhelm, and some are farfetched as in pastas called caesar salad, catch of the day and stir-fry. But locals like the Bank for its variety and value. And it remains rock-solid amid a changing array of downtown eateries.

(843) 522-8831. Entrées, $10.95 to $16.95. Lunch and dinner daily, from 11:30.

Diversions

The rather commercial Beaufort Visitors Center, relocated to the Conant House at 1106 Carteret St., dispenses information and makes reservations for a variety of town tours, including guided horse-drawn carriage, van, boat and walking tours. Guides add local color as they point out the film sites for major movies, embellish local history, share anecdotes and show the haunts of ghosts. Self-guided maps for walking and bicycle touring invite more leisurely exploration. Be advised: Most sights and tours do not operate on Sundays.

Historic Tours. Old Beaufort is laid out in a grid pattern like Savannah, with an occasional block or street that was never developed. Unlike Savannah's, these are not public squares but private parks. Most seem to belong to the adjacent properties. They were left open to maximize the breeze and provide a water vista, as indicated by the carved wooden signs at the end of many a street or alley: "This view preserved by the City of Beaufort." Actually there's not much to see besides marshes and water, and the adventurous visitor gets a feeling of trespassing.

The densest concentration of Federal, Georgian and Greek Revival houses is found on The Point, east of Carteret Street. Beaufort's oldest neighborhood, it's rimmed by water on three sides. About five dozen historic houses, most built with cotton profits, are of exceptional architectural distinction. Many have large yards and elaborate gardens, well screened behind thick greenery. An early morning walk through the area is delightful if somewhat haunting, with birds twittering, dogs barking, cats lurking and mysterious looking houses draped in spanish moss. Of particular interest are the substantial bayfront properties of the Fripps, the Verdiers, the Barnwells et al., variously called The Castle, Tidewater, Marshlands, the Oaks and Tidalholm. Most were used as film sites. From the Point, curving Bay Street runs west along the river. Its shops and mansions are an elegant front line, behind which lie narrow streets flanked by smaller houses and churches. Behind the downtown shops is the Henry C. Chambers Waterfront Park, a shady expanse of green with a playground, landscaped green and harbor promenade. Cruise ships, shrimp trawlers and sailboats dock here periodically.

Water Tours. The two-level Islander excursion boat, sailing daily from Waterfront Park, takes up to 125 passengers on river excursions and entertainment cruises. Two smaller outfits offer dolphin watching, environmental tours, sailing charters and coastal excursions from the Downtown Marina.

Historic Sights. Guides bring history to life in **The John Mark Verdier House**, 801 Bay St., a Federal-style house museum built about 1790 by a leading merchant/ planter. The Marquis de Lafayette was entertained here. During the Civil War, the house served as Union Army headquarters. It's open Tuesday-Saturday 11 to 4; admission $4. The **Beaufort Museum** is housed on the top floor of the 1798 Beaufort Arsenal at 713 Craven St. The arsenal is a tan, fortress-like structure built for the Beaufort Volunteer Artillery about the time the sea island cotton debuted and Beaufort entered its golden era. Among the exhibits of local memorabilia are Indian artifacts, Revolutionary and Civil War relics, and decorative arts. It's open daily except Wednesday and Sunday, 10 to 5; admission $2. **St. Helena's Episcopal Church,** 501 Church St., dates to 1712 and rises above interesting grave sites in the churchyard. The 1813 **Secession House,** 1113 Craven St., is where South Carolina's ordinance of secession from the Union was initiated.

Shopping. Bay Street and some of its intersecting streets have interesting stores and galleries. Low Country paintings by Nancy Ricker Rhett and bird carvings by William Rhett are featured at **Rhett Gallery**. Watercolorist Barbara Shipman shows her works at **Shipman Art Gallery.** Ceramic sculptures by Suzanne Longo and paintings by Eric Longo are displayed at **Longo Gallery.** Local artists also are shown at **Bay Street Gallery** and **Gallery One. Juxtaposition** features artwork, ceramics, handpainted furniture and gifts. **Waterside Place** offers gifts, gourmet foods and home accessories. **Bay Street Outfitters** carries fishing gear, travel goods, clothing and even cigars. **Rossignol's** is the place for decorative accessories. china, crystal and bridal gifts. **Plumage** is an elegant women's boutique. Fine linens and accessories are sold at **In High Cotton. A Tisket A Tasket** is a nifty garden shop and gallery. **Finders Keepers** stocks three rooms of collectibles. Collectibles, crafts and gifts also are found at **Southern Connections** and **The Craftseller.** Timeless toys for children of all ages are stocked at **Boombears. Firehouse Books and Espresso Bar** serves up coffee, sandwiches and books with a Southern accent in restored, atmospheric firehouse. **Cravings by the Bay** offers Southern specialty foods.

Extra-Special ——————————————————

The Gullah Culture.
Ancestral traditions of early African-Americans endure in the Sea Islands beyond Beaufort, especially on St. Helena Island. The Gullah language, a Creole blend of European and African tongues, arose in the holding pens of Africa's slave coast and matured on the isolated plantations of the Low Country.

Penn Center, Martin Luther King Jr. Drive, St. Helena Island.
After Union forces shelled the Port Royal area and occupied Beaufort in 1861, Northern benevolent societies helped support the Port Royal Experiment. It was the first large-scale government effort to help newly freed African blacks make the transition from slavery to freedom. Missionary teachers organized about 20 small schools across St. Helena Island. One was Penn School, the first school for freed slaves, now part of a 50-acre National Historic Landmark District called Penn Center. The 1862-vintage **York W. Bailey Museum** offers craft displays, tours, special lectures and such. The grounds are open for walking tours.
(843) 838-2432. Open Monday-Friday 10 to 4. Adults, $2.

Intricate Gullah handwoven sea-grass baskets and other wares are sold throughout the area. The Low Country's famed **Hallelujah Singers,** the lively choir in *Forrest Gump*, tell the Gullah story through song and dance, performing in their home area as well as around the country.

The Gullah House, 761 Sea Island Pkwy., St. Helena Island.
For a taste of traditional Gullah cuisine, head for this true establishment that catered for the *Forrest Gump* movie. A delicious Gullah concoction called Frogmore Stew (shrimp, sausage, corn on the cob, onions, potatoes and spices steamed together) is the specialty. Live entertainment is featured on Friday and Saturday nights.
(843) 838-2402. Open Tuesday-Thursday 11 to 9, Friday and Saturday, breakfast and lunch 7 to 3, dinner 5 to 10, Sunday 8 to 9.

Savannah, Ga.

Seductive Sense of Place

Long before author John Berendt made Savannah a choice destination for those who read his best-seller, *Midnight in the Garden of Good and Evil,* visitors were attracted to this seductive Southern belle cloaked in Spanish moss and mystery. Tourists came for its charm, history and architecture. Urbanologists studied it as a model city, both from its lofty beginning and its recent rebirth.

In 1733, British Gen. James E. Oglethorpe sailed up the Savannah River and laid out America's first planned city, eighteen miles inland from the Atlantic. He created a grid of streets interspersed with large squares after every second block.

Savannah's very layout is its biggest attraction. Along the riverfront is Factors Walk, the cotton exchange warehouse district where early Savannah fortunes were made. Beyond is the elegant grid of tree-lined streets interspersed with green spaces that slow traffic, let in sunshine and breezes, and yield tranquility. Moss-draped live oaks and colorful gardens, fountains and monuments are their hallmarks. Around the squares are richly varied and stately mansions and townhouses – many once near ruin but most now either beautifully restored or in the process.

Savannah dazzled from the beginning. When William Tecumseh Sherman marched through Georgia during the Civil War, he was so struck by its beauty that he billeted himself in the Green-Meldrim House. He spared the city and presented it to President Lincoln as a Christmas gift.

Savannah lapsed into obscurity for the next century or so. Cotton was no longer king and the city's downtown area was abandoned as life and commerce were reborn on the city's outskirts. As the landmark Davenport House was about to be razed for a parking lot, seven prominent local women rebelled and formed the Historic Savannah Foundation, a national leader in the preservation movement. Its revolving fund has helped save more than 1,200 historic structures. The 2.2-square-mile urban historic district is the nation's largest. Twenty-one of the original 24 squares remain (the others were given over to parking or buildings). They help give Savannah an international look with a rare – for this country – sense of place.

Lately two squares have come into fame of their own. Chippewa Square was the site of the famous bench in the movie *Forrest Gump.* Monterey Square was seen around the country when Bob Vila of the PBS television program *This Old House* renovated a home facing the square in 1996. It also was the site of an infamous fatal shooting in the mansion once owned by the grandfather of songwriter Johnny Mercer.

"The Book" and "The Movie," as

Balcony off guest room at Foley House looks onto impressive buildings facing Chippewa Square.

Midnight is called locally, not only recounts events surrounding the tragedy at the Mercer mansion. It reveals many of the secrets of local society, and has spawned a new outburst in tourism.

Things never will be quite the same in the city that Mercer called "a sweet, indolent place for a boy to grow up in." Yet Savannah has not been over-run by tourists nor junked up with *Midnight* paraphernalia. Even as trolleys and tour buses wind around the historic district, the city feels uncrowded.

Introverted Savannah, a city of 150,000, is no longer upstaged by its extroverted neighbor Charleston. It offers myriad delights for visitors. Within its historic district are architectural treasures, lush gardens, impressive homes, shops, restaurants and museums. Staying at an inn around one of the squares in the historic district is the best way to experience the community feeling envisioned by founder Oglethorpe.

Savannah is a hard city to leave. Its seductions tug at you.

Inn Spots

Inns and B&Bs have been evident in Savannah since the early 1980s, but have really come of age in the last few years. Almost all have new owners, who have raised the level of service and amenities, and most are in evidence. Be aware that parking is a consideration. A few inns have parking spaces, others give permits for free parking on the street, and still others leave guests to fend for themselves.

Most B&Bs have courtyards called "hidden gardens." Some of the most comfortable rooms often are on the lower or courtyard level that some folks shun as basement quarters (we generally find them warm and welcoming, often with brick walls and less of an austere feeling than in the high-ceilinged upstairs rooms). Parlors and dining rooms are usually on the second levels. The more coveted guest rooms with high ceilings often are on the parlor level and the floor(s) above.

The Ballastone, 14 East Oglethorpe Ave., Savannah 31401.

Restored in 1980 as one of the city's first B&Bs, this is arguably its most attractive, inside and out. The 1838 mansion is smack up against the sidewalk along broad Oglethorpe Avenue, Savannah's prettiest boulevard. Its gray facade presents bay windows, a wrought-iron curving stairwell, two balconies and intricate container plantings to the street. Behind the appealing exterior lies a world of sumptuous common rooms, comfortable guest rooms and an unusually high level of service that warrant one-word rave reviews ("fabulous," "perfection") in the lobby guest book.

To the left of the entry on the main floor is a tea room with marble-top tables for breakfast, lunch by reservation and afternoon tea. To the right is a formal parlor with full-length windows swagged in graceful draperies and a gold harp in a corner. Beyond is a lounge with an antique

Container plantings beautify entrance to The Ballastone.

bar, where hors d'oeuvres are served with evening beverages. It opens onto a small, lush side courtyard used for breakfast, drinks and idling.

At the rear of the main floor is a wing containing the Victoria Suite, with a king poster rice bed, Victorian sofa and chairs, fireplace and a double jacuzzi. Two suites with similar features are housed on the floors above. The China Trade, handsome in green and burgundy, has a step-up king bed enveloped in draperies. The Gazebo, its walls handpainted with intricate designs, harbors an antique birdcage beside a plush sofa and chair.

Elsewhere on the second and third floors are thirteen bedrooms, most with kingsize beds and fireplaces and all with TV/VCRs. Scalamandre wallpapers in Savannah colors are the decorative motif. Even the loveseat is canopied in fabric in the front-corner Scarlett's Retreat, one of the smaller rooms with a lace-canopied queen bed and a corner jacuzzi.

Owner Jean Claire Hagens, a retired oil company marketing executive who is a fifth cousin of Jefferson Davis, has raised the service level and prices since acquiring the Ballastone in 1997. A staff of eighteen caters to every whim, from complimentary pressing of clothing to delivering a nightcap at midnight. Rooms are furnished not only with terrycloth robes but with terry slippers. "We tie the men's with blue ribbons and the ladies' with red ribbons," says Jean. Towels are replaced and homemade chocolates and brandy are presented at nightly turndown.

A full Southern breakfast is prepared by a resident chef in the morning. The fare could be German apple pancakes, french toast or an egg casserole. The bill is enclosed in a copy of an artwork suitable for framing.
(912) 236-1484 or (800) 822-4553. Fax (912) 236-4626. Thirteen rooms and three suites with private baths. Doubles, $195 to $285. Suites, $315 to $345. Add $60 for October and March-May. Midweek discounts. Two-night minimum stay weekends. Children over 16. Smoking restricted.

The Gastonian, 220 East Gaston St., Savannah 31401.
The grande dame of Savannah's four-diamond inns and considered by some its most deluxe, this is known for its historic elegance as well as for Southern hospitality. Two adjacent mansions, built in the Regency Italianate style in 1868, are joined in back by a landscaped elevated walkway above a formal garden, with a wonderful large deck alongside.

Each of the seventeen guest quarters is distinctive. The feeling is old Savannah in the third-floor Mary Telfair with two poster double beds and crewel curtains and bedspreads, or in the Juliet Low with a queen brass bed, an original clawfoot tub and the inn's only private balcony. It's more contemporary in three newer street-level rooms with painted brick walls, hardwood floors and state-of-the-art bathrooms with jacuzzi tubs and large walk-in showers. The feeling is private in the snug rear Carriage House, with a queen bedroom upstairs containing a bright red "birthday tub" with hand-held shower and a small kitchenette/sitting room downstairs. And the feeling is positively decadent in the 40-foot-long Caracalla Suite, fashioned from a double parlor with two fireplaces. The front section has a canopied king bed and a few chairs, not exactly the kind to relax in. That's because you're meant to relax in the enormous whirlpool spa draped in fabric in the middle of the rear room, which looks like a Roman bath. The commode is in a tiny closet, there are two marble vanities, lots of mirrors and no shower. Those of us into showers had to go through contortions with a short, hand-held rubber extension that kept falling off the faucet while sitting in the midst of an empty ten-foot-square tub. And we'd better not even tell the story of trying to wash one's hair – suffice it to say that the whole area was drenched and we nearly broke a leg on the slippery wet floor. Whirlpool spa be cursed!

That was nothing compared to the small Japanese soaking tub in the Tomochichi Room. Part of the vanity in an alcove of the bathroom, the circular tub is three feet wide and four feet deep. It's billed as "designed for the agile" – an understatement, to say the least. Ladders are provided for access to similar but slightly larger, less formidable soaking tubs in the Eli Whitney and Mary Hilyer rooms. Interestingly, these three are by far the least expensive rooms.

Enough on baths. As refurbished by new owner Anne Landers, the accommodations are comfortable, the furnishings distinguished and the amenities first-rate. All have fireplaces and half have normal whirlpool tubs. TVs and telephones are standard. Silk/terrycloth robes are provided in the suites; the others get waffle-weave robes.

The restored side garden and a secret, walled garden are delightful. We basked beneath the moonlight on a warm November night with a peach schnapps on the rear terrace and relaxed the next morning on the front veranda outside the Caracalla Suite and watched Savannah get ready for work.

Gourmet treats gild the lily. The evening social hour and the communal breakfast

are among the best of their genre. Savories and sweets are put out with afternoon tea and wine, and guests generally sit in a circle around the antiques-filled parlor and chat. Evening cordials are available there at night. The next morning you join others at tables in a country kitchen and dining room for quite a repast: in our case, orange juice, baked grapefruit, muffins and an excellent spinach and ham quiche. As in the best hotels, the room bill comes with the newspaper outside the door.
(912) 232-2869 or (800) 322-6603. Fax (912) 232-0710. Fourteen rooms and three suites. Doubles, $195 to $275. Suites, $350. Two-night minimum weekends. Children over 12. No smoking.

Foley House Inn, 14 West Hull Street, Savannah 31401.
Two side-by-side, late 19th-century townhouses and a newer carriage house provide some of Savannah's most luxurious accommodations. Danish-born Inge Svensson Moore and her husband Mark moved from Connecticut to upgrade this B&B in 1995. Vivacious Inge is the innkeeper. Her husband, a money manager, "makes sure I can stay in business," quips Inge.

With great taste but no formal experience, Inge upgraded and redecorated everything in sight. Her favorite colors are shades of red, from the showy parlor to the main-floor Essex, the largest guest room. Rich in burgundy, the Essex is furnished with a king canopy bed, a day bed and a jacuzzi tub with a marble shower. All rooms are named after English counties, and have an antique map of the county and related pictures on the walls. "Learning on the job," Inge has become fond of other colors than her early reds. She says she takes the colors from the oriental rugs on the floors. The Easton Lodge with a king bed and bay window is attractive in gold and aubergine. Its large bathroom contains a double jacuzzi and a commode on a raised platform. The Stafford, a beauty in yellow with red accents, comes with a small front balcony from which occupants can look out onto Chippewa Square and the park bench where Forrest Gump sat and offered his box of chocolates. The room has a kingsize bed, a loveseat and two armchairs and a curved pine armoire, as well as a jacuzzi bath.

All rooms in the townhouses have fine antiques, fireplaces and kingsize beds except for five with two double beds. TV/VCRs, telephones and waffle-weave robes are standard. Four rooms in the newer carriage house across a rear courtyard are smaller and more contemporary. Inge apologizes for their shortcomings, but we quite like them and consider them good value.

Inge recently reopened the original double parlor, swathed in crimson with two fireplaces and lots of antiques. The rear portion had earlier been converted into a guest room. She turned the bedroom into a breakfast room and the bathroom into a small bar. Inge and her staff offer afternoon tea with delicious Danish anise cookies and chocolate cake, as well as canapés for wines that are for sale. Cordials are offered in the evening.

Breakfast, available from 7:30 to 10:30, is quite a treat. At our visit, a plate of melon and strawberries preceded a lavish french toast stuffed with bananas and walnuts. An egg, ham and spinach casserole with scones was on tap the next day.
(912) 232-6622 or (800) 647-3708. (912) 231-1218. Nineteen guest rooms with private baths. Doubles, $145 to $275. Smoking restricted.

Magnolia Place Inn, 503 Whitaker St., Savannah 31401.
There are palm trees out front, creeping fig vines climb the front staircase and

the only magnolia is an interloper, spreading across the side yard from the Georgia Historical Society property next door. This rare Steamboat Gothic structure was built in 1878 as a rather fashionable boarding house. Here, author Conrad Aiken was born to parents who boarded here while house-hunting. More recently, it has

been a favorite place to stay of author John Berendt during visits to promote "the Book."

That's not all that's unusual about the landmark house facing Forsyth Park. It's personally run by a trio of innkeepers, new owners Rob and Jane Sales from Atlanta and his widowed sister, Kathy Medlock from Houston. The original interior is virtually intact, except for the bathrooms, seven of which have jacuzzi tubs. The parlor is a rear portion of what had been a double parlor (the front is now a guest room). Tables in said parlor open for continental breakfast, with pastries obtained from a local bakery. Rare kimonos, one older than the house, are displayed above the curving

Palm trees shade verandas at Magnolia Place Inn.

staircase, which is topped by a skylight open to another skylight in the attic.

Interesting colors and arty accents prevail along with period pieces and parquet floors in the thirteen guest rooms in the main house. All but two have fireplaces – one tiled in Delft, and others with handpainted tiles – and all have TV/VCRs. Beds are king or queensize, many of them canopied. Most in demand is the top-floor General Nathaniel Green room, where author Aiken was born. Colorful in orange-red and green, it opens through Jefferson-style, climb-through windows onto the broad front balcony. Another prize on the top floor is the rear General Joseph Warren Room, striking in tangerine and green, with an extra-deep jacuzzi tub. It enjoys access to the back porch overlooking a landscaped courtyard with teak furnishings, a lily pond and fountain.

Five of the most appealing and comfortable rooms here are on the lower or courtyard level. Kathy's favorite is the queen-bedded James Oglethorpe, the smallest, but cheery in yellow florals. We liked the Andrew Jackson, colorful in orange and with a large circular bathroom underneath the front porch. Big opaque windows, ficus trees, tiled floors and a jacuzzi tub give it something of a spa look.

More surprises are evident in two new courtyard suites fashioned from what Rob called "a dungeon" beneath a house next door. More contemporary in English cottage style, the rear Courtyard Suite offers a kingsize bedroom, a queen sofabed in the living/dining area, and a bath with the commode enclosed in glass blocks

The President's Quarters occupies own city block facing Oglethorpe Square.

and a huge jacuzzi with a waterfall faucet and a shower overhead. The front Forsyth Park Suite is smaller and quirky, with a painted brick floor, a full kitchen, a queen bed and a bathroom with shower only.

Continental breakfast with sliced fruit, cereals and pastries from Express Café & Bakery is offered in the rear parlor of the main house. This room is notable for a handpainted tiled fireplace and butterfly prints on the walls and the rugs. The butterfly motif is the result of an antique cabinet imported from Europe. Unbeknownst to the buyer, its shelves were full of mounted butterfly collections.

Lemonade, tea and wine are offered in the afternoon. In the evening, coffee and dessert is served, perhaps cheesecake or key lime pie. Turndown service adds pralines and cordials.

(912) 236-7674 or (800) 238-7674. Fax (912) 236-1145. Thirteen rooms and two suites with private baths. Doubles, $145 to $240. Suites $180 and $250. No smoking.

The President's Quarters, 225 East President St., Savannah 31401.

This historic B&B, while not as splashy as some of its four-diamond peers, has a lot going for it. Location, for instance – occupying its own block facing Oglethorpe Square, surrounded by some of the city's finest mansions and closer than others to downtown and the riverfront. The inn faces a large, New Orleans-style courtyard and has its own parking lot. The bedrooms are extra-spacious, furnished in Federal style, some with balconies and lofts, and all with fireplaces. And the rates are lower than most others.

New owners Hank and Stacy Smalling moved from Jacksonville in 1997. After surveying inns from Asheville to Key West, they decided Savannah was the city in which they wanted to live.

They imparted fresh spirit to the twin Federal-style townhouses built in 1855 for Andrew Gordon Low, whose daughter-in-law was founder of the Girl Scouts. The four guest quarters on each floor are named for presidents who have visited Savannah. Presidential memorabilia, letters, photos and caricatures are scattered about the rooms and hallways. The Kennedy Suite with kingsize canopy bed and private balcony contains a portrait of Jacqueline Kennedy. Another balcony, a Victorian bed and a sofabed enhance the Carter Suite. The George Washington and Woodrow Wilson suites on the fourth floor have living/dining rooms down and loft rooms with king beds and jacuzzis upstairs. Beds are a mix of king and queensize, except for four rooms with two double beds. All have TV/VCRs hidden in armoires, writing desks, refrigerators and monogrammed terrycloth robes. Some of the most appealing accommodations are the three suites with queen beds in the inn's new annex across the street, one of Savannah's few street-level townhouses. The Smallings worked around the decorative ceilings handpainted by an early owner, a Norwegian artist. Each has a sitting room with fireplace and a bath with a jacuzzi. The street-level Ronald Reagan Room adds a private rear courtyard. The Ulysses S. Grant Suite has a private deck and a steam shower. The third-floor Abraham Lincoln Suite has a bath with fireplace and steam shower.

The Smallings put bowls of fruit in the rooms and offer substantial hors d'oeuvres and sweets with tea and wine in the small parlor off the lobby or on the bigger courtyard outside. Sweets and cordials are provided at nightly turndown. A continental breakfast, on certain days supplemented by quiche or belgian waffles, is taken in bedrooms or on the courtyard.

(912) 233-1600 or (800) 233-1776. Fax (912) 238-0849. Ten rooms and nine suites. Doubles, $137 to $157. Suites, $177 to $225.

Hamilton-Turner Inn, 330 Abercorn St., Savannah 31401.

Native Savannahians own and run this new B&B facing Lafayettte Square. That sets them apart from the others – guest diaries in each room testify to the personal hospitality dispensed by Charlie and Sue Strickland since the opening in 1998. Theirs is a fine example of a French Second Empire chateau, built in 1873, with a mansard roof topped in ironwork cresting like wedding lace. The Stricklands renovated and redecorated the home that had been owned and run briefly as a museum by Nancy Hillis, also known as Mandy (Joe Odom's girlfriend in "The Book.") She still lives here and works the desk at night to help the Stricklands, who are hands-on innkeepers.

Ornate signs bearing the names of famous Savannahians are on the doors of the fourteen rooms on four floors. Five rooms have working fireplaces, and four have jacuzzis (the rest are antique clawfoot tubs). Sinks are set into antique washstands. Furnishings are Empire, Eastlake and Renaissance Revival antiques. TV/VCRs are hidden in armoires, and telephones come with computer hookups. Down comforters cover the beds, most queen or kingsize except for two rooms with two double beds each. Oriental scatter rugs top the hardwood floors. Fresh flowers and bottled spring water are in every room.

The prized Oglethorpe Suite, cheery in a creamy mustard color, has a high queen sleigh bed awash in flouncy pillows in one corner, a jacuzzi bath with a canopy that matches the window treatments, and a sitting area with a set of fancy carved wood upholstered chairs facing a TV in the armoire. Guests can climb through Jefferson-style windows onto balconies on front and side. Next to the Oglethorpe in another front corner is the Noble Jones Room, handsome in a rich green with a king bed, fireplace and whirlpool tub. Green turns out to be a favorite decorative color, as evidenced by the chartreuse green walls in the rear Juliette Low Room, in which the white queen bed takes up most of the space. Rooms on the ground floor, with brick walls and carpeting, have outdoor entrances and convey a bit more warmth. The John Habersham, the smallest, is jaunty in white brick and Laura Ashley blue. The Eli Whitney is colorful in blue and yellow.

There's a small outdoor courtyard with a fish pond in back. Beyond is a two-bedroom carriage house apartment. The Stricklands designed it for families with children who want an inn experience.

The Stricklands cook a Southern breakfast, with changing variations. The day of our visit produced fresh orange juice, croissants and muffins, grits, scrambled eggs, sausage and hash browns. Charlie prepared Dutch apple pancakes the next day. The meal is taken in a tearoom containing six linen-covered tables for four. Tea with pastries is served here in the afternoon.

Guests gather in a majestic chandeliered parlor best described as sumptuous. It's notable for massive arched doors, pocket shutters and a white marble fireplace. One of the Empire sofas was acquired from the Mercer estate, and the gasolier lamp came from the Hunter estate. The Stricklands set out to restore the mansion to its former grandeur. "We even exceeded our expectations," said Charlie.

(912) 233-1833 or (888) 448-8849. Fax (912) 233-0291. Twelve rooms and two suites with private baths. Doubles, $160 to $235. Suites, $235 to $270. Carriage house, $300. Two-night minimum weekends. Children accepted. No smoking.

The Eliza Thompson House, 5 West Jones St., Savannah 31401.

When Carol and Steve Day detoured off the Interstate to visit Savannah the first time, "our mouths fell open and didn't close until we left," Carol says. "We fell in love with the city." They moved from Illinois in 1995 to buy this 1847 complex. It had opened in 1978 as one of Savannah's first B&Bs and was badly in need of refurbishing. A 40-foot container of antiques collected from their corporate travels around the world helped them furnish. Carol's warm welcome for guests earned her inn the local small business hospitality of the year award in 1998.

The Eliza Thompson is nicely situated in the heart of the historic district on a brick street that Southern Living called Savannah's most beautiful. It's more of a mixed bag than most B&Bs locally. For one thing it's the largest privately owned B&B (25 rooms), although it doesn't seem large. It has arguably the city's nicest hidden courtyard, a spacious brick and wrought-iron oasis colorful with hanging baskets, a crape myrtle older than the house and an artistic central sculpture fountain and pool full of koi. An arched breakfast colonnade faces the courtyard, and can be enclosed and heated in cool weather. On a mild November evening, this proved the best-lit place to catch up on some reading.

The Days tore up old linoleum, removed wall-to-wall carpeting and repainted rooms in stunning Savannah historic colors. Many of their antiques turn up in the small but gracious parlor. This is the setting for a spread of iced tea and sweets, wine and cheese and savories like peach-pecan dip with crackers, available from 5:30 to 7, as well as after-dinner coffee and dessert (carrot cake at our visit, cobblers or cookies) from 8:30 to 10.

More antiques were evident in our third-floor, front-corner room, with a queen poster rice bed beneath a twelve-foot-high ceiling draped in white fabric gathered into a medallion. A Victorian sofa, dressing table, ornate decorative fireplace, fancy swagged curtains and oriental rug dignified the room, which was the largest we saw. Its rather claustrophobic bathroom had to be one of the smallest, fashioned from what appeared to be a long closet or two. The bathroom for a parlor-level room with two queen poster beds is on two levels of a former stairwell. Altogether, thirteen widely varying rooms are on three floors of the main house. Less historic – but some might say more serviceable – rooms are out back in a wing and a carriage

Artistic sculpture fountain centers courtyard at The Eliza Thompson House.

house facing the courtyard. Most have french doors onto the courtyard or a balcony. The ones we saw had kingsize beds with wall canopies or tapestries and plush oriental rugs.

Breakfast is served buffet-style under the colonnade and may be taken to the courtyard. Ours began with juice, cereals and coconut-orange coffeecake. The main course was an exemplary baked pineapple french toast. Other morning's treats include sausage or ham quiche, eggs strata and baked eggs with cream cheese. Carol Day table-hops and chats with guests she hasn't met at the reception the evening before.

(912) 236-3620 or (800) 348-9378. Fax (912) 238-1920. Twenty-five rooms with private baths. Doubles, $99 to $210. Two-night minimum weekends. Children accepted. No smoking.

The Jesse Mount House, 207 West Jones St., Savannah 31401.

This 1854 brick townhouse, half of a double house, is luxurious and purposely small. "We could have bought the other half," says owner Rob Cunningham, "but our guests said no." They liked the intimacy, and also felt they were filling a missing niche in the local market. (The Jesse Mount has six rooms, where the norm is fourteen to twenty.)

Rob and his English-born wife Judy acquired the B&B in 1996 from a woman who was an interior designer "and did a wonderful job," says Judy. The Cunninghams simply continued to embellish and provide all the amenities of a first-class hotel, from gas fireplaces to environmental sound machines (with babbling brooks to lull you to sleep), from waffle-weave robes to 380-count sheets and feather quilts. Each room has a TV/VCR, telephone and original artworks. Four have whirlpool tubs.

The Cunninghams call "rustic" their charming street-level Peter Tondee Suite, which had been a utility room. British actor/producer Kenneth Branagh occupied its white-brick living room and queensize bedroom for three months and "said it felt like home," Rob reported. Behind it in the old kitchen facing the rear garden is the Africa Room. Its queen iron bed is canopied in white, with a steamer trunk and a leopard-skin rug at its foot, a sofa, a kitchen/dining alcove and a bath with an exotic double whirlpool waterfall tub. Across the garden courtyard in the carriage house is a cozy garden room with heart-pine floor, a queen canopy bed angled from the corner, and a plush white sofa and green chair.

Upstairs in the main house are three more guest rooms. Much in demand is Addie's Room, the original master suite. It's handsome in pale yellow, with a kingsize bed and a chaise lounge. A rear dressing room with a sofa and windows opens into a large bath with black marble floor and vanity, whirlpool tub, separate shower and a bidet. Rob's favorite is the smallest Jesse Mount Room, fourth-floor front, with a step-up canopy queen bed and a view into the branches of the live oak trees along Jones Street.

There's plenty of common space, "so people don't feel confined," says Rob. Beneath the Jesse Mount Room on the third floor is a library. The parlor floor has a rich red living room and dining room, each with crystal chandeliers hanging from gilt ceiling medallions. There are a rear deck and a brick courtyard below.

A proper English tea with homemade scones, shortbread and finger sandwiches is put out at 4 o'clock. Beds are turned down with a chocolate and a cordial.

Breakfast is served by candlelight in the fireplaced dining room or outside on the courtyard. The fare the day of our visit was fresh orange juice, muffins, a fruit course of warmed grapefruit with sorbet and mint, and a frittata with vegetables.

(912) 236-1774 or (800) 347-1774. Fax (912) 236-2103. Five rooms and one suite with private baths. Weekends, March-May and October: doubles, $195 to 240. Midweek, rest of year: $160 to $175. Two-night minimum weekends. Children over 12. No smoking.

Granite Steps, 126 East Gaston St., Savannah 31401.

This 10,000-square-foot mansion, built in 1881 and sold in 1998 for $2.1 million, is named for the double curved entry steps outside. Fancier names might be more appropriate, for there is nothing understated about the showplace opened in late 1998 by Donna Sparks, who moved here from suburban Atlanta. The property was acquired by her mother, Nancy Panoz, founder of Chateau Elan, a resort and winery outside Atlanta.

Local preservationist and antiques dealer Jim Williams of *Midnight* fame was renovating the house when he died, Donna advised. She and her mother finished the job. The public spaces lend themselves to functions. The double parlor to the right of the marble-floored foyer contains three crystal chandeliers overhead, two marble fireplaces and a grand piano in a bay window at one end. A morning-room/sunporch furnished in wicker adjoins it alongside. In back is a leather-clad library with a big TV. On the left side of the foyer, in what had been a ballroom, is an opulent dining room with wing chairs in the front bay, marbleized walls, draperies puddled to the floor and a handsome table set for ten. Off the state-of-the-art kitchen is a small breakfast room with palladian window and brass chandelier. The rear of the house opens onto a walled courtyard garden planted with boxwood and topiary.

Much of the rest of the space in the house is given over to three suites and two smaller guest rooms, all with fireplaces. The garden-level Abercorn Suite has a kingsize sleigh bed, a mirrored jacuzzi in an alcove, a living room with a fireplace and sleeper sofa, a wet bar in the private entry foyer and a marble bathroom with

Granite Steps is showy new B&B in restored 1881 mansion.

the commode in one side of a huge walk-in shower. The rear Telfair Suite on the second floor has a king poster bed with an iron fretwork canopy, a convertible loveseat/sleeper, a gas fireplace and access to the side balcony. Beyond a dressing area is an all-white bath with a double vanity, double jacuzzi and a skylit, walk-in shower. The front Oglethorpe Suite has a king sleigh bed, living room and an elaborate bathroom of Italian marble. There's an enormous shower, and the jacuzzi tub here is enclosed in library shelves and faces a TV.

Two guest rooms with queensize beds and access to the side balcony pale a bit in comparison, yet contain the luxurious furnishings, fresh flowers and a bottle of wine common to all other quarters. Turndown service produces peanut brittle candy, cookies or strawberries dipped in chocolate.

Tea or wine with hors d'oeuvres are served about 4:30. Breakfast is elaborate: perhaps eggs benedict with shrimp, scrambled eggs with smoked salmon or french toast stuffed with bananas and pecans. A pork tenderloin steak likely accompanies, as do a grits casserole, fresh fruit and muffins. The meal is served from 8:30 to 10:30. A continental breakfast is available earlier in the upstairs hallway.

Guests' comfort is foremost, says Donna. "I'd rather do five rooms really well than twenty rooms that are merely ordinary."

(912) 233-5380. Fax (912) 236-3116. Two rooms and three suites with private baths. Doubles, $250. Suites, $350.

Dining Spots

Elizabeth on 37th, 105 East 37th St., Savannah.

Elizabeth Terry and her husband Michael, the wine steward, have been drawing knowledgeable diners almost since they opened their restaurant in 1981. We found their handsome, turn-of-the-century mansion some distance removed from the historic district a gracious setting for a memorable dinner in Savannah many years back.

Elizabeth's fame has spread far and wide and she has won all kinds of awards since. Now assisted by daughters Alexis and Celeste, Elizabeth is in the vanguard of contemporary Southern cuisine, imparting sometimes stunning, sometimes subtle variations on classic local recipes. She has exhaustively researched Savannah cooking over the last two centuries for the most authentic nuances.

Dining here is pricey and worthy of special occasions, according to the local consensus. But visiting food lovers find the experience well worth it, and book far ahead for weekends.

Southern fried grits and black-eyed pea relish is the signature appetizer. It's available either with shrimp, country ham and red-eye gravy or, our choice, with goat cheese and red pepper. sauce.

A salad of mesclun greens accompanies the main course. Elizabeth might prepare grouper with a sesame-almond crust and serve it with peanut sauce. She roasts her chicken with ginger and pecans and serves it with creamed rice and pear-apricot chutney. Her beef tenderloin au poivre comes with madeira sauce and a fried green tomato. The pepper-crusted rack of lamb bears a mushroom and olive sauce and is accompanied by a potato cake and a spinach-stuffed tomato.

The changing desserts here are standouts. Among them are a Savannah cream cake similar to a trifle and a pear-almond tart.

(912) 236-5547. Entrées, $27.50 to $29.50. Dinner nightly, 6 to 9:30 or 10. Jackets required.

Bistro Savannah, 309 West Congress St., Savannah.

Contemporary bistro cuisine debuted in Savannah in this 1875 mercantile building across from the City Market. Original wood floors, brick walls showcasing local art, white lights wrapping around red ceiling ducts, and tan rattan chairs at marble tables add up to a Parisian look.

The seafood here is rated tops in Georgia, and the wine list is select, if pricey. One of us made a meal of appetizers. The corn, vidalia and sweet potato soup with smoked bacon and scallion greens was both filling and sensational. Also good were the ginger-glazed calamari with cucumber mint and crème fraîche and the crispy chicken livers with fried spinach over creamy risotto. The garlicky mussels and asparagus with risotto made a fine main course, and had a sauce to die for. Other choices ranged from coastal bouillabaisse over linguini and crispy flounder with apricot-shallot glaze to pecan-crusted chicken with blackberry-bourbon sauce and filet of beef tenderloin.

The raspberry-ginger crème brûlée and the liqueured berries over vanilla bean ice cream with short bread appealed for dessert. We shared the praline and almond basket bearing raspberry sorbet and fresh strawberries and savored every bite.

(912) 233-6266. Entrées, $12.95 to $21.95. Dinner nightly, 6 to 10:30, weekends 5:30 to 11.

Sapphire Grill, 110 West Congress St., Savannah.

A former chef and a manager from Bistro Savannah moved down the street in 1998 to open this highly rated restaurant and wine bar. Showy art on brick walls, pinpoint lighting from an exposed ceiling, metal columns and sapphire accents create a high-tech backdrop for the contemporary cuisine of owner Christopher Nason. The staff hustles back and forth between the main-floor dining room and bar, a kitchen on the second floor, and another dining room on the third.

"I don't need to go to aerobics class since I started working here," our waitress quipped. She served olive oil in a saucer into which she grated romano cheese and pepper, to go with two mini-loaves of chewy bread. Good starters were an appetizer of spicy shrimp on polenta and a tart salad of arugula, watercress and radicchio with grilled pickled green tomatoes, sweetened by mango-infused honey. Main courses ranged from an exotic pasta dish of grilled shrimp, pulled duckling and foie gras tossed with tomatoes and arugula to grilled muscovy duck breast and confit with caramelized mango demi-glace. Our oversize, decorated white plates held the signature local black grouper, encrusted in benne seed and ginger, teamed with jasmine rice and wok-seared vegetables, and mustard-seared yellowfin tuna with roasted golden tomato aioli, fried scallion wands and grilled vegetables.

The piratically priced wine list comes on a metal board that behaved like a magnet. It picked up a spoon or two as we studied the choices starting at $29, far more than the price of the most expensive entrée.

Among desserts were a cocoa crème brûlée and a praline basket filled with passionfruit sorbet and chocolate sauce.

(912) 443-9962. Entrées, $16 to $19. Dinner nightly, 6 to 10:30, Friday and Saturday 5:30 to 11:30.

The Olde Pink House, 23 Abercorn St., Savannah.

Facing Reynolds Square in the heart of the historic district is this 1771 Georgian mansion with Jamaican pink walls and a series of small, refined dining rooms appointed with antiques and Colonial portraits.

The wine cellars are situated in cast-iron vaults with dungeon-like doors harking back to the building's days as a bank. Pianist-vocalist Gail Thurmond, a local legend, entertains nightly in front of a seasonal roaring fire in the casual **Planters Tavern** downstairs.

Savannahians who live in the historic district are partial to the classic Southern cuisine and the elegant ambiance. The same menu is served in both the tavern and the restaurant. For starters, consider the she-crab soup laced with sherry, the caesar salad with crisp oysters or the artichoke fritters stuffed with goat cheese. Main courses vary from crispy flounder with apricot-shallot sauce to steak au poivre and grilled lamb loin with wild mushroom demi-glace. House favorites are roast duck with wild berry sauce and local black grouper stuffed with blue crab and topped with vidalia onion sauce.

Finish with Colonial apple pie, espresso and perhaps a brandy in the tavern.

(912) 232-4286. Entrées, $16.95 to $24.95. Dinner nightly, 6 to 10:30. No smoking.

45 South, 20 East Broad St., Savannah.

This is the high-style (make that very) adjunct to the famed Pirate's House, a more casual, touristy spot where our family enjoyed dinner in one of the fifteen nautical dining rooms on our first trip through Savannah in the 1970s. The Pirates' House is located on the site of the first public agricultural experimental garden in America. Its Herb House dining room, erected in 1734, is thought to be the oldest house in Georgia.

On a rather more grand scale is 45 South, which serves dinner only amid serene surroundings. Service is said to be unreliable unless you're with a regular patron. The contemporary menu features such starters as lump crab cakes (a menu fixture since the restaurant opened in 1977), grilled quail with chorizo, spring rolls of duck confit, and pork tenderloin with napa cabbage. Typical main courses are sautéed grouper encrusted with yukon gold horseradish potatoes, grilled ahi tuna with seared foie gras, confit of rabbit with mixed bean ragoût and sliced pheasant with wild mushrooms.

Afterward, adjourn upstairs to **Hannah's East** ("Hard-Hearted Hannah, the Vamp of Savannah"), a laid-back jazz bar. Owner-bassist Ben Tucker often plays duets with pianist Emma Kelly, "the Lady of Six Thousand Songs," another of the main characters in "The Book."

(912) 233-1881. Entrées, $19.50 to $31.50. Dinner, Monday-Saturday 6 to 9 or 9:30. Jackets required.

Seasons in Savannah, 315 West St. Julian St., Savannah.

This high-ceilinged expanse with an open kitchen alongside is located in the City Market area. With its white-clothed tables with flickering oil lamps amid ficus trees and exposed pipes, it's quite stylish..

It also has a great canopied sidewalk terrace, where we were seated at crisp-linened tables for an autumn lunch. The crab cakes with rémoulade sauce, yellow rice and vegetables were fine. But the Thai beef salad was a travesty – overcooked and tough the first attempt and barely better after being returned to the kitchen. Suavely and without being asked, the salad was removed from the bill.

We'd go back. The dinner menu appeals with dishes like bouillabaisse, shrimp and grits over greens, steelhead salmon rockefeller, pecan grouper and grilled brandied ribeye steak.

(912) 233-2626. Entrées, $16.95 to $21.95. Lunch, Monday-Friday 11:30 to 2:30. Dinner nightly, 6 to 10 or 11.

Mrs. Wilkes' Dining Room, 107 West Jones St., Savannah.

Who hasn't heard of this timeless establishment, a.k.a. Mrs. Wilkes' Boarding House? One of the most famous places for breakfast or lunch in the South, it's ensconced on the ground floor of brick row house with only the tiniest sign on the side door. Not that a sign is needed. Just follow the crowd that lines up long before Mrs. Wilkes gives the blessing at the first seating for lunch.

Mrs. Wilkes, still sprightly at 92, was the dressiest person there the day we lunched. Perched on a high chair near the cash register, she was natty in a green blazer as she signed her cookbook for doting patrons. Only reluctantly, we were told, did she agree to raise the tab for her prix-fixe lunch that for most people is dinner.

Every meal follows roughly the same format. You're seated at one of four communal tables for ten in either of two homey dining rooms. At lunch, a waitress pours iced tea and brings fifteen serving platters of food – fried chicken, beef stew, beans, carrots, beets, spinach, salad, coleslaw, biscuits and who knows what all at our visit – and plunks them around the table. They're meant to be passed, but inevitably you miss a few. We liked best the okra with tomatoes, the corn pudding and the cheese potatoes, as well as the small individual dishes of peach cobbler and banana pudding for dessert.

People said we wouldn't be able to eat dinner that night (having not pigged out, we surprised them). Our table mates at breakfast had skipped dinner and thought the whole experience remarkable. Others weren't all that impressed with what appeared to be a perfunctory performance for tourists. You're admonished if you fail to clear your plates, or happen to put them in the wrong place. Who's doing whom a favor, and paying for the privilege?

(912) 232-5997. Breakfast, $5. Lunch, $10. Breakfast, Monday-Friday 8 to 9. Lunch, Monday-Friday 11 to 3. No credit cards.

The Gryphon Tea Room, 137 Bull St., Savannah.

Tea is the raison d'être for this magnificent new tearoom transformed in 1998 from a one-time pharmacy by the locally ubiquitous and entrepreneurial Savannah College of Art and Design. It's an architectural showplace of rich Honduran mahogany paneling, mirrors and Tiffany glass. The ceiling is draped in fabric, oriental rugs top the tiled floors, and the rest-room walls are inscribed with quotes about tea.

Sit at marble-top tables for coffee or tea (in several variations, including full afternoon tea from 4 to 6 o'clock for $12). Order a deli sandwich, soup or a salad plate, from some interesting choices (how about paella salad?). The shrimp salad and chicken salad sandwiches on kaiser rolls that we took to eat in the car as we drove north made a fine lunch. The pastries, pies and cakes displayed at the counter look mouth-watering.

Enjoy them at tables and chairs along the sidewalk facing Madison Square – a great place to hang out.

(912) 238-2481. Open Monday-Friday 8:30 to 9:30, Saturday 10 to 9:30, Sunday 10 to 6.

Other restaurants worth knowing about: **Garibaldi's** in an old firehouse at 315 West Congress St., part of the Balish family chain (they also own the Pink House), gets high marks for neighborhood Italian fare. **The Lady & Sons** provides homestyle Southern cuisine with a menu and an open buffet at 311 West Congress St. Contemporary northern Italian is the forte of **Il Pasticcio,** a large and sleek space with an open kitchen in a former department store at 2 East Broughton St. Creative continental cuisine is offered at **17 Hundred 90,** a basement room reminiscent of an English cottage beneath an inn of the same name at 307 East President St. Tourists are attracted for casual dining along the riverfront in the Factor's Walk area to places like **The Shrimp Factory, River House Restaurant** and the **Boar's Head Grill & Tavern.** Facing Bay Street in General Sherman's 1864 military headquarters is a new steak and seafood dinner restaurant called **The Times on Bay.** Broughton Street, once the city's main shopping street, is being rejuvenated with ethnic restaurants like **Typhoon** (Asian fusion), **The Casbah** (Moroccan), **Sakura** (Japanese), **Juarez** (Mexican), **Tucson Grill** (Southwest) and **So-Soleil** (American/Fusion). Good downtown lunch spots are **City Market Café,** with a canopied patio, and **Express Café & Bakery.** Two British pubs of note are **Six Pence Pub** at 245 Bull St. and **Churchill's Pub** at 9 Drayton St. A new competitor for Mrs. Wilkes is **Nita's Place** at 140 Abercorn St., where Juanita Dixon dishes up coastal-flavored soul food to almost as wide acclaim. You can order à la carte, and she even has eight seats, plus a high chair, on the sidewalk outside. She's open daily from 11:30 to 3, which means weekenders don't go hungry.

Diversions

Most of Savannah's attractions are located in the 2.2-square-mile Savannah National Historic District, which is eminently walkable. Indeed, since parking is metered and traffic must keep moving, the best way to see and savor Savannah is on foot – once you've gotten your bearings. After considerable touring, Oglethorpe Avenue and Bull Street turned out to be favorite haunts for walking. Oglethorpe and Mercer proved to be the best located squares.

Orientation Tours. More than twenty tour companies offer bus, trolley, carriage and walking tours, most starting from the visitor center in the former railroad station at the edge of the historic district. Tours vary by company and guide. Among the best are Gray Line, Hospitality and Old Savannah. Some spend an inordinate amount of time along the not particularly inspiring riverfront area and Factor's Walk. Others expand the Historic District to include the rejuvenating Victorian District beyond. Most point out the key sites as well as eccentricities like downspouts carved like dolphins. One guide noted that most of his tour concentrated on churches and buildings associated with the ubiquitous Savannah Colleges of Arts and Design. SCAD has bought and renovated many an abandoned building for use as classrooms, dormitories and galleries. Special-interest tours are served by ghost walks and the "Book" tours" (see Extra-Special).

Historic Sites. More than 1,200 structures of architectural and historic significance – most built in the 19th century and restored since the 1960s – are located within the nation's largest urban historic district. Of all the mansions with guided tours, the most distinguished is the **Owens-Thomas House,** 124 Abercorn St., considered the finest example of Regency architecture in America. The sumptuous **Andrew Low House,** 329 Abercorn St., was built in 1848 by a cotton merchant and later was the home of his son and daughter-in-law, who founded America's first Girl Scout troop. The Regency-style **Juliette Gordon Low Birthplace,** 142 Bull St., is the restored birthplace of the founder of the Girl Scouts of the USA, which maintains it as a memorial and as a national program center. The 1830s **Green-Meldrim House** on Madison Square, now the parish house for St. John's Episcopal Church, is where General Sherman lived when he spared Savannah after his famous March to the Sea. The **Telfair Academy of Arts and Sciences,** 121 Barnard St., occupies an 1818 Regency mansion on the site of the early Royal Governor's residence in Georgia. Its Octagon Room is one of the finest period rooms in the country. A museum wing displays a wide-ranging American Impressionist collection. The "Bird Girl," who was photographed in Bonaventure Cemetery for the cover of "The Book," has been moved here.

Churches and synagogues also are of note in the historic district. The Gothic **Cathedral of St. John the Baptist,** Abercorn and East Harris streets, is one of the largest in the South. Its European-style twin spires can be seen all across town. The 1778 **Temple Mickve Israel** at 20 East Gordon St., the nation's only Gothic synagogue, looks like a Catholic church but with a Star of David over the front door. It houses the oldest Torah in America and a museum chronicling the illustrious history of the first Jewish congregation in the South. The imposing **Independent Presbyterian Church,** Bull Street at West Oglethorpe Avenue, is modeled after St. Martin-in-the-Field's in London. **St. John's Episcopal Church,** 1 West Macon St., was built in Gothic Revival style in 1852 and is famed for its chimes and stained-glass windows. **Christ Episcopal Church** at 28 Bull St., the first church established in the Georgia colony in 1733, bears a plaque honoring John Wesley, its first pastor, who founded the first Protestant Sunday school in the new world. He later founded the Methodist movement.

Monuments, historic markers and azaleas in Reynolds Square are typical throughout Savannah.

The Davenport House, 324 East State St., Columbia Square.

This is where Savannah's remarkable restoration movement started. Built by a Rhode Islander in 1815, the Federal house is arguably the most significant structure in Savannah. The historically beautiful city showed signs of neglect at mid-century, leading to Lady Astor's famous characterization of Savannah as "a beautiful lady with a dirty face." Outrage surfaced after the City Market was razed for a parking garage, and a year later the Davenport House was threatened. Seven prominent women banded together in the nick of time in 1955. They raised $22,000 to save the building, which had become a tenement, from being razed for a parking lot. Thus began the Historic Savannah Foundation, the nation's pioneering city preservation movement. It led to the preservation of hundreds of historic structures, primarily through a revolving fund that puts money into saving a house, selling it and then pumping the proceeds into another. It took the foundation seven years to ready the house for opening as a museum. The foundation ran it until 1997, when it turned it over to the Davenport Foundation. House tours show salient details, including an early painted "floor cloth" in the hallway. The museum shop dispenses preservation material and local lore.

(912) 236-8097. Tours daily every half hour, 10 to 4:30. Adults $5.

Factors Walk and Riverfront. Astride the bluff along the Savannah River are old cotton warehouses restored into shops, galleries, restaurants, bars and small hotels. Running parallel to broad tree-lined Bay Street, between parkland and warehouses, is Factors Walk, a cobblestone alley once traveled by farmers with buggies bearing cotton. Cotton brokers (called factors) walked overhead on a still-existing network of iron and concrete bridges connecting the buildings to the bluff, evaluating the cotton beneath. Below is River Street, where Georgia was founded in 1733. The cobblestone streets were once the ballast in sailing ships. Along the river is a pleasant, nine-block concourse of parks with plantings and benches for ship-watching (don't miss the statue of the waving woman).

The view across the river is not exactly inspiring, although that situation could change as a hotel and other buildings were under construction on the other side.

Shopping. Savannah has not been known as a shopper's mecca, but Broughton Street, the original main commercial street, is being rejuvenated lately. The original stores fled out Abercorn Street to outlying malls. In their place are emerging antiques stores, accessory and gift shops like **Willows,** and the odd apparel boutique like **Gaucho.** Otherwise, shopping of the tourist variety is centered on River Street and Factors Walk, down by the riverfront, and along Congress and St. Julian streets around the old City Market. Here you'll find all manner of stores, from a metaphysical bookstore to a gallery of vibrant Haitian art. We liked **The Hammock Company** for garden things, bird feeders and goods of that ilk.

Distinctive shops are scattered here and there throughout the Historic District, especially along Bull Street between Chippewa and Monterey Squares. The area around Madison Square is a favorite, from **E. Shaver Bookseller** to **Chutzpah and Panache** for fashions. Savannah College of Arts and Sciences has several good stores, including **Design Works** and **Ex Libris.** At Whitaker and Jones streets are more, including **Vernon C. Criner & Son,** right beside the Wilkes House, a trove of gift baskets, flowers, foods of the area and, at our November visit, wonderful Christmas things. Next to it, **The Market at Jones & Whitaker** has great cards, cookbooks and decorative accessories.

Extra-Special

"The Book" Tour.

The book *Midnight in the Garden of Good and Evil* is much more about a place than about a shooting. It has spawned a movie, a television documentary, bus tours and a gift shop. Native Savannahian Pat Tuttle started the original "By the Book" tours and now has six competitors. Her Hospitality Tours of Savannah are still considered best. We boarded her small bus to see Club One, where the Lady Chablis performed, the apartment where she lived and her doctor's office where she received her hormone shots. The bus passed Lee Adler's house (where he happened to be parking and getting out of his car), Clary's Cafe, the Oglethorpe Club and, of course, the Hugh W. Mercer House, the mansion in which antiques dealer and preservationist Jim Willliams lived and where he shot the hustler, Danny Hansford. The house, we learned, was left to his sister, who now lives there (and has it for sale for a cool $10 million) and is not happy about the tours coming by incessantly. We passed Troup Square where the University of Georgia mascot Uga was walked. We saw the offices of the lawyers who defended Williams, gazed upon the three houses in which Joe and Mandy lived and partied, and learned many tidbits about life in Savannah. After a stop at the Hospitality Shop, where hot cider and cookies were offered and where the merchandise is "Book" and Savannah-oriented, the tour departed for Bonaventure Cemetery, where John Berendt and Mary Hardy drank martinis on the memorial bench to Conrad Aiken, the Savannah-born writer. This was where guide Bob Newell really shone. He has made an extensive study of grave symbols and was writing a guide about them. The group tromped through what must be one of the most atmospheric cemeteries ever, draped in Spanish moss on a bluff by the river, and saw Johnny Mercer's grave, among many others.

(912) 233-0119. Tours daily at 10 and 2. Adults, $16.

Guests liken Greyfield Inn on Cumberland Island to staying in a movie set of the Old South.

St. Marys, Ga.

Nature's Refuge

Facing Florida's Amelia Island across Cumberland Sound, St. Marys remains essentially an historic fishing village amidst the hubbub of coastal development. Although it dates to the mid-1500s, it was established as a town by the British in 1787 and was the nation's southernmost port when Florida was a Spanish province. Ships docked here from many lands, and tales are still told of smuggling activities and skirmishes between the Spanish and British.

Tales also are told of the gilded age when the Carnegie family built lavish mansions just offshore on Cumberland Island, the largest and southernmost of Georgia's barrier islands. Now a national seashore preserve, its cachet soared after John F. Kennedy Jr. chose the island and its exclusive Greyfield Inn for his wedding in 1996.

St. Marys also gained national recognition that year when Money magazine named it No. 1 among America's hottest little boom towns. Its low-key lifestyle and prospering economy were cited. The area's traditional major employer, Gilman Paper Co., has been joined lately by the Kings Bay Naval Submarine Base, the East Coast home for Trident submarines.

Despite its sudden fame as one of America's most livable and fastest-growing areas, old St. Marys remains a small town at heart. The saying "See you in the funny papers" originated here after cartoonist Roy Crane arrived on the Doodlebug – now the Toonerville Trolley – and stayed at the Riverview Hotel. He spent his time sketching townspeople and landmarks that showed up a few months later in his nationally syndicated Wash Tubbs comic strip.

The center of the old town is relatively compact, stretching back from the riverfront. It seems far removed from the Naval Base, the new commercial strip out Highway 40 and the posh homes and fairways of Osprey Cove, a top-rated golf community.

The major draws for visitors are Cumberland Island, the largest wilderness national seashore accessible (barely) to the public, and Okefenokee Swamp, the largest national wildlife refuge in the East. Cumberland Island may be the attraction, but it allows only 300 visitors a day, which says something about the pace of tourism in this area. You can walk down the middle of St. Marys Street at 9 o'clock on a weekday morning and there's not a car in sight.

"People tire of the busy-ness of the Golden Isles and Amelia Island," says Mary Neff of the Spencer House Inn. They find a back-to-nature respite in this old, quiet town.

Inn Spots

Greyfield Inn, Cumberland Island, (Box 900, 8 North Second St., Fernandina Beach, Fla. 32035).

Long before John F. Kennedy Jr. even thought of getting married here in 1996, the estate owned by the Carnegies had drawn an international clientele of jet-set romantics and nature lovers. The much-publicized (after the fact) Kennedy wedding added to its mystique.

Not for glitz and glamour do well-heeled rusticators come to this storied inn of the old school. The private Cumberland Island property is accessed by the inn's shuttle boat (from Fernandina Beach, not St. Marys). There are no telephones, no televisions, no jacuzzis, no cars. Many of the guest rooms share baths and look as if they came from Grandma's summer cottage. Except for those in a couple of cottages, the only shower is located outside behind the inn. And yet, almost unanimously, guests cherish the experience of a stay here. Staying in a mansion and having an island almost to oneself are worth the expense, they say. The guest book is full of comments by people who liken it to living in a movie set of the Old South.

Thomas Carnegie, brother and partner of steel magnate Andrew Carnegie, bought property on Georgia's longest and southernmost barrier island in 1881 and built a lavish, 30-room mansion called Dungeness. He and Lucy Carnegie built Greyfield in 1901 as a home for their daughter, Margaret Ricketson. Her daughter, Lucy R. Ferguson, and her family opened Greyfield as an inn in 1960. Now run by Lucy's grandchildren, it is furnished as it was at the turn of the century, largely with possessions salvaged from the ruins of Dungeness, which was destroyed by fire in 1959.

Much of the first two floors of this rambling four-story house is given over to public areas: a dark paneled living room, a fireplaced library in which one could spend hours, a fireplaced dining room favored for communal eating and a more intimate dining porch. A favorite spot is the

Spencer House Inn has been a hotel most of the time since it was built as a residence in 1872.

honor bar, cozy and well-stocked, where you help yourself, sign a chit and then head out to the wide veranda. Complimentary hors d'oeuvres are served with cocktails at 6. The dinner bell rings promptly at 7. The service is what managing innkeeper Brycea Merrill (not one of the Carnegie descendants who often are around the property) calls "open seating." Dress is "informal for ladies and jackets for men are required." The three-course meal changes daily. The fare for the served, sit-down breakfast also changes, as does the picnic lunch that can be stowed in a basket and taken on a nature excursion, a hike or bicycle ride or to the beach.

Guest rooms are on the second, third and fourth floors of the main house and in a pair of cottages. One cottage has four bedrooms and one has two bedrooms. Each cottage has a shared living room and private baths. In the main house, three bedrooms have private baths and eight share three baths. The prized accommodation is the master bedroom with four-poster bed and private bath in the southeast corner of the house. Two new bedrooms with private baths in the fourth-floor attic were being readied at our visit, as were two more in a cottage. The house also was being air conditioned.

Other than savoring the old Southern way of life, the highlight for many is the complimentary four-hour nature tour in a jeep or army truck, conducted daily by the staff naturalist. The itinerary varies by conditions and the weather, but guests are assured of seeing lots of wildlife, including horses, turkeys, pigs, armadillos and, the day of our visit, an eleven-foot-long alligator lazing in a swamp.

(904) 261-6408. Fax (904) 321-0666. Three rooms and six cottage rooms with private baths; eight rooms with shared baths. Rates American Plan: doubles, $395 with private bath, $275 to $375 with shared bath. Children over 6. Smoking restricted.

Spencer House Inn, 111 East Bryant St., St. Marys 31558.
Built in 1872 by the collector of customs for the Port of St. Marys, this appealing pink structure with two-story verandas across the side has served as a hotel for most of its years. Now listed on the National Register, it was converted into a

B&B in 1990. Mary and Mike Neff from Houston, Tex., recently added the attractive front parlor and the breakfast room and are providing the caring oversight of live-in owners.

A staircase and a modern elevator – installed when this served as an office building – lead to fourteen guest rooms and a two-bedroom suite on the second and third floors. High-ceilinged rooms go off wide corridors and retain the original transoms above the doors.

The large front corner room adjoining the veranda possesses a kingsize four-poster bed, a settee, an armchair and a clawfoot tub. Our mid-size room was handsome with the dark green walls and white trim characteristic of the others. It came with a white iron queensize bed and floral comforter, a flouncy canopy treatment above the window, a modern tub-shower, thick towels, a single chair, a vase of fresh daisies and bedside chocolates. Furnishings are antiques or reproductions. TVs and clock radios are standard equipment.

There's lots of common space in which to mingle with other guests. Nowhere more so than on the upstairs veranda – "everybody's favorite spot," according to Mary – or in the large breakfast room where the sideboard is laden with fruits and juices, cereal, homemade granola, muffins and toasting breads. Mike cooks to order the morning's entrée, at our visit a three-cheese omelet. A fellow guest, who stays here frequently, said the Neffs are the most pampering hosts he knows.

(912) 882-1872. Fax (912) 882-9427. Twelve rooms and one two-bedroom suite with private baths. Doubles, $65 to $90. Suite, $115.

Goodbread Bed & Breakfast, 209 Osborne St., St. Marys 31558.

One of the better values along the East Coast is offered by Betty and George Krauss at the restored Victorian B&B they opened in 1992. Four large, comfortable guest rooms and substantial breakfasts are their hallmarks.

Front verandas upstairs and down face the main street in this house built about 1870 and furnished in Victoriana. Unusual archways on either side of the fireplace separate the pleasant living room and dining room. The latter is where a table for eight is set with colorful red mats, napkins and plates for breakfast. The fare was scrambled eggs, sausage and orange-date muffins the day of our visit. Pecan waffles were on tap the next day. Betty is known for homemade biscuits spread with fig preserves harvested from the fig tree in the back yard.

The former music room at the front of the house is now a guest room with king bed, TV and a bathroom with a small clawfoot tub and separate shower. The room is big enough to hold four chairs and "all the stuff that I didn't have room for elsewhere in the house," Betty advised.

Upstairs are three more large bedrooms. The Charleston with queensize bed has a huge, carpeted bathroom complete with fireplace and an upholstered chair. Another fireplace turns up in the bathroom of the Pine Room, which is furnished in pine and has a double poster bed. Both bathrooms, it turns out, were converted from former bedrooms and the fireplaces are among seven in the house. The rear Georgian Room has a kingsize bed, TV and two chairs. All rooms have access to the upstairs veranda with a glider swing overlooking Osborne Street.

(912) 882-7490. Four rooms with private baths. Doubles, $65.

Riverview Hotel, 105 Osborne St., St. Marys 31558.

Mayor Jerry Brandon grew up in this hotel owned by his family, and portraits of

Front verandas upstairs and down embellish facade at Goodbread Bed & Breakfast.

his three aunts who ran it in the early days hang over the fireplace in the lobby. It doesn't seem to have changed much since it was built in 1916, although Jerry has done some needed upgrading.

The spacious lobby offers seating and an old reception desk. Off one side is a coffee shop/bar with a side courtyard. Guests enjoy a complimentary continental breakfast here. In the afternoon and evenings, the bar becomes *the* local gathering spot. Off the other side of the lobby is Seagle's Waterfront Cafe, a leased steak and seafood restaurant.

The second floor holds eighteen bare-bones guest rooms with private baths and cable TV. Plastic glasses and a bar of soap are the bath amenities. All priced the same, rooms vary in size and come with one or two double beds. The ten outside rooms are most in demand for their river views; the interior rooms appeared quite dark. The prized corner balcony/river room comes with a double bed, a bureau and a single chair. A larger interior room we saw had two double beds and a desk with a chair, but no chairs for sitting. For seating, most guests head for the balcony with rocking chairs and swing overlooking the main intersection and the river "to see what's happening in the city," according to Gaila Brandon, the mayor's wife.

This is the same porch enjoyed by cartoonist Roy Crane, who stayed at the hotel in 1935 and depicted it, townspeople and the Toonerville Trolley in his comic strip Wash Tubbs.

(912) 882-3242. Sixteen rooms and one two-bedroom suite with private baths. Doubles, $50. Suite, $60 for four.

Dining Spots

Borrell Creek Restaurant & Lounge, 1101 Highway 40 East, St. Marys.
Unless you were looking for it, you'd probably miss this waterside establishment, considered the best and most versatile around. An Oriental family that also runs the Bamboo Restaurant in Fernandina Beach opened it in the early

1980s as a fine dining restaurant. A 1998 addition to the contemporary cedar building nearly doubled its size and added the Creekside Cafe and a large bar.

The original dining rooms are attractive with white tablecloths and sleek black chairs. You feel like you're on a boat on the enclosed porch, which extends out over wide Borrell Creek as it heads toward the St. Marys River and eventually the Intracoastal Waterway. A large new deck off the cafe also overlooks the water.

The cafe made a pleasant stop for lunch. One of us had a pasta with rock shrimp scampi, a specialty of the area. The other chose the cafe kabob, a dinner-size portion of steak, chicken, onions, green peppers, tomatoes and more. As we ordered the ubiquitous iced tea, our hostess suggested that we specify unsweetened – otherwise, sweetened comes automatically, "it's a Georgia thing."

The cafe menu, available day and night, offers a wide range of appetizers, salads, pastas, sandwiches and entrées from pecan-crusted flounder with tartar molasses sauce to ginger-lemongrass chicken. The dining room menu lists some of the same, plus heartier main dishes. Typical are shrimp provençal, seafood fettuccine, chicken with artichokes and mushrooms, and filet mignon with béarnaise sauce. Salads, vegetable, starch and rolls come with. No one leaves either venue hungry.

(912) 673-6300. Entrées, $10.95 to $17.95. Cafe, $8.95 to $10.95. Cafe open Monday-Friday 11:30 to 9, Saturday 3 to 9. Dining room, Monday-Saturday from 5.

Breaux's Cajun Cafe, 2710 Osborne Road, St. Marys.

This light and airy, hotel-style cafe at the GuestHouse Inn & Suites (a regional chain motel) draws visitors as well as locals for authentic cajun fare. It's run by Brett A. Breaux, an Acadian whose father is known in Louisiana cooking circles. Brett cooked at Fernandina Beach's acclaimed Beech Street Grill before opening his own place to share a part of his heritage. "Whatever is prepared, the cajun cook's heart, soul and heritage goes into every pot and pan," he says.

For dinner, that means bayou treats like crawfish pie, catfish stuffed with crabmeat and topped with crawfish étouffée, boudin nuggets and, "from the other side of the bayou," chicken and andouille gumbo, blackened chicken and Bourbon Street ribeye steak. Regulars say the white chocolate bread pudding is to die for.

Smaller portions and po-boys are offered at lunch. Blues piano music is played occasionally in the bar.

(912) 882-6250. Entrées, $7.25 to $15.25. Lunch, Monday-Friday 11 to 2. Dinner, Tuesday-Saturday 5 to 10.

Panorama, 123 Osprey Cove Drive, St. Marys.

The aptly named restaurant at the posh Osprey Cove golf clubhouse is where locals head for special-occasion dining. The dining room is elegant, even sumptuous, with a panoramic view of the golf course and marshlands from windows on three sides.

The fare is typical golf club by day and more inspired at night. For dinner, you might start with a portobello mushroom and sundried tomato pizza, lobster potstickers with newburg dipping sauce or escargots in puff pastry. Caesar salad is prepared tableside for two. Typical main dishes are ahi tuna with crème fraîche and caviar, fillet of grouper with lump crab gratin, herb-crusted cornish hen, tournedos of veal with porcini spaëtzle and pecan-crusted rack of lamb.

(912) 882-6575. Entrées, $15.95 to $19.95. Lunch, Tuesday-Friday 11:30 to 2:30. Dinner, Tuesday-Saturday 5:30 to 9 or 9:30.

The Greek Mediterranean Grill, 122 Osborne St., St. Marys.
This establishment occupies stylish space at the side of the French Quarter, a sophisticated shop for antiques, art and collectibles. Store owners Donna Boyette and Linda Allen ran it as the Golden Radish bistro for a time before leasing the space in 1998 to Evangelos Liapes, a native Greek, who maintained the ambiance and produced highly rated cuisine. The setting is a work of art. A local artist painted the wall murals patterned after the shopping bag from our favorite MacKenzie-Childs pottery in upstate New York. A twelve-year-old girl painted the clouds on the ceiling. Three multi-lamp chandeliers provide dim illumination, and gold tinsel shimmers behind tiny white lights in the windows.
The extensive menu offers a mixed bag of Greek and Mediterranean fare. For dinner, consider moussaka, spanakopita, kabobs, shrimp sadorini, chicken marsala or veal piccata. There are ample pasta dishes, and starters like grilled octopus, dolmades and Greek fried mushrooms. Salads include niçoise and taramasalata, which the owners describe as a caviar salad. Specialty desserts are baklava and Greek custard.
(912) 576-2000. Entrées, $7.95 to $14.95. Lunch and dinner daily, 11 to 9.

Pauly's, 102 Osborne St., St. Mary's.
A side courtyard is the dining venue of choice at this new restaurant, which in 1998 took over the space that was formerly Papa Luigi's. New owners Jim and Paul Watson retained the casual interior decor and offered a short menu of American fare with an Italian accent.
For dinner, expect such main courses as grilled yellowfin tuna with lemon-caper butter, grilled salmon with a lime-garlic-cilantro sauce, chicken florentine and grilled ribeye steak. Among pasta dishes are shrimp fra diavolo and ravioli primavera. Mussels fra diavolo and crab-stuffed mushrooms are typical appetizers.
Stuffed croissants and hefty sourdough subs are featured at lunch.
(912) 882-3944. Entrées, $8.50 to $11.95. Lunch and dinner daily, 11 to 9

Lang's Marina Restaurant, 307 West St. Marys St., St. Marys.
Here's a good place for a meal by the river. Seafood is the specialty, and there's a creative hand in the kitchen.
For lunch, you can get a grilled chicken salad, a smoked turkey or ham sandwich or a main dish of rock shrimp, blackened fish, quiche, chicken pot pie or even crêpes. The weekend dinner menu offers grilled, blackened or fried local rock shrimp or flounder fillets, grilled fish of the day, seafood platter and Southern-style fried chicken. Other fare includes shrimp or scallops linguini, chicken cacciatore and steak oscar.
(912) 882-4432. Entrées, $8.95 to $16.95. Lunch, Tuesday-Saturday 11 to 2. Dinner, Thursday-Saturday from 5.

St. Marys Seafood & Steakhouse, 1837 Osborne Road, St. Marys.
The ambiance is zilch and the menu predictable, but the locals pack this low-slung, gray roadhouse for heaping portions of fresh seafood (mostly fried) at pleasant prices.
The extensive menu offers more options and combinations than we could possibly enumerate. Suffice to say you can get a rock shrimp or oyster dinner (regular or large), a large fish platter (of catfish, snapper and trout), fish and grits, snow crab

legs, lobster or sirloin steak. The Saints platter for two – $21.50 for shrimp, oysters, scallops, deviled crabs, fillet of fish, hushpuppies, potatoes and coleslaw – is what has made the place famous. Other meals come with any two of the usual Southern sides. There's deep-fried alligator tail (for appetizer or lunch). Derby and peanut-butter mousse pie and strawberry cheesecake are the desserts of choice.
(912) 882-6875. Entrées, $5.25 to $23.95. Lunch daily, 11 to 4. Dinner, 4 to 9 or 10.

Two casual eateries are worth a mention.

Sweet Magnolia, a candy, ice cream and sandwich shop in the new Cumberland Post building along St. Marys Street, proved so successful in its first months it was expanding at our visit. Owner Patty Hay, a chef who was known for fine food at Seagle's at the Riverview Hotel before it downscaled in 1998, was planning an expanded menu and a coffee bar. Among sandwich offerings were rock shrimp salad, grilled vegetable and cajun chicken. The goat cheese salad (sautéed goat cheese over marinated blackeyed pea salad and mixed greens) is a specialty. We candied out on a sampling of the ten varieties of homemade fudge.

For our latte fix, we headed for **Whispers Coffee House & Cafe** at 302 Osborne St. Here folks gather for cappuccino and breakfast pastries, plus unusual soups served in bowls made of bread. It's a laid-back, old-fashioned place that's open from 7 a.m. to 8 or 10 p.m.

Diversions

Historic Sites. St. Marys dates to the 1500s and was settled as a town by the English in 1787. You know you've reached the historic district when the main drag, Osborne Street, separates into a boulevard shaded by live oaks and palm trees. Historic markers denote significant points from the 1800s and early 1900s along stately Osborne and residential side streets. There are cannons in the square in front of the old Riverview Hotel, and a pavilion is the site of special events along the riverfront. The ferry boat leaves here twice a day for Cumberland Island National Seashore. A detailed, self-guided historical walking tour is available at the visitor center, but is really unnecessary in that most of the sites are clustered around Osborne Street and are well identified by markers. An informative, fifteen-minute video program at the visitor center tells all. Don't miss the stark white interior of the pint-size First Presbyterian Church, built in 1808, the second oldest church in Georgia. The artist-drawn street signs along the main street are worth noting. If you happen to be here on a festival weekend, you'll likely see the Toonerville Trolley, the restored vehicle that shuttled passengers between St. Marys and Kingsland. Locally called the Doodlebug, it was made famous by cartoonist Roy Crane.

Orange Hall, Osborne and Conyers Streets, St. Marys.

The centerpiece of St. Marys is this handsome antebellum house museum and welcome center. One of the best examples of Greek Revival architecture anywhere, it was built in 1829 as a wedding gift for the minister of the First Presbyterian Church across the street by his wife's family. The house, with four large corner rooms on each floor, is furnished as if the couple were still living here. Curator Gerry Hernandez, who grew up in the house, was married here and spinned tales as she led a tour. She pointed out the Indian shutters and doors on the windows,

Orange Hall museum and welcome center is leading example of Greek Revival architecture.

inside and out, and the rare square baby grand piano in the music room. All kinds of collectibles are on display in the sewing room.

(912) 882-4000. Open Monday-Saturday 9 to 5, Sunday 1 to 5. Self-guided tours, $2.50.

St. Marys Submarine Museum, 108 St. Marys St. West, St. Marys.

Another aspect of St. Marys life – the nearby Kings Bay Naval Submarine Base of relatively recent vintage (1978) – is on display here. Most of the plaques, models and papers lovingly gathered by volunteers led by curator John Crouse, a retired Navy man, are of particular interest to those into submarine lore and history. But anyone would like the 40-foot-tall submarine periscope, lowered by crane through a hole in the roof of the former movie theater. The periscope magnifies up to six times and provides a wide-angle, closeup view of the sub base, Cumberland Island, downtown Fernandina Beach and three paper mills.

(912) 882-2782. Open Tuesday-Saturday 10 to 4, Sunday 1 to 5. Adults, $1.

Shopping. Collectibles, gourmet foods and all kinds of gifts are offered at **Blue Goose,** an enticing ramble of rooms in the 1821 Stotesbury-Johnson House, one of the town's oldest. The owners also offer nautical items in their new shop, the **White Pelican,** at Cumberland Post along St. Marys Street. Another destination for shoppers is the **French Quarter,** a New Orleans-looking emporium displaying Southern antiques, furnishings and artworks. Regional and Cumberland Island lore is offered at **Once Upon a Bookseller.** Outdoor gear, guided tours and boat rentals, including kayaks for access to Cumberland Island, are available at **Up the Creek Xpeditions.**

Cumberland Island National Seashore, Box 806, St. Marys.

The nation's largest wilderness island accessible to the public is separated from St. Marys and the Georgia mainland by several miles of river, marsh and Cumberland Sound. It extends eighteen miles north from Cumberland Sound opposite Fernandina Beach, Fla. The barrier island is inhabited by a few dozen residents and guests of the Greyfield Inn (see Inn Spots). Otherwise, access is limited to 300 visitors a day who get there by scheduled ferry service, charter boats or rented kayaks. The lush western side of the island is a shady refuge of live oaks, palmettos and pines. The eastern side has white sand beaches and dunes. The complex ecological system of forests, meadows, saltwater marshes and even a large freshwater swamp is home to 300 species of birds, armadillos, wild turkeys and herds of wild horses for which the island is famed. Most ferry visitors arrive at the dock near the Ice House Museum and walk a three and one-half mile trail past the ruins of the Carnegies' Dungeness mansion, a cemetery, marshlands and along the beach, and back to the Sea Camp visitor center for the return ferry to St. Marys. Some go off to observe the smoke-blackened chimneys and other ruins from early plantations. Others stay to camp. The 45-minute ferry trip aboard the Cumberland Queen leaves the park visitor center on the St. Marys waterfront at 9 and 11:45 a.m. daily, March-September, and Thursday-Monday rest of year. Return trips are at 10:15 and 4:45.

(912) 882-4336. Reservations: (912) 882-4335, Monday-Friday 10 to 2. Adults, $9.50.

The **Cumberland Island National Seashore Museum** was being developed in 1998 in an old bank building at Osborne and Bryant Streets. Plans were to feature rotating exhibits and provide a glimpse of life on Cumberland Island during its gilded age.

Crooked River State Park, 3092 Highway Spur 40, St. Marys.
This 500-acre park along the south bank of the Crooked River is another favorite of nature lovers. It offers a 1.5-mile nature trail as well as campsites, picnic shelters, a swimming pool and bathhouse. Nearby are the ruins of the famous tabby McIntosh Sugar Works mill built around 1825.

(912) 882-5256. Open daily, dawn to dusk. Park pass, $2 per vehicle.

Extra-Special

Okefenokee National Wildlife Refuge, off Route 121, Folkston.
About 45 minutes west of St. Marys is the exotic, strangely mysterious Okefenokee Swamp – the home of Pogo the possum of comic-strip fame – at the headwaters of the St. Marys and Suwannee rivers. Its 396,000 acres of bog were called by the Indians the "land of the Trembling Earth." Peat deposits up to fifteen feet thick cover much of the swamp floor. They are so unstable in spots that by stomping the surface you can cause surrounding trees and bushes to tremble. The main entrance near Folkston offers access into the heart of the Okefenokee via the manmade Suwannee Canal. The 4.5-mile Swamp Island observation drive, four miles of hiking trails, a 4,000-foot boardwalk into the swamp and two observation towers are available to view the abundant plant and animal life. A restored swamp homestead and visitor centers with dioramas are other attractions. You can take a guided one- or two-hour boat trip through the swamp, but to get the full experience rent a boat or canoe and venture along self-guided wilderness canoe trails into the swamp.

(912) 496-7836 or (800) 792-6796. Fee, $5 per vehicle. Open 7 a.m. to 7:30 p.m. daily in summer, 8 to 6 rest of year.

Pebble Hill plantation home outside Thomasville is one of largest in country.

Thomasville, Ga.

Plantations, Plus

Barely a century ago, the small southwestern Georgia city of Thomasville was celebrated as one of the most fashionable places in the world to visit. The railroad ended at Thomasville – "the best winter resort on three continents," according to Harpers magazine in 1897.

A dozen downtown hotels and 25 boarding houses beckoned Northern industrialists and socialites to spend the winter in the pine-scented uplands known as the Tallahassee Red Hills, away from the malaria-plagued Florida coast. They paid $4 a night for a room, but found they could buy an acre of land for $3. The sprawling old cotton plantations could be acquired for a song.

Early snowbirds built more than 50 grand houses along Hansell and Dawson streets in town, and turned the outlying plantation properties into quail-hunting and pleasure retreats. People like Cleveland steel magnate Howard Melville Hanna walked the red clay streets and bought two plantations in one day.

The resort era lasted three decades until the early 1900s. Henry Flagler's railroad opened up the Florida coast and construction of the Panama Canal proved how land drainage could reduce the breeding of yellow-fever and malaria-carrying mosquitoes. Southern Florida killed Thomasville's Hotel Era almost overnight.

Its plantations remain to this day, however. Seventy-one plantations cover about 300,000 acres – the largest such cluster in the country. All are still private residences, except for Pebble Hill, an outstanding museum, and Melhana, a swank new resort.

Although the old hotels are gone and the plantations generally hidden from public view, vestiges of the resort era beckon today's traveler to this city of 20,000 just twelve miles above the Florida state line.

The city has seven official historic districts, most reflecting its Victorian heyday. The grand houses represent an unusual variety of architectural styles. Among them is the magnificent Lapham-Patterson House, a quirky structure with no square rooms or right angles. The South's first indoor residential bowling alley is part of the outstanding local history museum. The oldest church drew Jacqueline Kennedy for solace after the president's assassination – she was a guest at John Hay Whitney's plantation – before it changed its affiliation from Catholic to Episcopal.

One of the historic districts includes the downtown, an early model for the national Main Street revival program. Most buildings were erected in 1886, and inscriptions reveal their original use. Locally owned shops and restaurants thrive in restored buildings that prompt visitors to look up and around. The elaborate walls and ceilings may be of as much interest as the merchandise and food.

More than 10,000 rose bushes bloom throughout the city during the annual Rose Show & Festival in late April and lead to the moniker, "The Rose City." There are twelve other parks, including one called Yankee Paradise. The oldest attraction is "The Big Oak," a downtown live oak that's wider than Niagara Falls is deep.

The railroad still runs at grade level through the streets, stopping through traffic in its tracks. Just as well. Thomasville is a languorous place in which to pause and, as its hospitable residents say, to stay a spell.

Inn Spots

Melhana Plantation, 301 Showboat Lane, Thomasville 31792.

When in plantation country, try to stay at a plantation. If you don't have friends who own one, surely this will do. Until lately it was part of a 7,500-acre tract known as the Melrose and Sinkola Plantations, owned by the Hanna families.

Charles and Frances Lewis of Thomasville purchased 40 acres and 30 historic buildings and set about creating "a grand plantation resort." They called it Melhana, for the previous owners – the Mel Hannas, senior and junior. Melhana opened in

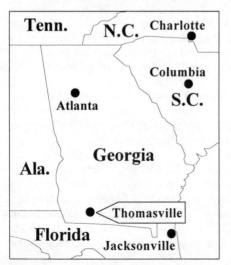

1998 with eleven guest rooms and a fancy restaurant in the original plantation home. A cottage with a kingsize bed and double jacuzzi in the former creamery and eight more jacuzzi rooms in the dairy barn in the working plantation village were opened later in the year. Fifteen more guest quarters were being readied in other out-buildings for early 1999. "We'll stop at 35 and see what happens," said Frederic H. Graham, who came aboard as general manager following a career with the Ritz-Carlton hotel chain – the level to which the Lewises aspired. His son Hill is the executive chef, and all the principals live on the property.

The concept is to "recreate the

Peacock wanders in front of main Pink House at Melhana Plantation resort.

feeling of a pleasure plantation, with service second to none," in Ric Graham's words. That includes 24-hour room service and a catering operation spread across 40 acres. The early stages of the developing resort focused on the antebellum home known as the Pink House, which belies its origin in 1825 as a four-room log cabin. Two cabin rooms now form the beautifully furnished living room, paneled in rare magnolia wood. Two elegant dining rooms comprise a 50-seat restaurant open to the public (see Dining Spots). A wide veranda richly furnished in wicker faces a marble fountain and a pond filled with koi.

Two single-story, ground-floor wings hold seven nicely secluded bedrooms in a variety of configurations and sizes. TVs, terrycloth robes, luxurious bathrooms and Melhana toiletries are standard. The Sevilla comes with a queen bed, fireplace and a club chair. Furnished in deep reds, the Winnstead has a double jacuzzi, kingsize poster bed and a single chair. The Melrose, with windows on three sides, is a knockout in florals and peach colors with a step-up kingsize canopy bed. An armchair and a settee face the gas fireplace in the sitting area. The bathroom comes with his and hers vanities and a jacuzzi tub. Our upstairs room in a hunting motif was rich in rusts and browns, the comforter on the step-up kingsize bed matching the wallpaper. It contained a chandelier, an armchair and a writing desk holding candies and a vase of roses. The tiled bathroom had a double vanity with a separate lady's dressing table and enough extra towels to outfit an army.

If seating seemed a shortcoming, there was plenty to be found in the living room, on the veranda and in the Hogan sitting room, an extra room at the end of the north wing. The Hogan is the setting for afternoon tea overlooking the restored boxwood and rose garden.

There's also lots of space around the plantation. The grounds are notable for wandering peacocks and old fire hydrants and hose carts (the Hannas were paranoid about fire). There are tennis courts, orange and tangerine trees and a greenhouse. The indoor pool house has one of the earliest heated pools, plus portholes for windows and a fireplace for warmth. The Showboat theater, paneled in pecky cypress, has solid mahogany benches. You reach it via a gangplank over a tiny pond, exactly as the Hannas' friends did when they attended the first screening of "Gone With the Wind," which plantation neighbor John Hay Whitney helped finance.

The eight bedrooms about to open in the dairy barn at our visit had brick walls and low portholes for windows. They looked rather snug and appeared dark, but would be "furnished to the nines," Ric said. More accommodations were planned in the superintendent's house, the calf barn and the bull barn. The stables have a small conference center, and an addition holds a two-bedroom presidential suite. There's a fitness center, and the superintendent's office harbors a gift shop. Golf carts are employed to transport people around.

Complimentary breakfast from a varied menu is offered in the main house. We enjoyed a cheese and tomato omelet with applewood bacon. Nighttime treats with turndown included a plate of cookies and a giant strawberry.

(912) 226-2290 or (888) 920-3030. Fax (912) 226-4585. Thirty-five rooms and cottages with private baths. Doubles, $250 to $350. Cottage, $450. Smoking restricted.

1884 Paxton House Inn, 445 Remington Ave., Thomasville 31792.

The recipe for a model B&B has been developed here by Susie Sherrod, a retired Army colonel/nurse. Indefatigable Susie, who was arranging flowers in the gazebo at our arrival, is a versatile, do-it-yourself dynamo with great taste.

Returning to her native Thomasville, she opened three suites in a Victorian house in 1991. She later converted a main-floor parlor into a suite with a queen poster bed and a sitting area with a loveseat and two chairs, a small sitting room with a loveseat and separate his and hers bathrooms. In 1994, she added four smaller rooms in a rear garden house beyond a shady, landscaped courtyard. (She made A Little Victorian Cottage into a shop where she sells the Victorian and lace button bags, wedding bags and sachets that she makes in her spare time.) The crowning touch was added in 1998: a guest cottage that adjoins a pool house with an indoor lap pool and a hot tub. All painted blue with white trim, the buildings enclose a large terrace and courtyard. A state preservation award attests to the authenticity and magnitude of her restoration.

Susie has thought of everything, from private telephone lines for each bedroom to unusual decorative accents, among them a collection of Hummel and Russian dolls in the main-floor suite. TVs, robes and bedside chocolates are standard.

The main house with wraparound front porch in the residential historic district appears deceptively small from the front. One side of the main floor contains a suite and the owner's quarters. The other side begins with a light and airy living room (Susie made the window treatments here as well as the bedspreads throughout). Beyond are a formal dining room, a second dining area in what had been the butler's pantry and a modern kitchen opening onto a sunporch overlooking the rear gardens and courtyard.

We'd happily stay in any of the guest quarters, which are smartly decorated in elegant 18th-century style rather than the frilly Victorian you might expect from the era. The second floor of the main house is given over to three suites. The Peach Suite has one spacious bedroom in peach and white with a kingsize fishnet canopy bed and two armchairs on a heart-pine floor, plus a second bedroom that is a mirror image but with a queen bed and a green color scheme. The Blue Suite takes its name from the blue porcelain china from East Berlin in one bedroom.

Cottages flank pleasant courtyard behind 1884 Paxton House Inn.

Susie and her mother hand-stitched the floral comforter on the bed to match the china. A second bedroom follows a flower garden motif. The 18th-Century Suite has a queensize fishnet canopy bed and a sitting room furnished in wicker and accented with more German china collections.

The secluded Garden Cottage also appears deceptively small. Besides a common room, the downstairs has two queensize bedrooms. Upstairs are a large kingsize room decorated in florals and the smallest room with queensize bed, two wing chairs and a view of the camellia trees.

Across the way is the new pool house with attached cottage. We took one look at the cottage and decided to stay. The large room beneath a vaulted ceiling contained a kingsize plantation bed, two armchairs served by strong reading lights, and a TV in an armoire thoughtfully positioned for watching from chairs as well as in bed. There were good artworks on the walls, a hidden kitchenette area and a large bathroom with separate vanity area and a whirlpool tub. Not that we used the whirlpool. We had only to open the door from the bathroom into the pool house – available to all by day, but private for the cottage at night – to swim in the lap pool or soak in the hot tub. The pool was so inviting we swam before dinner, before bed and before breakfast.

The cottage's porch faced a courtyard with lounge chairs and tables. We enjoyed the courtyard for a takeout dinner from a nearby restaurant. Susie poured a glass of wine, and we lingered under the stars on a mild autumn evening.

The next morning, she arose early to send us and a couple of regular businessmen/ guests on our way with a substantial breakfast of a monte carlo sandwich of Smithfield ham and cheese, garnished with exotic fruit. We can't wait to return to try her four-berry french toast and her turkey sausage quiche.

(912) 226-5197. Four rooms, four suites and one cottage with private baths. Doubles, $85 to $135. Suites, $165. Cottage, $185. Children over 12. No smoking.

Serendipity Cottage, 339 East Jefferson St., Thomasville 31792.

Kathy and Ed Middleton used to run a small B&B called Serendipity Court (because it was on Court Street in Luray) in Virginia's Shenandoah Valley. They sold it to retire to Florida, where "we were bored to tears," in Ed's words. They escaped to Thomasville for a getaway weekend and a change of seasons and fell in love with the town. So they moved into a 1906 house here, opened a B&B as a retirement project in 1993, and called it Serendipity.

They share their house – it's really much more than a cottage – with guests in three bedrooms and a variety of common areas. Off a huge front foyer is a formal Victorian parlor with a fireplace and a ticking grandfather clock on one side and a country-casual family room they call a keeping room with TV/VCR. An enclosed side porch contains a sitting area in one section and a dining area in another. There's also a large, formal dining room with a fireplace. A front porch adds a swing and more wicker seating.

Both excellent cooks, the Middletons serve a gourmet breakfast on unusual floral china on the sunporch, except for the few winter days when the temperature is too cold. Typical fare is their soufflé serendipity, a combination of cheeses, eggs and ham, surrounded by an array of fresh fruit and served with homemade cream biscuits. Other possibilities are Scandinavian pancakes, apple french toast laced with applejack and eggs Serendipity (like benedict, but with prosciutto instead of Canadian bacon).

The upstairs guest rooms come with private bath, TV and a decanter of sweet sherry. Chocolates are placed on the pillows at nightly turndown.

The Country Garden Room, its creaking floor covered by a hooked rug, conveys an "I Love My Garden" theme. There's a quilt on top and a trunk at the foot of the queensize brass bed. To the rear, Kate's Room with a fishnet canopy double bed is furnished more traditionally. The Victorian Rose is bright with wicker and florals.

The upstairs hall is a showplace of samplers. It turns out both Kathy and Ed do cross-stitching and produce the samplers.

The Middletons also bake scones and import devonshire cream for British afternoon tea, offered Friday and Saturday by reservation at 2 p.m. for $9.95. It's served in the sunporch or the dining room.

They offer guests golf privileges at the venerable Glen Arden Country Club.

(912) 226-8111 or (800) 383-7377. Fax (912) 226-2656. Three rooms with private baths. Doubles, $80. Two-night minimum peak weekends. Children over 12. No smoking.

Evans House Bed & Breakfast, 735 South Hansell St., Thomasville 31792.

This handsome yellow and white house with a wicker veranda faces 26-acre Paradise Park in the heart of an historic residential section in which two nearby B&Bs closed in 1998. This, too, had just changed hands at our visit and was in transition. New owner Gladys Deese had turned over management to an innkeeper. Neither was residing on the premises.

The Victorian parlor in front harbors a large-screen TV. The other front corner of the main floor holds the Rose Suite, with a private entrance and handicapped ramp, a double poster bed, a sitting area with a wicker chair and desk, and a kitchenette that hinted of its apartment heritage. The rear Regency Room offers two chairs at the foot of a kingsize bed. The side Library Room, light and airy, comes with a queensize bed with a fishnet canopy and quilt, an antique writing desk and a bath with clawfoot tub.

Serendipity Cottage occupies restored turn-of-the-century house.

Upstairs past gorgeous stained-glass windows embellished with roses are two suites. The Imperial offers a burled walnut kingsize bed, a sitting room with an antique daybed and a bath with footed tub and hand-held shower. The new B.W.'s Suite, formerly the owners' apartment, has a kingsize poster bed, a leather settee and an armchair with ottoman. It opens optionally into a front room with a queen bed that shares the bath to make a family suite. The suite also has a full kitchen with two stained-glass windows.

A full breakfast is served at a table for ten in the dining room. One morning might be Southern country fare, the next crêpes, the next pancakes and the fourth day innkeeper Theresa Mayo's "famous eggs benedict." She said her husband played the guitar for guests on the porch the previous weekend and everyone had such a good time that "no one wanted to leave."

(912) 226-1343 or (800) 344-4717. Fax (912) 226-0653. Two rooms and three suites with private baths. Doubles, $85. Suites, $85 to $165. No smoking. No credit cards.

The 1854 Wright House, 415 Fletcher St., Thomasville 31792.

Gray with white trim, this Greek Revival-style cottage on three acres south of downtown appeals with a columned front veranda and interesting architectural details. Dentil molding and twelve-foot ceilings dignify the interior.

Owners Peggie and Carl Wood converted their home of nine years into a B&B in 1998 "in anticipation of retirement," Carl said. They live upstairs, and turn over much of the downstairs to guests in two suites. Bedrooms can be rented separately from the sitting rooms, if guests prefer.

The configuration is unusual. What looks to be the main formal living room for the house turns out to be a sitting room for the "front suite." It opens into a bedroom with queensize bed, decorative oak fireplace and a wicker sitting area.

The "rear suite" has an antique double bed in a room done in pale yellow and blue florals. It adjoins a small bathroom with the smallest and shallowest tub you ever saw. Never mind. The rear sitting room adjoins a larger bathroom.

There's a front parlor furnished in rattan. A formal dining room is set with a table for four, plus two club chairs in a side bay window. Carl says they represent his wife's dream of sitting and staring out with nothing to do. A pair of binoculars is at the ready.

Breakfast the day of our visit was peach pancakes with bacon and Mexican quiche, plus tiny bran muffins served with strawberry butter. Another day might produce thick french toast made with homemade bread and country ham. Bagels with house-smoked salmon are a third option.

(912) 225-9922. Two suites with private baths. Doubles, $75; $65 without the sitting room. No smoking. No credit cards.

Dining Spots

You needed a scorecard to keep up with the merry-go-round of restaurant changes here in 1998. One venerable landmark abruptly closed. A grand new one opened. Almost none of the other players had the same name, the same owner or the same location as a year before.

Melhana Plantation, 301 Showboat Lane, Thomasville.

A changing weekly menu of "refined Southern cuisine" is offered in two elegant dining rooms at this new plantation resort. The table settings are as refined as the cuisine, jackets are required for men and service by white-gloved servers borders on the pretentious.

The food, as developed by 25-year-old executive chef Hill Graham, is at the cutting edge. Trained at the Pennsylvania Institute of Culinary Arts, he worked at Le Cirque 2000 in New York and garnered a four-diamond rating for the Ritz-Carlton Hotel in St. Thomas before joining Melhana.

The dinner menu is presented in three courses. The smallest amuse-gueule imaginable arrived with so complex a description we had no idea what it was – a thumbnail-size dollop of something or other. The shrimp and goat cheese bread salad with roma tomato was a delicate treat for $8.25. Our dinner partner started with the fried green tomato with roasted vidalia onion and buffalo mozzarella mousse, followed by a second course of ricotta gnocchi with oven-dried tomato and rapini, and pronounced both fine. She barely had room to finish her rack of lamb with rosemary custard and grilled asparagus. We, meanwhile, relished every last morsel of the grilled tenderloin of bison with marinated portobello mushroom and a dash of yukon gold potato puree. We longed for a bottle of wine, but it being Sunday night in Georgia it was not to be (waiters poured wine for those who apparently brought their own, but we were neither asked nor advised).

Desserts were marble cheesecake with amaretto sauce and a "crème" concoction with a fancy French name that the waitress muffed. It turned out to be exemplary courvoisier ice cream garnished with blueberries.

(912) 226-2290 or (888) 920-3030. Entrées, $23 to $31. Dinner nightly by reservation, 6 to 10. Jackets required.

Harrison's, 119 North Broad St., Thomasville.

Widely considered the best all-around restaurant in town is this versatile establishment housed in a former bank. Chef-owner Jim Mileo and his wife Barri, the hostess, closed their former Miamore restaurant in a restored Victorian home for a more central downtown location and a menu with more of a French accent. They named it for their first grandchild

The main dining room has well-spaced tables beneath an eighteen-foot-high ceiling. It's surprisingly attractive, given its height and walls of browns and grays. The bank vault now holds the wine cellar. A side room serves as a bar and lounge, with a rear dining area whose walls have been painted with an abstract cityscape. Good sourdough rolls preceded the arrival of our lunches. One of us enjoyed the succulent, herb-crusted grilled grouper, sauced with butter and lemon and served with a house salad tossed with raspberry vinaigrette. The other was intrigued by the "super salmon salad." It turned out to be an odd but tasty concoction of mixed organic greens topped with smoked salmon, capers and roasted garlic mayo. Tirami su, cheesecake, homemade flan and spumoni were the day's desserts.

The dinner menu is extensive. A house favorite is the fettuccine mileo, its alfredo sauce enhanced by prosciutto and peas. Choices range from stuffed shrimp, scampi, scallops and aforementioned grouper to meatloaf, veal vodka, grilled veal chop with merlot wine and caper sauce, steak béarnaise and "chirp and surf," lemon-pepper grilled chicken breast served with shrimp stuffed with crabmeat. Miamore cacciatore with Italian sausage, chicken and vegetables in a hearty tomato sauce with pasta is a holdover from Miamore days.

(912) 226-0074. Entrées, $10.95 to $18.95. Lunch, Monday-Saturday 11:30 to 2. Dinner, Monday-Saturday from 5:30.

The Terrace by Moonlight, 502 South Broad St., Thomasville.
This used to be known as The Grand Old House, a French restaurant that closed abruptly in 1998. It's still grand, but now it houses two restaurants with different names and owners. It seems it took two restaurateurs to pay the higher rent.

The Terrace is in the former basement tavern. It's owned by Deborah Heath, who had been running Melissa's restaurant (see below). The upstairs is Simply Delicious, which moved into elegant mansion rooms from a downtown location.

The Terrace, named for the brick terrace at the entry, retains a tavern look. A prominent bar and booths and tables covered with floral oilcloths give it a pubby feeling. The menu is a cut above. There are sandwiches, salads and appetizers from homemade potato chips with warm blue cheese to quesadillas and nachos. Grilled salmon with tomato, herb and garlic sauce was the seafood special at our visit. Other choices ranged from four pastas, served with soup or salad, to grill items, among them rosemary chicken, ribeye steak and beef tenderloin. Surf 'n turf combined a beef filet with a lobster tail.

The day's desserts were posted as cheesecake, pecan pie and twelve-layer chocolate cake.

(912) 228-9844. Entrées, $10.95 to $21.95. Lunch and dinner, Monday-Saturday 11 to midnight.

Richard's Evening Grill, 415 Smith Ave., Thomasville.
By day this is Henderson's, a long-running hamburger and fast-food joint. At night, owner Richard Henderson turns it into a grill, decked out in tropical island colors and festooned with colored Mexican and white lights. It's a large and casual place, much loved by the locals for a broad menu of fresh seafood and a small but well-chosen wine and beer selection at down-to-earth prices.

The evening menu opens with starters like crab cakes, green tomatoes, seafood gumbo and oyster stew. There are pastas and "fried favorites," as well as "special stuff" like shrimp creole and pork medallions with apple-pear chutney. You also can get a masterful cheeseburger with fries for an unheard-of $3. Most go for the grilled steaks or "fresh fishes" (grouper, salmon or tuna), each available in a variety of options. We liked the sautéed grouper with caribbean salsa, served with wilted spinach and saffron rice, accompanied by a house salad dressed with a sundried tomato vinaigrette. The key lime pie was a refreshing dessert.

(912) 226-3376. Entrées, $8 to $16. Dinner, Monday-Saturday 5:30 to 9 or 10. Henderson's, 6 a.m. to 3 p.m.

Melissa's, 134 South Madison St., Thomasville.
The recent history of musical chairs for local restaurants is no more pronounced than here. Melissa Summitt opened the cavernous brick building as a luncheon restaurant in 1990. She later sold the restaurant to Deborah Heath, who retained the name Melissa's. When the acclaimed Grand Old House closed across town in 1998, Deborah moved into its lower section and opened a dinner restaurant called The Terrace by Moonlight. Melissa returned to the warehouse to run Melissa's, with a new look and new accompaniments. Got it?

Under renovation at our visit, the place retained the flavor of the old laundry warehouse it once was, a cavernous space with exposed pipes and beams and funky furnishings. The restaurant was relocated to a raised side platform and a separate bar with dining area. Other spaces were being readied for a bed and bath shop plus a coffee and wine/cheese shop called The Idle Hours.

The menu offers an eclectic, extensive selection. Among "salads and plates" are grilled chicken and apple with blue cheese and mixed greens, chicken provolone over pasta, a sourdough bread bowl stew of curried ham, apples and dried cherries and a "poet's lunch" of soup, salad and half a sandwich. Sandwiches range from smoked turkey club to barbecued pork. The grill produces grilled chicken and a bacon-blue cheese burger on a french roll. The blackboard listed tropical semolina cake, buttermilk custard and a chocolate-coffee-banana sundae for dessert.

(912) 226-2929. Entrées, $4.95 to $6.95. Lunch, Monday-Saturday 11 to 3.

Simply Delicious, 502 South Broad St., Thomasville.
Newly relocated from a downtown location, Charlene McGalliard's well-regarded luncheon spot occupies the main floor of the mansion restaurant formerly known as The Grand Old House.

The setting in a variety of main-floor rooms is quite elegant. The extensive lunch menu ranges from the ubiquitous chunky chicken salad plate to cobb salad, from a grilled ham and cheese to a philly cheese steak sandwich, from a quiche of the day to an entrée of the day. A tea sandwich platter is served with fresh fruit salad and sherbet or cottage cheese.

Weekend dinners are more elaborate. One night's three-course menu offered a salad of baby greens, a choice of citrus-herbed Atlantic salmon with grilled vegetables or grilled beef tenderloin with marinated portobello on crushed yukon gold potatoes, and a dessert of macerated berries and vanilla ice cream with a crispy sugar tuile. The price varies depending on choice of entrée.

(912) 227-9428. Entrées, $9.95 to $16.95. Lunch, Monday-Saturday 11 to 2:30. Dinner, Friday and Saturday 6 to 10. Sunday brunch buffet, 11 to 2.

The Horse and Buggy, 125 North Broad St., Thomasville.
The name conveys the decorative theme of this lunch spot, an offshoot of a busy catering service. Indeed, lunch proved so popular that owner Mickey West moved in late 1998 into expanded quarters formerly occupied by Simply Delicious. Crab cakes are the specialty, and fans say there's nothing better than the open-face crab cake sandwich served with hollandaise on a toasted bun. The short menu also offers a chicken tart, a basil-tomato tart, a chilled roast beef salad and a salad of organic greens with mandarin oranges, avocado, tomatoes and red and yellow peppers. Specials and desserts change daily.
(912) 225-9600. Entrées, $6.95 to $8.50. Lunch, Monday-Friday 11 to 3.

Diversions

Plantations help define the Thomasville character. The area's 71 plantations represent the largest cluster in the country, covering more than 300,000 acres to the southeast and southwest and across the Florida state line. Although they were founded on cotton, the original owners could not afford their upkeep with the abolition of slavery following the Civil War. They sold the plantations primarily to wealthy Northerners who used them as seasonal residences and for quail-hunting. One is open to the public for tours (see below). Another has reopened as the Melhana resort detailed above. One plantation a year opens for an afternoon in April for the local hospital auxiliary's fund-raising tea.
President McKinley visited Marcus Alonzo Hanna, then the national Republican chairman, who had a house in Thomasville. His brother, Howard Melville Hanna, the Cleveland steel magnate and co-founder of Standard Oil, owned Melrose. Seventeen families related to the Hannas have plantations here, and private planes from Cleveland are a fixture at the municipal airport. The John Hay Whitneys owned Greenwood, and Mrs. Whitney wintered here until her recent death. President Eisenhower hunted quail at Milestone, owned by his Secretary of the Treasury George Humphrey, and golfed at Glen Arven Country Club, one of the nation's earliest. Today, the plantations are as low-profile as most of their owners, with the possible exceptions of Ted Turner and Jimmy Buffett.

Pebble Hill Plantation, U.S. Route 319, Thomasville.
Next door (so to speak) to Melhana, this is the most interesting plantation we've encountered in our travels. The entry road winds past woods and barns and outbuildings. The main house does not appear until after you reach the visitor center. It is so positioned and so screened from view that you don't appreciate its size until you're inside. "It's 3,000 acres of pure wealth," said our guide upon arrival.
The property was purchased in 1896 by industrialist Howard Melville Hanna, who gave it in 1901 to his daughter, Kate Smith Hanna Irland. She directed the construction of most of the buildings at Pebble Hill, including the main house, which replaced an 1850 house that burned. She left Pebble Hill to her daughter, horsewoman Elisabeth Irland (Poe), shortly after its completion in 1936. Known as Miss Pansy to one and all, she was married at age 49 to Parker M. Barington Poe. She lived there until her death in 1978 at age 81, and the property was willed to a foundation to be opened to the public.
The main house consists of 42 rooms, including a separate room just for table linens and a another that looks like a wet bar but is used for flower arranging. The eighteen bedrooms are supplemented by a five-room guest cottage for overflow.

The house was left as it would have been at the height of the winter season. It outshines better-known estates in terms of treasures *plus* livability. The main marble-floor hallway was designed to display 33 Audubon prints (more than in the Smithsonian), along with other wildlife and sporting works by artists who stayed here. The largest sitting room is paneled in a panorama of wildlife murals. Prized family antiques, porcelain, crystal, china and portraits are everywhere. So are unexpected treats: A lamp base made of three rifles, arrowheads, a stuffed bobcat, Pansy's incredible collection of horse show ribbons mounted on endlessly unfolding tiered boards. "If it moves you shoot it, if not you buy it," was said to be the slogan of this woman who lived for her horses and dogs.

The outbuildings and grounds hold unexpected sights as well. Tombstones are in front of the dairy where two prized cows are buried. Among the dozen wagons in the carriage house is the double-basket phaeton in which President Eisenhower hunted with a dog cage in back. You can see the dog hospital, the log cabin schoolhouse in which Miss Pansy was tutored, the Williamsburg-style stables and barns, and a wide brick garden cottage used as apartments for stablehands – an inn-goer would be quite happy to stay there today.

Pebble Hill is unusual in many ways, not the least of which is its relatively low profile for its size (its annual visitation is only about 25,000, a mere pittance for such an interesting destination). Isn't this the largest plantation in the country? No, it's not even the largest in Thomasville, various sources advised. "But it may be one of the biggest main houses." We know of none that is more fascinating.

(912) 226-2344. Open Tuesday-Saturday 10 to 5, Sunday 1 to 5. Gate fee $3. Guided tours of main house, $7.50.

Historic Districts.
More than 50 historic homes and buildings are detailed in a walking/driving tour booklet available for $1 from the visitor center. The major concentrations are along Dawson and Hansell streets on opposite sides of the downtown. Due to the varied tastes and wealth of the Northerners who built many of them, Thomasville has nearly every style of architecture represented. Hansell Street has been called Thomasville's Mason-Dixon Line because most houses on the east side were built by wealthy Southerners and those on the west side by Northerners.

Among the sites are tiny **All Saints Episcopal Church,** 443 Hansell St., the oldest original standing church (1881) in town. It was a Catholic church before it was moved to prevent its demolition. Jacqueline Kennedy attended Mass in the church while spending six weeks at the John Hay Whitney plantation following her husband's assassination. The **Hardy Bryan House** (1837) is the oldest two-story house in town. Restored in 1980, it is now a house museum opened Friday from 2 to 4. President Eisenhower attended services in the 1889 **First Presbyterian Church,** but almost everyone else seems to belong to the enormous First Baptist Church of newer vintage, facing the landmark 1858 **Thomas County Courthouse.** The Craftsman-influenced house in which Joanne Woodward was born is at 528 East Washington Street. She made her acting debut nearby on the old East Side School's stage, now the **Thomasville Cultural Center.** John Philip Sousa's band entertained in the old bandstand in **Paradise Park,** originally called Yankee Paradise because of all the Northerners who enjoyed its proximity to the early resort hotels.

The houses seem to get bigger the farther out you proceed along North Dawson Street. Two of the most imposing:

Lapham-Patterson House, 626 North Dawson St., Thomasville.

This monument to Victorian ingenuity was built in 1885 by C.W. Lapham, a prosperous Chicago shoe merchant who suffered lung damage in the Chicago fire of 1871. That explains why he installed fire extinguishers in all nineteen rooms of his winter vacation cottage. He also ordered 45 doors, including 24 to the outside. There are no rectangular rooms or right angles. The house was ahead of its time with hot and cold running water, indoor plumbing, its own gas lighting system and built-in closets. Among its peculiarities are fish-scale shingles, an oriental-style porch and a remarkable double-flue chimney with a unique walk-through stairway and a cantilevered balcony wrapping around the fire-place. The fireplace faces the dining room of what we

1885 Lapham-Patterson House was ahead of its time.

would call the front hall. "This one is in the English manor style," corrected Cheryl Walters Watson, curator of the state historic site. "There are no hallways here."

(912) 225-4004. Open Tuesday-Saturday 9 to 5, Sunday 2 to 5:30. Guided tours on the hour. Adults, $5.

Thomas County Museum of History, 725 North Dawson St., Thomasville.

As a local history museum, this is one of the best. The main J.H. Flowers House, a 20th-century Jeffersonian Revival building, replaces a structure that burned in 1923. The wrought-iron fence and the 1893 single-lane bowling alley are all that is left from the original. The bowling alley, housed in a Victorian cottage, is the oldest in the South, two years ahead of that at the Biltmore Estate. Of major interest are all the distinctive memorabilia from the plantations and the early hotel era. An entire wing is devoted to the plantations. You learn that one cotton plantation owner had to sell to a Northerner when her annual tax bill increased from $239 to $10,703 after the Civil War. Another owner funded the community hospital that turned Thomasville into a regional medical center. An 1897 register from the 300-room Mitchell House lists "Mr. and Mrs. C. Vanderbilt Jr. (NY)" and "Mrs. B.F. Goodrich & Maid." A section on famous Thomasville people touts Lt. Henry Flipper, a former slave, as the first black graduate from the U.S. Military Academy at West Point. The complex also includes a furnished 1877 Victorian cottage and an 1860 log house with detached kitchen. We found this museum so interesting it was tough to break away.

(912) 226-7664. Open Monday-Saturday 10 to noon and 2 to 5. Adults, $5.

Shopping. Thomasville's history extends to its downtown. Not only was it designated one of the first Main Street cities in the nation in 1982, it was honored as one of the top twenty in 1996 and 1997 and serves as a prototype for others wanting to join the program. All buildings are at least 100 years old, and most have been restored to their Victorian splendor. The brick-paved streets date to 1907. Period lampposts and tall, bushy pear trees line the sidewalks. Each corner has a sign listing the stores in that block. Signs on the buildings show their original use and date: telegraph office, millinery shop, barber – most in the 1880s.

This is definitely a downtown where things are looking up. You'll want to look up, too – at the architectural detail on the storefront facades, and inside at the ornate ceilings. Check out the original pressed-tin ceilings at **Neel's** department store, a fixture here since 1898. It's part of the original Mitchell House, a block-long hotel that did not burn and portions of which are still in evidence. Photos on a table at the entry testify to its history. The mezzanine level holds **Mitchell Coffee & Tea House. Jerger Johnson Jewelers,** the oldest store (1857), displays its wares in ornate cherry display counters and cabinets. A brass chandelier hangs from the ceiling of **Firefly,** which sells home furnishings and gifts. The impressive **Kevin's** outdoors store with a hunting theme is almost a museum with hardwood floors, brick walls and raftered ceilings. Pressed-tin ceilings enhance **J.T. Street's** apparel and **The Gift Shop.** Old photos top the shelves at **Thomasville Drug Store** (1881). The **Izzo Pharmacy** retains a soda fountain with swivel stools. **Hollybrook** in the 1882 Brokers & Exchange stocks home accessories and fine art. Also of interest are **Buon Appetito,** a kitchen shop offering coffees and tea; **Cargo Unlimited** and **The Wood World.**

Thomasville Rose Garden, Smith and Covington avenues. Above the waters of Cherokee Lake is this newish garden with more than 750 bushes planted around a Victorian gazebo. Thomasville had long been one of twelve test sites sanctioned by the National Rose Society. When its head gardener retired, the roses had to be plowed under. With its Rose City title at stake, the city jumped in and planted this garden. The roses start blooming in April in time for Thomasville's celebrated Rose Show & Festival, the oldest festival in Georgia (started in 1922 as a window exhibit in Neel's Department Store). The roses provide a succession of color until the first frost, usually in late January. Open daily. Free.

Extra-Special

The Big Oak, corner Crawford and East Monroe Streets.

To the uninitiated, Thomasville's oldest and most cherished landmark may not look like much. But consider the facts: The 317-year-old Quercus Virginiana, the largest oak tree east of the Mississippi, has a limb span of 162 feet. Holding hands, it took sixteen girls and fourteen boys to encircle the tree trunk. Cables criss-cross its limbs to stabilize the tree from heavy winds. As the tree grew, owners moved their houses rather than cut back its widening reach. One of the house occupants, a volunteer at the Thomasville visitor center, played in the tree as a girl – they called her Squirrel. The moss-laden oak is the centerpiece of the Elizabeth Irland Poe Park, which includes a gazebo. The oak was enrolled as a member of the National Live Oak Society in 1936. It has its own bank account, thanks to an anonymous donor who funded its maintenance.

Restored Windsor Hotel is Victorian centerpiece of downtown Americus.

Andersonville/Plains/Americus, Ga.

A Feeling for Humanity

A pair of two-bit hamlets with vastly differing historic sites of touching appeal are separated by a small city with a patriotic-sounding name.

One hamlet traces some of the tragedies of the Civil War. The other illustrates the rise out of nowhere of a populist president.

You may be vaguely familiar with Andersonville, the site of the infamous Civil War Prison called the Shame of the South. It's a place of stockades and monuments and gravestones, reminders of a tragic period revived by the movie "Andersonville" on Turner Network Television. The history endures in the new National Prisoner of War Museum, a haunting, state-of-the-art focal point of the nation's most controversial National Historic Site.

You surely are aware of Plains, the peanut-growing territory that spawned the Carter family and the 39th president of the United States. It really is a plain town of the plains, with a water tower and a peanut plant and mill that gives it something of the look a Kansas town. Lately endowed with restored sites associated with the Carters, it's a treasure trove of memorabilia that testifies to both the values and hardships of small-town America.

Unless you are familiar with Americus, you may not be aware that it is the home of one of the grandest restored Victorian hotels and a newly restored theater/opera house. It also is the birthplace and headquarters of Habitat for Humanity International, an appropriate organization to which both the Andersonville and Plains traditions contribute. Here a feeling for humanity is realized.

Andersonville and Plains, little more than dots on the map in southwestern Georgia, are the major attractions. Yet the attractions as they exist today are quite recent, so most of the usual accoutrements of tourism have only recently begun to surface.

Americus, the area's commercial center, seems smaller than its population of 16,500 would suggest. It is well placed to provide the bulk of accommodations, shops and restaurants an emerging area needs.

Inn Spots

1906 Pathway Inn, 501 South Lee St., Americus 31709.

Some of the area's most comfortable accommodations are offered in this 1906 mansion fronted by pillars and a curved porte-cochere. The previous owners did all the work and decorating when they converted the house into a B&B in 1994. So Chuck and Angela Nolan acquired a going operation when they moved from the Florida Keys in 1998.

The front of the main floor has both a formal parlor appointed in pale yellow for the ladies and a TV/music room favored by cigar-smoking gentlemen in the early days. Queen Anne furnishings and colorful stained-glass windows are in evidence in the parlor and in the chandeliered dining room.

The main floor also holds two guest rooms. The rear Bell Room, named for the original owners, has both a king bed and a sofabed. The former owner handpainted the ceiling and made the floral draperies. The side Roosevelt Room in which we stayed came with an elegant Victorian walnut queen bed whose bright red sheets coordinated with the color of the walls. A closet-size bathroom was augmented by a sink in the corner of the bedroom. A TV, telephone and turndown service with chocolates came with, as in all the rooms.

Upstairs are three larger guest rooms. The front Lindbergh Room, named for the aviator who flew his first solo flight nearby, offers a queen bed, jacuzzi tub and a private balcony over the front veranda. The kingsize Rosalynn Room, containing the former first lady's photo, is feminine and stunning in black and burgundy. A hunt theme prevails in the masculine Carter Room, which has a kingsize poster bed, a large bath with jacuzzi, and signed photographs of the former president.

Breakfast is served between 6:30 and 9 at a table for eight in the fireplaced dining room. Ours included eggs poached in a white wine sauce and a creation that Chuck termed a sausage ball. Wine and assorted beverages are offered in the evening.

(912) 928-2078 or (800) 889-1466. Five rooms with private baths. Doubles, $75 to $125. Children and pets accepted. No smoking.

Rees Park Garden Inn, 504 Rees Park, Americus 31709.

Don and Jodi Miles moved from Arizona to acquire this handsome antebellum mansion built in 1847. The residence had been converted into four apartments, so renovating it for B&B use took triple the time and expense

Pillars and curving porches grace facade of 1906 Pathway Inn.

they anticipated. Jodi designed the interior and Don executed the plans. They finally opened in late 1997 "and we're still not done," Don said at our visit a year later.

The house is a beauty. Gray with white gingerbread trim and a huge wraparound veranda, it sits on a large lot facing Rees Park. The long center hallway features a rare side staircase, with steps from an arched landing descending to the front and rear. It's similar to the Charleston exterior style, but rarely seen in an interior hall.

The living room is pleasant in mauves and greens and is accented with ceramic miniatures of European castles. More castles and an extensive collection of plates are displayed in the dining room, a most interesting space with a three-window bay along one side, three tables flanked by sleek restaurant-style upholstered chairs and, for good measure, two plush leather loveseats in front of the fireplace.

The rear corner of the main floor harbors the Veranda Room, colorful in greens and purples, with a king bed in the corner of the three-window bay, two armchairs and a sofa, and a bath with a garden tub for two. The room enjoys private access to the veranda. It also contains a live green vine growing on a trellis. "We found it growing through the baseboard from the outside and worked around it," Don explains.

Upstairs are three large guest rooms, each with TV and private telephone line. The rear Balcony Room with kingsize bed opens onto a private balcony. Here you'll find an oversize hammock in which some guests choose to sleep. The most popular room is Scarlett's, dramatic in jewel tones with kingsize bed, a loveseat and armchair in the bay window and a large bath with a garden tub and a separate shower. An adjoining room with two double poster beds turns Scarlett's into a two-bedroom suite. The Magnolia Suite is nearly a mirror image, with an antique queen poster bed and a smaller bath.

Each of the second bedrooms in the two suites have room for a separate bath, which Don was thinking of adding. He also was toying with the idea of converting his office on the front of the main floor into a seventh bedroom.

From the oversize kitchen, he prepares a breakfast of massive proportions. He warmed up for the job by opening the Windsor Gourmet Coffee House in the downtown hotel "before people here knew what cappuccino was." He closed it to

Rees Park Garden Inn is housed in restored antebellum mansion across from park.

concentrate on the B&B, but coffee equipment occupies prime space in the kitchen. The buffet sideboard is laden with treats like cheese biscuits, cheese omelet, bacon or ham, grits and a fruit plate.

The rear of the property contains a carriage house in which the owners live, as well as space for a gazebo, a goldfish pond and a putting green. Sidewalks found buried around the front and sides of the house were restored to recreate the original formal garden network.

(912) 931-0122. Two rooms and two suites with private baths. Doubles, $65 to $75. Suites, $95 to $105. Pets accepted. Smoking restricted.

The Guerry House, 723 McGarrah St., Americus 31709.

The 1833 raised cottage at Springhill Plantation is unusual for its classical Louisiana architecture generally associated with the lower Mississippi Delta. It's also unusual in that it's an enterprise of different ventures, from a B&B to a restaurant for private functions to a restoration in progress.

"Living history" is the theme in Sumter County's oldest antebellum plantation, a 26-acre, low-profile retreat of ponds, meadows and woods hidden only a few blocks northwest of downtown Americus. Owner Walter Stapleton Jr. did most of the ongoing restoration. His wife Pamela handles the B&B and the meals.

They opened in 1985 with a gourmet supper club for corporate and private parties on the lower floor of the historic plantation house, which is notable for brick interior walls and floors and beamed ceilings. They added the B&B in 1988, with one atmospheric suite on the lower floor of the main house and three rooms in the Overseer's Cottage. Walter made all the furniture for the suite, which offers a primitive handpainted queensize bed with matching armoire, a planter's desk and table, and a decided feeling of isolation. The two-story cottage out back has a wide porch overlooking the ponds. The two side-by-side rooms upstairs are snug with a queensize bed, a single chair, TV and telephone, and vanities in cupboards. The downstairs room with a private veranda has a double bed, antique loveseat and a jacuzzi garden tub. White lace curtains and oriental rugs accent the rough heart-pine interiors, which retain the look of the early 1800s.

Breakfast is served on the heart-pine table Walter made for the plantation's kitchen building. The meal includes fresh orange juice, ground Colombian coffee, granola, grits, eggs cooked to order, locally smoked bacon, homemade biscuits and preserves. Pamela hosts the cooking segment on a local TV show, for which she had made fudge pecan pies with pecans from their property the day of our visit. She averages three meals a week, for anywhere from 8 to 84 guests by reservation, and also serves candlelight dinners for as few as two overnight guests. She and her husband are also songwriters and have their own record album. He plays the banjo and guitar and she the mandolin They don period outfits to perform and sing for dinner guests. "We're re-enactors as well," explains Pamela.
(912) 924-1009. Four rooms with private baths. Doubles, $75 to $115.

The Windsor Hotel, 125 West Lamar St., Americus 31709.
A more beautiful brick structure, especially when bathed in sunlight or illuminated like a castle at night, is difficult to imagine. It was proclaimed the most elegant hotel in Georgia when it opened in 1892, and was restored a century later by the city and local investors.
The centerpiece of downtown Americus, the Windsor is a block-square masterpiece of turrets and niches, dormers and arched verandas. Inside, the atrium lobby of golden oak soars three stories high with balconies on all sides.
"We have a couple of ghosts in the hotel," says manager Mary Barfield, although they play second fiddle to the haute-Victorian architecture. The main floor offers a visitor information center and shops, including a retail branch of the famed Tog Shop, a local women's apparel mail-order business. On the second floor are a stately Victorian dining room (see Dining Spots) and a more casual pub.
The hotel's 53 guest rooms are on portions of three upper floors. They include 26 with one bed (mostly full-size but four with kings and a few with queens), nineteen with two double beds and six small suites with separate sitting areas. The ones we saw were simple and serviceable, decorated in the prevailing yellows and reds of the rest of the hotel.
Top of the line are two round suites in the tower. Decorated in pale yellow, the Carter Suite in the third-floor turret has a kingsize carved oak bed and a sitting area with a couch and two armchairs. The fourth-floor of the turret houses a bridal suite, decorated in champagne and rose, with a sitting area facing the windows for a panoramic view and a canopied king bed behind.
Common areas include arched verandas overlooking Lamar Street on the second and third floors. The second-floor veranda connects to Floyd's Bar, which offers drinks and a bar menu, served inside or on the veranda.
In late 1998, the city-owned hotel was acquired by Sharad Patal, owner of the local Ramada Inn. No immediate changes were planned.
(912) 924-1555 or (800) 678-8946. Forty-five rooms and eight suites with private baths. Doubles, $78 to $92. Suites, $99 to $159.

The Plains Bed & Breakfast Inn, 100 West Church St., Box 217, Plains 31780.
Talk about connections. Miss Lillian, Jimmy Carter's mother, rented a room here before her marriage in 1924. Jimmy Carter's campaign headquarters lives on in the depot almost across the street. Billy Carter's gas station stands abandoned nearby. The former president and first lady live in a house behind a gate just up the street. What there is of downtown Plains is across the railroad track.

At the heart of it all is this turn-of-the-century residence with wraparound porch and corner gazebo. Grace Jackson and her late husband sold their house to Billy and Sybil Carter in 1986 to buy this property to run as a B&B. Miss Lillian's picture hangs over the fireplace mantle in the small guest room named for her. The room has a queensize poster bed. A front corner guest room with twin beds has an in-room vanity, armoire and a single armchair. The rear honeymoon suite has a queen poster bed and is appointed in pink and black florals. Guests have a common area with a TV set at the end of the second-floor hallway.

Downstairs, the common rooms are given over to the **Magnolia & Ivy** gift shop and tea parlor, one of four in the area operated by sisters Terri Eager and Kay Snipes. Terri moved their Plains location here in 1998 and called it the perfect marriage between retailing and restaurant. She finds the B&B location ideal, although she says that "serving high tea in the middle of Bubbaville is ahead of the market."

The tea parlor serves as a breakfast room in the morning. Guests enjoy a full Southern breakfast of eggs, grits, sausage and toast.

As this book went to press, the inn was under contract for sale to a woman who owned a B&B in western North Carolina.

(912) 824-7252. Three rooms with private baths. Doubles, $65.

A Place Away Cottage, Oglethorpe Street, Box 26, Andersonville 31711.

Peggy Sheppard, a dynamo who virtually runs the Civil War Village of Andersonville, offers this quaint cottage for a B&B experience. A native Yankee school teacher who married a man from Americus, she and husband Fred live across the street in what was the schoolhouse. The cottage was the principal's house.

Flags flying out front identify the cottage, a gray house with a front veranda and a back deck, perched atop a rise and "a place away from the main drag, so it's nice and quiet," says Peggy. Two bedrooms with private baths share a common area likened to a country kitchen. One room has two double beds, and the other a queen and a twin bed. The rooms come with TV, coffeemaker and refrigerator.

Peggy checks guests in and gets them settled. She also stocks the kitchen with a continental breakfast of juice, fruit and homemade pastries like sour cream coffee cake and pumpkin bread.

(912) 924-2558 or 924-1044. Two rooms with private baths. Doubles, $50.

Dining Spots

The Windsor Hotel, 125 West Lamar St., Americus.

The area's only white-tablecloth dining is offered in the elegant – make that stately – Victorian dining room on the second floor of this restored hotel. A new chef took over the kitchen in 1998 and reduced the scope of the menu. Local people who had eaten there lately were thrilled with the food as well as the experience.

On an autumn weeknight our table and only two others (each with single diners) were occupied. Service was proper in effort if flawed in the execution, but the food was indeed good. The menu offered six choices from pecan-crusted salmon fillet with peach butter sauce to grilled chicken Windsor "smothered in tangy barbecue sauce." Spicy crab cakes with peach salsa and shrimp-stuffed mushrooms were among the appetizers. One of us liked the broiled filet mignon. The other took a chance on the Southern slow-roasted prime rib on condition that it be rare.

Plains Bed & Breakfast Inn faces Jimmy Carter's campaign headquarters in old depot.

It arrived well done, but a return to the kitchen produced a juicy, rare slab with the requested horseradish sauce. Good mashed potatoes and mixed sautéed vegetables accompanied. With a bottle of the house merlot, we were quite satisfied. Small cut-glass lamps graced the well-spaced tables, flanked by cushioned armchairs.

The dining room is generally open for three meals daily. Light fare is offered in Floyd's Bar.

(912) 924-1555. Entrées, $15.95 to $21.95. Lunch daily except Saturday, 11:30 to 2. Dinner nightly except Sunday, 6:30 to 9:30. Floyd's Bar, 4 to midnight.

Dingus MaGees, 120 North Lee St., Americus.

Beyond the Windsor, demanding diners are shortchanged in this area. A relative newcomer that one regular said was "a cut above Applebee's" is this place with a long bar, a small lower dining room and a mix of booths and tables amidst brick walls and whirring ceiling fans.

Like others of its ilk, it offers something for everyone, from six kinds of burgers to shrimp fettuccine to grilled prime rib. There are four chicken dishes, from "smothered" to teriyaki, plus barbecued baby back ribs, shrimp kabobs, fried shrimp, and steak and shrimp.

Start with a sampler of chicken fingers, Buffalo wings, cheese sticks and potato skins. Finish with the snicker bar cheesecake.

(912) 924-6333. Entrées, $7.99 to $13.99. Lunch and dinner, Monday-Wednesday 11 to 10, Thursday-Saturday 11 to midnight.

Forsyth 1889 Bar and Grill, 124 West Forsyth St., Americus.

This old-timer is all pine, from its booths to its paneled walls and its rear bar. The family-style menu is full of hearty food, dispensed with old-fashioned Southern hospitality.

The large menu covers the gamut, from "fried snacks" to grilled ribeye steaks. There are pasta dishes, Mexican items and sandwiches. Appetizers include potato skins, cheese-stuffed shrimp, stuffed jalapeños and deep-fried onion bloom.

Typical dinner entrées are grilled rainbow trout, chicken parmesan, chicken cordon bleu and grilled quail.

(912) 924-8193. Dinner entrées, $7.99 to $12.99. Open Tuesday-Friday 11 to 10, Saturday 5 to 10.

The Talking Bean, 142 South Lee St., Americus.

Coffees, lattes and fruit smoothies are featured at this corner coffeehouse at the edge of downtown. It's also a good place for breakfast sandwiches and waffles, interesting salads and sandwiches, and desserts. Consider one of the three chicken salads (the tropical with pineapple and oranges is a favorite) or the longhorn steak salad. The aztec chicken sandwich and a club sandwich combining steak, turkey, smoked bacon and cheddar cheese are among the specialties. Several vegetarian items stand out here in meat and potatoes country.

(912) 924-2299. Sandwiches and salads, $3.50 to $4.95. Open Monday-Thursday 7 a.m. to 9 p.m., Friday 7 to 10, Saturday 8 to 2.

Andersonville Restaurant, 213 West Church St., Andersonville.

This rustic restaurant in front of an RV trailer park occupies the town's oldest building, a residence built in 1847. It serves Southern-style lunches buffet style. Proceed through a cafeteria line that might offer a choice of sausage or beef tips over rice, black-eyed peas, butter beans, corn, potatoes and sliced tomatoes. The iced tea flows freely in an old camp of a building with communal tables inside and along a front porch. Peach cobbler is the dessert of choice.

This is also a popular place for Sunday dinner after church. For dinner on weekends, catfish and steak might be added to the fare.

(912) 928-8888. Lunch buffet, $5. Open Monday-Thursday 11 to 2, Friday-Saturday 11 to 9, Sunday 11 to 3.

Diversions

Andersonville and Plains are the focal points for most visitors. For emotional reasons, you might want to experience the traumas of Andersonville first. Plains serves as an inspiring sequel.

Andersonville National Historic Site, State Route 49, Andersonville.

This 495-acre park ten miles northeast of Americus consists of the new National Prisoner of War Museum, the site of the infamous Civil War Prison and the Andersonville National Cemetery. Begin at the museum, opened in 1998 to honor American prisoners of all wars, from the Revolution to the Persian Gulf, who "suffered captivity so that others could remain free." Anyone who spends the several hours required to fully appreciate the museum may never be the same.

A 27-minute documentary film, narrated by Gen. Colin Powell, sets the stage. Then proceed through a state-of-the-art museum of seven exhibition galleries, each an audio-visual wonderland of photos and graphics. They trace chronologically themes common to all POWs in American history, from capture through survival to freedom. Interactive databases detail stories that vary from poignant to horrifying. You see the intricate model sailing ship made of mutton soup bones by prisoners whiling away their time. You see and hear the unnerving accounts of loved ones who waited, often not knowing whether their prisoners were dead or alive or would ever return. The last gallery, "Escape to Freedom,"

Prisoner monument stands near rows of headstones in Andersonville National Cemetery.

ends on an uplifting note, such as it is. The visitor then proceeds outside to a rear sculpture garden and fountain, a "contemplative place" needed to counter the intensity within, according to Fred Boyles, site superintendent.

Andersonville is "the most controversial site in the National Park System," he said. "Here's where the book on war crimes was written." Beyond the sculptures are the reconstructed stockades and escape tunnels of Camp Sumter, the largest POW camp in the Civil War. In its fourteen months of operation, 45,000 Union soldiers struggled for survival in a 26-acre enclosure in conditions of extreme overcrowding, filth and disease. Nearly 13,000 died. Their bodies are buried shoulder to shoulder beneath tight symmetrical rows of headstones in the adjoining National Cemetery. A drive around the perimeter of the prison camp shows monuments to the victims erected by various states and the Providence Spring, so named because water miraculously gushed forth following a thunderstorm in answer to the prayers of desperate prisoners.

The site, despite its reminders of the horrors of war, is tempered by an educational theme and a landscape of beauty. The message is one of hope that reason and harmony may ultimately prevail.

(912) 924-0343. Site open daily, 8 to 5; museum, 8:30 to 5. Free.

Andersonville Civil War Village, State Route 49, Andersonville.

This humble village was the end of the rail line for Union prisoners transported here by train and marched the last quarter mile to Camp Sumter. The tiny village became the supply center for the prison. The train depot is now a visitor center and museum. A monument erected in the center of Church Street commemorates Henry Wirz, the Confederate captain in charge of the stockade, who was the only Civil War soldier to be tried and hanged as a war criminal. Some Southerners consider him a martyr who became a scapegoat for Northern outrage after the war. Peggy Sheppard, a Yankee transplant from Yonkers, N.Y., has spearheaded the village's restoration. Rustic antiques shops and eateries convey the feeling of the era. Well worth a visit is the **Drummer Boy Civil War Museum,** in which Gerry Lamby from New Jersey shares his remarkable collection of Lincoln memorabilia. Fifteen mannequins wear original uniforms, including those of drummer boys. Gerry spent nearly three years creating the intricate diorama of the prison stockade. Outside, a seven-acre pioneer farm contains animals and a dozen buildings relocated to the site. It's a favorite of the school and tour groups that flock here.

(912) 924-1558. Open daily, 9 to 5. Free.

Jimmy Carter National Historic Site, Plains.

"Any schoolboy, even one of ours, might grow up to be president of the United States," teacher-superintendent Julia Coleman is quoted as saying on a plaque at the entry to the former Plains High School. Jimmy Carter, Class of 1941, took her statement to heart. The high school was reopened in 1996 as a visitor center and museum with exhibits on Carter's life and times. A 25-minute orientation film, narrated by the late Charles Kuralt, is shown in the auditorium where Rosalynn Carter gave the valedictory speech in 1944.

Much of the town of Plains (population 700) is Carter land, as depicted by the National Park Service. Self-guided and group tours show the sites. Carter's boyhood farmhouse out the Old Plains Highway in Archery is undergoing restoration. Here is where 4-year-old Jimmy had to crawl through a window of their new home because his father had forgotten the keys. "It was the last time this house was locked," site supervisor Pat Recker advised. Young Jimmy used to walk the train tracks into Plains, "the big city," ten miles west of Americus. The small Plains train depot, which served as Carter's 1976 presidential campaign headquarters, now is a museum of campaign memorabilia. The Carters' current home, a 1960 brick ranch, is hidden in the trees behind Secret Service gates and a split-rail fence the former president built along Woodland Drive. (The house will pass to the park service upon their deaths.) The visitor can see the couple's first apartment, Public Housing Unit 9-A, and the Plains United Methodist Church where they were married in 1946. The former president still teaches Sunday school roughly three times a month at the outlying, 125-member Maranatha Baptist Church. This is not your ordinary Sunday school. Up to 600 people crowd the sanctuary and an overflow room served by closed-circuit television to hear the lesson at 10 a.m. Some stay for the 11 a.m. worship service, after which the Carters meet one and all and pose for photos.

Interesting Carter family sites abound. Brother Billy Carter's service station stands abandoned behind the Phillips 76 sign in the center of town. His widow Sybil manages the new Sun Point retirement home at one end of town. The Lillian G. Carter Nursing Center is at the other end. The Carter Worm Farm office and Hugh Carter's Antiques shop occupy two of the seven attached buildings that make up downtown Plains. The family's peanut and farm warehouses are the major landmark to the east. Our guide pointed out Rosalynn Carter's brother walking down the street. Such is life in Plains, "a haven" to which the worldly Carters always return.

(912) 824-4104. Site headquarters in high school, 300 North Bond Street. Open daily, 9 to 5. Free.

Other attractions appeal to diverse interests. The **Lindbergh Memorial Statue** commemorates the aviator's first solo flight at Souther Field, Route 49, Americus. The new **Georgia Rural Telephone Museum** in Leslie holds the largest collection of telephones and telephone memorabilia in the world. The historic **Rylander Theater,** West Lamar Street, Americus, was being restored for reopening in 1999 as one of the most technologically advanced theaters in the Southeast. Daily tours will be given of the 630-seat theater, one of only two in the nation with concert pipe organs. Visitors will enjoy a restored soda fountain in front as well as a choice of three rotating live performances on Andersonville, the Jimmy Carter Story and the Rylander Follies, a 1920s revue.

Shopping. Andersonville and Plains each have a handful of stores devoted primarily to antiques and collectibles. Most stores are centered in downtown Americus, in the block surrounding the restored Windsor Hotel. The **Americus Book Store** offers lots of room for browsing. **Mary Baldwin** purveys gifts, antiques and accessories. The **Tog Shop** in the hotel features women's sleepwear and bath products (its main outlet just north of town offers current and discontinued catalog items).

Extra-Special

Habitat for Humanity International, 322 West Lamar St., Americus.

It seems quite appropriate that this inspiring house-building ministry started and continues to be headquartered in Americus, between Andersonville and Plains. Young, self-made Alabama millionaire Millard Fuller refocused his life at Koinonia Farm, a Christian community at 1324 Highway 49, ten miles south of Americus. With Koinonia founder Clarence Jordan, Millard and Linda Fuller started building affordable housing for the poor in downtown Americus. Since its founding in 1976, Habitat has partnered with 70,000 families to build simple homes in every state and more than 50 foreign countries. With the goal of "a world without shacks," Habitat volunteers help low-income families build modest homes for an average of $38,000. The occupants pay back a 20-year mortgage averaging $168 a month to a revolving fund that finances the construction of more houses.

Habitat's tour department headed by George Keller, a former Habitat construction manager, operates out of a new tour center and museum at 417 West Church St.

He shows some of the 600 Habitat houses built in a week from scratch, clustered in three tracts and scattered about Americus. The first house, a modest two-bedroom bungalow at 245 East Church St., stands not far from the ordinary-looking house where the Fullers now live. Visitors view Millard Fuller's former law office and Habitat's first headquarters as well as the recently renovated headquarters complex, where the main lobby is an atrium with a three-floor view of housing facades. Here the Our House gift shop features Habitat-inspired books and gifts. Houses bearing names like Shalom and Joy provide temporary homes in the area for volunteers. The International Village exhibits five replicas of Habitat houses in Third World countries, including one built on stilts. Jimmy and Rosalynn Carter spend one or two weeks a year serving as some of Habitat's most dedicated volunteers, building houses and hope. "It s the most rewarding and joyful activity we are engaged in," says the former president.

(912) 924-6935 or (800) 422-4828. Guided tours, Monday-Friday at 8, 10, 1 and 3. Gift shop, Monday-Friday 8 to 6, Saturday 10 to 2. Free.

Warm Springs/Pine Mountain, Ga.
The Legacy of a President

Two men – good friends, but political antagonists – left their legacies in this region at the foot of a mountain in western Georgia.

One, of course, is Franklin Delano Roosevelt. He heard of the healing powers of the waters at Warm Springs and responded favorably to treatments in the pool here. Thus he was enabled to run for president and shape the New Deal, a turning point in world affairs.

The other is Cason J. Callaway, a textile magnate. He was picnicking with his wife Virginia at Blue Springs in nearby Hamilton when they discovered a rare late-blooming azalea species that turned out to be native to the area. They bought 2,000 acres, regenerated the depleted cotton fields, and planted native trees and other plants. Thus began Callaway Gardens, now a world-famous garden resort.

President Roosevelt became so attached to Warm Springs that he built the only home he ever owned here. It's forever known as the Little White House, the beloved place where he died in 1945 while posing for a portrait. The house has been opened to the public as a state historic site since 1948, prompting an influx of tourists to a simple village most had only heard of by name through news reports.

Cason Callaway and his wife opened their family retreat to the public in 1952, launching a garden empire and resort that their family continues to refine and expand. The 1996 death of Virginia Callaway freed up land for a planned tripling of the size of the gardens within the next few years.

The Little White House and Callaway Gardens are the chief attractions for visitors. But there are others: The tranquil F.D. Roosevelt State Park, Georgia's largest, atop Pine Mountain. The Pine Mountain Trail, a 23-mile-long hiking trail considered one of the Southeast's best. The antiques and collectibles shops of touristy Pine Mountain village (population 900) and of rustic Warm Springs (population 400).

Except for these commercial centers, this is a far-flung, mostly rural area embracing much of Harris and Meriwether counties. It stretches from Pine Mountain to Warm Springs, from Greenville to Waverly Hall. At its center is the Harris County seat of Hamilton, population 500, built around a quaint square.

What little wealth is in the area lies hidden. This area of Georgia is a world removed from the refinements of coastal Georgia and, only 70 miles away, boomtown Atlanta. The locals seek to keep it that way.

Inn Spots

Magnolia Hall, 127 Barnes Mill Road, Box 326, Hamilton 31811.

Kendrick and Dale Smith had looked for years for a potential B&B when they came across the abandoned 1890 high Victorian cottage that was the birthplace of the former Beth Walton, wife of Bo Calloway, head of Calloway Gardens. "It was in sad shape and had to be gutted down to the studs," Ken recalls.

You'd never know it today. A thoughtful renovation in 1994 turned the dark green cottage with red roof and white gingerbread trim into a gracious, five-room B&B that exudes character and personality. Dale has furnished with flair in "eclectic style." She favors Eastlake beds and family heirlooms, but comfort takes

Porch trimmed in gingerbread welcomes guests to Magnolia Hall.

precedence over clutter. All rooms have queensize beds, sitting areas and TVs hidden in armoires. Our quarters in the spacious rear Carrie's Corner on the main floor were typical: a tall walnut bed, a cream-colored sofa, a rocking chair, a bathroom with twin vanities and a shower with a built-in seat, and a walk-in closet big enough to double as a dressing area. The owners' attention to detail showed in the novel, three-way antique "touch lights" that turn on and off with the touch of a finger, the flashlight beside the triple-sheeted bed, the hair dryer and fine soaps in the bathroom, and the iron in the closet. Their devotion to heritage showed in the pictures and furnishings relating to Carrie Smith, the mother of Ken's father, who had occupied the room past his 100th birthday.

The T.L.C. continues in the front Walton Room, the original master bedroom with a bed in the three-window bay, a grandfather's desk, a collection of hat boxes and a shower big enough for two. Upstairs in what had been an unfinished attic are two suites. One has a four-poster bed and a sitting room with two Queen Anne-style recliners and a wicker rocker, plus an extra twin bed and a game table tucked into the dormers.

Family portraits are featured in the long central hall on the main floor. Up front are an elegant library/sitting room and a parlor with a grand piano, where Ken likes to entertain. Breakfast is served at a table for ten

House dating to 1833 is now Raintree Farms of Waverly Hall.

in the dining room. Ours was a feast of ethereal pancakes with strawberries, link sausages and a baked egg with havarti cheese, surrounded by Calloway speckled heart grits. "Have you ever heard of a mayor serving you coffee and then serenading you on the piano?" asked Dale. It turns out her husband is not only mayor of Hamilton but a child prodigy who chucked a potential career as a pianist for one as an accountant and financial planner.

Upon arrival, guests enjoy lemonade or a carafe of wine on the wraparound veranda shaded by a tall magnolia tree out front. Cream sherry and cookies are put out in bedrooms at nightly turndown.

(706) 628-4566. Three rooms and two suites with private baths. Doubles, $95. Suites, $115. No smoking. No credit cards.

Raintree Farms of Waverly Hall, 8060 Highway 208, Waverly Hall 31831.

A columned front porch spans the width of this two-story white clapboard house, built in 1833. Sandi Lee, only the sixth owner of the house, bought it in 1991 and opened it as a B&B two years later. She decorated with "an aura of elegance reminiscent of antebellum days long gone."

Step inside the wide center hall from a front veranda where your name is posted with a flourish on a "welcome" blackboard. On the right is a formal dining room. Here Sandi serves her elaborate gourmet breakfasts when the weather does not allow the use of the rear porch or the brick patio beside a fountain. Most of the furnishings reflect her ancestors, back to 1800. Her mother's settee, antique secretary and pictures dignify the front parlor. A veritable gallery of relatives' pictures spreads across a table in the master bedroom at a rear corner of the main floor. This large room has a double poster bed and a bathroom with a clawfoot tub tucked beneath an extra staircase rising to the infants' bedroom overhead. The stairs were built so the original parents could heed their youngsters' cries in the middle of the night.

The most popular accommodation is in the snug original kitchen, secluded off the new kitchen in the rear. It has a queen brass bed, a full bath and screen doors opening to a pastoral scene of an old cabin, pecan trees, fields and small pond. Upstairs are three rooms sharing two baths. They're generally rented as one room with private bath or as a two-room suite. One front bedroom has twin beds and another a double poster bed. Most lush is the rear Caroline's Retreat, with a queen canopy bed and a day bed. As in the rest of the house, they're dressed in Ralph Lauren comforters with matching window treatments. Sandi irons the sheets and hangs the bed covers outside on the shrubbery to bleach and dry. The upstairs hall is big enough to include a TV and games area, and space is available for an extra bedroom and private bath(s) in the future.

"Most guests don't come for the room but for the ambiance, the breakfast and to see me," says the gregarious hostess. They hang out in the keeping room off her big country kitchen, where old kitchen ware from her aunt's attic decorates a shelf, antique wash tubs adorn a wall and dishes stand upright in an open plate rack she designed herself. They gab with the cook as she prepares a substantial breakfast, perhaps apples sautéed in cinnamon and brown sugar, a cheese omelet with bacon and "heavenly hots" – pancakes with homemade syrup.

Outside, she proudly shows her new elderberry bushes, planted alongside the house to furnish the makings for elderberry flower fritters and elderberry tea. Full afternoon tea is served by reservation for groups of ten or more in her **Elderberry Tea Parlor.**

(706) 582-3227 or (800) 433-0627. Two rooms with private baths and three rooms with shared bath. Doubles, $125. Each additional in suites, $30. No smoking. No credit cards.

Georgian Inn Bed & Breakfast, 566 South Talbotton St., Greenville 30222. Folks used to come into her store in Warm Springs and say there was no place to stay except at Callaway. "So I'd bring them home with me," recalls Angela Hand. She offered one downstairs room in this 1914 pillared home for eight years before opening four more rooms in 1997.

Her spacious home is notable for eight fireplaces, high ceilings, stained-glass windows, and chestnut and heart-pine floors. It's a showcase for the decorating and floral design talents she employs at her store called the Veranda.

The main floor holds a sumptuous living room and a family room/den on either side of the center hall. Off the den is a spacious wicker sunporch that Angela calls "the best place in the house." And no wonder. We could barely remove ourselves from the gently rocking glider-swing.

Behind the den is Governor Terrell's Room, with a hand-carved mahogany poster bed, an Empire chest, marble-top dresser, TV ensconced in an armoire and double windows with plantation shutters overlooking the sunporch.

Similar attributes characterize four upstairs bedrooms, three with queen beds and one with a king. The rear Georgian Room is light and feminine with a white fainting couch at the foot of a bed whose floral comforter and shams coordinate with the window treatments. More masculine is the front Rhett Butler Room, with a plush loveseat at the foot of an antique mahogany and walnut bed angled from the corner and a portrait of Miss Scarlett overseeing *Gone with the Wind* memorabilia from its perch above the fireplace mantel. Every bed is topped with a tray stand bearing a single cup and saucer. That's for the gentleman of the party to serve his beloved her morning cup of coffee in bed, says Angela.

The heart of the house is the airy kitchen, with windows onto a backyard patio and gardens. Here is where her cook prepares what Angela calls "a killer good breakfast." The usual fare includes eggs, biscuits, grits, cheese soufflé, bacon, sausage and fresh fruit, served buffet style on a sideboard in the formal dining room. "People pig out and can't eat again until dinner time," says she. Or at least until the late afternoon, when Angela serves sweet iced tea, brownies or banana bread and the most delectable tea cakes we've tasted.

(706) 672-1600. Fax (706) 672-1666. Five rooms with private baths. Doubles, $125. No smoking.

Hotel Warm Springs, 47 Broad St., Box 351, Warm Springs 31830.

A relatively brief but illustrious history draws folks to the last of the area's summer hotels, a 1907 landmark on a prime corner of the crossroads that is downtown Warm Springs.

Gerrie Thompson, owner for ten years and a leading local promoter, renovated and redecorated fourteen rooms with private baths. Four on the first floor are reserved for smokers. Interspersed amid shops, their entrances are not particularly inviting. Better are those a bit removed from the action on the second floor. They go off an open common sitting room and a hotel-style corridor. They're furnished simply with antiques and an occasional decorative accent on the walls of plaster, with a queen poster bed here or two double beds there. Some of the English oak furniture was made in the factory that Eleanor Roosevelt established to help the unemployed on her property at Val-Kill, N.Y. Gerrie is partial to Room 104, which contains her grandmother's iron bed and furnishings, a washstand sink in the corner and a clawfoot tub in the bathroom. The simple side Presidential Suite has a sofabed in a sitting room with a corner washstand, and a queen poster bed and another corner washstand in a room beyond the connecting bathroom. The rear Honeymoon Suite comes with a kingsize bed, heart-shaped jacuzzi and separate shower. Most rooms have few amenities beyond TV sets.

"I baked nine loaves of banana nut bread this morning," Gerrie said as she led a tour. They were part of a substantial Southern country breakfast offered in the third-floor dining room.

The main foyer with its original tiled floor, stenciled walls and sixteen-foot-high ceiling contains the original telephone booth and cord switchboard plus a maze of gift items. An ice cream parlor occupies the corner site of the drug store where President Roosevelt used to come for ice cream. He was the only customer to get curb service, Gerrie said. Hotel rooms back then housed the press, Secret Service, visiting royalty and Hollywood celebrities.

(706) 655-2114 or (800) 366-7616. Twelve rooms and two suites with private baths. Doubles, $70 to $103. Suites, $120 and $145.

Aunt Stella's House Bed & Breakfast, Hamilton Square Street, Box 565, Hamilton 31811.

For a change of pace, consider this new B&B, a restored 1880s house that belonged to Leigh Rath's great aunt Stella. "The old home place was located on the other side of Pine Mountain," as Leigh tells it. The land was sold to the Callaway interests – "a familiar story around here" – and the house was dismantled piece by piece by her husband Bruce, a restorationist. He rebuilt it by the numbers on a wooded site facing the railroad track a block from Hamilton Square.

The job took two years and was finished in 1998. "We wanted to save the house and never thought about what to do with it," Lee said. Along came neighbor Ann Bacher, a retired minister's wife, who suggested a B&B and offered to manage it. Quickly it was a done deal. The Smiths from nearby Magnolia Hall (see above) filled it on weekends with their overflow.

The four-room house is a beauty, with floors, walls and ceilings of heart-pine, two stone fireplaces (also moved stone by stone), a kitchen and a modern bathroom in what had been a second bedroom. The front bedroom contains a double bed and two twins, all decked out in colorful quilts. The living room has a TV/VCR, a sofabed and chairs facing a fireplace. Conveniences include a telephone and a dish washer. A back porch looks out onto the woods. The front porch swing is where guests wait to watch one of the two trains a day go by.

Mrs. Bacher checks guests in and stocks the refrigerator with light breakfast items. After that, "the whole house is yours," according to the venture's brochure.

(706) 628-4733. A complete house with accommodations for two to six. Double, $115; each additional over age 12, $10. No smoking. No credit cards.

Callaway Gardens Resort, Highway 27, Box 2000, Pine Mountain 31822.

The 349 guest rooms and suites in the low-slung Callaway Gardens Inn structures betray their motor-inn origins. But the setting, across Highway 27 from the entrance to the gardens, is superior. Built around a flagstone courtyard and fountain, the red-brick and wood buildings painted taupe blend into the heavily wooded landscape. An interesting bird study area and a relaxing meditation section are focal points between room wings and the registration area and restaurants. Birds twitter and flowers bloom all around.

Recently renovated, our room with two double beds faced the lush courtyard and was quite comfortable. A mirror made the room appear larger. It was furnished in pine, with floral accents of bright blossom-print bedspreads and two framed garden scenes on the walls. An armoire held the TV and an honor bar. Callaway toiletries were in the bathroom. Other rooms have kingsize beds, and some overlook the pool. Large Roof Garden suites come with one or two bedrooms and a parlor.

Beside the motor inn, the resort offers 155 two-bedroom units in the Callaway Country Cottages on the north side of the property. Popular with groups and families, each comes with living and dining area, fireplace, screened porch and deck. The same amenities on a larger scale are available in the luxurious Mountain Creek Villas, near the Tennis Center and available for rent or sale.

The inn contains two restaurants (see Dining Spots), and five more are scattered about the resort property.

(706) 663-2281 or (800) 225-5292. Fax (706) 663-8114. Three hundred forty-nine rooms and suites with private baths. Mid-March through December: doubles $111, suites $160 to $310. Cottages, $185 to $295. Rest of year: doubles $96, suites $136 to $286. Cottages, $158 to $252.

Dining Spots

Fine dining restaurants are few and far between in this area where Southern buffets and barbecued ribs reign. One of the better, Bon Cuisine in Pine Mountain, closed abruptly in late 1998 when its rent was raised. Its owner was looking to reopen in smaller quarters nearby. Choices in Warm Springs range from the dark Victorian Tea Room ("all you can eat lunch buffet," $6.95) to Mac's Barbecue, a shanty where we enjoyed a tasty sliced pork tenderloin sandwich for lunch on a picnic table beside Mac's Steak House, a weekend dinner restaurant.

Oak Tree Victorian, Highway 27, Hamilton.
An 1871 Victorian – handsome in pale yellow with blue shutters and white gingerbread trim – is the area's finest all-around restaurant. Since 1983, veteran chef-owner Bob Cusic has been known for consistent food in plush surroundings. The interior exudes elegance, from its imported mantels and staircase to the enormous copper espresso machine at the entry. The sign out front stresses casual dress and dinner specials from $7.95.
Upwards of 150 people can be seated in three small dining rooms in front and a larger room with a bar in back. Giant chandeliers and plants hang overhead. Well-spaced tables are illuminated by shaded oil lamps.
The extensive "American-Franco-Italian" menu promises something for everyone, including aforementioned specials (fried catfish, lemon chicken breast and country fried steak, "suggested for the smaller appetite"). House-made rolls, salad, a bouquetière of vegetables and a potato croquette accompany the two dozen entrées, ranging from broiled orange roughy and stuffed prawns to chicken cordon bleu, duckling à l'orange, veal piccata or oscar, prime rib and steak diane. There are ten pasta dishes and sides like steamed broccoli with hollandaise for the traditionalists. This is probably the only area restaurant to offer broiled lobster, grilled veal chop and rack of lamb.
The captain's wine book displays the appropriate labels. Basic house wines can be ordered by the glass, half carafe or carafe.
(706) 628-4218. Entrées, $14.95 to $23.95. Dinner, Monday-Saturday from 6.

Marco's Italian Café, 9635 Highway 208, Waverly Hall.
People come from miles around to sample what some consider the area's best food. The draw is certainly not the ambiance. The rustic roadhouse still looks much like the pool hall it was until 1995. The walls are whitewashed cinder block, the green and white striped vinyl window swags match the banquette along one wall, and the bleached pine tables are set with cutlery rolled in paper napkins. Smokers are relegated to the rear bar section, which dispenses a modest selection of beers and wines. The ice water comes with a slice of lemon, a rarity hereabouts.
West Virginian Mark Maunz gave up a twenty-year sales career with Eastman Kodak to open "a little pizza place, just like back home." Assisted by a dishwasher, he prepared pizzas and pastas that attracted the throngs. One dish led to another, the pool tables were removed and hour-long waits for a table became common. Mark since has built a thriving catering business and turned kitchen duties over to a fulltime chef.
He was the genial host and waiter the slow weeknight we stopped in. He recommended the signature portobello mushroom for an appetizer, the penne alla vodka with prosciutto and tomato for a pasta dish and, for the main course, the gulf shrimp sautéed in creamy wine or lemon-butter sauces. We could not resist the "crazy fish," however. A novel dish, it turned out to be whitefish wrapped in angelhair pasta that was baked until crunchy and topped with a lemon-butter sauce, artichoke hearts and capers – sensational. The pesto bread that preceded came with by marinara sauce on the side, which was fortunate for the bread was so good it needed no embellishment. The house salad was dressed with a balsamic

vinaigrette. And, for good measure, garlic bread came with the main course, along with a superior pasta laced with spinach and cream sauce. A huge portion of tirami su, the dessert specialty, arrived on a plate drizzled with chocolate sauce. On Saturdays, Marco's adds lunch services, serving smaller portions of the dinner menu for half price. Oh yes, you can still get hand-tossed semolina pizzas. But most people opt for fancier dishes like sautéed grouper and veal saltimbocca. *(706) 582-3294. Entrées, $12.95 to $18.95. Lunch, Saturday 11:30 to 2. Dinner, Monday-Saturday 5 to 10.*

Cricket's Restaurant, Highway 18, Pine Mountain.
The exterior looks like a little red alpine chalet in the woods. Inside are a couple of dining rooms of rustic country décor and a kitchen run with devotion by chef-owner Mary Eason, whose husband John manages the front of the house. The Easons moved here from New Orleans, and their Cajun-Creole dishes proved so popular that they expanded from 40 to 100 seats over their first ten years. A pleasant front patio provides additional dining space when weather permits.

A sampler platter of gumbo, jambalaya, red beans and rice, crawfish étouffée, salad and parmesan bread appealed at our visit. Otherwise we would have been hard pressed to choose between them, not to mention grilled shrimp, catfish Orleans, blackened fish or roasted chicken, most served with brabant potatoes. The menu suggests wines for each choice. Smaller portions are available as appetizers. Also offered are a vegetable plate of the day and three sandwiches.

Favorite desserts are chocolate-pecan-praline cake, a warm chocolate brownie layered with buttercream or a light almond cream crêpe, a perfect ending for a hearty meal.

(706) 663-8136. Entrées, $7.95 to $15.95. Dinner, Wednesday-Sunday from 5.

The Bulloch House Restaurant, 47 Bulloch St., Warm Springs.
"Country with class" is the billing for this landmark, a Victorian house perched atop a hill and marked by a "fried green tomatoes" sign on the lawn out front and a gift shop alongside. Restored as a restaurant in 1990, it offers traditional home-cooked Southern meals of particular appeal to bus groups. Locals praise the food as some of the area's freshest and most consistent.

Tourists pour in at lunch time for a traditional Southern buffet spread. At our visit, the offerings were fried chicken, spaghetti with meat sauce, string beans, sweet potato soufflé, pinto beans, collard greens, fried okra and fried green tomatoes, plus a salad bar. Desserts were extra, but not to be missed: apple cobbler, strawberry shortcake and chocolate chip-pecan pie.

Much the same fare is available for the Sunday buffet and the weekend dinner buffet. An à la carte menu offers a variety from chicken salad plate and fried chicken basket to Mexican rollup and taco salad. Fried green tomatoes with Papa Garrett's stewed tomatoes can be ordered as a side dish. Many of the sides and specialties are packaged for sale.

(706) 655-9068. Buffet, lunch $5.95; evening and Sunday, $7.95. À la carte, $5.25 to $5.95. Lunch, Monday-Saturday 11 to 2:30. Dinner, Friday and Saturday 5 to 8:30.

Callaway Gardens Resort, Highway 27, Pine Mountain.
This well-known resort has seven restaurants, each with a character of its own. The spacious **Plantation Room** in the Callaway Gardens Inn features lavish

buffets for all three meals a day. The Friday evening seafood buffet for $19.95 is billed as a Callaway tradition. The night we were there, the full dinner buffet ($16.95) included scampi with linguini, Southern cottage pie, carved roast beef and turkey breast with giblet gravy, plus shrimp bisque, nine salads, four vegetables and four desserts. A light buffet was available for $8.95, as were four entrées ordered à la carte for $15.95 to $19.95. It being Sunday night in Georgia and no liquor available, (much of the state is dry on Sundays) we opted for room service and a bottle of wine we'd brought with us. An assertive chicken caesar salad with mesclun and the Callaway deluxe pizza with the works – and, not mentioned, the hottest jalapeño peppers ever – made a satisfying supper.

The inn's fancy **Georgia Room,** which was closed that night, offers upscale new cuisine, from sautéed chicken breast to sautéed veal chop. It's famed for a tableside preparation of bananas foster.

Inside the gardens proper are **The Gardens Restaurant,** featuring steaks, seafood and good lunch salads and sandwiches, and **The Veranda** for Italian cuisine. Both offer outdoor dining in season. Two other, more casual eateries are scattered around the property. The **Country Kitchen,** high up Pine Mountain in the Callaway Gardens Country Store, specializes in speckled heart grits, homemade biscuits, cured ham and muscadine sauce on a glass-enclosed porch overlooking the gardens.

(706) 663-2281 or (800) 225-5292. Plantation Room, entrées $15.95 to $19.95, open daily, 6:30 a.m. to 11 p.m. Georgia Room, entrées $17.50 to $24.95, dinner Monday-Saturday. Hours for other restaurants vary.

Diversions

Little White House State Historic Site, Highway 85, Warm Springs.
A stream of 88-degree water bubbling from the rocks at the base of Pine Mountain spawned an early resort favored by yellow fever victims. In 1924, news of the remarkable recovery of a young polio victim here reached a young New York lawyer who had been stricken with polio about the same time. Unable to find a cure, a despondent Franklin Delano Roosevelt headed for Warm Springs. In the pool he felt a tingle of life in his numb limbs and he grew stronger by the day. In 1927, he founded the Georgia Warm Springs Foundation for the treatment of fellow polio victims who could not afford such care, and became a pillar of what had been called Bullockville, helping to rename the village Warm Springs. He returned to New York and was elected governor of New York in 1928. Meanwhile, he frequently returned to Warm Springs for periodic pool treatments and started construction of a house, overlooking a deep wooded ravine above the spring. It was finished in 1932, shortly before he was elected president. He gave a house-warming party "for the residents of the village of Warm Springs" and patients and staff of the Warm Springs Foundation in what soon was to become known far and wide as the Little White House.

Visitors today start in a low-key museum, a surprisingly steep hike up the Walk of the States past the stones and flags of the 50 states. Here one views a twelve-minute, black and white movie. It reveals what the announcer intones is "something the public never saw," a rare picture of FDR with a leg brace over his clothing. The simple museum displays several wheelchairs, cases full of walking canes, the folk art of politics and an exhibit called the Years at Val-Kill in Hyde Park, N.Y.

The highlight, obviously, is the Little White House complex, down a slope from the entrance. In the garage beneath the Daisy Bonner Quarters, named for his

Little White House was Franklin D. Roosevelt's refuge in Warm Springs.

cook, is the president's 1938 Ford roadster. It still bears the 1945 Georgia license plate FDR-1 and is encased in glass so you can walk all the way around. Beyond is the six-room house, entered through the kitchen. An automatic audio recording describes the combination living/dining room, where the president worked at a desk on correspondence sent from Washington by overnight train. The unfinished portrait for which he was posing here at the time of his fatal stroke is shown on an easel. The sundeck he designed after the fantail of a ship leads to his secretary's bedroom on one side and the president's bedroom on another. Both are simple affairs paneled in pine, except for the president's bath with a raised commode and a tub separated from the wall so he could maneuver to get out. Eleanor's bedroom had two twin beds and occasionally housed guests, who otherwise were put up in the Guest House resembling the Daisy Bonner Quarters. Most of the furniture was made in the Val-Kill shops established by Mrs. Roosevelt to help the unemployed.

That's it for the Little White House, which really is little. "Everyone expects it to be much bigger," the park ranger acknowledged. There were no visiting dignitaries or lavish entertainments. This was FDR's getaway place, a simple refuge in which to renew himself to face the rigors of Washington and the world.

The restored hydrotherapy pools are about a mile away by car off Highway 27A, at the base of the ongoing Roosevelt Warm Springs Institute for Rehabilitation. The institute succeeds the original foundation he launched with the financial support of Cason Calloway and Edsel Ford.

(706) 655-5870. Open daily, 9 to 5 (last full tour at 4). Adults, $4.

Callaway Gardens, Highway 27, Pine Mountain.

In 1920, Cason J. and Virginia Hand Callaway came across a rare orange-red plumleaf azalea during a summer picnic at Blue Springs. The July-blooming azalea, native only within a 100-mile radius, inspired the Callaways to purchase the land in Harris County adjacent to Blue Springs and later to build Callaway Gardens, which opened to the public in 1952 and has been expanding ever since.

A new, centrally located visitor center was in the works as part of a major expansion initiated in 1998. Meanwhile, the best way to see the highlights of the sprawling, 14,000-acre property is to drive the five-mile-long, one-way Scenic Drive around Mountain Creek Lake. (Better yet, bike the 7.5-mile Discovery Bicycle Trail that parallels the road, criss-crossing it here and there. You get to cross the lake on a little ferry.) Even in mid-March, before much besides daffodils was in bloom, we were impressed with the picturesque woodlands, holly trees and lakes, and happened to spot deer and turtles.

The first major stop is the John A. Sibley Horticultural Center, one of the more innovative indoor-outdoor garden complexes in the world. Its five acres burst with seasonal flowers at their showy peak. An impressive shop has a garden theme, from floral mats and birdhouses to salt shakers and computer mouse pads.

Most novel is the Cecil B. Day Butterfly Center, the largest glass-enclosed tropical butterfly conservatory in North America. Fifty species and more than 1,000 individual butterflies flutter around between plants and trees amid tropical birds and ducks. You learn the average butterfly lives two weeks and some only a few days. We sat mesmerized by it all. Upon exiting, a signs advises: "Please check yourself for hitchhiking butterflies."

Another favorite stop is Mr. Cason's Vegetable Garden, three large, semicircular terraces that demonstrate the best techniques for growing more than 400 varieties of fruits and vegetables in the South. The home demonstration garden serves as an outdoor TV studio for the Southern segment of the PBS Series, "The Victory Garden."

For diversions, you can sun and swim at the largest manmade inland white-sand beach in the world (complete with a large outdoor playground), enjoy 63 holes of golf on four courses, play tennis on lighted courts and try your luck at fishing. The season extends from splashy camellias, azaleas, magnolias and rhododendrons in spring to Fantasy in Lights, the world's biggest light and music show, in late November and December.

If all the hype surrounding Callaway seems overly commercial, you may be surprised that the place really isn't.

(706) 663-2281 or (800) 225-5292. Gardens open daily, 7 to 7, late March through August; 8 to 5, rest of year. Adults, $10.

Pine Mountain. The mountain, as opposed to the village of the same name, is actually a high ridge extending some ten miles from Pine Mountain village and Hamilton to Warm Springs. It doesn't look like much, when viewed from below, but the rise is enough to provide stunning views from either side and prompt the need for a runaway truck ramp along Route 27. One of the best views is from the park visitor center at 2970 Highway 190. Scenic Route 190 traverses the crest of the flat-top mountain with observation pull-offs and some of the ambiance of the Blue Ridge Parkway. Most of the mountain is part of the 10,000-acre **F.D. Roosevelt State Park,** Georgia's largest park, which offers a swimming pool, two lakes for fishing and boating, 21 cottages and 140 campsites, and scenic picnic areas. Several structures in the park, including the stone swimming pool, were built during the Depression by Roosevelt's Civilian Conservation Corps. Above Kings Gap, a plaque marks Dowdell's Knob, where you can picnic at the president's favorite picnic spot with a panoramic vista of the valley below. The 23-mile-long **Pine Mountain Trail** meanders past unusual rock outcroppings and waterfalls. The trail is well maintained and divided into sections. The 4.3-mile

Dowdell's Knob Loop near the center of the trail is a favorite with day hikers. Some hikers consider the 6.5-mile Wolfden Loop one of the most scenic trails in the Southeast. Park open daily, 7 a.m. to 10 p.m. Day pass fee, $2.

On the south side of the mountain is a hamlet called Pine Mountain Valley, center of the **Valley Project,** an FDR federal reclamation project that provided public housing for low-income families. Those qualifying were given five to fifteen acres, a house and farm animals and taught how to live off the land. One park attendant likened it to an early commune; another called it the start of creeping socialism. We couldn't really see vestiges of the project, although we were told they are all around. An attendant at the Little White House site said her parents had lived in one of the houses.

Shopping. Almost all of the center of Warm Springs is given over to what ads proclaim are "65 shops and 9 restaurants." Most are concentrated along Broad and Bullock streets near the railroad depot where trains used to stop. The downtown was renovated in the 1980s, but still looks old and rustic. The shops are big on antiques and collectibles, many of them rather tacky, hidden down little alleys and around primitive courtyards. Among the best are **Sacks First,** which stocks upscale collectibles, and **Country Classics,** known for excellent buys on reproduction furniture and gifts. One shopper eyed a plump sofa for $1,691 and was told it had just been sold, but another could be ordered soon. Greenville innkeeper Angela Hand offers her floral designs, antiques and collectibles at the **Verandah.**

More shops are clustered in downtown Pine Mountain, where a railroad track runs down the center of the main street. There are a couple of galleries, an antiques mall and, our favorite, **Kimbrough Brothers General Store.** Its sign advertised "gifts, ready-to-wear, feed and seeds," with an emphasis on the former.

Extra-Special

Hamilton Square, Route 27, Hamilton.

Franklin Roosevelt was known as "the squire of Warm Springs," such was his impact on the area. But he also drove over in his hand-controlled Ford runabout to Hamilton Square in the county seat to talk with the locals – politicos and just plain folks. He knew the people, their joys and their problems, and from these associations evolved a concern for suffering and the common man that inspired the New Deal. Today, the square offers an enlightening glimpse of the Deep South. There are picnic tables beside the road and a little roofed pavilion with a detailed county map describing salient attractions. A plaque honors B.F. White, hometown song writer, teacher and editor, who published *Sacred Harp,* a "fa-sol-la" a capella singing school book "now in its fourth edition." A monument is inscribed "To Our Confederate Soldiers" on its north side. On the back facing south are the words "Fate denied them victory but crowned them with glorious immortality." The handsome, neoclassical courthouse of red bricks and white columns is by far the biggest building around. Flanking the square are small establishments with names like The Fillin' Station Restaurant (in an old service station), Juanita's Shop (antiques and collectibles with a traffic signal blinking out front), Marilyn's Styling Salon ("tanning beds available"), Hamilton Square BarBQ and the Pastime Café. Where better to find a slice of life?

Gold Museum in restored county courthouse is focal point of Dahlonega's Public Square.

Dahlonega, Ga.
There's Gold In Them Thar Hills

Native Americans and mountain wilderness prevailed here until 1828 when gold was discovered. Almost overnight, America's first major gold rush created a boomtown in the northern Georgia mountains and banished the Cherokees in a sorrowful exile known as the Trail of Tears.

The boom created the biggest gold plant east of the Mississippi and resulted in the opening of the first branch U.S. Mint in tiny Dahlonega (pronounced Duh-LON-a-ga). It lasted until 1848, when the California gold rush started and prospectors abandoned Dahlonega for another chance to strike it rich. The assayer of the Dahlonega mint pleaded from the County Courthouse balcony for the miners not to leave. He insisted in an expression that Mark Twain later translated in his *Gilded Age* into the legendary "Thar's gold in them thar hills."

Today, Dahlonega (an Indian word meaning yellow money or gold) mines not so much gold as tourists. The last commercial mine closed in 1906, although locals still pan for gold in nearby creeks and visitors try their luck at a couple of restored gold mines. Townspeople saved the beautiful 1836 courthouse in the Public Square from demolition in 1965 and paved the path for tourism. It became the fascinating Dahlonega Gold Museum, which tells the story of a town still impacted by gold today.

Around the town square – for good reason designated a National Historic District – are quaint shops in storefronts with arcades and porches that give the downtown area a look of the Old West. The former U.S. Mint is the site of the gold-steepled Price Memorial Building at North Georgia College and State University, home for the student Army Corps at the Georgia Military College.

Just off the square in this charming little college town (population about 3,500) are good B&Bs and restaurants, including one that has been a destination for family-style Southern cooking for years. New and larger inns occupy spectacular sites in the surrounding mountains.

Barely an hour's drive northeast of Atlanta, Dahlonega is a gateway to the Georgia mountains and the Chattahoochee National Forest. The 2,150-mile Appalachian Trail starts at Springer Mountain nearby. The East's highest waterfalls cascade more than 700 feet at Amicalola Falls. The area surprises with country stores, an antique rose garden, a huge pumpkin farm and a quirky art gallery.

There's more to these here hills than gold, it seems.

Inn Spots

Dahlonega has a couple of B&Bs right in town, but most are scattered in all directions in the surrounding mountains a few miles out of town.

The Blueberry Inn & Gardens, 400 Blueberry Hill, Dahlonega 30533.

"Four layers of mountains" are on view from the front porch – "our best room," says innkeeper Phyllis Charnley. Lined with 24 rocking chairs, the porch extends the width of the front and wraps around the sides of the house, which was built as in 1996 as a reproduction of a 1920s farmhouse. From suburban Atlanta, Phyllis and Harry Charnley looked at oceanside properties and old houses in disrepair for their dream inn. They finally decided to build from scratch in the mountains on a 55-acre site seemingly in the middle of nowhere, nine miles northeast of Dahlonega.

A long, bumpy road leads uphill past meadows, a stream and stocked fish pond before you reach the main inn, built to look like a house, and connected by an enclosed breezeway to a new barn.

"Guests come here for tranquility, to get away," says Phyllis. They get away in great comfort in common rooms, bedrooms and that great porch. The ground floor of the main house holds a "quiet" front parlor for reading. Beyond is a larger open parlor with the inn's only TV and big rear windows onto a nicely landscaped patio and garden. A spacious dining room contains three large tables. A butler's pantry is stocked with iced tea and cookies, wine and cheese. Phyllis

calls the sophisticated decor throughout "high country." The clean, crisp look is refreshing for those who tire of antiques and clutter.

Four guest rooms are upstairs in the main house and eight are in the attached barn. Nine have queen beds and three have twins. Baths are modern, with pedestal sinks. Rooms are the same size but are appointed quite differently. Comforters, window shams and even the chair fabrics match in each. One room has handmade quilts on the walls. Another harbors furnishings that belonged to Phyllis's grandmother. A fisherman's room sports the odd oar and a miniature twig chair.

Breakfast is served family style at 9. The fare is "never the same," Phyllis says. But fruit, juice, cheese soufflé, grits, biscuits and a sweet are typical. Scrambled eggs with country potatoes and broiled tomatoes, and dutch babies with fruit are other favorites. Harry Charnley makes blueberry pancakes on Sundays with berries picked on the property. At our late morning visit, Phyllis enticed us to try her banana-pumpkin bread and blueberry muffins – so good and so filling we barely could face lunch.

Because of the remote location, Phyllis will prepare simple dinners for two or more with advance notice.

(706) 219-4024 or (877) 219-4024. Fax (706) 219-4793. Twelve rooms with private baths. Doubles, $85 weekends, $75 midweek. Add $10 in October. No small children. No smoking.

Mountain Top Lodge, 447 Mountain Top Road, Dahlonega 30533.

A paved road winds uphill to this rustic cedar lodge, which really is at the top of the mountain. Expansive porches and decks flank the main lodge and stretch into the surrounding oaks, pines and dogwoods. Nine rooms are in the main lodge, and four more are down the slope in the secluded Hillside Lodge.

Changing seasonal decorative focal points and rustic implements on the front porch testify to an appealing mix of old mountain lodge and sophisticated amenities inside. Karen Lewan moved here from Chicago with her retired aunt and uncle in 1995 to take over a lodge established a decade earlier.

One end of the lodge is devoted to a spacious great room, with a guest kitchen enclosed in one corner, a library and game room in the loft above and a small TV room below, with a horseshoe pit and outdoor spa beyond. The other section contains guest rooms and, on the lower floor, a commercial kitchen, a breakfast room bearing a mountain mural painted by the previous owner and open shelves of colorful Fiestaware, plus a country dining room opening onto a walkout patio.

Paneled in cedar, the bedrooms vary. Numbered rather than named, all are nicely furnished with country antiques and flea-market finds. Two suites come with separate sunrooms and private decks. Another room has a sitting alcove with loveseat and chair and a private balcony. One room is decorated in Americana. Toys convey a children's theme in a snug room with a Jenny Lind double bed. Otherwise, beds are queensize (and two are kingsize). Three rooms contain an extra twin bed.

Much in demand are rooms with private decks in the secluded Hillside Lodge. Two upstairs with cathedral ceilings and exposed cedar beams have gas-log fireplaces and double jacuzzi tubs. We liked No. 9 with an Amish theme, a canopied queensize bed and twig rods hung with white curtains over the windows. A huge photo of an autumn mountain scene surrounded much of the circular jacuzzi in the bathroom. A mini-refrigerator is hidden in an old TV console in No. 10.

A hearty breakfast is served at 8:45 in the breakfast room, dining room or on the patio. Stratas, baked eggs elegante, farmer's casserole or yorkshire pudding with sausages might be the fare. Afternoon snacks and evening sherry are complimentary.

Fresh flowers from her gardens are displayed throughout the lodge. They are typical of personable Karen's caring touches.

(706) 864-5257 or (800) 526-9754. Eleven rooms and two suites with private baths. Doubles, $70 to $125; suites $80. Add $10 mid-September to mid-November. Deduct $10 midweek, January-April. Children over 12. Two-night minimum weekends in peak season. No smoking.

New Black Mountain Lodge was built from scratch on mountain top with panoramic view.

Black Mountain Lodge, Black Mountain Road, Box 540, Dahlonega 30533.
What to make of this large new facility, built by a Floridian with no previous
building experience on a mountain top with views that won't quit? It seems to be
mostly great hall and porches, swimming pool and recreation facilities, in-room
jacuzzis and outdoor tiki bar.

It's quite a place – and quite a story, as told by owner Jeff Wasserman. He and
wife Brenda sold their blue-plate-special restaurant and apparel businesses in
suburban Orlando, Fla., to move to Dahlonega to create an inn. "I built this myself
with two friends over two years," said Jeff, whose family of lawyers "thought I
was nuts" The design was a composite of ideas sketched on paper placemats at his
restaurant. The materials and technical advice came from Home Depot – "all my
questions drove them crazy."

He finished in time for a late 1997 opening, but meanwhile the Wassermans –
childless for the first ten years of their marriage – became parents of twin
daughters. Brenda broke her leg and was in a cast for seven months after the inn
opened. "Here, she had wanted to be the Bob Newhart innkeeper and I'd be the
maintenance man," recalls Jeff. "Now it's just the opposite. She's traveling to
visit family with the twins and I'm the innkeeper and loving every minute."

To see the impressive, 25,000-square-foot building today, few would realize
this was a do-it-yourself project. The major feature is a two-story high lobby with
a mass of plush seating areas all the same – burgundy wing chairs and chintz sofas
and loveseats on a carpet of green. The space is designed for weddings, but impacts
on the size and shape of the guest rooms on either side.

Our room, for instance, was far wider than it was deep, and furnished in light
pine. Most of the space was given over to a kingsize sleigh bed and an enormous
double jacuzzi, with a sink adjacent and a huge TV opposite. At the other end of
the room, a single wing chair with ottoman occupied an alcove off the bathroom,
which contained a shower for two. A mini-refrigerator was stocked with
complimentary soft drinks. A private balcony overlooked the woods and mountains
outside. The decor was an expanse of white and beige, from the patterned bed

comforter with six matching pillows to the potted plant of daisies on the dresser. A sign advised this is a non-smoking resort and warned of a $100 cleaning charge to be assessed any guest found smoking in the room or on the room porch.

The room turned out to be fairly typical, although suites added more seating. Finishing touches were still awaited a year after opening. A large bar of Ivory soap was the only toiletry and the table lampshade still bore its cellophane wrapping saying to remove before using. Jeff explained that bath amenities were on order and decorative embellishments had been on hold since twins and broken leg took his wife out of commission.

One does not spend much time in one's room here anyway. "Common space is what this is all about," said Jeff.

The far end of the lobby opens into a two-story-high dining room, where a full dinner (with two choices for main course) and a country buffet breakfast are included in the rates. A loft in the upper lobby contains tables for board games. The lower level has a coffee bar and library, a steam room and sauna, a complete Universal gym and a rec room with pool and ping-pong tables. Not to mention the Wasserman family quarters, which offer them more room than did their Orlando house.

A huge deck off the dining room overlooks an outdoor pool area to end all pool areas. Beyond is a tiki bar on a platform with a covered hot tub and an open deck. Nature trails wander about the property, which is surrounded by National Forest on all sides. A tennis court was being paved the day of our visit.

What prompted his inn to be full on an October weeknight when others were not? Jeff cited the tranquility and the extras: "Every room has a jacuzzi for two, breakfast and dinner are included, and with the National Forest on all sides we have no neighbors. You can't beat this for the price."

Never mind that dinner may be too early (6 o'clock) and breakfast too late (9 o'clock). This is a place to kick back in style and enjoy.

(706) 864-5542 or (800) 923-5530. Ten rooms and six suites with private baths. Rates MAP. Weekends, doubles $150, suites $175. Midweek, doubles $99, suites $124. Two-night minimum weekends. No smoking.

Royal Guard Inn, 65 Park St. South, Dahlonega 30533.

They operated a B&B in the Danish-inspired town of Solvang, Calif. So when they retired here to be near their son and fishing, John and Farris Vanderhoff bought a little gray cottage at the edge of downtown and built a large addition to open a B&B. "We should have called it Aunt Nine's" (for the wife of the town physician who once lived here), Farris said. But she decided instead to honor her Norwegian grandfather, who was a captain in the Royal Guard.

"We've tried to retire three times," said Farris, whose energy belies her years ("I'm 74 and John is 78"). "But I love to fuss and to entertain."

She has fussed over five guest rooms, each with private bath and TV. She designed the Viking's Den in front for Prince Valiant, while the dainty Gold Room nearby is "a queen's retreat" with gilt-framed artworks and a pink settee. The Captain of the Guard's Quarters are masculine. Top of the line is the rear Royal Suite in blue and white, with half-canopy bed, thick carpeting and a porch.

The main floor of the remodeled house is light and open. The common rooms flow from one to the other and into Farris's kitchen, the heart of the house. Here she prepares a breakfast that she likens to a brunch. One day's feast started with

Rear addition helped turn little gray cottage into Royal Guard Inn.

two kinds of melon, kiwi and strawberries. Then came an egg soufflé casserole and Norwegian pancakes, topped with strawberries and "real" whipped cream. She offers complimentary wine and a cheese tray every evening. Most guests enjoy it in the living room or on the big wraparound porch.

The Scandinavian accent in furnishings and ambiance makes a stay here like visiting a modern grandmother's house.

(706) 864-1713. Five rooms with private baths. Doubles, $75 to $85; October $85 to $90, winter $70 to $85. Two-night minimum for special events. No smoking.

Worley Homestead Inn, 168 Main St. West, Dahlonega 30533.

The old buggy out front is appropriate. Dahlonega's first B&B dates to 1845. The driveway in front of the pillared house that resembles a New England stagecoach tavern was once the old road to Atlanta. A new road was built on higher ground, hiding the structure below and conveying a sense that it has been bypassed by time.

Restored into a B&B in 1984 by the great-granddaughter of the original Worley family, the home definitely shows its heritage. New owners Frances and Bill Stumphf moved in 1996 from Marietta to acquire the Worley. Her mother, Christine Summerville, runs it when they are at work.

The furnishings are antiques. Frills, lace and frou-frou are everywhere, from the parlor to the upstairs veranda. The latter is a pleasant place for relaxing within the shadow of the gold spire of the Price Memorial Building on the foundation of the old U.S. Mint across the road. There's also a large side patio.

The eight bedrooms are named for Worley children. Maude's has a double sleigh bed and is one of three rooms with working fireplaces. Another fireplace is in Lee Anna's, which is paneled in pine, has a queen bed and an old galvanized tub. Will's room at the rear of the main floor has a double and a twin bed.

We were surrounded by antiquity in the Captain Worley Room, main-floor front. The bed along the front wall was close to the road, a writing desk was in the corner and a TV was on a dresser. The room was festooned with artificial flower arrangements, hung with historic pictures and photographs, and anointed with hats and costumes. We hesitated to empty our pockets at night for fear of losing the contents.

It turns out that Frances loves to decorate, and changes the decor with the seasons. Christine likes to cook, a propensity that turns breakfasts into gargantuan proportions. Rich, stick-to-your-ribs fare is served family style at a fancy table for fourteen in the chandeliered dining room. Ours included peaches and strawberries, butter grits, an egg casserole of sausage, cheese and peppers, baked french toast, and pineapple-banana bread pudding. You had to employ the boarding-house reach to indulge in all the goodies.

Frances sent us on our way with recipes for her mother's breakfast potato casserole and muscadine preserves. "No one ever leaves without saying how much they've enjoyed staying here," she said. "It's like going back to Grandma's house."

(706) 864-7002. Eight rooms with private baths. Doubles, $95 weekends, $85 midweek. Children over 12.

Mountain Laurel Inn, 135 Forrest Hills Road, Dahlonega 30533.

Frank Kraft has framed the letter in which the Bank of Dahlonega rejected his loan application for $25,000 to start a modest cabin colony in the mountains southwest of town. The idea was too risky and the location too remote, the bank wrote in 1977. So the former Florida utility company executive enlisted his family to help build five mountain cabins that quickly grew into a 150-acre spread of 55 buildings with 100 rooms in cabins, group lodges, an inn, restaurants, conference center and more that set for pace for lodging in northern Georgia.

The resort is officially called Forrest Hills Mountain Hideaway. It conveys a rustic, almost hokey air from its Gold City Corral stables near the entrance to a primitive River House used for weekly cookouts, reachable by horse-drawn wagon and lacking both electricity and plumbing. Behind the quirky veneer lie some of the most sumptuous accommodations and getaway cottages anywhere. They're part of the new Mountain Laurel resort, built for the 1996 Olympics.

Up the hill past group lodges and Frank Kraft's house is the Mountain Laurel Inn, a contemporary extravaganza complete with Blossoms restaurant, conference facilities and twelve enormous bi-level suites overlooking woods and mountain laurel. Each has a kingsize bedroom open to a whirlpool garden tub, plus an upstairs living area with a queensize sofa bed, entertainment center, efficiency kitchen and gas fireplace. Each suite opens onto a private deck on the main floor and a common deck with rockers off the second floor.

Some would think these accommodations to be the ultimate. But for the romantic getaways to which the resort caters, the ten new Cupid Cottages secluded off Honeymoon and Cupid lanes are preferred. These give new dimension to the word cottage – and not only in terms of their 1,000-square-foot size. Besides a kingsize bedroom, there's an elegant dining room that would do justice to a model home. In the plushly carpeted living room, a curving white sectional sofa faces a corner fireplace, with an entertainment center beside. On one side of the cottage is a circular whirlpool spa enclosed in a windowed garden room paneled in cedar. On another is a porch with a glider swing for two. It's all a tad nouveau, but there's nothing like having all the comforts of home and then some, in your own mountain hideaway. The resort offers modest pool and tennis facilities for those who can tear themselves away from their quarters.

The Blossoms restaurant serves a limited menu of four-choice, table d'hôte dinners, available to the public for $19.95, Monday-Saturday 6 to 9.

Remarkably, the prime accommodations rent for only $15 to $20 a night more

Worley Homestead Inn is decorated for holiday season.

than the basic and represent exceptional value. Package plans and "short-notice specials" reduce the prices further.

(706) 864-6456 or (800) 654-6313. Fax (706) 864-0757. Twelve suites, 30 cabins with hot tubs, three Victorian houses and four lodges with eight to sixteen bedrooms each for groups. Rates MAP. May-October: doubles, $188 to $208. Rest of year: $175 to $190.

The Smith House, 202 South Chestatee St., Dahlonega 30533.

For years, the Smith House has been a destination for diners seeking Southern dinners served family style (see Dining Spots). Less well known are the accommodations in a house built in 1884 by Capt. Frank Hall, a Yankee carpet-bagger who became the town's richest landowner, on top of one of its richest veins of gold ore.

Tan with green trim, the exterior of the house belies both its age and the fact that it serves up to 2,000 meals a day on busy weekends.

Guest rooms go off common porches and living rooms. They have an updated hotel look, with reproduction furnishings. A deluxe room comes with kingsize oak bed, a loveseat, two wing chairs and a floral comforter matching the draperies. The bathroom has a jetted tub with a shower and Caswell-Massey toiletries. A TV is hidden in an armoire. Other rooms are more basic. Two new efficiency "villas" are offered in the new Chestatee Crossing complex just up the street, facing the Dahlonega square.

The rooms appear comfortable and the common living rooms and porches appealing, but you get the impression they play second fiddle to the restaurant and country store. A complimentary continental breakfast of danish, bagels and donuts is offered in the reception lobby.

(706) 867-7000 or (800) 825-9577. Fourteen rooms and two villas with private baths. Doubles, $69 to $149. Villas, $149 to $275.

Dining Spots

Renee's Cafe & Wine Bar, 135 North Chestatee St., Dahlonega.
The historic red McGuire House became the culinary showcase in 1996 for Renee De Robertis. She relocated her tiny Nature's Cellar from Dahlonega Square and renamed the enterprise for herself.

The setting is simple: a couple of intimate main-floor dining rooms with dark green walls, green floral tablecloths and uncomfortable ladder-back chairs not designed for lingering. Upstairs is a wine bar, which was closed for renovations at our visit but is open weekends for tastings.

The Mediterranean-inspired food is first-rate. We'd heard great things about the Greek shrimp over saffron rice with artichoke hearts, plum tomatoes, carrots and feta cheese. But the chargrilled filet mignon topped with boursin cheese beckoned, as did a signature dish of crawfish tails tossed with spinach tortellini in a rich gorgonzola alfredo sauce. Assorted breads were served with lemon-herb olive oil in a saucer for dipping. Good house salads with honey-mustard and orange-hazelnut dressings came with.

Appetizers like nachos, muffuletta and black beans with saffron rice seemed redundant. We had to save room for dessert: an intense key lime pie and a decadent chocolate cream cheese brownie with chocolate syrup, chocolate chips and fudge ripple ice cream.

The area's best wine list is particularly strong on California reds.
(706) 864-6829. Entrées, $10.95 to $16.95. Dinner, Tuesday-Saturday 5 to 9 or 10.

Rick's, 47 South Park St., Dahlonega.
Once a partner at Renee's, Rick Whorf opened this lively restaurant in 1998 in a turn-of-the-century house that served for years as the office-residence of the town physician. He painted the walls of the small rooms green and hung them with folk art – a different artist in every room. White butcher paper tops the white-clothed tables.

It's a country charming setting for highly rated fare. Rick's house-smoked hen is a signature dish, turning up in a salad at lunchtime and served with homemade worcestershire sauce and Southern-style greens as an entrée at night. The crispy grouper sandwich is another favorite. We sampled a superior crawfish-corn chowder and chewy sourdough bread before digging into the smoked hen salad, an assertive mix yielding chilled hen, spicy tasso ham, swiss cheese, white beans and portobello mushrooms over chopped lettuces. The meal was so ample we had no room for dessert: a choice of apple ring cake with crème anglaise and cinnamon, oreo cookie mousse pie or strawberries in grand marnier over crème anglaise.

At night, appetizers range from crispy corn fritters with cayenne tartar sauce and grilled sesame shrimp with cucumber salad and fresh ginger to a novelty: homemade potato chips served with old-fashioned Hazel dressing. Main dishes vary from meatloaf and cheddar-smashed potatoes, to crawfish risotto cakes and chargrilled ribeye steak.
(706) 864-9422. Entrées, $9.95 to $15.95. Lunch, Wednesday-Monday 11:30 to 3. Dinner, Wednesday-Monday 5 to 9 or 10. Beer and wine license.

Wylies Restaurant & Coffee House, 19 North Chestatee St., Dahlonega.
Steve and Connie Wylie took over the old Coffee House in 1997 and upgraded

it into a full-fledged restaurant. They offer dining in a variety of venues: a main floor that retains its coffee shop heritage, with booths, white cloths at night and artificial greenery winding round the room. Downstairs is the Down Under Pub with entertainment. Out back is a wide porch that was about to be vastly expanded at our visit. The odd hours of service indicated the place was in transition. Like the facility, the menu suits a variety of tastes. For lunch, consider the emu burger ("fat-free red meat that is good for you"), a black bean garden burger, homemade quiche or a grilled chicken sandwich. The grilled chicken salad with honey-mustard dressing made a fine early supper, as did the enormous plate of black bean nachos with homemade chips. The dinner chef adds entrées like shrimp scampi over tomato-basil linguini, grilled Norwegian salmon, herb-roasted prime rib and locally raised emu filet, grilled and topped with mushroom sauce.

The dessert case holds treats like apple crumb cheesecake, deep-dish apple pie and death by chocolate.

(706) 867-6324. Entrées, $10.95 to $15.95. Lunch, Sunday-Wednesday noon to 8. Dinner, Thursday-Saturday 5 to 10.

The Smith House, 84 South Chestatee St., Dahlonega.

No one locally mentions the Smith House when asked what restaurants they recommend for dinner. They don't need to. This is an institution of 75-plus years, "world famous for Southern hospitality and mountain cooking."

Henry and Bessie Smith turned their home into an inn in 1922, and Mrs. Smith did all the cooking not only for her family but the hotel guests in a 22-seat dining room. The menu was basically the same as today: fried chicken, cured ham and lots of vegetables, served family style. The tradition continued under the Welch family, who took over in 1946 and grew the average daily customer count to more than 1,000. They refined the menu and enlarged the dining room to seat 260. Diners are seated at a table with about a dozen strangers, who help themselves to platters of fried chicken, beef stew, baked ham, angel biscuits, fried okra, banana fritters, candied yams and at least ten kinds of vegetables, nicely prepared and not steamed to smithereens. Fruit cobbler or strawberry shortcake usually ends the meal.

Although large and well kept, the Smith House "is not showy," says proprietor Fred Welch Jr. It's not a stretch for him to say: "After dining with us, you may feel as though you have attended a family reunion or a Sunday Camp meeting."

(706) 867-7000. Lunch and dinner buffets, $10.95. Lunch, 11 to 3. Dinner, 4 to 8. Closed Monday.

Caruso's Ristorante Italiano, 19B East Main St., Dahlonega.

This is of the genre that could be anywhere. But the fact it serves Curly's Pizza from next door sets it apart. So do the homemade pastas, served with salad and bread.

The place does a land-office business, particularly at lunchtime when it's a favorite of the downtown business crowd. Pizzas and submarines are the midday stars. We sampled the haystack antipasto, a veritable haystack of greens laden with ham, salami, olives, tuna, mozzarella and more. Choices on the extensive menu range from baked ziti to tortellini alfredo, from shrimp fra diavolo to veal marsala. Desserts run to spumoni ice cream and homemade cheesecakes.

The beer and wine lists are basic.

(706) 864-4664. Entrées, $8.95 to $12.95. Lunch, Monday-Saturday 11 to 4. Dinner, Monday-Saturday 4 to 9:30 or 10, Sunday noon to 8.

The Front Porch, 72A Public Square, Dahlonega.
This is called a glorified hot dog stand by some. But place your order and sit outside on a broad second-story front porch, shaded by a jungle of greenery overlooking the town square and the handsome Gold Museum. You almost feel you're in the treetops. The fare ranges from barbecue to knockwurst at modest prices.
(706) 864-0124. Open seasonally, 11 to 3. Closed in winter.

Diversions

Ever since deer hunter Ben Parks discovered gold in 1828, gold and Dahlonega have been synonymous hereabouts. The newspaper is called the Dahlonega Nugget, stores sell gold trinkets, and almost every woman wears gold jewelry fashioned from gold that she or her spouse/boyfriend panned.

Dahlonega Gold Museum, Public Square, Dahlonega.
Traces of gold were found in the bricks and mortar during the restoration of the unusually handsome 1836 county courthouse. Now Georgia's second most visited museum, the state historic site in the middle of the town square is the best place to begin a visit to Dahlonega. It tells the story of America's first major gold rush in terms both graphic and nostalgic. Dahlonega's was not really the first, but was the first *major* gold rush, site manager Sharon Johnson advised. At the entry is a 2,500-pound cast-iron safe holding thousands of dollars worth of gold, one nugget weighing more than five ounces and worth $7,000. Letters written by the Cherokee Indians, who were exiled by miners in their rush for gold, represent a sad part of local history. A 23-minute orientation film, "Gold Fever," is shown in the second-floor court chambers. It describes the mining techniques, hardships and lifestyles of early prospectors through interviews with members of their families. Our guide's husband is a part-time prospector – "he dredges and I get enough for a gold necklace," she said. Another guide and her husband turned the gold they panned into wedding rings. Manager Johnson topped both stories. She has a nugget and a necklace made from gold she panned.
(706) 864-2257. Open Monday-Saturday 9 to 5, Sunday 10 to 5. Admission, $2.50.

Consolidated Gold Mines, 125 Consolidated Gold Mine Road, Dahlonega.
Once your interest is piqued at the Gold Museum, head to the outskirts of town. Hidden down a hillside not far behind the Wal-Mart store is a different slice of life. Bushy-bearded guides who look and talk just like, well, gold miners demonstrate how things were done at the biggest gold mine east of the Mississippi. It turns out the guy behind the cash register was Johnny Parker, two-time world champion gold panner, since succeeded by sidekick Ronnie Gaddis, three-time champion. They'll show you how to pan for gold with a metal pan and a bunch of sand, shaking layers of sand and leaving the heavier gold at the bottom. The first-timer usually takes fifteen minutes before finding a few specks of glitter. The champions can do it in less than six seconds. On a 40-minute guided tour, you don a hard hat and descend 300 feet below ground into the deepest and longest tunnel of its kind in the world. Here you view the mine, as it appeared at the turn of the century. It's not for the faint of heart, for you'll see rising water that has to be pumped out periodically, sleeping bats and vestiges of explosives that turned some of the highly paid detonators into goners. The jagged tunnel with its original ore carts and track system extends 500 feet into the mountain. At our visit, crews

were excavating the far end so that tours would resurface at the gold processing plant and return above ground to the starting point and a quaint gift shop. *(706) 864-8473. Guided tours, daily 10 to 5, to 4 in winter. Adults, $10.*

Crisson Gold Mine, 2736 Morrison Moore Pkwy East (Hwy. 19-60), Dahlonega. Visitors pan for gold and gem stones at the oldest family-owned and operated gold panning place open to the public. Four generations of Crisson family have panned here. The Crisson mine includes a 115-year-old stamp mill, the only original working one of its kind in Georgia. The staff runs gold-bearing quartz through the noisy stamp mill once every hour. The mill crushes the quartz into sand, which separates out the gold. *(706) 864-6363. Open daily 10 to 6, to 5 in winter.*

North Georgia College & State University. Gold put Dahlonega on the map when the U.S. government built its first branch mint here in 1838. The mint closed at the outbreak of the Civil War, but through 1861 it coined more than $6 million in gold, representing only a fraction of the local gold production. The mint building and ten acres of property were donated to create the North Georgia Agricultural College, predecessor of this institution. The building later burned. Its original foundation is now the site of the college's Price Memorial Building, whose landmark spire is made of Dahlonega gold. The four-year, co-ed liberal arts institution is the home of the Military College of Georgia. The student Army Corps of Cadets is responsible for Reveille daily at 5 and taps at midnight. We happened by on a Monday afternoon and were treated to the weekly dress review on the drill field.

Shopping is a big attraction in and around Dahlonega. The downtown area flanking the Public Square is thriving, and any vacancies are quickly filled. The stores are particularly strong on collectibles, arts and crafts, and gold jewelry. Work your way around the square.

Golden Classics conveys an automobile theme, with collectibles and a cafe amid gum balls in a Texaco pump and a cash register in a red Chevy. Owner Tim O'Brien had plans for a sixteen-room hotel above his store. The **Dahlonega General Store** carries a little bit of everything, from marbles ($2.49 per cup) and tin signs to its own-label salsas, sauces and preserves. We sampled the coffee for five cents beside seven huge glass jars full of nickels and the odd dollar bill. Every day is Christmas at **Mountain Christmas.** At the **Ivy Cottage,** Linda Smith combines a dainty gift shop (linens and antique china) with a luncheon and tea room. The corner **Fudge Factory** speaks for itself, with twelve flavors plus peanut and pecan brittle and butter brickle crunch. The **Tasting Room of Habersham Vineyards** offers eighteen wines, including a sweet dessert wine called chambourcia. Everything a mountain outdoorsman needs is found at **Appalachian Outfitters Trading Co.** in the old 1858 Parker-Nix Storehouse. The potter was at work in his studio at **Brad Walker Pottery.** Mountain and nature themes prevail at the wonderful **Hummingbird Lane Gallery. Jones & Company** is a fine shop for gifts and accessories. In the new Chestatee Crossing complex, the **Cherokee Trading Post** mixes suave crystal and crafts, and **Chestatee Home Place** offers gifts and accessories.

Outside town are more shopping opportunities. The **Rockhouse Marketplace and Country Store** stocks everything from gourmet foods to home furnishings to outdoor accessories (here you'll find coffee for ten cents a cup – stash your dime in an oversize Coke bottle). Upstairs is **The Attic and Fruitful Vine,** where the creative artist-owner plies her wares and collectibles – she's so prolific a friend named her the fruitful vine.

The Antique Rose Emporium showcases easy-care and long-lasting roses in display gardens that bloom from the end of April until a hard frost. The roses are grown at the parent company headquarters in Texas. This four-acre site transformed from a forest in 1995 doubles as a nursery and education center.

It may not sound like all that much, but **Burt's Farm** is a big deal around here. Sixty-two acres of nearby pumpkin fields produce more than 70,000 pumpkins a year. They're on sale here, along with popcorn from corn grown on the farm. Tractor-drawn hay wagons take visitors on a two-mile loop ride around the farm. During the Christmas season, the farm is transformed with 500,000 lights and 35 animated scenes.

Amicalola Falls State Park, Dawsonville.

Fifteen roundabout miles west of Dahlonega is this 2,050-acre wilderness mountain park offering hiking, camping, a 57-room lodge and restaurant, and the highest waterfall east of the Rockies. It takes its name from the Cherokee Indian word for "tumbling waters." And tumble they do. From a wisp of a brook, a stream of water plunges over seven cascading falls a total of 729 feet. It appears from a distance to be one continuous drop, but only the upper part falls freely. The lower portion is six consecutive cascades through a steep, rocky creek. The best view is afforded from a strenuous, fifteen-minute hike uphill from a base area variously called a reflection pool and a trout pond. An easier but less rewarding view is obtained by driving up a paved road to the top of the falls and the lodge area. A bridge crosses the stream just before its main freefall. A sign warns visitors, "Beware. Fatalities have occurred." From the visitor center, an eight-mile approach trail leads to Springer Mountain and the southern end of the Appalachian Trail.

(706) 265-4703. Park open daily, 7 a.m. to 10 p.m. Daily pass, $2.

Extra Special

The Funky Chicken Art Project, 1538 Wesley Chapel Road, Dahlonega.

Sculptor Christina White finds art galleries stuffy and uncomfortable "for people who dress like me." So she and her painter-husband, James Sargous, moved from Dahlonega Square and established their own here in 1995. It's hardly your typical gallery, with a rustic barn-like structure for artworks and chickens clucking out back in a chicken house beside a sculpture garden. Nor is the art shown by more than 200 artists and craftsmen here typical. Much of it is offbeat, yet all is original and of surprising quality. A large marble piece on an island in the water garden, sculpted in her studio in Italy by Barbara Rheingrover, is world-class. Fine art and fun art are tucked into every nook and cranny. The draw is such that the gallery even has its own web site (www.funkychickenartproject.com). "We're now our own destination," says Christine. "We want visitors to slow down and really take it all in."

(706) 864-3938. Open Tuesday-Wednesday noon to 5:30, Thursday-Sunday 10 to 6. Free.

Porch off guest room at The Lodge on Gorham's Bluff looks across Tennessee River valley.

Mentone/Northeast Mountains, Ala.

Mother Nature, Pure and Simple

From the Gulf of Mexico, the cotton fields of Alabama gradually give way to the Cumberland Plateau and the beginning of the Appalachian Mountains in northeastern Alabama. You know you've arrived when signs of civilization thin out and Lookout Mountain looms high.

Lookout Mountain, which some associate more with Chattanooga, actually stretches 83 miles from the Tennessee city south to Gadsden in northeastern Alabama. It rises 2,000 feet and spreads one to ten miles wide, creating a mountaintop ridge of natural wonders in something of a time warp. Electricity and television came late to this impoverished area, and fast-food franchises and strip plazas – never. Bible-belt voters keep the county dry.

Log cabins, stone houses, humble antiques shops, tiny chapels, children's summer camps and old-fashioned signs accent the craggy landscape along a 100-mile-long Lookout Mountain Parkway that is not really a parkway but rather a meandering, two-lane road.

The surrounding wilderness abounds in nature's wonders: DeSoto Falls and state park, the Little River Canyon (deepest east of the Rockies) and the ancient rock formations and mirror-like lakes of Sequoyah Caverns.

The heart of the mountain area is the crossroads hamlet of Mentone (population 640), which flourished as a summer resort in the late 1800s and whose fortunes have gone downhill, so to speak. Mentone rests along "The Brow" of Lookout Mountain, where homes large and small overlook the valley below. Mentone claims the most children's summer camps, the coolest temperatures in Alabama and the southernmost ski resort.

At the foot of Lookout Mountain, almost a sheer drop beneath Mentone, is Valley Head, where the Winston family developed the railroad that brought early visitors to Mentone and Lookout Mountain.

Across the valley rises the Sand Mountain plateau, cresting at Gorham's Bluff, a visionary "new town in Appalachia" overlooking the Tennessee River.

The draw around here is Mother Nature, pure and simple.

Inn Spots

The Lodge on Gorham's Bluff, 101 Gorham Drive, Box 160, Pisgah 35765.

The centerpiece of the fledgling "new town in Appalachia" overlooks a watery spread of two creeks and the Tennessee River. From the 700-foot bluff, you can seemingly see forever. "The view is what gave us the audacity to do this," says Clara McGriff, referring to the new town she and her family are creating here. Her father owned acreage along the bluff, and she recalls picnicking over the years in the area now occupied by the lodge.

The three-story lodge with rooftop tower and double verandas was among the first structures built for the new town in 1995, after the amphitheater and the observation tower on each side. It doubles as the community's hotel and gathering spot and as a place for prospective homeowners to stay.

The main floor is given over to a plush living room and a TV room on one side and a twenty-seat dining room/restaurant on the other. Upstairs are six spacious guest rooms that define "elegant comfort," Appalachia style. Fireplaces, whirlpool tubs, sitting areas and private porches are among their attributes. Two rooms have kingsize beds, three are queensize and one has two doubles.

Clara McGriff did the decorating, endowing each room with a different character. She calls the style "classical but comfortable." Others call it sumptuous. Our quarters in the end King Suite were a high-ceilinged dream of dark blue walls, huge fieldstone fireplace and bookcase, an ornate gilded metal crown-canopy queen bed and matching dresser. The gold and gray colors of the bed and the fireplace were picked up in the bed covers and the floor-length draperies. The sitting area contained a chaise and three armchairs. It opened onto an awesome back porch, big enough for two green wicker chairs around a table, plus two white rockers. The expanse of stars above and the odd lights twinkling below created an unforgettable backdrop for a bedtime nightcap.

Rooms on the second floor come with porches. Two larger suites on the third floor have bigger sitting areas

Plush furnishings and porches typify rooms at The Lodge on Gorham's Bluff.

instead of porches, raftered ceilings and double fireplaces opening toward the jacuzzi tubs in the bathrooms.

Dinner was what Clara, the cook that night, called "a simple little country supper," served family style with the McGriffs and several guests in attendance. Simple turned out to be a buffet spread of oven-fried chicken, black-eyed peas, fried okra, cream-style corn and Sand Mountain tomatoes, followed by banana pudding. Iced tea accompanied. This typifies the fare offered at the popular Sunday afternoon lunch.

Breakfast the next morning in the pale yellow dining room trimmed in white started with a blend of orange-strawberry juice. A fruit plate contained cantaloupe, pineapple, strawberries and a fancy banana rolled in sour cream and toasted coconut. The main dish was a frittata, accompanied by bacon and sausage.

The restaurant operation was in transition at our visit, with Clara cooking weekdays and a caterer who had just bought property at Gorham's Bluff handling weekends.

Birmingham chef Chris Hastings, owner of one of that city's best new restaurants, was to assume management of the lodge's restaurant in 1999. His charge was to make it a destination for food. The McGriffs were enlarging the kitchen to accommodate the plans.

(256) 451-3435. Six rooms with private baths. Doubles, $135 to $175 weekends, $120 to $150 midweek. Children over 12. No smoking.

Winston Place, 353 Railroad St., Box 165, Valley Head 35989.

This 1831 mansion with quite a pedigree just keeps unfolding. It unfolds in layout, in décor, in history, in personality. Where to start? Bubbly innkeeper Leslie Bunch, the epitome of the Southern belle but "actually an Oklahoma army brat," came over from her nearby home with her three young sons in tow for breakfast the day of our visit to help unfold the tale.

Antebellum mansion with illustrious history is now Winston Place.

It seems that in 1946 her grandfather purchased the grand antebellum estate that had belonged to three generations of the illustrious Winston family from England, with connections to the Duke of Marlborough, Patrick Henry and Winston Churchill. (It also was the headquarters for 30,000 Union troops during the Civil War and was the site of the Cherokee Council Tree, where Sequoyah taught his alphabet.) Leslie's mother Jean grew up here. She and her husband, a retired Army and Civil Service officer whom everyone calls "Colonel," gave the house to Leslie and her husband Jim, a former football All-American at the University of Alabama, when Jim returned to the area to run a group of fast-food franchises.

Leslie was asked to open her new home in 1995 for a decorator showhouse as a fund-raiser for the arts. "I never intended to have a B&B – it just kind of happened." She thought she'd try one room. Her first guests turned out to be five people from England, who needed more than one room. Two more guest quarters had been opened when she got sidetracked with a teaching job and asked her parents back to run the B&B. The head of Crown Crafts in Atlanta then discovered the house and wanted to refurnish it for use as a photo backdrop for its fall catalog in 1997. (How he persisted in the face of Leslie's protestations is a tale in itself, but the results are there for all to see.) Now she has five opulently decorated rooms and suites, her parents as resident innkeepers and "a place that's still evolving. It's a happening."

The happening was obvious in our first-floor front room, a showplace in shades of reds, browns and greens. Pictured in the Crown Crafts catalog, it has a kingsize poster bed with at least fifteen plump pillows to remove and stash in a corner before retiring. Heavy fabric draperies puddle past Indian-shuttered windows onto the heart-pine floor. A leopard-skin rug is at the foot of the bed. Two wing chairs are placed beside a table set with elegant crystal and silver and bearing chocolates and a vase of long-stemmed roses. Only the closet-size bathroom fails to measure up.

Other guest rooms, all also with TV and fireplace, intrigue as well. One with two double crown-canopy beds has a bathroom draped in fabric, even the ceiling.

A rear upstairs room with two double beds and windows on three sides is showy in butterscotch and red. Magnolia patterns are everywhere in the front Magnolia Suite with two double beds, a two-part bath in the closets and access to the upper veranda. Also opening to the veranda are two bedrooms rented as a suite with a kingsize bed, another bed and lots of seating.

And then there are the public rooms. The parlor still has its original wavy glass windows, a fireplace of Italian quarry marble, a rare gooseneck rocker found in the barn, and a library of works by Leslie's great-uncle, who was Alabama's poet laureate. The downstairs TV den shines with Jim Bunch's football trophies. A contemporary kitchen serves the rear dining room, where bead-board walls painted deep red and a white ceiling set off a table for eight to good advantage.

Here is where breakfast is served to the accompaniment of classical music. In our case it included baked apples, scrambled eggs with ham, a cheese-potato casserole, watermelon garnish and biscuits.

The house has 2,700 square feet of porches, upstairs and down. They provide good vantage points for the outlying barn, former slave quarters, corn crib, shed and many varieties of trees, not to mention the whistling freight trains that rumble out front along the tracks of the railroad founded by one of the Winstons.

(256) 635-6381 or (888) 494-6786. Four rooms and one two-bedroom suite with private baths. Doubles, $125. Suite, $150. No smoking.

Raven Haven, 651 County Road 644, Mentone 35984.

Tony Teverino took early retirement from Southern Bell and, with his pert Irish wife Eleanor, bought this handsome rural residence on Lookout Mountain in 1994 and undertook a year's renovations to open as a B&B. "We've had fun with this place," Tony said. Their guests have, too.

The Teverinos offer four "theme rooms" and an abundance of common areas in a rambling, contemporary-looking stone and wood house on two levels. The first-floor Casablanca Room follows a Humphrey Bogart theme, right down to the book on the bed canopied in mosquito netting. Two wicker chairs add to an island motif, and the stenciled bathroom has a huge walk-in shower. Tony transformed three more bedrooms into the spacious Queen Anne Room, rag-painted the walls purple and placed a circular stained-glass window in a recessed ceiling above the bed.

Upstairs, the large Nautical Room with a boat motif comes with a side deck and private entrance. The captain's cannonball bed has a straw hat on the bed post and a fishnet behind. A rope hammock awaits beside the portholes, and a day bed and trundle are nearby. The newest room is underneath. The Little Room on the Prairie has the rough-hewn look of the garage it once was, with a fake window painted with a mountain scene and holding dried flowers. Two Amish vine rockers face a gas fireplace. Eleanor stenciled the floor and door. Tony built the large shower of local stones and blue glass blocks that he bought in Italy "because they were so pretty – I had no idea what I'd do with them." A philodendron plant thrives beneath its recessed floor light. The sliding door carved with a half moon symbolizes a prairie outhouse.

New Age music is piped into the bedrooms to awaken guests for breakfast. From a large, cathedral-ceilinged country kitchen come a variety of treats, perhaps Scotch eggs, or breakfast pizza, German pancakes or peachy french toast with amaretto. Two breakfast meats and a vegetable dish (zucchini or a mushroom casserole), grits and fruit accompany. It's served buffet style on a side table in the kitchen and enjoyed at a square table for eight in the dining room. Tony does most of the cooking and Eleanor the presentation.

The pleasant back yard has an attractive patio with a waterfall, two swings and a quarter-mile walking trail.

(256) 634-4310. Four rooms with private baths. Doubles, $70 to $85. Children over 14. No smoking.

The Secret, 2356 Highway 68 West, Leesburg 35983.

Inexplicably written in lower case as "the secret" in all its promotion, owners Carl and Diann Cruickshank call their Lookout Mountain-top retreat "the best kept secret in the South." Why, it's hard to imagine, although it's hidden from view so originally few people knew it was there. Perhaps it should be called The View, such is the panorama across Weiss Lake to the south, extending from Rome, Ga., to Gadsen, Ala.

The house was built of stone in 1965 by the owner of the local telephone company who liked to entertain and installed 48 phones inside. The Cruickshanks acquired the property at a bankruptcy auction and redid the entire house to open it as a B&B in 1995.

One wing of the house has four vaulted-ceilinged guest rooms opening onto decks. Two with kingsize mahogany rice beds face the view and two with two queen beds each face the woods. Each has a full bath and TV/VCR. The rooms are upstaged by the common areas. The principal one in season is the roof-top deck and swimming pool built on the bedroom level. The other is the enormous great hall/living room area with tall windows and vaulted ceiling. There's a lot going on here, from the porcelain doll collection in a glass display case behind the fireplace to the artificial flowers and plants over the front door. A life-like mannequin sits in a chair beside the leather seating area. Stuffed animals line the stairway to the bedroom area. Beneath the stairway is an eight-foot tall chair that turns adults into kids. The Cruikshanks photograph their guests in the chair as well as beneath the "kissing tree" outside.

Breakfast is served at 9 o'clock at a round table for twelve, so big that it had to be built on site. It's centered by a revolving lazy susan so that guests can reach the southern country breakfast treats set thereon, perhaps pecan pancakes and eggs or apple french toast.

After breakfast, folks go outside to feed the animals. Carl's menagerie includes llamas, whitetail and fallow deer, peacocks and a pair of albino wallabies imported from Australia.

Under construction for opening in early 1999 were what Carl called two small, steep-roofed "Hansel and Gretel" cottages beyond the pool. Each includes a deck, jacuzzi and fireplace. They join an older cottage with queen bedroom, kitchen and large deck.

(256) 523-3825. Fax (256) 523-6477. Four rooms and three cottages with private baths. Doubles, $95 to $115. Cottages, $135. No children. Smoking restricted.

Valhalla, 672 County Road 626, Mentone 35984.

This onetime B&B and cottage colony was in transition at our visit. In 1998, former nuclear engineer Karen Ormstedt purchased the property she had managed for eighteen months from the original owners, who had converted the 1930s farmhouse into a B&B and built four luxury cottages scattered along the side of a

Contemporary stone and wood house has been transformed into Raven Haven.

stocked fish pond in back. The former owner finished enclosing a rear porch with a hot tub an hour before the sale closed.

For Karen, Valhalla means the "Gates of Heaven." Surely it is an idyllic place for guests to stay, although breakfast no longer is offered. They can enjoy the main house with beautiful common rooms during the day and retire to their private cottage at night. Colorful "welcome" flags fly in front of the modern, barn-roofed cottages. Each is nicely furnished and has a living room with TV/VCR, dining area and kitchen, one to three bedrooms, screened porch and two hammocks overlooking the pond. Harmony is the biggest, with a king bedroom, a queen bedroom and two twins in the loft. Angel's Rest is the smallest, on a single level with a queen bedroom and a cozy living/dining area.

Field of Dreams is outfitted for the sportsman, with twig curtain rods and Smoky the Bear painted behind the wood stove. The upstairs loft has a queen poster bed on one side and two twins on the other. The bath in the middle has a sink fashioned from a barrel.

Cupid's Kiss, geared for romance, has more frou-frou. The headboard of the queen bed on the loft is a backlit stained-glass window and the footboard is a door painted with cherubs. The wash basin is in an old sewing machine. Couples sign their names to the hearts stenciled on the walls.

Each dining table is set quite elegantly as if for dinner. Guests bring their own food and can cook any fish they catch on the gas grills.

The twenty-acre property backs up to the Little River Canyon National Preserve. Trails lead to the canyon's edge a twenty-minute hike away.

Karen was thinking of reopening one bedroom in the farmhouse, as in the past. Meanwhile, she was enjoying the seclusion of her own valhalla.

(256) 634-4006. Four cottages with private baths; no breakfast. Doubles, $85 to $115; each additional $10. Two-night minimum stay weekends. Children welcome. No smoking.

Mountain Laurel Inn, 624 County Road 948, Box 443, Mentone 35984.
The mountain laurel along the bluff of the canyon below DeSoto Falls provides the name for this B&B. A gourmet breakfast is served in the main house and

guests stay in five rooms of a detached guest house that looks like a cottage in the woods. Sarah Wilcox and her golden retriever, Baxter, imbue it with a lively personality. Sarah, who camped at nearby Camp DeSoto and now is its accountant, bought the former Blossom Hill B&B in 1996. Besides changing the name, she redecorated the guest rooms. Two rooms are in the front of the outlying structure and two in back. A two-room apartment is upstairs.

Three rooms have queen beds and one a king and a twin. Each opens onto a front or back porch with rockers. Each has a TV, thick carpeting and a room diary in which guests share their thoughts. The Wildflower Room is pretty in wicker and has a subtle bunny theme. The Ski Room next door conveys a sports motif in dark blue and hunter green. Its bath is wallpapered to look like a library. The rear Deer Room is named for its deer heads and window treatments and a little family of the real thing that passes by periodically. The Bridal Room in a pink floral theme is so named for the Mentone Wedding Chapel next door.

The morning begins with coffee placed outside each guests' door. A substantial breakfast is served in Sarah's dining room beside big windows onto the woods and deck. Fresh fruit, bran muffins and eggs rancheros was the fare the day of our visit.

A ten-minute trail leads along the canyon to DeSoto Falls.

(256) 634-4673 or (800) 889-4244. Four rooms and a two-bedroom apartment with private baths. Doubles, $85, apartment $100 for two, $115 for four. Winter: doubles, $75; apartment $90 for two, $100 for four. Tax included.

Mentone Inn Bed & Breakfast, Highway 117, Box 290, Mentone 35984.

Built as a mountain hotel in 1927, this brown clapboard structure occupies a hillside perch near Mentone's main intersection. It's full of pine bead-board walls and rustic lodge touches, and retains the air of its hotel past.

The twelve guest rooms offered by owner Frances Waller vary. The Mentone Room, main-floor front, is simple and snug, with a queen poster bed, an in-room vanity and a clawfoot tub in the bathroom. The light and airy Needle Rock has a queen and a twin bed. Upstairs is the Cloud, with a queen sleigh bed and frilly curtain and spread. The corner Brow Room, a favorite overlooking the brow of Lookout Mountain, is bigger and has two double iron beds with colorful tufted comforters. The odd Eagle's Nest has one chair between two side-by-side double iron beds facing in opposite directions.

A two-bedroom cabin accommodates up to six with a double iron bed and two twins, a living room with futon and TV, and a kitchen.

The old hotel dining room, its walls and ceiling paneled in pine, holds ten tables. Guests get a full breakfast with several choices, including eggs any style, omelets or eggs benedict.

(256) 634-4836 or (800) 455-7470. Twelve rooms and one cabin with private baths. Doubles, $70. Cabin, $125. Closed in winter.

Mentone Springs Hotel, 6114 Highway 117, Mentone 35984.

Californians David and Claudia Wassom took over the Queen Anne Victorian hotel that had been abandoned at the crossroads of Mentone. They set about a gradual upgrade of the hotel built in 1884 by an ailing Pennsylvania physician who had visited Lookout Mountain and found his health improved after drinking the mineral spring water. At its height, the hotel offered 81 rooms, tennis courts and a nine-hole golf course.

An enormous porch stretches across the front of the hotel, and there's a large lobby with a central fireplace inside. Ten guest rooms have queen beds, and six feature fireplaces. Seven on the main floor retain their early look, including pull-chain lights and tongue and groove bead-board walls, ceilings and floors. They share a ladies' room, a men's room and several shower rooms. "This is my home, so the pictures and knickknacks are my personal things," said Claudia. The Wassoms have improved a portion of the second floor, which had no power, water or windows. Three bedrooms here now have those necessities as well as private baths. The honeymoon suite includes a settee facing the fireplace and a stenciled clawfoot tub in the bedroom. Claudia fashioned a fabric bed canopy with wood found in the building. Another bedroom has a bathroom big enough for a rollaway cot and clawfoot tub and yet lacks a shower. The largest suite has an oak bed in the bedroom, a loveseat and a new gas fireplace in the sitting room and a large bath beyond. Old-fashioned hair-curling irons and a bobbin for lace-making are displayed in the hallway. The latter reflects one of Claudia's hobbies.

David prepares a breakfast of the guest's choice in the hotel's dining room, big enough to seat 150. It becomes **Caldwell's Restaurant** at peak periods, serving lunch and dinner Thursday-Saturday in summer. A Sunday buffet for $7.95, including beverage and dessert, is offered most of the year.

(256) 634-4040 or (800) 404-0100. Two rooms and one suite with private baths and seven rooms with shared baths. Doubles, $69 to $79 with private bath, $54 to $59 with shared bath.

DeSoto State Park Lodge, 265 County Road 951, Fort Payne 35967.

In a mountain area where overnight accommodations vary, this state park adds to the potpourri.

The lodge in the heart of the park includes a large and quite good restaurant serving three meals a day (see Dining Spots). Nearby is a 25-unit motel with rear balconies outfitted with rocking chairs. Each unit has two double beds or one kingsize, cable TV and telephone. A B&B special of $49 for two is offered here midweek in winter. Off a winding road nearby are eleven recently renovated chalets sleeping four to six and eleven "rustic cabins" sleeping two to eight. Each is fully equipped and has a fireplace, cable TV, electric heat and air conditioning. The chalet we saw includes a comfortable living room, kitchen/dining area and double bedroom down and a twin bedroom upstairs. "It conveys a light and fresh look for a government operation," said our ranger guide, who called it "my idea of a getaway place." Three deer scampered across the road as we toured. The cabins, built by the Civilian Conservation Corps in the 1930s, definitely are rustic but were due for renovations. The park also has 78 improved campsites and additional wilderness campsites.

(256) 845-5380 or (800) 568-8840. Fax (256) 845-3224. Twenty-five motel rooms and 22 chalets with private baths. Motel $58 to $61 March-November, $53 to $56 in winter. Cabins, $65 to $75 in season, $61 to $71 in winter. Chalets, $82 in season, $78 in winter. Two-night minimum stay in chalets and cabins, May through Labor Day.

Dining Spots

Haute cuisine and fine dining are not what residents or visitors seem to look for in this area, although the revitalized restaurant at the Lodge on Gorham's Bluff seeks to fill that niche. This is mountain country in the foothills of Appalachia, so the dining options follow suit. A couple of dinner restaurants open on weekends only. As for alcoholic beverages, the county is dry, and whatever brown-bagging is allowed must be done discreetly. Most restaurants do not accept credit cards.

Dish, Highway 117, Mentone.

Hidden behind and beneath the Hitching Post antiques and crafts emporium is this new tearoom/café. It's a dish of a place, from the colorful dishes that decorate the walls to the fresh breads and food dished up by Terrence McCabe and Joe Hines. The pair left careers in Atlanta – Terry as a computer specialist and Joe as a house restorer – for the simpler lifestyle of Mentone. Both liked to cook and figured this was a way to make a living. They built a kitchen beside their little tearoom space and started offering lunches a few days a week.

Their menu is simple and changes weekly, depending on what's fresh and what Terry has picked up on his Wednesday trips to the market – "it takes a day and 150 miles just to shop," he explains. When we were there, the choices were Hungarian goulash, spinach and tomato quiche (both excellent) and a black bean burrito that sure looked good. The accompanying breads baked daily were so tasty we asked for seconds. Coconut custard pie was the day's dessert.

The partners keep a tight rein on their food inventory and often run out of a particular item. Any leftovers turn up in different presentations the next day. The weekend dinner menu includes a lot of carryover from the lunch, with the addition of a special entrée – one week, pork tenderloin; the next week, sirloin roast. Butternut squash, yams, carrots and potatoes accompanied the sirloin for a bargain $7.50. "We also do a lot of vegetarian things," Terry said.

The idea for the dish décor came from Terry's mother, who hung her handpainted china on a wall at home. Most of their decorative dishes are gifts "with stories behind them," Terry said. They provide a colorful backdrop for a convivial room that's small and intimate. The six tables are supplemented by a few on the flower-bedecked porch outside.

(256) 634-3669. Entrées, $5.50 to $7.50. Lunch, Thursday-Sunday 11:30 to 2. Dinner, Friday and Saturday 6 to 8. Dinner reservations recommended.

Little River Café, 4608 DeSoto Parkway, Fischer Crossroads.

Tony and Dana Goggans started this appealing-looking place as a sandwich and gift shop and coffeehouse. Tony, known as the Mentone troubadour, played the piano and so many folks came that family members took over the restaurant. He built the adjoining Lookout Mountain General Store and launched the wildly popular Barnyard Saturday Night hoedown (see Diversions).

Also locally popular and full of local color is this house built in 1927 around a stone fireplace. It's now run by Tony's niece's husband, Donny Baldwin, who added a second floor to seat 80 and was planning to add 50 to 75 more seats within a year. He does a land-office lunch business, and the café was filling up for dinner when we were there. Part of the reason was that Tony was playing and singing mellow Appalachian folk music in the corner. Another was the down-home Southern food. One of us tried the "great little chicken dinner" (grilled chicken breast, served with a side salad and fries). Another enjoyed the signature hamburger steak with sautéed peppers and onions with baked potato. Ribeye steak, western chicken, "smothered byrd" and chicken fingers rounded out the dinner entrées. Donny was planning to add grilled shrimp and grilled trout to the menu. Also available all day are quite a variety of appetizers, salads (a specialty is the cheesy chili chicken with mexicali dressing), sandwiches and burgers. The hot fudge brownie delight, topped with walnuts and vanilla ice cream, is enough for two or more to share. *(256) 997-0707. Entrées, $5.99 to $11.99. Lunch and dinner, Monday-Saturday 11 to 8:30 or 9:30.*

Log Cabin Restaurant & Deli, 6080 Highway 117, Mentone. This popular family restaurant in a log cabin dating to 1800 is Mentone's oldest restaurant and looks it. The cabin once was a trading post operated by Sequoyah, the Indian chief famed for inventing the Cherokee alphabet.

Collette Kerby took over what had been a sandwich shop in 1988 and added a full menu. She likes to show visitors the wide plank floors with the original saw marks, the log walls and the mountain rocks in the fireplace. Tables in the dark interior are made of cedar and some are enclosed in rustic fences. Collette added a side screened porch for semi-outdoor dining and enclosed lights in bushel baskets hung from the ceiling. For lunch, we shared the rustic front porch with two old-timers who happened to be costumed mannequins occupying a far table for posterity.

There's no deli as such, although the sandwiches live up to the description. And all the food is prepared from scratch. "We've kept the prices low because this is not a wealthy area," Collette acknowledged. The country ham dinner with red eye gravy, cornbread and choice of two side dishes tops the menu prices at $8.95. All others are under $5.50. For lunch, we were tempted by the cabin hobo, a thick fried bologna sandwich with onion, lettuce and tomato, but settled for the signature chili corn pone, a Mexican dish of cornbread topped with melted hot pepper cheese, chili, tomato and sour cream, served with nachos. It was super, especially teamed with Collette's specialty cabin cooler, Russian tea mixed with Sprite, served hot or cold. The cooler is a favorite of camp counselors who frequent the place, and also appealed to the cast of "Southern Heart," who ordered it for the screening party of the movie filmed around Mentone.

Fudge nut cake with ice cream is the dessert specialty. We preferred the peach cobbler with ice cream. *(256) 634-4560. Entrées, $5.25 to $8.95. Lunch and dinner, Tuesday-Sunday 11 to 9, to 7 weekdays fall to spring. Closed Monday.*

Mountain Inn Restaurant, DeSoto State Park Lodge, 265 County Road 951, Fort Payne.

The Civilian Conservation Corps built this rambling stone lodge in the 1930s to serve as the park's focal point for visitors. Green cloths cover the tables in the stone-walled dining rooms, and woods are on view from the rear windows.

The menu is surprisingly extensive for so remote a restaurant, but its size is an indication of its popularity. The dinner repertoire covers the basics from southern fried chicken and smoked ham steak with red eye gravy to spaghetti with meat sauce. Alabama catfish, fried or broiled flounder, prime rib and charbroiled ribeye steak also are available. So is a steamed vegetable platter, served plain or with cheese sauce. Seafood gumbo is the specialty starter. Desserts change daily.

The Sunday lunch buffet is a popular family outing, $7.95 for adults and $4.95 for children. *(256) 845-5380 or (800) 568-8840. Entrées, $5.95 to $13.95. Breakfast daily, 7 to 10. Lunch, 11:30 to 3. Dinner, 5 to 8 or 9.*

Cragsmere Manna & Gardens, DeSoto Parkway South (Route 89), Mentone. This Lookout Mountain landmark in an old stone and log farmhouse owned by Ronnie and Bonnie Barnett along the Brow offers fine dining by reservation, weekends only. She's the chatty hostess. They hire a chef to prepare a "a country gourmet menu" featuring seafood, fried chicken and steaks. Appetizers are few (fried mushrooms, cheese sticks and baked potato skins). Main courses come with soup or salad. Choices range from shrimp provençal to prime rib or filet mignon. Chicken comes in five presentations, from southern fried to cordon bleu. Desserts include New York cheesecake, chocolate derby pie and a "strawberry pizza" on a flaky crust with creamy filling and berry topping.

The dining venue of choice is the semi-enclosed back porch with two fireplaces and tables for 50. Another 50 diners can be seated in four small rooms of the house built in 1898. One room has a *Gone with the Wind* theme, and another with log walls has tables for two. Diners are allowed to bring their own drinks, which they discreetly pour themselves.

(256) 634-4677. Entrées, $7.95 to $16.95 Dinner by reservation, Friday and Saturday 5 to 9.

Diversions

Lookout Mountain. The mountain stretching 83 miles from Chattanooga to Gadsden is traversed by the scenic Lookout Mountain Parkway (generally Highway 89 in this area, but the route numbers change), a two-lane road. Houses are perched along the "brow" on either side of Mentone. The drive goes through DeSoto State Park. Every August, the parkway is part of the world's longest yard sale, when bumper-to-bumper traffic stops and shops for bargains offered by several thousand vendors. Diverse plant life abounds atop the mountain. Besides the predictable banks of rhododendron and mountain laurel, the landscape is notable for rare orchids, pink and white lady slippers and several varieties of trillium. The mountain gives birth to the Little River, the only one in the United States that forms and flows almost entirely on a mountain. Pure and unpolluted, it passes through upland forest backcountry until it reaches Little River Falls. It then flows through the "Grand Canyon of the East" before emptying into Weiss Lake.

Mentone. Located along the brow of Lookout Mountain, Mentone flourished in the late 1800s, when summer visitors arrived by train at Valley Head and were transported up Lookout Mountain by horse and buggy. Its resort bubble burst, first around the turn of the century and later with the Great Depression. The mountain became favored as a place for summer and year-round homes, particularly for people from Huntsville and Rome, Ga. It also claims more children's summer camps than any other area – twelve to fifteen, depending on who's counting. The summer camps define the tourist season, local restaurateurs and innkeepers say, especially on weekends when parents arrive to deliver or retrieve their charges. Camp DeSoto, Mentone's oldest summer camp, was founded in 1916 as a boys' camp and now is a Christian camp for girls. One of the biggest camps is the Comer Scout Reservation.

Among Mentone's attractions is the **Mentone Wedding Chapel,** a church in miniature in the woods at Shady Grove, near DeSoto State Park. Owner Linda Kilgore arranges wedding ceremonies every week – including four the weekend we were there – in a forty-seat chapel that she decorates to the hilt. Another attraction is the **Sallie Howard Memorial Chapel,** a larger chapel built around a boulder. Her ashes are interred inside the boulder, which serves as the pulpit.

Mentone's **Brow Park,** overlooking Valley Head and the Sand Mountain plateau, is the site of the Rhododendron Festival in May and the Mentone Colorfest in October. A Blessing of the Animals was scheduled here at our visit.

Little River Canyon National Preserve, Lookout Mountain.

Greenery adds color to Little River Canyon.

The feds took over operation of the 12,000-acre Little River Canyon wilderness preserve from the state in 1998. The narrow, winding **Canyon Rim Drive** (Highway 176), much of it without guardrails, hugs the canyon's western edge for about ten miles.

The spectacular canyon, up to 700 feet deep and 400 feet wide, is not barren like the Grand Canyon. Its sheer cliffs are lush with green vegetation. "I never dreamed there was anything like this in Alabama," a returning native gushed at one of the frequent lookout observation points. High points include Grace's High Falls and Umbrella Rock. Little River Falls is on view from a walking path off Highway 35 near its junction with the Canyon Rim Drive. World-class whitewater and rock climbing opportunities challenge the truly adventurous visitor.

(256) 845-9605. Open daily. Free.

DeSoto Falls State Park, Lookout Mountain.

Atop Lookout Mountain just south of Mentone is this 5,000-acre park billed as the "Home of Mother Nature." Chief among its far-flung attractions in two sections is DeSoto Falls, a 104-foot waterfall that was reduced to a trickle at out visit in the midst of a lengthy drought. The waterfall splashes into a pool beneath 150-foot cliffs. The Lookout Mountain Parkway, a scenic drive with overlooks, follows the west rim or brow for twenty miles. Eight miles of hiking trails laced with rhododendron pass many of the park's fifteen waterfalls. Unusual rock formations and rare forms of plant life are found. A new boardwalk trail leads to a beautiful view of the Azalea Cascade. In summer at the nature center, park rangers offer interpretive programs, from wildflower walks to exhibits of live birds of prey. A picnic area includes a playground, tennis courts and a swimming pool. A country store for camper check-in carries basic groceries, local crafts and souvenirs.

(256) 845-5380 or (800) 568-8840. Open daily, 7 a.m. to dusk. Free.

Sequoyah Caverns, 1438 County Road 731, Valley Head.

These remarkable caverns across from the base of Lookout Mountain are famed for their illuminated Looking Glass Lakes that look like mirrors. A guide turns on the lights as visitors wend their way a quarter-mile into the depths of the caverns, which end in an open, 100-foot-high "ballroom" where Cherokee Indians once gathered for ceremonies. Today, it plays host to the odd wedding and Scout overnights. We'll stick to the daytime tours along surprisingly manicured trails passing several extinct waterfalls. The amazing reflecting pools are so placid that you have to blow on them to make them ripple to prove they are water. The pools reflect the cavern's ancient fossils and rock formations, including the Golden Haystack, the largest stalagmite standing fifteen feet tall. The temperature inside the cavern is 58 degrees year-round. The half-mile circle tour ends back at a gift shop and farm, where you see white fallow deer, peacocks and a buffalo herd. The caverns are named for the Indian genius who while living nearby at Wills Valley invented the alphabet that allowed the Cherokee Nation to read and write. California's giant sequoia trees and Sequoia National Park also were named for him.

(256) 635-0024 or (800) 843-5098. Caverns open daily 8:30 to 5; weekends only, December-February. Adults, $6.

Fort Payne, the biggest town (population, 11,800) and county seat of DeKalb County, bills itself as "the sock capital of the world," thanks to all its hosiery factories. The **Depot Museum** in the 1891 train depot is the historical repository for Landmarks of DeKalb County. It's best known for Indian artifacts, pottery and baskets, but visitors will find other items of interest from a hosiery exhibit and campaign buttons to a foot warmer, homemade vegetable grater and an antique loom. Across Gault Avenue North is the restored **Fort Payne Opera House,** built in the town's 1890 boom days. The only opera house still in use in Alabama, it has a rare pump organ and local history murals that line the walls leading to the stage. Next to the opera house is an extravaganza of a different kind, "a block of socks" called **C.J.'s Wholesale Socks Outlet Store**.

Shopping. At the crossroads of Mentone, the recently renovated **White Elephant Galleries** in an annex to the historic Mentone Springs Hotel offers 24 rooms of antiques, gifts, crafts, books and collectibles for browsing. More shops and sheds surround the Log Cabin Restaurant & Deli on another corner, and still more are found at the **Hitching Post** antiques and crafts emporium on a third corner. Most shopkeepers are free-spirited and their hours vary, but they're generally open more days in summer and on weekends. One of the better shops is **Serendipity,** newly opened by two sisters to showcase "treasures for the home." Quite a novelty is the **Gourdie Shop,** where Sharon Barron creates dolls from gourds, burlap and a little paint.

Just across the George line on Highway 117 is **Mountain Mamas Pottery Studio,** where local and regional artists show pottery, jewelry, weaving, sculpture, fabric art and more. South of DeSoto State Park at Fischer Crossroads is the **Lookout Mountain General Store,** featuring gifts and necessities for home and garden and sponsor of Barnyard Saturday Night (see below).

Barnyard Saturday Night, DeSoto Parkway, Fischer Crossroads.

Mentone troubadour Tony Goggans spearheads this open-air Appalachian musical family event, a revival of the hoedown tradition. It's held in the open air outside the Lookout Mountain General Store every Saturday night that weather permits. The Malibous, the Tony Creek Girls and other mountain entertainers gathered by Tony present bluegrass, folk, gospel and country music. Fiddles, banjos, guitars, mandolins, dulcimers, harmonicas, washtubs, rub boards and a host of other Appalachian instruments provide foot-stomping music that varies with the performers and the night. The blurb says admission is free if you ride your horse, drive a buggy or wagon, ride your bicycle, drive your tractor or are under age 10 or over 80. Take a dollar off if you wear overalls, a top hat, a derby or a bonnet. Bring your lawn chair and enjoy. But take note: there's "absolutely no alcohol." *(256) 844-6500. Gates open, Saturday 6 to 10; music from 7 to 9. Admission, $5.*

Extra-Special _____

Gorham's Bluff, Pisgah.

You won't find it on the maps, and you'd need to know about this "new town in Appalachia" in order to seek it out. It's well worth a visit. Area residents Bill and Clara McGriff and daughter Dawn are executing their vision for the family-owned, 700-foot-high bluff overlooking the Tennessee River. The 153-acre project consists of a town center and 350 homesites for people interested in theater and the arts, a community lifestyle and a natural setting seemingly in the middle of nowhere, several miles north of the Jackson County hamlet of Pisgah. The project was inspired partly by the famed Seaside in Florida. The focus here is on the bluff, not the beach, and the lots here are twice the size and the architecture is Appalachian with porches, columns and towers. "We're building a town, not a planned community," said Dawn, an advocate of the New Urbanism. A performance amphitheater, a landmark observation tower, the Lodge on Gorham's Bluff and a public walkway along the bluff were finished first. The Gorham's Bluff Institute arranges music and theater festivals in what one leader likened to a mini-Chautauqua in the mountains. **Roseberry Mercantile** and **At Home** were early shops, and the **Shanty on the Bluff** dispensed weekend snacks for visitors. By late 1998, 70 residential lots had been sold, including all those available along the bluff. Twelve houses were up and occupied, three were under construction and ten more were about to start. Houses were rising around a lake and the McGriffs were erecting "speculation" homes and row townhouses in the center. Commercial buildings around the town green, artisan workshops in the old Pisgah School, a meeting house with the look of a church, a recreation complex and an assisted-living residence were being readied for 1999. By the end of the year, the McGriffs expected to have reached the critical mass necessary to turn wait-and-see skepticism into full-speed-ahead reality. Although the early going was slow, they remained hopeful their dream would be fulfilled within ten years.

(256) 451-3435. Follow signs off Jackson County Route 58, north of Pisgah.

Fairhope, Ala.

Utopia Along the Bay

On a wide, verdant bluff overlooking Mobile Bay lies a pleasing town founded on a utopian dream that was given only a "fair hope" of survival.

But survive it did. Fairhope was settled in 1894 by Midwestern idealists who established it as a single-tax colony. They gave up private land in favor of common ownership by a member-owned corporation, which leased it back to individuals for the good of the community. More than 100 years later, Fairhope thrives as a model community, the only one of its kind.

Fairhope is unusual for more than its utopian ideals.

It is one of the few shoreline communities located on a bluff, part of ridge that's the highest coastal point between Maine and Mexico. That gives it a hilly and green prospect uncommon for the Southeast coast. Fairhope also exudes an unmistakable air of prosperity, but it is leavened by a lack of showy pretension traceable to its humble beginnings. It has fine community-owned facilities, not the least of which are a mile-long waterfront park ahead of its time and a long pier stretching into Mobile Bay. Free-thinkers have built interesting homes, both substantial and modest. A creative spirit has spawned an uncommon number of authors and artists (the revered Fairhope Arts & Crafts Show draws up to 250,000 people annually the third weekend in March). The flourishing downtown, home to thriving shops and restaurants, changes its lavish floral landscape with the seasons. Fairhope's ties with New Orleans, from chefs to architecture, prompt some to call it "The Little French Quarter."

Why, Fairhope even has one of the folksiest-ever Web sites on the Internet, defining "All Things Southern."

Fairhope actually got a late start on what is now the good life. The area along the eastern shore of Mobile Bay developed first in the early 1800s around Point Clear, site of the venerable Grand Hotel. The antebellum hotels and cottages here and in Daphne, to the north of what is now Fairhope, were favored by wealthy Mobile and New Orleans residents for summer getaways. These areas flourished before Fairhope was founded in 1894 by 27 Northerners who arrived by bay boat to pursue the dream of economist/philosopher Henry George in a warmer clime. Their settlement based on collectivism grew and prospered.

Today the model community is home to small business entrepreneurs, academics, professionals and retirees (a national publication proclaimed Fairhope one of the nation's top ten retirement spots). It also has uncommon appeal for visitors who want to stay, eat, shop and explore the languorous shore of Mobile Bay. They, too, think they've found utopia, if only for a day or two.

Windows of Bay Breeze Guest House take full advantage of view of Mobile Bay.

Inn Spots

Bay Breeze Guest House, 742 South Mobile St., Box 526, Fairhope 36533.
A large, handsome house facing Mobile Bay. Three guest rooms and two cottage
suites that offer the utmost in comfort. Two living rooms, a sitting room and an
enclosed sunporch awash in wicker. Two outdoor terraces and a lush yard sloping
to the bay. A sandy beach and a long, well-equipped pier used for fishing or crabbing,
socializing and elaborate breakfasts. Gregarious owners that are the consummate
hosts.

You get all this and more at Bay Breeze, the family home of Becky Jones, a
Fairhope native who retired after 37 years of teaching, and her husband Bill, a city
councilman and pharmacy manager at the local hospital. Becky grew up in the
house, which started as four rooms across the street from a dairy farm and
underwent a lot of growth in 43 years. The Joneses built three cottages for elderly
parents and relatives at the front of the property (they call it the back, since the
house is oriented toward the bay and what they call their front yard). In 1991, with
all but one cottage unoccupied, they opened a B&B. They added another a year
later in her mother's house, now the Church Street Inn in uptown Fairhope.

"You've got five minutes to be company and then you're family," Becky advises
arriving guests. She puts them up nicely in the two cottages or in bedrooms in a
section of the stucco house facing toward the street. Our quarters in the Magnolia
Room came with a queensize iron and brass bed and an ante-room with a sitting
area and a day bed. The bed was quilted and triple-sheeted, the lamps were antiques
and the appointments included family portraits and heirlooms dating back five
generations. Nothing was particularly fancy – "that's not the Fairhope way," says
Becky – but everything was pleasant and supremely comfortable.

Not that we spent much time in our room, as Becky quickly sent us off to meet
other guests on the pier. No ordinary pier, theirs. Besides the predictable boat
docks and lounge decks, it has a massive, semi-enclosed mid-section that's a
veritable kitchen, pantry, dining and living area, complete with TV and piped-in
music. Here the Joneses prepare and serve drinks, hors d'oeuvres, occasional
dinners and their weekend tradition, "breakfast on the pier." Shrimp boats passed
in the distance and a menagerie of ducks quacked and fish jumped up close for
handouts as the hosts prepared their specialty crab omelets, served with sliced

tomatoes, honeydew melon, hash browns, toasted french bread and enough orange juice and coffee to sink a ship.

Some guests spend most of their stay on the pier, and few would question why. *(334) 928-8976. Three rooms and two cottage suites with private baths. Doubles, $95 to $105. No children. No smoking.*

The Porches, 19190 County Road 13, Fairhope 36532.

The name fits at this odd-looking, gray and white house in a quasi rural/ex-urban neighborhood just southeast of Fairhope. Eddie Levin from New Orleans always wanted a home with porches, so this was built to oblige. Twelve-foot-deep porches wrap around all four sides. Besides the usual furnishings, the porches contain a swinging full-size bed like a hammock, five pre-Civil War poplar benches that resemble church pews, a clawfoot tub filled with iced beverages for parties and a private hot tub for guests in a main-floor suite. As if the porches weren't enough, twelve pet lambs wander about what Mobile native Sandy Levin calls a hobby-sheep farm surrounded by five acres of meadows and pecan orchards.

The Levins opened their new, built-to-look-old house to guests in 1994 after they found themselves empty-nesters. The main floor contains a 70-foot-long center hall ten feet wide, seemingly mostly pine – from floors to walls to ceiling – except for a grand piano behind the staircase. A Victorian living room harbors a chandelier from Prague along with massive antique furnishings. Across the hall is a dining room with a table for twelve, where Sandy serves a country breakfast that includes juice, fresh fruit, garlic grits, eggs with chives or herbs, sausage and homemade blueberry muffins. Her huge kitchen produces afternoon treats like chocolate-chip cookies (yummy) and iced tea (refreshing). It's open to an expansive rear family/gathering room focusing on a Delft tile fireplace, designed to go with the antique mirror above.

Guest accommodations include the Shepherd Suite, the master bedroom at the rear of the main floor, across from the family room. It has a kingsize bed with a loveseat at its foot, facing a TV in an ornate carved oak armoire. Off a man's dressing area with antique sink is an eight-foot walk-in shower, with a mural of a pond scene painted on the ceiling and a door leading outside to the hot tub. A lady's dressing area adds an antique sink and a clawfoot tub. Next door is Rosie's Room, a pale pink guest room with a queen poster bed.

Upstairs are a TV/study with 200 videos and a huge office for Eddie's insurance business, whose facilities are available for business guests. Sandy touts the side Rainsong Room, with kingsize bed and big walk-in shower, named for the pitter-patter of rain on the sloping tin roof (the room has no windows in evidence). The front Sunset Suite is an expanse as large as the office. It comes with a kingsize bed, sitting area, exercise equipment, one of the few rugs in the house and a bathroom bigger than most bedrooms.

The atmosphere is convivial and relaxed, according to Sandy, and – except for the lambs – quite un-farm-like. For a different experience, the Levins rent out their new **Downtown Porches,** a two-bedroom, fully-equipped 1920s cottage at 102 North Church St. in Fairhope, where Sandy stocks the refrigerator for continental breakfast. Yes, it has porches – both enclosed, in front and back.

(334) 928-4754 or (888) 227-8291. Fax (334) 928-4793. Two rooms and two suites with private baths. Doubles, $85 to $99. Suites $115 and $189. Children restricted. No smoking. Downtown cottage, $125 for two, $135 for four; two-night minimum stay.

Century-old hotel has been converted into Magnolia Springs Bed & Breakfast.

Magnolia Springs Bed & Breakfast, 14469 Oak St., Box 329. Magnolia Springs 36555.

In 1996, David Worthington bought a small, century-old hotel built in Magnolia Springs, ten miles southeast of Fairhope on the way to the Gulf beaches, and fulfilled a fifteen-year dream. An Alabama native, he had traveled widely for eight years with an insurance company and had spent eleven years in restaurant management – experiences that served him well to run a B&B.

Except, perhaps, for its wide great hall, the National Register landmark resembles a residence more than a hotel. A heart-pine porch wraps around the front and side. A glass-paneled door with its original wavy windowpanes opens into the hall. Throughout, the walls and ceilings are of bead-board yellow heart-pine. The floors are tongue and groove heart-pine and most of the woodwork is rare curly pine, which includes the trim around the bathroom medicine cabinets and even extends inside. Only the rear den, outfitted with a comfortable sectional and a TV, departs from the prevailing dark pine. Here, the walls are paneled in white pine. A focal point is the central chimney, from which emanate three fireplaces, two facing the dining room and one the great hall, which doubles as a sitting area.

The main-floor McLennan room with kingsize iron bed contains a bath with a clawfoot tub that David retrieved from the back yard. It also has a rare elephant trunk toilet, whose base is shaped like an elephant trunk. Upstairs is the Harding suite with a queensize bed and a large sitting room. Two more rooms have queensize beds and one contains a double and a twin. All have TV and telephone are appointed with colorful linens, quilts and fresh flowers.

As good as the facilities are, one guest volunteered, "the best part is the host." Hospitable David opens his kitchen to guests who raid the stocked refrigerator for his acclaimed sweet ice tea. In the angular, fireplaced dining room with three tables for four, he serves a full breakfast of fresh fruit with low-fat yogurt sauce and a main course, meats and cheese. The main dish varies from baked french toast to breakfast pizza to spinach and mushroom quiche.

Old Fairhope Colony home is now Church Street Inn.

So involved in promoting the B&B business is David that he quickly joined the state B&B association and, within two years, became president-elect.

(334) 965-7321 or (800) 965-7321. Four rooms and one suite with private baths. Doubles, $94 to $104. Suite, $104. Children welcome. No smoking.

Church Street Inn, 51 South Church St., Box 526, Fairhope 36533.
If you'd like to stay in an old Fairhope Colony home, this one built of white stucco in 1921 at the edge of downtown fits the bill. "People coming to Fairhope want to stay either downtown or on the water," says owner Becky Jones, who also runs Bay Breeze Guest House. She can fulfill either desire.

This is a family home last occupied by her late mother. It has three guest rooms, an expansive living room, dining room and a kitchen stocked with all the makings for a self-serve continental breakfast. The house is much as her mother left it – with a green bead divider in a doorway and a living room full of sofas, chairs and even a window seat, all slip-covered in ruby fabric. Becky shows a scrapbook of her mother as an Ivory Soap girl. Her portrait over the fireplace was done by a young artist who broke his neck diving off a Daphne pier and painted with a brush between his teeth.

A front bedroom offers a queen bed, TV and an abundance of quilts – on the walls, draped across a chair and on an extra twin bed – plus a secret passage that goes all around the upstairs of the house. On the main floor are a side guest room with a Jenny Lind queen bed and a rear room with a king poster bed. All are outfitted with antiques and family heirlooms from five generations.

Guests make themselves very much at home in this grandmotherly home. Out back is a snug rear courtyard and a fountain.

(334) 928-8976. Three rooms with private baths. Doubles, $85.

The Fairhope Inn & Restaurant, 63 South Church St., Fairhope 36532.
Until 1998, this turn-of-the-century residence was one of Fairhope's first guest

houses, with a catering business on the side. New owners came along and reversed the priorities, turning the main floor into a restaurant of distinction and taking in overnight guests in four bedrooms and a cottage.

Above the restaurant are three bedrooms with private baths and TV. The Green Room has a queen bed, a big club chair and one window. The Blue Room with a king bed has more windows. We stayed in the front Yellow Room, perfectly nice with twin beds and windows covered in yellow florals, a plush chaise lounge, a TV in a pine armoire and green carpeting. The only drawbacks were the noise from the restaurant and the fact the bathroom was across the hall, smack between the other two bedrooms.

More appealing were the rear Garden Room, behind the kitchen on the main floor, with a queen iron canopy bed, a window seat and two little chairs, and the side Carriage House facing a dining courtyard. A queen poster bed, settee, stained-glass window and french doors onto a patio were among its attributes. Curiously, despite the difference between accommodations, all were priced the same.

There is no common area and we breakfasted alone the next morning in the empty restaurant dining room, a rather creepy feeling. A housekeeper put out a buffet breakfast of orange juice, grits, bacon and biscuits and said there were "eggs if you wish," before disappearing. We did wish, and received two scrambled eggs as we were about to leave.

(334) 928-6226. Five rooms with private baths. Doubles, $95.

Marriott's Grand Hotel, One Grand Boulevard, Box 639, Point Clear 36564. Just down the road from Fairhope is this landmark resort dating to 1847. It's situated on a grand triangle of a point with water on two sides in Mobile Bay. It was truly grand and a favorite of regulars and locals for years when it was owned by local investors. Eventually they turned it over to the Marriott corporation to manage, and then were bought out. The Marriott made it into a resort, conference center and golf club. Locals dismiss it as "a place for the newly wed and nearly dead."

We've heard that before and, in this case, consider it a bum rap. Although no longer a "grand old hotel" dispensing white-glove service, it has all the amenities for a four-diamond rating. The waterfront setting and subtropical landscaping are grand indeed.

The hotel survived twenty hurricanes in its first 151 years, including one in 1979 that closed it for six months. In 1998, the eight-foot storm surge from Hurricane Georges submerged much of the 550-acre resort under six inches of water. And yet, at our visit two weeks afterward, the place showed remarkably few effects from the battering, except for some lost piers.

The heart of the main building is a circular lobby around a central fireplace, with the pine walls, floor and ceiling typical of the area. Tea and cookies are served here every afternoon. Restaurants, lounges and guest rooms go off the lobby in various directions, most along the bayfront. Some of the better accommodations are in the newer, outlying Marine House and North Bay House, and villas overlooking the golf course and a marina. At our first visit, we were well pleased with our balcony room on the second floor of the North Bay House, with all Mobile Bay on view just outside. True, we had a special-value package rate and it was a typical hotel/motel room with all the Marriott amenities. Dinner in the Bay View seafood restaurant (a grade below the nouvelle continental Grand

Fairhope Inn & Restaurant adds dining to what was first guest house.

Dining Room) was quite satisfying if unmemorable but for the view. Walking back to our room along the bayfront path, we felt grand indeed.

(334) 928-9201 or (800) 544-9933. Three hundred and six rooms and suites with private baths. Peak season, doubles, $199 to $219 weekends, $139 to $159 midweek. Winter, $114 to $124 weekends, $104 to $114 midweek.

Dining Spots

Fairhope Inn & Restaurant, 63 South Church St., Fairhope.

Restaurateur Mike Pair and his wife Gayle acquired the old Fairhope Guest Quarters in 1998 and converted the main floor into an elegant restaurant. The main dining room is stunning in white and black, with walls painted the color of café au lait. There's more seating in a smaller front parlor room painted a bright burgundy and on a glass-enclosed wraparound porch overlooking an outdoor dining courtyard.

The Pairs also run a pair of restaurants in Mandeville, La., near New Orleans. Mike said he found that in Fairhope, "a restaurant like this was waiting to happen." Superb food priced right, polished service and a select wine cellar produced instant success.

The pan sautéed crab cakes with a tomato caper tartar sauce proved worthy of its billing as the signature appetizer. We also liked the wilted spinach salad with fresh peaches and candied pecans and the seafood pasta of shrimp, crawfish and fried oysters in a basil alfredo sauce. Other choices on the short menu included caramelized salmon on grilled peach salsa, grilled pork mignons with an orange-grand marnier demi-glace, and beef tenderloin stuffed with wild mushrooms and spinach ragoût. Desserts were vanilla crème brûlée, banana bread pudding with white and dark chocolate sauce, and dark chocolate brownies with vanilla ice cream and caramel sauce.

Similar fare, with an emphasis on salads, is offered at lunch. The Sunday champagne brunch menu features a shrimp and eggplant frittata, poached eggs with crab cakes and stuffed pain perdu.

(334) 928-6226. Entrées, $12 to $19. Lunch, Wednesday-Saturday 11 to 3. Dinner, Wednesday-Sunday 5 to 9 or 10. Sunday brunch, 11 to 3.

The Wash House Restaurant, Highway 98, Point Clear.

Unless you knew about it, you probably would not stop at this shed-like structure that was the old kitchen and wash house behind the Victorian Broadbeck House, now home of Punta Clara Kitchen.

Venture inside and prepare to be charmed. Norris the waiter puts on quite a performance as he takes and serves your order from an old-school menu that rarely changes. There's usually only one cook in the kitchen, so the meal is leisurely. The ambiance of white-clothed tables with low-vaulted ceiling, pine walls and fireplace is quite appealing.

Fried artichoke hearts are the appetizer specialty, although you also can choose spicy fried crawfish tails, stuffed mushrooms and "steak fingers" (sliced filet, deep-fried and served with a special cherry-mustard sauce). Main courses come with soup du jour or gumbo and salad. Choices are all seafood, except for prime aged steaks. They include broiled or fried gulf shrimp or bay oysters, sautéed shrimp on fettuccine, seafood platter, lump crabmeat over rice and a casserole of lump crabmeat and smoked provolone cheese.

Desserts are described as "Old South," the selection changing daily.

(334) 928-1500. Entrées, $15.95 to $22.95. Dinner nightly, 5 to 9 or 10.

Aubergine, 315 De La Mare, Fairhope.

It's strange how an architecturally distinguished restaurant with an appealing menu survives so well in a town in which we find no local people who would recommend it. High prices, paltry portions and attitude seem to be the common denominator of perceived shortcomings. The place is undeniably stately, and obviously not lacking a clientele. It's a high-ceilinged space, whose walls and ceilings are painted various colors. Pinpoint lighting illuminates showy art on the walls and single wild irises in tall glass vases on white-linened tables.

The ambiance is urbane and haute, as is the continental cuisine given regional accents by chef-owner Ann Curtright Bridgeman and her chefs. Starters could be a tropical shrimp martini (marinated with a papaya and mango salsa), seafood marguery en coquille, escargots bourguignonne and baked oysters foch. Soft-shell crabs stuffed with crawfish, served with red pepper-garlic sauce, is a seasonal main dish. Others include flounder stuffed with crab and shrimp, roast chicken in brandy-tarragon sauce, and roast leg of lamb with mild pepper jelly glaze.

Chocolate roulade and crème brûlée are staples on the dessert menu.

(334) 928-9541. Entrées. $16.95 to $23.95. Lunch, Tuesday-Saturday 11 to 2. Dinner Tuesday-Sunday, 5:30 to 9:30. Sunday brunch, 11 to 2.

Bahai, 184 North Section St., Fairhope.

In a small town with many good restaurants, this newcomer was creating waves upon opening in late 1998.

Gulf Springs restaurateurs poured a fortune into renovating an old downtown warehouse into a sophisticated Latin American bistro. Flaming torches and palm trees are out front. Inside is a colorful, barrel-ceilinged space with distressed-look walls, elegant table settings and a choice bar alongside.

The menu is novel for the area, from a signature paella valenciana dish to grilled tenderloin served with avocado dip and yuca with mojo. The chicken might be sauced with garlic and white wine and the grouper sautéed with citrus juice. Rice and beans are the standard accompaniments.

Fifteen tapas are touted in a special menu detailing "the art of eating leisurely at the bar." There's no better bar around.

(334) 929-1008. Tapas, $3.50 to $6. Entrées, $14 to $26. Dinner, Tuesday-Sunday 5 to midnight.

Church Street Café, 9 North Church St., Fairhope.
The largest restaurant in town, this 250-seat establishment was admittedly in need of an infusion of new blood.

Owners Martha and Fred Watkins cajoled Andree Burton, former owner of Andree's Wine, Cheese & Things deli here and fresh out of culinary school, to take over as chef. She delivered an extensive menu of updated regional specialties. Early reports were that the inconsistency that had plagued the restaurant had vanished.

Consider starters like crab and artichoke bisque or "citified tomatoes," crispy fried green tomatoes on a bed of roasted red pepper sauce, sprinkled with feta cheese. Or entrées like southwestern chicken linguini with spicy black bean sauce, coastal crab cakes, sautéed peppercorn-encrusted oysters over pasta, crawfish étouffée, veal piccata or grilled lamb chops with chorizo sausage chutney. Desserts range from bread pudding topped with bourbon sauce to an ethereal Bailey's Irish Cream and coffee sabayon.

All this may be enjoyed in a variety of venues, from the Board Room to the main Magnolia Room with a big artificial tree in the middle to the bar and bistro to the outdoor side deck. Live jazz is presented Thursday-Saturday nights.

(334) 928-6611. Entrées, $10.95 to $19.95. Lunch and dinner, Monday-Wednesday 11 to 9, Thursday-Saturday 11 to 9:30.

The Royal Oak, 14 North Church St., Fairhope.
The Union Jack flies along the American flag outside, a red British phone booth stands alongside and James Field's English accent mixes with wife Lisa's Mississippi drawl inside. The Fields started in 1995 with an English pub in a quaint 1930s cottage. It proved such a hit that they broadened its size and appeal in 1997 with a large front garden room and a "more Americanized" menu.

The extensive menu features English sandwiches and traditional pub food. Among the latter are fish and chips (augmented here with mushy peas), cornish pasties, and steak and mushroom pie. Evening additions to the all-day menu include four pasta dishes, seafood choices from coconut fried shrimp to broiled cod, and roasted Lancashire chicken, roasted Aylesbury duckling and grilled strip steak.

(334) 928-1714. Entrées, $11.95 to $18.95. Open Monday, Wednesday and Thursday 11 to 3 and 5 to 10, Friday-Sunday 11 to 10. Closed Tuesday.

Jus' Gumbo Bar & Eatery, 2 South Church St., Fairhope.
The name says it all, basically, at this simple place full of local color in the heart of suave, uptown Fairhope. The interior looks like a lunch room and bar from the Acadian countryside, where the gumbo is good and the beer flows freely.

On a pleasant day, we prefer the picnic tables beside the sidewalk out front. Here you sit, watching the passing sidewalk activity beside a wall painted with a mural of the downtown street scene. You feast on a spicy gumbo, served with tabasco and La Hot Sauce on the side, assuaged by Pigs Eye beer or iced tea. The gumbo is served over rice with French bread and crackers, in small or large portions. Ours was so assertive it called for a handkerchief. "You know the gumbo us really good when it makes your nose run," the lady in charge advised. Those not so inclined can order red beans and rice, turkey or roast beef po-boy sandwiches, or combinations thereof. That's about it.

We adjourned next door to Mr. Gene's Beans for a sample of the famed Fairhope Float, iced moccachino and frozen yogurt topped with shaved chocolate and cinnamon. Umm, good.

(334) 928-4100. Gumbo, $3.95 or $5.95. Open Monday-Friday 11 to 8, Saturday 11 to 6.

Lafittes, 805 South Mobile Street, Fairhope.

This low-slung building covered by live oaks had housed many a short-lived restaurant and stood empty for four years. Three men with 75 years of restaurant background between them teamed up to reopen it with 150 seats in late 1998. They named it for the pirate Lafitte and hired a chef from New Orleans to prepare seafood and steaks.

For dinner, cajun alligator and onion bloom are favorite appetizers. Snapper, swordfish, halibut and mahi mahi are available, grilled or broiled. An early winner was the treasure chest dinner: a hefty seafood platter bearing shrimp, oysters, scallops, deviled crab and more, for $14.99. The ribeye steak also gets good reviews.

Hot apple dumpling and blueberry delight are popular desserts.

(334) 928-1288. Entrées, $7.99 to $26.99. Breakfast daily, 7 to 11. Lunch, 11 to 4. Dinner, 4 to 10 or 11.

Mary Ann's Deli, 7 South Church St., Fairhope.

The consensus favors Mary Ann's as *the* lunch spot in town. Mary Ann and John Nelson cater some of Fairhope's best parties. They share their talents at midday in a couple of dining rooms with a gourmet food store backdrop and on a pleasant courtyard with wrought-iron tables, a setting that matches the dream New Orleans-style townhouse they built behind. Here you'll find an extensive selection of salad plates, quiches and deli sandwiches. The Fairhope Special combines chicken salad with bacon, lettuce and tomato on a croissant.

(334) 928-3663. Sandwiches and salads, $4 to $6. Lunch, Monday-Saturday 11 to 3.

Diversions

Like the rest of Alabama's Eastern Shore, Fairhope's tourist attractions are low-key and must be sought out. Most visitors come to shop, eat, walk the waterfront and play golf, according to tourism officials.

Yet Fairhope is centrally located in an area that invites exploration. To the north are residential Montrose, bustling Daphne and Historic Blakeley State Park and Spanish Fort (the sites of the last two Civil War battles). To the south are Point Clear, atmospheric Magnolia Springs, wildlife refuges, Fort Morgan and the Gulf of Mexico beaches. Across the bay are the famed Bellingrath Gardens and Home.

Fairhope Single Tax Colony. Central to enjoying Fairhope is an understanding of its beginnings as a utopian community more than a century ago. Eighteen adults and nine children arrived by bay boat in 1894 to settle a colony founded on reformer Henry George's principal of "cooperative individualism." They first purchased 150 acres, including a half mile along the bayfront, and later bought 200 acres of farmland in what is now the downtown area. Today, the corporation owns more than 4,000 acres, about sixteen percent of the municipality, including residential and business lots. It leases land for 99 years and the lessees pay rent to the corporation, which pays city and state taxes and funds community improvements. The rent is the only tax paid. The concept is interesting and may be explored in the library of the **Fairhope Single Tax Corporation,** with offices and a council room in prime downtown quarters at 336-340 Fairhope Ave., 928-8162, (open Monday-Friday 9 to 5). The concept is also controversial – some today tout it as the ideal mix between the extremes of capitalism and communism; others call it creeping socialism. Some lots are leased and others are deeded (owned), and the colony works closely with the municipal government.

You need a local guide to point out salient features of the colony. It basically consists of the downtown and two residential sections, laid out in lots of 66 by 66 feet or multiples thereof, close to the common bayfront park and pier. Modest bungalows, including two early Sears, Roebuck mail-order homes, prevail in what is dubbed the "Fruit and Nut Section" for its streets named Orange, Kumquat, Pecan and the like. Others flank streets named Prospect, Freedom, Liberty, Equity and Equality. More substantial houses, many on larger lots, are found along Magnolia and Bayview avenues. All are said to be in great demand. The founder's family still lives here, and the colony is an influential part of the broader community today.

Another vestige of the early colony is the **Marietta Johnson Organic School,** which flourished for years on the site of what now is the Fairhope campus of Faulkner State Community College. The old school, admired by John Dewey, did not adhere to traditional grade levels but rather the organic theory in which children developed like blooming rose petals, as one local historian described it.

The Fairhope Pier and Bayfront Parks. One of the colonists' earliest endeavors was to build a municipal pier in 1895 for the bay boats that connected the Eastern Shore with Mobile and brought visitors to the early hotels. Now a cement pier, it extends a quarter mile into the bay and contains the Yardarm Restaurant and a boat marina. It's a community gathering point or, as the sign says, a place "for walkers, talkers and fishermen." A fountain and gardens at the foot of Fairhope Avenue identifies the start of the pier. The colony donated the beach and land on either side for municipal parks, giving Fairhope an unusual amount of public access to the bayfront. Fairhope and adjoining beaches from Point Clear to Daphne are known for an unusual **Jubilee Phenomenon.** It occurs in summertime when complex early morning conditions force shellfish, flounder and other bottom-dwellers to swarm for oxygen on the beach surfaces. It's a jubilee for fishermen and spectators, but ends at sunrise.

Montrose adjoins Fairhope to the north along Scenic Route 98. It mixes palatial bayfront homes with antebellum landmarks beneath live oak trees draped in spanish moss. Now a national historic district, its board owns the community post office. An historic plaque describes **Ecor Rouge,** the highest coastal point between Maine and Mexico (120 feet above sea level). The red cliff, a mariner's landmark on Spanish maps of the 1500s, was named by French settlers in the 1700s.

Point Clear, adjoining Fairhope to the south, takes its name from the promontory that shelters much of the rest of the Eastern Shore from high winds and waves. The Grand is the last of the pre-Civil War hotels, and a **Confederate Memorial Cemetery** is part of its grounds. The Point Clear Historic District south of the hotel includes 28 notable homes built between 1850 and 1930. Cottages extend east along the shore to the **Brodbeck-Zundel Historic District.**

Signs at piers along Mobile Bay describe Gulf sturgeon and historic sites.

Punta Clara Kitchen, Scenic Highway 98, Point Clear.
The 1897 landmark known as Miss Colleen's House, a National Register site,
is the home of Punta Clara (Point Clear) Kitchen. It's owned by Miss Colleen's
niece, Dorothy Brodbeck Pacey, and her family. Three generations of Paceys
help staff the kitchen, which started in 1952 as a backyard hobby. Family recipes
are used to produce the fudge, pralines, covered pecans, preserves and jellies that
are sold here, in a downtown Fairhope shop and through a mail-order catalog.
This is a favorite stop for visitors, as much for the house interior as for the kitchen.
It's a veritable museum, furnished as it was at the turn of the century. You get to
peer into the clutter of the parlor, the bedroom once shared by four girls and the
master bedroom. Typewritten signs itemize the furnishings you're looking at.
(334) 928-8477 or (800) 437-7868. Open Monday-Saturday 9 to 5, Sunday 12:30 to 5.

Shopping. More than 75 shops are located across several downtown blocks
and courtyards centered around Fairhope Avenue and Section Street. Baskets of
hanging flowers cascade from lamp poles and sidewalk flower boxes, changing
with the seasons. Some of the sidewalks are flanked by memorial bricks, which
people purchase for $65 to have their say for posterity. They make for interesting
reading. We found a brick engraved with "Only a fool says there is no God '96"
next to one by "Two Musketeers, the Fearsome Fivesome and an Angel, 11/22/95."
The sayings keep people amused while their spouses shop. Women shoppers often
park their spouses in the rocking chairs outside Fairhope Hardware store.
Fairhope has no souvenir shops, as such. The **Fairhope Pharmacy** is the only
place to get a local postcard, and offers only three selections at that. Nor is there
a franchise store or restaurant in town, unless the new Orvis section at **Middle
Bay Outfitters** qualifies. Owner Jack West attracts attention as he gives fly-
fishing lessons on the corner of Fairhope Avenue and North Church Street. Beyond
East Bay Clothiers for Men is **Old Bay Mercantile,** a potpourri of antiques,
furniture, fine jewelry and collectibles. Nearby is **Bountiful Home,** a home
furnishings shop in a house that opened in 1986 as Fairhope's first B&B.
Art and craft galleries abound. Artists feature their own works at **Watercolors
by Willoweise** (Langham) and the new **Jim Gray Gallery**, where we picked up

a bird painting by daughter-manager Laurie Gray Schmohl. Potter Cathy Ginder has a studio at her home, and Tom Jones has a pottery east of town. We liked the hand-painted canoe paddles and Adirondack chairs outside **The Studio Over the Bay** and were enticed inside by all the whimsical, impressionist work by mostly Alabama artists. **Iron Age Gallery** specializes in an amazing variety of blacksmith and iron works.

Special interests are satisfied by **In the Company of Angels.** Lynn Boothe offers room after room of collectibles, figurines, fashion jewelry, dishware, cards and gourmet coffees at **Objects.** Carved pelican sculptures and local crafts caught our eye at **The Obvious Place.** Our favorite MacKenzie-Childs pottery is among the stock at **Christine's By the Bay. Over the Transom** carries rare books and self-publishes books for paying authors.

Fashion-conscious women of varying tastes are served at places like **The Colony Shop, C.K. Collection, M&F Casuals, Kathy Lambert's, Uptown** and **Dock of the Bay.** There's much more. We defy any shopper to leave Fairhope empty-handed.

Extra-Special

Magnolia Springs.
This picturesque old community hidden beneath oversize live oaks alongside the Magnolia River is one of the few remaining places to receive mail by boat. It's the Old South of vintage postcards, enjoying a new lease on life. First, the old hotel along Oak Street was converted into the Magnolia Springs Bed & Breakfast (see Inn Spots). Then came Charlie and Janie Houser, who renovated his grandfather's stately old riverfront homestead, known as the Governor's Club for the guests it hosted in years past. Charlie remembered the old Moore Bros. General Store where he used to charge his grandfather's account for penny candy and wanted to revive a community tradition. He bought the store (which had closed in 1993) and the abandoned post office and merged the two buildings. In 1998, **Moore Brothers Fresh Market** reopened with the best produce, butcher shop, bakery, deli, coffees and wines for miles around. The onetime post office was transformed into **Jesse's,** a 35-seat restaurant named for Jesse King, a fixture at Moore's store (it's said he never missed a day of work in 60 years). The fare cooked by a husband and wife team from New Orleans packs in the crowds, day and night. Indeed, the sea of cars overflowing from the parking lot into the roadway across from St. Paul's Episcopal Church and the 1894 Community Hall one Saturday noon turned out not to be for church or a festival. They belonged to shoppers and people waiting for tables in the restaurant or lunches for takeout from the deli. The lunch menu details fabulous deli sandwiches and salads. One big eater of our acquaintance said he ordered a Jesse's po-boy that turned out to be an entire loaf of French bread with a dozen oysters at one end and fresh shrimp at the other. It was so big he had to give half away. The dinner menu offers Louisiana specialties like shrimp or crawfish creole, stuffed mirleton and whiskey steak. Photographs of old Magnolia Springs along the walls add nostalgia.

Jesse's, 14470 Oak St., Magnolia Springs. (334) 965-6020. Entrées, $8.95 to $15.95. Lunch, Monday-Saturday 11 to 2:30. Dinner, 5 to 9.

Diverse flags that have flown over Amelia Island are unfurled along porch at Florida House.

Fernandina Beach/Amelia Island, Fla.
Isle of Eight Flags

The eight flags that have flown over historic Amelia Island are unfurled daily across the front of Florida's oldest surviving hotel.

They add color to the evocative, two-tone green and red facade of the Florida House Inn. And they add to the festive feeling of an island with a swashbuckling past, a developing present and a promising future.

Amelia Island is a thirteen-mile-long stretch of sand and palms northeast of Jacksonville. Separated from Georgia only by the Cumberland Sound, Florida's northernmost barrier island more resembles Georgia's Golden Isles than Florida in its climate, topography and lifestyle. Its location at what was the early frontier of Florida explains its shifting fortunes. Discovered by the French in 1562, it has been ruled by Spanish, British, pirates, patriots and Confederates – the only U.S. territory to have survived under eight different flags.

Touted as "The Queen of Summer Resorts" by American Resorts magazine in 1896, the island lost its initial luster as Henry Flagler's railroad drew tourists to the "new Florida" farther south. Fernandina Beach, the island's only town, became embedded in a Victorian time capsule – a Southern copy of what happened up north to Cape May, N.J.

Development occurred rather lately as the Amelia Island Plantation and Ritz-Carlton resorts lured vacationers for broad beaches and 90 holes of golf. The opening of the Ritz in 1990 gave the island cachet, and sleepy Fernandina Beach awoke with a flurry of upscale inns and B&Bs, restaurants and shops. With 450 ornate structures built before 1927 and few since, the 50-block historic district was ripe for the Victorian B&B experience.

The island is more a "feeling" than an array of tourist attractions. Other than golfing and beaching, the main pastime for visitors is to walk the streets of Fernandina's historic district, soaking up the richest concentration of Victorian architecture between Cape May and Key West. Besides the oldest hotel, the town offers Florida's oldest saloon and its only oral history museum. It's the shrimping capital of America, and stages an annual Shrimp Festival the first weekend of May.

Amelia Island is making up for lost time in terms of development, and locals wonder what the new century has in store. But the core town of Fernandina Beach will remain attached to its past, drawing visitors who prefer it that way.

Inn Spots

Elizabeth Pointe Lodge, 98 South Fletcher Ave., Fernandina Beach 32034.

David and Susan Caples got their start in 1980 with Amelia Island's original B&B and lodging service, the five-room 1734 House down the street. They knew exactly what to do when this oceanfront property harboring two dilapidated cottages became available.

"We built the shore house we always wanted," said Susan, a native Philadelphian who was partial to the beachy look of New England and the Jersey Shore. She and David, a New Yorker, favored the shingled, summery Nantucket look of The Wauwinet, a recently restored Nantucket resort, where they spent a fortuitous week.

Their 1890s Nantucket-style lodge with a maritime theme bears an unmistakable resemblance in look and feel to The Wauwinet. It has snug common areas and a breezy wraparound porch oriented toward the ocean on the main floor, plus twenty stylish guest rooms on two upper floors. Five newer accommodations are in two adjacent cottages. All share the personal service and amenities of a small boutique hotel.

Half the rooms in the main lodge yield head-on views of the ocean through big windows. All have oversize marble baths with tubs, eleven of the whirlpool variety. Beds are king or queensize. Decor in each is somewhat different. "David and I

each decorated half, and guests have fun trying to guess which one of us did which room," says Susan. They usually guess wrong. Each is light and airy, with understated fabrics and a nautical motif. Televisions are hidden in unusual pine armoires custom-made for the Jekyll Island Millionaires Club. Each armoire is identical in shape but stained differently to match the character of the room. Oceanfront rooms are on the small side, with only one chair for seating and no access to the outside. "Sunset rooms" facing the street are decidedly larger. Those we saw had two chairs and a chaise lounge.

Four suites in the Harris Lodge just north of the main structure come with sitting rooms and command top dollar. The Miller Cottage to the south offers two bedrooms and two baths and sleeps up to four.

Guests mingle in an angular living room/library open to the busy lobby but with a warming stone fireplace and windows onto the water. The staff serves complimentary wine, cheese and hors d'oeuvres during a nightly social hour at 6. Tea, lemonade and cookies are available much of the day. A light menu of soups, salads and sandwiches is offered from after breakfast until midnight.

The dining room with its big windows conveys the feeling of a ship. A friend built the cabinets around the perimeter to hold the substantial breakfast spread each morning. Domed chafing dishes contained Texas scrambled eggs, grits and cheesy potatoes the day we were there, and there were plenty of fruits and pastries alongside. The meal is taken at communal tables, or on white rockers on the porch facing the ocean beyond the dunes.

Owners David and Susan Caples at Elizabeth Pointe Lodge.

"We're so blessed with the location and being able to have the inn become what we wanted it to be," says Susan. Their success has given them considerable reputation in the lodging industry. They run monthly seminars for aspiring innkeepers and give pointers as consultants to their colleagues.

(904) 277-4851 or (888) 201-7618. Fax (904) 277-6500. Twenty rooms, four suites and one cottage with private baths. Doubles, $140 to $185. Suites, $160 to $215. Cottage, $235. No smoking.

The Amelia Island Williams House, 103 South 9th St., Fernandina Beach 32034.

Fernandina Beach's oldest house (1856) has become its most sumptuous B&B, thanks to the vision and resources of transplanted Northerners who were living in Palm Beach. Dick Flitz, a banker and sometime actor-director, and Chris Carter, a jewelry designer, took one look at the house and knew their dreamed-of B&B was meant to be. They made repairs, stripped and refinished the woodwork and hung 350 rolls of wallpaper in a six-month refurbishing that is portrayed in a fascinating photo album called "Before, During and After." Soon after opening in

1994, they acquired the rundown duplex house next door, gutted the interior and doubled their size from four rooms to eight.

The two houses offer some of the most elegant accommodations in the country, amid priceless antiques and pampering touches from nightly turndown service to gourmet breakfasts. Words and photos fail to do justice to the aura and accoutrements of this lived-in museum.

With his theater background and museum-quality collections passed through his illustrious family, Dick designed each guest room as a stage set to reflect a different country – the better to intrigue a worldly clientele.

The biggest is the Chinese Blue, a front-corner extravaganza. It has the inn's only kingsize bed, one of its five in-room working fireplaces, a loveseat in the bay window and a luxurious master bath across the hall. The smallest is the Camelot Chambers, an old English hideaway with a gauze-draped English wrought-iron canopy queen bed, a semi-open bathroom with the original built-in armoire and, crowning touch, a private porch beside a 500-year-old live oak, the oldest in town. Said porch comes with a whirlpool spa overlooking the garden and a cistern in which eighteen Japanese koi reside.

Amelia's Victorian Room is the partners' tribute to America. It has a nine-foot-high mahogany headboard, a Tiffany chandelier, a fireplace, marble-topped furniture and a bath with clawfoot soaking tub and two-person shower. It almost pales next to the Manchu Dynasty Suite, in which the headboard has been fashioned from a rare Chinese wedding bed. The rosewood lamp, desk and vase typify the stunning antiques throughout the house. The sitting room contains a 19th-century side lock chest, whose credentials are outlined in a yellowed newspaper clipping stowed in the top drawer. The bathroom, luxurious in red and gold, has a two-person shower. There's a rare bedroom set of black mahogany in the Leonardo Da Vinci Room.

Surely the Versailles Bridal Suite with a marble fireplace is the ultimate. The eight-foot-high headboard for the queen bed is a four-panel wooden French screen worthy of royalty. Its fourteen-by-sixteen-foot bath, bigger than most bedrooms, is complete with a white marble double jacuzzi, a two-person shower, a dressing table, a French loveseat, an oriental carpet and a crystal chandelier.

Lavish though the rooms are, creature comforts are not overlooked. Each room has a TV/VCR with extensive film library, hair dryer and ice bucket. And the most prized possessions with the rarest pedigrees are shared in public areas. The red and gold silk child's robe worn by the last emperor of China is displayed above the piano in the living room. Nearby are oriental cloisonnés, Japanese block prints and two Forbidden Stitches badges from the late 1500s. A rare prayer rug given by Napoleon to Dick's great-great-great grandfather hangs in the upstairs hallway. Another hallway holds two pictures of the Pilgrims, in which Dick points out "my ninth-great-grandfather," the first child born on the Mayflower. "It was almost prophetic that these pictures turned up at an antiques shop here in town," he says.

Most guests bring their cameras to breakfast. It's served from 8:30 to 10 in a remarkably elegant red and gold dining room. The intricate inlaid table is set with Royal Bristol china that belonged to Dick's grandmother. Typical fare might be broiled grapefruit on a fruit platter garnished with camellias and an egg quiche or blueberry-stuffed french toast. The afternoon brings refreshing iced tea laden with kiwis, strawberries and raspberries, plus homemade cookies and gorgeous cakes. Wine and cheese are offered from 5 to 8. When the triple-sheeted beds are

Dining room is set elegantly for breakfast at Amelia Island Williams House.

turned down at nightfall, expect to find a carafe of ice water and a swan card drawn by two angels bearing chocolate truffles and bidding sweet dreams.

Although the Williams House is dramatic and extravagant, it is neither overwhelming nor pretentious. Photos of the partners' families are displayed here and there to lend intimacy, and the hosts make guests feel at home. The difference is that this home is like a good museum. Guests keep coming back to take it all in.

(904) 277-2328 or (800) 414-9258. Fax (904) 321-1325. Six rooms and two suites with private baths. Doubles, $145 to $155. Suites, $165 to $205. Two-night minimum weekends. Children over 12. No smoking.

The Fairbanks House, 227 South Seventh St., Fernandina Beach 32034.

Its stunning architecture and the surrounding property attracted Theresa and Bill Hamilton to The Fairbanks House. "We'd been looking for an inn for four years and our search ended here," said Theresa. They persuaded founding innkeepers Nelson and Mary Smelker to sell in 1998.

They inherited a going operation and most of the furnishings, and kept everything the same for a year before handyman Bill, a former engineer/contractor in Maryland, started to undertake refinements.

The 1885 Italianate villa, created by famed architect Robert Schuyler and listed on the National Register, is an eye-popper that's impossible to miss. Converted from six luxury apartments, it sits back from the street on a property that takes up most of a square block, complete with a swimming pool, gardens and three cottages.

Off one side of the imposing entry foyer is a lovely pink and white living room with a rare Shakespearean tiled fireplace. The room opens through pocket doors

Fairbanks House cossets guests in stunning 1885 Italianate villa.

to a formal dining room with another tiled fireplace. Two guest rooms are on the opposite side of the foyer.

The house contains six bedrooms and three suites, all but one with working fireplaces. All come with fancy bathrooms, king or queensize beds, TV/HBO, telephone, hair dryers, irons, stocked refrigerators and in-room coffeemakers. Kitchenettes in most are rather startling vestiges of their apartment heritage. All decidedly different, they bear the ingenious and showy decor of the founding innkeeper, who made most of the canopies, bedspreads and window treatments herself. Antiques and oriental rugs prevail. Bathrooms have jacuzzi or clawfoot tubs.

We'd opt for one of the midsize rooms with sitting areas in the bay windows, or one of the rear suites with a fireplaced sitting room and a private porch overlooking the pool area. We would not particularly want to rattle around in the enormous third-floor Tower Suite, a low-slung apartment space with two bedrooms, a cozy reading room and an open kitchen/living/dining area, even with its access to the rooftop tower for a four-sided view around town. It served well as the former innkeepers' quarters.

Three appealing rear cottages are summery in wicker. Two have jacuzzis and one has two bedrooms.

The Hamiltons serve a sumptuous breakfast in the dining room or on the side porch. Expect to start with something like banana sorbet with kiwi sauce or spiced peaches with pecans. Florentine quiche with turkey ham or peach upside-down french toast could follow.

Hands-on innkeepers who live in a rear cottage, the Hamiltons offer wine and beer along with hors d'oeuvres at an afternoon social hour, plus a friendly atmosphere and great comfort.

(904) 277-0500 or (800) 261-4838. Fax (904) 277-3103. Six rooms, three suites and three cottages with private baths. Doubles, $125 to $175. Suites, $195 to $225. Cottages, $175. Children over 12. No smoking.

Bailey House, 28 South Seventh St., Fernandina Beach 32034.
Another architectural showplace listed on the National Register, this Queen Anne beauty was built by mail-order plans from architect George W. Barber of Tennessee. Owners Tom and Jenny Bishop matched the original in 1997 when they built a side addition that flows so well one cannot tell where old ends and new begins.

"This house drew us from Jacksonville," Tom said of their move four years earlier. They bought the property as a residence, converting the attic into family quarters, and inherited the existing B&B as a sideline. Tom's business foundered, Jenny's B&B took off "and now I'm working for her," Tom quipped.

Original heart pine floors, pine molding and wainscoting, fireplaces, pocket doors and stained-glass windows have been retained in the main house and added in the new. Furnished in stately Victoriana, the five original bedrooms appear larger than their new counterparts. Three have clawfoot tubs and two have fireplaces. Two add an extra twin or day bed, and one has two extra twin beds.

All four new rooms have marble fireplaces and two have whirlpool tubs. The Queen Anne offers a handcarved kingsize mahogany bed with an almost-matching carved antique dresser and armoire. A massive captain's chest is beside the door to Kate's Room. Bold wallpapers, oriental rugs and generally solid Victorian furnishings are the rule. TV sets are hidden in armoires.

Unusual antique brass corner plates catch the eye on each step of the two staircases to the second floor.

Breakfast is served in a small formal dining room and overflows into the adjacent parlor, where a table is sited in the turret. Sausage quiche was offered the day of our visit. Baked french toast and frittatas are other favorites.

(904) 261-5390 or (800) 251-5390. Nine rooms with private baths. Doubles, $95 to $140. Two-night minimum weekends. Children over 8. No smoking.

Hoyt House, 804 Atlantic Ave, Fernandina Beach 32034.
A spreading live oak screens this handsome pale yellow house with robin's-egg-blue trim from the town's main intersection. The house, built for a banker in 1905, is a replica of the Rockefeller Cottage on nearby Jekyll Island. A lawyer rescued it from demolition and turned it into a law office before John and Rita Kovacevich from New York happened by, saw the for-sale sign and converted the structure in 1993 into a welcoming B&B.

The Kovaceviches built a rear addition and put in eleven bathrooms. Rita decorated with great style the two living rooms, the formal dining room and the diverse guest rooms.

John's collection of giraffes – ranging from miniatures to more than six feet tall – is a focal point of the turreted living room. His wife's stuffed animals and dolls turn up everywhere else.

The bedrooms are markedly different in terms of decor – "a real collage," John calls it. A teddybear rests on a chair beneath a palm tree in the king-bedded room called Rainforest Green. The bathroom is wallpapered with bookshelves in the Regal Blue Room. The bed is in an unusual bay with four windows in the Desert Sunset Room. Some rooms have antique wash basins. All have TVs and telephones. Beds are king or queensize, as Rita insisted on comfort to accompany decor.

Her artistry shows up at the breakfast table, too. A baked omelet sandwich was the fare at our visit. Rita is also known for her bread pudding made with french bread and her hole-in-one eggs served in a hole in a bread loaf. The meal is taken at a table for eight beneath one of the chandeliers for which the house is notable. The shady, landscaped grounds include a garden gazebo.

(904) 277-4300 or (800) 432-2085. Fax (904) 277-9626. Ten rooms with private baths. Doubles, $104 to $144. No smoking.

Florida House Inn, 22 South Third St., Fernandina Beach 32034.

For an old tourist hotel, this offers exceptional comfort and charm.

Built in 1857 by the Florida Railroad, the oldest surviving hotel in Florida had housed Ulysses S. Grant and fed the Carnegies and Rockefellers before falling into disrepair. Bob and Karen Warner bought the 25-room boarding house in 1990 and closed for a year's renovations. They reopened with eleven guest rooms with modern baths and a restaurant serving boarding-house-style meals of wide renown (see Dining Spots).

"This is an old boarding-house hotel, not a B&B home," advises Karen. But the Warners have transformed it into the next best thing. They live on the hotel's third floor and oversee every detail with T.L.C.

They stripped countless coats of paint back to the original heart pine flooring and doors, and endowed their guest rooms with stunning, jade green Charleston tiled baths with clawfoot tubs or jacuzzis. Nine rooms have working fireplaces. Except for two rooms with twins, beds are queen or kingsize. Each is individually decorated in a crisp country look. Television, telephones, mints and bottled water are provided.

Karen's collection of more than 75 quilts – some made by her grandmother – are shown to good advantage on beds and walls. Two stored atop a tall armoire in an upstairs hallway made a plump resting spot for one of the house cats to observe the goings-on as we passed through. Another cat snoozed on a bar stool in the cozy pub, where Bob stocks quite an assortment of beers.

Verandas run the width of the first and second floors and offer the requisite rockers upon which guests relax and watch the world go by. The eight flags associated with Amelia Island's history fly overhead.

Behind the hotel is an expansive brick courtyard with wrought-iron furniture shaded by a live oak. In the restaurant, guests enjoy an ample Southern breakfast. The blackboard listed fruit salad, granola, blueberry pancakes, grilled ham, danish and apricot bread when we were there.

In 1998, the Warners added four deluxe guest rooms with king beds, two-person jacuzzi tubs and wood-burning fireplaces in an addition called Tree House Row. It's a new second story above the rear function room and overlooks the courtyard.

(904) 261-3300 or (800) 258-3301. Fourteen rooms and one two-bedroom suite with private baths. Doubles, $69 to $159. Suite $149. Children and pets welcome. Smoking restricted.

Dining Spots

The Beech Street Grill, 801 Beech St., Fernandina Beach.

This gingerbread-trimmed sea captain's estate with tiered wraparound verandas and a series of side annexes holds a ramble of dining rooms pretty in peach and green. Chase McQuarry's five-year-old restaurant is widely regarded as the town's best for fine wining and dining.

The fare is a testament to regional and contemporary cuisine. Look for starters

Abandoned bungalow provided charming home for French restaurant called Le Clos.

like Low Country seafood gumbo, chilled coconut and crab bisque, steamed dumplings with kim-chi or duck ravioli with an Asian beurre blanc and marinated seaweed salad.

Crab-stuffed local shrimp with tasso ham gravy, grouper encrusted with macadamia nuts, grilled duck breast with ancho chile and tropical fruit salsa, and roasted venison loin with black currant sauce typify the main dishes. Chived whipped potatoes, spicy Asian slaw and sweet potato hash are among the sides. Dessert could be chocolate truffle torte, white chocolate cheesecake or bread pudding with bourbon hard sauce. The 200-label wine list has been honored by Wine Spectator.

In 1998, Beech Street opened two other restaurants and briefly operated a third, our favorite Café Atlantis, when the original owner left. The new restaurants are the beachy **Terrace at the Beachside Commons,** 2900 Atlantic Ave., and **River Place Café,** a funky, cafeteria-style seafood haunt by the water off Route A1A at the Shave Bridge. Although the last in particular has many devotees, the grill remains the mainstay for fine dining.

(904) 277-3662. Entrées, $16.95 to $24.95. Dinner nightly, 5:30 to 10.

Le Clos, 20 South Second St., Fernandina Beach.

The most charming restaurant in town was opened in 1997 in a little yellow house by Katherine Ewing, a Le Cordon Bleu graduate who trained at the Ritz Hotel in Paris. She took an abandoned 1906 residence and transformed it into a welcoming restaurant resembling those of the French countryside.

"I always wanted to do this," she said as she distributed fresh flowers around the arty, gray and white dining room, where wine bottles and candles stand tall on each table. "I hate cute, but I became the queen of cute."

She produces provençal fare of considerable distinction. Start with her pork and chicken liver pâté or smoked Scottish salmon with traditional accompaniments.

Her fish of the day, scrawled in large letters on a huge blackboard, was crab cakes with pineapple relish at our spring visit. Other main dishes include scampi over homemade pasta, coquilles St. Jacques, poached chicken breast with Indian curries and spices, braised lamb shank and sautéed veal chop. A salad of organic field greens comes with.

Save room for one of Katherine's acclaimed desserts, among them French pastries, pear compote, chocolate mousse and crème caramel.

(904) 261-8100. Entrées, $17 to $23. Dinner, Tuesday-Saturday 5:30 to 9 or 9:30.

Joe's 2nd Street Bistro, 14 South Second St., Fernandina Beach.

Featuring new American cuisine with international accents, Joe Robucci's bistro opened to rave reviews in 1998. We weren't surprised, since his stylish Café Allègre had been wildly popular before it lamentably closed in our home area outside Hartford, Conn. Here you can eat by the fountain on a New Orleans-style courtyard, or at white-linened tables in an intimated, 60-seat dining room with an islands theme in a restored early 1900s house.

The dinner menu ranges widely from seafood paella, sautéed red snapper with sweet pepper coulis and shrimp étoufée to pecan-breaded breast of duck with spiced currant sauce, grilled leg of lamb with wine-honey glaze and filet mignon with chili sauce and fried oysters. The antelope au poivre with Szechwan peppercorns, wild mushrooms and scallion sauce sounds sensational.

Among starters are crab cakes with tropical tartar sauce and roast duck cappellini. Desserts are stellar, as they were in Hartford. Consider champagne sabayon, pecan-studded rum baba, chocolate banana bread pudding or grand marnier parfait.

The courtyard menu features focaccia pizzas and interesting light fare for dinner outside.

(904) 321-2558. Entrées, $17 to $23. Dinner nightly except Monday, 5:30 to 9:30.

The Southern Tip, 4802 First Coast Highway, Amelia Island.

Housed in one of the Southern-style structures in the Palmetto Walk shopping complex, this is a good bet for lunch as well as dinner. The setting is refined and the fare new American. Richard and Lisa Schmidt, who trained at the Ritz Carlton nearby, offer an intimate bar and downstairs dining room and a larger dining room upstairs.

The Cuban sandwich – roasted pork loin with spiced cheese and chipotle bean spread on a toasted hoagie roll – makes an unusual lunch. Or you can order a turkey BLT or a marinated Greek salad.

For dinner, expect main courses like seared mahi-mahi with pepper-mango sauce, herb-roasted chicken with olive-grape salsa, roasted pork tenderloin with cherry-fig chutney and grilled beef tenderloin with melted cambozola cheese and wild mushroom ragoût.

Dessert could be key lime pie with a trio of fruit sauces, chocolate-cappuccino mousse cake or pecan-crusted New York-style cheesecake.

(904) 261-6184. Entrées, $15.95 to $21.95. Lunch daily, 11:30 to 2. Dinner nightly 6 to 9.

Florida House Inn, 22 South Third St., Fernandina Beach.

It's fitting that Florida's oldest surviving hotel would reinstate the boarding-house dining room and down-home style that drew the Carnegies and Rockefellers in years past. The food is good, the price is right and the experience full of local color.

You sit at one of four communal tables for twelve in what looks to be a dining hall. Servers bring you a glass and a plate, along with pitchers of sweetened and unsweetened iced tea and a tray of relishes and munchies. The day's menu is posted on a blackboard, but there's always fried chicken plus a special (roasted quail when we were there). The food comes family style in heaping platters and bowls. Vegetables were collard greens, field peas, okra and stewed tomatoes, broccoli with cream sauce and honey-glazed sweet potatoes. Biscuits and cornbread accompanied. Desserts were fruit crumble or banana pudding. People come and go, and everyone gets more than enough to eat.

Cocktails, wine and beer from the cozy English-style pub may be enjoyed on the shady rear courtyard.

A slightly smaller version of the dinner extravaganza is available at lunch for $6.98.

(904) 261-3300 or (800) 258-3301. Dinner, prix-fixe, $11.98. Lunch, Monday-Saturday 11:30 to 2:30. Dinner, Tuesday-Saturday 5:30 to 9. Sunday brunch, 10:30 to 2.

Brett's Waterway Cafe, foot of Centre Street, Fernandina Beach.

The only in-town restaurant facing the Intracoastal Waterway, Brett Carter's contemporary establishment at the Fernandina Harbor Marina draws the tourists in droves. It drew us, too, for lunch at our first visit, before smaller restaurants emerged with more innovative fare.

Windows on three sides of the dining room take full advantage of the waterfront setting. The standard continental/American menu touches all the bases, from shrimp scampi and grilled chicken to steak au poivre.

If you have to wait for a table, check out the Carter Enterprises' **Front and Centre** store, full of unusual memorabilia.

(904) 261-0042. Entrées, $14.95 to $23.95. Lunch, Monday-Saturday 11:30 to 2:30. Dinner nightly from 5:30.

The Golden Grouper, 201 Alachua St., Fernandina Beach.

The McCarthy family got their start with their rustic Down Under seafood restaurant, ensconced since 1982 on the Intracoastal Waterway beneath the Route A1A bridge at the entrance to Amelia Island. They upscaled a bit at this large downtown newcomer, dressed in fishhouse decor and known for fresh seafood.

The namesake grouper is cajun-seasoned and baked in garlic butter, broiled in margarine or dusted with flour and deep fried in peanut oil. The fried shrimp is based on a signature Down Under recipe. Other dinner possibilities include soft-shell crabs, ginger-glazed tuna, baja mahi-mahi, fried oysters, Maine lobster and mixed grill of scallops, shrimp, grouper and crab cake. Stuffed chicken breast and charbroiled strip steak pacify the meat-eaters.

Spicy grouper fingers, grilled red pepper shrimp and conch fritters are among starters. Key lime pie is the favored dessert.

(904) 261-0013. Entrées, $13.95 to $20.95. Lunch, 11:30 to 3:30. Dinner, 5 to 9. Closed Monday.

Diversions

The ocean is the draw for many. The white Appalachian quartz beaches framed by magnificent dunes are mild in winter and cooling in summer.

Historic Fernandina. Billed as a quaint Victorian seaport, the 50-block historic district is listed on the National Register. The "seaport" today is not much more than a harbor marina and the home base of the nation's largest shrimping fleet. Nearly 80 percent of Florida's sweet Atlantic white shrimp are harvested in Amelia's waters. A bronze and copper monument to Fernandina shrimpers sits atop a twelve-foot tower of granite. Visitors may watch the return of the shrimp boats and tour the Burbank Trawl Makers (known as the Net House to locals), the world's largest producer of handmade shrimp nets. Next door to the Net House is Standard Marine (at North Second and Alachua), one of the largest marine hardware stores and suppliers of shrimping gear on the East Coast. Just east of the docks is the 1899 depot for Florida's first cross-state railroad, now the Chamber of Commerce visitor center, and a replica caboose.

More than 400 structures were built prior to 1927. A walking tour leads visitors past the most historic business buildings along Centre Street and the sherbet-hued, Victorian mansions of the Silk Stocking District. The latter are concentrated along South Seventh, North Sixth and Alachua streets. Adorned with the opulent gingerbread of the period, they include Queen Anne, Italianate, Chinese Chippendale, Florida Vernacular and Mississippi Steamboat masterpieces.

Replica gas lanterns, benches, floral planters bedecked with bright red begonias and cobblestone walks front the multi-hued brick buildings of palm-lined Centre Street, the main business thoroughfare. Among the landmarks is the Palace Saloon, Florida's oldest watering hole. Adorned with handpainted murals, it looks like a saloon of the wild west. A potent Pirate's Punch is dispensed from a 40-foot-long mahogany bar graced by handcarved caryatids. Up the street is the Nassau County Courthouse, built in 1891 and considered the finest surviving Victorian courthouse in Florida. Equally impressive is the 1912 post office, a three-story edifice. Beside it is the Lesesne House, a handsome Southern residence built in 1860. South Seventh is notable for the Tabby House, built of crushed oyster shells, and the four stunning Egmont houses, constructed in 1901 of lumber from the old Egmont Hotel on the site.

Horse-drawn carriage tours of the historic district are offered by Old Towne Carriage Co., 277-1555. Sea Horse Stable, 261-4878, offers beachside horseback riding.

Amelia Island Museum of History, 233 South Third St., Fernandina Beach.

The renovated 1935 county jail houses Florida's only oral history museum. Displays and live interpretation portray the island's history from aboriginal Indian settlements to 18th-century plantations to the present. The museum also conducts walking tours of the historic district Thursday and Friday afternoons at 3. *(904) 261-7378. Open Monday-Saturday, 11 to 2.*

Fort Clinch State Park, 2601 Atlantic Ave., Fernandina Beach.

This park has 8,400 feet of shoreline along the Atlantic Ocean, Cumberland Sound and the Amelia River. Its focal point is the brick outpost begun in 1847 by the federal government. It was occupied first by Confederate forces and then Union troops during the Civil War, and abandoned after the Spanish-American War. The walled fort's history comes alive as park rangers, clad in Union uniforms, carry out the daily chores of the garrison soldier and answer questions as if the year were 1864. Special full-garrison re-enactments and candlelight tours are offered periodically. The visitor center houses exhibits explaining the fort's history. The park is also home to unspoiled beaches, a nature trail that winds through a coastal hummock and around a manmade pond, a 1,500-foot fishing pier and the island's only campgrounds. *(904) 277-7274. Park open daily, 8 to sundown; fort, 9 to 5. Park admission: $3.25 per vehicle. Fort $1.*

Golf. Leading golf-course architects have incorporated Amelia Island's natural beauty – from ocean bluffs to intracoastal marshes – to create 90 holes of great golf. The 27-hole Fernandina Beach Golf Club is considered one of the finest public courses in the Southeast. Amelia Island Plantation, a 1,250-acre sanctuary on the island's southern tip, touts both a Pete Dye and Tom Fazio course combination of 45 holes and is recognized as one of the top twelve golf resorts in America. Gene Littler and Mark McCumber designed the eighteen-hole layout of the Golf Club of Amelia Island, located near the Ritz-Carlton.

Shopping. Centre Street is the home of the bulk of downtown stores, although newcomers are popping up on side streets. Housed in an 1873 building with hardwood floors and a pressed-tin ceiling, **Southern Touch** offers Battenberg lace and a potpourri of collectibles with a Victorian and French country ambiance. Wooden marionettes and crewel rugs are among the wares at **Southern Traveler.** Aptly named, **The Unusual Shop** is notable for jewelry, clothing and ceramic tiles. **The Ship's Lantern** offers wooden hand-carved sea life. **Celtic Charm** stocks unusual Irish gifts. Among clothing shops are **Tilted Anchor** and **Last Flight Out.** Pause for a pick-me-up – coffee, candy, ice cream or what have you – at **Fernandina's Fantastic Fudge, Amelia Island Gourmet Coffee** or **27 North.**

Other favorites are down island at **Palmetto Walk,** fifteen shops modeled after tin-roof school houses with verandas, and at the **Village Shops** adjacent to Amelia Island Plantation.

Extra-Special

The Main Squeeze, 105 South Third St., Fernandina Beach.

A delightful trellised outdoor terrace next to The Courtyard Florist is home to this juice bar and lunch spot headquartered in a small covered pavilion. The place has a California feel. On a sunny day, we paused for the day's special, a tuna salad pita with a side of macaroni salad and a refreshing mango iced tea. Other choices, nicely priced in the $4 range, included a taco salad and grilled chicken quesadilla. Juices from carrot to grapefruit are the main raison d'être, but beer and wine are also available. Quite a selection of breakfast items is available, too. There's no roof, so when it rains, everything is prepared to go. *(904) 277-3003. Open Monday-Saturday, 7:30 to 3.*

St. Augustine, Fla.
The Oldest City

Rather like a fine wine, the nation's oldest city improves with age.

The first time our family saw this town that's almost as much a part of America's consciousness as Plymouth Rock, it seemed to be one Niagara of tourist attractions after another. One son explored Ripley's Believe It or Not! Museum. Another went in search of baseball cards. Their elders wandered amid what seemed to be the relentless honky tonk of the historic area. We couldn't escape fast enough.

That was then. This is now.

Since the early 1970s, this city that seems bigger than its 15,000 population would suggest has capitalized on a readymade audience and spruced up its act. It's now one of our favorite places, an exotic bit of old Europe transplanted to the sub-tropics.

Not for naught did Florida empire-builder Henry M. Flagler envision St. Augustine as the start of America's Riviera. Co-founder with John D. Rockefeller of the Standard Oil Co., he erected fabulous Spanish Revival hotels and churches and built a railroad to bring turn-of-the-century tourists from New York to "the Newport of the South." Flagler's success inadvertently did him and St. Augustine in. As he built more railroads and more hotels farther south, travelers left St. Augustine in the lurch.

A century after St. Augustine's gilded age, this city that spans five centuries of history is on the rebound.

Some 28 inns and bed and breakfasts have opened in the last decade or so in the historic district. One of the original hotels was being reborn in 1999 as a luxury hotel. Nine historic properties were restored for opening in Old St. Augustine Village. The new World Golf Village, with a Golf Hall of Fame, resort hotel and convention center, catches the traveler's eye along I-95 just north of St. Augustine.

St. Augustine – the oldest, continuously occupied European settlement in the continental United States – was founded in 1565, 42 years before the English colonized Jamestown and 55 years before the Pilgrims landed at Plymouth Rock.

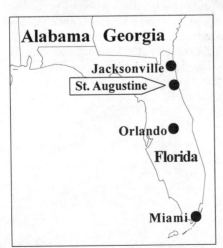

St. Augustine has always laid valid claims to the oldest: the oldest fortification, the oldest house, the oldest wooden schoolhouse, the oldest mission – even, less reliably, the oldest drug store (with a new Cyber Cafe beside) and the oldest live oak (surrounded by a Howard Johnson Express motel). There are 85 historic sites and attractions, many of them with a commercial hand out. Visiting each of the top twenty would cost more than $100, although family rates lessen the pain on the pocketbook for some.

A number of attractions and experiences, many of them associated with the Flagler vision, are first-rate.

Landmark Spanish Renaissance-style Ponce de Leon Hotel is now home of Flagler College.

Add the enticements of the nearby oceanfront, and the catchy local ad campaign – "72 miles of beaches – and the rest is history" – captures tourists of many persuasions.

St. Augustine harbors all kinds of treasures, and not all of them cost money. The historic district along the bayfront is relatively compact and made for walking. Much of the architecture is Spanish, the ambiance European, the courtyards and back alleys Mediterranean. The historian is in his element. The photographer has a field day. The browser encounters something different at every turn.

As darkness falls, church bells toll and vehicles give way to the clip-clop of horse-drawn carriages. Staying at a B&B in the Old City heightens the St. Augustine experience.

Inn Spots

Inns and bed and breakfasts are considered to be the lodgings of choice for St, Augustine visitors. Besides their personal touch, they are – with a few exceptions – the only accommodations within the historic district.

Casa de la Paz, 22 Avenida Menendez, St. Augustine 32084.

Its name – meaning "The House of Peace" – sums up what energetic innkeepers Donna and Bob Marriott try to do with this Mediterranean-style home on the bayfront, built in 1915 by a local banker. They provide a peaceful setting in six guest rooms and stylish common areas and pamper guests within an inch of their lives.

The Marriotts earned their spurs at a mountain B&B in North Carolina before purchasing this going concern in 1996. They're no relation to the hotel Marriotts. "No sir, we're a B&B," protests Bob. They undertook a total redecoration and upgrade "to make it sparkle," returning the casa to the heyday of the 1930s.

We'd heard great things about the casa through the years, so could only imagine its "total transformation" from what Bob called mismatched early K-mart decor. Now all is light and airy, tasteful and refined.

The new look begins at the side entry into a wonderful sunporch, full of wicker, palms and the peace lilies that are the symbols of the inn. Bathed in sunlight, with circular tables for two skirted in floor-length fabric, this is a place for an intimate breakfast with a view of the bay across the street. Beside it is a formal, chandeliered dining room with a ten-foot carved mahogany table set for eight. Breakfast the day of our visit began with fresh fruit, bagels and banana cake, and culminated in a ham and cheese quiche with grits. Raspberry-stuffed french toast was on tap the next day. The Marriotts are also known for their blueberry blintz soufflé, ginger pancakes with honey-maple-pecan syrup and homemade apple butter.

An English oak bookcase in the foyer is stocked with gift items from the inn's soaps and champagne to special coffee blended by the Marriotts' son. Beyond is a marvelous parlor with gleaming heart-pine floors, elaborate dentil molding and four windows onto the water. A coffee table holds a selection of cakes and baked goods all day long, and wine is offered in the afternoon. Beside is a turn-of-the-century fainting couch covered in brocade. Around the fireplace are built-in, leaded-glass cabinets holding some of Donna's 55 antique music boxes, which are ready for guests to play. Other antiques and collections are subtly on display nearby.

Three of the six upstairs guest rooms enjoy bay views. In front is the prized Ponce de Leon with fireplace and arched windows. It's regal in burgundy and gold. The queen bed is covered with a burgundy spread patterned with fleur-de-lis, a pattern repeated on the pillows. In the Queen Isabella, if you're so inclined, Bob says you can lie in bed and watch the lights on the Bridge of Lions at night. His favorite is the rambling, third-floor Captain's Quarters with a queen bedroom on the side and a sitting room in front. Two stools perched at high windows in the dormer are made for watching the moonrise. Donna is partial to the rear Santa Maria, one of three accommodations opening onto a side balcony. Light and cheery with a white wrought-iron bed, it takes its theme from Monet's "Water Lilies" print, which hangs near the entry. We'd opt for the adjoining Marco Polo suite with king canopy bed and small sitting room, but also are tempted by the Christopher Columbus. It's small but distinctive in 1930s beach style with matching floral splashes on the wallpaper borders, window treatments and demi-canopy over the bed.

Each bed is outfitted with 200-count linens and feather pillows. TVs are discreetly hidden in armoires, and telephones are reproduction hand-dials with push buttons. Each room comes with antique furnishings, stylish window treatments, the inn's own toiletries and a decanter of sherry,.

The rear courtyard is a pleasant retreat of tropical foliage and flowers, including a trickling St. Francis fountain and an orchid hanging from a tree. Beyond are six parking spaces for guests – a rare commodity in St. Augustine, but one typical of an inn where live-in owners give priority to guest comfort and service.

(904) 829-2915 or (800) 929-2915. Fax (904) 824-6269.Four rooms and two suites with private baths. Doubles, $149 to $189 weekends, $89 to $139 midweek. Suites, $159 to $174 weekends, $109 to $119 midweek. Two-night minimum weekends. Children over 15. No smoking.

Westcott House, 146 Avenida Menendez, St. Augustine 32084.
Local residents David and Sharon Dennison took over what had been a private

St. Francis fountain adds tranquility to tropical courtyard at Casa de la Paz.

residence built in the 1880s and converted it into one of St. Augustine's earliest B&Bs. Theirs is a handsome place, painted salmon with aqua trim. It claims arguably the best setting of any bayfront B&B, and certainly the quietest, least traffic-impacted location. Two front verandas facing the bay, a larger side porch decked out in pink geraniums and a spacious-for-St. Augustine side lawn and courtyard take full advantage.

Most of the common space is outside, as the Dennisons maximize the interior for guest rooms. All beds are kingsize, except for two with two queen beds each. The main floor holds the bayfront Menendez room with a fireplace, the side Rosalinda with a majestic burled Austrian bedroom set (one of several in the house) and the Esmaralda with two queen beds.

A stairwell centered by an elaborate glass chandelier leads to upstairs guest quarters. Among them is the Isabella with an imposing kingsize cherry four-poster bed. The cheery Elisa Maria room with two queen beds has windows on three sides and a sunporch look. Sharon did the decorating and made the pillow shams herself. The furnishings are Victorian, the antiques are European and American, and the decor crisp. Large TVs are prominent in each room, as is a clawfoot tub out in an attic bedroom.

The Dennisons, who live on the property, serve a continental breakfast of fruit, cereal and croissants, bagels and danish pastries, which guests take to the side porch or their rooms. Afternoon brings complimentary wine. Chocolates and a snifter of brandy are put out at nightly turndown.

(904) 824-4301 or (800) 513-9814. Nine rooms with private baths. Doubles, $150 to $175 weekends, $95 to $150 midweek. Children over 6. No smoking.

Touring horse-drawn carriage passes in front of Casa de Sueños Bed & Breakfast.

Casa de Sueños Bed & Breakfast, 20 Cordova St., St. Augustine 32084.
An arched side doorway leads into this grandly restored Mediterranean house built at the turn of the century. You'd never guess that it had been a professional office building as recently as 1994 or that its interior had been totally gutted. Or that owners Ray and Sandy Tool from Jacksonville had to take out five bathrooms and put in eight. But the rehab allowed the Tools to do the things that others only dream about in this, "the house of dreams." They say that staying here is like a dream come true.
A singer/guitarist who entertains guests here during happy hour on weekends and serenades them at breakfast painted the colorful rendering of the casa that graces the wall of the entry foyer. Miniatures often go home with guests as souvenirs.
Off the foyer is a charming sunroom/sitting room with chintz sofas and TV. Beyond is a plant-filled conservatory fashioned from an enclosed front porch with arched windows. Here is where the Tools serve a gourmet breakfast. "We both love to cook," says Sandy. Her husband is known for eggs Raymond, which he likens to eggs benedict but with the addition of gruyère cheese and spinach. She does things like spinach-mushroom quiche, pecan waffles and banana pancakes.
The main floor holds two guest rooms, one handicapped-accessible with one of the inn's four queensize beds, an outside entrance and an oversize, wheel-in shower. The prized Saragossa has a wood-burning fireplace, an oval jacuzzi in the corner and a separate shower in the bathroom. Roses are the theme here, from the photos done by a friend above the jacuzzi to the curtains to the bouquet resting on the queen bed at our visit. A TV/VCR, reproduction dial telephone with modem, a decanter of sherry, an assortment of toiletries, fresh flowers and a closet holding terrycloth robes are standard amenities.
Stylish decor that Sandy calls eclectic enhances the upstairs guest rooms as

well. The Castillo with an antique double spool bed has a wash basin implanted in an antique dresser. The blue and white Sevilla with king/twin bed has a whirlpool tub beneath a crystal chandelier. It shares an outside balcony with the largest Valencia Suite, whose whirlpool tub is in an enclosed balcony. The queen bed with a heart-shaped headboard in the Cordova Suite comes with a hand-crocheted spread and nine matching pillows. Thick carpeting graces most of the guest rooms. Oriental rugs dignify the shiny oak and heart-pine floors of common areas.

(904) 824-0887 or (800) 824-0804. Fax (904) 825-0074 or (800) 735-7534. Four rooms and two suites with private baths. Doubles, $105 to $165. Suites, $175 and $185. No smoking.

Casablanca Inn, 24 Avenida Menendez, St. Augustine 32084.

One of St. Augustine's earlier and more acclaimed B&Bs, this expanding operation centers around an unusual-looking, 1914 Mediterranean Revival home facing Matanzas Bay. Its broad porches are cooled by ocean breezes. The only inside common room is a small parlor off the lobby area where four armchairs encircle a coffee table holding a decanter of port.

The Casablanca is a place not for communal gathering but, as it names suggests, for escape and romance. The main house holds two rooms and ten suites, some of which aren't really two-room suites but are called that because of their sitting areas. Each offers outside seating on a private deck or porch. Beds are queensize and furnishings are mainly Victorian. Six have double jacuzzis, including one in the Butler Suite right in the bedroom, faced by a couple of wing chairs. Ceramic masks on the wall enliven the small parlor of the San Marco Suite, where the two-part bathroom was made from two closets. The two largest Anniversary and Celebration suites have double jacuzzis, decorative fireplaces and private porches with double hammocks.

In 1998, owners Tony and Brenda Bushell added eight more rooms on two floors of a restored coach house out back. These have queen beds, some with an extra twin, and jacuzzi tubs with a rubber ducky beside. They also have TVs and telephones, features lacking in the main house. Each opens onto a semi-divided porch or deck, smack up against Charlotte Street.

Homemade cookies are put out in the lobby every afternoon, and guests help themselves in the kitchen to beverages in a refrigerator stocked mainly for breakfast. The staff serves a two-course breakfast in an exotic, pillared dining room that spills outside onto the front veranda. The room, colorful in yellow and green, holds arty handpainted tables. Mirrors reflect the palms and waterfront scene outside.

(904) 829-0928 or (800) 826-2626. Fax (904) 826-1892. Ten rooms and ten suites with private baths. Weekends: doubles $129 to $179, suites $149 to $199. Midweek: doubles $89 to $139, suites $109 to $149. Two-night minimum some weekends. No smoking.

Casa de Solana, 21 Aviles St., St. Augustine 32084.

When Faye McMurry and her husband were seeking to move to St. Augustine to look for a home in which they could operate the city's first B&B, the realtor showed them only Victorian structures. She wanted something really old and indigenous, and finally found the 1763 Don Manuel Solana House, hidden behind

Historic Casa de Solana started local B&B phenomenon in 1983.

a walled front lawn and authentic as could be. She and her accountant husband made an offer and started the B&B phenomenon here in 1983.

The house is impressive, and definitely the McMurrys' home – as indicated by the sign at the entry to the effect that it is not a museum nor open for tours. Guests are escorted to one of four suites, each with a sitting room. They gather together only at 8:30 in the morning, when a lavish breakfast is served communally at a beautifully set table for eight in an expansive dining room. The room is notable for its beamed ceiling, gently ticking clock and a grand piano in one corner.

Two suites are on the first floor. One on the second floor, where the owners live, has a balcony overlooking the front courtyard. The last is on the third floor, with sloping ceilings and a great view of the bay from bedroom and sitting room. Bed configurations vary from one with antique twins joined as a king and one queensize to two antique doubles that simply proved incapable of being enlarged. Furnishings are antiques and family heirlooms from the Richmond area of Virginia, where outspoken Faye was given a proper upbringing as the daughter of a Southern Baptist minister and granddaughter of a judge. Amenities include TV, chocolates and a decanter of sherry.

Their longtime housekeeper, Doris, prepares the breakfast, which Faye helps serve. Fresh fruit followed by quiche lorraine with grits was the fare when we were there. It was served on part of an enormous collection of Faye's mother's china atop silver service plates. Individual pats of butter shaped like hearts or flowers accompany. "People can't believe we still do this, but we do," says Faye.

(904) 824-3555. Fax (904) 824-3316. Four suites with private baths. Doubles, $125 to $145. No smoking.

Alexander Homestead, 14 Sevilla St., St. Augustine 32084.

This 1888 Victorian, wrapped in tall trees and railed porches, was uninhabitable when Bonnie J. Alexander arrived on the scene in 1991. Five months of renovations turned it into a B&B that is the essence of Victoriana or, as her flowery brochure puts it, a legacy of the Romantic Age.

Bonnie digs out a photo to show the fireplace before she returned it to its original luster in the snug Victorian parlor. She had lots to do in four bedrooms, though you wouldn't realize it today. The Alexandria is a main-floor beauty with a hand-carved French walnut queen bed, woodburning fireplace, a modern bath with a double jacuzzi tub and french doors onto one of the porches with which this house abounds. Bonnie undertook considerable research to ensure that her furnishings were both high quality and authentic. The Queen Anne, upstairs in front, is dainty in pink with white lace bed covers, moiré swags and a clawfoot tub. Laura Ashley florals accent the Sweet William. Besides their calculatedly old-fashioned air, every bedroom has a queen bed, TV, private porch and amenities like waffle-weave robes and decanters of peach brandy and anisette.

Bonnie pampers guests with such afternoon goodies as raspberry-lemon bars or pound cake. Breakfast is served in a chandeliered dining room. Homemade granola with fresh fruit and vanilla yogurt precedes a substantial main course. The day of our visit it was baked apple french toast with little almond-poppyseed muffins. The next day's fare was strata and biscuits stuffed with cream cheese.

The hostess treats this very much like the homestead she calls it. It's in a quiet residential section where guests like to hang out on their porches and let the time go by.

(904) 826-4147 or (888) 292-4147. Fax (904) 823-9503. Four rooms with private baths. Doubles, $105 to $160. Two-night minimum stay on weekends. No smoking.

The Inn on Charlotte Street, 52 Charlotte St., St. Augustine 32084.

Flowers are the theme at this new B&B, as envisioned by the founding innkeeper who built a strong business in less than a year before her husband's business transferred them out of town in 1998. Vanessa Noel, an Englishwoman who worked at inns in Maine and New Hampshire for 30 years, was ready to move south after the ice storm of 1998. She took over a going concern and hoped to be joined soon by her husband David.

The flowers begin at the front entrance, where they're draped around the upstairs veranda and twine in garlands up the stairway banister. Floral fabrics are the theme of the colorful living room, where Vanessa offers wine, beer and soft drinks beside the coquina stone fireplace.

Upstairs in five guest rooms are more flowers – fresh in vases and splashy in huge artificial arrangements. Not to mention portrayed in fabrics and artworks employed throughout.

Flowers are stenciled in the bathroom of the rear Palm Room, itself cheery with a multi-colored quilt on the kingsize bed and a showy floral display. The front Matanzas Room with a fainting couch near the fireplace and a double jacuzzi in the corner has a king bed draped in a lace headboard scarf topped with a garland of flowers. A wrought-iron window frame screens the open bathroom from the rest of the room. The room opens onto a front veranda shared with the adjacent Lighthouse Room, nicely nautical in gray and navy. It has a clawfoot tub in the bedroom, as does the queensize Coquina Room.

Fresh roses and champagne are in every room. Vanessa serves a full breakfast of bacon and eggs or pancakes from 8:30 to 9:30 in the dining room.

(904) 829-3819. Fax (904) 810-2134. Five rooms with private baths. Doubles, $100 to $145 weekends, $75 to $125 midweek.

St. Francis Inn, 279 St. George St., St. Augustine 32084.
Built in 1791 as a private home and operated as an inn or boarding house since 1845, this versatile charmer wears its age with grace and authenticity. A super courtyard draped in bougainvillea faces the entrance, properly historic in white stucco with dark trim and an ornate, two-story veranda. One of St. Augustine's two inn pools lies around the side.

The main floor holds a variety of atmospheric common rooms, including a parlor/game room with gas fireplace and a beamed dining room. More seating is available in the upstairs hall and on the veranda. Most folks prefer to spread out on wrought-iron furniture in the idyllic courtyard, where a fountain trickles beneath a forest of bamboo. The courtyard is the scene of musical entertainment on Sunday evenings from April to October.

"The courtyard is what catches people," says owner Joe Finnegan. When he and his wife took over in 1985, the St. Francis was basically a boarding house featuring long-term rentals (in fact, his parents had stayed for three months some years earlier in what is now Elizabeth's Suite). The Finnegans reconfigured the layout into nine rooms and two suites. They upgraded the furnishings and services and, in 1996, renovated all the bathrooms with new tiling and brass fixtures. Six accommodations now come with whirlpool tubs (five of them double), and three of these have unusual electric-flame fireplaces – no heat but good for show. Three other rooms also have electric fireplaces. All but three rooms have queen or kingsize beds. Rooms, a few with kitchenettes harkening back to their boarding house days, are furnished with antiques, reproductions and family heirlooms. They convey a dated look appropriate for their age. Windows are shuttered and walls hold nifty recessed bookshelves and niches.

The Balcony Room with private porch overlooking St. George and Cordova streets and the Overlook Room above are particularly coveted. The adjacent Wilson House, originally the slave quarters and then the cookhouse, is a two-bedroom, two-bath cottage favored by families.

Rooms come with television sets (suites have two), telephones, green plants and fresh flowers. Chocolates are placed on the beds and postcards are stamped. There's a social hour with complimentary appetizers, beer and wine from 5:30 to 6:30.

A buffet breakfast is put out in the morning. Muffins and breads, granola and fresh fruit were supplemented at our visit by scrambled eggs.

(904) 824-6068 or (800) 824-6062. Fax (904) 810-5525. Nine rooms, two suites and one cottage with private baths. Doubles, $90 to $175 weekends, $65 to $135 midweek. Cottage for four, $175 weekends, $130 midweek. No smoking.

The Kenwood Inn, 38 Marine St., St. Augustine 32084.
Painted salmon and white, this tree-shaded structure looks like a house but reflects its heritage as a guest house and hotel since 1886. Among its attributes are a swimming pool partly screened from the street in front and a couple of living rooms, one a sunroom with TV. A pleasant walled courtyard is hidden behind the house.

The fourteen guest quarters in the rambling structure vary considerably. Some have one or two double beds and others have queens and kings. Club chairs provide comfortable sitting areas in most. The biggest we saw was a king-bedded room with two loveseats, an in-room vanity, a clawfoot tub and a TV. We're told a three-room suite with water view takes up the entire third floor. Some rooms have

Two-story veranda looks onto side courtyard at St. Francis Inn.

refrigerators and TVs. Hats on the doors, quilts and stenciling convey an old-fashioned, country look.

An extended continental breakfast is offered in the dining room by owners Mark and Kerrianne Constant or their staff. Fresh fruit, cereal and baked goods are the usual fare. Cookies and sherry are put out in the afternoon.

(904) 824-2116. Fax (904) 824-1689. Thirteen rooms and one suite with private baths. Doubles, $85 to $135. Suite, $175. No smoking.

Carriage Way Bed & Breakfast, 70 Cuna St., St. Augustine 32084.

Oklahomans Bill and Diane Johnson took over this B&B in 1992 as a retirement project. "We had three retail stores before, so find this very relaxing," explains Diane.

The house, built in the mid-1880s in the vernacular style with Victorian features, is modest both inside and out. There are narrow front porches upstairs and down, a small guest parlor on the side, and a dining room with a table for six. Guests gather here or on the front veranda for breakfast, perhaps waffles with sausage, omelets or pancakes, accompanied by homemade breads. Cakes and cookies are offered in the afternoon. A guest refrigerator is stocked with wine and beer, and evening cordials are put out near the TV in the parlor.

Three guest rooms are on the main floor and six upstairs. Two rooms have double beds and one has two doubles. The rest are queensize. Four of the bathrooms have clawfoot tubs with showers and the rest have showers only. Two are in the hallway a few steps from the bedroom. Rooms are simple in terms of furnishing and décor – a mix of antiques and reproductions with wreaths and dried floral arrangements for accents. The Masters Room, named for the builder of the house, has a queensize brass bed and a franklin stove and faces the upstairs veranda. So does its sidekick, the Pittman, with a queen brass bed in the corner. A bit newer in feeling is the prized Elizabeth Gould Room upstairs at the back. It comes with a queen four-poster bed, a cathedral ceiling with a pair of skylights, and a large walk-in shower.

The rooms are considered good value, At our visit, the Gould was the only one renting for more than $100.

(904) 829-2467 or (800) 908-9832. Fax (904) 826-1461. Nine rooms with private baths. Doubles, $69 to $130. No smoking.

The Casa Monica Hotel, 95 Cordova St., St. Augustine 32084.

The old Cordova Hotel in the heart of the old city was being restored for reopening in October 1999 as a 138-room luxury hotel. Orlando developer Richard Kessler, former head of the Days Inn chain, bought the property, last used as the St. Johns County Courthouse, to become one of his Grand Theme Hotels.

The original hotel formed part of a Gilded Age triangle with Henry Flagler's Ponce de Leon and the Alcazar across Cordova Street. It was built as the Casa Monica by Boston millionaire Franklin Smith. The hotel went bankrupt and was sold within four months to Flagler, who changed its name to the Cordova.

The five-story structure with turrets and towers is colorful in the Moorish Revival style. Four towers were being reconfigured as two-story suites. The seven-story corner tower was reserved for a three-story, two-bedroom penthouse. Accommodations feature the latest in hotel amenities, including three telephones. Spanish-style rod iron beds, white duvet covers, Spanish armoires, wicker lounge chairs and antique woven window treatments are among the appointments. Facilities include a fitness center, a courtyard with pool, and street-level shops.

Local chef John Compton planned to sell his acclaimed Old City House Inn & Restaurant next door to oversee the hotel's dining operation. He said the 120-seat dining room would offer "the choicest cuisine in St. Augustine."

(904) 827-1888 or (888) 472-6312. One hundred thirty-six rooms and suites with private baths. Doubles, $149. Suites, $200 to $600.

Dining Spots

Like most tourist towns, St. Augustine has a number of prominent, well advertised restaurants viewed locally as tourist traps. It also has a number of not so widely known places where you can get a good, perhaps exceptional meal at a fair price.

Bistro PJ, 8 Aviles St., St. Augustine.

They named it for their cat, Perrier-Jouet. Which tells you something about the playful spirit that Bob and Diane Sims impart to their stylish restaurant, reincarnated in the space they'd sold in 1996. After two years in Boca Raton, where their restaurant won top honors, they "tired of the South Florida rat race" and yearned for "laid-back St. Augustine." They reopened in late 1998 in the space where their original Champs of Avilas had evolved from a luncheon spot they began in 1988. They renovated the interior, rechristened it with the Boca name and added a wine cellar.

The theme is "artful contemporary cuisine." Chef Bob sautés his shrimp in vodka and vermouth, his yellowfin tuna in tequila and grand marnier, and his chicken in champagne and orange juice. The grouper riviera is poached with white wine, tomatoes, black olives and artichoke hearts. The filet mignon carries a complex bordeaux sauce. The osso buco is simmered in pinot noir.

Appetizers are exotic: an assertive black bean tart tempered with key-lime crème fraîche, a roasted garlic flan topped with scallop seviche, a portobello "pizza" stuffed with bruschetta and feta cheese. A pricey wine list offers plenty of exotic choices to accompany.

The setting is artistic as well. Showy paintings accent mint green walls above dark green wainscoting. Ficus trees separate a dozen well-spaced tables dressed in white linens over dark green undercloths. Tall, free-standing candles flicker. The stage is set for a memorable meal.

(904) 827-1010. Entrées, $16 to $28. Dinner, Wednesday-Saturday from 6.

Cortessés Bistro, 172 San Marco Ave., St. Augustine.

This promising newcomer opened in "uptown St. Augustine" in 1998 in the quaint, 1880s house in which proprietor Bonne Jones grew up. She and her Mexican husband, Jorge Talavera, the chef, transformed the structure into a stunning bistro. They later converted her parents' old Flamingo Bar out front into the chic Flamingo Room, the town's first martini and cigar bar. They joined the two structures with a outdoor dining courtyard that's inviting by day or night, and added a coffee and espresso bar.

The place is big yet intimate, flashy yet appealing. Tables in four small dining rooms in the house are set with tapestry mats, shaded oil lamps and, surprise, mismatched china. Check out the muse-like murals painted on the Garden Room walls by a sixteen-year-old girl.

The fare is Mediterranean. The all-day menu is strong on starters and light plates, from a signature tomato tart to focaccia of the day to a bistro cheese board to cobb salad "big city style." Pastas are served with crusty farm bread and salad. Dinner entrées include Minorcan fish stew, grilled three-peppered salmon over tomato coulis, grilled angus beef tenderloin and veal oscar. Desserts run from a fudge tart with warm mocha sauce to raspberry crème brûlée.

(904) 825-6775. Entrées, $13.95 to $19.95. Lunch, Tuesday-Friday 11 to 3. Brunch, Saturday-Sunday 10 to 3. Dinner, Tuesday-Sunday from 5:30.

Le Pavillon, 45 San Marco Ave., St. Augustine.

The ordinary looking house doesn't look like much, to say the least. Yet inside is a gracious old world atmosphere reflecting its European ownership and a tenure of serving lunch and dinner seven days a week for more than three decades. A local innkeeper frequently refers guests here, saying it's the only one he's never had a complaint about. "A Frenchman came back and said he had the best meal of his life here."

Similar accolades are heard frequently for the classic continental fare offered at prices about half what they would be in other areas.

Crêpes are a specialty, offered in four varieties as well as a combination of all four. The oysters rockefeller also comes highly recommended. Main courses cover the gamut from trout amandine to bouillabaisse, from sauerbraten to veal oscar, from chicken curry bombay to filet mignon with béarnaise sauce. But we've heard there's nothing better than the rack of lamb. Desserts include chocolate torte, cheesecake and creme de menthe parfait.

(904) 824-6202. Entrées, $13.95 to $18.95. Lunch daily, 11:30 to 2:30. Dinner nightly, 5 to 10.

Columbia Restaurant, 98 St. George St., St. Augustine.
A favorite of tourists, and deservedly so, is this venerable branch of a famed Tampa-based restaurant chain. It's Spanish, which is appropriate for St. Augustine, and is well located in the heart of the historic district. The complex with interior and exterior courtyards, bakery and takeout shop, gift shop and a wonderful, high-ceilinged main dining room surrounded by balconies makes it almost a sightseeing attraction.
That the food is so good and so consistent is a bonus, and these polished restaurateurs sure know how to handle the crowds. We always start with the Spanish bean soup that made the Columbia famous – a hearty concoction of garbanzo beans, smoked ham, potatoes and chorizo. Others say the Cuban black bean soup, served over a bed of white rice, is to die for. For lunch, nothing will do but Columbia's original 1905 salad, tossed at the table with an addictive mix of ham, cheese, romano cheese and garlic dressing – although we have succumbed occasionally to the Cuban sandwich. There are tapas, paella, Cuban platters and plenty of Spanish-inspired fish, poultry and meat dishes for dinner. The guava cheesecake is a worthy ending.
No visitor should leave St. Augustine without having savored the atmosphere and food at Columbia. It's as much an institution as the city itself.
(904) 824-3341. Entrées, $11.95 to $19.95. Open daily, 11 to 9 or 10.

A1A Ale Works, 1 King St., St. Augustine.
Imagine, the first microbrewery in the nation's oldest city offering some of its most exciting cuisine. We never would have guessed, and only a knowing few steered us this way. The fare is New World (the world of Columbus's discoveries) and, ye gads, there's no red meat on the menu. The food is au courant, and so is the huge upstairs dining room, a mix of tables and booths, with windows onto the waterfront and porches onto the street. The high-ceilinged dining room of brick and exposed pipes incorporates a decorative theme of fish with colors of aubergines and golds.
The cutlery arrives in a big washcloth that serves as the napkin, and a bottle of tabasco sauce is on each table. From an open kitchen comes a succession of treats from a menu that's made for grazing. For lunch, the roasted tomato-basil soup was fabulous, paired with a mango, jicama and red pepper salad and a side order of yucca fries with datil pepper mayo. The tuna picadillo sandwich with smoked gouda on Cuban bread was sensational, too. The Matanzas Bay berry ale hinted of raspberry, and the banana macadamia beignets for dessert were to die for.
The adventurous diner will find plenty to entice and expand his or her horizons. Others need not apply.
(904) 829-2977. Entrées, $10.95 to $18.95. Lunch daily, 11 to 4:30. Dinner nightly, 5 to 11.

La Parisienne, 60 Hypolita St., St. Augustine.
This whitewashed building with a welcoming little courtyard beneath an exotic, purple-flowering tree looks as if it has been transplanted from the South of France countryside. Ditto for the menu, a compendium of the classics skillfully executed, according to local consensus.
The Mediterranean fish soup, the smoked trout mousse and the snails in puff pastry are favorite starters. The bouillabaisse is Parisian; the shrimp étouffée is

rooted in the Louisiana Creole tradition. The chef prepares a New York strip steak au poivre and the veal chop "à la ancient city," with a forestière sauce. Desserts include chocolate mousse, crème brûlée and tarte aux noix. The prix-fixe dégustation menu – three courses with salad and choice of appetizer or dessert – is a good value for $26.

(904) 829-0055. Entrées, $14.50 to $24. Lunch, daily except Wednesday, 11 to 3. Dinner, Thursday-Sunday from 5.

Fiddler's Green. 2750 Anahma Drive, St. Augustine.
This oceanside grill overlooking the Atlantic and St. Augustine Inlet is a favorite of locals and visitors alike, for its food and setting as well as its courtesy pick-up service. A decor of green, pecky cypress paneling and a coquina stone fireplace reflect the site's heritage as the old Vilano Beach resort casino built in 1926.

The grill fare is thoroughly up-to-date, as in mahi mahi with key lime and bermuda onion aioli, blackened chicken with a cool citrus chutney, and a mixed grill of fresh fish, shrimp, scallops and oysters "rockefiddler" with pineapple-jalapeño salsa, Caribbean black beans and rice. Entrées come with crusty bread and caesar salad, as do a variety of pasta sautés. The grilled primavera salad with shrimp or chicken is a meal in itself.

Start with beer-battered conch fritters or fried blue crab claws with dill tartar sauce. Key lime pie is the dessert of choice.

(904) 824-8897. Entrées, $10.99 to $17.99. Dinner nightly, 5 to 9 or 10.

Among the myriad of other dining options: **Harry's Seafood Bar & Grill,** a new branch of a Jacksonville establishment started by a St. Augustine resident, offers New Orleans-style food and a large, festive tropical courtyard at the edge of the historic downtown. For a Caribbean waterfront feeling, try to snag one of the thatched-roofed tiki huts for a private lunch overlooking the bay at the **Conch House Restaurant and Lounge.** The conch chowder and fritters are almost as good as the view at this establishment run by descendants of the oldest Ponce family, out toward St. Augustine Beach. Florida coastal cuisine is served casually at the indoor-outdoor **Florida Cracker Cafe** in the heart of downtown. A good spot for innovative soups and sandwiches, although lacking in ambiance, is **Azalea's Cafe** hidden away on Aviles Street, the most atmospheric streetscape in town. A guitarist plays and the mood is dark and historic at **Cafe Alcazar,** offering an international lunch menu in the depths of what once was the world's largest indoor swimming pool at the rear of Henry Flagler's old Alcazar Hotel.

Diversions

As an old town laid out in Spanish style around a central plaza and with waters flowing here and there, St. Augustine may be a hard-to-fathom city for the visitor. Many streets, or portions thereof, are one-way. Parking can be difficult at peak periods. Your best bet may be to park at the visitor center ($3 all day) or at the sightseeing tour depots (free), and set out by trolley or foot.

To get your bearings, take a sightseeing tour first. Both the red **St. Augustine Sightseeing Trains,** 170 San Marco Ave., and the green **St. Augustine Historical Trolley Tours,** 167 San Marco Ave., follow roughly the same path and pass the same sites on narrated, hour-long tours of the old city. How informative they are depends on the driver. You will see a lot that looks worth going back to, and a lot that's not. At least you'll know which is which among all the attractions seeking your attention and cash. The tour ticket ($12) is particularly good for long-term visitors, since it allows on-and-off privileges at leading attractions and is good for three consecutive days.

Historic Attractions. Many are privately owned or owned by the city and not-for-profit organizations. That may explain their charm, which some find amateurish and others find refreshing. The attractions tend to come in clusters. One cluster is at the north end, outside the city gates. The Spaniards built **Castillo de San Marcos,** the largest coquina stone structure in the world, in 1672. The fortress, moat and all, squats along the bayfront, its cannon still perched along the sea inlet to defend the city. Although attacked more than once, it never fell in battle and endures as the nation's oldest fort. The nearby **Mission of Nombre de Dios,** a peaceful shrine where Don Pedro Menendez de Aviles landed in 1565, marks the beginning of Christianity in the United States. Follow beautiful, out-of-the-way **Magnolia Street,** canopied by towering live oaks, to the 21-acre **Fountain of Youth Archaeological Park.** The site where Ponce de Leon landed in 1513 contains the eternal spring reputed to be the Fountain of Youth. .

The heart of the old city is found beyond the **City Gate** (1808) in the area centering along the eleven pedestrian-only blocks of St. George Street. Plaques mark 18th-century Spanish Colonial structures that are now historic attractions or shops. Within the restored area lies the **Spanish Quarter Village,** a city-run representation of the original military garrison community. Visitors stroll from house to house and meet costumed interpreters busy at pastimes of the 1740s. The highlight is the twenty-minute tour of the de Mesa House, offered four times a day. The ticket-taker tipped us off to the fascinating story of the Minorcans, "my ancestors," as detailed in the Peso de Burgo-Pellicer House. (Village open daily, 9 to 6 or 7, weekends to 9; adults $6). The Spanish Quarter holdings also include the **Spanish Military Hospital** and the **Government House,** a museum tracing the history of St. Augustine, opposite the Plaza de la Constitution.

Another historic cluster is in the oldest residential neighborhood in the south end of the old city. Here the focus is the **Oldest House** complex, on a site occupied since the 1600s. The 1727 house, the area's oldest surviving Spanish structure, portrays the lifestyles of owners through three centuries and three cultures. Within the complex are ornamental gardens, the St. Augustine Museum of History and the Museums of Florida's Army. (All open daily 9 to 5, adults $5).

The **Ximenez-Fatio House** at 20 Aviles St., built in 1789 and long a boarding house, is of interest to those who want to see how early inngoers lived.

Old St. Augustine Village, 250 St. George St., St. Augustine.

A block-size collection of nine historic buildings was being painstakingly restored for opening as a microcosm of the oldest city in late 1999 or early 2000. The properties were assembled by Kenneth W. Dow, St. Augustine resident and heir to a Dow industrial fortune. One of the more recent structures was home to novelist William Dean Howells. Others date to 1790. Costumed interpreters and craftsmen will be on site for visitors to take self-guided tours in the manner of Colonial Williamsburg. Also on site is Ken Dow, a pony-tailed octogenarian who lives on the property and serves as consulting curator for the sponsoring Museum of Arts and Sciences.

(904) 255-0285. Open daily 10 to 5. Admission, $7.50 (estimated).

Flagler Landmarks. The west central part of the historic district focuses on the **Ponce De Leon Hotel.** The fabulous masterpiece of Spanish Renaissance architecture was built in 1888 by Henry M. Flagler as the first of the grand hotels intended to make this the American Riviera. The 400-room luxury hotel looks much as it did when Flagler catered to the Who's Who of the turn of the century with Tiffany glass, gold-leafed Maynard murals and electricity by Thomas Edison. It closed in the 1960s and became the home of Flagler College, a private liberal-arts college which – unlike its namesake – is known for value (all-inclusive yearly cost is $9,630). The sounds of student flip-flops punctuate the halls where well-heeled guests once tread. The mezzanine with windows by Lewis Comfort Tiffany, the interior decorator for the hotel, is off-limits to visitors. It's now a student lounge area. Visitors can view the great rotunda and steal a peak at the baronial arched dining room, where the hand-carved Austrian oak chairs original to the hotel flank red-clothed tables for four. Surely this must be the fanciest college dining hall anywhere. The multi-course prime rib dinner for $4.25, shown in an early menu in a display case in the rotunda, stands in contrast to the day's black-board menu, which listed a waffle bar, chicken fajitas and pepperoni pizza for dinner. Free guided tours are offered May-August daily on the hour, 11 to 4.

Behind the hotel is **Memorial Presbyterian Church,** built in 1890 by Henry Flagler in memory of his daughter Jennie, who died giving birth. He spared no expense and moved part of Venice to St. Augustine to create another monument to the Golden Age. Built in the Venetian Renaissance style in the shape of a cross, it is equal in size and grandeur to some of the great churches of Europe. This has a huge copper dome overhead and ornate terra cotta frieze work done by Italian artists. The woodwork is all hand-carved Santo Domingo mahogany. The kneeling benches beneath each pew are there because of the European tradition, a guide advised. Buried in the round mausoleum attached at the side of the church are Flagler, his first wife, his daughter and granddaughter. Also of interest nearby is Grace Methodist Church, another Flagler beneficiary, part of one of the most elaborate cohesive architectural complexes of the late 19th century in America.

Across from the hotel is the old **Alcazar Hotel,** which Flagler built a year later to attract the middle class. Not quite so tony but equally interesting, it's now home of the Lightner Museum (see Extra-Special). You'll understand why St. Augustinians, though they were proud of the Ponce DeLeon, loved the Alcazar. Beside the Alcazar is the old **Cordova Hotel,** purchased by Flagler after the original Casa Monica went bankrupt.

On the west side of the old Alcazar is **Zorayda Castle,** built in 1883 as his home by millionaire Franklin Smith, builder of the Cordova Hotel. The castle is a replica of the Zorayda tower of the Alhambra, Spain's most famous castle in Old Granada. The castle shows how Moorish kings lived, entertained and ruled Spain. It's open daily, 9 to 5; adults $5.

Shopping. Where to begin? The San Marco Avenue entrance to the city – a commercial strip that first struck us as tawdry – is being upscaled into an area increasingly worthy of its recent appellation, "Uptown St. Augustine." Most visitors think of downtown as St. George Street, eleven narrow, pedestrian-only blocks of palm trees and benches. Here you'll occasionally stumble across a treasure amid a sea of souvenir shops – a scene that has its own charms. Most specialty shops and art galleries are on side streets. Ads tout "the oldest city's original street of merchants," Charlotte Street. The consensus is that the best shopping is around the old plaza, the Alcazar courtyards and along Aviles Street, a lovely area with a decidedly European look. Sooner or later you'll likely end up at the St. Augustine Outlet Center, a better than average collection of more than 95 outlet stores strung out along I-95. It's so big a free trolley shuttles shoppers around the center.

World Golf Village, 21 World Golf Place, St. Augustine.

St. Augustine's biggest new attraction is quite a sight for arriving visitors along I-95, just north of the city. The 6,300-acre development rivals those of the Disney area southwest of Orlando. Here the main tourist attraction is the **World Golf Hall of Fame,** which expected to attract more than a million visitors in its first year. The hall and its IMAX Theater combine historic artifacts with interactive technology. Visitors walk across a replica of the famed Swilcan Burn Bridge from the 18th hole at St. Andrews and log on to survey highlights from golf action around the world. It's the first time all international golf organizations and pro tours have united in support of a single project. The first IMAX golf film shows the past, present and future of the sport through the eyes of two Scottish golfers. Built around Lake Kelly, the village also features a resort hotel, a convention center, a golf academy, an eighteen-hole championship golf course with two more on the way, shopping centers and residential communities.

(904) 940-4000. Open daily, 10 to 6. Hall of Fame, adults, $9. IMAX Theater, $6.

Extra-Special

The Lightner Museum, 75 King St., St. Augustine.

This is "the gem of St. Augustine," as proclaimed by no less an authority than our trolley tour driver, a know-it-all native. And so it is, for anyone with an interest in the Gilded Age and certainly for those into collections of the Victorian era. The museum was a gift to the city from Otto C. Lightner, a Chicago publisher and collector, who had crammed two fading mansions with relics of a bygone era. Moving here because of ill health, he bought the abandoned Alcazar Hotel to house his collections in the spirit of his idol, Henry Flagler. The old hotel and adjacent casino have their own fascinating story to tell as they showcase what's best described as a collection of collections. One of the country's most complete repositories of 19th-century life, it's been called the Smithsonian of the South. For connoisseurs, the major emphasis is on fine and decorative arts, with other collections of natural science, industry and anthropology. But some of the most fascinating are the oddball items from Lightner's original amateurish museum of "hobbies:" salt and pepper shakers and trivets, candles and keys, wooden nickels and cigarette lighters. One four-sided glass case holds a montage of shoes and boots. Matchbook covers and walking canes are displayed under the same roof as an 1873 Chickering piano from opera singer Amelita Galli-Curci. Winston Churchill's stuffed African lion and a 2,500-year-old Egyptian mummy occupy a room next to a collection of rare mechanized musical instruments. The lately restored Ballroom Gallery overlooks the old indoor swimming pool, now an antiques mall and cafe. Priceless vases and glassware are shown in what used to be the hotel's Turkish baths. Tiffany glass edifies an old massage room. Walk into the old Roman baths and come out to face an eight-foot-tall green malachite urn and pedestal from the Russian Czar's palace. You could be entranced for hours here.

(904) 824-2874. Open daily 9 to 5. Adults, $6.

Lighthouse at Grantham Point in Gilbert Park guides boaters to "Port of Mount Dora."

Mount Dora, Fla.

Land of Lakes and Hills

Where precisely is Mount Dora? the visitor might wonder, noting the T-shirts and bumper stickers that proclaim "I Climbed Mount Dora." It's the hill behind her inn, responds an innkeeper. It's just beyond the intersection of Highland and Fifth, surmises a Chamber of Commerce executive. It's on the crest above Donnelly Park, claims a merchant.

There is no specific site, apparently, that marks one of the highest points in Florida. Rather it is the name for the quaint town of 7,900 that rises 185 feet above the shores of Lake Dora. Mount Dora is not so much a place as an aura.

With its hills and lakes and unpretentious, old-fashioned air, the community looks as if it belongs in Wisconsin rather than Central Florida.

Centered by a lakeside inn that's as old as the town, Mount Dora claims the oldest inland yacht club and the second largest lawn bowling club in Florida as well as the state's oldest and largest bicycling festival. National magazines have touted it as one of the best places to retire, to raise a family and to vacation. Retirees say it reminds them of their hometown or the one they wish they'd had. Though known as "Festival City" for the special events that draw a million visitors annually, the town is happily untouristy and totally unspoiled.

Donnelly Park is the focal point, the New England town green if you will. Atop its crest is a white brick City Hall that reminds some of Tara in *Gone with the Wind.* Shuffleboarders play within sight of downtown shops and restaurants. Lake Dora is on view at the foot of the hill. The only franchise outlet is the corner Mount Dora Ace Hardware, about the largest store in town. Conspicuously missing are fast-food restaurants and shopping strips. Instead, Route 46 into Mount Dora from Interstate 4 is marked with enough bear-crossing signs to convince you they're not mere decoration.

Understated, turn-of-the-century homes on rather substantial lots flank streets leading away from Lake Dora. They share space with homes of more recent vintage and, but for the palms and orange trees, give the town the all-American look of the Midwest. Dozens of lakes large and small show why surrounding Lake County got its name.

Visitors have been lured to Mount Dora since the Lakeside Inn opened in 1883, the year the town was settled by thirteen families. Antiquers are drawn by the state's largest indoor antique market at the edge of town. More than 300,000 show up the first weekend in February for the annual Mount Dora Arts Festival. Weekenders escape to Mount Dora where the parking is free, where bells tinkle as you open shop doors and where the most photographed landmark is a doll-sized lighthouse beside a harbor. It's identified as the "port of Mount Dora."

Inn Spots

The Lakeside Inn, 100 North Alexander St., Mount Dora 32757.

One of five Historic Hotels of Florida and listed on the National Register, this started humbly as a ten-room lakeside hotel called the Alexander House. The inn was in its heyday in the Gatsby Era. It was expanded in 1930 to its present size with two annexes dedicated by Calvin Coolidge, who had just finished his presidency and spent the winter here. Subsequent owners undertook a $5 million renovation in 1985 to restore its vaguely English Tudor look. Today the Lakeside remains a focal point of Mount Dora, its distinctive yellow buildings with green roofs a reminder of days gone by.

Its 1883 founding date is emblazoned above the fireplace in the wide lobby that was originally used as a ballroom. The fireplace obviously had been in use the winter morning we visited, but the day had warmed up and guests were enjoying the rockers facing Lake Dora along the front veranda. Lavish displays of artificial flowers throughout the lobby testified to a faded elegance. The rest of the main floor is given over to Tremain's Lounge and the Beauclaire Dining Room (see Dining Spots).

Most of the inn's 88 guest quarters are located in the Gables and Terrace annexes, across the road from the main building. They face each other across a lawn sloping toward the lake. Rooms go off interior hotel corridors. Most come with king or

queensize or two double beds, a couple of chairs and a TV set. "Parlor rooms" add a sitting area with two chairs in the bay window and terrycloth robes in the closet. Top of the line are the Edgerton Suite upstairs in the main inn and ten "lakefront rooms" with views. Those we saw looked comfortable if unremarkable.

What the marketing department calls "an upscale continental breakfast" of fresh baked goods, cereals and yogurt is complimentary in the dining room. Lunch is available on the front veranda or in the renovated, covered poolside bar.

Spacious new Darst Victorian Manor faces Lake Dora.

Lately, the docks have been enlarged to add more boat slips and the pool area renovated and modernized.

(352) 383-4101 or (800) 556-5016. Fax (352) 735-2642. Eighty-seven rooms and one suite with private baths. October to mid-May: doubles, $150 to $180 weekends, $105 to $135 midweek; suite, $210 weekends and $160 midweek. Rest of year: doubles, $120 to $150 weekends, $90 to $120 midweek; suite, $210 weekends, $145 midweek.

Darst Victorian Manor, 495 Old Hwy. 441, Mount Dora 32757.

Jim and Nanci Darst from Fort Lauderdale looked up and down the East Coast before settling on Mount Dora as the place to realize their dream of a B&B. They checked a few historic structures that since have been converted into B&Bs, but decided instead to build. They obtained a prime property facing Lake Dora across the highway, within walking distance of downtown, and erected a 9,000-square-foot house full of modern comforts and Victorian fantasy.

A dream-like air pervades the property, partly because the structure is so new yet the decor is so frilly and flouncy. Prized antiques and furnishings came from Nanci's country Victorian retail shop in Fort Lauderdale. One gets the feeling the inn must have been her biggest customer.

Behind the requisite front veranda lie a dining room decorated within an inch of its Victorian life and an elegant living room of museum quality. The Darsts built its fireplace to fit their prized inlaid walnut mantelpiece, an ornate 1886 affair from the Pullman estate in Chicago. An 1880 pump organ occupies one corner, and an antique flying machine sculpture hangs from the ceiling. Dolls and bric-a-brac are displayed here and there. A table in the turret holds a complicated jigsaw puzzle forever in progress.

The structure is big enough to house twice as many guest rooms as the six the Darsts offer. But they reserved much of the space for their quarters.

A main-floor bedroom with a private side entrance contains the inn's only double bed. It's ever-so-decorated in designer Victoriana and black and rose florals. The second floor has three more guest rooms. Darin's Room, named for their son, is dressed in navy blue and white. Ornate Louis XV twin beds are separated by a nightstand hiding an antique potty from France. Judi's Room, named for Nanci's best friend, has a canopied queen bed in 1920s French deco style and two wicker chairs in the bay window. The Oak Splendor with Victorian oak queen bed, remote-controlled gas fireplace and lively florals offers a view of the lake.

Two suites take up the entire third floor. The Queen Anne, with queensize canopied four-poster, has a rear sitting room with a sofabed and a writing desk facing the lake in the front window. A canopied kingsize mahogany tester bed faces a gas fireplace in the Queen Victoria, which comes with a dining room and a substantial sitting room in the turret.

The lavish wallpapers and borders that brighten most rooms reach their apex in the Queen Victoria, which took 46 rolls to complete. Costumed dolls, Victorian doodads and long-stemmed roses are in each room, velour robes hang in the closets and the inn's toiletries top the pedestal sinks in the bathrooms. Noticeably absent are the TV sets and telephones that usually typify four-diamond properties as rated by AAA.

Breakfast is taken at tables for four in the chandeliered dining room. Banana-nut pancakes and sausage were served the morning of our visit. Nanci considers her specialty to be stuffed french toast. Stratas and egg dishes are also in her repertoire. Tea and fancy desserts are offered in the afternoon.

Out back, guests enjoy a swimming pool and hot tub. That is, when they're not taking in the view of Lake Dora from the front veranda.

(352) 383-4050. Fax (352) 383-7653. Four rooms and two suites with private baths. Mid-October to Memorial Day: doubles $135 to $175, suites $185 and $220. Rest of year: doubles $112.50 to $165, suites $162 to $200. Two-night minimum weekends. Children over 12. No smoking.

Magnolia Inn, 347 East Third Ave., Mount Dora 32757.

Named for the stately magnolia tree in front, this stylish B&B in a residential area is surrounded by showy gardens and an aviary, and comes with an unusual outdoor gazebo containing a wet bar and hot tub. New owners David Cook, a former chiropractor in Clearwater, and his wife Betty purchased the B&B as this book went to press. They offer comfortable bedrooms and plenty of common space and extra touches for their guests.

The Magnolia is decorated crisply and with flair in what the former owner called "Southern casual elegance from the 1920s and 1930s." The rear Magnolia Room with kingsize bed is a beauty in dark green and pale yellow. A showy border of magnolias wraps around the walls. A kingsize bed and armoire grace the Birds and Blooms Room, decorated according to its name. The front Rose Room is elegant with an Eastlake bed and furniture and polished floors. A queen bed juts from the corner of the rear Garden Room, furnished in wicker and florals. The Cooks turned the former owners' garage apartment into a cottage for guests.

The main floor harbors a large and elegant parlor with fireplace, a sunroom dressed in wicker and a comfortable TV room full of plush sofas and chairs. A formal dining room is the setting for some elaborate breakfasts. Eggs benedict was the fare the day of our visit, and blueberry french toast the next.

Later in the day, guests help themselves to beverages – wine and beer from the wet bar in the gazebo, and quite an assortment of sherries and cordials on display in the parlor. The side yard harbors decks and patios, flowering trees and an aviary with assorted parakeets, finches, cockatiels and lovebirds.

Brick and wrought-iron gate entry frames Magnolia Inn.

(352) 735-3800 or (800) 776-2112. Fax (352) 735-0258. Four rooms and one cottage with private baths. Doubles, $110 to $140 weekends, $90 midweek. Cottage, $150. No smoking.

The Emerald Hill Inn, 27751 Lake Jem Road, Mount Dora 32757.

Half a dozen roundabout miles southwest of town is this substantial 1940s home. Built by an orange grove owner, it's enveloped by the intoxicating odor from citrus trees, the mystery of spanish moss and the blooms of azaleas, camellias and such. The location is a shaded, two-acre "hill" of central Florida proportions facing tiny Lake Victoria, with two other lakes nearby.

If the lakeside grounds are exotic, the interior of the ranch house constructed of buff-colored Ocala limestone is spectacular. Interior designer Diane Wiseman, owner with her husband Michael, has embellished a 5,000-square-foot showplace. Two chintz sofas impart an elegant look to a lodge-like living room with a cathedral ceiling and a huge coquina rock fireplace. Beyond is an enormous, six-sided Florida room – all windows onto the grounds and lake. It has a wicker seating area in front of a fieldstone fireplace, a colorful floor of Cuban tiles and three tables set for breakfast. "I kept it understated because the view is so overwhelming," says Diane.

A rambling wing of the house contains four light and airy guest accommodations. A contemporary decorative flair enhances what Diane calls "lots of 1940s fun stuff," particularly in the bathrooms. The front queen-bedded Ruby Room with a 1940 tub is designed to be soothing. The front Sapphire Room, mellow in pale yellow, conveys a Laura Ashley/Ralph Lauren look. The rear Peridot Suite has a kingsize bed and a daybed in a room opening onto a patio, plus a walk-in glass shower open to the room and an adjacent sitting/TV room fashioned from a former nursery. The premier accommodation is the end Diamond Room, nicely removed from the rest of the house. It has windows on three sides, a solid wood queensize poster bed, a wedge-shaped bath with a curved glass-block wall, and a private lakeview patio. "You can sit in bed and look out at the lake," says Diane.

Breakfast is served in that great Florida room from a built-in service counter. The fare is healthful with a vegetarian bent. Fresh fruit, nuts and homemade muffins precede the main course – perhaps a blintz soufflé with blueberry sauce one day and an egg and cheese casserole with imitation sausage the next. Thus fortified, guests may move on to explore Mount Dora. Or they may succumb to what Diane calls the Emerald Hill syndrome and, despite the best of intentions, simply while away the day right here.

(352) 383-2777 or (800) 366-9387. Fax (352) 383-6701. Three rooms and one suite with private baths. Doubles, $99 to $139. Suite, $149. Two-night minimum festival weekends. Children over 10. No smoking.

Farnsworth House, 1029 East Fifth Ave., Mount Dora 32757.

Situated in a quiet residential section on the east side of town, this 1886 house is full of Southern charm and represents unusual value. Dick and Sandy Shelton renovated the onetime residence-turned-apartment house into a comfortable B&B.

The aroma of banana bread fills the combination living/dining room at arrival. "I always put a loaf of fresh bread in guests' rooms," Sandy advises. Beyond is a large screened porch made for enjoying mild evenings.

Upstairs in the main house are three suites, each with queen bed and a kitchenette and named for a grandchild. Pretty in pale yellow and blue, the Forever Amber has a pleasant sitting room with TV. It opens onto the bedroom and, beyond, a kitchen. The table there is set for breakfast and the refrigerator is stocked with wine, soft drinks, cheeses and a fruit basket, as is the case in all rooms. Forever Amber shares a big screened porch with the Richard Suite, actually one large room in which Sandy ingeniously created a floral canopy above the bed to hide the window to the porch. The rear John Joseph Suite has a sitting room with a loveseat that converts to a twin bed, and a rear porch. Decor varies from Ralph Lauren chintz to traditional to country homey.

Two tastefully decorated theme rooms in the rear carriage house mask their garage-like heritage. Each has a queen bed and a kitchenette. The St. Nicholas is done in red, green and white for a Christmas theme, right down to the bath toiletries. The adjacent St. Andrews, appointed in Danish modern, incorporates a golf theme.

A screened gazebo beneath a spreading camphor tree holds a hot tub.

Each accommodation is stocked with a continental-plus breakfast of cereal, pastries, fruit and juices, plus a loaf of Sandy's homemade bread.

(352) 735-1894. Fax (352) 735-0292. Two rooms and three suites with private baths. November-May: doubles $85; suites $115. Rest of year: doubles $75, suites $95.

Mount Dora Historic Inn, 221 East Fourth Ave., Mount Dora 32757.

You wouldn't think this snug yellow house with green and white trim at the edge of downtown would be big enough for owners Lindsay and Nancy Richards, let alone guests in four bedrooms with queen or kingsize beds and private baths. But looks are deceptive in the case of this 1886 structure. And the Richardses have managed to make the most of limited space.

Guests check in at an antique desk in a cozy common room that doubles as a breakfast area. The drop-leaf table in the middle opens in the morning to accommodate eight.

Upstairs in front are two bedrooms where the balconies were partly enclosed to provide space for bathrooms. On the main floor are a side guest room, the owners' quarters and a rear guest room with a 120-year-old brass bed and the B&B's biggest bathroom with a clawfoot tub and shower. The rooms are furnished

Mount Dora Historic Inn occupies house built in 1886.

with antiques – Lindsay has an antiques business as a sideline, and the house formerly was an antiques store before they converted it into a B&B in 1996. They've furnished it to the early 1900s period.

Wine and cheese are offered in the common room in the afternoon. The next morning, Lindsay serves a full breakfast of soufflé, casserole or quiche at 8:30. "We're known for our breakfasts as well as our antiques," he says.

(352) 735-1212 or (800) 927-6344. Four rooms with private baths. Mid-October to mid-May: doubles, $100 to $125 weekends, $75 to $85 midweek. Rest of year: doubles, $85 to $100 weekends, $65 to $75 midweek. Children over 12. No smoking.

Christopher's Inn, 539 Liberty Ave., Mount Dora 32757.

A farmhouse built in 1887, this Montgomery Ward prefab house was opened in 1994 as a B&B of the old school by Jack and Inez Simpson, who named it for a son who died. The living room holds a collection of old salt and pepper shakers and two cabinets full of Reader's Digests from the 1940s. Every bit of wall space is taken up by something or other.

The four upstairs guest rooms also are display areas for family possessions reflecting the Victorian era. All have TVs and private baths – three notable for redwood or western cedar paneling and one fashioned from a closet. A homemade fabric canopy matches the floral spread in the North Room, where the old Pontiac radio stands in contrast to the modern TV. Beds are queensize except in the East Room, which has a double bed, armoire, a bench and a TV on the dresser. The West Room offers a private balcony. Guests in other rooms share a large side deck off the second floor, a back deck and a gazebo.

Breakfast is taken in a homey dining room or on a side sunporch that appears jaunty by comparison. The sideboard holds a buffet spread of waffles, pancakes and french toast ready for warming in a toaster.

Jack is proud of the game room he fashioned from a musty side garage, its walls and ceiling paneled to the hilt with beaded boards. An old Studebaker car is parked out front, and two more are painted on the front of the building.

(352) 383-2244. Four rooms with private baths. Doubles, $95 weekends, $75 midweek.

Dining Spots

The Goblin Market, 331B North Donnelly St., Mount Dora.
Hidden in an alley off the tourist path is this culinary find, a favorite of those in the know. Shelves of books lend a library look to two small, dark dining rooms holding about a dozen tables. On nice days the dining locations of appeal are the sunny front courtyard or, our choice, the shady rear courtyard – an idyllic spot with four tables topped with canvas umbrellas and surrounded by lush greenery. It had to be idyllic to compensate for an inordinate wait for food to emanate from the tiny kitchen. Everyone else seemed to be in the same boat, waiting more than half an hour after placing an order for lunch to arrive. The goblin club sandwich of turkey, bacon and more stacked on sourdough, teamed with a chilled rice salad, was worth the wait. The "snobby" cobb salad lacked the traditional avocado but compensated with lots of cheeses and fresh mesclun. Desserts were lemon cheesecake and hurricane annie chocolate cake.

The evening menu offers a selection of new American fare. Smoked salmon napoleon, grilled portobello mushroom and escargots in puff pastry make good starters. Typical entrées are shrimp and artichoke pasta, grilled salmon served over couscous, potato-crusted black grouper on wilted spinach, and filet mignon with monterey jack and béarnaise sauce.

(352) 735-0059. Entrées, $15 to $19. Lunch and dinner, Tuesday-Saturday 11 to 3, Dinner to 9 or 10.

Ivy's, 439 North Donnelly St., Mount Dora.
Ivy and Matthew Dennis left the Lakeside Inn in 1998 to open their own restaurant in a former floral shop. Ivy, a Scottish woman who was in food and beverage management, oversees the 50-seat dining room. She designed it to be cheerful in yellow and "very European – clean and crisp." White linens and orchids are on each table. More seating is available outside on a partly enclosed patio that Matthew likens to a breezeway.

Matthew, the chef, features contemporary European cuisine. The extensive menu ranges from game (ostrich filet with a wild mushroom ragoût and venison in chocolate sauce) to vegetarian (roasted vegetable cassoulet and cashew nut roast). Among the main courses: Spanish paella, macadamia-nut-encrusted ahi tuna with black currant chutney, baked stuffed quail, osso buco, crabmeat-stuffed filet mignon and rack of lamb. Fine wines are available to go with.

Appetizers include escargots, smoked salmon timbales, goose liver pâté spiked with sauternes and grilled portobello mushroom with spiced apple and walnut relish.

The homemade desserts are exceptional. Among them are crème caramel, key lime tarts, "a very berry mile high cherry crumble," passionfruit and mango cheesecake, and chocolate macadamia nut torte.

(352) 383-4277. Entrées, $14.95 to $22.95. Lunch, Tuesday-Sunday 11 to 3. Dinner, Tuesday-Sunday 5 to 9.

The Cafe at Gourmet to Go, 321-1 North Donnelly St., Mount Dora.
The entrance is an old loading dock. A side wall holds shelves bearing containers full of seeds and nuts. Billowing fabric floats beneath the ceiling. Much of the rest of this laid-back establishment consists of tables and chairs and a kitchen area that produces some of the best food in town.

We first discovered this culinary gem down a side alley off Donnelly Street during a break from the arts festival, where we joined a few fellow discoverers at tables on a nearly empty side courtyard. The courtyard was strangely empty again on a mild winter Friday when the locals seemed to be gathered inside. At the counter, we ordered the popular Tennessee turkey sandwich piled high with apple slices, greens and gouda cheese and took a seat alone on the side patio. The sandwich arrived with a tall glass of mango iced tea, a side of potato salad, a melon slice and a strawberry, which served as dessert.

The cafe menu, available weekdays until closing, is the most innovative in town, with a variety of salads and sandwiches in the $4.95 to $7.95 range. On weekend evenings, the fare gets heartier. Starters could be Thai shrimp, mozzarella caprese or marinated portobello mushroom with the house soy-ginger dressing fanned over greens and garnishes. Typical main dishes are scallops mandarin, crab-stuffed shrimp, rosemary roasted duck, honey-pecan chicken and rack of lamb for two.

For wine or beer, select a bottle from the rack or cooler. The espresso is made in the old style from beans ground to order. "We do not offer lattes, shaved chocolate, whipped cream or any of the frou-frou lately associated with espresso," the menu advises. The cooks here prefer things their way.

(352) 735-0155. Entrées, $13.95 to $22.95. Lunch, Monday 11 to 3, Tuesday-Saturday 11 to 5. Dinner, Tuesday-Saturday 5 to 9 or 10. Sunday, cafe menu, 11 to 9, dinner, 5 to 9.

Park Bench Restaurant, 116 East Fifth Ave., Mount Dora.

Consistently good food and service are the hallmarks of Betty and Gary O'Neil's long-running restaurant. The main dining room and side sunporch are country pretty in pink and green.

The menu takes on continental flair with regional American overtones. Expect starters like french onion soup gratinée, spicy New Orleans barbecued shrimp, clams casino and oysters Louisiana. Main courses range from cioppino, a creole seafood medley over pasta and grilled yellowfin tuna with tomato-corn salsa to Santa Fe chicken, braised veal loin and filet mignon with béarnaise sauce. The signature Park Bench oscar is sautéed chicken with crab-stuffed shrimp and béarnaise sauce.

For lunch, consider a tuna, walnut and raisin salad plate, a veggie dagwood sandwich or a plate of pâté, fruit and brie.

(352) 383-7004. Entrées, $15.95 to $23.95. Lunch, 11:30 to 2:30. Dinner, 4:30 to 8:30 or 9. Closed Tuesday and Wednesday.

The Gables, 322 North Alexander St., Mount Dora.

A prime corner location opposite the Mount Dora welcome center draws the tourists to this large establishment with a couple of interior dining rooms and a nondescript front and side terrace for outdoor dining.

The continental/American menu yields such dinner dishes as shrimp scampi tossed with lemon pepper linguini, sea scallops broiled in citrus butter, chicken florentine, veal chasseur and pan-seared tournedos topped with jumbo shrimp and served with a port and mushroom duxelles.

Start with escargots, french onion soup gratinée or chicken liver pâté. Finish with one of the homemade desserts or, the menu suggests, an after-dinner liqueur. The roasted duck breast salad is the most innovative item at lunchtime.

(352) 383-8993. Entrées, $10.95 to $20. Lunch daily, 11 to 2:30. Dinner, 5:30 to 8:30.

Rocking chairs on porch at Lakeside Inn overlook inn buildings and Lake Dora.

Lakeside Inn, 104 North Alexander St., Mount Dora.

The grand dowager of area restaurants has been ensconced seemingly forever in the elegant cream and mauve Beauclaire Room here. Its reputation and atmosphere draw the dowagers, as it did the dowager of our family who treated us to lunch here on a day trip to Mount Dora some years back.

It's a shame the large room at the rear of the main inn does not offer a water view (for that, you can order a bar lunch on the front veranda). Instead, the windows look onto an emerging garden. The rest of the scene is a sea of tables.

Locals in the know say the food has its ups and downs, and the service inordinately slow. That does not seem to deter the throngs that pack the place for a leisurely lunch of, say, imitation crab and seafood salad in a pineapple boat, a corned beef reuben or chicken pot pie. Desserts are ice cream, sherbets and "selections from the bakeshop," displayed in a container near the entrance.

At night, the fare aspires to nouvelle heights. Starters could be crab bisque or brie en croûte. Among main courses are sesame-crusted rare ahi tuna, crispy Long Island duckling with raspberry-orange coulis and black angus New York strip steak. The crab cakes, filet mignon and prime rib come in small and large sizes.

(352) 383-4101 or (800) 556-5016. Entrées, $13.95 to $21.50. Lunch daily, 11:30 to 2:30. Dinner nightly, 5 to 9 or 10.

The Windsor Rose, 144 West Fourth Ave., Mount Dora.

In its own way, this English tea room and garden shop is as much an icon of Mount Dora as the genteel Lakeside Inn or even the noisy open-air Eduardo's Mexican-American cantina ("cold food and hot beer") are in theirs.

Here, in a quaint country cottage, lunchers sit in an ever-so-British timbered room full of photos of the Royals or a side courtyard with three tables near the garden shop. They sample cornish pasties, chicken and leek pie, a ploughman's lunch and English desserts. Or they pause for a spot of tea ($1.50) or full English tea ($17.50 for two) with the proper accompaniments.

(352) 735-2551. Entrées, $5.25 to $7.25. Open Sunday-Wednesday 10:30 to 6, Thursday-Saturday 10:30 to 8.

Shiraz, 301 Baker St., Suite 106, Mount Dora.

A Mediterranean look prevails at this new bistro and wine bar in the Sunset Square boutique shopping complex. Named for the grape shiraz, which originated as syrah in Persia, the place features fine wines and a selection of starters, pizzas, sandwiches, salads and desserts. Lately it has added a few more substantial items. Snack on a sampler platter of cheeses with fruit and baguette, bruschetta or a portobello mushroom pizza. Or try an Asian chicken salad, an applewood-smoked chicken sandwich or a sampler of smoked salmon or smoked trout. Dessert could be cheesecake, fruit plate or creamy chocolate cake.

(352) 735-5227. Entrées, $7.95 to $14.95. Open Tuesday-Saturday 11 to 9, Sunday 11 to 4.

Diversions

The lakes and hills, the historic ambiance and shopping are Mount Dora's major attractions. As one innkeeper said, "people from south Florida can drive four hours to Mount Dora for a weekend and think they're in New England."

Mount Dora Historic Tour. A map offered by the Chamber of Commerce, housed in the 1913 train depot, depicts for visitors a three-mile tour past 29 historic sites. Among them are the pink and white gingerbread Donnelly House, a showy Steamboat Gothic landmark named for the town's first mayor and situated across from the downtown park dedicated to his wife. It's now neither museum nor B&B but the fancy home of a Masonic lodge. Donnelly Park – the most prominent of many in this city of parks – has benches and shuffleboard courts. It is the focus of the annual Christmas Lighting of Mount Dora with 100,000 lights. Free concerts and other events take place on the park's entertainment platform known as "The Boards." The Mount Dora Historical Society displays local memorabilia in the tiny **Royellou Museum,** housed in the Old City Jail and Firehouse along a back alley called Royellou Lane. It's open Thursday-Sunday 12:30 to 3:30.

Narrated tours are good ways to savor the town's atmosphere and scenery. **The Mount Dora Trolley Co.,** 357-9123, gives hour-long tours from the Lakeside Inn and Country Cottage Craft daily at 11:30, 1 and 2:30; adults, $7. **Classic Carriages of Mount Dora,** 589-2555, offers half-hour rides – drawn by a Clydesdale named Shane – weekends from Fourth and Alexander; adults, $12.50.

Lakefront Tour. Within easy walking distance of downtown are the Lakeside Inn, the Mount Dora Yacht Club and trails through Gilbert Park to Grantham Point, home of a photogenic lighthouse built of bricks donated by residents. Its flashing beacon, standing all of 35 feet high, guides boaters to the "Port of Mount Dora." Beyond is **Palm Island Park,** where Florida's longest boardwalk allows visitors an up-close view of forested wetlands along the Lake Dora shoreline. Signs identify everything from cattails to rare camphor and Carolina trees. We saw blue herons, anhingas, ospreys and lots of fishermen, not to mention more ducks and geese in various guises than we knew existed. We did not see any of the alligators that signs warned against feeding. Nearby are more park play areas and picnic tables.

Boat Cruises. Local promoter Scott Alderman offers a variety of cruises on Lake Dora via his Rusty Anchor pontoon boat, 400 W. Fourth Ave., 383-3933. Tours and hours vary from a one-hour lakefront or sunset cruise ($8) to a three-hour lunch cruise ($15 plus meal) along the Dora Canal. The canal, actually a river, goes from Lake Dora to Lake Eustis and permits boats to get to Silver Springs and the Atlantic Ocean via the St. John's River. Locals proudly note that the canal was called the most beautiful mile of waterway in the world by sports . writer Grantland Rice. A variety of other cruises leave from the canal area. A paddlewheeler was being readied at our visit.

Antiquing. Mount Dora is full of antiques shops. By far the biggest is **Renninger's Antique Center,** on 115 acres along Highway 441 on the northeastern outskirts of town. Each weekend the place is wall-to-wall people looking for bargains offered by 500 dealers in more than 40,000 square feet of inside display areas. It's also the site of bigger antiques fairs roughly monthly from October to March, and full-fledged antiques extravaganzas in November, January and February. Otherwise, open Friday and Saturday 9 to 5. Free.

Shopping. Although antiques and collectibles are the main draw, plenty of other shopping opportunities present themselves along Donnelly, Baker and cross streets in an eight-block area between Third and Seventh avenues. The shops are locally owned – none of the "of Pinehurst and Palm Beach" syndrome – and there are plenty of sidewalk benches upon which to relax.

Some of the most interesting are clustered in the new Sunset Square complex. We liked the home furnishings and collectibles at **Coyote Flats.** Neat wreaths of vegetables in little clay pots caught our eye at **Instead of Flowers,** which stocks gifts, gourmet foods and children's things. **When Pigs Fly** draws shoppers into the Renaissance Building. Cappuccino accompanies books and cards at **Dickens-Reed Bookshop.** Some of the most interesting handmade crafts are at **Deborah & Friends.** The **Baker Street Gallery** is a haven for art lovers.

An antiques mall opened in 1998 in a former supermarket at Highland and Fifth streets. Other retailers followed as an "Uptown" shopping area began to develop.

Extra-Special

Mount Dora Arts Festival.

Staged annually the first weekend of February, this arts festival (with apologies to the Winter Park Arts Festival, considered tops in Florida) is the best of our acquaintance. Every year we join the throngs – now more than 150,000 each day – to view the works of 300 artists and craftsmen spread across fifteen downtown blocks around Donnelly Park. Fewer than one-third of applicants for the juried show are chosen, and more than half of those are from out of state. The artworks are a cut above the art show norm, and the walls of our Florida condo are hung with cherished pictures and prints we've bought here over the years. The food vendors also are a cut above, with all manner of ethnic offerings – from shish kabobs and caesar salads to falafel and apple strudel. So is the entertainment, especially the Perseverance Brass Band led by a very tall African American gentleman in tails, à la New Orleans, which parades through festival streets to much applause. The arts extravaganza is the biggest of the festivals that give Mount Dora its nickname of Festival City. But the October Crafts Fair is not far behind. The Antique Boat Festival in March, the Antique Auto Show in April and the October Bicycle Festival also have their fans.

Key West landmark at foot of Whitehead and South streets marks southernmost point in U.S.A.

Key West, Fla.
Tropical Paradise

Call it Tropical. Mysterious. Romantic. Debauched. Notorious. Captivating. Paradise. The Conch Republic. The Last Resort.

Call it what you will. The last of the Florida Keys cast its spell on notables as different as John Audubon, Ernest Hemingway, John Dewey, Tennessee Williams and Harry S. Truman. Not to mention the prosperous salvagers and merchants who preceded them and turned Florida's southernmost outpost into what for a time was the richest small town in America. Nor the artists, the VIPs and the multitudes who followed.

Key West is an island of contrasts. Pirates and novelists, sailors and adventurers, bootleggers and artists, treasure seekers and tourists live and languish side by side in a small town where the "world's longest street" stretches twelve blocks from the Atlantic Ocean to the Gulf of Mexico. Miami and the mainland are more than 150 miles distant. Cuba is a scant 90 miles across the horizon.

The sense of remoteness makes Key West "The Last Resort" – in more ways than one. So does the subtropical landscape and the lazy lure of a place where the ocean temperature varies only between 78 and 80 degrees and the air temperature not much more.

Since the first house in south Florida was built here in 1829, Key West has spawned its own culture, customs and cuisine. The descendants of early arrivals from the Bahamas are the island-born Key Westers known as Conchs. Their Bahamian-style homes and those of Cuban cigarmakers lurk between Victorian mansions built by New England sea captains. Bootlegging, shipwreck salvaging, shrimping, sponging, cigarmaking, artistry – all have helped create a small and swinging island city like no other.

The architecture and diversity of 3,100 structures in Key West's three historic districts alone are worth noting. So is the variety of enticements that allow one to snorkel along coral reefs, kayak through mangroves, parasail above idyllic beaches, tour historic homes and gardens, sample exotic cuisine, examine cross-currents of the art world, and take advantage of more attractions than a place its size has a right to offer.

Key West has had its ups and downs. Declines followed the destruction of Henry M. Flagler's overseas railroad in the 1935 hurricane and the closing of the Key West Naval Station in 1968. Belatedly, it turned to tourism. Historic landmarks became tourist attractions. Ramshackle boarding houses and decaying mansions were upscaled into inns and B&Bs. Bars and watering holes metamorphosed into restaurants. The pace decidedly quickened in the 1990s. The Key West that we first visited in 1984, when it was awakening from slumber, is quite different today.

There's more of everything, including residents and attractions and, especially, visitors. The lure of paradise grows stronger.

Inn Spots

The Key West Innkeepers' Association has 55 member properties, and there are countless other places to stay. Your choice may be determined not only by location, style and price but also by the sexual orientation of guests and the appeal of the courtyard/pool area that is so much a part of the Key West inn scene. Our selection here focuses on places that welcome couples and where the owners – or at least their tastes – are in evidence.

Simonton Court, 320 Simonton St., Key West 33040.

A brick lane and tropical gardens unite this rambling, two-acre complex that offers something for everyone. Guests stay in a two-bedroom manor house with a private lanai pool, two suites in a secluded townhouse with another private pool, six elegant quarters in a three-story mansion, nine smaller accommodations in an inn that was once a cigar factory or, our choice, in one of six charming pink and white cottages that housed cigar factory workers.

Hidden back from the street are two large pools and extensive gardens dripping with bougainvillea. In the midst of it all are the six cottages, each with front porch

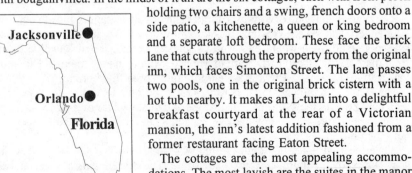

holding two chairs and a swing, french doors onto a side patio, a kitchenette, a queen or king bedroom and a separate loft bedroom. These face the brick lane that cuts through the property from the original inn, which faces Simonton Street. The lane passes two pools, one in the original brick cistern with a hot tub nearby. It makes an L-turn into a delightful breakfast courtyard at the rear of a Victorian mansion, the inn's latest addition fashioned from a former restaurant facing Eaton Street.

The cottages are the most appealing accommodations. The most lavish are the suites in the manor house behind the reception area and in the townhouse. The last includes the luxury Royal Palm

Three-story mansion backs up to breakfast area and pool at Simonton Court.

Suite with fourteen-foot-high skylit ceiling, king bed, wet bar, living room, Roman jacuzzi tub, private porch and a pool shared with the queen-bedded Bamboo Suite. Three high-ceilinged rooms on the second floor of the mansion are elegant in traditional style with queen beds, antique furnishings, refrigerators and outdoor decks or porches. Three on the third floor are outfitted in more tropical style. One has a jacuzzi, a sound system and access to a widow's walk with distant water views.

The original inn is in a structure that bears little resemblance to the factory it once was. Rooms here retain the old Key West flavor. They have king, queen or two double beds, some with additional loft or bunk beds. Four have kitchenettes and living/dining areas. All have the TVs, telephones and refrigerators standard throughout the complex.

Breakfast is put out in a covered bar behind the mansion near the main pool area. The spread when we were there included three kinds of juices, whole fruit, homemade biscuits and muffins, bagels and waffles.

A friendly staff works for the owners, who live in Kentucky most of the year.

(305) 294-6386 or (800) 944-2687. Fax (305) 293-8446. Fourteen rooms, five suites and six cottages with private baths. Mid-December through April: doubles $175 to $225, suites $225 to $275, cottages, $295 to $375. Rest of year: doubles $125 to $185, suites $155 to $235, cottages, $195 to $275. Minimum stays during peak season. No children.

Center Court Historic Inn & Cottages, 916 Center St., Key West 33040.

The two-block-long alley called Center Street is an anomaly – it's one of Key West's oldest and least gentrified neighborhoods, slumbering half a block away from busy Duval Street on one side and posh Simonton Street on the other. Seemingly singlehandedly, Naomi Van Steelandt is changing its nature. She restored a guest house and two adjacent cottages in 1994 into seven B&B accommodations, earning a couple of preservation awards along the way. Then she hopscotched along the street, buying three more properties as they – and the requisite transient licenses needed for nightly rentals – became available, adding seven more units. The day we visited, she had started renovating two more side-by-side cottages for a total of eighteen units. You got the feeling this one-woman dynamo was only beginning.

Naomi, a hands-on innkeeper from the get-go, offers quite a variety of accommodations. She also does things differently. Breakfast is self-serve from the main house kitchen at the hour you want. There's a convivial happy hour later in the day on the rear veranda or around the heated pool, spa and tropical gardens. Naomi's suites and houses are child- and pet-friendly. She adores local art, and decorates lavishly according to theme. "This is my underwater cottage," she advised during a tour, pointing out the unifying factor in all the artworks and accessories in the Cistern House, an efficiency unit with queen bed, porch and garden beside the pool. She lights a sculpture at night atop the well left open to view behind the guest house. Across the pool is an open-air "exercise pavilion" with workout equipment. In the two-bedroom Family House are a kingsize waterbed, a second room with double bed, a living room with a queen sofabed, a kitchen fully equipped with everything from gourmet utensils to a Cuisinart, a dining area ready for a dinner party, and a private deck in back.

Other accommodations vary from four simple but comfortable rooms with queen beds in the guest house to the self-contained Conch Cottage, a two-bedroom condo-style layout that, like the Family House, sleeps up to six. Here, wooden cats rest on a beam above the cathedral-ceilinged living room. An outdoor shower is hidden off the rear deck.

All accommodations have private baths, hair dryers, TVs, telephones, beach tote bags, in-room safes and wonderful art by a favorite Florida artist.

Naomi, a registered nurse who is also a notary public, performs weddings. She puts newlyweds up in the Treetop Studio, the top floor of the rare Eyebrow House down the street, which has a private rooftop deck with a jacuzzi, shower and gas grill. The main floor of the house holds a couple of two-room suites that share a rear deck outfitted with a hammock and a whirlpool spa.

We begged off on touring the three units in the Porchside Paradise, which Naomi described as "cute, cute, cute." Instead we reviewed her plans for two new "sister cottages," a few doors up Olivia Street. Former cigarmaker homes, these were to be "more cottagey in the Martha Stewart style." She envisioned these as rustic, with darker woods, crown molding and chair rails – "not so contemporary Caribbean" as the others.

We'll see them the next time, along with whatever else Naomi is up to. She's one of Key West's few innkeepers actually in residence, and may well be the life of the party.

(305) 296-9292 or (800) 797-8787. Fax (305) 294-4104. Four rooms and fourteen cottage suites with private baths. Mid-December-May: doubles $128 to $148, cottage suites, $158 to $328. Rest of year: doubles $88 to $108, suites $118 to $238. Children and pets welcome.

Heron House, 512 Simonton St., Key West 33040.
Unusual architectural and decorative touches as well as prolific orchids and rare plants elevate this 23-room complex a cut above. They testify to the efforts and ingenuity of Fred Geibelt and Robert Framarin, who vacationed in Key West in 1983 and never returned home to New Jersey.

Exotic tropical plants surround pool and guest quarters at Heron House.

Instead they purchased two old Conch apartment houses and converted them into seven simple guest rooms. A cardboard sign announced they were in business. They expanded and upgraded year by year by borrowing against the credit cards that kept arriving in their mail and paying them off as they went along.

Today, they offer quite a range of accommodations in four buildings surrounded by exotic tropical plants, most of which they propagated themselves. Robert is the orchid man, growing more than 100 species in an open-air "greenhouse" beside the courtyard bar. He also designs the artistic touches that Fred executes. These include the remarkable "wood quilting" on room walls – teak, oak or cedar designs in intricate patterns, no two of which are alike.

The visual treats begin in a new reception area, where the granite floor is a remarkable mosaic featuring four marble herons handcarved piece by piece.

Unusual touches abound. Stained-glass transoms above the room doors feature herons and orchids. Baths are of granite and marble. Original Key West watercolors hang on the walls and potted orchids are in each room. Striking traveler's palms from Madagascar fan out around the pool, the bottom of which is decorated with tiles in the shape of a heron. The common room is a plush outdoor retreat open on two sides. The walkways are of imported Chicago brick. A brick driveway is laid out in concentric circles, each brick cut to fit.

Rooms vary. Some are small, with double bed, private bath with shower and outside entry door. Some are mini-suites with king beds, sitting areas and private decks or porches onto the pool area. We sprung for a deluxe garden suite that turned out to be the latest and most deluxe, newly renovated atop the reception office. It was not beside the pool with the rest but rather upstairs across a large, clothing-optional sundeck full of unoccupied lounges that were better for prone sunning than upright reading or sipping of the complimentary champagne that came with the room. The interior was a large, angular but not particularly utilitarian space with a marble floor, kingsize bed, a desk, one wicker chair upon which to watch television, a couple of cushioned shelf seats tucked into alcoves and a wet bar. A full-length marble cabinet recessed in the foyer displayed a couple of fish sculptures. The jacuzzi tub/shower in the bathroom was encased in marble to the top of its vaulted ceiling.

Breakfast the next morning was a treat in the garden courtyard around a pool that seemed to be more for show than swimming. Cereals and prepared waffles and french toast ready for warming in a toaster supplemented the usual Key West fare of pastries, bagels and fresh fruit. Coffee and the day's paper were available first.

Although they finally finished upgrading the property to their standards in 1997, the partners were not done. They traveled to Thailand to buy furniture and linens and gather ideas for their next project: a tropical rain forest complete with waterfalls, streams, tropical fish and exotic plants along one side of the property. Stay tuned.

(305) 294-9227 or (800) 294-1644. Fax (305) 294-5692. Ten rooms and thirteen suites with private baths. Dec. 20 through April: doubles, $159 to $189, suites $259 to $289. Rest of year: doubles, $129 to $139 weekends, $119 to $129 midweek; suites, $179 to $199 weekends, $159 to $179 midweek. Children over 14. Two-night minimum stay required; five-night minimum holiday weeks. Smoking restricted.

Island City House Hotel, 411 William St., Key West 33040.

A substantial pool area and lush tropical gardens are the focal points of this small, family-friendly suite hotel located in a quiet residential section. "Hotel" is really a misnomer, for this complex personally overseen by Stan and Janet Corneal, former architects raising two children here, easily qualifies as a B&B inn – one of the more comfortable in Key West.

An eighteen-foot tiled alligator lurks along the bottom of the heated pool, one of Key West's largest and most inviting. A whirlpool spa awaits alongside. Palms, vines and other tropical flora tower overhead and sprawl throughout the jungly garden courtyard onto which the hotel's three buildings face. Scattered around the pool and gardens are outdoor breakfast and several sitting areas, for this is the hotel's bewitching common "room."

A hammock and two heavy wood chairs faced the pool area from the second-floor balcony outside our parlor suite, one of six in the three-story Cigar House built of red cypress on the site of a former cigar factory. Outfitted in tropical plantation style, the large living room had a full kitchen along one side, a rattan dining table in the center, and a rattan sofa with a coffee table in front and good reading lamps on either side. The full bathroom was small but serviceable (except for lack of a place to store one's toiletries) and the kingsize bedroom in the rear was quiet as could be, until we were awakened shortly before sunrise by a neighbor's noisy cockatiel and macaw – not a rare happening in Key West.

The majority of suites are in the original Victorian residence, built about 1888 and converted into a hotel in anticipation of the railroad's arrival in 1912. This landmark with three stories of wraparound porches holds ten one-bedroom and two two-bedroom suites, each individually furnished in Victorian style, some with antique pieces acquired by the Corneals from forays around their farm in northern Virginia. Notable for heart-pine floors and dark woods, each has a queen bed, kitchen and living/dining area that hint of their previous status as apartments. The

Suites in Cigar House overlook large pool at Island City House Hotel.

roof sundeck at tree-top level is open to all guests and gets full sun, which the shady courtyard area does not.

Four romantic studio suites are sequestered out of the way in the Arch House, the original carriage house and said to be the only one still standing in Key West. These second-story rooms are furnished in casual island style with queensize beds canopied in mosquito netting, loveseats, kitchenette and porch or deck overlooking street or gardens. Each comes with the TV, telephone and amenities standard throughout the complex.

One of the island's better continental breakfasts is put out in a charming horse wagon beside a fountain and fish pond in the garden. Juice, slices of fresh fruit, English muffins and all kinds of bagels for toasting, and addictive sticky buns filled the cart – not to mention the partakers – to overflowing.

(305) 294-5702 or (800) 634-8230. Fax (305) 294-1289. Four studio suites and eighteen parlor suites with private baths. Christmas week through April: doubles, $165 to $225. Rest of year: $95 to $155. Two-night minimum on weekends. Children welcome.

Eaton Lodge, 511 Eaton St., Key West 33040.

Collections from the owners' world travels are everywhere evident in this stylish B&B complex dating to 1832. One of Key West's first restorations as a guest house in the early 1980s, the classic 2½-story periwinkle Conch House had been boarded up in the 1990s. Two men renovated it and quickly sold it in 1995 to Carolyn and Steven West, who moved from Miami. "We furnished it with everything we ever had," said Carolyn, a well-connected New Yorker who had a great deal.

The Wests offer a variety of accommodations in three buildings around two hidden courtyards. All come with private baths, telephones and TV. Two have kitchenettes and all but one has a refrigerator.

The front parlor is furnished to the hilt in Victoriana. It's a stately contrast to the surprises beyond: a cluttered library/reception room, a rustic dining area open to the side yard and a spacious kitchen overlooking the rear pool and courtyard. The main floor also holds a small guest room in what had been a former doctor's office and two side guest rooms facing the oldest private garden in Key West.

Upstairs are four more guest rooms and a two-bedroom suite with three double beds. Other bed configurations vary from queen to kingsize. Each bears Carolyn's decorating touches and prized accessories. Two of the nicest are in the rear of this house that keeps unfolding. The Treetops Room comes with a queensize carved four-poster bed, Haitian paintings on the walls, Chinese garden stools for nightstands and a wicker balcony. Across the back of the house is the Sunset Room with a queensize bed, armoire, a colorful loveseat in the dressing room and balconies on either side, one overlooking a key lime tree from which Carolyn picked us a few samples. But for the rustic walls, you'd never guess that its bathroom is on one level of what had been a three-story concrete cistern, the island's tallest water reservoir.

The Victorian theme gives way to Caribbean in the rear carriage house, where four large rooms open onto the brick-paved courtyard. We were happily ensconced in the Saratoga, named for the racing town where Carol summered with her parents. It had a king bed, kitchenette, dining area and a wicker sitting area facing the TV, although we preferred to relax outside on our private brick patio beside the whirlpool spa. We even enjoyed a takeout dinner by candlelight on one of the courtyard tables for four. Never would we have guessed the setting could be so tranquil with busy Duval Street less than half a block away.

Seven parrots live around the courtyard and carry on a running conversation with anyone who will respond. They kept up a steady chatter with Steve West as he set out breakfast on the garden bar, where guests had helped themselves to an open bar during a cocktail hour the night before. Fresh fruit, bagels, croissants and boxed cereals were the fare.

Next door, the Wests also offer a pink three-bedroom house built in 1832, joined to the main property through the island's oldest garden. The garden is mulched not with wood chips but with scallop shells. Original paths wind past a fish pond fountain, tamarind and rare fruit trees, cascading orchids and other tropical goodies. Behind is a small swimming pool.

(305) 292-2170 or (800) 294-2170. Fax (305) 292-4018. Eleven rooms, one suite and three-bedroom house, all with private baths. Mid-December through April: doubles $139 to $189, suite $235, house $450. Rest of year: doubles $95 to $130, suite $189, house $325. No children. No smoking.,

La Mer and **Dewey House,** 504 and 506 South St., Key West 33040.

One of the more remarkable vistas in all Key West greets visitors as they enter the vestibule and common area of the new Dewey House. Ahead lies a designer living room with tiled floors, oversize chairs in splashy yellow and blue checked fabrics, tropical pillows and paintings. The room is open to the outside and a deck with a tiny dip pool, overlooking the palm-rimmed beach and the Atlantic.

The common area serves both the Dewey House, once the home of progressive educator John Dewey, and La Mer, two side-by-side Queen Anne-style gems opened by the owners of the Southernmost Motel. La Mer, the initial stage of this luxury B&B, holds eleven guest rooms, all with king or queen beds and four with ocean views.

The eight rooms in the Dewey House are more upscale. Each has a king or queen bed, a marble bath with jacuzzi tub, a custom-made armoire and a private porch. Three claim water views (two full and one partial). Those in front are close to the street. The rear rooms with lovely balconies are quieter.

Palm-rimmed beach is back yard for guests at La Mer and Dewey House.

Everyone in both houses shares the elegant Dewey House common area, where a continental breakfast buffet of croissants, pastries, bagels, cereal and yogurt is put out in the morning. It's taken to wrought-iron tables and chairs on the deck, or onto the sandy beach. Tea is offered in the afternoon.

A gazebo serves as the joint entry to the two properties.

(305) 296-5611 or (800) 354-4455. Nineteen rooms with private baths. Mid-December through April: doubles, $175 to $300. Rest of year: $125 to $220. No children. Two-night minimum weekends. No smoking in Dewey House.

The Weatherstation Inn, 57 Front St., Key West 33040.

A new luxury entry on the B&B circuit, this is unusual in several respects. It's set amid substantial residences in the former Navy Yard, now a private, gated community called the Truman Annex. Its rooftop deck enjoys a water view. And the handsome stucco residence built in 1911 looks more like an embassy than the government weather station it actually was until the 1950s. The latter function may explain the lack of an inside staircase (the second floor is accessed by an exterior stairway in the rear).

Local attorney Tim Koenig bought the structure, one of the few original structures still here and listed on the National Register, when the Navy sold all its property in 1987. He and his family lived here before converting it in 1997 into a B&B run by a manager.

The first and second floors hold four guest rooms each. Five have queensize beds, two are kingsize and one has two twins. Bahama shutters, gleaming hardwood floors and stylish furnishings convey a plush tropical theme. One main-floor room with a kingsize poster bed has a walk-in double shower. The room is dressed in pale yellow, while a neighboring room is appointed starkly in white and black.

Others upstairs vary from pale yellow with red accents to pale blue or pale green. Two have access to a side balcony. The largest room, second-floor front, has a queensize mahogany poster bed with duvet cover and its own balcony atop the pillared front porch. Armoires hide the TV sets. Guests hang up clothing on a lineup of coat hooks on the wall.

A common room in the basement was in the works at our visit. The only other common area was a rooftop sundeck, reached by a dizzying exterior spiral staircase – with an ocean vista above the buildings in back and a view of visiting cruise ships as well as the evening sunset. The nicely landscaped yard includes a plush side courtyard with a tiny pool.

A continental breakfast of fresh fruit and pastries is taken on a rear deck or beside the pool.

(305) 294-7277 or (800) 815-2707. Fax (305) 294-0544. Eight rooms with private baths. Mid-December to mid-May: doubles, $195 to $315. Rest of year: $150 to $215. Children over 12. Two-night minimum weekends. Smoking restricted.

Bananas Foster, 537 Caroline St., Key West 33040.

Bananas Foster – don't you love it? Foster Meagher converted a classic Revival house, built by one of Florida's first millionaires along Mansion Row, into a small B&B with considerable style in 1994. He sold it in 1998 to Ron Hoiberg and John Winslow, who became in-residence innkeepers. They don't serve bananas foster, the New Orleans dessert, but John, a chef, prepares homemade brioche, croissants, banana bread, coffee cake and even white chocolate macadamia-nut cookies and cherry crumble cake to go with the five kinds of fresh fruit put out for continental breakfast in the garden. He makes two different appetizers every afternoon for happy hour, when complimentary wine and beer are offered. He also occasionally offers dinners for holidays and special occasions.

The rooms exhibit a decorative flair that is unusual for Key West, as executed by the founding owner, an architectural designer. Off the living room on the main floor, the English Hunt Room is dark and masculine with mahogany molding and wainscoting, a queen poster bed and thick carpeting – rare for Key West. It is quite a contrast to its neighbor, the nautical Nantucket Room, pale yellow and white with a rocker of distressed wood and a queen poster bed wrapped in a picket fence at head and foot.

An antique game table occupies a corner of the living room. The polished wood floor is left uncovered here, as well as in the dining room.

Two rooms in a cottage behind the house open onto the garden, where a combination jacuzzi/dip pool occupies an old cistern and an intimate terrace holds a few tables for breakfast. The Mardi Gras Room has a king bed and a day bed, interesting paintings and a walk-in, double-headed shower.

An exterior staircase leads upstairs in the main house to two larger rooms sharing the front veranda. One with a 19th-century Parisian motif is elegant in beige and cream tones. Its tapestry-look draperies and swagged windows match the canopy surround behind the kingsize bed.

All rooms have king or queen beds, TVs and telephones. Four have refrigerators. Parking is provided.

(305) 294-9061 or (800) 653-4888. Fax (305) 292-9411. Six rooms with private baths. Mid-December to mid-April: doubles, $165 to $195. Rest of year: weekends $120 to $145; midweek, $110 to $130.

The Conch House, 625 Truman Ave., Key West 33040.
The fourth and fifth generations of the original owners imbue this 1889 house with a sense of local history. Listed on the National Register, the house was converted into a B&B in 1993 by Francine Delaney Holland, great-granddaughter of the original owner, and her son Sam Holland Jr., who oversees it today. His octogenarian grandfather, who lives next door, occasionally joins overnight guests for breakfast and tells stories of Key West's early days.
The family home is the essence of early Key West architecture. Its seaside Victorian styling with Bahamian influences is characterized by spindled wraparound porches, wood shutters, high ceilings and picket fences. A similarly styled cabana alongside faces the pool area.
The main house contains a formal reception room and a small breakfast room with wicker furniture and tiled floor. Sliced fruit, cereal and homemade banana-apple bread, cinnamon rolls and Cuban breads are offered here in the morning.
Also on the main floor are two bedrooms, furnished like the rest of the house with Victorian antiques. The largest has a queensize bed with picket fence headboard, marble-topped tables and a sofa and easy chair. Upstairs are three more bedrooms, plus a small upstairs sitting area facing the balcony. Two beds are kingsize; the rest in the house and in the cabana are queensize. A cache of toiletries is wrapped in towels standing tall on each bed. Telephones and TVs are standard equipment.
Outside by the small, sunny pool area are two more guest rooms, one up and one down, in the aforementioned cabana. They're furnished in tropical wicker. In between the cabana and the main house is another little cabana house with a double bed and a walk-in shower.
(305) 293-0020 or (800) 207-5806. Fax (305) 293-8447. Eight rooms with private baths. Mid-December to mid-May: doubles $128 to $178. Rest of year: $88 to $138. Two-night minimum in winter and weekends year-round. No children. No smoking.

La Pensione, 809 Truman Ave., Key West 33040.
Built in 1891 as the residence of a leading cigarmaker, this Classic Revival mansion was restored in 1991 into a nine-room B&B. Pale yellow with green shutters and white trim, it is notable for intricate gingerbread, hand-planed walls of the locally ubiquitous Dade County pine and shuttered french doors opening onto wraparound verandas.
Nine guest rooms, all with kingsize beds, are individually appointed in the Key West style. Some with wicker furnishings and loveseats in the bay windows open onto verandas. The one we were shown, said to be among the largest, was furnished in what the manager called Ethan Allen country classic style. It had two recliner chairs and more of a motel look than most Key West inns.
Breakfast is extended continental, which the day of our visit included a special quiche. Belgian waffles are served on other occasions. The meal is taken in a breakfast room or by the sunny pool.
La Pensione offers off-street parking, an asset in Key West.
(305) 292-9923 or (800) 893-1193. Fax (305) 296-6509. Nine rooms with private baths. Doubles, $148 to $168, Christmas to mid-May; $88 to $98 rest of year. Two-night minimum on weekends. No children.

Master suite of Gardens Hotel looks out onto pool, courtyard fountain and cottage with guest rooms.

Small Hotels/Resorts

The Gardens Hotel, 526 Angela St., Key West 33040.

Among the many, no more exotic lodging property can be found in the heart of Key West than this acre of tropical gardens that once was the island's largest private estate. The home and garden, nurtured from the early 1930s by Peggy Mills as a labor of love, is now the site of a small luxury hotel. It was opened in 1993 by New Yorkers Bill and Corinna Hettinger.

Bill designed and supervised the construction of a seventeen-room complex in five small buildings. For the interiors, his wife chose furniture and fabrics from around the world.

Guests enter a private world through the main house, an 1870s Conch masterpiece listed on the National Register. Upstairs are two small rooms with queen beds and gold-plated bath fixtures and a huge master suite. The last has a king bed and a settee in a bedroom alcove, a sitting room with queen sofabed and a skylit marble bathroom with bidet, jacuzzi, cedar sauna, steam shower and double vanity. Triple french doors open onto a cloistered deck overlooking pool and gardens.

Mere mortals would be quite content in the Bahamian-style Eyebrow Cottage off by itself in a far corner of the property. Here beneath a cathedral ceiling are a kingsize bed, marble bath with jacuzzi, private porch and all the trimmings of the rest of the accommodations: TV, telephone, stocked minibar, waffle-weave robes, hair dryer and Nina Ricci toiletries from France. Rooms are decorated in aqua and pink florals and chintz, furnished in imported yew or mahogany, and enhanced with original oil paintings of Key West scenery by New Zealand artist Peter Williams.

The other original building, called the Carriage House, holds a poolside bar for guests. Upstairs are two widely separated bedrooms with jacuzzi baths. They could be rented individually but are booked as a suite, since guests in the first accommodation wouldn't want to hear occupants of the second traipsing down the hall late at night, we were advised.

Two buildings were erected in 1993 on what had been a tennis court. With wraparound porches facing pool and gardens, they contain twelve additional guest rooms.

Peggy, the resident blue and gold macaw named for the original owner, comes out of her cage in the garden for breakfast with guests in the solarium at the rear of the main house. Fresh flowers are on individual tables, and the buffet is laden with fruits, cereals, cheeses, croissants and pastries, perhaps including Key West beignets.

Besides the lush tropical pool area, guests enjoy wandering the brick paths through the restored gardens that had been opened to the public in the 1970s. Hidden from the street behind brick walls, they are illuminated at night and contain intimate seating areas and a tiered Georgian fountain. They also hold four rare tinajones, one-ton earthenware containers imported from Cuba for collecting rainwater.

(305) 294-2661 or (800) 526-2664. Fax (305) 292-1007. Fourteen rooms, two suites and one cottage with private baths. Dec. 20-April: doubles $245 to $335, cottage $465, suites $555 and $675. Rest of year: doubles $155 to $275, cottage $295 to $395, suites $385 to $595. Two-night minimum on weekends. Children over 7.

The Marquesa Hotel, 600 Fleming St., Key West 33040.

The Marquesa is the one that started the small luxury hotel boom. Local builders Richard Manley and Erik deBoer purchased an 1884 Greek Revival residence that had been a boarding house and developed a fifteen-room boutique hotel with a restaurant in 1988. In 1993, the property was basically doubled in size. A carriage house was built from the ground up with covered parking beneath. Twelve "junior suites" emerged, and an existing pool was added to the kitty.

Except for the original structure, the word hotel is misleading. The complex backs up to a tropical courtyard, and the look is distinctly residential. Porches with a breakfast table and two rattan loungers front the junior suites, spread around the rear perimeter of the property. They have living rooms or sitting areas and kingsize bedrooms with unusual mod faucets in the deep soaking tubs. Decor mixes West Indies-style reproductions with modern fabrics and accessories. Four-poster iron beds, 400-pound sleigh beds from Indonesia, planter's chairs, teak tables from the Philippines and yew wood armoires from England are among the furnishings.

The original standard hotel rooms were described by our guide as "more charming because they're historic." They were fully occupied the night we were there in a switch from the high-end norm where the best rooms usually go first.

Each guest room comes with a marble bath with hair dryer, waffle-weave robes, mini-safe, TV, telephone and a stocked minibar. The stock was unusual here in that it was all on jarring display on a table top somewhere in each room. Orchids are placed in every room prior to guests' arrival. Chocolates are presented during nightly turndown. Continental breakfast is available for $7.50 in the morning.

Spectacular floral arrangements welcome guests in the formal reception room, a mix of Federal furnishings in gleaming mahogany and burnished cherry. The front desk is hidden behind closed doors.

The 48-seat Cafe Marquesa in the front corner of the hotel is considered one of Key West's best restaurants (see Dining Spots).

(305) 292-1919 or (800) 869-4631. Fax (305) 294-2121. Fourteen rooms and thirteen suites with private baths. Mid-December to mid-April, doubles $225 to $265, suites $340. Mid-April to Memorial Day and mid-October to mid-December, doubles $200 to $235, suites $300. Rest of year: weekends, doubles $170 to $200, suites $245; midweek, doubles $145 to $175, suites $220. Two-night minimum on weekends. Children over 12.

The Paradise Inn, 819 Simonton St., Key West 33040.

Shel Segal left Detroit in 1974, opened the island's largest florist business and bided his time. In 1995, he built from scratch in a field behind his original floral shop an eighteen-room inn complex and called it, not inappropriately, paradise.

"We wanted a residential feeling in a residential neighborhood," said Shel, who achieved his goal in spades. Behind an automatic gated parking area lie two Bahamian-style houses holding eight mini-suites and seven full suites, plus three cigarmaker cottages with one or two bedrooms each. The pool, the spa, the lotus pond, the sculptures, the heron fountain and the exotic gardens – each species identified by a sign – are so attractive that guests are reluctant to leave this hidden island within an island.

The accommodations are outfitted with distressed pine and light oak furnishings in Bahamian style. Shel calls the yellowish walls "linen white." All beds are kingsize. Full suites and cottages add queensize sofabeds. Each comes with TV, phone, safe, sitting area or sitting room, porch and a marble bar with refrigerator beneath. Marble baths feature jacuzzi tubs, a shaving mirror in the showers, hair dryers, monogrammed robes and a second telephone for "the telephone call that can't wait." The two-bedroom, two-bath Royal Poinciana Cottage comes with its own porch and private garden hideaway alongside. A handicapped-accessible mini-suite has its own parking place.

Three herons spout water into a fountain beside the pool, and Japanese koi swim in the lotus pond on terraces tiered toward a hidden spa. Shel's green thumb produced a state award for the landscaping.

A continental breakfast is put out in the front reception area. The fare includes fresh orange juice, croissants, pastries and Cuban coffee. Room service dinners are available from the Siam House restaurant next door.

(305) 293-8007 or (800) 888-9648. Fax (305) 293-0807. Fifteen suites and three cottages with private baths. Dec. 20 to mid-April: suites $250 to $315, cottages $350 to $495. Rest of year: suites, $165 to $250; cottages $240 to $375. Two-night minimum on weekends. Children over 7.

A Tropical Island Resort

Little Palm Island, 28500 Overseas Hwy., Little Torch Key, 33042.

For a touch of Tahiti, take the fifteen-minute shuttle Escape to this five-acre offshore island resort. It's 28 miles back toward the mainland from Key West, but a world apart.

Here, on a tropical island where presidents once fished, sun-starved celebrities bask in Relais & Chateaux-style comfort. Fourteen thatched-roof villas contain two side-by-side "bungalow suites" each, none very far from the water. Rope hammocks are strung between swaying palms. A wraparound deck envelops each living room with a sofabed and two rattan chairs and a bedroom with mosquito-netted kingsize canopy bed. Taking center stage in the middle is the bathroom, with dressing area and vanity in one section, a jacuzzi tub in another other and, outside, a private shower screened in bamboo.

There is electricity, thanks to Warner Brothers having selected Little Palm with its South Seas ambiance for the filming of *PT 109,* the movie about John F. Kennedy's wartime experiences. There are no telephones except for a phone booth in President Truman's former outhouse and only a few televisions are available. The theme is summed up by the resort's 800 GET-LOST phone number.

Suite offers bedroom, living room and porch at The Paradise Inn.

Pampered by a friendly staff, sybarites can indulge 24 hours a day in a lagoon-like pool and waterfall, use complimentary sailboats and canoes, snorkel along the shallow coral reef out toward the open Atlantic, or swim and fish along the shore-side harbor channel. Sauna and spa services are available. A sunset sail with wine and cheese is offered every evening before dinner.

Meals are bigtime here, thanks to the many glamorous, open-air dining areas and the cooking of acclaimed chef Michel Reymond, who has been with the much-honored resort since its 1988 opening. Redwing blackbirds begged for scraps during our memorable lunch, taken beside the sliver of a sandy beach. An unusual avocado gazpacho, a lobster-crabmeat salad, a sensational rare tuna steak with roasted wasabi crust and a couple of glasses of chardonnay set us back a cool $65.

The tab was worth it to have gotten as close as you can to a South Pacific idyll within the continental United States. Think of the air fare one saves.

(305) 872-2524 or (800) 343-8567. Fax (305) 872-4843. Twenty-eight suites with private baths. Suites: Christmas-March: $750 to $850 weekends, $600 midweek. Late spring and fall: $550 to $700 weekends, $450 to $550 midweek. June-September: $450 to $550 weekends, $350 to $450 midweek. Add $125 daily per person for MAP, $140 for AP. Two-night minimum on weekends, three to five nights on holidays. Children over 16.

Lunch or Sunday brunch by reservation, 11:30 to 2:30. Dinner by reservation, 7 to 10:30. Entrées, $26.50 to $34.50.

Free shuttle for those with reservations leaves Dolphin Marina at Milepost 28.5 hourly on the half hour, returning on the hour, from 7 a.m. to 11 p.m.

Dining Spots

Key West has more than 150 restaurants, but, according to locals in the know, only a dozen or so worthy of the name. The problem for the visitor is that, except for a few, there is little consensus on precisely which ones those dozen are. Be advised: the best are far from the touristy establishments around lower Duval Street and Mallory Square.

Cafe Marquesa, 600 Fleming St., Key West.

Tops on most lists for fine dining is this sophisticated, 48-seat cafe in a corner of The Marquesa Hotel. The intimate, L-shaped room with coffered ceiling has stippled yellow walls, tall windows, rich mahogany molding and four large mahogany mirrors making the room seem bigger. A wonderful trompe-l'oeil kitchen scene surrounds an opening into the actual kitchen, where executive chef Susan Ferry prepares award-winning "food of the Americas," a blending of cuisines.

Her menu changes nightly. Typical main courses are sesame-crusted yellowfin tuna with miso rémoulade, buttermilk-marinated hog snapper with pomegranate vinaigrette, roasted duck breast and confit leg with raspberry jus, and New Zealand lamb with a compote of roasted bananas and papaya. Exotic accompaniments vary with the dish.

You might start with a trio of the day's soups, a grilled cajun shrimp caesar salad or salmon tostada with habañero salsa, crème fraîche and caviar. The dessert of choice is key lime napoleon with tropical fruit.

North and South American wines are featured.

(305) 292-1244. Entrées, $23 to $30. Dinner nightly, 6 to 11, 7 to 11 in summer. No smoking.

Cafe des Artistes, 1007 Simonton St., Key West.

This highly rated restaurant appears to share a building with Duffy's Steak and Lobster House. But the similarity ends there. The small and intimate interior is très French in the country style, with white arches and adequately spaced tables dressed with white linens and shaded candles. There was no sign of an outdoor terrace the night we were there.

The ambiance is appropriate for Provence, but not quite what most are looking for in Key West. Nor are the fancy food and hefty prices. Connoisseurs, however, appreciate the contemporary French fare with a tropical accent.

To start, consider a roulade of goat cheese, smoked salmon and caviar or roast quail stuffed with armagnac-soaked apricots and foie gras. Main courses range widely from black grouper braised in champagne and lobster flamed in cognac with mango and basil to steak au poivre, roast veal with garlic and double lamb chops in tarragon sauce. Classic French desserts follow suit.

Owner Tim Ryan planned to open a contemporary Italian restaurant in the quarters vacated in 1998 by the late Palm Grill at 1208 Simonton St.

(305) 294-7100. Entrées, $22.95 to $38.95. Dinner nightly, 6 to 11.

Louie's Backyard, 700 Waddell Ave., Key West.

This was our favorite Key West restaurant for lunch at our first visit in 1984, a year after it opened, and it remains so today. Little has changed in the interim – how could it, given the idyllic back terrace tiered from the dining room open to the rear down open decks beneath a flowering mahoe tree to the tropical Afterdeck Bar beside the ocean? It's one of the most attractive restaurant settings anywhere. Locals caution that the food is inconsistent and the service arrogant at dinner, but everyone seems to love this high-end place for a leisurely lunch. Perhaps the staff has gotten the message. At a weekday lunch they were inordinately apologetic for delays in taking our order and delivering a stellar napoleon of grilled vegetables with asiago cheese and a superior grilled sirloin salad with roasted garlic vinaigrette, maytag blue cheese and mixed greens. Conch fritters with hot pepper jelly and wasabi accompanied. The piña coladas and margaritas here are considered the best in town, although ours were nothing exceptional. But the ocean view is, especially at lunchtime when all the little boats are skittering about, parasailers soar overhead and a cruise ship departs for points unknown.

The dinner menu yields dishes like "snapper behind bars," wrapped in sliced potatoes with spiced mango-rum sauce, and stuffed filet of beef in puff pastry with a white peach and green peppercorn sauce.

(305) 294-1061. Entrées, $25 to $32.50. Lunch daily except September, 11:30 to 3. Dinner nightly, 7 to 10.

A&B Lobster House, 700 Front St., Key West.

A fixture for 51 years, the A&B Lobster House was vastly upgraded in 1998 by local restaurateur Paul Tripp. Already the owner of three waterfront eateries along Restaurant Row in the historic Key West Bight marina area, he saw the need for an upscale seafood restaurant. When the nearby A&B became available, he took over and transformed the upstairs into an elegant, 200-seat dining area with indoor and outdoor seating along the water. Adjacent is Berlin's, a cocktail lounge and cigar bar. Downstairs is a smaller, casual oyster bar called Alonzo's.

The with-it fare gets rave reviews. A house specialty is black grouper oscar stuffed with crabmeat and stone crabs, topped with mango béarnaise and served with asparagus and coconut-pecan rice. Citrus grilled dolphin, grilled Key West pink shrimp, cioppino pasta, grilled veal chop and steak au poivre are other favorites. Maine and Florida lobster comes in seven variations, including pasta, newburg, and surf and turf.

Stews, pan roasts and bisques are featured starters. How about an oyster pan roast with oysters, leeks, chili sauce and paprika? Or roasted saffron and ginger mussels?

(305) 294-5880. Entrées, $19.50 to $35. Berlin's, dinner, Monday-Saturday 6 to 11; Sunday brunch, 11 to 4. Alonzo's, Monday-Saturday 11 to 11.

Antonia's, 615 Duval St., Key West.

This old-timer, rebuilt to resemble the original following a 1995 fire, is almost everyone's favorite locally. Perhaps it's the fine northern Italian fare and consistent service offered by Antonia Berto since 1978. Perhaps it's the urbane, New Yorkish bistro setting that some see as a welcome break from Key West's relentless tropical backdrop. Wine bottles and olive oils displayed in the windows indicate Antonia's priorities.

Fabulous seafood and beef tenderloin dishes are hallmarks, especially the yellowtail snapper braised with watercress, belgian endive, radicchio, arugula and artichokes. Veal marsala and sliced chicken piedmontese are other favorites. The pastas are deceptively simple, and the antipasti first-rate. We'd go for the

cinque crostini, five slices topped variously with goat cheese and herbs, marinated eggplant, sundried tomatoes and such, or the carpaccio, the preparation of which varies. Among salads are one with sixteen blanched vegetables served warm and tossed with baby lettuces, olive oil and champagne vinegar.
(305) 294-5662. Entrées, $15.50 to $22.50. Dinner nightly, 6 to 10.

Alice's on Duval, 1114 Duval St., Key West.
The world cuisine of chef-owner Alice Weingarten is highly rated. We tried to eat here, but faced a half-hour wait for a table near a window late on an otherwise slow Tuesday night and refused to subject ourselves to the smoky though convivial atmosphere. The walls and pillars in the high-ceilinged interior are painted in pastel shades, and floral cloths top the close-together tables. But oh, for a breath of fresh air.

Alice's menu is our kind of menu, original and categorized by small plates, cold plates, large plates and sweet plates. It's perfect for grazing. We could make a meal from such exotic small plates as Mexican potstickers with tequila salsa, conch and green chile fritters, sticky hoisin duck shumi and Moroccan gyoza dumplings. Heartier eaters are sated by "Aunt Alice's magic meatloaf," if they don't first succumb to pistachio-crusted grouper with coconut rice, Mediterranean roasted chicken or papaya-marinated skirt steak.

Black bottom key lime pie and tropical fruit shortcake with passionfruit chantilly cream are refreshing endings to the assertive fare.
(305) 292-4888. Entrées, $12.95 to $25.75. Dinner nightly, 6 to 11.

Latitudes Beach Cafe, Sunset Key, Key West.
Dine under the stars at this new, open-air restaurant beside the Gulf on exclusive Sunset Key. An eight-minute shuttle boat ride takes you from the Key West Hilton to its deluxe cottage colony and residential complex on a private island. The restaurant is operated by the Hilton for cottage guests and residents, but is open to the public as well.

Tables are on flooring beside the water and on the beach. Part of the dining area is covered by awnings and may be shielded by windscreens. Tiki torches are lit at night, and the ambiance is magical. The contemporary dinner menu is decidedly upscale. You might start with sesame-seared yellowfin tuna with Asian dipping sauce, oak wood-smoked salmon with tobiko caviar and toast points, or goat cheese and portobello mushroom in phyllo with frizzled greens. Main courses include lobster and scallop tempura with Caribbean fruit salsa, Asian-seared mahi mahi, grilled veal chop with thyme-maple jus and beef tenderloin with gorgonzola-scallion butter.

The breakfast and lunch menus are similarly innovative. "Frozen libations" are the drinks of choice.
(305) 292-5394. Entrées, $22.95 to $30.95. Breakfast daily, 7 to 11. Lunch, 11 to 5. Dinner, 5 to 10 or 11. Reservations required.

Cafe Blue, 1202 Simonton St., Key West.
Affordable Mediterranean cuisine and a quiet, covered outdoor dining terrace commend this new eatery, the third offered by veteran local restaurateur Gail Brockway. Wrought-iron rails stripe the windows of the side bar/dining room, while painted branches with mirrored leaves fan out Italian condo style along the

interior wall of the terrace. Vestiges of a gallery occupy a large inside room that leads to the lavatories.

Dinner fare ranges from pastas and couscous through such dishes as shrimp scorpio, dolphin piccata, paella and lamb kabobs. Panzanella Sicilian bread salad, mussel soup seasoned with saffron, spanakopita and lamb kofte are possible starters. The lunch menu yielded a superior salade niçoise and a zesty grilled lamb burger with mint yogurt sauce. The waiter neglected to say they had run out of pita bread for the lamb burger, however, substituting unwanted sourdough, and forgot to bring the sample of garlic soup he offered when we questioned whether it was the real thing. When we ordered the key lime napoleon, only to find out it wasn't available that day, we decided we had had enough. Alas, good service is a perennial Key West problem. Yours could be better than ours.

(305) 296-7500. Entrées, $14 to $18. Lunch daily, 11 to 3. Light fare, 3 to 6. Dinner, 6 to 11.

Cafe KaRUMba! 1215 Duval St., Key West.
Man-about-town Eliot Baron, who put the immensely popular Mangia Mangia pasta house on the local restaurant map, went Caribbean with this pale pink stucco restaurant and bar in 1997. Palm murals adorn the walls and the ceiling is a painted sky in the downstairs dining room. Upstairs in a tropical bar, the island's widest selection of rum drinks starts where the Wine Spectator award-winning cellar at his Italian eatery leaves off.

We headed outside to the jaunty rooftop deck overlooking the Duval Street action – at least what there was of it in this quieter section of upper Duval. With artistic, handpainted tables and a laid-back atmosphere it was the perfect setting for a late-night dinner. A varied menu of Caribbean specialties ranged from Cuban roast pork and calypso stew chicken over rice to grilled tuna and steak martinique with sweet-potato fries. Quite satisfying were the sautéed conch with pineapple and ginger, an excellent house salad of mixed greens with haricots verts and the crispy yucca pancake topped with a skewer of grilled spicy shrimp, pineapple and pepper. Great sides of Caribbean rice and vegetables accompanied, as did a $16 bottle of Oregon riesling. The specialty mojita, billed as a mint julep with rum rather than bourbon, began this enjoyable evening. We finished with a dish of frozen key lime yogurt from Flaming Crossing Ice Cream down the street.

(305) 296-2644. Entrées, $10.95 to $13.95. Dinner nightly, 5:30 to 11.

Seven Fish, 632 Olivia St., Key West.
Some of the best food in town is served at affordable – make that unbelievable – prices in this 40-seat corner roadhouse. Sculptures of seven fish hang in a window. Red molded school chairs are at yellow tables beneath a raftered ceiling. A bar at one end holds vintage wines.

All is very small and intimate for a with-it crowd that applauds simple but stylish cooking. The menu offers meat loaf with "real mashed potatoes" and grilled vegetable egg foo yung among more substantial fare priced mainly in the low teens. Typical are grilled mahi mahi with black pepper dijon, shrimp scampi with asparagus spears, grilled chicken with pear and caramelized walnuts and a mixed grill of skewered chicken, shrimp and vegetables. Salads come in small and large sizes, and the three-cheese caesar can be ordered with grilled chicken or crab cake.

Start with a spicy tuna roll, wild mushroom quesadilla or a crab cake with ginger garlic. Finish with bananas flambé or apple pie with ice cream and cinnamon. *(305) 296-2777. Entrées, $9 to $17. Dinner nightly except Tuesday, 6 to 11. No smoking.*

Blue Heaven, 729 Thomas St., Key West.
The reputation of this quirky restaurant in the center of Bahama Village, home of Key West's Afro-Caribbean community, preceded our visit. So did word of the roosters that stopped our car as they skittered around the middle of Thomas Street. The restaurant supposedly was closed for three days of kitchen renovations, but we could find neither kitchen nor any sign of renovation.

Only open, so to speak, was the Blue Heaven Bake Shop with a sign saying "Serving sin on a fork since 1997 – this will impress you in 20 years." The only person inside exerted himself from the couch enough to point the way to an unlocked gate to enter the restaurant property. We spotted a couple of cats snoozing here and there amid the colorful picnic tables spread around a dirt courtyard. We also caught a glimpse of the Rooster Gallery, the Rooster Cemetery, the Blue Heaven Gift Shop and the Blue Heaven Showers ("$1, to watch $2"). The door of the Bordello Galleria upstairs was open, but we couldn't find a way up.

Although we couldn't truly experience this popular place considered the essence of the old Key West, we hear the seafood benedict is sensational for breakfast. The dinner menu lists such entrées as Caribbean barbecued shrimp, Jamaican jerk chicken, pork tenderloin with chutney and curry butter, vegetarian specials and grilled strip steak with cracked pepper-mango butter. The signature dessert is banana heaven – banana bread with flamed bananas, spiced rum and homemade vanilla bean ice cream.

(305) 296-8666. Entrées, $8 to $16.50. Breakfast and lunch, 8 to 3. Dinner, 6 to 10:30. Closed Monday.

Diversions

All the assets of a tropical island combine with the advantages of a diverse small city to keep visitors busy for a weekend, a week, a month – even forever, should they decide as so many do to stay. We can only cover some don't-t-miss highlights.

Parking is limited and the meters expensive. Bicycles and mopeds are the preferred means of transportation locally. The historic Old Town area that is of most interest to visitors is reasonably compact. The best way to see and savor the real Key West is on foot.

Conch Tour Train, Front Street, Key West.
The first-time visitor should get oriented by boarding Key West's signature Conch train. It covers fourteen miles and 100-plus attractions in about 90 minutes. The driver narrates as he goes, with a few whistle toots and some Disneyesque audio hoopla along the way. Sit up front and slide back and forth on the bench to take pictures on whichever side is of most interest. Be really quick or you'll miss that Kodak moment. The train toots around the busy Mallory Square area before winding through the streets of Old Town, out busy North Roosevelt Boulevard and back past fascinating Houseboat Row, East Martello Fort & Museum, the beaches along the south side of the island, and the attractions of upper Duval and

Audubon House is named for ornithologist who stayed here while painting birds of the Florida Keys.

Whitehead streets. At tour's end, you'll be informed of interesting Key West tidbits and ready to concentrate on those sites and areas of particular interest. *(305) 294-5161. Tours daily, 9 to 4:30. Adults, $14.*

More specialized interests are served by the architectural, cemetery, bicycle and personalized city walking tours offered by Sharon Wells of **Island City Heritage Trust,** (305) 294-8380 or 294-5397. State historian in Key West for seventeen years, she now writes and publishes the annual *Walking and Biking Guide to Historic Key West,* a free 60-page booklet that's the most enlightening and lively of its kind.

Among her tours are one of **Nancy Forrester's Secret Garden,** a stroll through one save-the-planet advocate's remarkable rainforest and botanical garden at the end of Free School Lane, in the heart of Old Town. The day we tried to tour the owner was caring for an ailing bird and we were left to our own devices. The "$6 greens fee per primate" hardly seemed worth it for the few minutes we had available. We'd already seen our fill of gumbo limbo trees, hanging orchids, exotic palms and cages of cockatiels and scarlet macaws.

Another interesting tour is of the **Key West Cemetery,** sixteen feet above sea level on a modest rise called Solares Hill. Vaults are above ground because an 1847 hurricane disinterred bodies from the town's first burial ground near Southernmost Point. The whitewashed tombs of pet terriers and the inscriptions on the headstones tell something of the quirkiness of Key West. One woman's memorial to her philandering husband reads: "At least I know where you're sleeping tonight."

Audubon House and Gardens, 205 Whitehead St., Key West.
An exceptionally good audio tape guides visitors at their own pace through the

wonders of this imposing house in which ornithologist John James Audubon stayed while painting the birds of the Florida Keys in 1832. Actually, he was only a guest in the family home of Capt. John H. Geiger, master shipwreck salvager, whose prized antiques and furnishings are of considerable merit in their own right. Here, Audubon added eighteen new species to his Birds of America engravings. They include the white-crowned pigeon, painted on a branch of an orange-blossomed Geiger tree from the gardens and one of 28 first-edition Audubon works displayed in the house. The voices of Geiger family members guide visitors throughout the house, which is well worth seeing. The tour ends in the gardens, which gave Audubon some of his inspiration. There's an excellent museum shop.

(305) 294-2116. Open daily, 9:30 to 5. Adults, $7.50.

Ernest Hemingway Home and Museum, 907 Whitehead St.. Key West.

Key West's most visited attraction is the imposing 1851 Moorish-influenced mansion the author was given in 1931. The house is set in a tropical garden he designed and planted. The guided tour is a nostalgia trip for Hemingway devotees, especially in the cottage studio where he wrote 300 to 700 words a day on the small typewriter on view. Others are entranced by the six-toed cats descended from Hemingway originals and visible everywhere, including in a cat hospital behind the gift shop. "We have 69 cats on the property named after old movie stars," advised our guide. "No, not James Dean," she responded to a young girl. Check out the penny embedded in the concrete at the head of Key West's first swimming pool, a gift to the author from his wife. When he discovered the pool's $20,000 price tag, he took a penny from his pocket, pressed it in the wet cement and told his wife, "You may as well take my last penny, too."

(305) 294-1575. Open daily, 9 to 5. Adults, $6.50.

Little White House Museum, 111 Front St., Key West.

Opened in 1991, this is a fascinating stop for anyone with an interest in President Harry S. Truman and how he turned the unlikely looking Navy commandant's house on the Naval Base into the Little White House. "I've a notion to move to Key West and just stay," he advised wife Bess on one of his first visits, according to the ten-minute film that begins the tour. You see the president's bedroom where he napped on a day bed, the South Porch where he played poker and drank Kentucky bourbon, and the living room in which an original copy of the Chicago Tribune's erroneous front page, "Dewey Beats Truman," is on display with five lines upside down. The place is full of mid-century nostalgia, but is as up-to-date as its changing special exhibits and the guest book signed by ex-President Jimmy Carter and family at their 1997 New Year's visit, when the Presidential Gates leading to the Little White House in what is now the privately developed Truman Annex were opened once again.

(305) 294-9911. Open daily, 9 to 5. Adults, $7.

Art Galleries are a principal Key West attraction, and a brochure lists two dozen of the best. **Gingerbread Square Gallery** is Key West's oldest; its offerings certainly are stylish and colorful. **The Gallery on Greene** is among the newest. A tiger-skin motorcycle caught our eye in the window of the exotic **Caribbean Gallery.** We liked the contemporary pieces at **Kokopelli,** and the great dolphins and marine creatures at the two **Wyland Galleries of Key West,** whose young namesake artist painted a stunning "whaling wall" mural in just three days on a building in the Seaport district. The tiny **Haitian Art Co.,** crammed with primitive art, is worth the trek to 600 Frances St. Our all-around favorite was the **Island Arts Co-op Gallery** at 1128 Duval, to which we returned every chance we could to find yet another little acquisition.

Shopping. The touristy stores are concentrated in the Mallory Square area along Front and Green streets and lower Duval Street, chockablock full of raunchy T-shirt and souvenir shops. We prefer the stores in the Historic Seaport District near the marina known as Key West Bight and those farther out Duval Street, plus a few on parallel Simonton Street and cross streets like Fleming.

Don't miss **Fast Buck Freddie's,** a mini-Bloomingdale's known for its window displays. Inside is an incredible emporium of treasures, from clothes to pottery to cards, Christmas items and a special section for the gay clientele. Quite unexpected is the suave **H.T. Chittam & Co.**, something of an L.L.Bean South, with a bright red seaplane hung beneath a soaring ceiling and a log facade fronting the sportswear section.

With its two-story high interior, the **Compagnie International Express** is the most striking, especially at night. **Hot Hats** carries all kinds of sun hats and blessedly few baseball caps. Pick up a Conch Republic towel at **Towels of Key West,** or some Frette towels at **John Kent** next door. **Cuba! Cuba!** speaks for itself. **Pandemonium** offers colorful everything, from hundreds of tiles to vases to juggling balls to license plate albums to painted furniture, all very avant-garde. A convertible covered with tiles is parked next door in front of **Glass Reunions,** featuring lovely glass from paperweights to jewelry to mobiles.

In the Harborwalk/Seaport area, we like to stop at the **Key West Aloe Co.** and its nearby factory outlet, though the prices have soared in recent years. **Key West Handprint Fashions and Fabrics** offers the splashy designs popularized by Suzy dePoo and Lily Pulitzer, whose shop is nearby. **Mac's Sea Shanty** holds Key West appeal for tourists. We picked up a key lime pie ($10 whole, $2.75 a slice) to take home from **Key Lime Pie Co.**, and acquired all the key lime goods we could ever need at the **Key West Lime Shop,** which featured a frozen chocolate-dipped key lime pie slice on a stick.

The **Pelican Poop Shoppe** at 304 Simonton offers Caribbean arts and crafts with a bird theme in three rooms in the National Register-listed Casa Antigua, where Ernest Hemingway first settled in to write *Farewell to Arms.* A $2 self-guided tour of the lush tropical garden in back is free with a $10 purchase. **Plantation Potters** exhibits good American crafts beside a sculpture garden at 521 Fleming St.

Extra-Special

Mallory Square Sunsets.
A Key West spectacle known as applauding sunset has grown into a unique tradition. The old pier where steamships docked is transformed nightly into a stage for an ever-changing lineup of artists, acrobats, fire-eaters, palm readers, performing animals and food vendors. Called "buskers," they work for tips and a dollar in their hats helps sustain the evening ritual that for many is the essence of the Key West experience. The frenzied scene often upstages the sunset.

Index

A

A&B Lobster House, Key West, FL 361
A1A Ale Works, St. Augustine, FL 328
Abbingdon Green, Asheville, NC 108
Ackland Art Museum, Chapel Hill, NC 60
The Aerie, New Bern, NC 24
Aiken County Historical Museum, Aiken, SC 148
The Albemarle House, Edenton, NC 18
Albemarle Inn, Asheville, NC 114
Alexander Homestead, St. Augustine, FL 322
Alexandra's Inn, Georgetown, SC 154
Alice's on Duval, Key West, FL 362
Amelia Island Museum of History, Fernandina Beach, FL 314
The Amelia Island Williams House, Fernandina Beach, FL 305
Amicalola Falls State Park, Dawsonville, GA 274
Andersonville Civil War Village, Andersonville, GA 247
Andersonville National Historic Site, Andersonville, GA 246
Andersonville Restaurant,, Andersonville, GA 246
Andrew Low House, Savannah, GA 212
Annie's Inn, Montmorenci, SC 144
Anson, Charleston, SC 176
Antonia's, Key West, FL 361
The Asheville Urban Trail, Asheville, NC 122
Ashley Inn B&B, Charleston, SC 174
Aubergine, Fairhope, AL 297
Audubon House and Gardens, Key West, FL 365
The Augustus T. Zevely Inn, Winston-Salem, NC 78
Aunt Stella's House Bed & Breakfast, Hamilton, GA 254

B

B 900 and The Cellar, Winston-Salem, NC 84
Bahai, Fairhope, AL 297
Bailey House, Fernandina Beach, FL 309
The Ballastone, Savannah, GA 198
Bananas Foster, Key West, FL 354
The Bank Waterfront Grill & Bar, Beaufort, SC 193
Barnyard Saturday Night, Fischer Crossroads, AL 288
Battleship North Carolina, Wilmington, NC 47
Bay Breeze Guest House, Fairhope, AL 291
Bay Street Inn, Beaufort, SC 188
Beaufort House, Asheville, NC 112
The Beaufort Inn, Beaufort, SC 189 and 191
The Beech Street Grill, Fernandina Beach, FL 310
Bellamy Mansion, Wilmington, NC 45

The Best Cellar, Blowing Rock, NC 101
The Big Oak, Thomasville, GA 238
Biltmore Estate, Asheville, NC 120
The Bistro, Asheville, NC 118
Bistro de Jong, Beaufort, SC 192
Bistro PJ, St. Augustine, FL 326
Bistro Savannah, Savannah, GA 208
Black Mountain Lodge, Dahlonega, GA 265
Black Walnut Bed and Breakfast Inn, Asheville, NC 115
Blossom Café, Charleston, SC 177
The Blowing Rock, Blowing Rock, NC 103
Blue Heaven, Key West, FL 364
The Blueberry Inn & Gardens, Dahlonega, GA 263
"The Book" Tour, Savannah, GA 214
Borrell Creek Restaurant & Lounge, St. Marys, GA 219
Brasington House Bed & Breakfast, Charleston, SC 172
Breaux's Cajun Cafe, St. Marys, GA 220
Brett's Waterway Cafe, Fernandina Beach, FL 313
The Briar Patch, Aiken, SC 143
Brookgreen Gardens, Pawleys Island, SC 163
Brookstown Inn, Winston-Salem, NC 81
The Bulloch House Restaurant, Warm Springs, GA 257
Burgwin-Wright House, Wilmington, NC 45

C

The Cafe at Gourmet to Go, Mount Dora, FL 340
Cafe Blue, Key West, FL 362
Cafe des Artistes, Key West, FL 360
Cafe KaRUMba! Key West, FL 363
Cafe Marquesa, Key West, FL 360
Caffe Phoenix, Wilmington, NC 42
Callaway Gardens, Pine Mountain, GA 259
Callaway Gardens Resort, Pine Mountain, GA 255 and 257
The Cannonboro Inn, Charleston, SC 174
Captain's Quarters Inn, Edenton, NC 17
Carolina CrossRoads, Chapel Hill, NC 58
The Carolina Hotel, Pinehurst, NC 68
The Carolina Inn, Chapel Hill, NC 54
Carolina's, Charleston, SC 176
Carriage Way Bed & Breakfast, St. Augustine, FL 325
Caruso's Ristorante Italiano, Dahlonega, GA 271
Casa de la Paz, St. Augustine, FL 317
Casa de Solana, St. Augustine, FL 321
Casa de Sueños Bed & Breakfast, St. Augustine, FL 320
The Casa Monica Hotel, St. Augustine, FL 326

South by Southwest, Winston-Salem, NC 85
Southbound Bistro & Grille, Winston-Salem,
    NC 84
Southeastern Center for Contemporary Art,
    Winston-Salem, NC 90
A Southern Season, Chapel Hill, NC 61
The Southern Tip, Fernandina Beach, FL
    312
Spanish Quarter Village, St. Augustine, FL
    330
Spencer House Inn, St. Marys, GA 217
Sweet Basil, Southern Pines, NC 74
Sweet Magnolia, Savannah, GA 222
Sweet Magnolia, St. Marys, GA 222

T

The Talking Bean, Americus, GA 246
Tanglewood Manor House, Winston-Salem,
    NC 82
Telfair Academy of Arts and Sciences,
    Savannah, GA 212
La Terrace, Southern Pines, NC 73
The Terrace by Moonlight, Thomasville, GA
    233
Thalian Hall, Wilmington, NC 45
Theos Taverna, Pinehurst, NC 72
Thirty-Six Meeting Street, Charleston, SC 173
Thomas County Museum of History,
    Thomasville, GA 237
Thomas Wolfe Memorial State Historic Site,
    Asheville, NC 122
Thomasville Rose Garden, Thomasville, GA
    238
Toad Hall, Highlands, NC 127
Top of the Hill, Chapel Hill, NC 59
Town & Country Inn, Aiken, SC 144
Trestle House Inn, Edenton, NC 16
Tryon Palace Historic Sites and Gardens,
    New Bern, NC 31
Tufts Archives, Pinehurst, NC 75
Twenty-Seven State Street Bed & Breakfast,
    Charleston, SC 172
Twig's Restaurant & Lounge, Blowing Rock,
    NC 100
Two Meeting Street Inn, Charleston, SC 165
TwoSuns Inn Bed & Breakfast, Beaufort, SC
    186

U

Up Your Alley, Aiken, SC 145

V

Valhalla, Mentone, AL 280
The Verandas, Wilmington, NC 36
The Village Bed & Breakfast, Chapel Hill, NC
    52
The Village Café, Blowing Rock, NC 101
The Vineyards Restaurant, Winston-Salem,
    NC 86

W

The Wash House Restaurant, Point Clear, AL
    297
Waterman's Grill, Edenton, NC 19
The Weatherstation Inn, Key West, FL 353
Wentworth Mansion, Charleston, SC 169
West End Café, Winston-Salem, NC 87
Westcott House, St. Augustine, FL 318
Weymouth Center for the Arts & Humanities,
    Southern Pines, NC 75
Weymouth Woods Sandhills Nature Preserve,
    Southern 75
Whispers Coffee House & Cafe, St. Marys,
    GA 222
The Willcox Inn, Aiken, SC 141
Wilmington Adventure Walking Tour,
    Wilmington, NC 47
Wilmington Railroad Museum, Wilmington,
    NC 45
Wilmington Trolley Co. Tour, Wilmington,
    NC 44
The Windmill European Grill/Il Pescatore,
    Asheville, NC 119
The Windsor Hotel, Americus, GA 243 and
    244
The Windsor Rose, Mount Dora, FL 342
Winkler Bakery, Old Salem, NC 90
Winston Place, Valley Head, AL 277
Wolfgang's on Main, Highlands, NC 137
World Golf Village, St. Augustine, FL 332
Worley Homestead Inn, Dahlonega, GA 267
The Worth House, Wilmington, NC 40
The Wright Inn, Asheville, NC 112
Wylies Restaurant & Coffee House,
    Dahlonega, GA 270

Z

Zebulon Latimer House, Wilmington, NC 45
Zevely House, Winston-Salem, NC 85
Zorayda Castle, St. Augustine, FL 331

Also by the Authors

Inn Spots & Special Places in New England. The first in the series, this book by Nancy and Richard Woodworth tells you where to go, stay, eat and enjoy in New England's choicest areas. Focusing on 35 special places, it details the best inns and B&Bs, restaurants, sights to see and things to do. First published in 1986; fully revised and expanded fifth edition in 1998. 524 pages of timely ideas. $16.95.

Inn Spots & Special Places / Mid-Atlantic. The second volume in the series, this book by Nancy and Richard Woodworth covers 35 special areas in the Mid-Atlantic region from New York to Virginia. First published in 1992; fully revised and expanded third edition in 1998. 536 pages of timely ideas. $16.95.

Getaways for Gourmets in the Northeast. The first book by Nancy and Richard Woodworth appeals to the gourmet in all of us. It guides you to the best dining, lodging, specialty food shops and culinary attractions in 22 areas from the Brandywine Valley to Montreal, Cape May to Bar Harbor, the Finger Lakes to Nantucket. First published in 1984; fully update fifth edition in 1997. 570 pages to read and savor. $18.95.

Waterside Escapes in the Northeast. This new edition by Betsy Wittemann and Nancy Woodworth relates the best lodging, dining, attractions and activities in 36 great waterside vacation spots from Chesapeake Bay to Cape Breton Island, from the Thousand Islands to Martha's Vineyard. Everything you need to know for a day trip, a weekend or a week near the water is told the way you want to know it. First published in 1987; revised and expanded third edition in 1996. 474 pages to discover and enjoy. $15.95.

Weekending in New England. The best-selling travel guide by Betsy Wittemann and Nancy Woodworth details everything you need to know about 24 of New England's most interesting vacation spots: more than 1,000 things to do, sights to see and places to stay, eat and shop year-round. First published in 1980; fully revised and expanded fifth edition in 1997. 448 pages of facts and fun. $16.95.

The Originals in Their Fields

These books may be ordered from your local bookstore or direct from the publisher, pre-paid, plus $2 shipping for each book.

Wood Pond Press
365 Ridgewood Road
West Hartford, Conn. 06107
Tel: (860) 521-0389
Fax: (860) 313-0185
E-Mail: woodpond@ntplex.net
Web Site: www.getawayguides.com.

ON LINE: Excerpts from these books are found at www.getawayguides.com. Check out this web site for updates on some of our favorite inns, B&Bs, restaurants and attractions in destination areas around the East.